Literature FOR YOUNG ADULTS

BOOKS FOR CONTEMPORARY READERS

and more

Joan L. Knickerbocker

ASHLAND UNIVERSITY

Martha A. Brueggeman

ASHLAND UNIVERSITY, PROFESSOR EMERITUS

James A. Rycik

ASHLAND UNIVERSITY

H·H·P

Holcomb Hathaway, Publishers
Scottsdale, Arizona

Library of Congress Cataloging-in-Publication Data

Knickerbocker, Joan L.
   Literature for young adults : books (and more) for contemporary readers / Joan
L. Knickerbocker, Martha A. Brueggeman, James A. Rycik.
      p. cm.
   ISBN 978-1-934432-43-3 (print book) — ISBN 978-1-934432-82-2 (ebook) 1.
Young adult literature–Study and teaching 2. Teenagers–Books and reading. I.
Brueggeman, Martha A. II. Rycik, James A. III. Title.
   PN1008.8.K55 2012
   809'.892830712—dc23

                      2012019249

**Credits and Acknowledgments can be found on p. 418,
an extension of the copyright page.**

Holcomb Hathaway, Publishers, Inc.
8700 E. Via de Ventura Blvd., Suite 265
Scottsdale, Arizona 85258
480-991-7881
www.hh-pub.com

10 9 8 7 6 5 4 3 2 1

Print ISBN: 978-1-934432-43-3
Ebook ISBN: 978-1-934432-82-2

Printed in the United States of America.

CONTENTS

Changing Literature, Changing Readers, Changing Classrooms   1

Bringing Young Adults and Literature Together   29

❸

The Language of Literary Conversations   63

Realistic Fiction   97

LITERATURE REFLECTING LIFE

Historical Fiction   133

THE PAST IN PERSPECTIVE

Traditional Literature   165

RETELLING AND REINVENTING TALES

Fantasy and Speculative Fiction   197

IMAGINARY WORLDS AND WORLDS THAT MIGHT YET BE

Nonfiction   231

ARTISTRY AND INFORMATION

Poetry, Short Stories, and Drama   261

THE OTHER LITERATURE

The Art of Literature   295

COVER ART, PICTURE BOOKS, ILLUSTRATED LITERATURE, AND GRAPHIC NOVELS

Film   327

EXPANDING THE LITERATURE CURRICULUM

Literary Criticism in the Classroom   361

Appendices

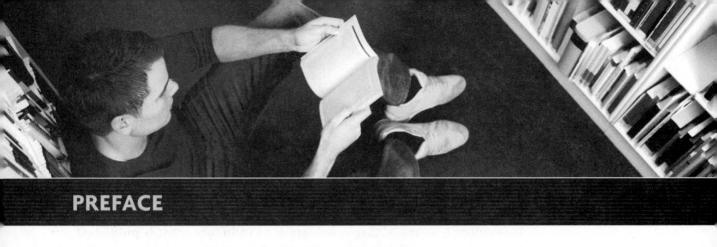

*T*his book is written by three book lovers, but it is about more than books. It is also about readers, specifically young adult readers, who are choosing and using literature in the early part of the 21st century. The challenges and concerns faced by today's adolescents may resemble those of past generations, but today's readers inhabit an increasingly diverse and technological world. In our discussion of literature for young adults, we acknowledge those realities, which influence how literature is chosen and consumed as well as what readers seek and receive from literature. We highlight works that can expand young adults' awareness of all kinds of diversity, and we provide glimpses of the ways in which young adults can access literature instantaneously and share ideas online with readers all over the globe.

Like most book lovers, we have a profound respect for the works of literature that have provided a foundation for generations of readers and writers to build on. We have tried to do justice to those works. Nevertheless, our particular emphasis in this book is on contemporary works and on the ways in which contemporary readers access, interpret, and share those works. This emphasis is reflected in some of the distinguishing characteristics of this book:

- **We highlight recent developments in literature that are characterized as postmodern or metafictive.** We believe that metafictive techniques that defy traditional narrative conventions and postmodern attitudes of skepticism about authority are particularly well-suited to the natural inclinations of adolescents, so we include works that exemplify these characteristics throughout this book.

- **We examine the implications of a critical literacy stance.** For us, critical literacy involves seeing a literary text, like any other text, both as the product of a particular culture and as a potential influence on that culture. Critical literacy often focuses on the relationship between texts and social factors such as race, class, and gender, and we recognize these as issues that young adults will face.

- **We analyze the role of visual elements such as graphics, color, and typography in contemporary literature for young adults.** We examine how these visual elements are used in interpreting graphic novels, illustrated books, and picture books, and we consider how visual elements in book covers are integral in communicating both a work's intended audience and its overall meaning.

- **We link literary theory to classroom practice.** The concluding chapter of this book reviews the major theories that have been used to describe how literature should be interpreted. It then connects each of those theories to particular classroom literacy routines and suggests works that would be especially appropriate for putting a particular theory into action.

- **We explore how marketing considerations influence what is published and how young adult readers engage with literature.** Author websites, tie-ins between books and movies, and the opportunity to post reviews of books online are just a few examples of a changing marketplace that allows young adults to become active consumers of literary products as well as students of literature.

In our attempt to highlight contemporary works meaningful to today's young adults, we also devote attention to "nonbook" forms of literature, particularly feature films. In addition to including discussions of films where appropriate in most chapters, we devote Chapter 11 to the basic elements of film study and to exploring the wide range of films that are available for young adults. We also expand traditional concepts of literature to include varieties of books, such as graphic novels, that continue to grow in popularity.

In addition to being lovers of literature, we are career educators, and this book reflects our concern with bringing young adults together with literature in ways that will make them lifelong readers. In Chapter 2, we present a number of classroom literacy routines, each of which offers unique advantages for supporting young adults' development as readers. Additionally, each chapter contains one or more **Classroom Scenarios** designed to help teachers visualize how young adults can be guided to engage with a literary work.

Other special features in the book include the following:

- **Focus Questions** preview the content of each chapter and may be used for post-reading discussion and review.

- **Featured Author** boxes supply biographical information about authors who have made significant contributions to literature for young adults and provide insights into their bodies of work.

- **Focus Novel** boxes provide in-depth analysis of a work that is representative of major concepts discussed in the chapter.

- **"A Sample of . . ."** boxes provide annotated lists of books and films, so that readers can explore a particular theme or focus in greater depth.

As three long-time book lovers and educators, we wrote this book as a showcase for the quality and variety of literature currently available to young adults. Whether you are a prospective teacher, a practicing teacher, a librarian, or simply a fan of literature for young adults, we invite you to join us in exploring the literary works contained here and to consider your role in helping young adults to understand and appreciate all that this literature has to offer.

The Website: "Literature and Literacy for Young Adults"

As an additional teaching tool and resource for your education students (and you!), we have created the website "Literature and Literacy for Young Adults" (www.hhpcommunities.com/youngadultlit). This site serves as a companion to this book and will introduce educators to new books and to quality books they may have missed. Instructors, you may read more about this online resource/companion website on page xvi. Please also direct your students to that page so they can take full advantage of the site.

Contact us at info@hh-pub.com or via your Holcomb Hathaway sales representative if you wish to set up an individual class forum at the site. On the forum, your class can share insights, recommendations, information, and resources about the growing body of contemporary and classic literature for young adults.

ACKNOWLEDGMENTS

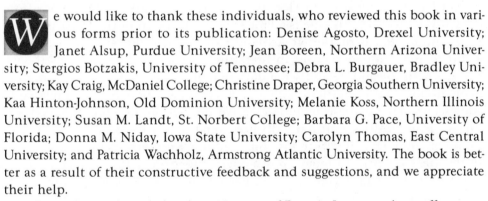 e would like to thank these individuals, who reviewed this book in various forms prior to its publication: Denise Agosto, Drexel University; Janet Alsup, Purdue University; Jean Boreen, Northern Arizona University; Stergios Botzakis, University of Tennessee; Debra L. Burgauer, Bradley University; Kay Craig, McDaniel College; Christine Draper, Georgia Southern University; Kaa Hinton-Johnson, Old Dominion University; Melanie Koss, Northern Illinois University; Susan M. Landt, St. Norbert College; Barbara G. Pace, University of Florida; Donna M. Niday, Iowa State University; Carolyn Thomas, East Central University; and Patricia Wachholz, Armstrong Atlantic University. The book is better as a result of their constructive feedback and suggestions, and we appreciate their help.

We wish to acknowledge the assistance of Bonnie Lowery, whose efforts as a proofreader and online researcher made a difficult task that much easier. We want to thank Sarah Grace Landis for lending her expertise on dramatic literature, and our students, Katie DeMarco, Ashley Haines, Jessica Kidder, Amanda Largent, and Stephanie Rambeau, who assisted us with several portions of this book.

Finally, our deepest appreciation to Nick Knickerbocker, who taught us important lessons about young readers, to Jim Bruggemann for his patience and support, and to Mary Rycik, a valuable colleague to all of us and an invaluable spouse to one of us.

ABOUT THE AUTHORS

Dr. Joan L. Knickerbocker received a B.S Ed. in English Education from the University of Wisconsin River Falls, her M.A.T. in Reading Education from the University of Wisconsin Superior, and her Ph.D. specializing in literacy from the University of Illinois. She is a Professor of Education in the Department of Curriculum and Instruction at Ashland University, where she teaches undergraduate and graduate courses in literature for young adults, literacy theory, and methods for middle and secondary school teachers. She has presented at many national and international conferences on a variety of topics related to adolescent literacy; these include creative nonfiction, developing electronic literacy communities, culturally diverse literature, author studies, and changes in contemporary literature for young adults. Knickerbocker has published in the areas of critical literacy, postmodern literature, and the literary development of young adults, and she has been a longtime reviewer for the *Middle School Journal*.

Dr. Martha A. Brueggeman received a B.S. in Education from Valparaiso University, her M.Ed. in Special Education from Kent State University, and her Ph.D. in Education from the University of Akron; in addition, she completed work in literacy at Virginia Tech. She is a Professor Emeritus of Ashland University, having taught both graduate and undergraduate literacy courses there. Before teaching at Ashland, Brueggeman taught a variety of grade levels in both private and public schools. She has published in state and national journals, including *Literacy Research and Instruction*, *Journal of Reading*, and *American Secondary Education*, and has presented at national and international conferences including the Association of Literacy Educators and Researchers, International Reading Association, Midwestern Educational Research Association, and the United Kingdom Reading Association. Brueggeman is currently a member of the Central Ohio Regional Literacy Team, through which area universities and agencies work together to provide information and direction for state literacy initiatives.

Dr. James A. Rycik received a B.S.Ed. degree from Ohio University and M.Ed. and Ph.D. degrees from Kent State University. He was a middle grades reading specialist and language arts teacher in the Cleveland area for 20 years before going to

Ashland University, where he is a Professor of Education in the Department of Curriculum and Instruction. Rycik served for five years on the Commission on Adolescent Literacy of the International Reading Association and was one of the co-authors of the Commission's *Position Statement on Adolescent Literacy*. He is the editor of the journal *American Secondary Education* and is a member of the Editorial Review Board of the *Journal of Adolescent and Adult Literacy*. He has collaborated on three previous books on literacy, including *Teaching Reading in the Middle Grades* with Judith Irvin. Besides literature for young adults, Dr. Rycik's ongoing scholarly interests include inquiry literacy and the multiple literacies of adolescents.

Visit the "Literature and Literacy for Young Adults" Site!

Publishers are releasing new literature for young adults at an unprecedented rate. As a teacher, librarian, or other fan of this literature, you may find it challenging to keep abreast of promising new releases. The "Literature and Literacy for Young Adults" website (www.hhpcommunities.com/youngadultlit) that serves as a companion to this book will introduce you to new books and to quality books you might have missed.

On the site, you will find brief "book talks" about the many titles the authors continue to discover and identify as high quality literature for young adults. You will be able to search the reviews by genre, subject area (especially important for informational books and content area teachers), author, title, and book format (e.g., "graphic novel") to find titles suited to your needs and the needs of your students or patrons. These authors are experienced educators working with literacy and literature for young adults, ensuring that the books reviewed on the site are of high quality and suited to this audience.

Visit the site for more information about its features and content, and to explore!

Changing Literature, Changing Readers, Changing Classrooms

Literature for young adults is always evolving, constantly changing. Young adult readers, too, are constantly changing. This chapter defines contemporary young adult literature and describes its early history. We explore changes in the content and structure of contemporary literature and in the way it is marketed to young adults. The chapter discusses some characteristics of contemporary young adult readers and concludes by highlighting key elements of a contemporary literature classroom: teaching with diverse literature; encouraging a critical perspective; and incorporating graphic texts, technology, and film effectively.

FOCUS QUESTIONS

1. What is contemporary literature for young adults?

2. How has literature for young adults changed over the years?

3. How can teachers design instruction to most effectively support students' interactions with young adult literature?

DEFINING LITERATURE FOR YOUNG ADULTS

introduction

Defining literature for young adults seems like a good place to start, but determining what constitutes literature for young adults—compared to literature for children or literature for adults—isn't as simple as it might appear. Stephenie Meyer's *Twilight* books, for instance, have been listed as children's literature in *Publishers Weekly* (Roback, 2007), but they have also been included in a weekly list of literature popular with college students (*Chronicle of Higher Education*, 2009).

To distinguish literature for young adults from adult literature that teachers frequently select to be read in secondary school, Nilsen and Donelson (1985) defined young adult literature as that which children between the ages of 12 and 18 choose to read (p. 9). That definition is still widely accepted, but does it work with today's literature? Or, as Crowe (1998) suggested, should literature for young adults include only works written for and marketed to young adults? That would eliminate works by authors such as Bruce Brooks, whose *The Moves Make the Man* (1984) began as a novel for adults, or Robert Cormier, whose popular novels, including *The Chocolate War* (1974), were conceived for an adult audience but redirected by publishers.

Teachers need a definition of literature for young adults in order to select and recommend books for young adult readers, and we need to define it to clarify the scope of this book. Remember, however, that any definition needs to be flexible, even if it is a bit fuzzy.

Blurred Lines and Fuzzy Definitions

Marc Aronson, editor, author, and expert on publishing, points out that "young adult literature" is a paradox because it maintains its own identity even though it overlaps every genre of literature, from books for children to those clearly targeted to adults (2001). Picture books, for example, seem to be intended for children. Nevertheless, many contemporary picture books are so sophisticated and complex that this genre can no longer be seen as entirely for young children (Anstey, 2002).

The phenomenon of picture books for young adults may have begun with author Jon Scieszka and illustrator Lane Smith's *The True Story of the 3 Little Pigs* (1989). It was followed by their *The Stinky Cheese Man and Other Fairly Stupid Tales* (1992), which the American Library Association (ALA) selected as both a Caldecott Honor Book and one of the Best Books for Young Adults (Cart, 2001). The blurring of age boundaries continued with Brian Selznick's *The Invention of Hugo Cabret* (2007), a novel of over 500 pages with 158 black and white drawings. It won the highly prized Caldecott Medal, an award that has often been given to picture books intended for young children.

Tom Feelings' book, *The Middle Passage: White Ships/Black Cargo* (1995), was reviewed as an "adult book for young adults" (Hawkins, 1996). Except for the introduction, it is a wordless picture book of heart-wrenching black and white illustrations that depict the fate of captured West Africans as they were transported to lives of slavery. Clearly, young children were not the intended audience for this picture book.

The line between adult literature and literature for young adults is also blurry. Each year the ALA presents the Alex Award to ten books that were published for the adult market but appeal to readers ages 12 to 18. Sometimes sophisticated young adult novels such as *The Astonishing Life of Octavian Nothing, Traitor to the Nation* (Anderson, 2006), and *This Is All* (Chambers, 2006) are referred to as "crossover" novels because they also appeal to adults (Hunt, 2007). These books, written by well-established authors of young adult literature, have gained extensive literary recognition. They are long, complex in language and style, and sometimes indistinguishable from the best adult literary fiction (Hunt, 2007).

Who can categorize a work such as *The Book Thief* (Zusak, 2006), which was originally published in Australia as an adult book but marketed in the United States as a book for adolescents (Sutton, 2007)? What about *Emil and Karl* by Yankev Glatshteyn, a Yiddish language book written in 1940 and translated into English by Jeffrey Shandler in 2006? It may be impossible for readers to know for whom a novel was originally published, but it may not matter.

Definitions of literature for young adults are often fuzzy, partly because of who is doing the defining. Publishers, librarians, teachers, reviewers, and booksellers (Aronson, 2002) each have their own ideas as to what constitutes literature for young adults. Some definitions identify literature for young adults according to who *should* read it, while others focus on who actually buys it and reads it. There may be a considerable difference between the selections that adults make on behalf of adolescent readers and these readers' own preferences (Aronson, 2002).

Roger Sutton (2007) suggested that readers' choices should determine what constitutes literature for young adults, but he also pointed out that those choices change depending on the individual reader and the era. A definition that depends on readers' choices raises the question, "Which readers?" It seems apparent that the traditional 12–18-year-old range no longer describes contemporary young adult readers (Cart, 2004). Some young adults read literature published for an adult audience, and some adults read literature generally thought of as written for young adults. The increased number of multigenerational books has pushed the upper age of young adult readership to 25 (Cart, 2001), or even perhaps as high as 35 (Cart, 2004). Concurrently, the lower end of the age range is edging downward, partially due to the emergence of very sophisticated picture books.

One final source of fuzziness in defining literature for young adults comes from answering the question, "What is literature?" Lukens and Cline (1995) defined literature as that which can "provide pleasure and increase understanding," and they noted that literature for young adults will help them "to explore and to understand their own typical concerns" (p. viii). Literature can also be defined in terms of genres, the identifiable patterns of subject matter and form that are often used to categorize creative works. Most readers would readily name realistic fiction, historical fiction, folk tales, fantasy, and poetry as genres of literature. They might not be quite so unanimous about nonfiction, but works such as biographies, autobiographies, and historical accounts are certainly literature when they provide pleasure, understanding, and information to their readers. Readers might not agree at all, however, about some current works that do not fit any traditional genre.

When the International Reading Association (IRA) and the National Council of Teachers of English (NCTE) published their *Standards for the English Language Arts* in 1996, many teachers were puzzled by the statement that students should "read a wide range of print and non-print texts" (IRA/NCTE, 1996, p. 3). What, they wondered, was a text that had no print (and how does one "read" it)? In the years since then, however, the term has proved useful as a way to describe works in nontraditional forms such as wordless picture books and graphic novels, enhanced ebooks and multimedia/online sources, as well as "non-books," such as feature films and television shows. Nevertheless, these works are not universally accepted as literature, and although young adults may buy them and read them, they are not necessarily included in all definitions of literature for young adults.

Literature for Young Adults: A Contemporary Definition

We have chosen to use the term "literature for young adults" rather than the more familiar term "young adult literature" for the works that are described in this book. This reflects a decision to include not only the literature that writers, publishers, and translators have marketed to an audience of people who are not yet considered adults, but also literature written for adults that has found an audience with younger readers.

Although readers of young adult literature may range from age 10 to 25, or perhaps older (Cart, 2001; 2004), the readers we consider in this book are between 10 and 18. This reflects our dual focus on literary works and on the ways in which teachers can introduce readers in grades 4 through 12 to literature that matters to them.

We believe that the author's intended audience for a work, the demographic to which it is marketed, and the age range of those who buy and read it are all part of defining a work as literature for young adults. More importantly, however, we believe that such literature has at its center the voice and perspective of young adults. It may reveal the realities of their world or present avenues for escape and fantasy, but it connects with a reader's search for a sense of self, and it provides a way of knowing the world that transcends personal experience. Contemporary readers are diverse, with eclectic interests and tastes, so contemporary literature for young adults is eclectic and available in a multitude of formats.

Although we acknowledge that our definition, too, may seem fuzzy, it guided the writing of this book: **Contemporary literature for young adults** *includes print and nonprint works that bring pleasure and understanding to many readers between the ages of 10 and 18 by providing ways of exploring their own identities and of discovering their place in the contemporary world.* The majority of the works described in this book have been written during the 21st century, and many have characteristics that were not commonly found in literature for young adults written in earlier decades. We also have included literature written before the beginning of this century if it continues to resonate with young adults or if it is particularly useful for helping contemporary young adults connect to the world of literature or to the world around them.

CHANGING LITERATURE FOR YOUNG ADULTS

Literature for young adults is in a constant state of change (Aronson, 2001). A variety of influences have had an impact on both the content and structure of literature. The next section provides a brief overview of the history of literature for young adults beginning with the emergence of realism. Then we will explore three major trends that have shaped literature for young adults: the changing literary market place, postmodernism, and increasing diversity.

New Realism

Prior to World War II, the literature recommended to young adults tended to be either classic stories with a young protagonist, such as *Treasure Island* (Stevenson, 1883/1925) or escapist adventures such as the mysteries featuring Nancy Drew (originally published by Grosset & Dunlap beginning in 1930) or the Hardy Boys (created by Edward Stratemeyer in 1927), which bore only the slightest resemblance to the lives of actual adolescents. Arguably, contemporary literature for young adults began in the 1950s with the publication of the coming-of-age work *The Catcher in the Rye* (Salinger, 1951). Although published as an adult novel, it rapidly became popular with young adults. Its cynicism and frank language signaled the shift to a new realism that would later emerge in literature written specifically for young adults.

Realistic fiction became a dominant force in literature for young adults (Campbell, 2004) in the late 1960s, beginning with *The Outsiders* (Hinton, 1967), and continuing with *The Contender* (Lipsyte, 1967), and *Mr. and Mrs. Bo Jo Jones* (Head, 1967). In place of implausible adventures or minor conflicts with adults, the protagonists of these new books confronted poverty, violence, and teenage pregnancy, often with little or no support from parents who were either ineffectual or absent. In *The Pigman* (Zindel, 1968), for instance, teenagers John and Lorraine take turns describing the dismal relationships they have with their parents and narrating the story of the friendship they develop with elderly Mr. Pignati, who becomes a sort of surrogate parent to them.

As new topics appeared during the 1960s, a broader range of characters also emerged. In addition to *The Contender*, which focused on an African American young man in Harlem, *Sounder* (Armstrong, 1969) and *The Soul Brothers and Sister Lou* (Hunter, 1968) included people of color portrayed in difficult social and economic situations. John Donovan's *I'll Get There. It Better be Worth the Trip* (1969) marked the first novel for young adults with gay characters (Cart & Jenkins, 2006).

During the 1970s and 1980s, sometimes referred to as the "golden age of adolescent literature" (Nilsen, 1993), authors such as Robert Cormier, Walter Dean Myers, and Lois Duncan, to name only a few, wrote well-crafted and challenging literature for young adults (Owen, 2003). The plots took the form of *young adult problem novels*, dealing with social issues and coming-of-age situations. The authors mentioned above, as well as Judy Blume (see the Featured Author box), Paula Danziger, and M. L. Kerr, gave a voice to the issues and concerns of adolescents, and in return, some of them became celebrities.

Postmodern Influences: Disbelief and Experimentation

The end of World War II brought changes in attitudes, styles, and academic disciplines that are collectively referred to with the term **postmodernism** (Goldstone, 2004). The dominant attitude in postmodernism (Gregson, 2004) is disbelief. This disbelief is often reflected by a reluctance to accept the official version of what is true or the prevalent rules concerning how things must be done (Knickerbocker & Brueggeman, 2008). After witnessing the power of propaganda in Hitler's Germany and the devastation of war, many people developed an understandably suspicious attitude toward authority in the postwar era; thus arose the desire to throw off old ways of doing things in favor of experimentation. Postmodern ideas and attitudes became influential in adult art and literature, and they also were incorporated into literature for young adults.

By the 1960s and early 1970s, postmodern thought had influenced literature in three ways (Lambert, 2001). First, a distrust of the dominant culture led to increased attention to people who were outside the mainstream. The political effect of that increased attention was support for movements such as the civil rights movement and the women's movement. In literature, authors raised issues about cultural representation, so that multicultural and feminist literature proliferated and eventually edged into the school curriculum.

A second postmodern influence was an increasing use of media and electronic texts. As more and more people used and produced such works, the concept

Judy Blume

In many ways, Judy Blume is the author who best represents the golden age of literature for young adults. Beginning with *Are You There God? It's Me Margaret* (1970), Blume turned out a string of hit books that made her a superstar author on a scale that would not be matched until J. K. Rowling rocked the publishing world almost 30 years later. Blume has sold 80 million books, and her work has been translated into 31 languages.* Throughout the 1970s, Blume continued to produce novels such as *Then Again, Maybe I Won't* (1971) that reflected the sometimes stark realism of the golden age, even when they were set in nice suburban neighborhoods.

Blume's work illustrates the wide age range encompassed by literature for young adults. Her humorous books such as *Freckle Juice* (1971) and *Tales of a Fourth Grade Nothing* (1972) appealed to an audience at the lower end of the age spectrum. *Blubber* (1974) featured characters in the middle grades, but it was not at all humorous. It portrayed the cruelty that is all too common in middle schools. Jill, a typical fifth-grade girl, inadvertently brands her classmate Linda with the dreadful nickname Blubber. Once the damage is done, however, Jill finds her own status enhanced, and she must make some difficult decisions about what she values and who she wants to be.

Blume's books for older readers, including *Are You There God? It's Me Margaret* (1970), *Deenie* (1974), and *Forever* (1975), addressed topics of puberty and sexuality that were becoming more common but were still controversial in literature during the 1970s. She related a story, for instance, about some reactions to her first book:

> When *Margaret* was published in 1970, I gave three copies to my children's elementary school but the books never reached the shelves. The male principal decided on his own that they were inappropriate for elementary school readers because of the discussion of menstruation (never mind how many fifth- and sixth-grade girls already had their periods). Then one night the phone rang and a woman asked if I was the one who had written that book. When I replied that I was, she called me a communist and hung up. I never did figure out if she equated communism with menstruation or religion.

During the 1980s Blume continued to produce successful new books that dealt with serious personal and social issues. In *Tiger Eyes* (1981), a girl named Davey Wexler deals with the murder of her father during a robbery, and *It's Not the End of the World* (1972) portrays the emotional conflicts experienced by sixth grader Karen as her parents begin a divorce. Blume's willingness to address their real-life concerns resulted in an unprecedented popularity with adolescent readers. In return, she received hundreds of letters asking for her advice, some of which she published in *Letters to Judy: What Kids Wish They Could Tell You* (1986). The book has become part of an ongoing campaign by Blume to help children and adults communicate with each other (Notable Biographies.com, n.d.).

Media tie-ins to literature for young adults have become commonplace, but Blume was a pioneer in that area, as Fudge, a character in her five-book Fudge series, became a Saturday morning children's show in 1995 (IMDB, 2010). Blume was also a pioneer in creating a website that allowed her to share her writing process with readers. The website has also served as a vehicle by which she reacts to storms of criticism and censorship of her work. According to her website, Blume's belief in young people's freedom to read led her to edit the book *Places I Never Meant to Be: Original Stories by Censored Writers* (1999), and she has continued to work with the National Coalition Against Censorship.

*Except where otherwise cited, the author's website is our source.

of textuality expanded. *Text* no longer referred only to written words, but also to illustrations and other visual renderings. Today, the term *text* may refer to combinations of visual and written modes, as it does in product advertisement. It may also refer to the audio mode for a podcast or to the audio, visual, written, and gestural modes used with interactive multimedia games (Anstey & Bull, 2006).

Third, a general distrust of authorities led to less concern for the opinions of literary experts about the value of a work and more respect for readers' opinions. Roland Barth, a French literary theorist and cultural critic whose writings on postmodern literary theory greatly impacted U.S. thought, referred to this change as the decline or death of the author's authority over the literary process. For Barth, the question to ask of literature was no longer, "What does this mean?" but rather, "How does it work or function?" (Lambert, 2001). Less concern for the opinions of authors and other literary professionals widened the debate about what books should be included in the canon, the body of literature that is considered worthy of study and respect. Many began to question whether great works by women, members of minority groups, and non-Western authors had been overlooked.

Taken together, postmodern influences resulted in literature that is more aware of the underlying cultural assumptions of both authors and readers. It is also less bound to the "rules" of traditional genres as authors push the boundaries and challenge the reader's expectations of how literature, including literature for young adults, should look and how it should be read.

New Forms and Topics

The young adult problem novel that was so characteristic of the 1970s became less prominent as mass media such as talk shows, cable television, and the Internet began to offer teenagers other forums for exploring their concerns (Aronson, 2001). At the same time, other genres began to emerge. Nonfiction, for instance, has become increasingly diverse and important. Publisher Dorling Kindersley has introduced quality narrative or literary nonfiction that is enhanced by sophisticated use of visuals and written by accomplished authors such as Russell Freedman, James Cross Giblin, Milton Meltzer, and Rhoda Blumberg (Cart, 2001).

Multimodal and graphic texts

Disregard for the conventions of traditional genres has opened the door for creating new genres, particularly **multimodal texts** that combine the language

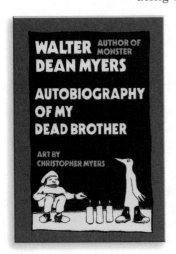

and structures of traditional genres with images and perhaps sound and links to online content, in the case of some ebooks. *Autobiography of My Dead Brother* by Christopher Myers (2005) combines comic strip art and realistic graphic novel-like illustrations with text written by his father, Walter Dean Myers. Each component, visual and textual, adds a layer of meaning in this multigenre work. Mark Schultz's *The Stuff of Life: A Graphic Guide to Genetics and DNA* (2008) uses black and white illustrations to inform readers about genetics in the context of the story of a scientist from another planet coming to earth to learn how to save his people.

Blue Lipstick: Concrete Poems (Grandits, 2007) is, as the title suggests, a book of poems told in text and drawing. The poem "Missing" is written on the various sides of a milk carton to illustrate a sleepy student's "missing" brain. The carton is labeled with "Stupor Farms,

2% Awake" and the company's logo, a sleeping cow. Other text on the carton includes "Missing: Have you seen Jessie's brain?," "Last known activity: Staying up all night instant messaging Lisa," a recent "drawing" of her brain and a computer simulation of what it looks like now, and "If you find this missing brain, contact Jessie immediately." Text printed next to the carton admonishes Jessie to wake up and eat her cereal. As with all the poems in this book, this poem requires both words and images to be understood.

Comics and **graphic novels** represent another major change in the content and form of literature for young adults. Graphic novels are "book-length comic books that are meant to be read as one story" (Weiner, 2003, p. xi). Graphic novels are not a separate genre; rather they are an art form that can be adapted to many story forms from realistic fiction to fantasy. *Maus: A Survivor's Tale* (Spiegelman, 1986), for example, is a graphic novel that is part memoir, part historical fiction, and part fable. The clear black and white drawings in this tale about surviving the Holocaust depict Jews as mice, Polish people as pigs, and the Germans as cats in a way that is personal, tragic, and moving. *Maus: A Survivor's Tale* earned a special Pulitzer Prize for literature in 1992. The popularity of the Maus books increased through the 1990s, and in some schools they became required reading (Gorman, 2003; Weiner, 2003).

More recently, *American Born Chinese* (Yang, 2006) was a finalist for the National Book Award in the young people's literature category, and it won the 2007 Michael L. Printz Award for excellence in young adult literature. It is not unusual for a book to receive more than one commendation, but it is newsworthy when a graphic novel wins a literary award, such as the ones mentioned above, that is not designated for graphic works. *American Born Chinese* focuses on three characters, a monkey called The Monkey King, a boy of Taiwanese parentage, and a TV-sitcom teenager. All three must come to grips with their own identities and the prejudice of others. The *Absolutely True Diary of a Part-Time Indian* (Alexie, 2007) also won a National Book Award. The story is told in text and 65 illustrations by Ellen Forney that add an important dimension of insight into the main character's struggles and successes.

Metafictive literature

Even a literary work for young adults that is recognizably a novel may deliberately break the rules of the genre. The plot may be nonlinear, or it may have no resolution. The setting may be unclear because multiple times and places are intertwined. Characters may be inconsistent or fluid, and their voices may have multiple and contradictory viewpoints. Multiple narrators might cloud the reader's interpretation of reality, and experimentation with form and structure may take precedence over any recognizable theme.

Many postmodern books employ stylistic devices that are sometimes labeled metafictive (Waugh, 1988). Unlike traditional fiction, which seeks to immerse readers in the story so they lose awareness of the act of reading, **metafictive literature** intentionally reminds them that they are reading and interacting with words, images, and other elements (Cashore, 2003). Pantaleo (2004) suggested that the reader of a metafictive novel should have a sense of "getting the inside joke" and an awareness of the ways in which the novel is playing with traditional beliefs and forms.

Understanding the stylistic devices that characterize postmodern literature for young adults can help teachers to appreciate these works and to guide their students to understand and appreciate them as well (Knickerbocker & Brueggeman, 2008). Some of the most important metafictive attributes are described in Chapter 3 and illustrated with examples from literature for young adults.

Increasing diversity in literature

Globalization has affected literature as much as it has other aspects of contemporary life. Books by non-Western authors are now commonly translated and published for the adult market in the United States and Europe. Another important influence on literature has been the postmodern "discovery" of minority cultures and of people who are poor and powerless. Contemporary stories often depict events from the point of view of cultural outsiders, those who live on the margins of society. These influences and others have combined to make literature for young adults increasingly diverse.

We will use the term **diverse literature** instead of multicultural literature to describe works that help readers to cross boundaries and see the world from new perspectives. This choice acknowledges that readers differ in many ways, including language, sexual orientation, and social position, as well as ethnicity or cultural background. In the following section, we identify some of the ways in which literature for contemporary young adults reflects the increasing diversity of its audience.

The number of English language learners in the United States has been steadily rising in recent decades. One approach of diverse literature is to offer the work in dual languages. *Sisters Hermanas* (Paulsen, 1993) tells the story of Traci, a girl from the suburbs, and Rosa, an undocumented Mexican. The same book contains both the Spanish and English versions; readers choose which end of the book is "up" and thus are able to read the language they prefer. Another approach is to provide a glossary of non-English words, such as those provided in *Red Hot Salsa: Bilingual Poems on Being Young and Latino in the United States* (Carlson, 2005) and *Buried Onions* by Gary Soto (1997). Books written in heavy dialects or those that have profanity may increase authenticity, but they may add a layer of interpretation and perhaps resistance for readers not familiar or comfortable with such language.

Diverse literature may portray unfamiliar worlds in unfamiliar ways. For example, lack of a common language plagues Adam, an Australian boy living in a fictional city in the Middle East, and Walid, a boy from Bangladesh, in *Camel Rider* (Mason, 2007). The story is told in alternating voices that intensify the cultural differences. Sarah Mussi's *The Door of No Return* (2007) is the story of an English teenager of African descent who travels to Africa to unravel the events leading to the death of his grandfather. Readers may be unfamiliar with England's history of slavery and surprised to learn of its similarities with the United States. Various formats are used to tell the story, including letters from lawyers, newspaper clippings, and old diaries.

Clashes of cultural identity may arise if a character experiences conflict concerning the differing values and beliefs of the various microcultures to which he or she belongs. For example, in *The Fold* (Na, 2008), a young girl of Korean descent considers plastic surgery on her eyelids to make herself look more "American," even though the boy she wants to charm is also of Korean descent. The title *Mexican White Boy* (2008) by Matt de la Pena describes Danny, who is a non–Spanish-speaking, half-white, half-Mexican boy struggling with his identity and his place in both sides of his family.

Sometimes cultural clashes are defined less by heritage or language and more by place and time. In *Homeboyz* (Sitomer, 2007), the main character comes from a middle-class, African American family. His dad runs his own business, and both older siblings are in college, but Teddy becomes enmeshed in the world of gangs after his younger sister is killed in a drive-by shooting. In this novel, the clashes of culture are steeped in socioeconomic status, reflected in language, and are also products of individual values and beliefs. Religious conflicts are at the center of *Does My Head Look Big in This?* (Abdel-Fattah, 2007). Fashion-conscious Amal decides to wear the hijab, the traditional head covering, and her more liberal Muslim family members discourage her from making this decision.

Sexual identity, as compared to sexual stereotyping, was broached as a topic in 2004 with Julie Anne Peters' *Luna*. *Luna* was the first novel for young adults that addressed transsexual/transgender issues (Cart & Jenkins, 2006). Between 2000 and 2004, 66 young adult titles with gay, lesbian, transgendered, and/or queer questioning content were published, compared to 70 titles from the entire decade of the 1990s (Cart & Jenkins, 2006). It is likely that interest in, and growth in the number of, GLBTQ titles will continue.

The Changing Marketplace

Changes in literature for young adults may reflect both lasting social change and temporary fashion trends, much like those in popular music and clothing. They may also reflect significant changes in the literary marketplace. Since the 1960s, businesses of all kinds have become increasingly aware of teenagers as a desirable market segment. Record companies and fashion designers may have been quicker to see the potential in this market and to capitalize on elements of youth culture, but the publishing industry has clearly launched its response. New genres have been developed for the youth market as have new ways of bringing literary products to the customer.

During the golden age, young adults discovered books featuring new voices and new perspectives, but the explosion of new titles for young adults was undoubtedly fueled in part by the availability of inexpensive paperbacks, often sold in schools through book club catalogs. By the 1980s, Scholastic book clubs began the large-scale packaging of paperback series (Nilsen, 1993). The Baby-sitters Club series (1986–2000) appealed especially to middle school girls. Romance series, most notably the Sweet Dreams books (1981–1996), followed by the Sweet Valley High Romance series, were also hugely popular (Aronson, 2002).

Series books have remained a mainstay of the market place. *A Series of Unfortunate Events* (Snickett, 2006), consists of 13 volumes relating the darkly comic tribulations of the Baudelaire orphans. The Joey Pigza books by Jack Gantos are another popular example. Beginning with *Joey Pigza Swallows the Key* (1998), the series tells how Joey learns to live with ADHD. He finds who he really is as he faces the threat of being put into a special education school and the challenge of reconnecting with the father who left him.

Like movie sequels, series books provide a publisher with a dependable audience. Multivolume works such as *The Chronicles of Narnia* (Lewis, 1950) have long been the norm in the fantasy genre, predating the massive success of the Harry Potter novels. Potter, in turn, paved the way for other franchise books, most recently Meyers' Twilight books and all of their vampire relations. Notice that all three of these franchises have been adapted for movies. Films, especially those with sequels, have in fact come to play a major role in the literary marketplace.

At times books deliver an audience for the movie, but just as often a successful film creates interest in the written story. *The Princess Diaries*, directed by Garry Marshall (2001), introduced many young readers to the book of the same name (2000) by Meg Cabot. Cabot credited the film with helping to create a demand for her books about Mia Thermopolis, an ordinary ninth-grader who finds out that she's a princess and must adapt to the sudden status change from student to royalty (Cabot, n. d.). The Princess Diaries series currently consists of ten books.

Writing has always been both an art and a business, but the connection between the creative process and the marketplace seems to be growing more obvious and more explicit. Well-established authors of adult books have been sought by publishers to write for the young adult audience (Cart, 2004). Ace Books, a mass-market fantasy publisher, for instance, did not wait for inspiration to strike an author in order to publish a set of full-length classic folktales. They commissioned a group of established writers of fantasy to create the Fairy Tale series (de Vos & Altmann, 1999). Ace highlights the trend toward selecting or even engineering literature that can be marketed to a target group of young readers. Although such commercialism may seem crass, it has resulted in an unprecedented diversity of form and content, as shown in the box on the facing page.

Literature for young adults, particularly those works with movie tie-ins, often are prominently displayed at commercial bookstores. Young adults can purchase books there or just sit and read a wide range of literature. They can also read a novel without ever touching paper by using ebooks and audiobooks. Google intends to digitize seven million titles over a six-year period, and both Stanford University and Oxford University have plans to digitize their respective libraries (Webb, 2007). These and similar developments should greatly broaden the number of works available for young adults and their teachers. With a few taps on the keyboard, readers can also locate extensive plot summaries, reader reviews, and even critical analyses. The marketplace has never been so friendly to readers.

Highlights in the Marketing of Literature for Young Adults

1990s

- MTV, a television network with an extensive young adult audience, begins publishing books geared toward their viewers (Cart, 2004).

- Fast-paced miniature novels (under 100 pages) are designed for the struggling high school reader to replace condescending "hi-lo" books with controlled vocabulary (Campbell, 2004).

- Crossover novels, such as Philip Pullman's *The Golden Compass* (1996), become bestsellers (Cart, 2004).

- Publishing houses establish imprints aimed at specific ethnic audiences; for example, Rayo, which publishes literature for the Latino market (Cart, 2001).

- Japanese comics or manga, such as Kamio's *Boys over Flowers* (1992–2003), particularly popular with preteen and teenage girls, emerge as a major area of graphic novels (Weiner, 2003).

2000s

- Self-publishing sites proliferate and result in well-known works such as *Beowulf* (Hinds, 2007) and *Eragon* (Paolini, 2003), later published by Candlewick Press and Knopf, respectively.

- Graphic Universe Line publishes *Graphic Myths & Legends* and *Twisted Journeys*—books that let readers pick from multiple plot outcomes (*Publishers Weekly,* 2009).

- Teenage authors such as Amelia Atwater-Rhodes, Christopher Paolini, and Flavia Bujor become popular.

- Through a co-publishing arrangement, Tokyopop adapts HarperCollins books into manga format (Kinsella, 2006).

- In *Dark Dude* (Hijuelos, 2008) Atheneum editors declare their commitment to publishing the "finest literature of Latino inspiration."

- HarperCollins (2009) promotes Lauren Conrad's *L.A. Candy* through a cell phone app. Books serve as publicity for movies; HarperCollins publishes Candace Bushnell's *The Carrie Diaries* (2010) to coincide with the release of the film *Sex in the City 2.*

- Harlequin launches an African American imprint, Kimani Tru, with Monica McKayhan's *Indigo Summer* (Pride & Reid, 2008).

- Scholastic creates book video trailers, dedicated book sites, and author blogs, and also develops a relationship with teens via social networking to market their books (Pride & Reid, 2008).

CHANGING READERS

*A*ll of these changes in literature for young adults are, to some extent, reflections of changes in readers. Contemporary readers of young adult literature are increasingly diverse. They have typically grown up in a culture that is saturated with media, and they have more ways of accessing print and nonprint text than any previous generation. As a result of all these factors, they also may have less patience with traditional literature than any previous generation. In this section, we will consider the characteristics of contemporary readers and their implications for teachers.

Reader Diversity

For readers as well as for books, we consider diversity to include the broad range of characteristics that show differences among young adults. These characteristics include race, ethnicity, and religion; language; socioeconomic status; gender and sexual orientation; and special needs. All individuals belong to several cultural groups that influence their values, beliefs, behaviors, and world views. For example, Jeff, a preservice teacher, is gay, politically conservative, and a science geek who grew up in a predominately Slovak community in an urban area. For Jeff, as for other young adults, elements of diversity do not function in isolation. They rather create a complex mix of characteristics that influence an individual's response to the world as well as to literature (Allan & Miller, 2005).

Digital-Age Readers

Dresang (1999) pointed to the "digital age," beginning with the influence of television in the 1960s and 1970s, as the driving force behind a change from verbal to visual communication. She contended that digital technology has changed both text and reader, resulting in a "societal landscape that has gradually emerged as computers have become more commonplace and as the Internet has become a locale where children can learn and play" (p. 6).

In the digital age, contemporary readers can engage with literature in expanded and altered ways. The Harry Potter books, for example, generated complex websites, online chat rooms, reviews, commentaries, and more. FanFiction (www.fanfiction.net/book) allows readers to create their own stories featuring their favorite characters. Harry Potter has close to 400,000 entries. Composition genesis websites allow readers to gain insights into the author's writing process (Unsworth, 2008). The official website of Stephenie Meyer (www.stepheniemeyer.com) links to a wealth of information. Links may include movie promotions, a list of the songs she listens to in her head as she writes, pictures of the cars mentioned in the novels, and links to fan sites, including some in German and French.

Like many author websites, Sharon Draper's site (http://sharondraper.com) provides access to her blog and Twitter feed. Draper, a former teacher, includes links to study guides, homework help, information on contacting her for school visits, and links to a site to buy her books. There is also a link to an IRA podcast, where readers can hear her talk about her work.

Students can now share their interests with a global audience. Social networking sites, discussion forums, online games, and interactive fan fiction provide opportunities for individuals to control their own identity they create for an audience (Williams, 2008). Blogs, originally thought of as online journals, can focus on books and authors in a school environment (Wang & Hsua, 2008). They also provide adolescents with an out-of-school venue for sharing their thoughts about anything they choose. The days of writing a response to literature for an audience of a teacher and classmates may soon be past. Literature is available in auditory, visual, and interactive formats and can be accessed and responded to through a variety of handheld and digital devices. Many of our students are already taking advantage of these choices, as shown in the following box.

Real-Life Examples of Electronic Access to Literature

- On a recent vacation Shanna told her family that she had to get her reading done for class. Because she was going to do a large part of the driving, they agreed to listen to *Copper Sun* (Draper, 2006), a book about slavery, while traveling.

- Alex was having difficulty with the formal style of *The Astonishing Life of Octavian Nothing, Traitor to the Nation* (Anderson, 2006) and checked out a CD from the library to listen to as he read along in the novel.

- Michaela lamented her forgetfulness because she failed to charge her laptop computer and therefore hadn't finished reading her novel.

- Danny prefers to do his reading on a tablet computer, which has a screen larger than his cell phone and looks more like paper than like a computer. The text-to-voice feature allows him to listen while he exercises.

- David downloads books from the library to his tablet computer. He especially likes the way it allows him to see the visuals in books in full color.

- Joe is confident that he has read a novel that none of his friends have read. The novel is from Online Originals (www.onlineoriginals.com), a publisher of ebooks that have not been previously available in any other format.

Contemporary Readers: New Challenges

Contemporary readers have an unprecedented access to a wide array of literary texts, from inexpensive paperbacks, to electronic downloads, to movies on television. That does not mean, however, that their teachers will not face challenges. The National Endowment for the Arts (NEA; 2004) reported a steady trend of decline in the percentage of Americans reading literature, from 56.9 percent in 1982 to 46.7 percent in 2002 (p. ix). The report concluded that

> Literature reading is fading as a meaningful activity, especially among younger people. If one believes that active and engaged readers lead richer intellectual lives than non-readers and that a well-read citizenry is essential to a vibrant democracy, the decline of literary reading calls for serious action. (p. ix)

Sadly, the most dramatic decline in literary reading is among those who have just left high school. Among 18-to-24-year-olds, the percentage who read literature dropped by 17 percent in just 20 years.

The Alliance for Excellent Education (2009) continually updates information regarding adolescent literacy at its website (www.all4ed.org/). Such information can help teachers understand the students they are teaching now and will be teaching in the future. Among low-income eighth graders, only 15 percent read at or above a proficient level. Minority and low-income students trail their peers by 22 to 28 percentage points on national reading and writing assessments. On average, African American and Hispanic twelfth-grade students read at the same level as white eighth-grade students. Over 10 percent of students enrolled in U.S. schools are English language learners who do not have adequate proficiency in English to succeed on their own in an English-speaking classroom.

Online technologies may have students reading and writing in ways they never did before, and perhaps they are reading and writing more than they were a decade ago (Williams, 2008), but those same technologies may contribute to a reluctance to read conventional text.

Teachers will encounter students who are avid readers, students who struggle, students who are unable to read English proficiently, and students who are able to read the literature in the curriculum but are unwilling to do so. It stands to reason that a changing population of readers will need a literature program that accommodates their increasingly diverse needs and interests. This means that both the literature that adolescents are asked to read and the ways they engage with that literature in the classroom may have to change.

CHANGING CLASSROOMS

I n 1999 the IRA published a *Position Statement on Adolescent Literacy* (Moore, Bean, Birdyshaw, & Rycik). It asserted that "Adolescents deserve access to a wide variety of reading materials that they can and want to read," and "instruction that builds both the skill and desire to read increasingly complex materials" (pp. 14–15). Similar principles were affirmed in a later statement issued by the IRA and the National Middle School Association (2001). The goals outlined in both statements suggested a need for change in many language arts classes where adolescents were limited to a fixed canon of classic novels and classroom activities that focused narrowly on traditional literary analysis and essay writing. Nevertheless, a gap persisted between the experiences provided for adolescents in school and in the media-saturated, technological, global world outside the school doors (Rycik, 2008).

The Common Core State Standards for the English Language Arts (National Governors Association Center for Best Practices, Council of Chief State School Officers, 2010) were not developed specifically for young adults, and they do not focus only on reading literature, but they do have an impact on discussions about what adolescents should be reading and what they need to learn. The Common Core State Standards (CCSS) endorse a broader view of literacy and literature that is consistent with ideas that have already been mentioned in this chapter, as is evident in the following:

> Students who meet the Standards readily undertake the close, attentive reading that is at the heart of understanding and enjoying complex works of literature. They habitually perform the critical reading necessary to pick carefully through the staggering amount of information available today in print and digitally. They actively seek the wide, deep, and thoughtful engagement with high-quality literary and informational texts that builds knowledge, enlarges experience, and broadens worldviews. (p. 3)

The CCSS include a description of range, quality, and complexity of materials that should be read in grades 6–12, which includes stories, poetry, and drama as well as literary nonfiction. The list of suggested texts that accompanies this standard, however, heavily favors British and American works written before 1980, and almost all of those works were written for an adult audience. Though these books have traditionally been part of the language arts curriculum, educators are likely to find that the many diverse forms and genres of text now available will also play an important role in developing skills as well as the motivation to read.

Throughout this book, keep in mind that in an ideal literature program all students will "experience a seamless curriculum that empower[s] them to grow increasingly fluent as readers, increasingly able to employ the strategies to interpret complex texts, and increasingly willing to read more challenging texts" (Knickerbocker & Rycik, 2002, p. 196). We advocate approaches that support contemporary readers and texts such as those identified in a Policy Research Brief from the NCTE (2007), which states that "Sustained experiences with diverse texts in a variety of genres that offer multiple perspectives on life experiences can enhance motivation, particularly if texts include electronic and visual media."

In the remainder of this chapter, we identify five elements necessary for effectively engaging contemporary readers with literature: teaching with diverse literature; using metafictive literature; encouraging a critical stance; integrating technology; and incorporating graphic, multimodal, and media forms of literature. We also present the first of many Classroom Scenarios, which are designed to help shape your approach to teaching and learning about literature.

Teaching with Diverse Literature

Bishop (1997) defined multicultural literature as "works that reflect the racial, ethnic, and social diversity that is characteristic of our pluralistic society of the world" (p. 3). This definition works as long as "social diversity" is broadly defined and given equal status to the other microcultures that influence our individual identities. Often, however, multicultural literature has seemed to focus only on the largest racial and ethnic microcultures in the United States: African American, Asian American, Latino, Jewish, and Native American. Other issues of diversity, such as poverty or gender, often seem to have been relegated to a lesser status.

Every minority group includes a wide variety of differences concerning family history, cultural customs, religious beliefs, and personality traits. Do not assume that matching a single cultural characteristic portrayed in a text, such as race, to a particular reader will guarantee that the reader will be receptive to the book. As explained earlier, we chose the term *diversity*, and not *multicultural*, to describe the broad range of differences between human beings and the literature that reflects these differences.

Many teachers hesitate to use literature from cultures with which they are unfamiliar or uncomfortable (Landt, 2006). Those same teachers may select literary works from the canon, however, such as *Beowulf* or a play by Chekov, without extensive knowledge of the culture that produced these works (Soter, 1999). Perhaps, then, it is not unfamiliarity that deters teachers from including culturally diverse literature as much as it is personal levels of discomfort. White readers sometimes resist the political messages in multicultural texts if those messages threaten their values and identities (Ketter & Lewis, 2001). White teachers may also feel resistance or wish to avoid making any of their students feel uncomfortable.

Resistance or avoidance may be particularly pronounced with literature about gender issues, but as many as two million adolescents are harassed each year for appearing to be gay, lesbian, bisexual, or transgendered (Kloberdanz,

2001). And while there are differences in reading preferences between boys and girls, one should not assume that all boys prefer nonfiction and graphic novels (Smith & Wilhelm, 2002) or that all girls like romance series. On the other hand, trustworthy information about reading preferences categorized by gender is readily available and can play a role in selecting or recommending literature. Many libraries sort books by popularity with boys or girls, as do commercial online bookseller sites. Teachers can also rely on their own reading and observations of their students to develop lists of books or authors likely to interest either the boys or girls in their classrooms. Aronson and Newquist, for example, made their target audience very clear in *For Boys Only: The Biggest, Baddest Book Ever* (2007).

Cultural authenticity, an issue related to cultural diversity, remains an often contested topic. Accepting only literature written by a member of the culture identified in a particular literary work is, in Kathryn Lasky's opinion, "a kind of literary version of ethnic cleansing" (cited in Hinton & Dickinson, 2007, p. 6). Russell Freedman responded to a question about the appropriateness of someone outside of a culture writing about that culture by saying that the message should not be confused with the messenger (Virginia Hamilton Conference, April 11, 2008). He pointed out that he had written about Crazy Horse; he isn't a Native American. He wrote about Marian Anderson; he isn't a woman. And he had written about Lincoln without being a Republican. The cultural authenticity of a work lies in the work itself, not the heritage or orientation of its author. Cultural authenticity and other issues relating to diversity in literature are discussed further in Chapter 4.

A metaphor of literature as both a mirror and a window has often been used to describe multicultural or diverse literature. The metaphor implies that such literature provides a way for readers to learn about both themselves and people unlike themselves. Galda (1998) acknowledged the usefulness of this metaphor but pointed out that a person looking through a window is likely to focus first on the world outside and only gradually become aware of his or her reflection. In the literature classroom, diverse literature certainly helps young people to understand people and places in worlds that differ from their own. Ultimately, though, such literature also helps them to understand themselves. Diverse literature should highlight the unique attributes of a character or community while also illuminating universal experience. Every genre of literature for young adults has culturally diverse characters and settings, and we will continue to discuss culturally diverse literature throughout this book.

Teaching with Metafictive Literature

The number of literary works with diverse characters, settings, and situations has increased, and so has the number of postmodern works containing metafictive characteristics. Taking pleasure in the challenge of postmodern literature depends on the reader's understanding and appreciation of its metafictive devices (Anstey & Bull, 2006). Metafictive devices are described in Chapter 3.

Instruction in the metafictive devices helps readers understand novels having these characteristics and also helps students develop concepts about authorship that apply to all literature. Because metafiction purposely "draws attention to the writing as an artefact in order to pose questions about the relationship between fiction and reality" (Waugh, 1988, p. 2), readers must consider the author's writing decisions in a direct way. Describing and evaluating the literary elements that are used in metafictive literature will help students understand these books, and it will help them understand, through contrast, how the fiction they typically read works.

An additional benefit of reading metafictive literature may be that students become more patient and strategic readers (Coles & Hall, 2001). A student's ability to tolerate ambiguity is fundamental to his or her growth as a reader (Meek, 1988; Spiro, Coulson, Feltovich & Anderson as cited in Pantaleo, 2005). Metafictive books create opportunities for students to work through a story that does not easily make sense, often by making them realize that their confusion was deliberately created by the author. Subsequent discussions can focus on both the cause of the confusion and how this makes them feel as readers (Philpot, 2005).

Puhr (1992) suggested that "sharing postmodern works with students makes them aware that fiction continues to evolve and authors continue to experiment, testing the limits of the novel's form and of their reader's intellectual acumen" (p. 66). Simply put, instruction in postmodern literature provides "literature to think with" (Geyh, 2003, p. 12). See the Classroom Scenario on p. 20 featuring discussions about a metafictive novel in an eleventh-grade English class.

When familiar schemata of how a book works, especially one written for young adults, fails to result in immediate understanding, our confidence as teachers may be threatened, and a common response is avoidance or dislike (Anstey, 2002). Teachers tend to choose books for students based on their own reading (McClay, 2000), so they need to consciously make an effort to read literature with metafictive elements. Literature with metafictive characteristics will be included throughout this book.

Teaching with a Critical Perspective

Postmodern attitudes of disbelief and suspicion about the source of information are sometimes referred to as taking a critical stance as a reader or simply as critical literacy. Definitions of **critical literacy** vary (Green, 2001), but a critical literacy perspective involves engaging readers with literature in a way that encourages them to examine beliefs about society and language. A critical perspective focuses on the ways in which texts are constructed in social, political, and historical contexts. Such a perspective encourages readers to consider the ways in which these contexts position both readers and texts and how these contexts influence, and even endorse, particular interpretations of the text (Serafini, 2003).

When focusing on critical literacy, select your choice of texts and instructional approaches with the goal of expanding your students' literary experiences beyond the surface of texts and individual reader response. Encourage students to explicitly consider the author's choices in constructing the text and how they, as individuals, are influenced during their reading (Bean & Moni, 2003). By doing this, some power is pulled away from the author and given to the reader,

classroom scenario

Text Discussions with a Metafictive Novel

AS YOU READ, consider how The Book Thief's *unusual narrative strategies have encouraged students to be conscious of the author's literary choices as well as the factors that influence their response to the work.*

In an eleventh-grade English class, students are reading *The Book Thief* (Zusak, 2006). Each day their teacher, Mr. Rey, invites them to react to what they have read, especially to those features of the novel that puzzle or bother them. Some students find the novel challenging because it defies their expectations. It is told in flashbacks and flash forwards, and students argue about this technique. Some of them get upset, for instance, when the narrator says that one particular character is going to be killed many chapters before it actually happens. They also question Zusak's use of Death as the narrator and his decision to include a separate "story within a story" written by a character in the novel. All these techniques contradict their previous experiences with narration.

One day a student named Elena notes that this is the first novel she has read about German villagers being victimized by the Nazis. This remark prompts a discussion regarding the perspectives that are

included and excluded in the novel. A girl named Alice remembers stories passed down in her family about German relatives fleeing Germany and the difficult time they had after coming to the United States. She tells about a relative living in the Midwest who was asked to sign a loyalty oath because the members of his family who had remained in Germany made his allegiance questionable. Jake, who is Jewish, says that the notion of innocent Germans is preposterous, and a brief argument follows that ends with the students talking about how their different backgrounds have influenced their responses to the novel.

Through their discussions about the text, the students identify some of the metafictive characteristics of the novel, such as its nonlinear plot and its nontraditional structure and format, and they consider how the author's choice of narrator and plot structure has affected their interpretations. When they finish reading the novel, Mr. Rey raises the question of the author's motives for writing it. He directs the students' attention to the short biographical note in the book and then instructs them to further investigate Zusak's background. They discover that his parents grew up in Nazi Germany and told him of the things they had seen. They saw Jews marched through towns on their way to concentration camps, but they also saw Germans helping Jews.

The students in Mr. Rey's class have taken a critical perspective by examining the social and cultural factors that influenced the author when he was creating the novel as well as the factors that influence their reactions to it. They also note how the novel stresses the importance of literacy and how that factor might impact a librarian's decision to buy it or a teacher's decision to assign it.

creating a more balanced relationship that allows the reader to go beyond the uncritical acceptance of the words on the page.

When teaching from a critical perspective, guide students to consider the motivation of the author; the devices the author uses to lead the reader's interpretation of the text in a particular direction, alternative perspectives to the author's, and perspectives independent from those in the text (Molden, 2007). Because books with metafictive characteristics are often deliberately constructed to make readers aware of the author's act of storytelling, such books are often particularly well-suited for teaching with a critical perspective. Critical literacy is also discussed in Chapter 12.

Integrating Technology into Teaching

Integrating technology into teaching with literature for young adults does not require a great deal of technical expertise or a large budget for hardware or software. It is more a matter of drawing students' attention to the many ways they can access resources that will support their understanding and enjoyment of literature. They can, for example, find extensive literary analyses on author, publisher, or bookseller websites. They can obtain author information from a multitude of sources through a quick online search. Fan fiction sites will encourage them to engage in dialogue about a literary work and even to rewrite scenes.

ClassBlogmeister (www.classblogmeister.com), a free interactive journal site designed for teachers, is a useful tool and a good place to begin exploring technology in teaching. Your ClassBlogmeister page can be kept private for you to use with a specific class, or it can be opened up to other classes and schools. Students can blog about a literary work with individuals who have self-selected or been assigned to participate in a conversation about a particular literary work. They can share original writing.

ClassBlogmeister also allows students to post podcasts, such as an audio broadcast of oral reading or a readers' theater production. Another possibility for opening up conversations about books is a wiki, a collection of web pages that allows anyone with access to add information or opinions for the rest of the community, or the whole Internet, to see (Spivy, Young & Cottle, 2008).

The possibilities for using technology to enhance the study of literature may seem endless, but some teachers have yet to integrate these resources into their classrooms. More examples of using technology as a tool for understanding and appreciating literature for young adults will be included throughout this book.

Teaching with Graphic, Multimodal, and Media Texts

We may not agree that "the centuries-long domination of texts and words in culture, particularly Western culture, has come to an end" (Mitchell, 1995, cited in Felten, 2008), but we do agree with Dresang (1999), who believes that the boundary between pictures and words has become less certain and that a greater understanding of the relationship of print and graphics is needed nowadays. Contemporary young adult readers are comfortable with nontext visual media, and they are generally at ease with reading the combination of words and pictures used in graphic-style formats (Gorman, 2003).

James Bucky Carter suggested that "There is a graphic novel for virtually every learner in your English language arts classroom" (2007, p. 1)—hesitant readers, gifted readers, and everyone in between—but visual and multimodal texts have made their way into the classroom mainly as scaffolds, as temporary support for later learning that is thought to be more difficult in terms of content and literacy requirements. They are seen as motivators and a means for enticing reluctant readers (Jacobs, 2007), but such a view does not acknowledge that reading a visual or multimodal text is an acquired skill.

We live in an image-saturated world, but as Peter Felten (2008) pointed out, this does not mean that students, let alone teachers, have developed a sophisticated visual literacy. He points out that being surrounded by images does not ensure an ability to interpret, evaluate, or create images any more than listening to music guarantees that listeners will critically analyze it or create their own.

We believe more emphasis should be placed on graphic novels as multimodal texts. Such texts can be thought of as "complex textual environments" (Jacobs, p. 22) that require a new and unique understanding of textual, visual, auditory, gestural, and spatial elements. Graphic novels are a means to help students engage critically with ways of making meaning that exist all around them (Jacobs, 2007). In Chapter 10 we focus on graphic novels and other printed texts that rely heavily on visual elements.

Teaching with Films in the Literature Classroom

People watch movies for the same reasons they read books: to vicariously experience a story. They critique a movie using criteria that are much the same as those that they use to judge a novel: the characters must be interesting and act in thought-provoking or interesting ways that create an emotional response. Films and novels share the literary devices of plot, characters, setting, themes, point of view, imagery, and symbolism.

In the classroom, films have been used as a reprieve from teaching, as entertainment, or as a reward, sometimes resulting in complaints from administrators and parents (Hobbs, 2006). Nevertheless, films in the classroom are a good idea if they are used effectively and purposefully (Vetrie, 2004). Films provide glimpses into our nation's past and other cultures of the world, resulting in increased understanding of history and culture. They are also excellent vehicles for teaching critical literacy when used to demonstrate how to separate fact from fiction and interpretation from reality.

Film excerpts can illustrate specific elements, or entire movies can help students understand the interplay of the literary characteristics (Teasley & Wilder, 1997). Film can illustrate traits particular to a genre. Foreshadowing and perspective used to create suspense are elements of classic Alfred Hitchcock movies. Some elements of fiction may be more readily understood through a visual medium. A film set in the 19th century, for example, can create a sense of setting that otherwise may elude a reader. Literary devices such as the flashback or self-reference may also be more apparent in film.

Students' familiarity with film may encourage them to engage in lengthier discussions and to consider the work beyond a literal understanding. They may feel more confident, motivated, and willing to consider concepts that had remained unattainable to them through written texts (Smilanich & Lafreniere, 2010). Students may be eager to learn about cinematic techniques so that they can better understand a favorite film or an adaptation of a required reading. The result may be a young adult audience that is more discriminating and conversant about what they view.

Teachers may hesitate to add film to their curriculum because they may feel unschooled in film language and techniques, or they may be concerned about ratings and censorship issues. Time is also a concern. The more movies watched, the fewer books read. Determining the most effective balance between written and visual texts, or deciding which movie is most appropriate for a particular purpose, can be daunting. Chapter 11 focuses on the content and form of film and how to connect it to print literature.

In the past few years, publishing companies have shown a renewed vigor in formatting and selling literature for the young adult audience. In the *ALAN Review* (2005) Jeffery Kaplan commented:

> Today, we face a plethora of young adult books that represent every conceivable genre and literary style. To be sure, we are on the precipice of reinventing ourselves because our young adult books are constantly in search of the new and revealing so that more and more young people will find their way to the delectable hallways of good and engaging reads. (p. 11)

The number of books appealing to young adults published each year has never been higher. Contemporary young adults reflect every conceivable combination of diverse backgrounds, reading abilities, and interests. The content and structure of their literature illuminates that diversity. Technology provides us with new avenues for accessing and engaging with literature. Reconsidering how we teach print and nonprint literature may help us more effectively bring young adults and their literature together. We hope that Michael Cart's declaration that we are in the midst of a new golden age of literature for young adults (2001) continues to be true. It is an exciting time to be a teacher of literature for young adults.

conclusion

BIBLIOGRAPHY OF LITERATURE FOR YOUNG ADULTS

Abdel-Fattah, R. (2007). *Does my head look big in this?* New York: Orchard Books.

Alexie, S. (2007). *The absolutely true diary of a part-time Indian.* (E. Forney, Illus.). New York: Little, Brown.

Anderson, M. T. (2006). *The astonishing life of Octavian Nothing: Traitor to the nation. Volume I, The pox party.* Cambridge, MA: Candlewick Press.

Armstrong, W. H. (1969). *Sounder.* New York: Harper & Row.

Aronson, M., & Newquist, H. P. (2007). *For boys only: The biggest, baddest book ever.* New York: Feiwel and Friends.

Beddor, F. (2006). *The looking glass war.* New York: Dial.

Blume, J. (1970). *Are you there God? It's me, Margaret.* New York: Dell.

Blume, J. (1971). *Freckle juice.* New York: Four Winds Press, 1971.

Blume, J. (1971). *Then again, maybe I won't.* New York: Dell.

Blume, J. (1972). *It's not the end of the world*. New York: Bradbury Press.

Blume, J. (1972). *Tales of a fourth grade nothing*. New York: Dutton.

Blume, J. (1974). *Blubber*. Englewood Cliffs, NJ: Bradbury Press.

Blume, J. (1974). *Deenie*. Englewood Cliffs, NJ: Bradbury Press.

Blume, J. (1975). *Forever*. Englewood Cliffs, NJ: Bradbury Press.

Blume, J. (1981). *Tiger eyes*. Englewood Cliffs, NJ: Bradbury Press.

Blume, J. (1986). *Letters to Judy: What kids wish they could tell you*. New York: Putnam.

Blume, J. (Ed.). (1999). *Places I never meant to be: Original stories by censored writers*. New York: Simon & Schuster.

Brooks, B. (1984). *The moves make the man*. New York: Harper & Row.

Bushnell, C. (2010). *The Carrie diaries*. New York: Balzer & Bray.

Cabot, M. (2000). *The princess diaries*. New York: HarperCollins.

Carlson, L. (2005). *Red hot salsas: Bilingual poems on being young and Latino in the United States*. New York: Holt.

Carroll, L. (1865, 1871, 2000). *Alice's adventure in wonderland and through the looking glass*. New York: Signet Classics/Penguin.

Chambers, A. (2006). *This is all*. New York: Amulet Books.

Conrad, L. (2009). *L.A. candy*. New York: HarperCollins.

Cormier, R. (1974). *The chocolate war*. New York: Pantheon.

Crutcher, C. (2005). *The sledding hill*. New York: Greenwillow Books.

Cullen, L. (2007). *I am Rembrandt's daughter*. New York: Bloomsbury Children's Books.

de la Pena, M. (2008). *Mexican white boy*. New York: Delacorte Press.

Donovan, J. (1969). *I'll get there. It better be worth the trip*. New York: Dell.

Draper, S. (2006). *Copper sun*. New York: Atheneum Books for Young Readers.

Feelings, T. (1995). *The middle passage: White ships/black cargo*. New York: Penguin.

Fields, T. (2007). *Holdup*. New Milford, CT: Roaring Brook Press.

Gantos, J. (1998). *Joey Pigza swallowed the key*. New York: Farrar, Straus and Giroux.

Glatshteyn, Y. (2006). *Emil and Karl* (J. Shandler, Trans.). New Milford, CT: Roaring Book Press.

Grandits, J. (2007). *Blue lipstick: Concrete poems*. New York: Houghton Mifflin.

Gruber, M. (2005). *The witch's boy*. New York: HarperTempest.

Head, A. (1967). *Mr. and Mrs. Bo Jo Jones*. New York: Signet.

Hijuelos, O. (2008). *Dark dude*. New York: Atheneum Books for Young Readers.

Hinds, G. (2007). *Beowulf*. Cambridge, MA: Candlewick Press.

Hinton, S. E. (1967). *The outsiders*. New York: Viking.

Hunter, K. (1968). *The soul brothers and sister Lou*. New York: Szebiench's Sons.

Kamio, Y. (1992–2003). *Boys over flowers*. San Francisco, CA: Viz Media.

Lasky, K. (2004). *Blood secret*. New York: HarperCollins.

Lewis, C. S. (1950). *The lion, the witch and the wardrobe*. New York: HarperCollins.

Lipsyte, R. (1967). *The contender*. New York: Harper & Row.

McKayhan, M. (2007). *Indigo summer*. New York: Kimani Tru Harlequin.

Marshall, G. (Dir.). (2001). *The princess diaries*. United States: Walt Disney Pictures.

Mason, P. (2007). *Camel rider*. Watertown, MA: Charlesbridge.

Mussi, S. (2007). *The door of no return*. New York: Margaret K. McElderry Books.

Myers, W. D. (2005). *Autobiography of my dead brother*. (C. Myers, Illus.). New York: HarperTempest.

Na, A. (2008). *The fold*. New York: G.P. Putnam Juvenile.

Paolini, C. (2003). *Eragon*. New York: Knopf.

Paulsen, G. (1993). *Sisters hermanas*. Orlando, FL: Harcourt Brace.

Peters, J. A. (2004). *Luna*. New York: Little, Brown.

Pinkey, A. D. (2011). *A bird in a box*. (S. Qualls, Illus.). New York: Little, Brown.

Pullman, P. (1996). *The golden compass*. New York: Knopf.

Salinger, J. D. (1951). *The catcher in the rye*. Boston, MA: Little, Brown.

Schultz, M. (2008). *The stuff of life: A graphic guide to genetics and DNA*. (Z. Canon & K. Cannon, Illus.). New York: Hill & Wang.

Scieszka, J. (1989). *The true story of the 3 little pigs*. (L. Smith, Illus.). New York: Viking Kestrel.

Scieszka, J. (1992). *The stinky cheese man and other fairly stupid tales*. (L. Smith, Illus.). New York: Viking.

Selznick, B. (2007). *The invention of Hugo Cabret*. New York, NY: Scholastic Press.

Sitomer, A. L. (2007). *Homeboyz*. New York: Hyperion Paperbacks for Children/Jump at the Sun.

Snickett, L. (2006). *The complete wreck: A series of unfortunate events, books 1–13.* (B. Helquist, Illus.). New York: HarperCollins.

Soto, G. (1997). *Buried onions.* New York: HarperCollins.

Spiegelman, A. (1986). *Maus I: A survivor's tale.* New York: Pantheon.

Stevenson, R. L. (1883). *Treasure island.* New York: Scribner.

Yang, G. L. (2006). *American born Chinese.* New York: First Second.

Zindel, P. (1968). *The pigman.* New York: Harper & Row.

Zusak, M. (2006). *The book thief.* New York: Knopf.

WEBSITES WITH ANNOTATIONS

Blume, Judy • **www.judyblume.com**

The author's official website, including summaries of works, personal writing tips, and resources for educators.

ClassBlogmeister • **www.classblogmeister.com**

A free interactive journal site designed for educators. A teacher's page can be kept private for use with a specific class or opened up to other classes or schools. Students are able to blog, share original writing, and post podcasts.

Draper, Sharon • **www.sharondraper.com**

The author's official website, including summaries of works, links to study guides, and information about school visits.

Encyclopedia of World Biography • **www.notable biographies.com**

Presents biographical sketches as well as information regarding the significance of the individual.

Fan Fiction • **www.fanfiction.net/book**

Allows readers to offer criticism of posted works or create new chapters for numerous titles.

Meyer, Stephenie • **www.stepheniemeyer.com**

The author's official website, including summaries of works, movie promotions, personal playlists, and links to fan sites.

Online Originals • **www.onlineoriginals.com**

A publisher of ebooks that have not been previously available in any other format.

REFERENCES

Allan, K. K., & Miller, M. S. (2005). *Literacy and learning in the content areas: Strategies for middle and secondary school teachers* (2nd ed.). New York: Houghton Mifflin.

Alliance for Excellent Education. (2009). Fact sheet: Adolescent literacy. Retrieved March 1, 2009, from http://www.all4ed.org/files/AdolescentsLiter.

Anstey, M. (2002). "It's not all black and white": Postmodern picture books and new literacies. *Journal of Adolescent & Adult Literacy, 45,* 444–457.

Anstey, M., & Bull, G. (2006). *Teaching and learning multiliteracies: Changing times, changing literacies.* Kensington Gardens, Australia: Australian Literacy Educators Association, and Newark, NJ: International Reading Association.

Aronson, M. (2001). *Exploding the myths: The truth about teenagers and reading.* Lanham, MD: Scarecrow Press.

Aronson, M. (2002, February). Coming of age: One editor's view of how young adult publishing developed in America. *Publishers Weekly,* 82–86.

Bean, T. W., & Moni, K. (2003). Developing student's critical literacy: Exploring identity construction in young adult fiction. *Journal of Adolescent & Adult Literacy, 46,* 638–648.

Bishop, R. S. (1997). Selecting literature for a multicultural curriculum. In V. J. Harris (Ed.). *Using multiethnic literature in the K-8 classroom* (pp. 1–19). Norwood, MA: Christopher-Gordon.

Blume, J. (n.d.) Judy Blume. Retrieved from www.judyblume.com.

Cabot. M. (n. d.). The princess diaries. Retrieved from www.megcabot.com/princessdiaries/about.php.

Campbell, P. (2004, January/February). The sand in the oyster: YA biblio-bullish trends. *Horn Book,* 61–65.

Cart, M. (2001). From insider to outsider: The evolution of young adult literature. *Voices from the Middle, 9*(2) 95–97.

Cart, M. (2004, December). Carte blanche: What is young adult literature? *Booklist,* 734.

Cart, M., & Jenkins, C. A. (2006). *The heart has its reasons: Young adult literature with gay/lesbian/queer content, 1969-2004.* Lanham, MD: Scarecrow Press.

Carter, J. B. (2007). *Building literacy connections with graphic novels page by page, panel by panel.* Urbana, IL: National Council of Teachers of English.

Cashore, K. (2003). Humor, simplicity, and experimentation in the picture books of Jon Agee. *Children's Literature in Education, 34*(2), 147–181.

Chronicle of Higher Education. (2009, January 9). What they're reading on college campuses. *Chronicle of Higher Education, 55*(18), A6.

Coles, M., & Hall, C. (2001). Breaking the line: New literacies, postmodernism and the teaching of printed text. *Reading Literacy and Language, 35*(3), 111–114.

Crowe, C. (1998). What is young adult literature? *English Journal, 88*(1), 120–122.

de Vos, G., & Altmann, A. (1999). *New tales for old: Folktales as literary fictions for young adults.* Englewood, CO: Libraries Unlimited.

Draper, S. (n.d.). Welcome to Sharon Draper. Retrieved from www.sharondraper.com.

Dresang, E. (1999). *Radical change: Books for youth in a digital age.* New York: H. W. Wilson.

Felten, P. (2008, November/December). Visual literacy. *Change, 40*(6), 60–64.

Galda, L. (1998). Mirrors and windows: Reading as transformation. In T. E. Raphael & K. H. Au (Eds.), *Literature-based instruction: Reshaping the curriculum* (pp. 1–12). Norwood, MA: Christopher-Gordon.

Geyh, P. E. (2003). Assembling postmodernism: Experience, meaning, and the space in between. *College Literature, 30*(2), 1–29.

Goldstone, B. P. (2004). The postmodern picture book: A new subgenre. *Language Arts, 87*(3), 196–204.

Gorman, M. (2003). *Getting graphic: Using graphic novels to promote literacy with preteens and teens.* Worthington, OH: Linworth.

Green, P. (2001). Critical literacy revisited. In H. Fehring & P. Green (Eds.), *Critical literacy: A collection of articles from the Australian Literacy Educator's Association.* Newark, DE: International Reading Association.

Gregson, I. (2004). *Postmodern literature.* London: Arnold.

HarperCollins. (2009, June). Corporate press release. Retrieved from www.harpercollins.com.footer/release.aspx?id+802&b=&year=2009.

Hawkins, B. (1996, February). Review of The Middle Passage: White Ships Black Cargo. *School Library Journal, 42*(2), 132.

Hinton, K., & Dickinson, G. K. (2007). *Integrating multicultural literature in libraries and classrooms in secondary schools.* Columbus, OH: Linworth.

Hobbs, R. (2006). Non-optimal uses of video in the classroom. *Learning, Media and Technology, 31*(1), 35–50.

Hunt, J. (2007, May/April). Redefining the young adult novel. *Horn Book,* 141–147.

International Reading Association & the National Council of Teachers of English (1996). *Standards for English language arts.* Newark, DE: Author.

International Reading Association & the National Middle School Association (2001). *Supporting young adolescents' literacy learning: A position paper jointly adopted by International Reading Association and National Middle School Association.* Newark, DE: Author.

Internet Movie Database (2010). *Fudge.* Retrieved from http://www.imdb.com/title/tt0111971/.

Jacobs, D. (2007). More than words: Comics as a means of teaching multiple literacies. *English Journal, 96*(3), 19–25.

Kaplan, J. S. (2005, Winter). Young adult literature in the 21st century: Moving beyond traditional constraints and conventions. *ALAN Review,* 11–18.

Ketter, J., & Lewis, C. (2001). Already reading texts and contexts: Multicultural literature in a predominately white rural community. *Theory into Practice, 40*(3) 175–183.

Kinsella, B. (2006, May). Diversifying: Tokyopop launches teen prose line. *Publishers Weekly,* 8.

Kloberdanz, K. (2001, September/October). Out on the shelf. *Book,* 90–91.

Knickerbocker, J. L., & Brueggeman, M. A. (2008). Making room on the shelf: The place of postmodern young adult novels in the curriculum. *American Secondary Education, 37*(1), 65–79.

Knickerbocker, J. L., & Rycik, J. (2002). Growing into literature: Adolescents' literary interpretation and appreciation. *Journal of Adolescent and Adult Literacy, 46,* 186–208.

Lambert, G. (2001). Literature studies. In *The Encyclopedia of Postmodernism* (pp. 227–230). London: Routledge.

Landt, S. M. (2006). Multicultural literature and young adolescents: A kaleidoscope of opportunity. *Journal of Adolescent & Adult Literacy, 49,* 690–697.

Lukens, R. J., & Cline, R. K. (1995). *A critical handbook of literature for young adults.* New York: HarperCollins College.

McClay, J. K. (2000). "Wait a second . . .": Negotiating complex narratives in Black & White. *Children's Literature in Education, 31*(2), 91–106.

Meyer, S. (n.d.). Official Website of Stephenie Meyer. Retrieved from http://www.stepheniemeyer.com.

Mitchell, W. J. (1995). *Picture theory: Essays on verbal and visual representation.* Chicago, IL: University of Chicago Press.

Molden, K. (2007). Critical literacy, the right answer for the reading classroom: Strategies to move beyond comprehension for reading improvement. *Reading Improvement, 44*(1), 50–56.

Moore, D. W., Bean, T. W., Birdyshaw, D., & Rycik, J. A. (1999). *Adolescent literacy: A position statement for the Commission on Adolescent Literacy of the International Reading Association.* Newark, NJ: International Reading Association.

National Council of Teachers of English (2008). *NCTE Position Statement. The NCTE definition of 21st century literacies.* Retrieved from www.ncte.org/positions/statements/21stcentdefinition.

National Council of Teachers of English (2007). *Adolescent literacy: A policy research brief.* Urbana, IL: Author.

National Governors Association Center for Best Practices, Council of Chief State School Officers (2010). *Common core state standards for English language arts & literacy in history/social studies, science, and technical subjects.* Washington DC: Author.

National Endowment for the Arts (2004, June). *Reading at risk: A survey of literary reading in America.* Retrieved June 10, 2009, from http://www.nea.gov/pub/ReadingAtRisk.

Nilsen, A. P. (1993). Big business, young-adult literature, and the Boston Pops. *English Journal, 82*(2), 70–75.

Nilsen, A. P., & Donelson, K. L. (1985). *Literature for today's young adults* (2nd ed.). Glenview, IL: Scott, Foresman.

NotableBiographies.com (n.d.). Judy Blume biography. Retrieved from www.notablebiographies.com/Be-Br/Blume-Judy.html.

Owen, M. (2003, March). Developing a love of reading: Why young adult literature is important. *Orana,* 11–17.

Pantaleo, S. (2004). The long, long way: Young children explore the fabula and syuzhet of shortcut. *Children's Literature in Education, 35*(1), 1–20.

Pantaleo, S. (2005). Young children engage with the metafictive in picture books. *Australian Journal of Language and Literacy, 28*(1), 19–37.

Philpot, D. K. (2005). Children's metafiction, readers, and reading: Building thematic models of narrative comprehension. *Children's Literature in Education, 36*(2), 141–159.

Pride, F., & Reid, C. (2008, December), More and better books for black teens. *Publishers Weekly, 255*(49), 28–32.

Publishers Weekly (2009, March). Comics grow at graphic universe, 256(9), 8–9.

Puhr, K. M. (1992). Postmodernism for high-school students. *English Journal, 81*(1), 64–66.

Roback, D. (2007, September). Children's series best sellers. *Publishers Weekly,* 20.

Rycik, J. A. (2008). Secondary education news & views: A decade of adolescent literacy. *American Secondary Education, 27*(1), 62–64.

Serafini, F. (2003, February). Informing our practice: Modernist, transactional, and critical perspectives on children's literature and reading instruction. *Reading Online, 6*(6). Retrieved from www.readingonline.org/article/art_index.asp?HREF=serafini/index.html.

Smilanich, B., & Lafreniere, N. (2010). Real time teaching. Reel teaching = real learning: Motivating reluctant students through film studies. *Journal of Adolescent and Adult Literacy, 53,* 604–606.

Smith, W. W., & Wilhelm, J. D. (2002). *Reading don't fix no Chevys: Literature in the lives of young men.* Portsmouth, NH: Boynton/Cook.

Soter, A. O. (1999). *Young adult literature and the new literary theories.* New York: Teachers College Press.

Spivy, M., Young, D., & Cottle, A. (2008). Bridging the digital divide: Successes and challenges in the implementation of 21st century skills. In K. McFerrin (Ed.), *Proceedings of Society for Information Technology and Teacher Education International Conference* (1534–1539). Chesapeake, VA: Society for Information Technology and Teacher Education.

Sutton, R. (2007, May/June). Problems, paperbacks, and the Printz: Forty years of YA books. *Horn Book,* 231–243.

Teasley, A., & Wilder, A. (1997). *Reel conversations: Reading films with young adults.* Portsmouth, NH: Heinemann.

Vetrie, M. (2004). Using film to increase literacy skills. *English Journal, 93*(3) 39–44.

Unsworth, L. (2008). Multiliteracies, e-literature and English teaching. *Language and Education, 22*(1), 62–75.

Wang, S., & Hsua, H. (2008). Reflections on using blogs to expand in-class discussion. *TechTrends, 52*(3), 81–85.

Waugh, P. (1988). *Metafiction. The theory and practice of self-conscious fiction.* London: Routledge.

Webb, A. (2007). Digital texts and the new literacies. *English Journal, 97*(2), 83–88.

Weiner, S. (2003). *Faster than a speeding bullet: The rise of the graphic novel.* New York: Nantier, Beall, Minoustchine.

Williams, B. (2008). Tomorrow will not be like today: Literacy and identity in a world of multiliteracies. *Journal of Adolescent & Adult Literacy, 51,* 682–686.

CHAPTER TWO

Bringing Young Adults and Literature Together

chapter overview

This chapter explores strategies teachers can use for choosing young adult literature and for bringing readers together with those books. First, we identify three broad criteria for book selection: developmental, social, and literary significance. Next, we describe typical stages in the development of literary appreciation and identify ways to support that development. We provide five different classroom "literacy routines"; each of these broad approaches for organizing instruction provides a unique environment for guiding students' interactions with literary texts. We examine tools teachers can use for gathering needed information about students. The chapter concludes with a discussion of issues related to censorship.

FOCUS QUESTIONS

1. What criteria should teachers and librarians use in selecting appropriate literature for young adults?
2. What professional resources and techniques can they use to select appropriate literature?
3. How can they support the development of young adults' appreciation for literature?
4. How can teachers organize instruction so that diverse groups of students can engage successfully with a wide range of literature?

introduction

In the previous chapter we pointed out that young adults have many new ways to access literature, so they are less dependent on librarians and teachers than they once were. That does not mean, however, that all students in middle school and high school are ready to navigate the media marketplace or to use online networks of readers in order to find the literature that is right for them. A study by Hughes-Hassell and Rodge (2007) showed that at that time most students were still getting their reading materials from three primary sources: the school library, the public library, and the classroom. These findings suggest that if students don't get their books at school they might not get them at all.

Some young adults may be prepared to choose books with little or no guidance, but many will need a "matchmaker," someone who knows a wide range of literature for young adults and also understands the interests and needs of adolescents. Unfortunately, there is troubling evidence that many students are failing to find compatible books in their English classes. Numerous studies summarized by Lenters (2006) suggest that a lack of interest in the reading materials that are provided for adolescents is resulting in widespread resistance to reading.

Research by Reeves (2004) revealed that students go to great lengths to avoid reading assigned materials, often substituting study aids and film versions in place of reading to pass tests. Guthrie and Davis (2003) found that, even in the middle grades, many students have disengaged from the literacy curriculum in school. Similar to Reeves' findings, their study indicates that young adolescent students are already reading passively or trying to avoid reading altogether. Fifth grade students in the study noted that their opportunities to make choices in their reading were decreasing and that few of their English language arts teachers used a variety of texts for instruction.

All teachers hope to inspire in their students a lifelong love affair with books. This chapter explores effective matchmaking by examining ways to pick the right books, to make introductions that successfully break the ice, and to guide young readers into meaningful and satisfying relationships with books.

SELECTING LITERATURE FOR YOUNG ADULTS

Teachers do not always have complete control over the literature they use in their classrooms, but they should be prepared to use whatever influence they do have to advocate for the best possible selections for their students. Thinking about the qualities of appropriate literature is also a way to rediscover the value of the literature that is already in the classroom. In their *Standards for the English Language Arts* (1996), the IRA and the NCTE suggest criteria for selecting literature for classroom study:

> In choosing texts, teachers and students should consider relevance to students' interests and other readings; relevance for students' roles in society and the workplace; literary quality; and balance and variety in form, style, and content. Complexity is another important criterion. Students benefit from reading texts that challenge and provoke them; they also benefit from simpler texts that promote fluency. (p. 28)

Rycik and Irvin (2005) emphasize that the literature young adults engage with in the classroom should have three kinds of significance: developmental, social, and literary. These three characteristics overlap, as shown in Figure 2.1, but we

Criteria for selecting literature for young adults.

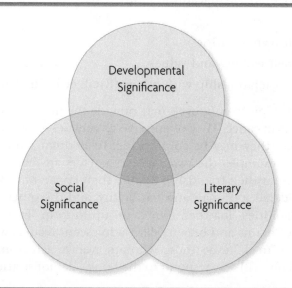

will examine them separately in order to show their implications for choosing and using literature. It is important to remember, however, that in truly excellent literature the three kinds of significance interact to provide a literary experience that is both pleasurable and memorable for young adult readers.

One approach that teachers and others can take to find likely matches for their students is to seek out works that have received awards recognizing their merit. We describe various awards and list winning titles in Appendix A, but in this chapter we connect a few of the awards to each type of significance. Many of the awards, it should be noted, can certainly be placed on more than one list.

Developmental Significance

Obviously, young adults have a lot going on in their lives (Lounsbury, 2009). In addition to rapid and often disconcerting physical changes, they face an evolving relationship with their parents, new expectations from other adults, increased academic demands, and the challenge of renegotiating their roles and status in relation to peers of both sexes. Adolescents seem unlikely to value anything unless it connects with this pressing agenda; literature for young adults, however, has a great potential to make the connection. Cart (2008) notes that,

> [The value of literature for young adults] is to be found in how it addresses the needs of its readers. . . . By addressing these needs, young adult literature is made valuable not only by its artistry but also by its relevance to the lives of its readers. And by addressing not only their needs but also their interests, the literature becomes a powerful inducement for them to read, another compelling reason to value it. (p. 2)

Literature for young adults that makes a successful connection to the common interests and concerns of adolescents has **developmental significance.** In particular, developmentally significant literature usually provides opportunities for readers to:

- Explore their own identities
- Reflect on their feelings and values
- Consider their relationship with others (Rycik & Irvin, 2005, p. 138).

Contemporary "problem" novels may provide the most obvious examples of developmental significance. They often serve as vehicles for adolescents to work through the issues they may be confronting. In Rodman Philbrick's *Freak the Mighty* (1993), for example, the two main characters are both outcasts, which becomes the basis for their friendship despite their apparent differences. One of the boys is considered too small and too brainy, and the other is too large and has learning disabilities. Together, they team up to form "Freak the Mighty," a perfect mixture of brains and brawn. Many adolescent readers will relate to the feeling of being a "freak," even those who are average achievers in school and typical in size. Many will also respond to the book's demonstration of the power of friendship.

Readers can find developmental significance in many kinds of literary works. Nonfiction such as Anne Frank's *The Diary of a Young Girl* (1947/2001), for instance, allows readers to explore identity by considering how they might measure up to the challenges faced by young people in the past, and fantasy novels often speak to an adolescent's desire to do great things in the world. Although they are more likely to be associated with time traveling or epic battles, many fantasy novels touch on the changing family dynamics that are common in adolescence. In Madeleine L'Engle's fantasy *A Wrinkle in Time* (1962), for instance, 12-year-old Meg comes to see her father as a person with limitations, and she begins to feel more love and responsibility for her younger brother.

Cart (2008) argues that literature can help young adults to find role models, construct a personal philosophy, and develop a realistic picture of the world that equips them for impending adulthood and citizenship. Literature can also be a way for adolescents to clarify their values and, perhaps, to consider potential careers. Jon Skovron's *Struts & Frets* (2009), for instance, focuses on a young man considering a career in music. Skovron's protagonist, Sammy, wants to be a rock star but must deal with an unsupportive mom who wants him to go to college, a floundering band, a changing relationship with his best friend, and the increasing dementia of his musician grandfather. An on-the-air music competition goes badly, but when encouraged to play at an open mike night, Sammy comes to realize that it isn't fame he wants but rather the chance to keep playing. He decides that college could be a place to learn more about music. The novel includes a bonus playlist that can serve as the soundtrack for the book.

Although adolescents may need to work through some general developmental issues, teachers cannot assume that their students will readily engage with any story that focuses on young adult characters or problems. The identity of a particular individual consists of much more than his or her age group. Like all people, young adults may actually be thought of as having multiple identities. They are sons or daughters, boyfriends or girlfriends, artists or athletes, members of a religious or ethnic group. Each of these identities may affect their views about literature or their interest in a particular literary work.

Nevertheless, teachers should be aware of some general developmental patterns that have emerged from decades of research on young adults' reading interests. G. Robert Carlsen's research (1980) revealed that early adolescents, ages 11 to 14, like to read about animals, adventures, mysteries, sports, the supernatural, fantasy, stories set in the past, stories about home and family, and stories about coming of age in other cultures. Middle adolescents, ages 15 and 16, select nonfiction, historical novels, adventure, romance, and stories of adolescent life. Late adolescents, around 17 and 18 years old, select literature that focuses on personal values, social questions, strange experiences and unusual circumstances, and the transition to adulthood.

More recent research by Hopper (2005) indicates that the patterns of students' leisure reading have remained relatively stable over the decades, although, of course, the actual books have changed. This study also shows, however, that other factors besides their age are involved in determining what they find interesting. Hooper found that adolescents typically pick books their peers have enjoyed, which validates reading as a peer group cultural experience. This suggests that interest depends, in part, on who else is in the room.

A study of the leisure reading of urban adolescents (Hughes-Hassell & Rodge, 2007) confirmed previous research by reporting that 72 percent of the primarily Latino and African American students surveyed engaged in reading as a leisure activity and that female adolescents read more than males. The study did, however, report some interesting differences from earlier research. In previous studies, girls indicated a preference for realistic fiction, mystery, and fantasy, while boys preferred adventure and action texts. In this study, gender differences were much less pronounced. Both genders expressed an interest in reading about other adolescents, and both females and males showed a strong preference for magazines. Their least favorite topic was historical figures.

A great variety of compiled reading lists, including lists of books that have won awards and honors, serve to guide teachers toward books with developmental significance. Here are a few such lists:

- **Young Adult Library Services Association (YALSA) Teens' Top Ten and the IRA's Young Adults' Choices** reading lists both involve young adults in identifying the works that are recognized. The works selected for these lists include both fiction and nonfiction across a wide range of topics. Adolescents connect to them and recommend them to other adolescents. Among the books on these lists are *Wintergirls* (2009) by Laurie Halse Anderson, a book about the pressures girls face to be thin, and *Identical* (2008) by Ellen Hopkins, which deals with the darker side of family relationships. Both books, which are discussed more fully in Chapter 4, are examples of novels that address issues that often surface in the teen years.

- **YALSA's Alex Award** was established in 1998 to recognize literature written for adults that has special appeal for young adults. The award reflects the organization's understanding that many young adults are developmentally ready to read contemporary adult literature. Reading literature that is intended for adults may facilitate adolescents' transition into the adult world. *The Talk-Funny Girl: A Novel* by Roland Merullo (2011) is about 17-year-old Marjorie who lives in rural New Hampshire. She has been isolated from society, abused by her family, and speaks a strange dialect. With the help of a relative she is able to escape. She finds the courage and resilience to meet the challenges of a different life.

- **YALSA's Quick Picks for Reluctant Young Adult Readers** is a list of fiction and nonfiction titles that have the potential to encourage young adults who do not usually care for reading. Quick Pick titles are not typically structurally or stylistically complex, but they all contain themes that appeal to teenagers' emotions. Paul Volponi's *Rikers High* (2010), a story about a boy in jail, and *Sex: A Book for Teens: An Uncensored Guide to Your Body, Sex, and Safety* (2010), a nonfiction book by Nikol Hasler, were selected as Quick Picks.

Social Significance

The IRA/NCTE Standards for the English Language Arts (1996) note that reading literature can offer students "perspectives which may contrast and conflict with their own experiences and invite them to reflect critically on alternate ways of knowing and being" (p. 29). Literary works that are especially likely to give the reader new perspectives about society and its diverse members have **social significance.**

Paolo Friere developed an entire approach to teaching and learning literacy by focusing on literacy as a tool for empowering individuals who had been forced by poverty into the margins of society. His philosophy is often summarized by the statement that literacy requires "reading the world" as well as "reading the word" (Friere & Macedo, 1987). Literary works with social significance can help students to become better world readers. The characters, conflicts, and themes that are explored in such works provide substance that will inform and challenge adolescents' understandings of the world and of their place in it. A socially significant work will generally have some or all of the following characteristics:

- Draws attention to issues of power and powerlessness
- Helps readers to see the perspective of individuals or cultural groups who are unlike themselves
- Helps readers to identify ways of promoting justice and equity
- Engages readers emotionally in ways that can help them take action.

Literary works that include minority characters or cultures often meet the criteria of social significance, as long as the characters play a significant role in the story and the cultural setting is more than just a backdrop. Walter Dean Myers' *The Beast* (2003), for example, is a novel that explores both the tensions that are associated with being a member of a cultural minority and the horrors associated with drug abuse. Anthony, known as "Spoon," comes home after four months at an exclusive prep school and is shocked to find his girlfriend, Gabi, once a vivacious, aspiring poet, has become a thin, wasted drug addict. She has lost her way in the world and fallen victim to "the Beast."

In literature classes, books with social significance are particularly well suited to the critical literacy stance that we described in Chapter 1. Powell, Cantrell, and Adams (2001) point out that critical literacy actually has the potential to promote a more democratic society.

> Literacy instruction in a democracy ought to help students to communicate effectively with all persons in a multicultural society and to see the value of literacy for their own lives and for social, political, and economic transformation. We would argue that a democratic agenda requires a critical literacy—one that acknowledges the differentials or power in society and seeks to realize a more equitable, just, and compassionate community. (p. 77)

Critical literacy may involve disapproval or disappointment with one's own culture, but a critical literacy approach is more about raising questions than feeling guilty or assigning blame. In almost any social group, some people have more influence, possessions, or privileges than others. The members of the group may or may not be content with these differences, but they should be aware of them. Literature with social significance can help raise that awareness.

Many awards are given for literature with social significance. Some of these specify a culture or type of diversity. These awards help teachers identify works that genuinely engage readers with other cultures or with significant social issues. The following awards and books demonstrate the wide range of socially significant literature for young adults. (Appendix A includes lists of additional awards based on specific cultural considerations, including the Pura Belpré Award, the Arab American Book Award, and the American Indian Youth Services Literature Award.)

- **The Coretta Scott King Book Award,** first awarded in 1970, is given to African American authors and illustrators. Rita Williams-Garcia was the recipient of the 2011 author award for *One Crazy Summer* (2010). The Black Panthers, hippies, political unrest, and social change frame the setting of this story of three young sisters visiting their absentee mother. Their mother, a poet who is heavily involved in social change, has little time for them. The history of the Black Panthers is revealed beyond the headlines of the time. The girls quickly realize that many of the social and educational services in the community are provided by the Black Panthers. Through the eyes of a child, the summer of 1968 in Oakland, California, unfolds, telling a story of political, social, and personal change for three young African American girls and the world around them.

- **The Schneider Family Book Award** is presented to a work that conveys the disability experience to young adult audiences. Piper, the main character in *Five Flavors of Dumb* (2010) by Antony John, has been deaf since she was six. Her preferred means of communicating is signing, but she also is a good lip reader. Her baby sister, Grace, has a cochlear implant that was paid for with the college fund left to Piper by her deaf grandparents. Her parents revel in Grace's development as a hearing child; she is perfect. Piper is not. In order to make money to go to Gallaudet, a university specializing in education for the deaf and hard of hearing, Piper becomes the manager for a rock band called Dumb. Through this experience her inner "rock" emerges, and she comes to understand that not being able to hear is part of who she is but does not define her or who she will become.

- **Notable Books for a Global Society** recognizes works that increase understanding of people and cultures throughout the world. *All the Broken Pieces* (2010), a book in verse by Ann E. Burg, concerns Matt Pin, son of an American soldier and a Vietnamese mother, who was airlifted from Vietnam and now lives with an American family. Although he is loved and cared for, he cannot erase the horrific images of his mother and brother who were left behind. He meets Jeff, a veteran of the Vietnam War, who carries his own haunted past. The book explores the long-lasting and far-reaching effects of war, which are never fully erased.

- **The Stonewall Children's and Young Adult Literature Award** is bestowed on works of merit relating to the gay, lesbian, bisexual, and transgendered experience. Brian Katcher's *Almost Perfect* (2009), the 2011 recipient of the award, is a story of a transgendered girl told from the perspective of the straight boy who loves her but fails to support her when he discovers she was born a male. The novel realistically portrays her struggle with her sexual identity and the reactions of family members, friends, and strangers.

Literary Significance

Literature for young adults has **literary significance** when it provides an opportunity for students to gain experience with the forms and techniques of literary writing. A work of literary significance may be either classic or contemporary, but it will exhibit one or more of these characteristics:

- Demonstrates the literary devices and language of exemplary writing
- Facilitates the study of authors
- Exemplifies trends and influences on literary writing (Rycik & Irvin, 2005, p. 138).

A work may have literary significance because over time it has become part of a society's cultural heritage; these are works that many, if not most, well-read individuals in that particular society will have read—or read about. Collectively, these works of literature are sometimes referred to as the **literary canon.** Works in the canon were not written specifically for young adults, and few would be considered contemporary from the standpoint of their initial publication date. Nevertheless, they have stood the test of time because their artistry, characters, and themes transcend a particular era. Such books have a place in the literature for young adults. One example is *To Kill a Mockingbird,* which is our Focus Novel (see p. 38).

The works of Shakespeare may be the first that come to mind when the literary canon is mentioned. Changes in language and customs from Shakespeare's time to today certainly present some obstacles for students, especially when the works are only read and not viewed or performed, but these obstacles can be overcome when the plays are taught in ways that combine their literary qualities with their personal and social relevance for young adults.

In recent years, many new works have been created that can either prepare young readers for Shakespeare or give them the pleasure of rethinking or revisiting a play they have already seen or studied. *Enter Three Witches* by Caroline Cooney (2007) is one of the best examples. The book retells the story of Macbeth from the point of view of 14-year-old Lady Mary, who is a ward of Lord and Lady Macbeth. She witnesses the play's events from vantage points ranging from the kitchen to the throne room.

The addition of a youthful protagonist adds an element of developmental significance. Not surprisingly, Mary has a love interest in the story, but she is in danger of being forced to marry a member of Macbeth's inner circle, a man who wants her only for the wealth she will inherit. Mary experiences the kind of

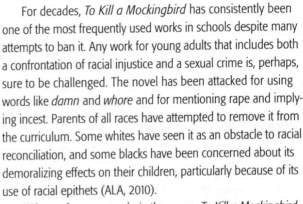

To Kill a Mockingbird by Harper Lee (1960) is an example of a work that combines all three kinds of significance for young adults. Most Americans acknowledge the literary significance of both the book, which won a Pulitzer Prize in 1961, and the film (Mulligan, 1962), which was nominated for three Academy Awards. The story also has developmental significance for young adults as a coming-of-age story, and social significance in that it has continued to be relevant to national debates about race and social justice even 50 years after its initial publication.

To Kill a Mockingbird is set during the Great Depression in the rural community of Maycombe, Alabama. The story focuses on a lawyer named Atticus Finch, a widower who is raising two children, Jem, age 12, and Jean Louise, known as Scout, age 9. The plot of the book centers on the trial of Tom Robinson, an African American man who has been accused of raping a white teenager. Atticus agrees to act as Tom's lawyer even though he knows the racist community will find him guilty.

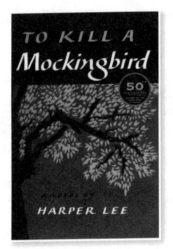

To Kill a Mockingbird was assumed to be based on the Scottsboro Case, an actual 1931 trial in which nine African American teenagers were convicted of raping two white women despite highly questionable evidence. The book has social significance, both for candidly addressing racism and for its theme of courage in confronting injustice. It is important to remember the context in which the book was published; it was set 25 years before it was published in 1960, but even in 1960 the subject matter was timely. The civil rights movement was just beginning; legal segregation still prevailed across most of the South; and economic and social segregation still characterized much of the North.

Within the context of this social landscape, Lee's novel is the story of two children who are reassessing their relationships with their family and their community as events push them to grow up in a hurry. Scout is looking back from the perspective of an adult as she relates the events of the summer in which she grew out of her childhood assumptions about her father and her neighbor, Arthur "Boo" Radley, whom she regards as a kind of bogeyman. She also learns about what she truly should fear: violence, bigotry, and ignorance.

For decades, *To Kill a Mockingbird* has consistently been one of the most frequently used works in schools despite many attempts to ban it. Any work for young adults that includes both a confrontation of racial injustice and a sexual crime is, perhaps, sure to be challenged. The novel has been attacked for using words like *damn* and *whore* and for mentioning rape and implying incest. Parents of all races have attempted to remove it from the curriculum. Some whites have seen it as an obstacle to racial reconciliation, and some blacks have been concerned about its demoralizing effects on their children, particularly because of its use of racial epithets (ALA, 2010).

As is true for many works in the canon, *To Kill a Mockingbird* acquires a new kind of social significance if it is approached from a critical literacy perspective. As we saw in the previous chapter, such a perspective includes considering how cultural identity and cultural assumptions affect both authors and readers. Contemporary readers might examine how Harper Lee's identity as a white Southerner and as a woman influenced the way she told the story. They might also question why the story tells so little of the thoughts and feelings of Tom Robinson, the black man who is unjustly accused of rape and wrongly convicted. One might, in fact, argue that with the possible exception of Calpurnia, the family's housekeeper, most of the African Americans in the story play a role that is limited to the type of dignified resignation that Atticus Finch admires.

Contemporary readers might also consider how their own identities influence their interpretation of the story. White readers might find, for instance, that the story allows them to feel a sense of satisfaction that such racism is a thing of the past, a perception that is made more likely by the author's choice to tell the story as a remembrance. African American readers, on the other hand, might feel some resistance to the notion that racial progress came through the efforts of concerned white people rather than through the social activism of African Americans. The point of such critical discussions is not to emphasize social divisions or to question an author's integrity. The point is to make readers aware of their own cultural filters and, by doing so, to add another layer to their appreciation of complex works.

confusion and powerlessness young people often feel in the midst of upheavals in the adult world. Her presence in the story also gives fresh dimension to the horror that the audience is meant to feel. Because of her youth and inexperience, Mary is genuinely shocked by the King and Queen's ruthless violence, and she is frantic to do something to help. Her attempts to warn Lady MacDuff of the imminent danger to herself and her children are particularly poignant, especially when she finds out later that they have all been murdered.

Each chapter of Cooney's story begins with a quote from the play, although the quote may be taken from a point earlier or later in the play. The language of the book avoids modern colloquialisms, but only suggests Elizabethan English. In the author's note at the end of the book, Cooney explains that just as Shakespeare transformed the story of the real Macbeth that was told in Holinshed's Chronicles, she has elaborated on Shakespeare's version. She concludes with a message to readers that might also serve as a message to teachers:

> Now read Shakespeare's *Macbeth*. A play is a boring thing when read silently because those lines are intended to be spoken. Read Shakespeare out loud. Act as you go. It's more fun when the whole class does it, and everyone takes a part or trades parts, but you can do it alone.... When a line doesn't seem to mean anything saying it out loud a few times usually gives you the sense of it. (p. 280)

Cooney's book is only one of many recent novels that illuminate Shakespeare's world and that of his works. These works are highly respectful of the plays and often display their own literary artistry even as they attempt to add an element of developmental significance. See the accompanying box for a sampling of these books.

Clearly, adolescent readers should have opportunities to encounter some of the great literary works of their culture (Jago, 2000). Teachers play an important role by breaking the ice to introduce students to these works. It is also clear, however, that "arranged marriages" with classics will not be the way most young adults form satisfying and lasting relationships with literature.

Many works written specifically for a young adult audience incorporate sophisticated and complex literary techniques that are also found in classic literature. *Blue Plate Special* (2009), for example, is a challenging novel by Michelle Kwasney that combines a nonlinear plot with multiple narrators, who each use a distinctive form or style. The story shows three generations of women and the long-term effects of the choices they made during their teen years. Not until several chapters into the novel does the reader learn that these women are grandmother, mother, and daughter.

Madeline, an overweight daughter of an alcoholic, grew up in the 1970s, has cancer, and wishes her daughter and granddaughter would visit her in the hospital. Desiree, her daughter, tells her story in short lines of free verse. Desiree was raped by Madeline's boyfriend, resulting in her pregnancy. Madeline's boyfriend is murdered by the man that Desiree's child, Ariel, believes is her father. Ariel, Madeline's granddaughter, is in an unhealthy relationship with a possessive and controlling boy. The multiple voices, differing styles, and non-chronological events allow the reader to experience the unique adolescence of

. . . OF LITERATURE RELATED TO
THE TIME AND PLAYS OF WILLIAM SHAKESPEARE

Dating Hamlet: Ophelia's Story. Lisa Fiedler, 2002. This book began as a poem that the author wrote while she was in college. Although many elements of the play are maintained, this modern retelling attempts to correct Shakespeare's often minimal attention to female characters. (This shortcoming was at least partly the result of laws that prohibited women from appearing on stage in Shakespeare's time, necessitating that women's roles be played by young boys.) In this story, Ophelia becomes the narrator, a witness to many of the play's events, and more of a partner in Hamlet's struggles. Ages 14 and up.

Interred with Their Bones. Jennifer Lee Carrell, 2007. This literary murder mystery revolves around a possible manuscript of Shakespeare's lost play, *Cardenio.* Shakespeare scholar Kate Stanley is drawn into a twisted plot that has her criss-crossing the country between actual centers of Shakespearean study as she tries to discover who is systematically destroying First Folio editions of Shakespeare's plays and killing Shakespeare experts. Interspersed with the plot is a series of historical flashbacks and a running debate about the many candidates who have been reputed to be the true authors of the plays. Ages 16 through 18, especially those already familiar with some of Shakespeare's works.

King of Shadows. Susan Cooper, 1999. This story involves time travel, but it is strictly secondary to an extraordinarily detailed picture of the Elizabethan theater. A young actor named Nat Field finds himself unexpectedly transported from the New Globe Theater to the original Globe. He becomes an apprentice and observes Richard Burbage, Will Kempe, and the rest of the Lord Chamberlain's Men, including Shakespeare himself, as

they prepare to stage *A Midsummer Night's Dream.* Ages 10 and up.

Manga Romeo and Juliet. Richard Appignanesi and Sonia Leong, 2007. Most of Shakespeare's best-known plays have been adapted into manga, a Japanese form of graphic novel. In this book, the authors set the story in modern Tokyo rather than Verona and create two warring Yakuza families in place of the Montagues and Capulets. Nevertheless, this version uses Shakespeare's plot and his language. Although some lines are cut in this adaptation, it retains about 70 percent of the original script and runs over 200 pages. Ages 14 and older.

Romeo's Ex: Rosaline's Story. Lisa Fiedler, 2006. This novel retells the story of Romeo and Juliet from the point of view of the girl Romeo has a crush on at the beginning of the play. Rosaline, who is Juliet's cousin, falls in love with Benvolio and finds herself drawn into the feud between the Montagues and the Capulets. Rosaline's first-person narration suggests Elizabethan English and contains some actual lines from the play. Ages 14 and up.

The Shakespeare Stealer Series. Gary Blackwood, 2000, 2002, 2006. This three-book series paints a vivid picture of all aspects of life in Elizabethan England and features Shakespeare as a recurring character. Widge is a lowly apprentice to a printer, but he has the rare talent of being able to write. He is sent to London to attend performances of *Hamlet* and then transcribe the script from memory so that other companies can perform unauthorized versions of the play. Soon he becomes an actor and a special assistant to the Bard himself. Ages 11 to 14.

each woman, as well as their later interconnectedness. Like many works with metafictive characteristics, in *Blue Plate Special* the author's artistic choices create much of the story's emotional power.

Teachers seeking other recent works with literary merit might begin with the winners of major awards. We have selected a few to discuss in this section. There are also awards for specific genres, such as mysteries, science fiction, poetry, historical fiction, and nonfiction. Additional awards are listed in Appendix A.

- **The Michael L. Printz Award for Excellence in Young Adult Literature** is based solely on literary merit. John Corey Whaley's *Where Things Come Back* (2011), a recent recipient of the Printz award, intertwines plot lines dealing with drug overdose, spotting a bird thought to be extinct, suicide, kidnapping, missionaries in Africa, romance, and friendship. Deaths, and the lives forever changed by those deaths, and a missing brother create a tone of sadness and despair, but underlying this depression is hope. The uniqueness of each of the numerous characters, alternating points of view, and the underlying mystery propel the story forward.

- **The Newbery Medal** is given to a distinguished work for children up to and including age 14. The 2011 medal winner, Clare Vanderpool's *Moon Over Manifest* (2010), shifts back and forth from 1936 Depression-era Missouri to the Great War of 1918. Twelve-year-old Abilene, left by her father with strangers in what she thinks must be his home town, researches her father's past and discovers the town's history. Abilene's first-person narrative is intertwined with newspaper columns, letters from World War I soldiers, and stories told by an old Gypsy woman. The language and dialect is consistent with the time, place, and characters, and the multiple narrative devices create an interesting tale.

- **The National Book Award for Young People's Literature** is selected by a panel of professional writers and is considered a "preeminent literary prize" (National Book Foundation, n.d.). The 2011 recipient, *Inside Out and Back Again* by Thanhha Lai, is a novel in verse about the relocation of a young girl, her siblings, and mother from war-torn Vietnam to Alabama. The sparse language evokes images of the beauty of her homeland and culture, as well as the emotional upheaval experienced differently by each family member. The novel is based on Lai's personal experience.

THE DEVELOPMENT OF LITERARY APPRECIATION

As is true with other aspects of human development, various models have been created to describe how a reader's appreciation of literature grows and changes over time (Early, 1960; Nilsen & Donelson, 1985). These models describe predictable stages that readers pass through on their way to literary appreciation, although they differ in the number and names of the stages. The models also assume that satisfying literary experiences are required in order to move from one stage to the next. If properly supported, growth in literary appreciation will parallel the growth adolescents experience in other aspects of their lives as they create a personal identity and find their place in the world.

Stages of Literary Appreciation

Accepting a stage model of literary appreciation does not mean that teachers should not challenge students, but rather that students need to be comfortable with the literature they read. A class may have readers at several levels of development, so the challenge for the teacher is to determine a reader's level and help him or her move forward. The following descriptions of **stages of literary appreciation** should help teachers to recognize students' progress and support their growth.

Unconscious delight

This stage is typical in young adolescent readers and occurs when the reader derives personal satisfaction in the reading experience. The reader does not think about why a work is worth reading; it simply is. Literary experiences characteristic of this level usually occur with literature that is at the reader's **independent reading level,** the level that he or she can read fluently and with ease. A young reader who is functioning at this stage often becomes lost in the reading and looks forward to the next opportunity to continue. Readers at this stage enjoy fantasy novels and series books, anything they can disappear into. This stage of **unconscious delight** is prerequisite for all later stages. Moreover, reaching this stage depends greatly on the amount of literary reading that an individual does. Those who are school-only readers may never experience this stage, or it may be experienced much later (Nilsen & Donelson, 1985).

Self-conscious development

Early (1960) identified the next stage of literary appreciation as **self-conscious development.** Typically, readers at this stage are seventh through ninth graders who are trying to find themselves through reading realistic fiction and contemporary problem novels. They are struggling with their own identity and, in turn, are developing a critical perspective on the motives that influence literary characters. For readers at this stage of development, the pleasure of reading is enhanced by their growing ability to relate to characters they are reading about as they vividly imagine themselves in the place of a character and consider what they might do in a similar situation.

Conscious delight

For readers who have reached a higher level of literary appreciation, often referred to as **conscious delight,** part of the pleasure of the literary experience comes from understanding the craft of the writing. Readers at this stage value literature with social and literary significance. They take pleasure in style, structure, symbolism, and other literary or metafictive characteristics. They are looking for where they fit in the world, so they seek out literature such as science fiction and social issues fiction. At the highest level of this stage, an individual reads a wide range of literature, and literature is a well-established value in this reader's life.

Influences on Literary Appreciation

Many factors influence how far and fast readers will develop their appreciation for literature. Time spent reading is related to comprehension, attitudes toward reading, and acquisition of knowledge of the world (Moore, Bean, Birdyshaw, & Rycik, 1999), and it is also one of the most important elements in developing appreciation. Students who do not read outside of school may not have the opportunity to lose themselves in literature, and the more advanced stages of development may come much later for the student who does not engage in recreational reading.

Family also plays a crucial role in the development of enthusiastic and sophisticated readers. Consider, for example, 8-year-old Nick, who has been interested in all things related to witches and wizards ever since preschool. His grandmother was aware of this interest and began reading to him Joseph Delaney's *The Last Apprentice: Revenge of the Witch* (2005). Even though the book was indicated as suitable for readers ages 10 and up, she knew he would enjoy it. Nick loved the book, and he and his grandmother were excited to discover that *The Last Apprentice* is a series. It became a family ritual that each trip to a book store began by searching the shelves for the next novel in the series.

The novels have exciting (and often frightening) black and white illustrations at the beginning of each chapter. Nick studied the pictures closely before beginning each book and again at the beginning of each chapter. He often predicted what would happen next. By the middle of third grade, Nick and his grandmother took turns reading passages from the books aloud. As a fourth grader, Nick reread all the novels by himself.

Eventually, Nick independently read Delaney's *The Last Apprentice: The Spook's Tale and other Horrors* (2009), a smaller book of brief background stories about the characters who appeared in the series' five previous novels. He was excited to share with his grandmother how these stories explained why the Witch assassin was so evil. Nick experienced a strong sense of pleasure and was able to consider the motivations of the novels' characters, and perhaps those of others as well.

Nick, at the age of 10, consistently showed the characteristics of the unconscious delight stage of appreciation. His experiences illustrate how skills and strategies of reading grow along with a love of literature. They also suggest some approaches that teachers can adapt to support the development of literary appreciation for groups of readers in a classroom setting. Nick's enjoyment of the *Last Apprentice* series began with listening to his grandmother read to him. Listening allowed him to become "lost" in the story without concern for difficult words or sentence structures.

Eventually, Nick's enjoyment of the stories and his familiarity with the characters, plot lines, and language helped him to read parts of the stories himself. In turn, his successful reading added to his enjoyment of the stories. Because they foster this cycle of skill and enjoyment, stories published in a series are especially useful for building reading independence, and most adults who become avid readers have worked their way through at least one such series.

Nick's story illustrates many characteristics of readers who are on their way to high levels of literary appreciation, and it shows some of the ways in which adults can support that journey. The challenge facing classroom teachers, however, is to support literary development in classes of diverse readers. Remember that stages of appreciation are not precise. Just as young adolescents often have moments of childish behavior and moments of maturity, readers do not leave earlier stages behind wholesale, and they occasionally show traits of a higher stage, especially when they experience a supportive classroom environment.

Note that Nick's willingness to reread the stories indicates that he is on his way to becoming an avid reader. His second reading allows him to savor details and to notice patterns that he might have missed in his initial immersion in the stories. Notice too, that his enjoyment of the literature is intertwined with his relationship with his grandmother. Sharing the reading experience gave it a particular power. Moreover, it was her knowledge of his interest in witches and wizards that led her to introduce Nick to books that were supposedly beyond his level.

Teachers, like parents and other family members, play a large role in moving students through the stages of literary appreciation. In order to assist students' development, teachers need to choose appropriate books and also guide students' interactions with those books. They need to address the diverse needs and interests of the student population, and they need to create classroom experiences that are appropriate developmentally, socially, and academically. Orchestrating instruction that blends all of these considerations would be impossible without some kind of organizing structure. The following sections describe five broad approaches, or literacy routines, that can provide such a structure.

LITERACY ROUTINES FOR BRINGING STUDENTS AND LITERATURE TOGETHER

The IRA states that "Adolescents deserve instruction that builds both the skill and the desire to read increasingly complex material" (Moore, Bean, Birdyshaw, & Rycik, 1999, p. 102). Skill and desire (or the will to read) develop together as readers acquire vocabulary, learn strategies for deriving meaning, and gain experience with a wide range of literary genres and styles. Teachers support the development of both skill and will by ensuring that all students have opportunities to read, interact with peers, and reflect on the meaning of literature in their lives.

Because students are diverse, their development is not uniform, so no single approach will be appropriate all the time for everyone. We suggest that teachers employ a variety of classroom literacy routines to ensure the proper balance of experiences. A **literacy routine** is a pattern of materials, procedures, and activities that fit together to meet a particular literacy goal. Figure 2.2 provides an overview of five literacy routines that can be used for bringing students and literature together. Each of the routines is especially appropriate for students at a particular stage of literary appreciation and promotes a particular kind of classroom interaction with literature. We provide a brief description of each as well as one Classroom Scenario demonstrating a teacher read-aloud in the context of a mediated listening–thinking activity (discussed below) and another modeling the use of literature circles.

Teacher Read-Alouds

Reading aloud is a well-established and often-promoted practice that has the potential to increase both understanding of text and student engagement (Albright & Ariail, 2005; Blessing, 2005; Lesesne, 1996). Even though many teachers do not see reading aloud as a valuable teaching strategy with adolescents, **teacher**

Literacy routines for bringing students and literature together.

figure **2.2**

LITERACY ROUTINE	PURPOSES	TEACHER ROLES	STAGES OF APPRECIATION	KEY SELECTION CRITERIA
Teacher read-aloud	• Explore new genres and authors • Model fluency • Guide comprehension • Introduce vocabulary • Build interest in reading	• Model fluency and comprehension • Lead text discussions • Introduce vocabulary	• Unconscious delight • Self-conscious development	• Developmental significance • Literary/social significance
Guided literature study	• Read aesthetically from classic and contemporary literary texts • Learn terms and tools of literary analysis • Acquire new vocabulary	• Guide discussions about meanings within texts and between texts • Introduce concepts of literary analysis • Give background knowledge • Teach vocabulary	• Self-conscious development • Conscious delight	• Literary significance • Social or developmental significance
Literature circles	• Gain independence and experience • Acquire new vocabulary • Develop literary tastes	• Establish groups and procedures • Monitor text discussions	• Unconscious delight • Self-conscious development • Conscious delight	• Developmental, literary significance
Reading workshop	• Gain independence and experience • Acquire new vocabulary and "book language" • Develop favorable attitudes	• Establish procedures • Monitor text discussions	• Unconscious delight • Self-conscious development	• Developmental significance • Social significance
Unit-centered reading	• Read literature to explore a topic or theme • Learn new vocabulary • Develop concepts and attitudes	• Identify topics and themes for study • Make curriculum connections	• Unconscious delight • Self-conscious development • Conscious delight	• Social significance • Literary significance

read-alouds can be effective both for modeling fluent reading and for providing a satisfying communal experience with literature that takes advantage of adolescents' natural desire to be part of a peer group. Some teachers have students follow along in their own copies of the text during a read-aloud, a process that is referred to as **shared reading** (Allen, 2000).

Whether or not students read along, however, a read-aloud should not allow them to become passive. Because all the students in the group are hearing the same material at the same time, read-alouds present a unique opportunity for diverse students to discuss literature on a level playing field, where students who struggle or read more slowly can fully participate. One way to actively involve students in text discussions is through a **mediated listening–thinking activity (ML–TA),** a technique in which the teacher reads up to a meaningful stopping point in the text. Students are then invited to make predictions about and point out connections within the story and explain their reasoning (Combs, 2003).

classroom scenario

A Mediated Listening–Thinking Activity, with Read-Aloud

This scenario describes an example of an ML–TA using Ray Bradbury's short story, "All Summer in A Day" (1954). AS YOU READ, think about how well the ML–TA framework meets the needs of both the stronger and the weaker readers in the class.

Ms. James decides to begin a unit on science fiction with the short story "All Summer in a Day" by Ray Bradbury. She chooses the story mainly for its literary significance. Bradbury is an important science fiction author, and the story illustrates how the setting of a science fiction story is often crucial to the conflict. The story takes place in a futuristic colony on Venus, and that setting is the cause of a conflict between Margot, who has had the experience of seeing the sun in the sky when she lived on Earth,

and the children born on Venus, who could not remember having seen it. Although the story was not written specifically for young adults, it has developmental significance. It is set in the familiar realm of a school and deals with an incident of bullying, a problem too many adolescents have experienced.

Ms. James decides that a mediated listening–thinking activity will support her students' interaction with the story. She predetermines points to stop the read-aloud and prompt the students for predictions about possible events and outcomes. These predictions will encourage students to draw inferences by making connections between events in the story and by connecting the story to their own knowledge and experience.

Before reading, Ms. James asks, "Have you ever heard of Ray Bradbury?" She shares information about the author and mentions that his best known works are *The Martian Chronicles* (1950) and *Fahrenheit 451* (1953). She then asks, "What characteristics does science fiction usually have?" Students mention technology, futuristic settings, and science fiction movies they have seen. Ms. James asks them, "Based on the title of the story and knowing that it is science fiction, what do you think will be the setting for the story?" They suggest that it will be somewhere where summer only lasts a day and that it might be on another planet.

Ms. James also asks what predictions students can make about what might be the problem or conflict in the story. A student responds that "People probably aren't going to like having only one day of summer." Ms. James asks "Why do you think so?" She listens to other students' predictions and occasionally asks them to elaborate, but she carefully avoids indicating whether their predictions are right.

Ms. James instructs her students, "While I am reading, listen closely to the description and visualize the setting. That means to try to make a mental picture of what the story is describing. There will be some surprises." She reads far enough into the story to establish the setting of the Venus classroom and then stops to invite students to share what they have pictured. They mention the near-constant rain and the sound it makes. She resumes reading and stops again after the passage, "They hated her pale snow face, her waiting silence, her thinness, and her possible future." Ms. James asks the students to describe their picture of Margot and how that image affects their feelings about her.

Ms. James summarizes the conversation by saying, "We know that her classmates don't like her and that they are jealous of her. Thinking about her problem, what can we predict will happen?" Their predictions include, "She is going to be much better after the summer day," and, "Her classmates will do something mean to her." Ms. James continues reading the story, stopping at strategic moments for students to make connections to real life and to other science fiction books and movies they have experienced. She also asks them to visualize new elements of the setting.

The end of the story reveals that the children have locked Margot in a closet so she cannot see the sun. Ms. James asks students to discuss their response to the story's ending, which does not tell what ultimately happens to Margot as a result of the children's cruelty. She also asks them again to relate what images of the setting they thought were most memorable.

If most students in a class are at a stage of unconscious delight, the material chosen for a read-aloud might emphasize developmental significance, and the discussion might focus even more on students' personal responses and connections rather than literary elements. But Ms. James' lesson is appropriate for her diverse class. The setting on an alien planet and the problem of jealousy provide elements conducive to unconscious delight, but her guidance via open-ended questions and predictions nudges those students toward more self-conscious development, and the attention she draws to literary elements, such as the characteristics of the genre and the vivid description of the setting, is appropriate for those students who are closer to the stage of conscious delight.

Guided Literature Study

The *Common Core State Standards for the English Language Arts* (National Governors Association Center for Best Practices, 2010) call for students to read increasingly complex literary and informational texts as they progress through school. In order to meet this standard, many students will require direct instruction and well-developed scaffolding or support. Guided literature study is a literacy routine designed to meet these needs.

Compared to other literacy routines, such as reading workshops, **guided literature study** is characterized by a high degree of teacher oversight and control. The teacher often selects both the literary work to be studied and the objectives to be met. Those objectives can range from learning about specific literary elements and terminology to broader goals such as engaging in a particular approach to literary analysis, exploring genre characteristics, reading critically, or increasing engagement and the desire to read.

The instructional activities typical in guided literature study tend to be teacher-centered. Often, they are designed to provide guidance from the teacher before, during, and after reading. That guidance might involve providing necessary background information about the text or author, posing oral or written questions, demonstrating strategies for interpreting texts beyond a literal level, or expressing an appreciation for the beauty of the language or the significance of a theme.

Guided literature study puts literary significance and conscious appreciation of literature in the forefront; however, that does not mean it should be confined to a dry technical analysis. Students can and should be guided to engage with social and cultural issues raised by literary works, and they certainly should be invited to make personal connections. Guided literature study can be enlivened considerably when teachers choose literature with metafictive characteristics (see Chapter 3) as a vehicle for exploring literary technique, and classic literature can gain a new relevance when it is approached from a critical literacy perspective, as was demonstrated in the discussion of *To Kill a Mockingbird* earlier in this chapter. A Classroom Scenario in Chapter 3 will provide an example of a guided literature study.

Unit-Centered Literacy Routines

Unit-centered literacy routines can take several forms. Genre units, author studies, or explorations of literary themes are organized to create connections among literary texts. Ms. James, for instance, could follow up her ML–TA lesson on "All Summer in a Day" with a unit on short stories, a unit on the science fiction genre, or a unit that included other classic and contemporary works that explore jealousy and persecution.

Unit-centered reading may also involve students in reading and viewing a wider range of material, including fiction, nonfiction, movies, and informational texts. Ms. James could collaborate with a social studies teacher to connect Bradbury's story to a unit on the 1960s that focuses on the cold war, and a science teacher might be involved with activities connected to researching science fiction movies, the early days of the space program, or technological advances of the era. Ms. James could also create an integrated unit that does not focus on any academic discipline. Integrated units, also known as interdisciplinary units or thematic units, are often built around points where the personal and social needs of students intersect (Beane, 1995, 1997). Ms. James could, for instance, create a unit around the theme "facing the future" that explores fictional visions of the distant future as well as students' imaginings of their own futures and the future of our planet.

Literature Circles

Daniels (2001) identifies the two key elements of **literature circles** as *voice* and *choice*. In literature circles, students carry on discussions about books that they have chosen from a number of suggestions. Teachers must provide careful guidance to prepare students to lead these discussions for themselves. Often the groundwork is laid in other literacy routines that are more teacher-directed, such as guided literature study or read-alouds. Generally, students are directed to prepare ahead of time so they are ready to participate in the group. They might, for instance, make entries in a reading log, a notebook in which they record their reactions to each section of a book, including their likes, their dislikes, and their questions.

Some teachers recommend or even assign a particular book for particular students, usually on the basis of the book's difficulty. Teachers may also fold a literature circle routine into a larger unit. The Classroom Scenario on p. 50 models use of a literature circle.

Reading Workshop

The two main components of a **reading workshop** are student choice and significant time in class to read silently. The choices for a workshop may be any school-appropriate material, but students can also be limited to broad categories; for example, any novel or any book-length work, fiction or nonfiction, related to World War II. Ivey and Broaddus (2001) find that students considered the time spent in silent reading to be one of the two best uses of class time, along with teacher read-alouds. Students do not see the time they spend in silent reading as "practice" or a "literary workout" that will make them stronger readers. They see it rather as a way to make more sense of the text at hand and to "concentrate, comprehend and reflect without being disturbed or distracted by some other task" (Ivey & Broaddus, 2001, p. 367).

The reading workshop is an environment that is suited to developing or sustaining unconscious delight through extensive reading of developmentally significant books. Teachers typically provide little direct instruction, and discussions might be limited to occasional small group sharing of students' responses to their books. Often, as part of a reading workshop, teachers or students will give a **book talk,** a brief introduction to a work that aims to entice readers, as an aid to choosing books.

For example, Cari, a student in one of our classes, presented a first-person book talk on the historical fiction novel, *Chains* (2008) by Laurie Anderson. Cari came barefoot, dressed in a long denim skirt, with an old rusty chain wrapped around her body. On her cheek was a jagged red "I." She told, in first person, the story of Isabel, a young slave during the Revolutionary War. She ran her fingers across the "I" but didn't immediately explain what the letter meant. Cari showed the cover of the book while she talked about the story for about 10 minutes, then read a bit of the book aloud. The very last thing she explained was that she had been branded with an "I" for insolence to her loyalist mistress, but to her the "I" stood for Isabel, and it was a symbol of her strength.

As Cari's talk demonstrates, good book talks convey more than information. They are a way for the talker to share personal interpretations and evaluations with potential readers. Ruth Clark suggests (2007) that book talks for adolescents have some entertainment value and vary in style from reading an excerpt, to talking about a character or event in the book, to becoming a character in the book. Clark surveyed 1,500 students in grades six through twelve and found that they preferred the first-person approach. In this approach, the book talker chooses a part of the book that has the potential for creating interest and writes a script speaking in the voice of one of the characters. That was Cari's approach. When she gave her book talk in a seventh-grade class, she was pleased how

classroom scenario

Understanding Diversity through Literature Circles

In this scenario, the teacher chooses books for her literature circle primarily on the basis of their social significance. She then offers students a limited number of choices. AS YOU READ, consider how Ms. Garcia uses literature circles as a way to move her students from the stage of unconscious delight toward the stage of self-conscious development.

Ms. Garcia teaches a ninth-grade English class in a small-town middle school. She wants to take advantage of the power of literature to expand her readers' world, so she plans an experience that will add to her students' understanding of city life. She selects four novels about contemporary urban life and organizes the class into literature circles by having them sign up for one of four novels. Two of the choices have female protagonists. In *Call Me Maria* (Cofor, 2004), the 15-year-old main character has left her mother in Puerto Rico and come to live with her father in a New York City barrio in hopes of receiving a better education. Like many immigrants, Maria finds herself torn between two worlds as she struggles to make friends and adjust to the gritty life of a big city. She expresses her conflicts in poems as well as prose.

Sketches by Eric Walters (2008) is a novel that takes readers into parts of the world they might prefer to avoid. It tells the story of 14-year-old Dana who has fled her home because her mother's second husband has sexually abused her. As a runaway, Dana lives on the streets of Toronto for months, panhandling and scavenging food from dumpsters. Eventually, she finds her way to Sketches, a center for homeless youth where she learns to use her artistic ability to earn money and self-respect. Despite its hopeful ending, *Sketches* provides a realistic picture of the humiliation and fear that come with homelessness.

Ms. Garcia also provides two choices with male protagonists. *The Hoopster* (Sitomer, 2006) is a book about an urban high school student who is African American and a basketball player. In the story, he confronts racism and must deal with changing relationships with family and friends. *The Death of Jayson Porter* (Adoff, 2008) is about a young man who lives with his abusive mother in a housing project in Florida. Jayson cannot fit in at his predominately white school, and he is struggling to maintain a relationship with his father, who is a drug addict. Jason wants to believe things will get better, but nothing seems to change, and he is unable to cope with the harsh realities of his life.

Ms. Garcia is pleasantly surprised when, based on brief examinations of the books, some of the male students sign up to read books with female protagonists. They say their choices are based on an interest in New York City, concern about the problem of homelessness, or an interest in art. Several female students also sign up for books with male protagonists.

Ms. Garcia hopes that because her students are about the same age as these characters, they will be able to see the characters as individuals whose lives include human relationships and occasional joys and achievements in addition to the gangs, drugs, and violence that are so prominent in media portrayals of city life.

Ms. Garcia asks students to do some journaling as they read in order to encourage them to think more deeply about the feelings and motivations of the characters and the challenges that are posed by their environments. The journal entries become a starting point for small group discussions, and the students become increasingly comfortable sharing their ideas. Ms. Garcia drops in on each group discussion and builds on their responses. In the group discussions and in her replies to their journal entries, she empha-sizes that every reader responds personally to literature and that diverse responses are to be respected.

Eventually, Ms. Garcia asks the students to do some double entry journaling (Yopp & Yopp, 2001). She begins by dividing a piece of paper in half vertically. On the left, she writes specific passages she wants students to respond to. Students write their responses on the right side of the paper directly across from the text passage. Ms. Garcia occasionally guides their attention to passages that describe elements of urban life that are not commonly portrayed in the media. After students become comfort-able with the double entry format, they select passages themselves and discuss with their literature groups why these passages are meaningful to them.

When the students finish reading their novels, each group selects a way to share with the class. The *Sketches* group decides to create or find online examples of art works that might have been drawn by Dana to show what homelessness is like and to represent her concerns for two friends who resist com-ing in off the streets. The Jayson Porter group creates a report on Jayson's case that might be given to a suicide prevention group.

The literature circles that Ms. Garcia designs emphasize readers' personal perceptions and reactions to their novels. The journal entries require the reader to stand back and examine the elements of the story, but the process of analysis grows out of students' reflections and discussions rather than follow-ing a formal pattern. Some students in this class have experienced obstacles to entering the stage of self-conscious development. Although they have had some experiences of unconscious delight, their history of reading fiction is not extensive enough for them to move on to the next stage of appreciation. For that reason, an emphasis on analyzing fiction in a very formal manner would probably be premature. Notice that the groups not only choose their books but also the way they want to present their books to the class. Their results reflect the social significance of the books in forms that come more easily to these contemporary ninth graders than essay writing would.

many students asked her questions about the novel. Later, the teacher reported that many students requested the novel for their next literature selection. Book talks such as the one Cari did can give students useful support for choosing their own books, an important component of any reading workshop.

Teachers and students may find the guidelines developed by Kelley Worman (2005), under the auspices of the U.S. Institute of Museum and Library Services, helpful for preparing and giving book talks. Worman suggests that the three key elements to good book talks are the *hook*, the *content*, and the *cliffhanger*. The **hook** grabs the audience's attention; for instance, the presenter may use props, sound, connections to a movie, or read an interesting part of the story out loud. In our example above, Cari wore a costume and spoke as she imagined the charac-ter would talk. She presented the content of the book though a first-person telling of the setting and events. She ended with a cliffhanger, calling attention to the brand on her face, but not explaining what happened next.

Numerous websites also provide models of book talks. Scholastic's video book talks (www.scholastic.com/librarians/ab/booktalks.htm) offer samples done by professionals. Samples of book talks by students can be found at Nancy Keane's Book Talks: Quick and Simple (http://nancykeane.com/booktalks/student.htm).

TOOLS AND RESOURCES FOR MATCHMAKING

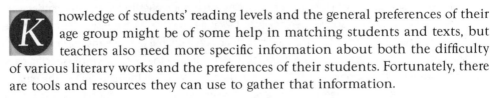nowledge of students' reading levels and the general preferences of their age group might be of some help in matching students and texts, but teachers also need more specific information about both the difficulty of various literary works and the preferences of their students. Fortunately, there are tools and resources they can use to gather that information.

Interest Surveys

Like questionnaires people fill out for dating services, students can supply information about themselves that will help a teacher to predict whether they are likely to "hit it off" with a particular piece of literature. Dozens of these **interest surveys**, or inventories, are available to gauge students' interests, reading preferences, and habits. Sometimes they take the form of a list of activities (like playing baseball or listening to music), and students rate each of the items according to how likely they are to do them. Items such as "reading magazines" or "reading a novel" are usually included with the list. One caution about this kind of list is that interest in an activity does not necessarily translate into a preference for reading about it. Students who rate swimming highly as an activity, for example, may have no interest at all in reading about swimming.

Pitcher et al. (2007) created a rather lengthy inventory designed to find out what motivates adolescents to read. This inventory can be used as is or modified to include a wider perspective of contemporary literature. Another approach to gathering data from students is a critical incidents survey, which invites students to share their actual experiences with books through open-ended prompts. Here are some examples:

- Briefly tell about a time when you read a book that you really enjoyed.
  - What was the book about?
  - How did you find it?
  - What made it so good?

- Briefly tell about a time when you read a book that you didn't enjoy at all.
  - What was the book about?
  - How did you find it?
  - What made it unpleasant to read?

Although written responses are certainly valuable, the critical incidents survey is much more effective if students are invited to share their individual stories orally. The class can then draw some conclusions about the group as a whole such as, "We read books recommended by friends," or "We don't like long books."

Matching by Readability

Readability, the reading ability needed to read a particular work, is certainly one factor to consider when arranging matches between young adults and literature. A student may be very interested in a book, but if it is too difficult, the overall experience will not be satisfying. Readability is often expressed by a grade level number. For example, a novel with a readability level of 7.2 suggests that the book can be comfortably read by a typical student in the second month of seventh grade. These grade levels are calculated with a formula that takes into account the difficulty of the vocabulary and the length of sentences.

The combination of word length and sentence length is fairly useful for a rough prediction of how hard a text is. Long words may be harder to decode than short words, and they are often labels for ideas that are complex and abstract, such as *democracy* or *polynomials*. Shorter words, on the other hand, are frequently used for familiar objects like *food* or *desk*. Similarly, long sentences are often more difficult not only because they have more words, but also because they require readers to make connections between several ideas. Information on readability formulas as well as easy-to-follow directions for using several well-known formulas can be found at the website Readability Formulas (www.readabilityformulas.com).

It is tempting to try matching students with literature by comparing a readability number to a student's grade level, but that creates some problems. First, not all students read at grade level. Even if they do, that does not mean that books below that level will be too easy. Often, the experience of getting lost in a story only comes with a story that is easy to read. On the other hand, many readers have had the experience of successfully reading a book far beyond their supposed reading level because of a strong desire to do so. Second, readability formulas do not consider the prior knowledge and experience of the reader, or the context in which the literature will be experienced. A reader who has seen the movie version of *Frankenstein*, read a great deal of science fiction, and discussed ideas related to the book with a group of friends will find the book to be more readable than someone who has not had those experiences.

Book Sampling

Neither of the previous methods we have described for gathering information involves readers handling books. If reader surveys are like the questionnaires for an online dating service, **book sampling** is like speed dating. In speed dating, men and women sit down at a table face-to-face and get to know each other. After a few minutes, a bell rings and everyone shifts to a new partner. The idea is that this brief acquaintance is enough for people to decide whether they want to learn more about each other. In *book sampling*, readers have brief interactions with books in order to make a rapid decision about which ones they might have a future with.

Book pass

Allen (2000) describes a **book pass** activity in which the class sits in a circle and each student receives a different book. After the starting signal they have about three minutes to examine the jacket of the book, read the first page, and sample a few passages. They then fill out a form that asks for the book title, author, and a comment or rating indicating how likely they are to read the book. When the teacher calls out, "book pass," everyone passes their book to the right. The process repeats until time runs out or everyone has seen all of the books. Allen recommends that students have the opportunity to tell about the books they definitely want to read. Their book pass form gives them a record of some books they might like to read in the future, and it can easily be shared with the teacher.

Book sorts

Unlike the book pass, which is done in a whole class setting, **book sort** is done by individuals or small groups. A student receives a stack of about 6 to 10 books and allowed to peruse each for a few minutes before sorting them into three piles along the lines of "definitely, maybe, and no way." The teacher asks the student to explain his or her reasoning either while the sorting is in process or after all the books have been placed in piles. The student then looks again at the "definitely" pile and talks about what those books have in common. Finally, the teacher can ask which one book the student would like to read first.

In the small group variation of the book sort, a pile of books is placed in front of three students who try to reach a consensus about how to sort them. When time is up, the group is asked to report to the class its three "most definitely" books, its biggest "no way," or the book that was the hardest to agree about. Talking about the books is a key element in both of these sampling activities. The conversation tells the teacher a great deal both about what the class likes and doesn't like and about the strategies the students use for selecting books. At the same time, students are given a view of the wide range of possibilities available to them, and they become more able to articulate their own preferences.

Using Outside Recommendations

Several book distributors have websites that display a wide range of literature and provide data that teachers can use to decide which books particular readers might enjoy. Accelerated Reader (www.arbookfind.com) and Scholastic Book Wizard (http://bookwizard.scholastic.com/tbw/homePage.do) are two free commercial sites that provide interest and reading level information on thousands of books. As is the case with all the other tools and resources we have mentioned, the question with these websites is to what extent teachers should rely on them in making recommendations to students. It is interesting, for instance, to compare what two sites have to say about the same books.

Accelerated Reader indicates that *Surrender* (Hartnett, 2005) is of interest to the upper elementary grades and estimates the book's reading level at 4.9. Scholastic gives an interest level of ninth through twelfth grade and a grade level equivalent of 5.2. Interestingly, when our undergraduate students read this novel last year, several of them found it confusing and even stressful because of metafictive characteristics, such as a nonlinear plot and unreliable narrators. Thus, it seems unlikely that a student in fourth or fifth grade would comprehend it, regardless of its readability.

Fat Kid Rules the World (Going, 2003) is considered interesting to older students by both Accelerated Reader and Scholastic, which give it a reading level of 4.7 and 4.3 respectively. However, neither the readability nor interest level prepares a reader for the extensive profanity and depth of despair experienced by some of the characters.

Professional book reviews play a role in making literature selections, because they show what experienced professionals think about the quality or literary merit of a particular work. Compare these two reviews of the same audio version of *Fat Kid Rules the World* to see if they give different impressions. The first says, "Sexual references, negative portrayals of adults for most of the novel, and excessive use of expletives, especially the 'f' word, make this novel most appropriate for individual listening" (Gonzales, 2003, p. 74). The other says, "Filled with self-deprecating humor, the first-person novel is skillfully narrated by Lillard, . . [who] perfectly captures the punky teen. He emphasizes just the right words and pauses in just the right places to involve listeners in the lives of these troubled friends" (Austin, 2003, p. 445). Recommended grade levels in various reviews for *Fat Kid Rules the World* range from grades seven to ten to grades ten to twelve.

Professional book reviews provide impressions and insights beyond a recommended grade, but teachers may want to seek a second opinion rather than relying on any one review because, like all professional opinions, the reviewers might not agree. *School Library Journal, Publishers Weekly* and *Horn Book* are excellent sources for reviews. *The English Journal* and the *Journal of Adolescent and Adult Literacy* also include reviews of young adult literature. Young Adult Book Reviews (http://youngadultbookreviews.com) and Featured Teen Book Reviews at Young Adult Books Central (www.yabookscentral.com) are reliable and current online review sources.

SELECTION, CENSORSHIP, AND CHALLENGES: ISSUES OF INTELLECTUAL FREEDOM

Roald Dahl's *Charlie and the Chocolate Factory* (1964), Philip Pullman's *The Golden Compass* (1995), and Neil Gaiman's *Coraline* (2002) are recognizable as movies or as movies based on literature read by children and young adults. These novels have something else in common; they have been challenged or banned in a library or classroom setting (University of Illinois, 2010). Challenged books include all types of literature, contemporary publications as well as classics, children's picture books and literature for young adults, and both popular titles and award winning literature.

Intellectual Freedom for Teachers and Students

The American Library Association (ALA) (2010) defines a **challenge** as an attempt to remove or restrict materials from the curriculum or library based on the objections of a person or group. A successful challenge results in a **banning,** the removal of those materials. Removing a work or restricting access to it by its intended audience is also called **censorship.**

The ALA considers the removal of materials a breach of the First Amendment because it restricts intellectual freedom by limiting an individual's right to hold any belief on any subject and to convey those ideas in any chosen form. The ALA (2011) interprets the amendment as meaning all individuals have the right to unrestricted access to information and ideas regardless of the medium used and the content and the viewpoints of author or receiver of the information. The

National Council of Teachers of English (2010) considers the right of any individual to read whatever he or she wants basic to a democratic society.

A counter argument to this interpretation of the First Amendment is based on the belief that children are not developmentally capable of making the same decisions as adults and therefore should not be given the same rights as adults. Kevin Saunders proposes that society should be allowed to shield its youth from harmful elements such as those found in "violent materials, vulgar or profane materials, and the hate-filled music used to recruit the next generation to supremacist organizations" (Saunders, 2005, p. 26). He further argues that it is in the best interests of society to limit the access of authors, film producers, and computer programmers to a juvenile audience. He does not dispute their right to create whatever they want, but, in his opinion, they should not have the right to make their work accessible to children (Saunders, 2005).

Challengers and Challenges

Parents challenge books more than any other group of people. The intent of these challenges is usually to protect children from controversial ideas or opinions that are thought to be dangerous. Sex, profanity, and racism are the primary categories of challenges and occur most often in schools and school libraries (Doyle, 2010). The ALA's policy concerning access to information supports parents' right to restrict library resources, but only for their own children (ALA, 2010).

The number of challenges each year is significant. Between 2001 and 2010 there were 4,659 challenges with the majority of those challenges occurring in classrooms and school libraries. Interestingly, challenges were also made to institutions with an adult audience such as college classes and academic libraries (ALA, 2011). In addition to these reported incidents, perhaps as many as 85 percent of the challenges to library materials receive no media attention (Doyle, 2010). Although exact figures are not available, censorship is apparently extensive and presumably so are its consequences.

Even failed attempts at censorship can lead to voluntary restriction of works by teachers, librarians, and others. Seventy percent of teachers will alter texts, including award-winning books, when reading aloud if something might be offensive, and 60 percent will not purchase books considered risky (Agee, 1999). They are, in essence, self-censoring.

Data on the amount of self-censorship by librarians and teachers is limited. A survey of librarians by the *School Library Journal* found that 70 percent of respondents said they will not buy controversial materials because of fear of parental response. Twenty-three percent of the librarians said their own personal objections would influence their purchasing decisions. Sexual content is the most frequent cause for censorship, followed in descending order by objectionable language, violence, homosexual content, and religion (Whelan, 2009).

Librarians see censorship and challenges as real threats, justifiably so. Forty-nine percent of the survey's respondents said they had dealt with a book challenge in the past. Jobs have been lost because of controversy over materials (Whelan, 2009). Teachers may be more prone to censor work if they do not feel they have support from peers, administration, or their school board. Without

Chris Crutcher

An Author Confronting Challenges and Censorship

Censorship or the threat of censorship may influence the work and careers of authors. Many of Chris Crutcher's novels have been selected as best books for young adults by the ALA; four were selected as *Booklist*'s 100 best books of the 20th century. He has been honored with the Margaret A. Edwards Award for outstanding literature for young adults and the ALAN Award for a significant contribution to adolescent literature. His novels also appear frequently on challenged and banned book lists. The ALA identified Crutcher as one of the most frequently challenged authors of the 21st century. Several of his novels are included in the top banned/challenged books for the last two decades. Crutcher states that controversy isn't his goal, but he believes that as an author he must tell the truth. He trusts his readers to interpret his work (Teenreads, 2003).

In an interview for *Teacher Librarian* (Price, 2009) Crutcher talked about his audience: "I know who I write about and I get responses that say they are appreciative, so that's all I need. The people who suffer personally are the teachers and librarians who know that certain kinds of books are 'healing' to certain kids and for that reason, stand up for the books. They take the direct hit, and I feel a huge need to support them" (p. 71). Crutcher also states that teachers and librarians should have the support of administrators to enable them to "operate in a theater of safety" (p. 71).

Crutcher has been a teacher, therapist, and child advocate, and in those positions he has witnessed firsthand children who are victims of horrible circumstances and crimes. These realities frame his novels. He believes, however, that he balances the tragic with the humorous (Follos, 2006). Readers of his novels do confront racism, abuse, incest, bullying, and homophobia. They also experience victims who fight back and are aided by peers and adults, often teachers. His work is frequently about sports, being loyal, and sometimes becoming a hero (Aronson, 2007). His protagonists are most often male, seniors in high school, gifted athletes, and intelligent.

Crutcher's first novel for young adults, *Running Loose* (1983), set the stage for the issues explored in many of his later novels and short stories: prejudice, love, sex, relationships between adults and adolescents, death, and faith. *Running Loose* also forecast Crutcher's use of explicit language and frank descriptions of adolescent experiences. Louie Banks, the protagonist of *Running Loose,* is kicked off the football team for taking a stand against his coach after he directs his players to purposely injure an African American player on a competing team. Louie's first love ends tragically with the death of his girlfriend, and he struggles with his anger and sorrow.

In *The Sledding Hill* (2005), Crutcher, as himself, visits a school to speak on behalf of his fictitious novel, *Warren Peece,* which has been challenged. This event mirrors Crutcher's actual experiences. He often goes to schools where his books have been challenged to answer people's questions. If a book does get banned, he responds by sending multiple copies to the nearest public library. He also lets local media sources know he has done so (National Coalition Against Censorship, 2009). *The Sledding Hill,* arguably Crutcher's most ardent attack on censorship in his literature for young adults, contains no profanity.

Crutcher's *Deadline* appeared on a list of books challenged in 2009–2010 along with *Mein Kampf* by Adolf Hitler, *To Kill a Mockingbird,* and the *Merriam-Webster Collegiate Dictionary* (Doyle, 2010). He would probably consider being lumped together with *To Kill a Mockingbird* an honor; it was the only book he enjoyed reading in high school (Follos, 2006). Crutcher responded to the questions regarding the censorship of *Deadline* by saying, "A book finds its place" (Pierce, 2007).

Crutcher's work continues to be found in the hands of young adults, and his efforts to advance intellectual freedom have been recognized and appreciated. He was the first person to receive the NCTE Slate Intellectual Freedom Award, which was established in 1996. He won for his efforts to promote anti-censorship of books for young adults (Aronson, 2007). He also is a recipient of the Intellectual Freedom Award from the National Coalition Against Censorship.

support, they may feel isolated and may succumb to their fears by selecting a less controversial literary work (Freedman & Johnson, 2001).

Teachers may also avoid using nonprint literature as a way to defray potential controversy. The NCTE suggests that the teacher's role in the discussion of nonprint literature is to mediate conflicts in viewpoints. "The discussion of controversial topics or works does not imply endorsement or approval of the views or values suggested by those works or expressed by students in discussion of those works" (2004, p. 3). The NCTE further suggests that the integrity of a work be maintained by presenting it whole and uncut.

Challenges and Choices

Literature evokes, and sometimes provokes, emotional and intellectual responses. Differing opinions about what literature should be read by a specific group of students are to be expected. Disagreements over literary works can be less daunting if the educator is prepared. Figure 2.3 offers recommendations that may help teachers select and support their decisions.

 *figure* **2.3**   Recommendations to help teachers select literature for their classroom and support their decisions.

- Communicate. Talk with other teachers, school librarians, public librarians, and administrators. Do not place a colleague or supervisor in the position of being caught off guard by a complaint.

- Consider how a literary work is to be incorporated into the curriculum. Read or view completely any literary work, print or nonprint, intended for whole class instruction and write a rationale for it. Selections for independent reading, literature circles, reading workshops, or recreational reading can be presented as part of a collection or grouping so students have choices.

- Use professional resources. NCTE's *Rationales for Challenged Books, Volume 2* (2005), provides rationales for literature for students in grades 4–12. The NCTE Anti-Censorship Center and the ALA provide a wealth of information about legal issues and support. Lists of banned books and guidelines for selection and reporting are included in their materials. Herbert N. Foerstel's *Banned in the U.S.A.: A Reference Guide to Book Censorship in Schools and Public Libraries* (2002) provides an overview of major book banning incidents, pertinent laws, descriptions of well-known banned books, and comments from authors of literature for young adults.

- Read reviews, both professional and public. Book lists can also be helpful, but are not without opposition. YALSA's yearly "books that won't make you blush" list (www.ala.org/yalsa/) can be seen as an aid for selecting materials, but in an inclusionary list there are inherent questions about the works that are excluded. A caution when using this type of list is that it implies a moral judgment, and this type of judgment is not impartial or unanimous (Pattee, 2007).

- Don't dismiss a film based solely on rating. Courts have ruled that ratings by the Motion Picture Association (2010) are not relevant for instructional purposes because those ratings are made without regard for artistic and educational value (NCTE, 2004).

- Be respectful of parents and community members or groups inquiring about a literary work. Not everyone questioning a selection has a nefarious intent. Challenges may come from individuals or groups hostile to free inquiry, but they also may come from misinformed or misguided people, or from well-intentioned individuals who fear that a particular work imposes a potential danger to some segment of the community (NCTE, 1998–2010).

- Discuss the motives and consequences of censorship with students. Reading altered texts, such as Alan Gribben's revised version of Twain's work, *Mark Twain's Adventures of Tom Sawyer and Huckleberry Finn: The NewSouth Edition* (2011), and comparing them to the originals encourages critical literacy. Picture books that have been challenged, such as *Winnie the Pooh* (Milne, 1926), *The Very Hungry Caterpillar* (Carle, 1994), or the *Tale of Peter Rabbit* (Potter, 1902) provide another approach for discussing censorship.

- Establish a policy, based on adherence to the principles of intellectual freedom for the selection of materials, print and nonprint. Establish a written procedure for any inquiry or challenge regarding a literary work. The NCTE's "Citizen's Request for Reconsideration of a Work" is included in Appendix B.

Literature should engage young adults in deep, critical thinking and guide them to consider ideas and opinions other than those they already have. Avoiding controversy is not the answer, and neither is being required to read or teach a specific literary work. "There is a distinction between censorship—suppressing speech because of the disapproval of the content—and editorial, academic, or artistic judgment about what to publish, teach, or show in a museum" (Heins, 2001, p. 13).

Each community, school, class of students, and teacher is different. The most appropriate selection of literary works may be specific to a time and place, purpose, and reader. NCTE recommends that each school develop its own criteria for selecting curriculum materials. These materials should have a clear connection to educational objectives, but they should also address the needs of students.

conclusion

I vey and Broaddus (2001) surveyed 1,765 diverse sixth-grade students and asked them how their reading needs were being met in school. Students reported that their worst reading experiences were related to assigned reading. The findings showed that sixth-grade students were willing to read, but they wanted to read personally interesting materials, and they wanted some control over what they read. Teachers sometimes need to suggest or assign literary works, but in order to develop a sense of themselves as independent readers, students also need to choose texts for themselves. As they discuss their reading selections with their teachers and peers, students gain insight into their reading preferences and learn to evaluate the importance of different kinds of texts.

In Chapter 1 we defined literature by what it can do; it makes readers feel and think. The first task of the teacher is to find literature that activates students' feelings by connecting with their daily lives and also helps them to think deeply about the world around them and the world of books. The second task is to create a classroom environment that allows diverse readers to find their own "entry point into literacy" (Brozo, 2002, p. 15). Teachers will never make every student happy all the time, but by balancing considerations of developmental, social, and literary significance and incorporating a variety of classroom literacy routines, they can greatly improve the odds that students will find a lasting match with literature.

BIBLIOGRAPHY OF LITERATURE FOR YOUNG ADULTS

Adoff, J. (2008). *The death of Jayson Porter.* New York: Jump at the Sun/Hyperion.

Anderson, L. H. (2008). *Chains.* New York: Simon & Schuster Books for Young Readers.

Anderson, L. H. (2009). *Wintergirls.* New York: Viking.

Appignanesi, R., & Leong, S. (2007). *Manga Romeo and Juliet.* New York: Harry N. Abrams.

Blackwood, G. (2000). *Shakespeare stealer.* New York: Puffin.

Blackwood, G. (2002). *Shakespeare scribe.* New York: Puffin.

Blackwood, G. (2006). *Shakespeare spy.* New York: Puffin.

Bradbury, R. (1954, March). "All summer in a day." *The Magazine of Fantasy and Science Fiction,* 6(3).

Bradbury, R. (1950). *The Martian chronicles.* New York: Doubleday.

Bradbury, R. (1953). *Fahrenheit 451*. New York: Ballantine.

Burg, A. (2010). *All the broken pieces*. New York: Scholastic.

Carle, E. (1994). *The very hungry caterpillar*. New York: Philomel.

Carrell, J. L. (2007). *Interred with their bones*. New York: Penguin, Plume.

Cofor, J. O. (2004). *Call me Maria*. New York: Orchard Books.

Cooney, C. B. (2007). *Enter three witches: A story of Macbeth*. New York: Scholastic.

Cooper, S. (1999). *King of shadows*. New York: Margaret K. McElderry.

Crutcher, C. (1983). *Running loose*. New York: Greenwillow Books.

Crutcher, C. (2005). *The sledding hill*. New York: Greenwillow Books.

Crutcher, C. (2007). *Deadline*. New York: Greenwillow Books.

Dahl, R. (1964). *Charlie and the chocolate factory*. (J. Schindelman, Illus.). New York: Knopf.

Delaney, J. (2005). *The last apprentice: Revenge of the witch*. (P. Arrasmith, Illus.). New York: Greenwillow Books.

Delaney, J. (2009). *The last apprentice: The spook's tale and other horrors*. (P. Arrasmith, Illus.). New York: Greenwillow Books.

Fiedler, L. (2002). *Dating Hamlet: Ophelia's story*. New York: Holt.

Fiedler, L. (2006). *Romeo's ex: Rosaline's story*. New York: Holt.

Frank, A. (2001) *The diary of a young girl: The definitive edition*. (O. Frank & M. Pressler, Eds.; S. Massotty, Trans.). New York: Doubleday.

Gaiman, N. (2002). *Coraline*. New York: HarperCollins.

Going, K. L. (2003). *Fat kid rules the world*. New York: Putnam.

Hartnett, S. (2005). *Surrender*. Cambridge, MA: Candlewick Press.

Hasler, N. (2010). *Sex: A book for teens: An uncensored guide to your body, sex, and safety*. San Francisco, CA: Zest Books.

Hopkins, E. (2008). *Identical*. New York: Margaret K. McElderry.

John, A. (2010). *Five flavors of dumb*. New York: Dial.

Katcher, B. (2009). *Almost perfect*. New York: Delacorte.

Kwasney, M. D. (2009). *Blue plate special*. San Francisco, CA: Chronicle Books.

Lai, T. (2010). *Inside out and back again*. New York: Harper.

Lee, H. (1960). *To kill a mockingbird*. Philadelphia, PA: Lippincott.

L'Engle, M. (1962). *A wrinkle in time*. New York: Ariel Books.

Merullo, R. (2011). *The talk-funny girl*. New York: Crown.

Milne, A. A. (1926). *Winnie the Pooh*. (E. H. Shepard, Illus.). London: Methuen.

Mulligan, R. (Dir.). (1962). *To kill a mockingbird*. USA: Universal.

Myers, W. D. (2003). *The beast*. New York: Scholastic.

Philbrick, W. R. (1993). *Freak the mighty*. New York: Blue Sky Press.

Potter, B. (1902). *The tale of Peter Rabbit*. London: Frederick Warne.

Pullman, P. (1995). *The golden compass*. New York: Knopf.

Sitomer, A. L. (2006). *The hoopster*. New York: Hyperion.

Skovron, J. (2009). *Struts and frets*. New York: Abrams Amulet.

Twain, M. (2011). *Mark Twain's Adventures of Tom Sawyer and Huckleberry Finn: The NewSouth Edition*. (A. Gribben, Ed.). Montgomery, AL: NewSouth Books.

Vanderpool, C. (2010). *Moon over Manifest*. New York: Yearling.

Volponi, P. (2010). *Riker's high*. New York: Viking.

Walters, E. (2008). *Sketches*. New York: Viking.

Whaley, J. C. (2011). *Where things come back*. New York: Atheneum.

Williams-Garcia, R. (2010). *One crazy summer*. New York: Amistad.

WEBSITES WITH ANNOTATIONS

AR BookFinder • **www.arbookfind.com/default.aspx**
Offers summaries of and interest levels and reading levels for thousands of books.

Booktalks • **http://nancykeane.com/booktalks/ student.htm**
Author Nancy Keane provides samples of book talks by students.

Lee, Harper • **www.harperlee.com/**
The author's official website includes summaries of works, biographical information, and online resources.

National Council of Teachers of English • **www.ncte. org/positions/statements/censorshipofnonprint**
Links to the "NCTE Guidelines for Dealing with Censorship of Nonprint and Multimedia Materials."

Readability formulas • **www.readabilityformulas.com**
Information on readability formulas and directions for using several well known formulas.

Scholastic Booktalks • **www.scholastic.com/librarians/ab/booktalks.htm**
Provides models of video book talks done by professionals for use in classrooms.

Scholastic Book Wizard • **www.scholastic.com/bookwizard/**
Provides summaries of and interest and reading levels for thousands of books. Includes book talks, lesson plans, author studies, videos, and discussion guides.

REFERENCES

Accelerated Reader Book Finder (n.d.). Retrieved from http://www.arbookfind.com.

Agee, J. (1999). There it was, that one sex scene: English teachers on censorship. *English Journal, 89*(2), 61–68.

Albright, L. K., & Ariail, M. (2005). Tapping the potential of teacher read-alouds in middle schools. *Journal of Adolescent & Adult Literacy, 48,* 582–591.

Allen, J. (2000). *Yellow brick roads: Shared and guided paths to independent reading 4–12.* Portland, ME: Stenhouse.

American Library Association (2010). Banned and challenged books. Intellectual Freedom. Retrieved from www.ala.org.

American Library Association (2011). American Library Association. Retrieved from www.ala.org.

Aronson, D. (2007). Profiles: Chris Crutcher's stories resonate with young readers. Retrieved from http://www.debaronson.com/profiles/chris_crutchers_stories_resonate_with_young_readers/.

Austin, P. (2003). Review of *Fat Kid Rules the World. Booklist, 100*(4), 445.

Beane, J. A. (1995). Curriculum integration and the disciplines of knowledge. *Phi Delta Kappan, 76*(8), 616–622.

Beane, J. A. (1997). *Curriculum integration: Designing the core of democratic education.* New York: Teachers College Press.

Blessing, C. (2005). Reading to kids old enough to shave. *School Library Journal, 51*(4), 44–45.

Brozo, W. G. (2002). *To be a boy, to be a reader: Engaging teen and preteen boys in active literacy.* Newark, DE: International Reading Association.

Carlsen, G. R. (1980). *Books and the teenage reader: A guide for teachers, librarians and parents* (2nd ed.). New York: Harper.

Cart, M. (2008). The value of young adult literature. Retrieved from http://www.ala.org/ala/mgrps/divs/yalsa/profdev/whitepapers/yalit.cfm.

Clark, R. C. (2007). Become the character! First-person booktalks with teens. *Library Media Connection 26*(2), 24–26.

Combs, M. (2003). *Readers and writers in the middle grades* (2nd ed.). Upper Saddle River, NJ: Merrill Prentice Hall.

Daniels, H. (2001). *Literature circles: Voice and choice in book clubs and reading groups* (2nd ed.). Portsmouth, ME: Stenhouse.

Doyle, R. P. (2010). Books challenged in 2009–2010. Retrieved from http://www.ila.org/pdf/2009banned.pdf.

Early, M. (1960). Stages of growth in literary appreciation. *English Journal 49*(3), 161–167.

Foerstel, H. N. (2002). *Banned in the U.S.A.: A reference guide to book censorship in schools and public libraries.* Westport, CT: Greenwood Press.

Follos, A. M. G. (2006). Author profile: The 3 C's of Chris Crutcher. *Library Media Connection, 25*(3), 40–43.

Freire, P., and Macedo. D. (1987). *Literacy: Reading the word and the world.* South Hadley, MA: Bergin and Garvey.

Freedman, L., & Johnson, H. (2001). Who's protecting whom? I hadn't meant to tell you this, a case in point in confronting self-censorship in the choice of young adult literature. *Journal of Adolescent and Adult Literacy, 44*(4), 356–369.

Gonzales, K. C. (2003). Review of *Fat Kid Rules the World. School Library Journal, 29*(11), 74.

Guthrie, J. T., & Davis, M. H. (2003). Motivating struggling readers in middle school, through an engagement model of classroom practice. *Reading and Writing Quarterly, 19,* 59–85.

Heins, M. (2001). *Not in front of the children.* New York: Hill and Wang.

Hopper, R. (2005). What are teenagers reading? Adolescent fiction reading habits and reading choices. *Literacy, 39*(2), 113–120.

Hughes-Hassell, S., & Rodge, P. (2007). The leisure reading habits of urban adolescents. *Journal of Adolescent & Adult Literacy, 51,* 22–33.

International Reading Association & the National Council of Teachers of English (1996). *Standards for the English language arts.* Newark, DE: Author.

Ivey, G., & Broaddus, K. (2001). "Just plain reading": A survey of what makes students want to read in middle school classrooms. *Reading Research Quarterly*, 36(4), 350–377.

Jago, C. (2000). *With rigor for all: Teaching classics to contemporary students*. Portsmouth, NH: Boynton/Cook.

Kane, S. (2011). *Literacy and learning in the content areas*, 3rd ed. Scottsdale, AZ: Holcomb Hathaway, p. 24.

Keane, N. (2009). Nancy Keane's book talks. Retrieved from http://nancykeane.com/booktalks/student.htm.

Lenters, K. (2006). Resistance, struggle, and the adolescent reader. *Journal of Adolescent & Adult Literacy, 50*, 136–146.

Lesesne, T. S. (1996). Reading aloud to build success in reading. In K. Beers & B. Samuels (Eds.), *Into focus: Understanding and creating middle school readers*. Norwood, MA: Christopher Gordon.

Lounsbury, J. H. (2009). Understanding and appreciating the wonder years. Retrieved from http://www.nmsa.org/moya/PlanYourCelebration/PRResources/WonderYears/tabid/1198.

Moore, D. W., Bean, T. W., Birdyshaw, D., & Rycik, J. A. (1999). Adolescent literacy: A position statement for the Commission on Adolescent Literacy of the International Reading Association. *Journal of Adolescent & Adult Literacy, 43*, 97–111.

Motion Picture Association of America (2010). Film ratings. Retrieved from http://www.mpaa.org/ratings.

National Coalition Against Censorship (2009). The Kids' Right to Read Project interviews author, Chris Crutcher. Retrieved from http://www.ncac.org/The-Kids-right-to-Read-Project-Interviews-Author-Crutcher.

National Council of Teachers of English (2004). NCTE guidelines for dealing with censorship of nonprint and multimedia materials. Retrieved from http://www.ncte.org/positions/statements/censorshipofnonprint.

National Council of Teachers of English (2005). *Rationales for challenged books, Volume 2*. Urbana, IL: Author.

National Council of Teachers of English (2010). NCTE guideline on the students' right to read. Retrieved from http://www.ncte.org/positions/statements/righttoreadguideline.

National Governors Association Center for Best Practices (2010). *Common core state standards for English language arts & literacy in history/social studies, science, and technical subjects*. Washington, DC: Author.

Nilsen A. P., & Donelson, K. L. (1985). *Literature for today's young adults* (2nd ed.). Glenview, IL: Scott, Foresman.

Pattee, A. (2007). Rethinking "racy reads." *School Library Journal, 53*(1), 30–31.

Pitcher, S. M., Albright, L. K., Delaney, C. J., Walker, N. T. Seunarinesingh, K., Mogge, S., et al. (2007). Assessing adolescents' motivation to read. *Journal of Adolescent & Adult Literacy, 50*, 378–396.

Powell, R., Cantrell, S., & Adams, S. (2001). Saving Black Mountain: The promise of critical literacy in a multicultural democracy. *Reading Teacher, 54*(8), 772–782.

Pierce, J. B. (2007). Redemptive reading: Chris Crutcher talks about teens and authenticity. *American Libraries, 38*(11), 68.

Price, J. (2009). Teacher, therapist, free speech advocate: An interview with Chris Crutcher. *Teacher Librarian, 37*(2), 70–72.

Readability Formulas (n.d.). Retrieved from http://www.readabilityformulas.com.

Reeves, A. R. (2004). *Adolescents talk about reading: Exploring resistance to and engagement with text*. Newark, DE: International Reading Association.

Rycik, J. A., & Irvin, J. L. (2005). *Teaching reading in the middle grades: Understanding and supporting literacy development*. Boston, MA: Pearson.

Saunders, K. W. (2005). Censorship should be used for the protection of children. In A. C. Nakaya (Ed.), *Censorship: Opposing views*. Detroit, MI: Thompson Gale.

Scholastic (n.d.). Booktalks. Retrieved from http://www.scholastic.com/librarians/ab/booktalks.htm.

Scholastic (n.d.). Book wizard. Retrieved from http://bookwizard.scholastic.com/tbw/homePage.do.

Teenreads (2003). Author profile: Chris Crutcher. Retrieved from www.teenreads.com/authors/au-crutcher-chris-2.asp.

University of Illinois at Urbana-Champaign (2010). S-collection. Challenged children's Books. Retrieved from http://www.library.uiuc.edu/edx/challenged.htm.

Whelan, D. L. (2009). A dirty little secret: Self-censorship is rampant and lethal. *School Library Journal, 55*(2), 26–30.

Worman, K. (2005). Booktalking guidelines and resources. *Infopeople Project*. U.S. Institute of Museum and Library Services. Retrieved from http://infopeople.org/sites/all/files/past/2006/teens/bktalking_resources_cg.pdf.

Yopp, R. H., & Yopp, H. K. (2001). *Literature-based reading activities* (3rd ed.). Boston: Allyn & Bacon.

CHAPTER THREE

The Language
of Literary
Conversations

chapter overview

Young adult readers develop their appreciation for literary works by reading and reflecting on them and sharing their ideas with others. Terminology that describes similarities and differences between literary texts and identifies important elements within texts greatly aids this reflection and sharing. In this chapter, we consider the implications for selecting, interpreting, and discussing literature in terms of genre. Next, we define literary elements in conjunction with classroom activities that help readers use these concepts in discussion and in writing. The final section of the chapter focuses on the terminology of contemporary metafictive literature and shows how teachers can use the technique of bridging between texts to add richness to literary conversations.

FOCUS QUESTIONS

1. How do various literary genres affect the way students select and respond to literature?

2. What are literary elements and how do they influence readers' interpretations and discussions about literature?

3. What are metafictive characteristics and how do they influence the interpretation of a literary work?

4. How does bridging make use of intertextual connections to scaffold the study of literature?

introduction

*I*f you went to a mechanic who examined your car and declared that your "whatchamacallit" didn't seem to be in sync with the "thingamajig," you would probably look for another mechanic. Good mechanics have learned the specialized vocabulary that explains how automobiles work. That specialized vocabulary helps them talk about automotive problems and explain them to others. In a similar way, literary terminology helps young adult readers to think and talk about literature. Just as car buyers use categories such as SUV, sedan, van, and sports car to describe differences between vehicles, readers use genres to choose and understand literature. Identifying the parts, or elements, that authors use to construct literature and the labels used to categorize it can help readers to join conversations that increase the pleasure and understanding they gain from literature. The Common Core State Standards for the English Language Arts (2010) affirm the importance of being able to listen to others and to build on their ideas, and advocates participation in the kinds of conversations that are featured in this chapter.

> To become college and career ready, students must have ample opportunities to take part in a variety of rich, structured conversations—as part of a whole class, in small groups, and with a partner—built around important content in various domains. They must be able to contribute appropriately to these conversations, to make comparisons and contrasts, and to analyze and synthesize a multitude of ideas. (p. 48)

In this chapter, we discuss how literature is categorized into genres and the terminology that is used to describe the elements of literature. We emphasize, however, that the language of literature is only a tool, not an end in itself. We are certainly not suggesting that teachers assign a weekly list of literary terms and give a quiz on Friday. That will not bring readers any closer to the goal of literary appreciation. Rather, we are suggesting that young adults should have opportunities to develop this language naturally as they read, view, discuss, and respond to literature in a classroom or in a larger community of readers.

GENRE

Both authors and readers are involved in a constant process of grouping works with similar characteristics into categories and then labeling those categories. Those categories are called **genres.** Pavel (2003) noted that "genre helps us figure out the nature of a literary work because the person who wrote it and the culture for which that person labored used genre as a guideline for literary creation" (p. 202). Recognizing the genre of a work helps readers know what to expect, even though authors may still spring an occasional surprise. Genre labels can also act as a kind of shorthand that makes it easier for readers to converse about works they have read.

In recent years the term *genre* has been applied to "any type of discourse that possesses typified, distinguishable, conventions of form, style, or content in recurring contexts" (Harris & Hodges, 1995, p. 96). Based on this definition, text messages, parking tickets, and recipes are all genres because they have differing content, forms, contexts, and purposes. We have narrowed our focus to genres that categorize literary texts, but genre remains a sometimes confusing concept. Part of the complexity of genre study is that people disagree on how to categorize literature. The same literary work may be placed in more than one category, and the names and the numbers of categories will vary depending on who is doing the categorizing. We identify three different approaches to categorizing literary works, and each of those approaches has some impact on the ways that writers create texts and the ways that readers select, interpret, and evaluate them.

A Traditional Approach

A traditional approach to defining genres may also be called an academic approach, because literary critics and professors are often responsible for defining the elements of form and content that characterize each category. Eventually, a category *description* may become a *prescription*, a set of conventions or rules that writers observe when they are creating texts and that discerning readers use when they evaluate the quality of a particular work.

Librarians as well as scholars may deal with literary texts that span hundreds of years, so both groups find an advantage in genre labels that are stable and slow to change. Nevertheless, conventions in literature do change over time, just as conventions in dress or manners change. Even as genre labels change, however, new sets of recognizable conventions develop (Spohrer, 2009). Recognizing the conventions that are used in writing a traditional genre may help students to comprehend that genre and to recognize deliberate deviations from each genre's typical structure, content, or purpose.

A Marketplace Approach

Because publishers, like all business people, are constantly looking for products that will sell, they tend to connect new literary works to some proven commodity. The marketplace approach to categorizing literary works can be seen in the system used at web-based retailers that links works together with the phrase, "Customers who purchased this item also bought _____." The marketplace approach is also obvious in large chain bookstores, where the paperback version of a book that has been adapted into a movie may show the stars of the movie on its cover and be displayed next to the movie DVD, a pictorial book on the making of the movie, a biography of the author, and several similar books that are popular with the same age group.

Carrie Ryan is the author of young adult fantasies such as *The Forest of Hands and Teeth* (Ryan, 2009), which is on the ALA list of best books for young adults. On the website Magical Words (2010), Ryan discussed the effect of the marketplace on writers:

> [When I was writing for the adult market] people would say to write the book of your dreams, but always be aware that when you go to sell it, the bookstore needs to know where to shelve it. I think this is something that genre writers are very aware of—when to bend the rules, when to break them, and when to adhere to them. (unpaged)

According to Ryan, booksellers and publishers may divide literature for young adults into realistic and fantasy genres, but they do not create the hard and fast categories that they do for adult literature. "To me, this is one of the greatest thrills writing (and reading) YA. I don't have to worry where my book is going to be shelved or how the booksellers will be pitching it."

A Reader-Based Approach

A reader-based approach to categorizing literature is closely related to the marketplace approach simply because readers are, in fact, the market for literature. In this view, however, the focus shifts from the connections sellers make between works to the connections that readers make between works as well as the connections they make with other readers.

Individual readers often categorize books according to their own idiosyncratic connections. A reader might, for instance, connect Linda Sue Park's story of the Japanese occupation of Korea, *When My Name Was Keoko* (2002), with other books that describe diverse cultures. However, another reader might connect it with other literary works that have a historical setting or with works that use metafictive techniques. *Impulse* (2007), Ellen Hopkins' novel about three young adults who have tried to kill themselves, might be connected with other realistic fiction, with a documentary film dealing with the same topic, or with other novels told in free verse such as *Out of the Dust* (Hesse, 1997).

Readers' choices of particular kinds of literature may connect them with other readers or, at least, reflect connections they already feel. Individuals may consciously engage with particular media content to convey an image to others (Hall, 2007). If the people that an individual wants to be associated with are talking about a particular, movie, television show, book, or game, the appeal of that material will be enhanced. Conversely, people may downplay their interest in genres that they perceive to have negative social implications, as was evidenced in studies regarding perceptions about people who read romance novels and science fiction. Teachers must consider how genre functions as a social construct for contemporary readers. This means they need to understand how a young adult reader might be affected by how their peers evaluate what he or she is reading or viewing (Hall, 2007).

Classroom Implications

Whether the categories are reader-based or traditional, such as epic poems or historical fiction, genres are always based on the concept of **intertextuality,** the process of interpreting any text in relation to another previous text (Cairney, 1996). Anne Lundin (1998, as cited in Latham, 2008) explained that "texts draw upon texts, which themselves are based on yet different texts. The meaning is produced from text to text; new worlds are made out of old texts." Although scholars have debated the difference between intertextuality and influence (Landwehr, 2002), authors are certainly influenced by what they have read and experienced, so no text can be completely free from intertextual influence, even if the author wants it to be (Latham, 2008). Understanding the intertextual nature of literature is part of a young adult's growing sophistication as a reader, so genre discussions are an important part of the literature program.

Library Journal launched a program in 2006 to create a mechanism for librarians to stay abreast of books and genre classifications. It combined factors from all three approaches to genres. The program includes a traditional approach of studying broad classifications of literature and narrower subgenres within those categories, and it identifies key authors and titles. The approach also considers reader-based factors, however, such as the appeal of a particular genre, how readers respond to works in that genre, and how they talk about those works (Wyatt, 2008).

Students can be guided to better understand the nature and functions of genres through market-based and reader-based activities that highlight intertextual connections. Teachers might, for instance, have students look up some of their favorite books on an online bookstore and try to identify what characteristics their book shares with those recommended by the website. Students can also be asked to identify the typical content and form of popular culture genres such as "chick flicks," "monster movies," or "reality competitions." The last category's characteristics might include team challenges, allowing contestants to talk to the camera about their hopes and other contestants' weaknesses, and dramatic pauses before the announcement of a contestant's elimination.

Genre labels, like other literary terms, are useful tools that help students to make and share comparisons between literary works. Literary conversations can also be enhanced by equipping students with the language that identifies and describes the component parts of a literary whole. Those components are called *literary elements.* In this chapter, we focus on the literary elements found in fiction, but many of these same elements appear in nonfiction, as will be seen in Chapter 8.

THE ELEMENTS OF FICTION

The language of literature is extensive and complex. Understanding literary concepts allows readers to use literary terms in meaningful literary conversations. Focusing your instruction on literary elements as they are used both to describe and evaluate literature will not only help students understand a particular literary work, but it will also help them to better understand how fiction works in general. The terms used to describe fiction have been surprisingly consistent from generation to generation and from source to source. We have found that various references such as Lukens and Cline's *A Critical Handbook of Literature for Young Adults* (1995), *The Longman Dictionary of Literary Terms: Vocabulary for the Informed Reader* (Kennedy, Gioia, & Bauerlein, 2006), and *Merriam-Webster's Encyclopedia of Literature* (1995) generally agree on which terms should be included in a discussion of the elements of fiction, and their definitions are given below.

Character

Memorable stories depend on memorable characters. A vividly drawn character like Sherlock Holmes or Ebenezer Scrooge can live in generations of readers' imaginations. A young adult reader who closely identifies with one or more of the characters in a story is much more likely to have a satisfying reading experience. Most often, this identification is with the **protagonist,** the central figure in the story, but readers can identify with all kinds of characters, even villains. Identifying with a character is not the same as hero worship. It is more a matter of a reader recognizing points of similarity or sympathy with a character while imaginatively "trying on" a set of personal traits and "trying out" a particular way of living.

Round vs. flat characters

Identifying with a character comes more easily if the character is portrayed as a complex individual with a range of traits, strengths, and weaknesses. Such solid and three dimensional characters are called **round characters.** Authors create round characters by providing descriptions of how each character looks, talks, and acts. Readers also glean information about characters from the responses and comments of other characters. Almost everyone responds to Ebenezer Scrooge with fear, for instance, but his nephew Fred says he feels sorry for him because he has chosen to make himself miserable.

In contrast to round characters, readers are unlikely to identify with **flat characters** because the author provides too little information for that character to be well developed. Often, these characters are given one or two characteristics, such as bright red hair or a habit of being late. Bob Cratchit is certainly more lovable than Scrooge, but readers usually don't think much about him as a person, even if they have sympathy for his situation.

The minimum in character development comes with a type of flat character called a **stereotype.** Stereotypes are characters reduced to a single trait, often by categorizing them as belonging to a particular group such as "nerds," or "rednecks." In life, stereotyping is usually viewed negatively, but in literature stereotypes may be necessary to quickly introduce a minor character. Readers can readily call to mind a picture of stereotypes such as "Wall Street tycoon" or "soccer mom" because they represent categories that are common in a particular culture. **Archetypes** are similar to stereotypes, but rather than representing a particular era or culture, archetypes are the kind of universal figures often found in mythology and legends, such as the brave hero or the wise old man.

Dynamic vs. static characters

A character that changes during the course of a story is called *dynamic.* A **dynamic character** changes in response to events that occur during the story. A **static character,** on the other hand, remains essentially the same in personality and behavior and is most often a minor character. The protagonists of most stories, especially book-length stories, are both round and dynamic. The reader comes to know these characters well enough to see how they change, even if those changes are subtle. The **antagonist,** the person or force that is directly opposed to the protagonist, on the other hand, may be either round or flat.

Fairy tales are one of the few genres in which the protagonist can be somewhat flat and static. A reader knows little about Cinderella at the beginning of the story except that she is very good and very miserable. At the end of the story, she is still good, but she is no longer miserable; only her circumstances have changed.

Activities for learning about characters

Teachers can help the learning process by frequently using terms such as *dynamic* and *static, protagonist* and *antagonist, round* and *flat.* Such terms are internalized over time as students hear them and are encouraged to use them in literary conversations. Teachers can also engage students in other activities to reinforce the concepts behind the terms. Here are some examples:

Graphic organizers. Janet Allen (2000) created a graphic organizer that features a drawing of a skeleton surrounded by prompts for certain kinds of character traits (see Figure 3.1). "Thoughts" and "plans," for example, appear next to the skeleton's head, and a line to the chest is labeled "feelings." Students fill in relevant information for each of the prompts. This organizer develops students' understand characterization visually.

Graphic organizer for fleshing out a character's thoughts, feelings, actions, strengths, and weaknesses.

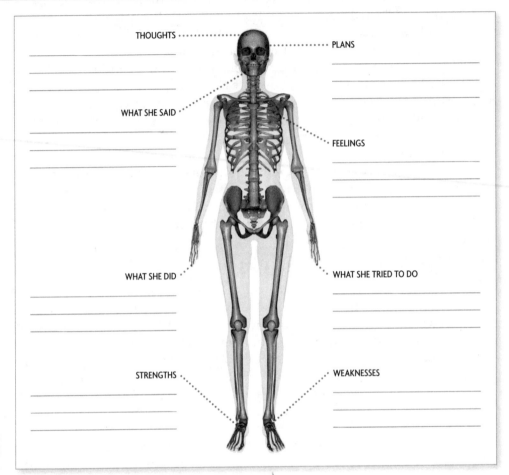

THOUGHTS ············   ············ PLANS

WHAT SHE SAID ··

··· FEELINGS

WHAT SHE DID ··   ·· WHAT SHE TRIED TO DO

STRENGTHS ··   ·· WEAKNESSES

Recreated based on
J. Allen (2002). Used
with permission.

Character continuum. Students can work in groups to make a character continuum on large paper by drawing a line with "flat" written on one end and "round" on the other, and then placing each of the characters along the continuum to reflect how developed they are. For *A Christmas Carol*, for instance, Scrooge would probably be placed at the "round" end of the continuum, but Tiny Tim might be placed toward the "flat" end because all readers know about him is that he has a sweet disposition despite his illness.

Character chart. Have students create a chart for a main character that is divided into three columns marked "self," "others," and "narrator." As they read a story, they can periodically record statements the characters make about themselves, statements other characters make about them, and statements the narrator makes. Students may need to put a question mark next to statements made by rival or enemy characters if they have reason to doubt the veracity of those statements.

Change statements. Choose a dynamic character and have students reflect on how that character's actions and ideas have changed. Students then write as if they were that character, making statements following the form, "I used to _____, but now I _____. Ebenezer Scrooge, for instance, might say "I used to think Christmas was a humbug, but now no one celebrates it better than I do."

Setting

Setting is the time and place in which the action of a story occurs. We can also think of setting as including the culture and context in which a story takes place (Smith & Wilhelm, 2002). The importance of a setting depends on the genre of the literary work. The setting in historical fiction is critical, for instance, because actual events and people may provide the context for the story, and characters must speak and behave as people did during that time and place if the story is to be believable.

Symbolic settings

A setting can be a **symbolic setting**—it comes to represent something other than a literal place and time. In Terry Pratchett's *Nation* (2008) a small tropical island devastated by a tsunami is the context for the survival story of Mau, an island boy, and Daphne, a girl related to British royalty. In a sense, the island is also a character because Mau sees it as a living enemy he must conquer. The aftermath of the storm reveals evidence that an ancient advanced society once existed on the island, so the setting also represents the building of a new civilization, a new Nation.

Integral vs. backdrop settings

In photography, a backdrop is a screen that is placed behind the subject to provide the illusion of a different setting. A **backdrop setting** in literature is much the same. It may provide pleasant scenery, but it attracts little notice and could be changed without significantly altering the events of the story. In some stories, however, the time and place are essential to the story and thus are referred to as an **integral setting.** These have a major influence on the events, characterization, or theme of a story. Victorian London is an integral setting in the Sherlock Holmes stories. Holmes' deductions often depended on his knowledge about the appearance and behavior of people from various social classes in that era, and the foggy, innumerable, twisting lanes of London often added to the difficulty of his cases.

Activities for learning about setting

The following classroom activities direct students' attention to the features of setting and encourage them to consider the importance of the setting to the story:

Setting transplant. Have students list all of the ways in which the story would change if it were transplanted to their home town and current time period.

Would the characters' attitudes and values be different? Would some of the events become impossible?

Travel brochures. Students create a brochure that plays up the good points of the setting and downplays the bad points. For *To Kill a Mockingbird* (Lee, 1960), for instance, they might write, "Maycomb, Alabama, is an old-fashioned community with helpful neighbors and an excellent sheriff's department. Don't miss the County Courthouse, scene of many historic trials, and enjoy our annual Target Shooting contest."

Mapping. In this activity, students use the descriptions in the text to make a map, diagram, or drawing that shows either the overall setting of a story or that of a particular scene. Have them mark and label parts of the drawing that were important to the action of the story. In mapping *To Kill a Mockingbird*, for instance, they would include Atticus Finch's house, the Radley place next door, the Courthouse where Tom Robbins is tried, and the schoolyard where Scout is attacked.

Plot

The basic ingredients of a **plot** are what the characters do (actions), what happens to them (events), and the sequence of those actions and events (the narrative order). The narrative order can be chronological, where the story is told in the order the events occurred, or it can be told in flashbacks and flash forwards that disrupt the story's chronology. The plot of a story is not independent from setting and character. Often it grows out of particular traits of the main character or the circumstances of the setting.

In Lois Lowry's novel *The Giver* (1993), for example, Jonas, the protagonist, has an inborn ability to see things that the rest of his community cannot. The plot of the story begins when Jonas is formally selected at the age of 12 to become the new Receiver of Memories for the community. The plot depends both on character, Jonas' unique abilities, and on the setting, the peculiar nature of his community where children have their life's work chosen for them by a council, and no one but the Receiver has any record or memory of the past. Throughout the book, both Jonas' character traits and the community's way of life continue to drive his actions.

Conflicts

Plots revolve around a **conflict,** a struggle between the protagonist(s) and some other force. Four kinds of conflict can appear in a story, either alone or in combination.

Interpersonal. The first and most common conflict is an **interpersonal conflict** that pits person against person. In literature for young adults, such conflicts are often between the protagonist and peers or adults the protagonist believes are interfering or dominating.

Internal. The second kind of conflict is an **internal conflict,** also called a "person against self" conflict. It occurs when a character is struggling with a personal issue such as a choice between opposing values. Often internal conflicts are found in combination with other kinds of conflicts. A teenager might, for instance, be tempted to abandon a long-held value in order to fit in better with a group of hostile peers. A conflict that is internal may also be resolved internally. The character may undergo some personal change such as making a decision, learning to adapt to the situation, or accepting what cannot be changed.

Person against nature. A character who is pitted against impersonal forces, particularly elements of nature such as a storm or rugged environment, is involved in a **person against nature conflict.** The setting may become the antagonist in a person against nature story, as the Alaskan wilderness is in *The Trap* (Smelcer, 2006). Often this type of conflict is found in stories set in a harsh and threatening natural landscape, but survival stories can also take place in urban areas with the city as the source of the conflict.

Person against society. Battling hatred, prejudice, or other forms of social injustice is a **person against society conflict.** Such conflicts can occur on a grand scale with thousands of people demanding social change, as the people of India do in the film *Gandhi* (Attenborough, 1982). Sometimes, however, a conflict with society can be difficult to identify because it focuses on the protagonist(s)' internal discomfort with the values and mores of their society. In *The Giver,* the information that Jonas receives about his community creates a moral and emotional dilemma for him. He finally decides that he must leave the community in order to save the life of a child the people are planning to "release" in a form of mercy killing.

Types of plot structures

Progressive. A **progressive plot** or narrative structure begins with an exposition that provides background. This may consist of describing the setting, introducing the protagonist and antagonist, and establishing the protagonist's goals. By the end of the exposition, a conflict has been introduced and leads to a time of **rising action** in which the conflict is further developed, usually with additional complications or obstacles that thwart the protagonist's efforts. The rising action eventually reaches a **climax,** or turning point. The climax is not always a particularly dramatic event, but it is the moment in which the outcome of the story becomes inevitable. The climax is followed by **falling action,** in which the conflicts are worked out and most or all of the questions raised in the story are answered as the plot reaches a **denouement,** sometimes called the **resolution.** Progressive plots are often represented by a diagram that looks like a triangle with the left side representing rising action and the right side falling action leading to the resolution.

A story with a definite resolution will leave readers with a sense of closure or completeness. An open-ended conclusion is one where the author does not provide closure, and the reader has to speculate on what happened to the main characters. Some readers were dissatisfied with the ending of *The Giver* because it is unclear whether Jonas and Gabriel, the child he is trying to save, actually survive their attempt to flee through the countryside in the middle of winter. Readers of *The Giver* do not obtain a sense of closure, although the sequel, *Gathering Blue* (Lowry, 2000), does indicate that Jonas has survived and become an important leader in a new community.

Episodic plots. The forward momentum of a progressive plot is missing in an **episodic plot,** which presents a series of incidents that are loosely tied together. The events in episodic stories gradually reveal significant aspects of the setting or characters, but the main characters may only react to events instead of initiating them in an attempt to reach a particular goal. Episodic novels work in the same way as some long-running television shows. Each episode is a story that stands on its own, but it also contributes to the viewer's overall understanding of the characters and their relationships.

Episodic plots are evident in Richard Peck's Grandma Dowdel series. In *A Long Way from Chicago: A Novel in Stories* (1998) and *A Year Down Yonder* (2000), Mary Alice and her younger brother Joey make extended visits to see their eccentric Grandmother Dowdel. They observe a series of humorous incidents that reveal their grandmother's cleverness, fierce independence, or carefully concealed kindness. The incidents are told in the order in which they happened, but Grandma does not face a particular conflict from one story to the next, nor is she trying to achieve any particular goal other than living her life exactly as she sees fit.

Peck's last book about Grandma Dowdel, *A Season of Gifts* (2009), follows the same pattern, although it is about the preacher's family, the Barnharts, who move next door to Grandma Dowdel. The adventures can be read as separate short stories that focus on the various members of the family, but collectively they explore the setting through the family's encounters with the local townspeople.

Other structural devices

An **author's narrative strategy** is the overall plan for *how* the story will be told (as opposed to *what* will happen). This strategy includes decisions about whether to use devices such as a prologue, flashbacks, or an epilogue. Each of those devices extends the story beyond the events of the main narration.

Prologues. Authors occasionally provide a **prologue** at the beginning of the novel to briefly describe events that occurred before the plot begins. In *Jellicoe Road* (2006), Melina Marchetta uses the heading "Prologue" to set apart an initial flashback which is printed entirely in italics. The subheading of the first chapter, "Twenty-Two Years Later," further explains the leap in time between the description of a terrible car accident in the first few pages of the novel and the beginning of the plot.

Flashbacks. One way of showing how past events are connected to the plot's current events is to insert a brief glimpse of a past event. Such an interruption is called a **flashback,** and the technique is used in films as well as print. The main narrative of Harry Potter and the Sorcerer's Stone, for instance, begins when Harry is old enough to attend Hogwarts School, but the film (Columbus, 2001) uses a flashback to show the night Harry's parents died when he was just an infant.

Epilogue. An author can summarize events that take place after the end of a story by using an **epilogue** to clarify certain issues or provide a sense of closure. *A Step from Heaven* (Na, 2001) concludes with an epilogue in which Young Ju reflects on the sacrifices her mother made to raise her children in an unfamiliar country after the family immigrates to the United States from Korea. This epilogue evokes a sense of love and well-being that contrasts with the harshness and violence depicted in the main plot.

Point of View

Deciding who will tell the story and how much will be revealed to the reader is another part of the narrative strategy, called the story's point of view. **Point of view** (sometimes abbreviated POV) is the perspective, the voice, or the narrator an author uses to tell the story. Point of view in written literature can be used to keep readers at a distance or to draw them in to identify with the characters. The different kinds of point of view are described in terms of the pronouns that an author would be using for each of them.

First person point of view

With a **first person point of view,** the pronouns "I" and "me" predominate, and the story is told from the perspective of one character, usually—but not always—the protagonist. The "I" character can only relate those aspects of the story that are experienced directly by that character. A first person point of view can create an intense connection between reader and character, because the reader knows everything the character is experiencing, thinking, and feeling. In the Newbery honor book, *Al Capone Does My Shirts* (Choldenko, 2004), the narrator is 12-year-old Moose Flanagan, who comes to live on the island of Alcatraz in 1935 when his father becomes a guard at the famous maximum security prison. Moose's older sister Natalie suffers from an unnamed developmental problem that would now be recognized as a disability on the autism spectrum. The first day they are on the island, Moose is asked how old his sister is:

> "Ten," I answer. Natalie's age is always ten. Every year my mom has a party for her and she turns ten again. My mom started counting Nat's age this screwy way a long time ago. It was just easier to have her younger than me. Then my mother could be happy with each new thing I did, without it being another thing Natalie couldn't do. (pp. 11–12)

Moose steadfastly refuses to talk about Natalie to the other characters, but readers see the embarrassment he feels and the strain on his family, particularly his mother, who refuses to give up hope and is desperately searching for a school that can help Natalie.

With first person narration, readers share the narrator's emotions, but they may also share the narrator's confusions about the significance of various events. Readers do not know for sure whether Natalie has autism because Moose himself does not know. In Arthur Conan Doyle's Sherlock Holmes stories, Holmes' friend Dr. Watson tells each story in a way that reflects his own mystification about the case that is unfolding. He always sees the clues but remains clueless, and that allows the reader to enjoy the mystery as well.

Authors may also use a device called an **unreliable narrator** in order to add a layer of interpretation for the reader. Edgar Allan Poe's classic story "The Tell-Tale Heart" (1843), for instance, begins with the narrator calling his own sanity into question. A more recent example is Josh Lieb's 2009 novel *I Am a Genius of Unspeakable Evil and I Want to Be Your Class President*. In that story, a 12-year-old boy named Oliver Watson describes how he has amassed a huge fortune and a private army. He then reveals his elaborate plan to become class president, which includes deposing the dictator of an unnamed South American country. The story is obviously not meant to be taken as realistic, but the reader is given no clue until the very end that all of the events may be figments of the imagination of an ordinary and unhappy boy.

Third person point of view

The use of the pronouns "he," "she," or "they" signals a **third person point of view,** which can be either limited or omniscient.

Limited. When a story is told from one character's perspective and the other characters' perspectives are unknown, the story is being told from a **third person limited point of view.** In *The Giver*, the focus is on Jonas throughout the story, so the reader knows only those events in which Jonas is participating and those that the Giver tells him about. Readers are sometimes told what Jonas is thinking, but they do not hear his thoughts in his voice, and they do not know the thoughts of other characters. The limited point of view reflects Jonas' limited understanding of his society and the people around him.

Omniscient. When the thoughts and actions, past or present, of many characters are revealed, an author is using an **omniscient point of view.** An omniscient viewpoint allows the author to include events or insights the main character did not experience or notice. In *A Christmas Carol* (Dickens, 1843) the narrator knows all of Scrooge's secrets as well as those of his deceased partner, Jacob Marley, even what happened to him after he died. The omniscient narrator also knows the future and tells what will happen to Scrooge and Tiny Tim long after the events of the story.

Second person point of view

Although student writers sometimes like to use it, a **second person point of view** is rarely found in published literature. A second person viewpoint makes the reader the main character of the story. A second person story might begin,

"You walk slowly down the dark hallway with your hands outstretched feeling for a light switch. Your heart is hammering a mile a minute. You know someone is in the darkened house with you." Such a point of view can be intense, but it is difficult to sustain that intensity for a whole story, and there is little opportunity to develop characters since the protagonist is "you."

Activities for learning about point of view

Modeling POV shifts. Rewriting scenes from a book into a different viewpoint helps students understand the concept. But first teachers should model the process. You might, for instance, rewrite the scene in which Moose Flanagan first meets the other kids on the island into an omniscient point of view in order to tell what the other children are thinking about Natalie and to explain the pressure Moose feels to never say anything negative to or about his sister.

Retelling personal narratives. Suggest possible topics for students to use in writing a personal narrative, a true story that happened to them. They might, for instance, write about an incident that involved taking care of a younger sibling or about a family outing that was especially enjoyable or disastrous. Then have students rewrite that story substituting their own name (or he/she) for every instance of "I." Have them discuss which version they like better and why. Then discuss how their preference relates to the decisions authors make about point of view.

Movie POV. Show a scene from a movie and ask students whether the camera stays close to the action or removed from it and how involved they feel. Discuss the scene by asking questions such as, "Whose story is this?" and "How does that person feel about the events that just happened?" The opening scene of *Star Wars* (1977), directed by George Lucas, is a good example. The audience views a battle in space from a great distance. Viewers have a broad picture of everything that is going on, but they do not yet identify with anyone in the story. Within five minutes, however, the camera gradually closes in on a desperate Princess Leia, and the viewer is drawn into her story. Similarly, in many of the following scenes, the camera, and thus the viewer's attention, is focused closely on the other protagonist, Luke Skywalker, as he tries to rescue Leia.

Theme

The concept or proposition that gives a story its significance is its **theme.** Theme reflects the author's perspective or purpose for writing the literary work. It is what a literary work is about, its values and truths, and the questions it raises that go beyond the context of a specific plot. Different readers might identify different themes in the same literary work. Some readers might, for instance, see the theme of *A Christmas Carol* to be an optimistic message that people can always change for the better. Others might see it as a rejection of materialism or as a tribute to the value of loving families. A reader's interpretation of themes might be influenced by both the experiences the reader has had and by the nature of the reader's engagement with a particular text.

Explicit vs. implicit themes

Themes can be either explicit or implicit, and one story may include both kinds. **Explicit themes** are directly stated in the story by the narrator or by one of the characters. In the movie version of *The Wizard of Oz* (Fleming, 1939), for instance, Dorothy explains what she has learned in Oz and concludes with an explicit statement that "there's no place like home." In contrast, **implicit themes** emerge from what characters do, the decisions they make, and the motives behind those decisions. The actions of Dorothy and her companions support the conclusion that evil can be defeated by intelligence, courage, and the love of friends and family, but none of the characters ever says that in so many words.

Activities for learning about literary themes

Because themes are so open to interpretation, they are excellent for sparking literary conversations. On the other hand, some students may be frustrated by questions for which there are no clear "right" answers. Teachers can help by guiding students' discussions about themes with techniques such as the following:

Theme lists. Provide a list of themes that appear repeatedly in literature and let students decide which of them, if any, apply to the story they have just read. A theme list, like the list of four kinds of conflicts, helps students to see recurring patterns in literature, but it should not be used as a shortcut to a "right" answer. It should rather be used as a starting point for discussions in which students will explain and support their choices, and multiple interpretations should be expected. The list might be made up of questions such as

- "Are individuals sometimes more important than the group?"
- "Is freedom more important than security?"

It could also be in the form of phrases such as

- "Coming of age"
- "Finding one's true self"

In either case, the list should be considered a temporary scaffold to be used only as long as it is needed.

Reaction guides. This type of post-reading guide is similar to a theme list, but with two differences. The format presents a series of complete sentences, and students can write "A" for agree or "D" for disagree according to whether they believe the statement reflects an idea from the story. Instead of a universal list of themes, the guide contains statements that are specific to a particular work. For *The Giver*, for example, the guide might include the statement, "Giving up pain and conflict also means giving up joy and love." Students would then discuss how, or if, this statement is connected to the events of the story.

Book defense. Students can be guided to consider a work's significance by taking on the role of a defense attorney who must argue against the book being "erased." The issue is not censorship of objectionable material, but rather, "Does this book somehow make a reader's life richer? Does it, for example, help readers understand themselves and others?" Students can write or orally deliver a closing statement making their case to the "jury."

Style

The actual language used in the literary work is its **style,** and this is the final element in an author's narrative strategy. Style is made up of diction and word choice, sentence structure (syntax), and the tone an author uses. Authors can use language that is formal or informal, contemporary or historical, challenging or easy. Some authors have a characteristic style that is used in all of their works. Others adapt their style to the characters and setting of a particular story.

Diction

One of the main tools authors use to create a distinctive style is **diction,** the level of formality in the language used by the narrator and the characters. Levels of diction range from very formal, such as the language in technical books and textbooks, to informal (colloquial), to slang and profanity. Word choice is a major part of diction, but not the only part. In literature for young adults, authors must decide how much dialogue should reflect the type of language teenagers use. They must also decide whether to reflect the regional speech that goes with the setting. Han Nolan's use of a colloquial level of diction, including dialect, in *Born Blue* (2001) creates an image of Janie, or Leshaya as she calls herself, and the harsh environment in which she lives.

> I had a lot to think on that day, but weren't nothin' 'bout Mama Linda. I weren't gonna let what she done to me—trading me for drugs—get inside me. I just wrapped myself up in one more rock-hard layer of I-don't-care-'bout-nobody and sat in the living room, waiting for Daddy Mitch. I wanted to know for sure if Daddy Mitch be my real daddy or not. I never did ask before 'cause of how he had such a temper, but this time I had the temper, and I wanted to know 'cause I figured if he wasn't, I gonna run away somewhere. (p. 76)

Imagery and figurative language

Authors often use language to create a picture in the reader's mind. **Imagery** is a frequently used style device that creates a strong impression in the reader's mind by appealing to all the senses through descriptions of sight, sound, smell, touch, and taste. In **figurative language,** words are used in a non-literal way so that readers can draw on a familiar object or experience in order to understand something less familiar. Similes and metaphors are commonly used types of figurative language. **Similes** are comparisons using "like" or "as," and **metaphors** are implied comparisons between two dissimilar things that have some trait in common. **Personification,** another commonly used form of figurative language, is assigning human traits to nonhuman things. Dickens plays with figurative language in the opening of *A Christmas Carol,* and he also displays the humorous wordiness that was characteristic of his style:

> Old Marley was as dead as a door-nail. Mind! I don't mean to say that I know, of my own knowledge, what there is particularly dead about a door-nail. I might have been inclined, myself, to regard a coffin-nail as the deadest piece of ironmongery in the trade. But the wisdom of our ancestors is in the simile; and my unhallowed hands shall not disturb it, or the Country's done for. You will therefore permit me to repeat, emphatically, that Marley was as dead as a door-nail. (Dickens, 1985, pp. 3–4)

Dickens pokes gentle fun at the commonly used simile, partly by pointing out that doornails do not actually live or die.

Symbolism

Authors use symbolism when they want a depth of meaning beyond the surface or literal definition of words. A **symbol** is an image in words, but it tries to do more than create a strong sense impression. It uses the image to represent an abstract or figurative meaning. The New England town of Monument in the short story "Mine on Thursdays" by Robert Cormier (1980), for instance, represents an old, staid, and inflexible way of life to the divorced father who is telling his story.

Allusion

In "Mine on Thursdays," the narrator, who has finally realized his failure as a father, peers into the funhouse mirrors at a carnival. As he studies his distorted image he, "thinks of himself as a poor man's Dorian Gray" (p. 36). He is referring to *The Picture of Dorian Gray*, a novel by Oscar Wilde (1890/1998), in which the main character remains young and beautiful, while a painted portrait of him slowly transforms into an ugly reflection of his life of debauchery and evil. Such a reference to another literary work is called an **allusion.** In addition to mentioning other stories, an allusion can refer to an event in history, to contemporary people and places, or to popular culture.

Tone

The narrator's language conveys an attitude, or **tone,** toward the characters and events of story and, perhaps, toward the readers. Tone is conveyed through word choice and perspective. A reader might describe the tone of a work as humorous, sarcastic, serious, or poignant. Kathi Appelt builds tension and a sense of seriousness through the lyrical repetition of phrases in *Underneath* (2008). "Go back a thousand years, to this same spot along the creek, here beneath the stars. Go back to the moment Grandmother slithered along the bank, in search of her granddaughter, the little girl who glimmered" (p. 206). In *The Spectacular Now* (2008) by Tim Tharp, readers readily perceive an irreverent and cocky attitude in the main character through the use of profanity, slang, and hyperbole, or exaggeration. This early impression contrasts with the serious, almost sad, tone of the novel when the character is revealed to be a self-centered alcoholic sliding further and further into oblivion and despair.

Literary Elements in *Trouble* by Gary D. Schmidt

Although we provide examples for each of the literary elements, it is easiest to understand them when we see how they are used in a single work. Recognizing and describing this interplay of elements is the ultimate goal of literary conversations. The following analysis of the novel *Trouble* (Schmidt, 2008) shows how these elements can be used to describe a literary work.

The importance of the **integral setting** in *Trouble* is established in the first sentence as the **third person narrator** informs the reader why the family does not live in the town of Trouble: "Henry Smith's father told him that if you build your house far enough away from Trouble, then Trouble will never find you. So the Smiths lived where their people had lived for exactly three hundred years, far away from Trouble, in Blythbury-by-the-Sea" (p. 1).

The **personification** of the town of Trouble throughout the novel gives it character-like qualities, and Henry's confrontations with Trouble in its many forms is the basic plot. Henry and his sibling go to Longfellow Prep and Whittier Academy "with kids whose names were so Anglo-Saxon that King Richard the Lion-Hearted would have recognized them all" (p. 3). This statement **foreshadows** one of the **conflicts,** the racism that is creeping into this part of Massachusetts.

Henry's older brother, Franklin, dies from injuries suffered in a car accident. The presumed driver, Chay Chouan, a Cambodian teenager from a nearby town, is arrested, but not convicted of any crime. Chay's release stirs the racial unrest in the community. Racial tension becomes a direct **person against person** conflict in a fight scene between Chay and Henry, in which Chay does not fight back, and in a physical confrontation with working men who see Chay as the reason their economic situation is bad.

Beginning in chapter two, the first of a series of **flashbacks** signals that the story will be told from an **omniscient point of view** but that it will not be told chronologically. From these short glimpses of the past, the reader gradually pieces together a story that Henry does not know. It is the story of a boy and girl falling in love, an accident, a father's cruel act fueled by racism, and the end of any hope for reconciliation.

Henry sets out to climb Mount Katahdin, a feat Henry's brother Franklin had frequently taunted him he would never accomplish due to his lack of courage. He is accompanied by his friend Sanborn, an ironic, witty, and often abrasive sidekick, and

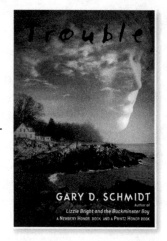

by a stray black dog that appeared at his house one day. Perhaps too coincidently they are picked up by Chay, who is running away from home. He was not guilty of Franklin's death; he was, however, guilty of arson. As Chay's background is revealed, readers learn that he is a result of rape, a survivor of the Khmer Rouge, and hated by his father. The reader, who knows that the flashbacks have been foreshadowing Chay's story, can't help but see the strength in this character, and by contrast, the weaknesses in the others. Even Henry's father casts doubt on his dead son's character when he asks Henry if Franklin would have been a good man.

Symbols are abundant in this novel. The mountain looms high, waiting to be conquered in both the literal and figurative sense. A wreck of an ancient and mysterious slave ship appears in the cove near Henry's house. Black Dog, a marred and injured stray, remains hopeful and faithful. It is Black Dog who holds out her paw in reconciliation. And the act of arson becomes a cleansing of Chay's past.

The revelation for Henry that it was his sister driving the truck, not Chay, is followed quickly by the **climax** in the next chapter, when the fishermen appear at the boys' campsite. Henry is shot, and Chay goes for help and disappears. Henry, Sanborn, Louisa, and Black Dog climb Mount Katahdin, knowing they will find Chay. Chay's rescue and his and Louisa's realization that they must tell the truth and deal with the Trouble that will follow provide the **resolution** and final closure.

Henry has come to realize "The world is Trouble . . . and Grace. That is all there is. . . . It was time to get home. No matter what happens, there is always the business of the world to attend to" (pp. 296–297). This explicit **thematic statement** brings the story full circle. You can't hide from trouble, but when trouble appears—and it will—it can be tempered with mercy and kindness. Henry climbed the mountain not to prove his manliness, but to save the life of another and redeem his own.

There is certainly more to be said about *Trouble,* but this analysis clearly illustrates two points. First, literature for young adults is as sophisticated and complex as any other literature, and second, the terminology of literary analysis is indispensable for discussing such rich and complex literature—inside or outside of the classroom. Using literary language with ease takes time, however, and it is most likely to occur when students can discuss literature in a supportive environment with a skillful teacher.

classroom scenario

Guiding a Grand Conversation

Grand Conversation is a term used by Peterson and Eeds (1990) to describe how readers can uncover deeper layers of meaning as they share their ideas about a text. Unlike some other forms of discussion, the teacher does not direct a Grand Conversation toward predetermined issues or conclusions. Instead, the teacher guides the conversation by listening carefully and interjecting a few carefully chosen remarks, particularly those that supply students with the language of literature. The process is illustrated by the following case, in which Mr. Gabrielli's eighth-grade class has an open-ended Grand Conversation about their responses to the Newberry award-winning novel Criss Cross *(Perkins, 2005), a book that follows the intertwining stories of 14-year-old Debbie, her neighbor Lenny, and their friend Hector throughout one apparently uneventful but still memorable summer.*

AS YOU READ, notice how the teacher enters the conversation just a few times, carefully choosing moments when he can draw students' attention to issues and elements that appear in many literary works. As you will see, he uses the conversation to further his students' use and understanding of literary elements.

The students in Mr. Gabrielli's class, who have almost finished reading the book, are arranged in one big circle and invited to say something about the novel. Laryssa begins by mentioning that she likes the way Debbie's lost necklace keeps turning up and getting passed from one person to another, and she adds a prediction that sooner or later it will come back to Debbie.

Sofie says, "I thought Debbie was going to be the main character, but then Hector started being more important." Several students then chime in on the main character question. After a few minutes, Mr. G. asks if it is possible for a book to have more than one protagonist and whether they can think of a book or movie that might be an example. Eventually, Curt suggests *The X-Men*, and there is a general agreement because the characters in the movie "kind of take turns" being the focus of the story.

Jake takes the conversation in a new direction. He seems annoyed with the book because "nothing seems to happen." Other students agree that in much of the book the friends "just hang out," but Laryssa says, "that's just like real life. Sometimes nothing big happens." Again, Mr. G. poses a question. He asks them to think about the four kinds of conflicts and to identify any conflicts the characters might be facing.

Students mention Debbie's mixed feelings about Colin, a boy from out of town she meets while he is visiting family. They also mention Hector's pursuit of a girl in his guitar class and several other examples. They conclude that the conflicts are "pretty much internal." Mr. G. follows up by asking, "Do you see any changes in the characters as the book goes on?" Students name a number of examples such as Debbie's new understandings about love and some new skills that the characters are developing. Curt sums up by saying, "something is happening, but not anything very dramatic."

Various students take their turns saying something about the book, with many of their remarks identifying incidents that they particularly liked. Marcee then says that she was confused about the scene where the narrator relates Debbie's thoughts as she is reading the book *Wuthering Heights*. Marcee explains that she went online and found out that Wuthering Heights was about a young woman who is trying to decide which of two men she really loves. She says that she then understood that "Debbie was thinking about which one was better, Colin or Hector, so it sort of made sense."

Mr. G. adds that there is a name for what the author was doing in that section. He writes *allusion* on the whiteboard, and he explains that the author, Lynn Rae Perkins, was making an allusion to another book hoping that some readers would "get it" and that it would help them understand something about Debbie. As the conversation winds down, Mr. G. leaves the class with a question. "Why is the title of this book *Criss-Cross*? What does it tell you about what the author thinks is happening in this book?"

Notice that the students' conversation touches on many elements of fiction literature. Using terms such as *protagonist* and *plot* makes their conversation easier. In some places, though, they need assistance. Mr. G. supplies the term *allusion* because it is useful in the context of what Marcee was trying to explain. He does not use the term *episodic plot*, but he does mention the concept. His closing questions lay the groundwork for introducing the term during the next day's discussion. In conversations such as this, students gradually incorporate the vocabulary that will support their appreciation of both conventional and metafictive literature.

USING METAFICTIVE TERMS IN LITERARY CONVERSATIONS

Some of the difficulties the students experience in understanding *Criss-Cross* are undoubtedly caused by its differences from many of the other books they have read. It does not seem to fit into any particular genre, and that makes it harder to predict where it is heading or to see the pattern that holds the incidents of the plot together. As we discussed in Chapter 1, many contemporary books for young adults are deliberately designed to thwart readers' expectations. These works are often labeled *metafictive*, and the usual terminology may not adequately describe them. In the following section, we examine some of the language that is useful to teachers and students as they engage in discussions about metafictive texts.

Nonlinear Plots and Multiple Settings

Nonlinearity means that rather than following a straight line through a series of events, the narrative text veers off in different directions. The plot of a novel like *Trouble* is basically chronological even though it employs flashbacks to fill readers in on events that happened in the past. The flashbacks create occasional brief interruptions, but the reader is still able to discern the flow of the main plot. Some plots, however, are nonlinear; they do not follow a chronological straight line long enough for readers to be sure about either the order or the direction of events. Nonlinear stories may have multiple and extensive jumps in time. In addition to flashbacks, they may have **flash forwards** that allow the reader to know the outcome of an event before it happens.

An example of a nonlinear novel is Lynn Cullen's, *I Am Rembrandt's Daughter* (2007). The story is told through numerous flashbacks and flash forwards, narrated by the protagonist. A date is established in the prologue, which is then followed by a chapter set three years earlier. The pattern of moving both forward and backwards in time is framed around particular works by Rembrandt. Kathryn Lasky's *Blood Secret* (2004), a story chronicling the history of Sephardic Jews, is also nonlinear. It shifts back and forth from specific events in history to a modern setting. Each shift to another historical event features a first person narrator living in that time.

Rebecca Stead's Newbery honor book *When You Reach Me* (2009) is another example of a nonlinear plot. At first it seems like a straightforward story set in the 1970s, about a young girl living with her divorced mother and trying to maintain her relationships with friends. When inexplicable events and mysterious messages begin to appear, readers react by looking for suspects among the characters. It is not until the last chapter that they realize that the events of the story have actually been shaped by influences from many years in the future. In effect, readers must completely revise their understanding of the order and meaning of events after they read the last page.

Self-Reference

When a novel exposes the process of creating the book or acknowledges the existence of the author, readers are reminded that they are immersed in fiction, and the book is said to be **self-referential.** Occasionally this technique takes the form of an author speaking directly to the reader, but in *The Sledding Hill* (2005), Chris Crutcher actually puts himself in the story. As himself, he visits a school where a fictional book authored by him is being censored. The book jacket notes that Crutcher "is wrestling with writer's block."

Multiple Points of View

The use of **multiple points of view** is one of the more prominent metafictive devices found in contemporary literature for young adults. Different voices may be used in postmodern texts to acknowledge that no one has a monopoly on truth and that the meaning of events depends greatly on the person who observes them. At times, instead of a single story, a metafictive novel will contain multiple narratives told from different points of view. In Andrea Davis Pinkney's *Bird in a Box* (2011), three children tell their separate first person stories. Their names—Hibernia, Willie, and Otis—are used as chapter titles. Some chapters portray their individual lives, but others are about their shared experiences and their love for the boxer Joe Louis.

Multiple narrators can provide differing perspectives on the same events, or they may each provide separate pieces of a whole narrative that the individual characters alone are not privy to. In *Sweetgrass Basket* (2005) by Marlene Carvell, two young Mohawk sisters, Sarah and Mattie, are sent by their father to live at the Carlisle Indian Industrial School. Their story is told in a prose poetry style using alternating voices. The use of multiple narrators is signaled both by including the teller's name in the chapter titles and by the typography of the chapters. The typeface for Mattie, the elder but smaller sister, is bold, but the chapters from

Sarah's perspective are written in lighter print. In the early chapters, the sisters are responding to the same events, but in later chapters their experiences begin to diverge. Using character names as chapter titles and varying the typefaces are devices that make the alternating voices immediately obvious.

Not the End of the World by Geraldine McCaughrean (2004) is a stark picture of survival and death on Noah's ark. All of the chapters are told in the first person, but the perspective shifts from chapter to chapter among various narrators, both human and animal. The cast of characters is listed at the beginning of the book, and most of the chapters identify the narrator in the title. The first chapter, however, is simply titled "Day One," and the reader does not fully realize who the narrator is until she is addressed by name, Timna. She becomes the primary narrator, and whenever she resumes the story the chapter title includes "Timna Continues."

The Sisterhood of the Traveling Pants by Ann Brashares (2001) tells the individual stories of four friends as a pair of pants are sent from one girl to another. The narrator of each chapter is not identified in the chapter title, but her identity is revealed in the context of the first sentence. The novel begins with a first person prologue explaining the purchase of the pants, as told by Carmen, and an explanation of the girls' relationship. The epilogue is also in Carmen's voice as she reflects on their summer experiences, their friendship, and, of course, the pants.

With multiple points of view, questions about the credibility of the narrator are also multiplied. The reader must carefully consider which of the tellers, if any, is trustworthy. *The Secret Twin* by Denise Gosliner Orenstein (2006) has two characters: Noah, a surviving conjoined twin, and Grace, the nurse hired to care for his grandmother while she recovers from plastic surgery. At least that is what the reader is told by Noah, whose first person voice is the first that the reader encounters. Grace's chapters are told in third person. Noah's inability to face reality is not revealed until the end of the story when the reader learns that his grandmother is actually dead.

Dead Connections by Charlie Price (2006) features various characters relating the events surrounding the murder of a teenage girl. The multiple voices include a boy who hears dead people, an alcoholic police officer, and a mentally unstable adolescent. The unreliable narrators provide a heightened sense of mystery as the reader must determine the veracity of each voice. The multiple viewpoints do not clarify events; they actually obscure the truth to allow the mystery to unfold.

Experimentation with Style

Authors of contemporary literature for young adults show a willingness to experiment that is part of a postmodern attitude. They employ almost every conceivable style, including some that might be called "retro." In the Newbery award winning *The Tale of Despereaux* (2003), Kate DiCamillo's narrator adopts a device that is a throwback to earlier centuries by directly addressing the reader in an elaborately courteous style: "The world is dark, and light is precious. Come closer, dear reader. You must trust me. I am telling you a story."

VanSickle (2006) noted that using free verse in a novel rather than regular prose is a postmodern stylistic innovation that is especially captivating for a young adult audience. Sullivan (2003) summed up the appeal of this style by pointing out that poetry lends itself well to introspection and intense emotion and that verse has the practical attraction of short lines and lots of white space.

Ellen Hopkins has written several verse novels that successfully combine a poetic style with harsh realism. *Impulse* (2007) is the story of three adolescents who have tried to kill themselves and are now in a residential facility. Each of their stories is told in their individual voice in varying styles of free verse that differ visually and rhythmically. Although each chapter is identified by the character's name, this soon becomes unnecessary as the reader comes to recognize each character by his or her style of verse.

Mixing and Inventing Genres

Combining or even inventing genres is a metafictive technique that has become increasingly common in contemporary literature for young adults. The breaking of genre conventions is often reflected in nontraditional structures or in unconventional design layout and typography. Electronic books offer additional opportunities to go beyond the traditional printed page, but even a traditional printed book today uses various unexpected and descriptive formats to help tell a story. Walter Dean Myers' *Shooter* (2004), for example, incorporates multiple formats, such as police and counselor interviews, newspaper and police reports, and diary entries, as part of the investigation of a school shooting. A yellow strip reading "Police Line Do Not Cross" adorns the cover of the novel to foreshadow its content.

In another example, the first part of *Holdup* by Terri Fields (2007) is told in a typical narrative format, although from multiple perspectives. In the next section, the location of the action is identified as specific spots at the Burger Heaven restaurant, such as the parking lot, the back booth, or the door. Multiple print media, such as a school paper, newspaper interview, speeches, e-mails, and letters are used to draw closure to each character's life.

The entire story of *ttyl* by Lauren Myracle (2004) is written in instant messages sent between three sophomore girls; see Figure 3.2 for an example. The title, which is texting jargon for "talk to you later," is indicative of the language throughout the book. Each page of the book suggests the shape and typography of a computer screen. Color, as well as vocabulary and sentence structure, are used to distinguish the three writers, so the name of the writer becomes unnecessary. *Nothing but the Truth: A Documentary Novel* by Avi (1991) combines classroom discussions, diaries, newspaper articles, school memos, and announcements, and yet a reader has no difficulty responding to the overall novel as realistic contemporary fiction. Although the mixed elements create a format that differs from the expected, the content does not. It tells a fairly familiar story of a contemporary adolescent male having a conflict with a teacher and trying to get out of her class.

A page from *ttyl,* written in instant messages.   *figure* **3.2**

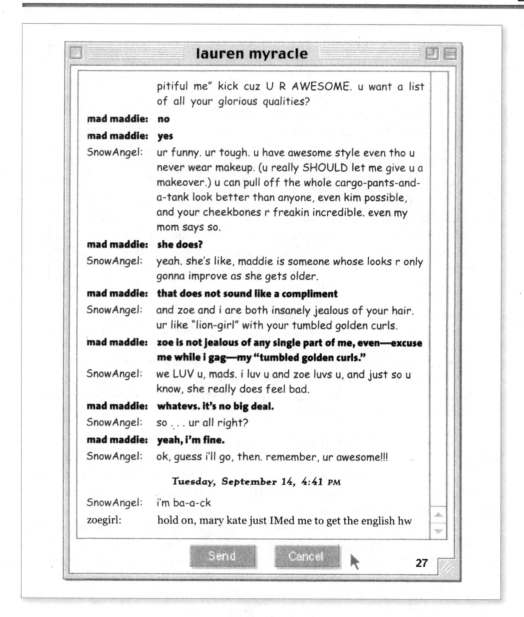

	lauren myracle

> pitiful me" kick cuz U R AWESOME. u want a list of all your glorious qualities?

mad maddie: **no**

mad maddie: **yes**

SnowAngel: ur funny. ur tough. u have awesome style even tho u never wear makeup. (u really SHOULD let me give u a makeover.) u can pull off the whole cargo-pants-and-a-tank look better than anyone, even kim possible, and your cheekbones r freakin incredible. even my mom says so.

mad maddie: **she does?**

SnowAngel: yeah. she's like, maddie is someone whose looks r only gonna improve as she gets older.

mad maddie: **that does not sound like a compliment**

SnowAngel: and zoe and i are both insanely jealous of your hair. ur like "lion-girl" with your tumbled golden curls.

mad maddie: **zoe is not jealous of any single part of me, even—excuse me while i gag—my "tumbled golden curls."**

SnowAngel: we LUV u, mads. i luv u and zoe luvs u, and just so u know, she really does feel bad.

mad maddie: **whatevs. it's no big deal.**

SnowAngel: so . . . ur all right?

mad maddie: **yeah, i'm fine.**

SnowAngel: ok, guess i'll go, then. remember, ur awesome!!!

Tuesday, September 14, 4:41 PM

SnowAngel: i'm ba-a-ck

zoegirl: hold on, mary kate just IMed me to get the english hw

Send   Cancel   27

Intertextuality in Metafictive Literature

As noted previously, all literary works show some level of intertextuality, because all literature is influenced by the works that have come before. Some texts, however, include more consciously intertextual references than others. In particular, metafictive texts may be deliberately connected to other works in ways that go far beyond allusion. As a metafictive device, intertextuality implies that a new work is created and understood largely through its relationship to a previous work or works. The newer work may be an extension that invites readers to build on their experiences with an earlier work, or it may be a reinvention that stimulates readers to reexamine the previous work or to reconsider their interpretations of it.

Dark Sons by Nikki Grimes (2005) is a young adult novel that provides a striking example of intertextuality as a narrative device. It simultaneously tells two stories: the biblical story of Ishmael and the modern story of Sam, a child of divorce. The characters have no physical connection to each other, yet both share similar emotions and experiences. In the final chapter, Sam reads the Genesis account of Ishmael and makes the connection that he and Ishmael are like brothers, two dark sons. In order to fully understand Sam, the reader needs to be aware of the biblical story of Abraham and Ishmael.

Several kinds of intertextuality are evident between Rebecca Stead's *When You Reach Me* (2009) and Madeleine L'Engle's *A Wrinkle in Time* (1962). In an interview, Stead explained that she had loved L'Engle's book as a child and as an adult still admired its insight into human emotions and fragility combined with fearlessness in taking on life's big questions (Stead, n.d.). Initially, Stead simply made an allusion to *Wrinkle* as the favorite book of Miranda, her main character, but that initial connection grew.

> As my story went deeper, I saw that I didn't want to let the book go. I talked about it with my editor, Wendy Lamb, and to others close to the story. And what we decided was that if we were going to bring L'Engle's story in, we needed to make the book's relationship to Miranda's story stronger. So I went back to *A Wrinkle in Time* and read it again and again, trying to see it as different characters in my own story might (sounds crazy, but it's possible!). And those readings led to new connections.

Stead's finished novel included several conversations about *Wrinkle* between Miranda and a mysterious new boy at her school who eventually plays a crucial role in the plot. In fact, those conversations and her understanding of L'Engle's book are the means for Miranda (and the reader) to piece together the actual chain of events that has occurred.

The young adult novel *The Looking Glass Wars* by Frank Beddor (2006) is intertwined with Lewis Carroll's classics *Alice's Adventure in Wonderland* (1865) and *Through the Looking-Glass* (1871). In Beddor's novel, Carroll's novels are treated as fiction, but Alice is treated as real. The novel includes other characters from the original books, such as the Queen of Hearts (Aunt Redd) and the Cheshire Cat. In *The Witch's Boy* by Michael Gruber (2005), many separate intertextual connections to traditional tales are intricately woven throughout the novel. Near the end, the tale of Rumpelstiltskin is revealed to be the underlying narrative that connects to the major theme of the novel, but the book's intertextuality creates connections to multiple folk tales.

Literary conversations about books with one or more metafictive traits require both teachers and students to acquire both a new vocabulary and new tools for interpretation. The following classroom scenario suggests one way to begin that process.

classroom scenario

Introducing Metafictive Novels with Picture Books

Using picture books with older children is a well-established instructional approach for teaching concepts, content, genre, and reading strategies (Billman, 2002; Fingerson & Killeen, 2005; Zambo, 2005). In the following Guided Literature Study, Ms. Andrews pairs picture books that exemplify metafictive traits with novels that have the same characteristics. AS YOU READ, consider how picture books are used to stimulate literary conversations that make it easier to understand longer works later on.

Ms. Andrews begins by writing "Metafictive Literature" on an interactive whiteboard. Under this heading she adds "intertextuality, nonlinearity, self-reference, multiple perspectives, and nontraditional structure or format." She explains that the class is going to be reading novels that don't follow the rules of how novels usually work. To help them understand these characteristics, they first are going to read some picture books. The students laugh and comment that this should be easy.

Ms. Andrews projects the fixed-layout ebook version of David Macaulay's *Black and White* (1990) on the whiteboard and reads the first few pages. Her students mutter that the book does not make sense. When asked why, they reply that the pictures do not go together and they cannot figure out who the story is about or what is happening. Josh comments that the "warning" on the cover page said there might be four stories or there might only be one. Ms. Andrews suggests that they look at the entire book first and maybe that will help them decide how to read it. When they finish, several students comment that they did not expect a picture book to "take so much thinking" to read and that the unusual format was difficult to follow.

Next, Ms. Andrews holds up the picture book Macaulay's *Shortcut* (1995). Katie comments that the book is by the same author and they had better be prepared to be tricked again. Ms. Andrews responds that the book is nonlinear, so they will not be able to follow the events of the story in chronological order. Therefore, they may have to reread some of the chapters before they can figure out the relationship between what appear to be disconnected events. Afterward, the students create a chronological timeline of the events.

Over the next few days, Ms. Andrews continues to introduce metafictive characteristics. *Once Upon a Fairy Tale* (Starbright Foundation, 2001) contains many traditional fairy tales; however, each story is told from multiple perspectives. While the class listens to the CD that came with the book, Ms. Andrews shows the pictures. Audio versions of each character's perspective are narrated by famous people, including Hugh Grant, Mike Myers, Oprah Winfrey, and Conan O'Brien. The class discusses how the multiple perspectives change the traditional versions of the stories. Samantha says that "Wolf von Big Baden" is hilarious and she never thought about the wolf at all in the original story, but the picture of him dancing around in Granny's robe and rabbit slippers made her laugh. Ms. Andrews tells the class they are making "intertextual connections," or thinking about one story or version of a story in contrast to another.

In *Do Not Open this Book!* by Michaela Muntean, illustrated by Pascal Lemaitre (2006), Pig continually reprimands the reader for turning the page. He reveals that he needs more time to think, and he has not decided on a genre. Pig leaves blanks in the story and invites the reader to fill them in. Following

(continued)

Ms. Andrew's read-aloud of the book, the students discuss how the author is calling attention to the writing process. One of the students responds that this must be the trait called *self-referential*. Ms. Andrews asks him why, and Mike explains that the author is referring to himself.

Ms. Andrews shares with the class *The Three Pigs* (2001) by David Wiesner. This book has several metafictive traits. The pigs talk directly to the reader; they fly out of the book, and they fly in and out of different stories. These stories are written and illustrated in different styles. One is a nursery rhyme, the other uses very formal language. The students label each of these traits with the corresponding metafictive term and discuss what they think about the story.

The last picture book the students look at is *Snowflake Bentley* (1998) by Jacqueline Briggs Martin, illustrated by Briggs Martin and Mary Azarian. This book combines a fictionalized biography of snowflake expert Wilson Bentley with nonfiction information presented in side panels. Ms. Andrews places additional picture books around the room and encourages students to look at them during their Reading Workshop time.

A day or two later, Ms. Andrews introduces the novels the students will be reading. Because she knows her students need to focus on metafictive traits, she has selected a variety of novels at their independent reading levels: *Out of Order* (Hicks, 2005) uses multiple narrators; *Project Mulberry* (Park, 2005) has a self-referential discussion between one of the characters and the author; *Victory* (Cooper, 2006) uses two narrators and a nonlinear time line; *Letters from Rapunzel* (Holmes, 2007) makes an intertextual connection to Rapunzel and uses a nontraditional format, and Gary Paulsen's *The Legend of Bass Reeves* (2006) mixes genres.

Each day the students read the novels silently and keep reading logs in which they respond to questions related to the metafictive characteristics. Students who are reading the same novel meet in Literature Circle after they have read a few chapters. They meet again to share their reading log entries midway through the book and after they have finished.

Throughout this unit, students' conversations as a whole class and as members of small groups are an important element in their developing understanding of metafictive elements. These conversations, are, moreover, supported by their knowledge of the language of literature.

Encouraging Intertextual Connections through Bridging

Ms. Andrew's unit provides an effective example of an approach called bridging that draws connections between literary texts in order to highlight elements they have in common. The term was introduced in Sarah Herz's influential book *From Hinton to Hamlet: Building Bridges Between Young Adult Literature and the Classics* (1996). Herz proposed that literature for young adults could be a bridge that crossed the gap between the intended curriculum and students' actual literary knowledge and skills. "By linking YAL with the classics," Herz wrote, "we can see our students become developing readers, connecting, comparing and drawing parallels about the elements of literature they discover independently" (p. 25–26).

Ms. Andrews' unit used bridging from short illustrated texts to novels and from teacher read-alouds to independent small-group reading of novels. We have expanded the concept of **bridging** to take in any pairing or grouping of literary works for the purpose of creating intertextual connections. Defined in such a way, bridging is a highly useful and flexible approach for developing literary concepts.

Bridging to works in the canon

Using literature for young adults to scaffold students' understanding of more complex classical or canonical works has become a well-established practice. Joan Kaywell's four volume reference set, *Adolescent Literature as a Complement to the Classics* (1993, 1995, 1997, 2000), for instance, identifies literature for young adults from the 1990s that can support students' reading of canonical works. A bridge may be based on similarities in either the content or the form of the two works. A novel for young adults might be deliberately chosen to introduce a setting, conflict, or theme that also appears in a more challenging work.

Reading *If I Should Die Before I Wake* (Nolan, 1994), for example, could prepare students for Elie Wiesel's *Night* (1960), a novel considered by Jago (2000) to be a required classic. Both novels force the reader to examine the protagonist's struggle to maintain faith and the will to stay alive. Nolan's book juxtaposes the story of a contemporary neo-Nazi girl with that of a young Jewish girl struggling to survive in a World War II death camp. *If I Should Die before I Wake* may be easier to read than *Night*, which was written for an adult audience, but its descriptions of concentration camps are no less horrific. If students are to read a canonical work with mature themes, then the novel for young adults that is used as a bridge must also have a mature treatment of the circumstances and theme.

Karen Hesse's Newbery Medal winner *Out of the Dust* (1997) provides another example of a novel for young adults that can be an effective bridge to a classic story with mature themes and a rather grim setting. Both Hesse's novel and *The Grapes of Wrath* (1939) by John Steinbeck examine the impact of the dust bowl of the Great Depression by focusing on one family. *The Grapes of Wrath* details the Joad family's struggle to survive as they try to relocate from dust-ravaged Oklahoma to California. *Out of the Dust* tells a story of a young girl whose family remains in Oklahoma but is plagued by poverty, illness, and a horrible accident that kills the mother and her unborn child. Both novels deal with mature themes presented with vivid imagery and challenging language and style.

Latham (2008) pointed out several intertextual connections to challenging adult works in David Almond's young adult novel *Skellig* (1998). The story is about a boy who encounters an owl-like creature that may be an angel and may be responsible for saving his seriously ill baby sister. Almond's story has many parallels to Gabriel Garcia Marquez's short story "A Very Old Man with Enormous Wings" (1972), and he has acknowledged the influence of Marquez's work on his writing. Although *Skellig* contains no direct allusion to Marquez's work, it could be used as a bridge to Marquez's story or to other stories that fit within the narrative tradition known as magic realism. In magic realism, the realistic world is convincingly real, but fantastical elements emerge in a way that may make the reader question what is real and what is not. Students might need some assistance with magical realism because it usually fuses fantasy and reality without any clues to signal which are the fantastical aspects of the story.

Skellig also contains numerous quotations from William Blake's poetry. Although Blake is mentioned, the novel includes none of his poems in its entirety. Instead, pieces of the poetry are included in the regular prose in what Latham (2008) calls a collage. Readers might ignore the bits of Blake, but if they are guided carefully they will encounter some remarkable new literary experiences. They will also gain an additional understanding of the themes in *Skellig* that can enhance their literary conversations. Almond invites his readers "to become active participants in the making of meaning" (Latham, p. 225). Teachers can support this sort of "co-authoring" by creating appropriate bridges between texts.

Reverse bridging

Using a young adult novel as a scaffold to a work in the literary canon is only one form of bridging. The process could also be structured as a **reverse bridging** so that students read a challenging work with a great deal of teacher assistance, and that work then becomes a bridge to less challenging literature that young adults will read more independently (Knickerbocker & Rycik, 2002). A teacher using the guided literature study routine that we introduced in the previous chapter could, for example, introduce the historical context of *Night* and guide students to consider themes of faith and resilience. Students could then move into literature circles or a reading workshop routine in order to read related literature for young adults, including *If I Should Die Before I Wake* (Nolan, 1994).

Reverse bridging fosters teaching for independence by using a gradual release of responsibility model (Pearson & Gallagher, 1983) that moves from teacher modeling and heavy scaffolding with a work in the literary cannon to guided practice, and then to student application of literary concepts and strategies for interpretation in the young adult novel. Such an approach allows a teacher to assess students' ability to interpret developmentally appropriate literary texts rather than their memory of what they were told about a work in the canon. Reversing the usual sequence of bridging also allows students to see that the themes and techniques of canonical literature endure and continue to have relevance for contemporary readers and writers.

Other forms of bridging

By comparing works that have literary elements, themes, or other aspects in common, teachers can create scaffolds in which each work supports the understanding of another. In this way, the underlying intertextuality of literature becomes more apparent. Various forms of literature, both print and nonprint, can be paired or grouped in many ways to make useful bridges. The following are just a few examples:

Bridging by literary elements. Novels written in a more traditional style and structure can be paired with metafictive novels by genre, theme, author, or a particular literary device in order to encourage comparisons. If the focus is on novels with metafictive characteristics, books can be grouped based on a particular element, such as multiple perspectives.

Bridging by author. Author studies are another way of highlighting intertextual connections. In addition to *Skellig* other works by David Almond also have explicit and implicit intertextuality. Reading his *Kit's Wilderness* (1999) and *Clay* (2005) in addition to *Skellig* provides an opportunity to investigate intertextuality more thoroughly by comparing and contrasting these novels.

Bridging with media. Bridging between film and print literature is discussed at length in Chapter 11. Television shows can also be effective bridges for focusing on a particular literary element. In *Malcolm in the Middle* (Boomer, 2000–2006), Malcolm talks directly to the audience, thereby breaking the wall between story and audience, and Michael Weston, a deposed spy, uses a similar technique in *Burn Notice*, created by Matt Nix (2007). Both shows provide opportunities to consider how point of view affects a literary experience.

Bridging by issues or characters. Multiple works that present an issue or social situation may elicit more reader engagement than any single selection could. We have mentioned several novels in previous chapters that have protagonists who are young males from minority cultures. The following grouping contains a graphic novel, illustrated novels, novels with metafictive characteristics, and novels written in a traditional narrative: *American Born Chinese* (Yang, 2006); *Buried Onions* (Soto, 1997); *Homeboyz* (Sitomer, 2007); *The Death of Jayson Porter* (Adoff, 2008); and *The Absolutely True Diary of a Part-time Indian* (Alexie, 2007). Regardless of the order in which these works are read, readers will likely find their understanding of racism growing as they make intertextual connections.

In this chapter, we have highlighted the importance of talk as an approach to teaching and learning about literature. Involving young adults in literary conversations has the obvious advantage of tapping into their natural inclination to be social, and may in turn foster the kinds of rewarding experiences that can stem the threat of aliteracy described in the first chapter. Teachers do not have to choose, however, between fostering positive attitudes and academic growth. As stated earlier, the Common Core State Standards for the English Language Arts (2010) affirm the importance of being able to listen to others and to build on their ideas, and advocates participation in the kinds of conversations that are featured in this chapter.

In this chapter, we also explored the concept of intertextuality as it is applied to genre study, metafictive literature, and the instructional technique of bridging. The instructional applications of intertextual connections will continue to be important throughout the rest of this book.

In Chapters 4 through 9, we will examine major genres of literature familiar to most teachers, beginning with the fiction genres. Realistic fiction refers to stories that could be possible. Historical fiction denotes realistic stories set in a past time and place that influences all aspects of the plot. Traditional or folk literature consists of stories told, retold, and sometimes revised from generation to generation. Fantasy is a genre that often takes place in an imaginary setting and depicts events and characters that may defy the laws of physics. Following

conclusion

the fiction genres, we examine literary nonfiction. This consists of texts, including biography and autobiography, that present factual information using many of the devices that characterize good fiction. The distinct features of poetry and drama are considered in Chapter 9. For each of these genres, we describe useful groupings of literary works that highlight connections in content and form. We also present teaching activities that are embedded in a range of classroom literacy routines.

BIBLIOGRAPHY OF LITERATURE FOR YOUNG ADULTS

Adoff, J. (2008). *The death of Jayson Porter.* New York: Hyperion.

Alexie, S. (2007). *The absolutely true diary of a part-time Indian.* New York: Little, Brown.

Almond, D. (1998). *Skellig.* New York: Dell Yearling.

Almond, D. (1999). *Kit's wilderness.* New York: Delacorte.

Almond, D. (2005). *Clay.* New York: Delacorte Press.

Appelt, K. (2008). *Underneath.* (D. Small, Illus.). New York: Atheneum.

Attenborough, R. (Dir.). (1982). *Gandhi.* United Kingdom/India: Goldcrest Films/Columbia Pictures Corporation.

Avi. (1991). *Nothing but the truth: A documentary novel.* New York: Orchard Books.

Beddor, F. (2006). *The looking glass war.* New York: Dial.

Boomer, L. (Creator). (2000–2006). *Malcolm in the middle.* [Television series]. Los Angeles, CA: Fox Network.

Brashares, A. (2001). *The sisterhood of the traveling pants.* New York: Delacorte.

Bronte, E. (1847/1983). *Wuthering Heights.* New York: Bantam Classics.

Carroll, L. (1865). *Alice's adventures in Wonderland.* London: Macmillan.

Carroll, L. (1871). *Through the looking-glass.* London: Macmillan.

Carvell, M. (2005). *Sweetgrass basket.* New York: Dutton Children's Books.

Choldenko, G. (2004). *Al Capone does my shirts.* New York: Scholastic.

Columbus, C. (Dir.). (2001). *Harry Potter and the sorcerer's stone.* USA: Warner Brothers.

Cooper, S. (2006). *Victory.* New York: Margaret K. McElderry Books.

Cormier, R. (1980, 1995). "Mine on Thursdays." In *8 plus 1.* St. Louis, MO: Turtleback.

Crutcher, C. (2005). *The sledding hill.* New York: Greenwillow Books.

Cullen, L. (2007). *I am Rembrandt's daughter.* New York: Bloomsbury U.S.A.

DiCamillo, K. (2003). *The tale of Despereaux.* (Timothy Basil Ering, Illus.). Cambridge, MA: Candlewick Press.

Dickens, C. (1843/1985). *A Christmas carol.* London: Hancellor Press.

Fields, T. (2007). *Holdup.* New Milford, CT: Roaring Brook Press.

Fleming, V. (Dir.). (1939). *The wizard of Oz.* U.S.A.: Warner Brothers.

Garcia Marquez, G. (1972). "A very old man with enormous wings." In *Leaf storm, and other stories.* (G. Rabassa, Trans.). New York: Harper, pp. 105–112.

Grimes, N. (2005). *Dark sons.* New York: Hyperion.

Gruber, M. (2005). *The witch's boy.* New York: HarperTempest.

Hesse, K. (1997). *Out of the dust.* New York: Scholastic.

Hicks, B. (2005). *Out of order.* Milford, CT: Roaring Brook Press.

Holmes, S. L. (2007). *Letters from Rapunzel.* New York: HarperCollins.

Hopkins, E. (2007). *Impulse.* New York: Margaret K. McElderry.

Lee, H. (1960). *To kill a mockingbird.* Philadelphia, PA: Lippincott.

Lasky, K. (2004). *Blood secret.* New York: HarperCollins.

L'Engle, M. (1962). *A wrinkle in time.* New York: Farrar, Straus & Giroux.

Lieb, J. (2009). *I am a genius of unspeakable evil and I want to be your class president.* New York: Penguin.

Lowry, L. (1993). *The giver.* Boston, MA: Houghton Mifflin.

Lowry, L. (2000). *Gathering blue.* Boston, MA: Houghton Mifflin.

Lucas, G. (1977). *Star wars.* U.S.A.: 20th Century Fox.

Macaulay, D. (1990). *Black and white.* Boston, MA: Houghton Mifflin.

Macaulay, D. (1995). *Shortcut.* Boston, MA: Houghton Mifflin.

Marchetta, M. (2006). *Jellicoe Road.* New York: HarperTeen.

Martin, J. B. (1998). *Snowflake Bentley.* (M. Azarian, Illus.). Boston, MA: Houghton Mifflin.

McCaughrean, G. (2004). *Not the end of the world.* New York: HarperTempest.

Muntean, M. (2006). *Do not open this book!* (P. Lemaitre, Illus.). New York: Scholastic.

Myers, W. D. (2004). *Shooter.* New York: HarperTempest.

Myracle, L. (2004). *ttyl.* New York: Amulet Books.

Na, A. (2001). *A step from heaven.* Asheville, NC: Front Street.

Nix, M. (Producer/Creator). (2007). *Burn notice.* [Television series]. Miami, FL: USA Network.

Nolan, H. (1994). *If I should die before I wake.* San Diego, CA: Harcourt Brace.

Nolan, H. (2001). *Born blue.* San Diego, CA: Harcourt.

Orenstein, D. G. (2006). *The secret twin.* New York: HarperTeen.

Park, L. S. (2002). *When my name was Keoko.* New York: Clarion.

Park, L. S. (2005). *Project mulberry.* New York: Clarion.

Paulsen, G. (2006). *The legend of Bass Reeves.* New York: Wendy Lamb.

Peck, R. (1998). *A long way from Chicago.* New York: Dial.

Peck, R. (2000). *A year down under.* New York: Dial.

Peck, R. (2009). *A season of gifts.* New York: Dial.

Perkins, L. (2005). *Criss cross.* New York: HarperCollins.

Pinkney, A. D. (2011). *Bird in a box.* (S. Qualls, Illus.). New York: Little, Brown.

Poe, E. A. (1843). "The tell-tale heart." Retrieved April 10, 2012, from www.-literature.org/author/poe-edgar-allan/tell-tale-heart.html.

Pratchett, T. (2008). *Nation.* New York: HarperCollins.

Price, C. (2006). *Dead connections.* New Milford, CT: Roaring Brook Press.

Ryan, C. (2009). *The forest of hands and teeth.* New York: Delacorte.

Schmidt, G. (2008). *Trouble.* New York: Clarion.

Sitomer, A. L. (2007). *Homeboyz.* New York: Hyperion.

Smelcer, J. (2006). *The trap.* New York: Holt.

Soto, G. (1997). *Buried onions.* New York: HarperCollins.

Starbright Foundation. (2001). *Once upon a fairy tale.* New York: Penguin.

Stead, R. (2009). *When you reach me.* New York: Wendy Lamb.

Steinbeck, J. (1939). *The grapes of wrath.* New York: Viking.

Tharp, T. (2008). *The spectacular now.* New York: Knopf.

Wiesner, D. (2001). *The three pigs.* New York: Clarion.

Wilde, O. (1890/1998). *The picture of Dorian Gray.* New York: Random House.

Wiesel, E. (1960). *Night.* (S. Rodway, Trans.). New York: Hill & Wang.

Yang, G. L. (2006). *American born Chinese.* New York: First Second.

WEBSITES WITH ANNOTATIONS

Magical Words • **www.magicalwords.net/**
Writing tips and publishing advice for aspiring novelists.

Schmidt, Gary D. • **www.hmhbooks.com/schmidt/index.html**
The author's official website, including summaries of works and resources for educators.

REFERENCES

Allen, J. (2000). *Yellow brick roads: Shared and guided paths to independent reading, 4–12.* Portland, ME: Stenhouse.

Billman, L. W. (2002). Aren't these books for little kids? *Educational Leadership, 60*(3), 48–51.

Cairney, T. H. (1996). Pathways to meaning making: Fostering intertextuality in the classroom. In L. B. Gambrel & J. F. Almasi (Eds.), *Lively discussions! Fostering engaged reading* (pp. 170–180). Newark: DE: International Reading Association.

Fingerson, J., & Killeen, E. B. (2005). Picture books for young adults. *Teacher Librarian, 33*(4), 32–34.

Hall, A. (2007). The social implications of enjoyment of different types of music, movies, and television programming. *Western Journal of Communication, 71*(4), 259–271.

Harris, T. L., & Hodges, R. (Eds.) (1995). *The literacy dictionary: The vocabulary of reading and writing* (pp. 95–96). Newark DE: International Reading Association.

Herz, S. K. (1996). *From Hinton to Hamlet: Building bridges between young adult literature and the classics.* Westport, CT: Greenwood Press.

Jago, C. (2000). *With rigor for all: Teaching the classics to contemporary students.* Portland, ME: Calendar Islands.

Kaywell, J. E. (Ed.) (1993, 1995, 1997, 2000). *Adolescent literature as a complement to the classics. Volumes 1–4.* Norwood, MA: Christopher Gordon.

Kennedy, X. J., Gioia, D., & Bauerlein, M. (2006). *The Longman dictionary of literary terms: Vocabulary for the informed reader.* New York: Pearson Longman.

Knickerbocker, J. L., & Rycik, J. (2002). Growing into literature: Adolescents' literary interpretation and appreciation. *Journal of Adolescent and Adult Literacy, 4,* 196–209.

Landwehr, M. (2002). Introduction: Literature and the visual arts; questions of influence and intertextuality. *College Literature, 29*(3), 1–16.

Latham, D. (2008). Empowering adolescent readers' intertextuality in three novels by David Almond. *Children's Literature in Education, 39,* 213–226.

Lukens, R. J., & Cline, R. K. J. (1995). *A critical handbook of literature for young adults.* New York: HarperCollins.

Lundin, A. (1998). Intertextuality in children's literature. *Journal of Education for Library and Information Science, 39,* 210–213.

Merriam Webster's Encyclopedia of Literature (1995). New York: Author.

Magical Words. Special guest stars: Carrie Ryan. Retrieved from http://magicalwords.net/specialgueststars/special-guest-stars-carrie-ryan/.

National Governors Association Center for Best Practices, Council of Chief State School Officers (2010). *Common core state standards for English language arts & literacy in history/social studies, science, and technical subjects.* Washington, DC: Author.

Pavel, T. (2003). Literary genres as norms and good habits. *New Literary History, 24,* 201–210.

Pearson, P. D., & Gallagher, M. C. (1983). The instruction of reading comprehension. *Contemporary Educational Psychology, 8,* 317–344.

Peterson, R., & Eeds, M. (1990). *Grand conversations: Literature groups in action.* Richmond Hill, ON: Scholastic Canada.

Smith, M. W., & Wilhelm, J. D. (2002). *"Reading Don't Fix No Chevys": Literacy in the Lives of Young Men.* Portsmouth, NH: Heinemann.

Spohrer, E. (2009). Not a gay cowboy movie?: *Brokeback Mountain* and the importance of genre. *Journal of Popular Film and Television, 37*(1), 26–33.

Stead, R. (n.d.). *A Q&A with Rebecca Stead.* Retrieved from http://www.amazon.com/When-You-Reach-Rebecca-Stead/.

Sullivan, E. (August, 2003). Fiction or poetry? *School Library Journal, 49*(8), 44–45.

Van Sickle, V. (2006). Subcategories within the emerging genre of the verse novel. *Emerging Scholars & New Voices, 10*(3). Retrieved from http://tlg.ninthwonder.com/rabbit/v20i3/emerging.html.

Wyatt, N. (November, 2008). Keeping up with genres. *Library Journal, 133*(3), 30–33.

Zambo, D. (2005). Using the picture book *Thank you, Mr. Falker* to understand struggling readers. *Journal of Adolescent & Adult Literacy, 48,* 502–512.

CHAPTER FOUR

Realistic Fiction
LITERATURE REFLECTING LIFE

chapter overview

In this chapter we define realistic fiction and explain why it remains a dominant force in literature for young adults. Works of realistic fiction are grouped both by themes and by subgenres. The chapter then focuses on works that explore gender and sexual diversity and cultural diversity in the United States and beyond. We also describe examples of realistic fiction with metafictive characteristics. Last, we discuss authenticity and accuracy as criteria for selecting realistic fiction for young adults.

FOCUS QUESTIONS

1. What are the defining characteristics of realistic fiction?
2. Why is realistic fiction popular with young adults?
3. How does realistic fiction help adolescents explore the diversity in the world?
4. What criteria should be considered when selecting diverse literature?
5. How are metafictive characteristics used in realistic fiction?

introduction

*T*he previous chapter defined a *genre* as a collection of texts that are related by audience and purpose as well as by form and subject matter. In this chapter, we focus on a genre of literature for young adults that has been dominant since the 1960s and 1970s, **realistic fiction** (Campbell, 2004). Readers expect the characters in realistic fiction to behave in a recognizably human manner, and they expect the situations and circumstances confronted by the protagonist to be possible in real world settings. In works of realistic fiction, there are no supernatural events and no magic to solve problems.

The events reflected in realistic fiction must be plausible; they do not have to be probable or common. For example, in Ellen Hopkins' novel *Identical* (2008), the protagonists are twins, Raeanne and Kaeleigh. They seem to live a life of privilege, but their father, a district court judge, is addicted to alcohol and OxyContin, and he has sexually abused Kaeleigh since early childhood. The twins' reactions to the abuse and neglect include eating disorders, self-mutilation, drugs, alcohol, and promiscuity. *Identical* is told from alternating first person points of view. Kaeleigh's attempted suicide begins the unraveling of the story toward the climactic revelation that Raeanne was killed in a car accident several years earlier. Kaeleigh, who suffers from dissociative identity disorder, is actually the only narrator.

The events in *Identical* are certainly uncommon. Realistic fiction does not have to portray the everyday world that most young adults experience, but the elements of a realistic story may well be someone's reality. Hopkins (ellenhopkins.com, n.d.) explained that the idea for *Identical* began with her realization that three of her friends were abused as children. Their ability to survive and become strong women prompted Hopkins to write about the long-term effects of sexual abuse. Hopkins has succeeded in turning facts of real life into realistic fiction.

WHAT IS REAL IN REALISTIC FICTION?

arc Aronson asserts that "contemporary fiction for young adults is real, not because it is typical or normal, but rather it is real because it goes beneath the surface, because it tells a truth people don't want to see, because it doesn't settle, it provokes" (2001, p. 82).

Realistic fiction might be thought of as the literary counterpart of reality television. Young adult viewers understand that the producers of reality survival shows are not going to let people die and that the island where they compete is not really deserted. But they also recognize the authenticity of the contestants' behavior. Just as reality television "accentuates a voyeuristic gaze among audiences" (Moorti & Ross, 2004, p. 203), realistic fiction allows teens to become spectators of events that may be beyond their own experiences and that are most likely more dramatic than their own. As Aronson notes, "those art works take you to places in yourself you did not even know existed. I can think of no greater service to teenagers than to give them the experience of delving deeper into themselves so that they find resources that they did not know they possessed" (2001, p. 83). Arguably, it is realistic fiction that is at the heart of what Patty Campbell (2004) calls the central theme of literature for young adults—finding the answer to the question "who am I, and what am I going to do about it?"

Contemporary realistic fiction ranges from **problem novels** reflecting the most negative circumstances of contemporary life to lighter fare focusing on more readily solved problems. From an adult perspective, realistic fiction may sometimes seem to exaggerate the problems faced by adolescents, and problem novels have occasionally been criticized as formulaic and overly negative. Although problem novels dealing with social issues and coming-of-age situations are still popular, realistic novels that reflect the more typical aspects of life for young adults are gaining ground (Koss & Teale, 2009). The tone of realistic fiction can vary from disturbing and depressing to light and humorous. The resolution of a story may leave the reader feeling secure with a sense of well-being, or it may be open-ended, leaving the reader with uncertainty and unanswered questions. Literature for young adults "does not (and should not) have to mirror a singular version of youth" (Pattee, 2004, p. 243).

THEMES IN REALISTIC FICTION

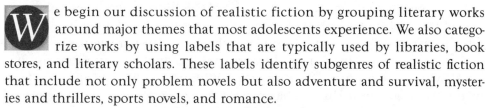e begin our discussion of realistic fiction by grouping literary works around major themes that most adolescents experience. We also categorize works by using labels that are typically used by libraries, book stores, and literary scholars. These labels identify subgenres of realistic fiction that include not only problem novels but also adventure and survival, mysteries and thrillers, sports novels, and romance.

Separating realistic fiction into subgenres suggests that each category differs significantly from others in content, tone, setting, or some other element, but these categories present a conundrum: How scary must a story be to be a thriller, or how much sports does a novel need to include to be considered a sports novel? Chris Crutcher's *Whale Talk* (2001) is frequently categorized as a sports book because the swim team is a central element, but it also is a novel about racism, child abuse, love, and forgiveness. Remember that genres are fluid. Literature can be described, sorted, and categorized in many ways, and these groups are not mutually exclusive. We will use the subgenres as a supplement to the theme-based groupings below.

Challenges

Realistic fiction allows readers to vicariously experience realities other than their own. Young adults may wonder how it would feel to climb a mountain, persevere against terrible odds, defeat a villain, or solve a crime. They also want to explore social, political, cultural, and ethical issues and to consider how they will confront those issues as adults. Adolescents are developing the ability to think abstractly, and many of their thoughts are about themselves. They are learning to interact with their environment in a more complex way, to reflect on their choices, and to form a self-identity (Barnett, 2009). "Trying on" different characters in a variety of situations helps young adults discover who they are and who they want to be. The challenges encountered during adolescence are reflected, literally and figuratively, in realistic fiction.

The challenge to survive

In realistic **adventure** and **survival stories,** the main character will always face an external challenge that is often a matter of life and death. The danger may come from the natural environment or from other people, but meeting the challenge results in personal growth and self-discovery. A popular example of a survivor adventure is Gary Paulsen's *Hatchet* series (1987), in which a boy named Brian survives in the Canadian wilderness following a plane crash. In each of the sequels, *The River* (1991), *Brian's Winter* (1996), *Brian's Return* (1999) and *Brian's Hunt* (2003), Brian must overcome new challenges in the wilderness. In the process he acquires the skills and attitudes that make him a mature, self-reliant young man.

In Roland Smith's *Peak* (2007), Peak Marcello is trying to become the youngest person to reach the summit of Mt. Everest. Survival against nature is Peak's central challenge as he deals with obstacles of the mountain, which include cold, lack of oxygen, and the discovery of icy corpses in his path. Peak must also overcome human obstacles such as his competitors, his unscrupulous father, Chinese officials, the media, and a controversy over the use of Tibetan Sherpas as guides.

The Winter Road by Terry Hokenson (2006) is another adventure survival novel with a protagonist battling nature. Willa is a 17-year-old licensed pilot who is flying solo near Hudson Bay when her plane crashes. She must contend with the stark reality of her surroundings, her feelings of desperation, and her low sense of self-worth during an 18-day struggle to survive. This book provides a gender counterpoint to the *Hatchet* series.

In Madaline Herlong's *The Great Wide Sea* (2008), Ben's father is having a difficult time dealing with the death of his wife and decides to take his three sons on a year-long sailboat trip. The father disappears overboard, a storm damages the boat, and the boys are stranded on an island. They find food and water and manage to survive for three months. Then Dylan falls over a cliff while hunting for bird's eggs and is seriously hurt. Ben, the eldest brother, must face the sea again if Dylan is to live.

Sometimes a young protagonist is challenged by villains, known or unknown, rather than by the impersonal forces of nature. Both **mysteries** and **thrillers** are characterized by a tone of urgency and a sense of impending danger. The difference lies in the level of suspense. In a mystery, the reader is waiting for something to be revealed. The significant event has already occurred and the protagonist must figure out who is responsible (Smith, J., n.d.). In a thriller the reader is waiting for something significant to happen. The protagonist's job is to prevent the terrible thing from happening.

The line between a suspenseful thriller and a mystery can be hard to draw, but Peter Abrahams' *Reality Check* (2009), winner of the 2010 Edgar Award for best young adult mystery, exemplifies the elements expected in a mystery for young adults. Abrahams, author of the popular middle-grade *Echo Falls* mystery series, writes for an older audience in this novel. Sixteen-year-old Cody is investigating his girlfriend Clea's disappearance. A letter from Clea provides the first clue, and Cody puts himself in great peril to find her. A red herring, or misdirection, keeps the outcome from being easily guessed. Cody discovers the surprise villain and solves the crime. His situation as an injured athlete and dejected boyfriend adds to the novel's appeal for adolescents.

John Green's *Paper Towns* (2008), also an Edgar Award-winning mystery for young adults, is about a missing girl and the boy who has loved her since they found a dead body together when they were children. The girl, Marge, has left clues to her whereabouts, and Quentin and his friends embark on a road trip intent on finding her, even though they are not sure if she has run away or committed suicide. The clues lead them to a town that doesn't exist; it is a fictitious town placed on a map as a copyright trap. Quentin finds Margo and discovers who she is and not who she has pretended to be.

If the Witness Lied (Cooney, 2009) is a mystery about a long-lost relative who shows up to care for the Fountain orphans. She arranges for them to be on a reality show, which leads to their wanting to know the truth about their father's death. The novel rotates through multiple perspectives. In *Chasing Vermeer* (Balliett, 2004), one of Johannes Vermeer's famous paintings goes missing, and two sixth graders take it upon themselves to find it. Art, math, and puzzles are all part of their efforts to recover the painting from a thief who threatens to destroy it.

Code Orange (2005), a thriller by Caroline Cooney, is both suspenseful and gruesome. While working on a biology project, Mitty finds an envelope containing smallpox scabs. He fears he has become contagious and could cause an outbreak of the terrible disease. Without thinking, he uses the Internet to make inquiries, which leads to him being kidnapped. The course of the disease is explicitly described so the reader knows the impending death Mitty is facing.

Runner (Deuker, 2005) exemplifies a fast-paced action approach to the thriller. Chance and his alcoholic father live on a small, dilapidated sailboat, but even the small boat costs more than they have. Chance decides to make fast money picking up and delivering suspicious packages, which places him in imminent danger. The reader is aware from the get-go that they contain something suspicious and probably illegal. Suspense intensifies when the nature of the packages changes, and the man who hired Chance dies. SWAT teams and terrorists abruptly appear, creating an action-packed climax.

Graham McNamee's *Acceleration* (2003), an Edgar Award-winning novel, blends the characteristics of mystery and thriller. Duncan finds a diary at the Toronto subway lost-and-found where he works. Suspense escalates with each bit of information he pieces together from the diary. Slowly he figures out that the author of the diary is a deeply disturbed serial killer whose aberrant behaviors have escalated over time. The police will not get involved. Duncan, spurred on by his guilt over an accidental death, knows that he must take on the role of the detective and track down the murderer before something terrible happens again.

Personal challenges

Young adults want to know that their problems and concerns are shared by other adolescents. The protagonists described in this section are dealing with an intrapersonal or internal struggle. These person-against-self conflicts include physical and mental challenges and facing the consequences of past choices.

Challenges of mind and body. Realistic fiction provides an avenue for young adults to critically and sensitively consider a wide range of physical, mental, and emotional disabilities. The National Institute of Mental Health (NIMH) determined that about 20 percent of youth experience some type of mental disorder during their lifetime, and that many of these problems begin in childhood and adolescence. These conditions include anxiety disorders, attention deficit hyperactivity disorder, autism spectrum disorders, borderline personality disorder, depression, eating disorders, schizophrenia, and suicide (NIMH, 2010). The Schneider Family Book Award (see Chapter 2) is a helpful resource for selecting literature about the experience of living with a disability or being a friend or relative of the person with the disability. Literature for young adults includes books about physical disabilities, as well as books about autism, learning disabilities, developmental disabilities, illnesses, Tourette syndrome, Down syndrome, and cerebral palsy.

Humorous and lighthearted, *Rules* (2006) by Cynthia Lord is a recipient of the Schneider Family Book Award and a Newbery Honor book. Twelve-year-old Catherine has developed a set of rules, such as "keep your pants on in public," to help her younger brother who is autistic make his way in the world. While the story is about siblings and friendship, it also shows how Catherine's feelings about her brother have an impact on her relationships and her own sense of self-worth.

Sharon Draper's (2010) *Out of My Mind* presents the life of 11-year-old Melody, a girl with cerebral palsy. The first-person point of view provides an inside look at what it must be like to have an excellent intellect but be unable to communicate. In the book, Melody receives a voice synthesizer and is able to live up to her abilities. Melody's triumphant success makes this novel appealing to readers who are Melody's age.

Shawn, the narrator in *Stuck in Neutral* (Trueman, 2000), also has cerebral palsy, and, like Melody, he is very intelligent. Shawn considers his life fulfilling because he is totally aware of his surroundings, and he can remember everything he has ever heard. But he is afraid his father is going to kill him because he believes Shawn is severely challenged mentally and must be suffering greatly. The novel's ambiguous ending offers no resolution to Shawn's dilemma.

Wintergirls (2009) by Laurie Halse Anderson, recipient of the Margaret A. Edwards Award, takes a hard look at the impact of eating disorders on two teenagers: Cassie, who is bulimic, and Lia, who is anorexic. The two girls were once friends but became estranged, and Cassie died painfully and alone as a result of excessive binging. Lia's guilt at not responding to the many phone calls from her estranged friend leaves her caught between real and unreal. Lia's first-person, present-tense narration alternates between normal descriptions and conversations and a stream of consciousness that is sometimes shown in italics and crossed-out lines of text as she censors herself. Flashbacks fill in the extent of Lia's illness and her past hospitalizations. Anderson shows the devastating results of bulimia and anorexia, not just for the individuals with these eating disorders, but for their families and friends as well.

Nothing (2008) by Robin Friedman provides a gender balance for *Winter Girls*. The male protagonist, Parker Rabinowitz, 17, struggles to be the perfect son, get into the perfect college, and become the perfect Jewish doctor. He begins binging as a way of maintaining control over one aspect of his life. His first person narration alternates with his sister's free verse poetry, providing insights into the perspectives of both a person with an eating disorder and a person who loves him and envies his outward perfection.

In *Break* (2009) by Hannah Moskowitz, 17-year-old Jonah has too many responsibilities in his dysfunctional family, including caring for his younger brother, Jesse, who has life-threatening food allergies. Following a car accident in which Jonah discovers that broken bones mend stronger, he sets out on a personal mission to break every bone in his body. Jonah's sense of responsibility for Jesse is so intense that, following an allergic episode that Jonah could have prevented, he breaks all his toes with a hammer.

Jerk California (2008) by Jonathan Friesen portrays the life of recent graduate Sam Carrier, who has Tourette syndrome, a neurological disorder characterized by involuntary vocal and motor tics. His feelings about himself and his hatred toward his dead father, whom he blames for his disease, have been shaped by his abusive stepfather. Sam sets off on a cross-country trip and along the way meets many people who cared deeply about his father, including his grandmother. Sam, who is actually named Jack, comes to terms with his condition through his journey of self-discovery. A video trailer (www.spike.com/video/jerk-california/3023386) provides a glimpse into Jack's life, his romantic interest, and some of the significant symbols found in the novel.

The consequences of past choices. Another personal challenge adolescents experience is facing the consequences of their choices. The challenge facing Martin Stokes in Paul Volponi's *Rikers High* (2010) is not one faced by many young adults. Martin is incarcerated for an act he did not know was illegal, and every day is a struggle to stay unharmed. Martin is unintentionally caught between two fighting boys and suffers a deep cut from a razor blade, marking his time in prison forever on his face. The book presents a candid depiction of Martin's world, including violence, racism, masturbation, and suicide. Author Volponi's experience as a teacher at Rikers Island, a New York City correctional facility, lends credibility to the language and actions of the boys and the people in charge.

Story of a Girl (Zarr, 2007) portrays the consequences of a single sexual act. Thirteen-year-old Deanna's reputation is ruined after her father catches her having sex with 17-year-old Tommy. Tommy boasts of his conquest and gives Deanna a bad reputation in school. Two years later, even though Deanna has not even kissed another boy, her father still refuses to talk to her and she is continually harassed in her small hometown. The theme of consequences is further developed through Deanna's older brother, who is a teenage parent and husband.

After by Amy Efaw (2009) recounts, in bits and pieces of flashback, the story of 15-year-old Devon who left her newborn infant in a dumpster. Afterward, she mentally disassociates from the events and is unable to remember what happened. During her pretrial she remembers what she has done and pleads guilty to abandoning the baby. The movie *Plain Truth* (Paul Shapiro, 2004), based on the Jodi Picoult (2000) novel of the same title, is a similar story about a young Amish girl who has denied giving birth. In this story, the baby is dead and a trial ensues.

The film *Juno* (2007), written by Diablo Cody and directed by Jason Reitman, won the Academy Award for best original screenplay. The film chronicles the life of quirky, smart 16-year-old Juno, who accidently becomes pregnant. She decides to give the baby up for adoption and answers a newspaper ad from an infertile couple. Juno's pregnancy and her decision to go through with the adoption are realistically portrayed.

Pregnant Novalee Nation knows she will keep her baby, even after her boyfriend abandons her. *Where the Heart Is* (2000), directed by Matt Williams, is based on the novel of the same name by Billie Letts (1995). Novalee perseveres partially because of her own fortitude, but also because of the kind and supportive people she encounters. Several years pass before she recognizes her own value to others.

Relationships and Expectations

Adolescence is a time for redefining relationships within a family, with friends and peers, and with society. During this period, alliances shift from parents to friends and peers. Close same-sex friendships are very important in early adolescence (12–14), as are peer relationships and group identity in middle adolescence (14–17). Love relationships change frequently in middle adolescence. Feelings of love and passion emerge, as do concerns about sexual attractiveness and sexual identity. By late adolescence, sexual identity is usually solidified and serious relationships are the goal (South Carolina Department of Mental Health, n.d.). All of these shifting relationships are frequent subjects in literature for young adults.

Understanding family

Not surprisingly, understanding family is a key theme in literature for young adults because relationships with families often change significantly during adolescence. *Surviving the Applewhites* (2002) by Stephanie Tolan, a 2003 Newbery Honor book, pits 13-year-old Jake Semple, a reputed arsonist with spiked hair, against E.D. Applewhite, the 12-year-old hyper-organized daughter of an eccentric and artistic extended family. Through Jake and E.D.'s alternating perspectives, outrageous family members are humorously described. Jake becomes a part of this individualistic bunch, and E.D. comes to recognize her own talents and decides being part of her family isn't so bad.

Although not as large, the family in *The Big Game of Everything* (2008), a National Book Award finalist by Chris Lynch, is every bit as strange as the Applewhites, and while not as raucously funny, this novel is humorous and touching. Jock ponders what is important in life. His parents eschew material goods while his grandfather measures a person's success by his wealth. The novel begins with Jock's ambivalence, "You have to love your family. You do, even if you don't, right?" Jock finds an answer to his question.

Shattered (Baron, 2009) describes not only Cassie's splintered violin, as represented on the book's cover, but also her relationship with her father, who has become increasingly erratic and violent. Cassie comes to understand that her father's behavior is due to the fact that he was abused as a child by his own father. Through this revelation, her family begins the healing process. Musical metaphors are used throughout the novel, and the final chapter is titled "Coda," the term for a closing section of a musical composition. Cassie's new-found relationship with Nick, an ardent baseball player, mixes the metaphors of their chosen forms of expression: "Goddess music calls to his baseball soul. I'm my own version of home plate. Trusting my hands, I'm taking a swing. Bow on string, like bat to ball. I'm playing on" (p. 260).

Unlike *Shattered*, the parents in *Why I Fight* (Oaks, 2009) make no attempt to understand or change their destructive behaviors. Wyatt Reeves, arsonist and runaway, pours out his story to an unidentified stranger on a bus. Memories flood over him, and through a disjoined narrative he relays how he came to be on his own. When Wyatt was twelve, he burned down his family home and moved in with Uncle Spade. Spade then became his manager of sorts, dragging Wyatt around the country to compete in illegal bare fisted fights. Over several years, Wyatt's anger and hatred grow. His attempt to reconcile with his parents has failed, but he realizes that he will be all right on his own. Wyatt's story is open ended but hopeful.

The disintegration of a family after the disappearance of its youngest daughter is tempered with first love in Jillian Cantor's *September Sisters* (2009). In the opening scene, set two years after Becky's disappearance, Abby's father comes to school to inform her that her sister has been found, thus revealing the mystery. A few paragraphs later, the time frame is established. This foreshadowing also broadcasts what will happen to this family: "The night before Becky disappeared was amazingly normal; it could've been any night in my life, any night the summer before my thirteenth birthday" (p. 20). Abby's first-person narration describes the painful breakup of her family and her memories of her sister. She also tells of meeting her new neighbor, Tommy, and their deepening relationship as they share their personal losses with each other.

Peer relationships

Along for the Ride (Dessen, 2009) is about family and peers but features no parental abuse, explicit sex, or illegal behavior. It focuses on the everyday problems of losing a loved one, parents divorcing, and facing new relationships. Socially awkward Auden, the daughter of two very flawed academics, decides to spend her last summer before college with her dad and his new wife and baby. During this time she comes to understand herself and family members, value new friendships, and trust in a first love. The characters are well developed and the issues are meaningfully explored without cliché or stereotypes. High school readers will appreciate the multilayered issues along with the denouement. The following fall Auden again encounters Eli, the young man she fell in love with during the summer when she went "along for the ride."

In *Every Soul a Star* (2008) by Wendy Mass, three very different middle grade students are brought together at the Moon Shadow campground that specializes in astronomy. The novel is told in alternating voices, and each character has very different levels of interest in and knowledge about astronomy. Jack has failed science; Ally lives for it; and Bree just wants to be a model. Science is laced throughout the story, but the characters' brief friendship is the captivating aspect of the novel.

Friendships take a dark turn in *Black Rabbit Summer* (2008) by Kevin Brooks. The story is a murder mystery. It also is an intense examination of present and past friendships and secrets. The summer after graduation, Pete, the son of a police officer, becomes involved in an alcohol- and drug-laden reunion with former school friends. The friends include Stella Ross, a local celebrity who winds up dead, and Raymond, who goes missing. As Pete searches for Raymond, he wonders how his friendship with Raymond remains so much a part of him.

John Green's *An Abundance of Katherines* (2006) is a witty coming of age road trip story that includes many mathematical formulas, footnotes, anagrams, and flashbacks. The story's protagonist, Colin Singleton, is a former child math prodigy who recognizes that what made him special as a child is not so extraordinary in young adulthood. The title is based on his belief that he has been dumped by nineteen girls, all named Katherine. He embarks on a road trip with his best friend Hassan. During their travels, Colin works on a mathematical theorem on dating, meets interesting people, and concludes that there is more to life than being a genius.

Romantic relationships

Romantic relationships are a central aspect of life for many young adults. By the tenth grade, interactions with romantic partners are more frequent than those with other friends, siblings, or parents. These early relationships influence attitudes toward intimate relationships in adulthood and help the young adult to separate from the family and develop autonomy (Bouchey & Furman, 2003).

Romance is a widely recognized subgenre of realistic fiction. The Romance Writers of America (n. d.) suggests that two basic elements comprise a romance novel: a central love story and an emotionally satisfying and optimistic ending. Although subplots can be numerous, the love story is the central focus. There are no restrictions on style, tone, setting, or levels of sensuality.

Elizabeth Eulberg's *The Lonely Hearts Club* (2010) is all about the struggle to balance romance with other relationships in a teenage girl's life, especially when the romance is new and exciting. Maintaining relationships with girlfriends while also having a boyfriend is high school junior Penny Lane Bloom's problem. After romance disappoints, Penny begins a Lonely Hearts Club. The club's cardinal rule is that members must swear off boys. Eventually the club rules are amended to allow dating, but girlfriends cannot be sacrificed for a boy. This underlying reminder of the importance of sisterhood is told with fast-paced humor.

Kissing the Bee (Koja, 2007) combines romance with science and folklore. Dana, a high school senior, is studying bees for her senior biology project, and her notes punctuate the first-person narrative. Dana has fallen in love with Emil, who unfortunately is the current boyfriend, or drone, of Avra, the queen bee in Deanna's friendship circle. Emil declares his love for Dana but cannot detach himself from Avra. The book concludes with the myth that the sting of a bee on the lips brought poetry to humans. The phrase "kissing the bee" means the pain inflicted by the sting is equal to the wisdom the bee imparts.

Romances are not always written from a girl's perspective. *The Summer I Got a Life* (2009) by Mark Fink is a fast-paced, sometimes humorous "boy romance" that also includes sports, sibling rivalry, male bonding, and acceptance of differences. Californians Andy and his older brother Bradley spend part of their summer with free-spirited relatives in Wisconsin. Andy meets Laura, an independent, talented, and attractive girl who uses a wheelchair. Her disability is dealt with in a straightforward manner, and their relationship is typical of young teenagers experiencing first love.

Nick Burd's *The Vast Fields of Ordinary* (2009) is included in lists of the top ten romances for youth. Dade Hamilton falls in love with Pablo, a young man who publically denies his homosexuality, and with Alex, an openly gay adolescent. The emotions experienced are those experienced by all adolescents, regardless of their sexual orientation. This story combines a disintegrating marriage, jealousy, friendships, self-acceptance, and the disappearance of a child into a tale of summer love.

Romance novels may be a single title or part of a series (Romance Writers of America, n.d.). Lists of novels are available on several websites, including www.youngadultromancewriters.com and http://www.goodreads.com, under "Young Adult Romance."

A few of the highly successful writers of popular romance series for young adults are Hailey Abbott, *Summer Boys*; Ann Brashares, *Sisterhood of the Traveling Pants*; Ally Carter, *Gallagher Girls*; Zoey Dean, *The A List*; Sara Shepard, *Pretty Little Liars*; and Cecily Von Ziegesar, *Gossip Girls*.

School Culture

Young adults are intimately familiar with school as setting; after all, most are in the midst of at least twelve years of school. Thus, the social rules, relationships with peers and adults, expectations, and perceived norms of the school milieu are the context for many books and films.

School is central to the plot and theme in *Cheater* (Laser, 2008). A group of students called the Confederacy recruit the brilliant Karl Petrofsky into their high-tech cheating scheme. Karl, wanting to be part of a popular crowd, convinces himself that by joining the cheaters he is undermining the unreasonable and vindictive vice principal. This satire of contemporary school life and business and academic ethics makes cheating and lying seem commonplace. Karl's parents purposely mislead people in their jobs, and the vice principal blackmails students. A mayoral candidate is willing to conspire with the cheaters so that SAT scores will be higher, thus giving the school a better reputation and increasing property values. The outlandish events and the self-deprecating tone of Karl's narration provide balance for the novel's serious issues.

Jaime Adoff's *Names Will Never Hurt Me* (2004) is about school, fitting in, and the consequences of not fitting in. The culture of school is intensified as the entire book takes place in one day, on the one-year anniversary of a school killing. Multiple narrators relay what school is like. Images of bullies, boring teachers, sexual harassment, unscrupulous administrators, and a hierarchy of heroes and zeros create a picture of the school. Student interviews with a newscaster, dialogues between the principal and several different people, and students' writings are interspersed throughout the novel.

Senior prom may be second only to graduation as a high school rite of passage. In *Prom* (2005) Laurie Halse Anderson captures the importance of this event to many students at an urban high school, but not for Ashley Hannigan. Her post–high school aspirations are limited to moving out of her parent's house into an apartment with her high school dropout boyfriend. When a teacher embezzles the prom funds and Ashley's best friend breaks her leg, Ashley has to step up and do whatever it takes to have a prom. A secondary theme focuses on family. Ashley's parents actually like each other, and this "normal" working-class family gets through the day by accepting and counting on each other.

One of the roles of school is to prepare young adults for more school (college). "Type A" personality Kate Malone loves calculus, chemistry, and physics, and her goal is to go to MIT. Laurie Halse Anderson cleverly weaves science concepts throughout *Catalyst* (2002). Chapter titles such as "Statis," "Relative Density," and "Transition Element" can be appreciated by readers with even a limited knowledge of chemistry. When MIT rejects her application, Kate has difficult realities to face about herself, her family, and her future. An excellent companion to *Catalyst* is the television movie *Acceptance* (2009), directed by Sanaa Hamri and based on the book *Acceptance* (2007) by Susan Coll, which also explores the pressure to get into the right school.

School is especially significant when the school is a boarding school and students live in a world seemingly free from adult interference. *Jellicoe Road* (Marchetta, 2006), *Looking for Alaska* (Green, 2005), both winners of the Printz Award, and *The Disreputable History of Frankie Landau Banks* (Lockhart, 2008), a Printz honor book, illuminate the mystique of the boarding school culture.

Taylor Lily Markham, the protagonist of *Jellicoe Road*, is the leader of the students who live in her dormitory at Jellico School. Their longtime rivals are the townies, the kids who live in town and go to public school, and the cadets, boys who come from Sydney to participate in an outdoor training exercise for six weeks every year. They engage in elaborately organized and potentially dangerous "territorial wars" in the nearby woods without adult intervention. Taylor has lived at the school since her mother left her on the road when she was 11, and a young woman, Hanna, picked her up. Taylor's history is slowly revealed through a manuscript Hanna is writing.

The Disreputable History of Frankie Landau Banks begins with a letter by Frankie to the headmaster of Alabaster Preparatory Academy, in which she confesses to wrongdoings against the school. Frankie's elevated status in school, which allows her to sit at the right table and hang out with the right clique, is based on her relationship with her popular boyfriend. Frankie figures out a way to manipulate an all-male secret society. She also comes to learn the consequences of a girl outwitting the boys in a male-dominated culture.

The setting for *Looking for Alaska* is a southern prep school. Miles Halter, a new student, gets filled in by his roommate, the Colonel, about the cool kids. The Colonel also suggests that if Miles, dubbed Pudge, because he is so thin, were a "hot shit" in public school he wouldn't want to be friends with him. Miles informs the Colonel that he wasn't hot shit, he was just "regular shit." The Colonel introduces Miles to Alaska, a girl he immediately finds exciting and sexy. Typical adolescent behaviors of smoking, drinking, breaking curfew, and pranks ensue. The novel is divided into "Before" and "After" sections, which refer to the days before and after the climatic event of Alaska's death.

The movie *Mean Girls* (2004), directed by Mark Waters, is about the social cliques of a public high school. Home-schooled Cady Heron, played by Lindsay Lohan, returns from Africa having never attended an American school and is naíve about the social pecking order. Her desire to belong is compelling, and as Cady learns how social groups function, she becomes as mean as the "Plastics" were to her when she first met them. The final scene focuses on the junior girls who will become next year's top Plastics.

A comedy/drama with a high school setting, *Charlie Bartlett* (2008, directed by Jon Poll), depicts the fears and frustrations felt by many teens, as well as the ongoing quiet desperation of the principal. Charlie, who has been kicked out of several exclusive schools, now faces public education. His intimate knowledge of psychiatry and his seemingly unending supply of prescription drugs result in Charlie's becoming the school's de facto therapist. He becomes an integral part of the school's social structure as students begin to count on him for advice and support. Restroom "confessional" scenes portray the myriad problems faced by contemporary young adults. The movie contains profanity and brief nudity.

Sports Culture

As with school, most adolescents are very familiar with sports; most have been involved in playing or watching sports throughout their school years. Sports fiction includes literature focusing on the game action, books that blend character development with the game, and stories where the main character is an athlete, but the sport is only loosely connected to the story (Crowe, 2001).

John H. Ritter, a writer of sports fiction for young adults, explains how he sees his books fitting into the larger genre of realistic fiction. He believes his books are about kids dealing with hard choices.

> To me, that's the definition of YA lit. They're stories about the first time in life when one has to stand on one's own two feet, make a life-altering decision, then live with the consequences of that choice. If it happens to be on the ball field, fine. But usually it doesn't. It's just that the events on the ball field may lead up to that moment and help shape the kid so that one day he can take his stand. (Interview with Chris Crowe, 2000)

Front and Center (2009) by Catherine Gilbert Murdock is the final book in the "Dairy Queen" trilogy that also includes *Dairy Queen* (2006) and *The Off Season* (2007). Football player and basketball star D.J. is facing the pressure of family, friends, coach, and recruiters as she decides which college to attend. The story blends family crises, romance, and sports. D.J. struggles with not being a good player and also with her lack of desire to be a leader.

Mike Lupica, sports columnist and ESPN reporter, and Tim Green, former NFL player, write from the insider's viewpoint. Lupica's *The Batboy* (2010) begins in Comerica Park during a Detroit Tiger's home game. The description of the game in progress is similar to a play by play, with added color. Brian, the batboy of the title, struggles with his relationship with a previously suspended player, his absentee father, his own feelings about playing, and his ongoing batting slump.

In *Baseball Great* (2009) Tim Green introduces Josh, a 12-year-old who wants to stay in one place and play ball. His father, a minor league ball player, insists that Josh play for a very competitive team, the Titans, coached by a man who wants to win no matter what it takes. *Rivals* (2010) continues Josh's story as his team makes it to the national tournament in Cooperstown, New York. The plot focuses on some of the nastier aspects of winning at all costs, and Josh struggles with the ethics of sports. Josh confronts the bad guys, leading to a high-speed escape in a motorboat.

Realistic sports fiction is a popular subgenre. Additional works categorized as sport fiction by publishers are listed below. This grouping includes books about different sports with female and male protagonists.

Ball Don't Lie. Matt de la Pena, 2007. The only thing that Sticky has going for him is his basketball talent. His mother died, he is in foster care, and he spends most of his time in a run-down gym with other homeless people. With the help of the basketball court and his new girlfriend, Sticky is determined to overcome his past. Ages 14–18.

Black and White. Paul Volponi, 2005. Marcus and Eddie, also known as Black and White, make good decisions on the court, but off the court they break the law. Marcus is caught and ends up serving time, while Eddie goes on to college. The story is told from alternating voices and focuses on basketball and racial issues. Ages 12 and up.

Center Field. Robert Lipsyte, 2010. Mike has finally won the center field position until a new kid from the Dominican Republic challenges him. The authentic baseball play-by-play, girl problems, and a mystery about his coach move the story along quickly. Ages 14 and up.

Game. Walter Dean Myers, 2008. Drew is a skilled basketball player who attends Harlem High School. The only way he will make it to college is by earning a basketball scholarship. When his high school coach ends up favoring another player on the team, Drew's future is threatened. He has to do whatever it takes to stay out of the streets and make it to the NBA. Ages 12–18.

Gym Candy. Carl Deuker, 2008. Mick's father did not make it to the NFL, and Mick is not about to repeat that mistake. He wants to be bigger and stronger, to beat out the competition. He resorts to steroids and suffers the consequences: acne, depression, uncontrolled anger. The on-field action is authentic. Ages 14 and up.

Open Court. Carol Clippinger, 2007. Carol is a tennis prodigy who truly loves the game. At age 13, she has already outgrown her hometown competition. Her dad wants to send her to an academy and take full advantage of her talent, but Carol isn't so sure she can measure up against tougher competition, especially as personal relationships are changing. Ages 11 and up.

Open Ice. Pat Hughes, 2005. Nick is only a sophomore, but he is already the star on the hockey team. He is a tough kid, but after a concussion everyone tells him that he is done for good. The long term effects of head injuries are realistically presented. Nick experiences a sexual relationship. Ages 15–18.

The Ring. Bobbie Pyron, 2009. Mardie has gotten in trouble with the law and is being forced to go to the gym with her stepmother. She joins a girls' boxing class where she learns to channel some of her anger about her dead mother, distant father, and gay brother into the sport. Ages 12 and up.

Take Down. (*Winning Take Down* Series, #8). Rich Wallace, 2007. Donald is in seventh grade and after seeing a high-school wrestling match, he is excited to join the middle school team, but he has to control his temper if he wants to win. Ages 10–12.

FILMS

Bend It Like Beckham. Directed by Gurinder Chadha, 2002. In this film English Jess Bhamra loves to play soccer, but her Indian parents find this unacceptable for a girl. She gets to play and finds romance. PG-13.

The Blind Side. Film. Directed by John Lee Hancock, 2009. This film, a fictionalized account of the story of Michael Oher, who became an All-American football player, focuses on his high school years when he is taken in by a family and tutored so that he can qualify for NCAA Division I athletics. PG-13.

DIVERSITY IN REALISTIC FICTION

*I*n Chapter 1 we introduced *diversity* as the term we would use to describe the many ways readers differ from each other in terms of language, sexual orientation, social position, and ethnicity or cultural background. The two areas of diversity addressed in this section are gender and sexual diversity and cultural diversity. Cultural diversity within the United States is discussed separately from cultures in other countries.

Gender and Sexual Diversity

Michael Cart (2004) suggests that a significant function of young adult literature, especially for those youth who are often identified as outsiders, is "the
life-saving necessity of seeing one's own face reflected in the pages of a good
book and the corollary comfort that derives from the knowledge that one is
not alone" (p. 46). One group of outsiders that has remained largely invisible is
gay, lesbian, bisexual, transgender, and questioning (GLBTQ) teenagers. In 2004
Cart found only 150 titles dealing with issues specific to this group published
since the first novel written for young adults dealing with homosexuality, *I'll
Get There. It Better Be Worth the Trip* (1969) by John Donovan.

GLBTQ themes, however, are more common in literature for young adults
than Cart's findings would suggest. Koss and Teale's (2009) analysis of high quality, popular books for young adults published between 1999 and 2003 revealed
that in about 10 percent of the books there was at least one GLBTQ character.
Each of these books contained a main character focusing on a GLBTQ issue, and
in no title in their sampling was a GLBTQ character a part of the story without
the issue of sexuality being a significant aspect of the story (p. 567).

The Printz Honor Award recipient, *Hard Love* (1999), by Ellen Wittlinger,
is the story of a friendship built around an interest in "zines," or self-published
magazines. John or Gio, as he likes to present himself, is a troubled teenager trying to deal with his parent's divorce and his mother's imminent remarriage. He
meets and falls for Marisol, who has made it very clear from the onset of their
relationship that she is a lesbian. He invites her to prom. She realizes that dressing up is fun and that being a lesbian does not mean she cannot be pretty. The
novel explores the fragile line between friendship and love, and relationships
between straights and gays.

Julie Anne Peters' *Luna*, (2004), a National Book Award finalist, is told from
the first person point of view of Reagan, the sister of Liam, who is a transgender
person. *Luna* is as much about Reagan's challenge of loving and supporting a
transgender person as it is about Liam's journey to become Luna. Liam's conflict is revealed through a series of flashbacks to early childhood. Ultimately, he
leaves home with the goal of having sexual reassignment surgery.

Debbie Harry Sings in French (Brothers, 2008) breaks ground by featuring
a transvestite, heterosexual protagonist. Due to his small stature and reserved
manner, Johnny is often perceived as gay. He questions his sexual identity,
but as his relationship with an unconventional girl develops, he realizes he is
straight. He also realizes he likes to dress in girls' clothing. Johnny comes to the
realization that he can be a guy who likes girls and also be a guy who likes to
dress like a girl.

The Last Exit to Normal by Michael Harmon (2008) looks at the impact of
having a gay parent. Ben Campbell has been getting in trouble ever since his
dad announced he was gay and Ben's mom left. His Dad, his partner Edward,
and an angry Ben move to Montana to stay with Edward's mother. After 20
years of not seeing each other, Miss Mae greets her son by asking him if he is
still "funny." The significance of Edward's response, "Gay as the day I was born"
has an impact on Ben's acceptance of his father. *The Last Exit to Normal* is about

Jacqueline Woodson

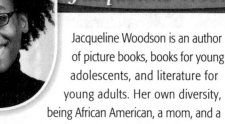

Jacqueline Woodson is an author of picture books, books for young adolescents, and literature for young adults. Her own diversity, being African American, a mom, and a lesbian, is reflected in her work. When asked about the controversial subjects she writes about, she responds, "I write realistic fiction. If I was writing realistic fiction and I wasn't dealing with real stuff, then I would be lying. The characters and situations wouldn't seem real. There are all kinds of people in the world. If I leave out queer people, if I leave out people of color, if I leave out deaf people, I can go down the line, then I wouldn't be speaking the truth to the people" (Kathy Belge, n.d.). Woodson wants to use literature as a means of changing how people think and act. Her goal is to impact the greater good of this world (Pepper, 2005).

Woodson writes about difficult social issues such as prejudice, sexual abuse, poverty, violence, and interracial relationships (Taylor, 2006). She also has written historical fiction featuring strong women of color as a means to show her daughter and all readers that women of color do not have to be nor have they been invisible (Rochman, 2005). However, she always tempers the perspective in her books with hope. She believes books for young people should show them that sometimes when a situation is difficult, just surviving is an accomplishment (Schneider, 2008).

Woodson wrote *If You Come Softly* (1998) to show how hard first love is. She views her characters as a modern day Romeo and Juliet. Friends and family disapprove of the relationship of Miah, who is black, and Ellie, who is white. Their alternating voices, Ellie in first person, Miah in third, provide insights into their individual situations, as well as their grow-

ing feelings for each other. *The House You Pass on the Way* (1997) is also about how hard it can be to love someone. Staggerlee, who is biracial, is disappointed when the girl she has a relationship with falls for a boy. The prejudice within the black community toward Staggerlee's sexual experimentation is a central theme.

Hush (2002) asks the question, what if? When Toswiah's police office father tells the truth about white policemen killing an unarmed black youth, her family is placed in the Federal Witness Protection Program. Shifting between past and present, Toswiah, now Evie, must reinvent herself as she and her family are dealing with the loss of friends, family, community, and personal identity.

Woodson considers rapper and performer Tupac Shakur to have been an influential activist. *After Tupac & D Foster* (2008) is about this influence. Two neighborhood girls, an unnamed narrator and Neeka, develop a friendship with D, a foster child who seems to be from nowhere. Their shared love of rapper Tupac Shakur and his music brings them together. The opening and closing chapters refer to the musician's death, which proves to be a defining moment for them.

Woodson's *Locomotion* (2003), a National Book Award finalist, and *Peace, Locomotion* (2009) are about 11-year-old Lonnie, whose parents died in a fire and who has been separated from his little sister. Lonnie finds an outlet for his emotions writing poetry. Woodson wrote the sequel because she wanted Lonnie to find peace.

Woodson is a recipient of the Margaret A. Edwards Award for lifetime achievement and has received dozens of other literary awards, including a Newbery honor citation, a National Book Award, and a Coretta Scott King Author Award. *Miracle's Boys* (2000), a story of three orphaned brothers trying to survive, was made into a miniseries directed by Bill Duke and Spike Lee (2005).

teenage romance, parent child relationships, issues of child abuse, letting go of the past, and dealing with bullies. It is also about being gay.

Michael Cart and Christine Jenkins' *The Heart Has Its Reasons: Young Adult Literature with Gay/Lesbian/Queer Content. 1969–2004* (2006) provides excellent resources for teachers interested in finding literature with GLBTQ content for their students. Additional online resources are available at Alex Sanchez's

. . . OF BOOKS ABOUT GLBTQ CHARACTERS

Absolutely, Positively Not . . . David LaRochelle, 2005. Turn the cover page and the word "Gay" appears. This is a humorous account of 16-year-old Steven's attempts to prove to himself that he is heterosexual, followed by a fairly uneventful revelation to himself and others that he is gay. Ages 12–16.

Geography Club. Brent Hartinger, 2003. A group of gay teens forms a fake club as a pretense to get together. As part of both growing up and coming out, Russell, the story's narrator, and other members of the club gain insights into who they are and where they fit in the world. The club is renamed the Gay Straight Bisexual Alliance. Ages 13 and up.

My Heartbeat. Garret Freyman-Weyr, 2002. In this Michael Printz honor book, Ellen has not really thought about the relationship of her older brother, Link, and his close friend, James, until someone asks if they are a couple. James tells Ellen that he is bisexual, and they start to date. Ellen's first-person, present-tense story is about sexual conflict and sexual awareness, but it is also about families, friendships, and first loves. Ages 12 and up.

Parrotfish. Ellen Wittlinger, 2007. Transgendered Grady is trying to present who he really is to his family and peers. His journey, beginning with asking his family to call him Grady instead of Angela, and cutting his hair and donning male clothes, ends with a high level of acceptance from a variety of family members, old and new friends, and a supportive teacher in a short amount of time. Ages 15 and up.

FILM

Doing Time on Maple Drive. Directed by Ken Olin and written by James Duff, 1992. In this television movie about a dysfunctional family, Matt, a college student, tries to kill himself in a car accident because he cannot deal with being gay. He goes so far as to propose marriage and brings the girl home to meet his family. NR.

"Great Gay Teen Books," www.alexsanchez/gay_teen_books.htm, a site with over 50 fiction titles as well as several nonfiction resources. The American Library Association includes a GLBTQ Rainbow List (http://rainbowlist.wordpress.com) as does www.pinkbooks.com.

In May of 2009, the *English Journal* devoted an issue to "Sexual Identity and Gender Variance." This issue includes a glossary (Chase and Ressler, 23–24) and excellent overviews of novels (Letcher, 123–126) identified for middle and secondary readers (Curwood, Schliesman, and Horning, 37–43). In the accompanying box, we have selected a few contemporary titles to highlight literature dealing with GLBTQ content.

Cultural Diversity

Noted author and poet Nikki Grimes states that what disturbs her most about multicultural literature is its "ghettoization." By this she means the relegation of multicultural literature to specific time frames such as Black History Month, Chinese New Year, and Cinco de Mayo. She also indicates that too often African American literature is read only in classrooms where African American students predominate and that this also contributes to a pattern of marginalization (2005, p. 23).

The lack of quality, culturally diverse literature may have contributed, in the recent past, to limited use of literature in schools about cultures in America that are not Eurocentric. More recently, however, publishers have established imprints geared toward literature about a variety of American cultures. The Diversity in Publishing Network (www.dipnet.org.uk) provides lists of websites and blogs that are helpful for identifying publishers, authors, and critics of multicultural literature. The African American community, unlike most demographics groups, is experiencing a surge in readership, attributed partially to the growth in urban, or street, fiction also called "hip hop lit." These stories focus on the culture of the streets and provide realistic portrayals of crime, violence, sex, drugs, and music of the streets. The market for this type of fiction is significant, and major publishing houses such as Simon and Schuster have created divisions exclusively for urban writers (Meloni, 2007). Some cultural groups, such as Native Americans, remain underrepresented, particularly in contemporary realistic fiction (Smith, C. L., n.d.).

No list can be representative of all the literature written about the diverse people who live within the United States, let alone in the rest of the world. Therefore, the literature included in this section is only a very small sampling of literature for young adults about diverse contemporary cultures. The titles selected are intended to reflect the sentiment conveyed by author and editor, Naomi Shihab Nye, "Literature is one of the best bridges among us. And it is a beautiful bridge without a toll" (2005, p. 39).

Cultural diversity within the United States

Walter Dean Myers' novel in script form, *Monster* (1999), illustrated by Christopher Myers, received the first Michael L. Printz Award for excellence in young adult literature. In 2012, Myers was named by the Librarian of Congress as Ambassador for Young People's Literature in part because of his substantial contribution to young people's literature and his highly revered status by readers and peers (Library of Congress, n.d.). Myers' novels often portray urban black young men caught in a life of crime and neglect that may end with incarceration. This is the theme in *Lockdown* (2010). Reese, a 14-year-old African American who has grown up in New York with a drug addicted mother and an abusive father, is serving time in a detention center. He learns that survival is more than winning fights; it is a choice.

Nora Raleigh Baskin's *The Truth about My Bat Mitzvah* (2008) explores the importance of heritage and religion for a girl growing up in a nonreligious Jewish family. Meeting relatives at her beloved Jewish grandmother's funeral, being given her grandmother's Star of David, and the impending Bat Mitzvah ceremony of a friend prompt Caroline to examine what it means to be Jewish, both personally and as perceived by society. Caroline comes to realize that a Bat Mitzvah is the girl, not the celebration. A glossary includes definitions of Jewish customs and terminology.

The cover of *Tyrell* (2006) by Coe Booth shows the back of the head of an African American boy with braided hair. He is looking out over a littered yard to old apartment buildings. Fifteen-year-old Tyrell's dad is in jail, and his mom has been convicted of welfare fraud. He is torn between his obligations to others and self-preservation as he faces the unrelenting challenges of homelessness, poverty, crime, drugs, sexual frustration, and struggling to stay in school. The first-person narrative captures the voice of an urban youth and includes street language.

Viola Canales won the Pura Belpré Award for *The Tequila Worm* (2005). It uses short episodes to portray Sophia, a young Latina girl, from early childhood through her teen years. Sophia shares stories from her childhood that illuminate aspects of her culture, such as the Day of the Dead, a holiday to honor dead loved ones, and a cousin's quinceañera, a celebration of a girl's transition to womanhood. Sophia struggles to balance pride in her Mexican American heritage with her desire to succeed in the broader Texan culture. A final chapter, years later, brings Sophia back to the barrio where she confronts the urban decay of her childhood community.

The fast-paced *Borderline* (2009) by Allan Stratton includes images that could easily be taken from of a popular television show. Fifteen-year-old Sami Sabiri is accustomed to being taunted and bullied at school because he is a Muslim, but what happens to his family goes beyond simple cultural differences. The FBI breaks into his house and arrests his Iranian-born father for collaborating with Islamic terrorists. Sami, an American citizen, is interrogated and kicked out of school. When Sami realizes the full impact of the government's position and power, he goes undercover to find out the truth. Stratton adeptly portrays the everyday life of an Islamic American family until racism and hatred turn it upside down.

Ask Me No Questions by Marina Budhos (2006) features a similar theme. Fourteen-year-old Nadira and her family immigrated to New York from Bangladesh and have kept their illegal status a secret for years. Everything changes after 9/11 when a failed attempt to get to Canada leads to the father's detainment.

Sherman Alexie's semi-autobiographical *The Absolutely True Diary of a Part Time Indian* (2007) explores what it means to be an Indian and won the National Book Award for Young People's Literature. Junior and his family live on the Spokane Indian Reservation. Poverty and alcoholism permeate their lives. Junior decides that he has to go to a better school than the one on the "rez." He experiences racism from both expected and unexpected sources.

Justina Chen Headley's *Nothing but the Truth (and a Few White Lies)* (2006) explores the struggles of being biracial. High school sophomore Patty Ho is "hapa," half Taiwanese and half white, but does not feel comfortable in either culture. Her white father is absent, and her mother is "all about being Taiwanese" and is determined that Patty attend a prestigious college. When a fortune teller predicts Patty will marry a white man, her Taiwanese mother sends her to math camp at Stanford. Patty discovers that math is not so bad and neither are the boys she meets. Patty's witty, first-person narrative and her search for identity transcend a cultural context.

The subject matter in Rita Williams-Garcia's *No Laughter Here* (2004), female genital mutilation, is difficult to think about; however, the novel brings to light differences between cultures. Victoria has not been the same since she returned from her native Nigeria. When confronted about the emotional change

Efrain's Secret. Sofia Quintero, 2010. Seventeen-year-old Efrain is smart and driven to succeed but caught in the poverty, crime, and violence of South Bronx. He succumbs to the temptation of selling drugs to make fast money to pay for SAT tutoring. His first-person narration conveys the Spanish slang of his Latino neighborhood. Each chapter begins with a Spanish vocabulary word linked to the college placement exam. Ages 13 and up.

Between the Deep Blue Sea and Me. Lurline Wailana McGregor, 2008. This recipient of the 2010 American Indian Youth Literature Award tells the story of Moana Kawelo, a museum curator living in Los Angeles. When she returns to Hawaii for her father's funeral, she undergoes an introspective examination of her identity as a Native Hawaiian. Ages 13 and up.

Jumped. Rita Williams-Garcia, 2009. Fashionista Trina has unknowingly insulted Dominique, a tough basketball player, and Letica has overheard Dominique's plan to "jump" Trina at the end of the school day. Told in teenage lingo from alternating perspectives, Dominique's reasons for bullying, Letica's hesitancy to get involved, and Trina's oblivion to others are placed in the context of an urban high school where girl-on-girl violence is depicted as commonplace. Ages 12 and up.

A Step from Heaven. An Na, 2001. This Printz Award recipient tells the story of a Korean immigrant family. Young Ju's narrative begins in her childhood and ends when she is on the verge of adulthood. This immigrant story of promises kept and promises broken concerns a father who cannot adapt to American culture and a son who seeks refuge in gangs. Young Ju and her mother persevere. Ages 13 and up.

FILMS

Save the Last Dance. Directed by Thomas Carter, 2001. Following the death of her mother, Sara moves in with her father on Chicago's Southside. As a white girl in a predominately black neighborhood, she finds it difficult to establish relationships, especially a romantic relationship with a black classmate. PG-13.

Smoke Signals. Directed by Chris Eyre, 1998. The film, written by Sherman Alexie, echoes several of his novels. Set on a reservation, a main character is a basketball player whose life is impacted by alcoholism. Friends must come to grips with their differing views about their culture. PG-13.

in Victoria, her brother explains that this surgery is their custom and someone outside of their culture has no right to judge. An author endnote explains that 2 million girls are subjected to this custom each year even though it is banned by law in several African nations.

The National Association for Multicultural Education (www.nameorg.org) offers excellent resources for developing a curriculum that is culturally sensitive. The awards for literature of social significance discussed in Chapter 2 also can be helpful resources.

The world beyond the United States

The National Geographic–Roper Public Affairs 2006 Geographic Literacy Study indicated that young adults are sorely lacking in knowledge about the world. For example, they found that two-thirds of 18- to 24-year-olds could not find Iraq on a map. Nearly three-fourths thought English was the most widely

classroom scenario

Responding to Diverse Literature

AS YOU READ, consider how and why the teacher is using a critical perspective with culturally diverse literature. Evaluate the student's journal response in relation to the teacher's goals.

Mrs. Grant wants to provide her eighth-grade students with opportunities to experience literature about a wide range of cultures, although she knows that this will not, in and of itself, create respect for cultural differences (Glazier & Seo, 2005). She expands the journal prompts she typically uses to enhance critical perspectives. She asks her students to consider why the author wrote the work and what assumptions the author is making about the readers. She also asks her students to consider their own responses and to analyze why they respond as they do. In a handout, she provides the prompts shown in Figure 4.1.

 **4.1**   Journal prompts with a critical perspective for responding to diverse literature.

What assumption does the author make regarding readers' values, experiences, habits, and familiarity with stylistic devices?

- What does the reader have to know about society, politics, or culture?
- What does the author assume the reader knows about places, people, or events?
- How does the author use language to affect the reader?

What characteristics about you or your past experiences may have influenced your response to this novel?

- Did cultural factors influence your response?
- Did you find yourself accepting the text or resisting it?
- How have your own background and personality influenced your response to the text?

spoken native language in the world (National Geographic Education Foundation, 2006). Literature has the potential both to create interest in global awareness and to provide information about cultures and people beyond the borders of the United States.

War, particularly the role of the United States in contemporary wars, is the focus of *The Day of the Pelican* (2009) by Katherine Paterson, *Purple Heart* by Patricia McCormick (2009), and *Sunrise over Fallujah* (2008) by Walter Dean Myers. Paterson's protagonist is Meli Lleshi, an 11-year-old Albanian living in

Mrs. Grant's class has been reading *The First Part Last* (2003) by Angela Johnson and researching the author. They have discussed how readers' backgrounds and experiences can affect the way they respond to a novel, and she reminds the students to consider why they react to a novel the way they do. In response to the prompts provided, Jenny writes this journal entry:

October 9th

I found out in my background reading that people really liked Bobby in Heaven *(1998) and wanted to know more about him. Ms. Johnson said she saw a boy on a train with a baby so she decided to write about Bobby. I think that probably influenced her, but she likes to write about true to life situations and I think that mattered more. I also think she wanted to tell the story of teenage pregnancy, but from a different perspective. I think she is attacking the stereotype of black teen fathers neglecting their babies. She wants teenagers to think about the consequences of what they do. It wasn't judgmental about Bobby and Nia having sex, but it was very apparent that Bobby had to give up a lot, and Nia is in a coma, maybe forever. The cover shows Bobby holding the baby, but he isn't looking at her. He seems to have a dazed look on his face as if his mind is a long way away.*

In order to understand this book the reader has to know how flashbacks work and to keep track of the jumping back and forth in time. It helped that the chapters were titled "Then" and "Now." There were some swear words, but not the really bad ones so it didn't bother me and I think that is how Bobby would talk. It would help to know about New York and what it is like to live there and not have much money. I have never been there, but I knew about Brooklyn from movies.

While I was reading I kept thinking about my cousin. She had a baby when she was a teenager and the father never even sees the baby. I was angry with Nia for not being a good mother, but at the end of the book you find out what happened to her and then I felt bad. I guess I was influenced by my cousin's situation. Even though Bobby did some dumb stuff, he was nurturing and I wondered how many teenage guys, black or white, would really be that way.

After the students write in their journals, they meet in small groups to compare their reactions to the novel and to consider why their opinions are similar or different.

Kosovo in the late 1990s. When the Serbians escalate the violence and brutality against minority groups, Meli and her family attempt to find safety. After deprivation and loss, they finally arrive at a refugee camp. After the war, Meli and her family immigrate to the United States where difficult adjustments begin anew. The attack on the World Trade Center causes classmates to judge her and her brother as Muslims above all else, and therefore as an enemy. Several years pass during the story, illuminating the long-term hardships experienced by many Albanian Muslims.

Purple Heart focuses on the personal cost of war for an 18-year-old American soldier fighting in Iraq. Matt Duffy has witnessed something awful, but because of a traumatic brain injury from being shot, he cannot remember what. The scenes in the hospital, with military personnel, and with the soldiers he serves are realistic and brutal. The plot explores the complex and often dangerous interactions of solider and civilian.

Myers' *Sunrise over Fallujah* (2008) illuminates the futility of war through 18-year-old protagonist Robin Perry, who is the nephew of Richie, the young soldier fighting in Vietnam in Myers' award winning *Fallen Angels* (1988). In 2003, Robin is sent to Baghdad to participate in Operation Iraqi Freedom. Initially, he feels excited and committed to the cause, but gradually, through the everyday experiences of war, including killing someone, he changes. His changes are related in his first-person narration, letters, and e-mails home. As in *Fallen Angels*, many of the soldiers in this novel are young, poor, and from a minority culture.

In Tammar Stein's *Light Years* (2005) Maya Laor has left Israel to study astronomy at the University of Virginia. Chapters alternate between her past life as an Israeli soldier, which includes the vivid memory of the death of her boyfriend by a Palestinian suicide bomber, and her current life as a college student adjusting to a new culture. Maya comes to realize that although her past is light years away and she wants to leave the horrible memories far behind, Israel will always be her home.

Sold (2006) is a bold novel about a young girl from Nepal who is sold into prostitution. Patricia McCormick writes in first-person, present-tense free verse, which punctuates the stark revelations about the lives of the girls in such brothels. McCormick spent several months in Nepal and India researching the sex slave industry, and the book contains many details of the surroundings and circumstances of Lakshmi's life.

Deborah Ellis' *I Am a Taxi* (2006) and the sequel *Sacred Leaf* (2007) explore issues related to cocaine production in Bolivia. Twelve-year-old Diego lives with his mother and sister in the women's prison where he earns money as a "taxi" running errands for inmates. When he makes a mistake that puts an end to his taxi job, he turns to working in the cocaine pits. The portrait of the sinister drug smugglers intensifies the horrible effects of the drug; however, these novels are more than simplistic tales of the evils of cocaine. Ellis also portrays Bolivian culture, politics, and traditions.

Randa Abdel-Fattah, an Australian Muslim, was prompted to write about Muslim teenage girls because in her own youth she found Muslim women depicted as either oppressed or as terrorists. Referring to her book *Does My Head Look Big in This?* (2007) she explains, "I wanted to write a book that gave a young Muslim teenager a voice and allowed her the chance to dispel stereotypes and shock readers into realizing that teenagers, no matter their faith or culture, have common experiences; that there is more in common than there is different; and that the differences should be respected, not feared" (Rochman, 2007).

Two of Abdel-Fattah's books, the previously mentioned *Does My Head Look Big in This* (2007) and *Ten Things I Hate about Me* (2009) provide contrasting pictures into the lives of two Muslim teenage girls. In the former novel Amal is a fashion-conscious Australian of Palestinian heritage who decides to wear a hijab, or head scarf, to show her commitment to her faith. She struggles with responses from friends and family, as well as all the typical challenges a teenager faces. In *Ten Things I Hate About Me*, a girl who is Lebanese-Australian eschews all identifiable aspects of her heritage. She dyes her hair, wears blue contact lenses, and has people call her Jamie, because she believe that high school is no place to be "ethnic." At home she becomes Jamilah, a devout Muslim daughter who attends madrasa, her Islamic school, where she studies Arabic and plays the darabuka drums. Somehow, she must reconcile these two parts of her life.

Finding Nouf (2008), an Alex Award-winning mystery by Zoe Ferraris, is set in contemporary Saudi Arabia. Sixteen-year-old Nouf's body has been found in the desert, raising many questions. The story is told in alternating voices from the perspective of Nayir Sharqi, a devout Palestinian Muslim, and Katya Hijazi, a forensic technician and a modern Saudi woman. The novel focuses on Islamic practices and interpretations of those practices across gender, age, social class, and culture.

REALISTIC FICTION WITH METAFICTIVE CHARACTERISTICS

Many contemporary novels already mentioned in this chapter have metafictive traits, previously described in Chapter 3. The following works have been chosen as examples of realistic fiction that incorporates metafictive techniques such as multiple narrators, nonlinear plot, mixed genres, and nontraditional styles.

Multiple Narrators

Multiple narrators may emphasize that the meaning of an event depends greatly on who is observing and interpreting what is happening. Multiple or shifting narrators also provide different perspectives and insights into character development and plot.

In Carolyn Mackler's *Tangled* (2010), four young adults narrate the stories of their lives over a four-month period. Multiple characters describe the events in their lives that overlap, and each character also relates events known only to that individual. This use of multiple narrators provides insights into each character's feelings and private experiences as well as a balanced perspective of what happened to them when they were together. Chapters are renumbered beginning with each narrator. The novel has strong romantic undertones.

Alternating chapters reflect the differing voices of authors Rachel Cohn and David Levithan in *Nick & Norah's Infinite Playlist* (2008). Cohn wrote Norah's chapters and Levithan wrote Nick's, resulting in two distinct characters and perspectives. Nick and Norah, bonded by music and the trials of adolescence in general (relationships, parents, sexuality, etc.), fall in love over the course of a single night spent roaming Manhattan in search of a band playing a late-night gig.

In a similar vein, John Green collaborated with David Levithan to write *Will Grayson, Will Grayson* (2010). There are two Will Graysons: a straight, smart, nerdy guy written by Green; and a gay, clinically depressed teen, written by David Levithan. The two authors create two unique characters who have the same name, but very different lives. Lower case is used for one of the Wills in order to identify which Will is narrating. The two Wills accidently meet half way through the story at a porn shop. Although the Wills narrate the story, it is very much the tale of Tiny Cooper, a three hundred pound, flamboyantly gay football player, friend of one Will, in love with the other. Straight relationships, gay relationships, and friendships are all complicated, and yet Tiny brings them together through song.

Nonlinearity

A text is nonlinear if it does not follow a straight line through a series of events. An author may choose to sequence events out of chronological order to emphasize an event, to highlight a character's way of thinking, or to add interest.

If I Stay by Gayle Forman (2009) is the story of Mia, a gifted classical musician. The chapters alternate between what happens during the 24 hours leading up to and after a car accident in the present, and chapters about her past. The scenes in the present, starting with the morning of the accident, are identified by time and progress in chronological order. In one scene, Mia has an out-of-body experience. She watches everything around her, including the medical crew working on her and her brother's bodies. The other sections are untitled, nonlinear, and resemble the flashes of memory someone might have looking back on life.

The nonlinearity of *Shift* (2008) by Jennifer Bradbury intensifies the story of two friends who begin a cross country bike ride after graduation only to have it end with one boy, Win, disappearing and the other, Chris, being interrogated by the FBI. Alternating chapters flash back to events during the trip then forward to Chris's life at college after Win's disappearance. Win's wealthy, tyrannical father hires detectives to find his son, and he threatens to terminate Chris's father's job if Chris refuses to tell him about the bike trip and his son's disappearance. Eventually, Chris locates and confronts Win. In finding his friend and coming to terms with the nature of their friendship, Chris finds himself.

Mixed Genre/Unique Style

Some authors mix different types of writing or use nontraditional structures. Combining genres may provide a mechanism for including information or insights that would not be revealed using a single type of literature.

Jeanette Ingold infuses historical fiction throughout a contemporary story in *Paper Daughter* (2010). Maggie, a high school student, becomes involved in an investigation of government corruption that somehow is connected to her recently deceased father. Maggie is determined to find out the truth about her father, who was a reporter, and in doing so she learns about her own cultural history. Although the majority of the novel is Maggie's story, it alternates with the story, written in italics, of two teenage siblings who illegally immigrated to the United States from China in 1932.

Julia Alvarez explores the complex issues surrounding migrant workers and the survival of the family farm in *Return to Sender* (2009) through the use of letters, diaries, and third-person narration. Tyler's father has been injured, and the only way his family can keep their Vermont farm is to hire undocumented Mexican laborers. The other main character is Mari, a daughter of one of the migrant workers. Tyler's third-person narration is juxtaposed with Mari's letters and diary entries. The use of letters as a story telling device emphasizes her family's situation. Mari's letters remain unsent because mailed letters can be used to locate workers and lead to deportation. Spanish words are interspersed throughout the story as are Mexican history and customs. Tyler wrestles with what is illegal as compared to what is immoral.

Punkzilla (Rapp, 2009), a Printz honor book, uses first-person letters to chronicle a part of the life of 14-year-old Jamie. Most of the letters are written by Jamie, but some are written to him. Bits and pieces of his life are revealed, not in the order of occurrence, but rather as Jamie thinks of them. Jamie, a runaway, wants to visit his brother who is dying from cancer. Along the way he becomes involved with thieves, delinquents, and a prostitute. Jamie's motives and desires, both when he is sober and when he is on drugs, are revealed. The language Jamie uses is explicit, and the descriptions of life on the streets and the people he encounters are realistic and, at times, gut wrenching.

The first paragraph of *Shattering Glass* (Giles, 2002) reveals a murder. The reasons for the murder unfold through the first-person narrative of Young Steward, an aspiring writer, and quotes from members of his clique, his classmates, and adults. Placed at the beginning of each chapter, the quotations, some from years later, provide insights into the boys' thoughts and behaviors as they set out to transform the school nerd. The boys in the clique resort to brutal, violent behavior when true personalities and intents are revealed.

Nikki Grimes' *Bronx Masquerade* (2002), a Coretta Scott King Award winner, meshes first-person narratives with a variety of poetic styles. A teacher sets up an open microphone, and students are invited to recite their own poetry. Tyrone, a recurring voice, uses urban slang such as "homey" and talks about the white folks. Tyrone's comments reveal additional information about each student.

Intertextuality

Intertextuality implies a connection between two or more literary works. As stated previously, it may be used as a device in a particular work to take advantage of readers' experiences with a similar text. The interpretation of the more recently read work is influenced by the previously read work.

Goth Girl Rising (2009), a sequel to *The Astonishing Adventures of Fanboy and Goth Girl* (2006) by Barry Lyga, presents Kyra, or Goth Girl, as the narrator. Following the death of her mother and a suicide attempt, Kyra is hospitalized in a mental ward for several months. During this time, her friend Fanboy has had his graphic novel published in a literary magazine, elevating his status with his peers and changing his relationship with Kyra. Kyra's nonlinear narration is interspersed with unsent letters to her hero, Neil Gaiman, the author of the graphic novel *Sandman* (1995). She tells Gaiman that she wishes life could be easy, like in one of his comics. She wants it to fit together like panels and word balloons on a comic book page. Kyra mentions several of Gaiman's works and describes her experiences reading them. The reccurring references obviously connect to his work in particular, but they also create a connection to graphic novels in general.

AUTHORITY, AUTHENTICITY, AND ACCURACY IN REALISTIC FICTION

Authority, cultural authenticity, and accuracy are significant issues when selecting and teaching realistic fiction, especially literature of diversity. **Authority** refers to the question of whether or not an author can write accurately about a cultural group if he or she is not a member of that group. Some educators and authors believe that authors of culturally diverse literature should belong to that culture (York, 2008); however, this may be too limiting. Perhaps a better approach is to examine **cultural authenticity,** the ability of the author to portray all aspects of a story accurately. This perspective assumes the reader is knowledgeable about the culture depicted and is capable of reading critically (Wilfong, 2007).

The level of **accuracy,** the exactness or correctness of the characters, situations, or settings has been an issue with realistic fiction for young adults since its inception, The discussion of how much is too much has been reinvigorated by the popularity of hip hop fiction, mentioned earlier. Hill, Perez, and Irby (2008) placed street fiction in the context of its relationship to popular culture. Such fiction may feature coarse language and sexual and violent content, yet they believe that the reader's connection to urban young adults makes hip hop fiction a valuable addition to the literature curriculum. Familiarity with urban street fiction enables a teacher to bridge between school and out-of-school texts (Marshall, Staples & Gibson, 2009).

Websites, particularly blogs and reviews on commercial sites, provide a multitude of viewpoints that readers can consider as they develop their own opinions regarding the authority, cultural authenticity, and accuracy of a work. For example, the HappyNappyBookseller.com review (2009) of *The Orange Houses* (2009), a well-received novel by Paul Griffin, evaluates the book as lacking authenticity. A main character is described as an "African" refugee, not a refugee of a particular country. The reviewer contends that this results in a character devoid of culture. Similarly, a reviewer, identifying herself as having lived in India for 24 years, responded to the award-winning *Homeless Bird* by Gloria Whelan (2000) as misleading and fraught with inaccuracies about India. Whelan did not, in fact, travel to India before writing the book (Isaacs, 2001). The point is not whether these reviewers are correct or incorrect in their opinions; it is that they offer additional insights into the authenticity of a work of fiction portraying a culture not native to the author.

An additional layer of evaluation is necessary for culturally diverse litera-ture in audiobook format. *Book Links* (2004, p. 31) poses the questions, "what is the cultural and linguistic background of the narrator? Does it match the book's setting and characters?" Perhaps the question should be, "does the voice of the narrator match the linguistic and cultural background of the character?" Another consideration when judging the authenticity of audiobooks is if the other auditory elements, music and sounds, also reflect the culture (*Book Links,* 2004).

Professional resources also can be helpful in determining the quality of realistic fiction. For example, a checklist for evaluating literature about Arab Americans developed by Tami Craft Al-Hazza and Katherine Bucher and pub-lished in the *Reading Teacher* (2008) can be accessed online. Their checklist can serve as a prototype for evaluating any culturally diverse literature.

Paulette Molin's *American Indian Themes in Young Adult Literature* (2005) provides insights into the frequent lack of authenticity found in works about native peoples, often in well received books by award winning authors. For example, she asserts that Robert Lipsyte's *The Brave* (1991), *The Chief* (1993), and *Warrior Angel* (2003) perpetuate stereotypes, beginning with the titles and continued in his "clichéd torn-between-cultures theme" (p. 5). She states, "Lip-syte frames and defines American Indian identity issues from an outsider's perspective, not in tribal terms of sovereignty, culture, enrollment, descent and upbringing, which are far more complex" (p. 5). Molin recommends works by Joseph Bruchac, Michael Dorris, Susan Powers, and Cynthia Leitich Smith for their authenticity and sensitivity.

Michael Cart and Christine Jenkins (2006) remind readers that when evalu-ating stories about GLBTQ teens, authenticity and inclusiveness are important, but first and foremost the work should be evaluated as literature. Are characters multidimensional? Are settings rich in verisimilitude? Is the voice not only authentic but also original? Are the insights into GLBTQ issues fresh? Are the narrative strategy, structure, and themes innovative? In other words, evaluation of authority, authenticity, and accuracy belong within the context of the evalu-ation of the literary work as a whole.

Teaching Ideas ▪ REALISTIC FICTION

Preparing students to experience literature, especially realistic fiction with mature themes, unfamiliar dialectics, explicit language, uncomfortable or unfamiliar situations, or cultures dissimilar to their own may require more deliberate use of pre-reading activities. Pre-reading activities should motivate, spark curios-ity, establish background, and enhance the likelihood that young adults will connect on a personal level with the literary work. The following pre-reading activities are easy to construct, with the caveat that the learning activity should match the literature at hand as well as the readers.

Anticipation guide. Create a series of statements that are thematically or topically related to the literature. The statements should be opinion-based. Students respond to the statements individually, usually by agreeing or disagreeing, followed by discussion. Here is an example for *Prom* (Anderson, 2005):

AGREE   DISAGREE

  ○   ○   Students should conform to the school's rules and traditions.

  ○   ○   Prom is an expensive, outmoded, high-school tradition.

  ○   ○   Relationships matter more than personal goals.

  ○   ○   Getting by is enough for normal kids.

  ○   ○   Parents are a necessary but often embarrassing part of life.

Predicting. Have students look at a book's front and back covers. Consider the cover illustration and possible interpretations of the title. Discuss what the students know about the author and if anyone has read other books by this author. If yes, talk about those books and consider similarities in plot, characters, style, and theme. How might this novel be like other novels written by this person? What are the students' expectations about the book's genre?

Scenarios. Create a scenario similar to one in the novel and ask students what they would do if they were in the same situation. An example with *Code Orange* could be: "You open a envelope and white dust billows out. You don't know if it is harmless, dangerous, or lethal. What do you do?" Students can write in their journals or discuss the question in small groups.

Author research. Have students research the author, including a visit to his or her official website. This may provide insight into the author's purpose for writing and clues about the intended audience. For example, on her home page, Jacqueline Woodson (www.jacquelenewoodson.com) explains when, where, and why she wrote each of her books.

conclusion

Realistic portrayals of young adults in the contemporary world mean that some literary works will feature explicit language, violent acts, and sexual situations. Marc Aronson points out the chasm that may exist between the goals of authors who write for young adults and the beliefs of the adults who evaluate and select the literature for classrooms and libraries. This gulf is often widened by their differing views of adolescence (2001, p. 3).

Amy S. Pattee (2004) relates an incident that illustrates some of the tensions that often surface when realistic fiction for young adults is brought into the classroom. The adults enrolled in her course on literature for young adults vehemently objected to the novel *When Jeff Comes Home* (1999) by Catherine Atkins. Jeff, the main character in *When Jeff Comes Home*, is kidnapped while on a vacation with his family. He is held captive in a dark basement for over two years and abused emotionally, physically, and sexually. The story of Jeff's experience and that of his desperate family is told with brutal realism.

The adult students in the class considered the novel to be inappropriate for adolescent readers because it was too graphic and frightening. Their responses prompted the instructor to ask two questions: "What does young adult literature do, and what do we think young adult literature is supposed to do?" Those questions go to the heart of most disputes about realism. Fiction that portrays sociopathic characters and elements of society that are disturbing and dysfunctional serves no purpose if literature written for young adults is a means of "guiding youth through the social processes that lead to culturally determined maturity as well as a means of socializing youth" (Pattee, 2004, p. 245). Such a view assumes, however that young adult readers are essentially clay, waiting to be molded by the vicarious experiences fiction provides.

Pattee suggests that perhaps adults have difficulty with literature that depicts brutal and violent situations because adults want to maintain an idealized view of youth (2004). We agree with Pattee. We are not suggesting that young adults read only realistic fiction that portrays the harsher aspects of life. But we are suggesting that young adults, like all readers, may sometimes seek to understand the darker aspects of human behavior.

BIBLIOGRAPHY OF LITERATURE FOR YOUNG ADULTS

Abdel-Fattah, R. (2007). *Does my head look big in this?* New York: Orchard Books.

Abdel-Fattah, R. (2009). *Ten things I hate about me.* New York: Scholastic/Orchard Books.

Abbott, H. (2004). *Summer boys.* "Summer Boys" series. New York: Scholastic.

Abbott, H. (2005). *Next Summer.* "Summer Boys" series. New York: Scholastic.

Abbott, H. (2006). *Last Summer.* "Summer Boys" series. New York: Scholastic.

Abbott, H. (2007). *After Summer.* "Summer Boys" series. New York: Scholastic.

Abrahams, P. (2009). *Reality check.* New York: HarperTeen.

Adoff, J. (2004). *Names will never hurt me.* New York: Penguin.

Alexie, S. (2007). *The absolutely true diary of a part time Indian.* (E. Forney, Illus.). New York: Little, Brown.

Alvarez, J. (2009). *Return to sender.* New York: Knopf.

Anderson, L. H. (2002). *Catalyst.* New York: Viking.

Anderson, L. H. (2005). *Prom.* New York: Viking.

Anderson, L. H. (2009). *Wintergirls.* New York: Viking.

Atkins, C. (1999). *When Jeff comes home.* New York: Puffin.

Balliett, B. (2004). *Chasing Vermeer.* New York: Scholastic Press.

Baron, K. (2009). *Shattered.* Lodi, NJ: WestSide Books.

Baskin, N. R. (2008). *The truth about my Bat Mitzvah.* New York: Simon & Schuster.

Booth, C. (2006). *Tyrell.* New York: Push/Scholastic.

Bradbury, J. (2008). *Shift.* New York: Atheneum.

Brashares, A. (2001). *The sisterhood of the traveling pants.* New York: Delacorte.

Brashares, A. (2003). *The second summer of the sisterhood.* New York: Delacorte.

Brashares, A. (2005). *Girls in pants: The third summer of the sisterhood.* New York: Delacorte.

Brashares, A. (2007). *Forever blue: The fourth summer of the sisterhood.* New York: Delacorte.

Brooks, K. (2008). *Black rabbit summer.* New York: Scholastic.

Brothers, M. (2008). *Debbie Harry sings in French.* New York: Holt.

Budhos, M. (2006). *Ask me no questions.* New York: Atheneum.

Burd, N. (2009). *The vast fields of ordinary.* New York: Dial.

Canales, V. (2005). *The tequila worm.* New York: Wendy Lamb/Random House.

Cantor, J. (2009). *September sisters.* New York: HarperTeen.

Carter, A. (2010). *Only the good spy young.* "Gallagher Girls" series. New York: Hyperion.

Carter, A. (2010). *Don't judge a girl by her cover.* "Gallagher Girls" series. New York: Hyperion.

Carter, T. (Dir.). (2001). *Save the last dance.* USA: Paramount.

Chadha, G. (Dir.). (2002). *Bend it like Beckham.* UK: Film Screen.

Clippinger, C. (2007). *Open court*. New York: Knopf.

Cohn, R., & Levithan, D. (2008). *Nick & Norah's infinite playlist*. New York: Knopf.

Coll, S. (2007). *Acceptance*. New York: Farrar, Straus & Giroux.

Cooney, C. (2005). *Code orange*. New York: Delacorte.

Cooney, C. (2009). *If the witness lied*. New York: Delacorte.

Crutcher, C. (2001). *Whale talk*. New York: Greenwillow Books.

Dean, Z. (2008). *California dreaming*. "A-List" series. New York: Little, Brown.

Dean, Z. (2007). *Beautiful stranger*. "A-List" series. New York: Little, Brown.

Dean, Z. (2007). *Heart of glass*. "A-List" series. New York: Little, Brown.

De la Pena, M. (2007). *Ball don't lie*. New York: Delacorte.

Dessen, S. (2009). *Along for the ride*. New York: Viking Penguin.

Deuker, C. (2005). *Runner*. Boston, MA: Houghton Mifflin.

Deuker, C. (2008). *Gym candy*. New York: Graphia.

Donovan, J. (1969). *I'll get there. It better be worth the trip*. New York: Dell.

Draper, S. (2010). *Out of my mind*. New York: Atheneum.

Duke, B., & Lee, S. L. (Dirs.). (2005). *Miracle Boys*. USA: Feral Films.

Efaw, A. (2009). *After*. New York: Viking.

Ellis D. (2006). *I am a taxi*. Toronto, ON: Groundwood Books.

Ellis D. (2007). *Sacred leaf*. Toronto, ON: Groundwood Books.

Eulberg, E. (2010). *The lonely hearts club*. New York: Point Scholastic.

Eyre, C. (Dir.). (1998). *Smoke signals*. USA: Miramax.

Ferraris, Z. (2008). *Finding Nouf*. New York: Houghton Mifflin.

Fink, M. (2009). *The summer I got a life*. Lodi, NJ: WestSide Books.

Forman, G. (2009). *If I stay*. New York: Dutton/Penguin.

Freymann-Weyr, G. (2002). *My heartbeat*. New York: Houghton Mifflin.

Friedman, R. (2008). *Nothing*. Woodbury, MN: Flux.

Friesen, J. (2008). *Jerk California*. New York: Speak/Penguin.

Gaiman, N. (1995). *The sandman. Vol. I: Preludes and nocturnes*. (Sam Kietch, Mike Dringenberg, & Malcolm Jones III, Illus.). New York: DC Comics.

Giles, G. (2002). *Shattering glass*. Brookfield, CT: Roaring Brook Press.

Green, J. (2005). *Looking for Alaska*. New York: Dutton.

Green J. (2006). *An abundance of Katherines*. New York: Dutton.

Green, J. (2008). *Paper towns*. New York: Dutton.

Green J., & Levithan, D. (2010). *Will Grayson, Will Grayson*. New York: Dutton.

Green, T. (2009). *Baseball Great*. New York: HarperCollins.

Green, T. (2010). *Rivals*. New York: HarperCollins.

Griffin, P. (2009). *The orange houses*. New York: Dial.

Grimes, N. (2002). *Bronx masquerade*. New York: Dial.

Hamri, S. (Dir.). (2009). *Acceptance*. USA: All In Entertainment.

Hancock, J. L. (Dir.). (2009). *The blind side*. USA: Alcon Entertainment/Fortis Films.

Harmon, M. (2008). *The last exit to normal*. New York: Knopf.

Hartinger, B. (2003). *Geography club*. New York: HarperTeen.

Headley, J. C. (2006). *Nothing but the truth (and a few white lies)*. New York: Little, Brown.

Herlong, M. H. (2008). *The great wide sea*. New York: Viking.

Hopkins, E. (2008). *Identical*. New York: Margaret K. McElderry.

Hokenson, T. (2006). *The winter road*. Asheville, NC: Front Street.

Hughes, P. (2005). *Open ice*. New York: Laurel Leaf.

Ingold, J. (2010). *Paper daughter*. Boston, MA: Houghton Mifflin.

Johnson, A. (1998). *Heaven*. New York: Simon & Schuster.

Johnson, A. (2003). *The first part last*. New York: Simon & Schuster.

Koja, K. (2007). *Kissing the bee*. New York: Farrar, Straus & Giroux.

Kwasney, M. (2009). *Blue plate special*. San Francisco, CA: Chronicle.

LaRochelle, D. (2005). *Absolutely, positively not*. New York: Arthur A. Levine.

Laser, M. (2008). *Cheater: A novel*. New York: Dutton.

Letts, B. (1995). *Where the heart is*. New York: Warner.

Lipsyte, R. (1991). *The brave*. New York: Harper Trophy.

Lipsyte, R. (1993). *The chief*. New York: Harper Trophy.

Lipsyte, R. (2003). *Warrior angel*. New York: HarperCollins.

Lipsyte, R. (2010). *Center field*. New York: HarperTeen.

Lockhart, E. (2008). *The disreputable history of Frankie Landau-Banks*. New York: Hyperion.

Lord, C. (2006). *Rules*. New York: Scholastic.

Lupica, M. (2010). *The batboy*. New York: Philomel.

Lyga, B. (2006). *The astonishing adventures of fanboy and goth girl*. Boston, MA: Houghton Mifflin.

Lyga, B. (2009). *Goth girl rising*. Boston, MA: Houghton Mifflin Harcourt.

Lynch, C. (2008). *The big game of everything*. New York: HarperCollins.

Mackler, C. (2010). *Tangled*. New York: HarperCollins.

Marchetta, M. (2006). *Jellicoe Road*. New York: HarperCollins.

Mass, W. (2008). *Every soul a star*. New York: Little, Brown.

McCormick, P. (2006). *Sold*. New York: Hyperion.

McCormick, P. (2009). *Purple heart*. New York: HarperCollins.

McGregor, L. W. (2008). *Between the deep blue sea and me*. Mililani, HI: Booklines Hawaii, Ltd.

McNamee, G. (2003). *Acceleration*. New York: Wendy Lamb.

Moskowitz, H. (2009). *Break*. New York: Simon Pulse.

Murdock, C. G. (2006). *Dairy queen*. Boston, MA: Houghton Mifflin.

Murdock, C. G. (2007). *The off season*. Boston, MA: Houghton Mifflin.

Murdock, C. G. (2009). *Front and center*. Boston, MA: Houghton Mifflin.

Myers, W. D. (1988). *Fallen angels*. New York: Scholastic.

Myers, W. D. (1999). *Monster*. (C. Myers, Illus.). New York: HarperCollins.

Myers, W. D. (2008). *Game*. New York: HarperTeen.

Myers, W. D. (2008). *Sunrise over Fallujah*. New York: Scholastic.

Myers, W. D. (2010). *Lockdown*. New York: Amistad HarperTeen.

Na, A. (2001). *A step from heaven*. Asheville, NC: Front Street.

Oaks, J. A. (2009). *Why I fight*. New York: Atheneum.

Olin, K. (Dir.). (1992). *Doing time on Maple Drive*. USA: Fox.

Paterson, K. (2009). *The day of the pelican*. Boston, MA: Clarion.

Paulsen, G. (1987). *Hatchet*. New York: Bradbury Press.

Paulsen, G. (1991). *The river*. New York: Delacorte.

Paulsen, G. (1996). *Brian's winter*. New York: Delacorte.

Paulsen, G. (1999). *Brian's return*. New York: Delacorte.

Paulsen, G. (2003). *Brian's hunt*. New York: Wendy Lamb.

Peters, J. A. (2004). *Luna*. New York: Little, Brown.

Picoult, J. (2000). *Plain truth*. New York: Washington Square Press.

Poll, J. (Dir.). (2008). *Charlie Bartlett*. USA: Metro-Goldwyn-Mayer.

Pyron, B. (2009). *The ring*. Lodi, NJ: WestSide books.

Quintero, S. (2010). *Efrain's secret*. New York: Knopf.

Rapp, A. (2009). *Punkzilla*. Somerville, MA: Candlewick Press.

Reitman, J. (Dir.). (2007). *Juno*. USA: Mandate Pictures.

Shapiro, P. (Dir.). (2004). *Plain truth*. Canada/USA: Muse Entertainment.

Sachar, L. (1998). *Holes*. New York: Farrar, Straus & Giroux.

Shepard, S. (2010). *Heartless*. "Pretty Little Liars" series. New York: HarperTeen.

Shepard, S. (2010). *Killer*. "Pretty Little Liars" series. New York: HarperTeen.

Shepard, S. (2009). *Wicked*. "Pretty Little Liars" series. New York: HarperTeen.

Smith, R. (2007). *Peak*. Orlando, FL: Harcourt.

Stratton, A. (2009). *Borderline*. New York: HarperTeen.

Stein, T. (2005). *Light years: A novel*. New York: Knopf.

Trueman, T. (2000). *Stuck in neutral*. New York: HarperCollins.

Tolan, S. (2002). *Surviving the Applewhites*. New York: HarperCollins.

Volponi, P. (2005). *Black and white*. New York: Penguin.

Volponi, P. (2010). *Rikers high*. New York: Viking Penguin.

Von Ziegesar, C. (2009). *I will always love you*. "Gossip Girl" series. New York: Little, Brown.

Von Ziegesar, C. (2009). *It had to be you*. "Gossip Girl" series. New York: Little, Brown.

Von Ziegesar, C. (2007). *Don't forget about me*. "Gossip Girl" series. New York: Little, Brown.

Wallace, R. (2007). *Take down*. New York: Puffin.

Waters, M. (Dir.). (2004). *Mean girls*. USA: Paramount.

Whelan, G. (2000). *Homeless bird*. New York: HarperCollins.

Williams, M. (Dir.). (2000). *Where the heart is*. USA: Twentieth Century Fox.

Williams-Garcia, R. (2004). *No laughter here*. New York: HarperCollins.

Williams-Garcia, R. (2009). *Jumped*. New York: Amistad/Harper Teen.

Wittlinger, E. (1999). *Hard love*. New York: Simon & Schuster.

Wittlinger, E. (2007). *Parrotfish*. New York: Simon & Schuster.

Woodson, J. (1997). *The house you pass on the way*. New York: Delacorte.

Woodson, J. (1998). *If you come softly*. New York: Putnam.

Woodson, J. (2000). *Miracle's boys*. New York: Putnam.

Woodson, J. (2002). *Hush*. New York: Putnam.

Woodson, J. (2003). *Locomotion*. New York: Delacorte.

Woodson, J. (2008). *After Tupac & D Foster*. New York: Putnam.

Woodson, J. (2009). *Peace, locomotion*. New York: Putnam.

Zarr, S. (2007). *Story of a girl*. New York: Little, Brown.

WEBSITES WITH ANNOTATIONS

Alex Sanchez's Great Books for Gay Teens • **www.alex sanchez.com/gay_teen_books.htm**

Sanchez is an author of novels for young adults featuring GLBTQ themes. This website lists teen novels, poetry anthologies, and nonfiction books with gay, lesbian, bisexual, and transgender characters and themes written by other authors.

American Library Association • **http://rainbowlist. wordpress.com**

Provides a GLBTQ Rainbow Book List for children and teens.

Diversity in Publishing Network • **www.dipnet.org.uk**

Provides lists of websites and blogs that are helpful for identifying publishers, authors, and critics of multicultural literature.

Hopkins, Ellen • **www.ellenhopkins.com**

The author's official website, including summaries of novels, poetry, video interviews, and tips on writing and publishing.

National Association for Multicultural Education • **http://nameorg.org/**

Provides resources to help teachers develop a culturally aware curriculum.

Rainbow Book List • **http://glbtrt.ala.org/rainbow books/**

Hosted by the Rainbow Project, including an annual bibliography of quality books with significant and authentic GLBTQ content, recommended for people from birth through 18 years of age.

Woodson, Jacqueline • **http://jacquelinewoodson. com/bio.shtml**

The author's official website, including summaries of works and resources for educators.

Young Adult Romance Writers • **http://youngadult romancewriters.com/**

Features reviews of romance novels written for young adults, along with links to author websites.

REFERENCES

Al-Hazza, T. C., & Bucher, K. T. (2008). Building Arab Americans' cultural identity and acceptance with children's literature. *Reading Teacher, 62*(3), 210–219.

American Library Association. (n.d.). GLBTQ rainbow list. Retrieved from http://rainbowlist.wordpress.com.

Aronson, M. (2001). *Exploding the myths: The truth about teenagers and reading.* Lanham, MD: Scarecrow Press.

Barnett, R. (2009). Helping teens answer the question "who am I": Cognitive development in adolescents. Family, Youth and Community Sciences Department, Florida Cooperative Extension Service, University of Florida. Retrieved from http: edis.ifas.ufl.edu/fy769.

Belge, K. (n.d.). *An interview with Jacqueline Woodson.* Retrieved from http://lesbianlife.about.com/od/artistswritersset1/a/JWoodson.htm.

Book Links (2004, January). Choosing multicultural audio books, 13(3), 31–30.

Bouchey, H. A., & Furman, W. (2003, March/April). Dating and romantic experiences in adolescence. In P. Campbell, The sand in the oyster: The outsiders, Fat Freddy, and me. *Horn Book,* 177–183.

Campbell, P. (2004, May/June). The sand in the oyster: Our side of the fence. *Horn Book, 80*(3), 360–362.

Cart, M. (2004). What a wonderful world: Notes on the evolution of GLBTQ literature for young adults. *ALAN Review, 31*(2), 46–52.

Cart, M., & Jenkins, C. A. (2006). *The heart has its reasons.* Lanham, MD: Scarecrow Press.

Chase, P., & Ressler, B. (Guest Eds.). (2009). Sexual identify and gender variance. *English Journal, 98*(4).

Chase, P., & Ressler, B. (2009). Sexual identity and gender variance: Meeting the educational challenges. *English Journal, 98*(4), 15–22.

Crowe, C. (2000). More than just sports novels: An interview with John H. Ritter. *ALAN Review.* Retrieved from http://www.johnritter.com/interviews-ALAN-Review-2000.html.

Crowe, C. (2001). Young adult literature: Sports literature for young adults. *English Journal, 90*(6), 129–133.

Curwood, J. S., Schliesman, M., & Horning, K. T. (2009). Fight for your right: Censorship, selection and LGBTQ literature. *English Journal, 98*(4), 37–43.

Diversity in Publishing Network. (n.d.). Retrieved from www.dipnet.org.uk.

Ellenhopkins.com (n.d.). Retrieved from http://www.ellenhopkins.com.

Glazier, J., & Seo, J. (2005). Multicultural literature and discussion of mirrors and windows. *Journal of Adolescent and Adult Literacy, 48,* 686–700.

Grimes, N. (2005). The common denominator. *English Journal, 94*(3), 22–24.

HappyNappyBookseller (2009). *The Orange Houses Paul Griffin*. Retrieved May 16, 2010, from http://thehappynappybookseller.blogspot.com/2009/11/orange-houses-paul-griffin.html.

Hill, M. L., Perez, B., & Irby, D. (2008). Street fiction: What is it and what does it mean for English teachers? *English Journal*, 97(3) 76–81.

Isaacs, K. (2001). Flying high. *School Library Journal*, 47(3), 52–55.

Kane, S. (2011). *Literacy & learning in the content areas* (3rd ed.). Scottsdale, AZ: Holcomb Hathaway.

Koss, M. D., & Teale, W. H. (2009). What's happening in YA literature? Trends in books for adolescents. *Journal of Adolescent & Adult Literacy*, 52(7) 563–572.

Letcher, M. (2009). Off the shelves. *English Journal*, 98(4), 123–126.

Marshall, E., Staples, J., & Gibson, S. (2009). Ghetto fabulous: Reading black adolescent femininity in contemporary urban street fiction. *Journal of Adolescent and Adult Literacy*, 53, 28–36.

Meloni, C. (2007). Attracting new readers with hip hop lit. *Library Media Connection*, 25(5), 38–40.

Molin, P. F. (2005). *American Indian themes in young adult literature*. Lanham, MD: Scarecrow Press.

Moorti, S., & Ross, K. (2004). Reality television: Fairy tale or feminist nightmare? *Feminist Media Studies*, 4(2), 203–231.

National Geographic Education Foundation and Roper Public Affairs. (2006). Final report: National Geographic–Roper Public Affairs 2006 geographic literacy study. Retrieved from http://www.nationalgeographic.com/roper2006/pdf/FINALReport2006GeogLitsurvey.pdf.

National Institute of Mental Health (2010). National survey confirms that youth are disproportionately affected by mental disorders. Retrieved from www.nimh.nih.gov/science-news/2010/national-survey-confirms-that-youth-are-dis.

Nye, N. S. (2005). From one friend to another. *English Journal*, 94(3), 39–41.

Pattee, A. S. (2004). Disturbing the peace: The function of young adult literature and the case of Catherine Atkins' *When Jeff Comes Home*. *Children's Literature in Education*, 35(3) 241–255.

Pepper, R. (2005). Jacqueline Woodson speaks on her 'youthful' writing. Windy City Media Group. Retrieved from http:www.windycitymediagroup.com/gay/lesbian/news/ARTICLE.php?AID=7189.

Prater, M.–A. (2003). Learning disabilities in children's and young adult literature: How are characters portrayed? *Learning Disabilities Quarterly*, 26(1), 47–62.

Romance Writers of America. (n.d.). The romance genre. Retrieved from http://www.rwanational.org/cs/the_romance_genre.

Rochman, H. (2005). The *Booklist* interview: Jacqueline Woodson. *Booklist*, 101(11), p. 968.

Rochman, H. (2007). The *Booklist* interview: Randa Abdel-Fattah. *Booklist*, 104(6), p. 54.

Sanchez, A. (n.d.). Great gay teen books. Alex Sanchez website. Retrieved from http://www.alexsanchez/gay_teen_books.htm.

Schneider, D. (2008). Talking with Jacqueline Woodson. *Book Links*, 17(5), 28–30.

South Carolina Department of Mental Health (n.d.). Get the facts on mental illness: Adolescent development. Retrieved from www.state.sc..us/dmh/adolescent_facts.htm.

Smith, C. L. (n.d.). Native American themes in children and young adult books. Cynthia Leitich Smith website. Retrieved from http://www.cynthialeitichsmith.com/lit_resources/diversity/native_am/NativeThemes_intro.

Smith, J. (n.d.). Mystery vs. suspense thriller book genres. MysteryNet.com. Retrieved from www.mysterynet.com/books/testimony/mystery-vs-thriller/.

Taylor, D. (2006, June). Jacqueline Woodson. *School Library Journal*, 52(6), 42–45.

Wilfong, L. G. (2007). A mirror, a window: Assisting teachers in selecting appropriate multicultural young adult literature. *International Journal of Multicultural Education*, 9(1) 1–13.

Woodson, J. (n.d.). Jacqueline Woodson: Author of books for children and young adults. Retrieved from www.jacquelinewoodson.com.

York, S. (2008). Culturally speaking; Booktalking authentic multicultural literature. *Library Media Connection*, 27(1), 16–18.

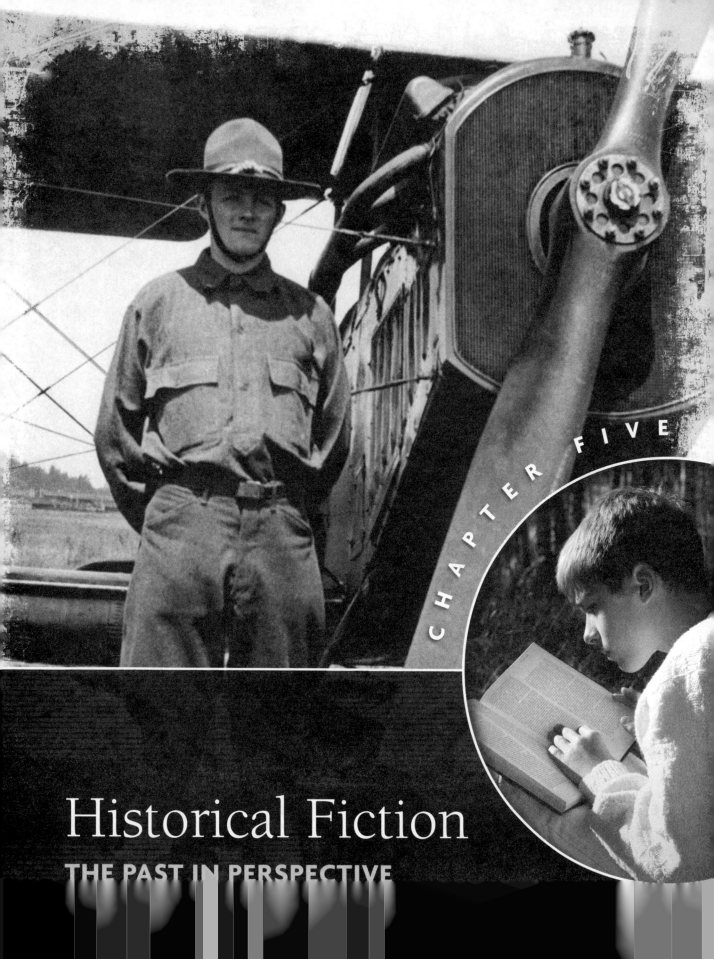

CHAPTER FIVE

Historical Fiction

THE PAST IN PERSPECTIVE

chapter overview

Historical fiction brings together history and imagination. It helps young adults connect the facts of history with characters they can identify with on a personal and emotional level. In this chapter, we describe the characteristics of historical fiction and group collections of works in three different ways. First, we organize works around themes and social issues that teachers may want to explore with young adults. Next, we present works organized by time periods. In the third group we focus on historical fiction that contains metafictive traits. In the final two sections of this chapter, we examine issues of accuracy and offer teaching suggestions.

FOCUS QUESTIONS

1. What are the characteristics of historical fiction?

2. What are common themes found in historical fiction?

3. What are the major issues with historical fiction?

4. What are approaches for teaching historical fiction?

5. How do metafictive characteristics influence a reader's interpretation of historical fiction?

introduction

Los Alamos in 1943 is a place hidden behind a strict wall of secrecy. Inside, however, the inhabitants are excited by the rumors they hear about the gadget that is being completed by strangers in their midst. Early on the morning of July 16, 1945, a picnic atmosphere prevails as spectators await the first demonstration of the atomic bomb. Just a few weeks later, 11-year-old Dewey turns on her radio and hears through the static, "Japanese city of Hiroshima." Tired of war news, Dewey quickly turns the dial. That is the ending of Ellen Klages' novel *The Green Glass Sea* (2006).

The title of Klages' book refers to a new element created by the intense heat of the atomic blast, a blast that changed the world forever. The novel received the Scott O'Dell Award for historical fiction, and it illustrates many of the characteristics that define the genre. According to *The Longman Dictionary of Literary Terms*, historical fiction is that "in which the narrative is set in another time or place with marked attention to historical accuracy. In historical fiction, the author attempts to recreate a faithful picture of daily life during the period, letting it serve as the backdrop for the local action" (Kennedy, 2006, p. 77).

Throughout her book, Klages blends fictional characters with real people, such as scientists Richard Feynman and Robert Oppenheimer. She pays meticulous attention to detail as she describes the objects that were part of everyday life in the 1940s: oilcloth tablecloths, Captain Marvel comics, Ovaltine, and the *Saturday Evening Post*. Her characters speak the slang of the day, such as "later alligator."

Careful historical research gives Klages' story an authentic sense of time and place, but the book offers more than that. It gives insights into the thoughts and feelings of two adolescent daughters of scientists who tell their stories from alternating third-person perspectives. Like all of the best historical fiction, *The Green Glass Sea* brings together time, place, characters, and events in a way that allows readers to understand a bygone era by helping them to imagine it.

ARE ALL STORIES SET IN THE PAST HISTORICAL FICTION?

Michael Cart (2009) comments that history is a moving target and historical fiction is a "relative and fugitive term" (p. 36). How far in the past must a story be set before it is categorized as historical? *Sunrise over Fallujah* (2008) by Walter Dean Myers, which we described in Chapter 4, is set in 2003. The war in Iraq is certainly still part of America's contemporary consciousness, but for how long? As time passes will this novel be considered historical?

Is historical fiction set in the author's past, or the reader's? In the early 1900s, Upton Sinclair came to Chicago with a mission. Supported by a socialist newspaper, he wanted to expose the exploitation of workers in the meatpacking industry. He published *The Jungle* in 1906 as a sensational account of contemporary political and social corruption. Sinclair wrote *The Jungle* to change his present, but readers today see it as a chronicle of the past. Brown and St. Clair (2006) suggest that the distinction between works set in the past and those set in the present fades as time passes so that eventually both take place in a historical period. What is thought of as the past will be ever changing as the distance between the fictional setting and the time in which the work is read continues to expand.

At a panel discussion on historical fiction at the Associated Writing Programs annual conference in 2002, Sarah Johnson stated that "above all historical fiction is a genre of controversy and contradiction" (2002, p. 1). The influence of the historical context varies considerably in such works and opinions differ greatly as to how much history a story must have in order to be labeled historical fiction. Clearly, announcing that "the year was 1941" on the first page does not make a book historical fiction—at least not good historical fiction.

Brown and St. Clair (2006) maintain that the historical fiction label should only be attributed to literature about a clash between opposing sociopolitical powers (p. 11). *Fire from the Rock* (Draper, 2007), for instance, is the story of an individual student, but it is also the story of a political struggle between people demanding change and those who were determined to preserve the inequalities of the past. Sharron McElmeel (2009) contends that the term **period fiction** rather than historical fiction should be used when a book is set in the past but has a plot that addresses universal themes that are not specific to the period.

Continuum of Historical Contexts

As seen in Figure 5.1, the influence of a historical setting may be thought of as a continuum. At one end is a narrative in which historical references establish a social, political, and cultural backdrop without tying the characters to any specific event. At the other end are fictionalized stories about real people and/or

 **5.1**   A continuum of historical contexts.

PERID FICTION ←		→ HISTORICAL FICTION
Main characters are all fictional and may interact with each other in ways that seem contemporary.	Main characters are fictional but may interact with actual historical figures.	Main characters may be a combination of fictional and historical figures who interact in a plausible way.
Objects, customs, events, and people of the period are mentioned.	Objects, customs, and language of the period are portrayed accurately and consistently.	Objects, customs, and language of the period are interwoven with the action.
Neither the plot nor the themes depend on the specific historical context.	Main characters are aware of historical events and respond to them in some way.	Characters influence specific or representative historical events or respond to them in depth.
The consciousness and concerns of the characters are recognizably contemporary rather than historical.	Readers become aware of details of daily life, the effects of historical events, or the issues that were prominent in the era.	Readers are able to imagine the consciousness of historical characters and to experience events of the period vicariously.

real events in which substantial information about historical events is provided in great detail.

A continuum indicates an almost infinite number of points between two opposites. Read the descriptions of the three books described below and decide where you would place each on the continuum.

Tales of the Madman Underground: An Historical Romance 1973 (2009) by John Barnes, is, as the title indicates, set in 1973. The 532-page story covers six days of Karl Shoemaker's senior year. Language from this time period ("stoner," "nerd," "groovy boy," "J.D." [juvenile delinquent]), as well as references to the Kent State shootings and Vietnam, create a historical flavor, and yet, the novel has a contemporary feel. The depiction of small-town life in Ohio, an alcoholic, cat-loving, conspiracy-freak mother, a gay friend, sexual encounters, profanity, and a focus on school and students in group therapy create a sense of *now* as much as *then*. Time and place do influence the characters and events, but teachers and readers expecting significant historical insight into the deep social upheaval of the era are likely to be disappointed. Those looking for a poignant coming-of-age novel that realistically depicts troubled young adults who happen to live in another time will appreciate Barnes' story much more.

A Voice of Her Own: Becoming Emily Dickinson (Dana, 2009) imagines the young life of the American poet from a first-person perspective. Nineteenth-century language and detailed description of the minutia of Dickinson's life, including the impact of her illnesses, physical and mental, create the authenticity of time and place and provide both historical and personal context for her poetry. Dana has meticulously documented both her research process and resources, as would be expected from well-written historical fiction about an actual person, and identifies the origin of specific lines from poems and correspondence.

Sharon Draper's *Fire from the Rock* (2007) places fictionalized characters in the middle of the struggle for civil rights and school integration. Eighth grade honor student Sylvia is one of the African American students chosen to integrate Central High in Little Rock, Arkansas, in 1957. If she agrees, she will become part of history. She also knows the danger involved and what she will leave behind. Her story is revealed through a third-person narrative alternating with diary entries. The fictionalized characters allow the author to include imagined feelings, thoughts, and conversations. An author's note explains what happened to the actual students.

Tales of the Madman Underground: An Historical Romance 1973, would probably be placed on the left of the continuum. The setting adds interest but does not heavily influence the story or the characters. A *Voice of Her Own: Becoming Emily Dickinson* would probably fall somewhere in the middle. Even though the time and place is accurately portrayed and certainly would have influenced Dickson's life, the use of first person requires the author to interpret Dickinson's thoughts and feelings. *Fire from the Rock* would fall to the right of the continuum. The setting depicted in this novel is not only integral to the events in the story, it could be debated that the time and place caused the events or at least greatly contributed to them.

The point of the continuum is not to segment historical fiction into subcategories that must be labeled and learned by young adult readers; rather, it is to demonstrate the complexity and variability in historical fiction. For our purposes, a simple definition works best. **Historical fiction** is a fictional story set in the past. The past will influence the events and characters in varying degrees. Johnson (2002) suggests that the lack of an exact definition should not prevent readers from appreciating the genre.

Historical Fiction: A Critical Perspective

Historical fiction frequently reflects the postmodern or critical perspective discussed in Chapter 1. A critical perspective requires considering the social and cultural forces that influence both authors and readers. A critical stance involves looking beyond the surface of the story to see who is on the margins of an event and what role they may be playing.

Contemporary historical fiction is likely to depict the role of women and members of cultural minorities, especially when doing so can help to balance the "official" or traditional view of events (Brown & St. Clair, 2006; Macleod, 1998). For example, *Flygirl* (2009) by Sherri L. Smith is about a young African American woman who passes for white so she can join the Women Air Force Service Pilots during World War II. This novel adds both women and people of color to a story that has typically focused on white men. It also highlights the racial inequality that existed during the war, which became more visible in later decades.

As indicated above, stories of real and imagined people and events are influenced by the social and cultural mores of the author. Anne Scott MacLeod (1998) illustrates how authors' interpretations of the past are influenced by their own time by contrasting Esther Forbes' *Johnny Tremain* (1943), *My Brother Sam Is Dead* by James and Christopher Collier (1974), and *Hang for Treason* by Robert Newton Peck (1976).

Esther Forbes wrote *Johnny Tremain* in the midst of World War II. The novel presents the Revolutionary War as a struggle for political freedom, echoing the patriotic American sentiment toward the war raging in the author's day. *Johnny Tremain* ends with the hopeful belief that the righteous Colonists will prevail against a powerful, oppressive enemy that seeks to limit freedom. In contrast, the Collier brothers and Peck were writing at a time when the country was divided over the war in Vietnam. By this time war was no longer idealized, and these books concentrate on the negative aspects of war. All three authors wrote historical fiction based on documented evidence; however, their interpretations of events reflect attitudes that were shaped by a social and political climate.

A critical perspective also suggests that the interpretation of historical events is influenced by the social and cultural background of the reader and by the circumstances in which a particular work is read. Readers will often resist historical interpretations that contradict the views of their own cultural tradition, and they may interject the present into historical settings by ascribing contemporary motives to historical characters. They might, for instance, assume that a silversmith apprentice like Johnny Tremain would see his work as drudgery, when Johnny saw it as a great opportunity.

COMMON THEMES IN HISTORICAL FICTION

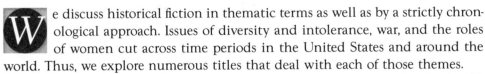

We discuss historical fiction in thematic terms as well as by a strictly chronological approach. Issues of diversity and intolerance, war, and the roles of women cut across time periods in the United States and around the world. Thus, we explore numerous titles that deal with each of those themes.

Social issues often overlap and interact, so the novels we describe do not necessarily belong exclusively in one category. For example, *Flygirl* (Smith, 2009) could be included in the section on diversity and intolerance because it is about racism. It is also about the psychological impact of war and strong female protagonists and fits in with those collections. Several of the novels described in the thematic sections have unusual stylistic aspects, but a collection of novels with metafictive characteristics is also described separately later in the chapter.

Diversity and Intolerance

In Chapter 1 we shared Lukens and Cline's notion that literature can be defined by what it can do, which is to "provide pleasure and increase understanding" (1995, p. viii.). Historical fiction can play a significant role in helping readers understand diversity and tolerance.

It is difficult for a young adult to develop a sense of social responsibility—an investment in the well-being of others and a sense of civic responsibility—without first understanding the past (Wolk, 2009). Historical fiction provides a chance for young adults to view those they might otherwise find threatening from a safe distance. Entering imaginatively into the past struggles of people who have often been the target of intolerance may be the most effective inoculation against hate that young adults can receive. The following novels are examples of the thousands of works of historical fiction for young adults about a group with power marginalizing or even enslaving another group based on culture, ethnic origin, or religion.

Slavery and racism in the United States

The novels described in this section are narratives about people of color in the United States. The settings span over one hundred years of American history, but the problems of limited opportunity and damaged self-worth caused by racism have changed little from era to era. For example, Ida Mae, the protagonist in *Flygirl* (Smith, 2009) wants so desperately to join the Women Air Force Service Pilots that she alters her father's license to look like her own and alters her appearance to pass for white. The personal cost of her hidden identity is demonstrated when her mother comes to tell her that her brother is missing in action. Ida Mae guardedly pretends that her mother is her childhood maid.

Sharon Draper's *Copper Sun* (2006), a Coretta Scott King Award winner, chronicles the story of 15-year-old Amari, whose story begins in 1738 when a group of pale strangers visits her African village. The strangers are with warriors from the Ashanti tribe, so they seem safe. The harrowing scene that follows tells a part of the story of slavery not frequently portrayed—the horrific slaughter of Africans at the hand of both European slavers and other Africans. No elder or child survives the attack on Amari's village. Amari is kidnapped into slavery and eventually purchased as a birthday gift for a landowner's son.

The remaining chapters alternate between Amari and Polly, an indentured servant, presenting the contrast between those in servitude who can earn their freedom and those who cannot. The girls escape and head south to Florida, which is a Spanish colony and therefore a safe haven. Cruelty on a personal and intimate level underscores the institutionalized cruelty of slavery. An afterword by the author includes information about Fort Mose, which became the first free black town in the United States.

Chains (2008) by Laurie Halse Anderson, winner of the Scott O'Dell Award for historical fiction and a National Book Award finalist, creates an authentic view of New York City on the dawn of the Revolutionary War. It depicts the stark contrast between the world of wealthy loyalists, in which proper ladies "slept late, wrote letters, and picked out melodies on a badly tuned spinet," and the lives of servants and slaves. Thirteen-year-old Isabel is a slave who is sold, beaten, branded, and starved. She turns her allegiance to the patriot cause. Her invisibility as a slave makes her the perfect spy. No one pays attention to her as she listens at doors and moves about the city on errands. She soon discovers that both loyalists and patriots support slavery. Each short chapter begins with a historical quote; this one from Benjamin Franklin underscores the economics of slavery: "Our slaves, Sir, cost us money, and we buy them to make money by their labour. If they are sick, they are not only unprofitable, but expensive" (p. 157).

The Adventurous Deeds of Deadwood Jones (2008) by Helen Hemphill is the story of Prometheus Jones, age 14. Prometheus is the child of a slave, but he is fortunate enough to be born on the day Abraham Lincoln signs the Emancipation Proclamation. Prometheus wins a horse in a raffle and heads out West on a cattle drive. The typical ingredients of a cowboy story—stampede, Indian raids, gunfights, horse stealing—are layered over a post–Civil War history. In an author's note, Hemphill states that more than 5,000 African Americans worked as cowboys and that a real cowboy, Nat Love, inspired the story.

Lesley M. M. Blume's *Tennyson* (2008) is set in Louisiana during the Great Depression. The once grand and opulent Aigredoux, a magnificent antebellum plantation, has succumbed to ruin. The ceilings are falling on its occupants, and its furnishings and fixtures have been sold. Eleven-year-old Tennyson and her younger sister are left at the mansion in the care of their aunt while their father searches for their runaway mother. During a series of dreams Tennyson visualizes the former grandeur of the plantation and the lives of her ancestors, all built on slavery. She sees her relatives hiding jewels and silver and hoarding goods in expectation of Union soldiers. Slaves fight with their masters in battle. Tennyson confronts her relatives about living in a past they have concocted as an illusion of their former glory. She chastises her aunt and uncle for sustaining a "temple that your family built to worship itself."

The Watsons Go to Birmingham, 1963, by Christopher Paul Curtis (1995) was the first of his historical fiction works to focus on the African American experience. In this book, in order to remove their oldest son from the violence and gangs of 1960s Michigan, the Watsons head South to their grandmother's house in Birmingham, Alabama. They may not be allowed to stop anywhere en route, and the trip underscores the pervasive racism in the South at that time. Curtis blends historical fact with fiction as the fictional Watsons experience the bombing of a church in which children are killed. This event is based on the actual bombing of the Sixteenth Street Baptist Church in 1963, in which four young girls were killed and many others wounded.

Other books by Curtis about African Americans include *Bud Not Buddy* (Curtis, 1999), a Coretta Scott King Author Award recipient. Set in 1936 Michigan, the story highlights the lives of jazz musicians, while exploring the deep-seated racism and the far-reaching impact of the Great Depression. In *Elijah of Buxton* (Curtis, 2007), Elijah is the first child born into freedom in Buxton, Canada, a real settlement for free blacks. Even though the Civil War is still raging, he ventures into the United States and witnesses firsthand the brutality of slavery.

The Rock and the River (2009) by Kela Magoon takes place in 1968, the year Dr. Martin Luther King was assassinated. The story focuses on 14-year-old Sam and his fictional family. Sam's father, a civil rights activist, is a minister and a close associate of King. Sam's older brother joins the Black Panther Party, a group who rejected passive resistance for a more self-determined route of social change. The violence, underlying racism, and oppression blanketing Chicago at this time are realistically depicted. After Sam witnesses police brutality and experiences violence on a personal level, he chooses his own direction.

Code Talker: A Novel about the Navajo Marines of World War Two by Joseph Bruchac (2005) is told from the perspective of a grandfather telling his grandchildren about his experiences as a young marine during World War II. Navajo Kii Yazhi was given the name Ned Begay at the government-run boarding school he was sent to as a child. At school he and the other Navajo children were forbidden to speak their native language or follow their traditions. Ironically, his ability to use an unbreakable code based on his native language was instrumental in the Allies winning World War II.

Immigration was central to the settling of the United States, beginning with the first colonists in the 1600s. Some people came to America to escape hardship and suffering, while others were searching for adventure and fortune. Once they arrived, however, many suffered discrimination, fear, hatred, and all too often—violence. Much of the immigrant-themed literature for young adults focuses on these issues.

The impetus for Donna Jo Napoli's *Alligator Bayou* (2009) was a news article about the lynching of five Sicilians in 1899 Louisiana, a time when Jim Crow segregation was the law of the land. The Italians live separately from both blacks and whites and are called "dagoes," "mafia," and "more monkey than people." Bigotry is a significant part of this story, and it ultimately leads to a lynching. *Alligator Bayou* also explores the underlying economic motivations behind the lynching. White customers are appalled that the Sicilian grocers serve customers as they come in, and not by a predetermined "social order." Calogero, the 14-year-old protagonist learns the dangers of befriending someone outside his cultural group. He escapes a mob chasing him by running through a swamp filled with alligators and snakes.

The Alex Award-winning *Night Birds* (2007) by Thomas Maltman is a richly detailed story of German immigrants who leave Missouri to settle in Minnesota during the 1800s. The story is told from the alternating perspectives of Hazel and her nephew, Asa. Hazel marries a Dakota tribesman, and the Dakota culture is seen through her eyes. Asa's view, one generation later, reveals the changes in the Minnesota landscape. The Civil War rages, Native Americans and settlers fight for land and life, and "law abiding" citizens clash with the James–Younger gang. Life is depicted as an ongoing struggle to win the land, a struggle that the European settlers believe is theirs to win.

Cynthia Kadohata explores the persecution of Japanese Americans in *Weedflower* (2006). Even before the Japanese attack on Pearl Harbor, 12-year-old Sumiko was rejected and ridiculed by her classmates. After the United States declares war on Japan, Sumiko and her family are sent to the Poston camp, a real internment camp on the Mohave Indian reservation. Sumiko befriends Frank, a Mohave boy, and she comes to realize that they, too, have been sorely mistreated. *Weedflower*, a recipient of an award from the Jane Addams Peace Association, considers the loss of property and civil liberties and how easily the protection of citizenship can be taken away.

Graham Salisbury's *Eyes of the Emperor* (2000) also spotlights the racism toward Japanese Americans during World War II. Eddy, a second-generation Japanese American citizen living in Honolulu, enlists in the army following Pearl Harbor. After enlisting, he experiences racism, hatred, isolation, and confinement. His military assignment is to work with attack dogs, not to train them but rather to be the bait so they will learn the "smell of the enemy." Salisbury's research included numerous interviews with Japanese American veterans.

Kadohata's Newbery Medal recipient *Kira Kira* (2004) is set in the 1950s. Katie's family has joined a few other Japanese American families in Georgia to work in the poultry business. The racism they experience is established early in the novel when they check into a motel. They are only allowed in one of the backrooms, which costs more than the regular motel rooms. Katie's father has the rare skill of being able to identify male chicks from females. Even so, her parents work in horrendous conditions in the nonunion poultry plant. Told from Katie's perspective, the story centers on the illness and death of Katie's sister from lymphoma and the degrading, poorly paying work her parents must do. The Japanese culture frames the family's customs, habits, and beliefs.

Prejudice against Jews continues in post-World War II America in *What I Saw and How I Lied* (2008) by Judy Blundell, a National Book Award for Young People's Literature winner. Fifteen-year-old Evie, her mother, and stepfather Joe take a hastily planned vacation to Florida after Peter, a war buddy of Joe's, shows up. Joe and Peter smuggled Jewish artifacts out of Europe after the war, and Peter wants his cut. Evie becomes enthralled with Peter, but so does her mother. Peter disappears while on a boating trip with Evie's parents, and Evie must testify at her parents' trial. After the trial she tries to return the money from the stolen artifacts to the Jewish people. She fears that if she cannot right this wrong, her family is doomed. Anti-Semitism slowly seeps into the story in the same way that racism often did in the South during this time.

Prejudice and inequality in other cultures

Hatred and oppression of one group of people by another and resistance to change are not limited to any country, people, or time. *Tiger, Tiger* (2005) by Lynne Reid Banks, for example, shows why Christians were persecuted in ancient Rome and depicts how Christianity played a role in Rome's downfall.

Julius Caesar's daughter, Aurelia, learns that all societies have hierarchies and that the Christian slaves in the Roman empire have no responsibilities or concerns. "They only have to do what they are told, and live out their simple lives in peace and order" (p. 16), her elders tell her. She is further reminded that the Christians placed their all-powerful god above the Roman gods and this threatens the existing order of Rome. Two tigers, one trained to kill Christians, the other pampered and privileged, serve as a metaphor for describing the power structure and class system in ancient Rome.

Kathryn Lasky's *Broken Song* (2005) is a fictionalized narrative based on the early life of her Russian grandfather and depicts anti-Semitism in Russia. The novel is divided into four sections. Part I, the longest section, is set in Russia in 1897. Fifteen-year-old Reuven is becoming a superb violinist. In one of the frequent Cossack raids on the Jews, most of his family is murdered. Reuven and his baby sister survive but are forced to leave their home. In the next section, set in Russia 1900, Reuven becomes part of the Jewish Worker's Federation, where he is a key player in the fight against Jewish persecution. In two final sections, "America, Ellis Island, New York, 1904" and the "Epilogue," Reuven is united with his sister in America and becomes a famous violinist.

Literature about the Holocaust is a genre of historical fiction that continues to grow in popularity (Cory, 2005). Many young adults have been exposed to the Holocaust through films such as *Schindler's List* (1993), directed by Steven Spielberg and based on the novel *Schindler's Ark* (1982) by Thomas Keneally. The book and film depict the acts of an actual German businessman, Oskar Schindler, who helped over 1,000 Jews to survive World War II. Like *Schindler's List*, director and screenwriter Mark Herman's *The Boy in the Striped Pajamas* (2008) depicts the atrocities of the Holocaust, but also portrays glimpses of humanity in the midst of horror. The film is based on the novel of the same name by John Boyne (2006). Despite being the son of the camp commander, eight-year-old Bruno does not understand that the enclosed area at the back of the garden is a concentration camp. He befriends a young imprisoned boy through the barbed wire that surrounds the camp. The boy must wear a uniform of "striped pajamas" while awaiting extermination. While attempting to help his friend find his father, Bruno crosses to the other side of the wire and meets the same fate as the prisoners.

Jerry Spinelli's *Milkweed* (2003) vividly portrays life in the Warsaw ghetto during the Nazi occupation. The narrator is a young orphan boy who does not know his name, his parents, or where he is from. He is taken in by Uri, the leader of a group of Jewish street children who survive by stealing. Uri makes up an identity for the boy, and he becomes Misha Pilsudski, a Russian gypsy. Misha and Uri are herded into the ghetto with the other Jews and undesirables. Misha's small stature enables him to sneak in and out of the wall to smuggle in food. Misha's naiveté eventually gives way to the grim realization that the train he so badly wants to ride is transporting people to the gas chambers. Years later in the United States, Misha takes on his final identity, as his granddaughter's "Poppynoodle."

In contrast to the Nazi Holocaust in Europe, persecution of Koreans by the Japanese before and during World War II is not often included in the history textbooks for U.S. students. This persecution is the focus of Linda Sue Park's *When My Name was Keoko* (2002). Park was inspired by family stories to write about life in Korea during the Japanese occupation. During the time period covered in the novel, 1940 to 1945, the emperor of Japan forces all Koreans to adopt Japanese customs. It is illegal to read anything not written in Japanese, and all Koreans must assume Japanese names. Ten-year-old Sun-hee and older brother Tae-yul alternate narrating this story. The novel and the author's note personalize the victimization of the Korean people.

Elephant Run (2007) by Roland Smith portrays the far-reaching impact of the Japanese invasion of Burma. At the height of the London Blitz, Nick's mother sends him to Burma to be with his estranged father, where he will ostensibly be safer. Then the Japanese invade, commandeer the plantation, and imprison his father in a labor camp. Nick and his new friend Myra set out on an elephant to rescue his father and Myra's brother. Colonization, Burma's desire for independence, and the cruel treatment of the Burmese people at the hands of the Japanese are explored. Details of the culture and elephant training are included.

Padma Venkatraman's *Climbing the Stairs* (2008) is a richly layered story set in India during World War II. The caste system, British control and domination of India, the subservient and repressive roles of women, Gandhi's movement of nonviolence, religious beliefs, and the impending threat of Japanese invasion all merge in this insightful portrayal of the life of privileged Brahmins, one of the upper castes in India. The story is told from the perspective of 15-year-old Vidya. After her father is severely beaten by the British, she is forced to live with wealthy conservative relatives during a period of cultural and social upheaval. They do not believe, as her father does, that women should be educated and make decisions about their own lives. Vidya struggles to achieve her personal goals in a household that disapproves of those goals.

The first time nonwhites were allowed to vote in South Africa was 1994. The pervasive persecution and prejudice resulting from South African Apartheid is the focus of *Afrika* (2008) by Colleen Craig. Kim, a 13-year-old Canadian, accompanies her expatriate journalist mother, a South African native, to South Africa where she will report on the Truth and Reconciliation Commission. The political history of Apartheid is revealed through testimony at hearings of the commission and from the personal histories shared by the people Kim and her mother meet. Kim seeks out her own history. For the first time she meets her father and comes to understand why he remained in South Africa. She learns why truth must be followed by reconciliation if there is to be a future for Kim, her family, and for South Africa.

The Alex Award-winning *The Kite Runner* (2003) by Khaled Hosseini is the story of Amir, a young boy in Kabul who befriends the son of his father's servant. The novel covers the fall of the monarchy in Afghanistan and the Soviet invasion that resulted in the migration of thousands of Afghan people to other countries, including the United States. The story focuses on religious and political persecution in Afghanistan and the rise of the Taliban, as well as the difficulties of trying to make a new life in another country.

The Effects of War

Sometimes recorded history seems to consist of little more than a series of wars punctuated by brief periods of peace. Chronicles of war name heroes and battlefields and count up casualties, but they do not tell the stories of the parents, women, and children who mourn their lost loved ones and struggle to survive in the resulting chaos. The novels in this section describe the effects of war from the perspectives of these non-combatants.

Two Girls of Gettysburg (2008) by Lisa Klein is the story of two cousins, one living in Gettysburg, Pennsylvania, the other in Richmond, Virginia. The story is told in alternating points of view. Lizzie's first-person perspective details life in Gettysburg beginning in 1861 and continuing to Lincoln's Gettysburg Address in 1863. After her father and brother have joined the army, Lizzie must take over the family butcher shop and give up her plans to continue her education. Rosanna's voice is revealed through diary entries. She hastily marries a dashing Confederate soldier and follows him to the battlefield as a nurse. The two girls reunite at the Battle of Gettysburg. Their stories illuminate the effect of the war on families and communities as people try to carry on with their day-to-day lives while war rages around them.

Richard Peck's Scott O'Dell Award-winning *The River Between Us* (2003) begins in 1916 as two sons travel with their father in a Model T to visit his Illinois hometown. The novel shifts to 1861 and explores issues of race and identity as the boys learn of their father's real parentage. The book highlights the plight of army doctors during the Civil War, the reality of war camps, and the roles of black and white women during this war.

Susan Campbell Bartoletti, author of *Hitler Youth: Growing Up in Hitler's Shadow* (2005), also wrote *The Boy Who Dared* (2008). The latter is based on the true story of Mormon Helmuth Hubener, a German schoolboy who defied the Nazis and paid the ultimate price. The novel begins with Helmuth awaiting execution in Plotzensee Prison in Berlin in 1942. Through a series of flashbacks, the author portrays a world in which propaganda and lies, the loss of freedom, and the persecution of innocent people are becoming part of everyday life. Helmuth's brother declares that he is not a Nazi but will stand by his country, while Helmuth wants to know what kind of a man fights for something that he knows is wrong. The author includes a map, photographs, lengthy notes, a Third Reich timeline, and a bibliography.

Karen Lasky includes historical notes explaining the rise of Hitler at the beginning of *Ashes* (2010). Gaby Schramm's father, a Jewish professor at the University of Berlin, is a good friend of Albert Einstein and other celebrated scholars and writers. While they intellectualize their course of action, Gaby experiences the everyday impact of the Nazi movement. She fears the brown-shirted thugs, the growing influence of the Hitler Youth, and the changes at her school. The family moves to their summer home but cannot escape from what is happening to their country. Each chapter begins with quotes from famous writers whose works were destroyed in book burnings. The opening quote by Heine, "Where they burn books, they will end by burning human beings" foreshadows the horror that Gaby experiences.

War Games (2009) by Audrey Couloumbis and her husband Akila Couloumbis is a fictionalized account of Mr. Couloumbis' wartime memories of a childhood in occupied Greece during World War II. Twelve-year-old Petros and his family must hide all connections to their former home, the United States, when a German officer commandeers their house for his personal quarters. Tension mounts as Petros' family hides a Greek resistance fighter. Eventually, Petros begins to like the commandant and see him as more than a German soldier. The third-person point of view keeps the central focus on Petros' actions. It also accommodates information about life in rural Greece during World War II, the causes of war, and the ordinary people who fought against Nazi invasion.

Postcards from No Man's Land (1999) by Aidan Chambers, a Carnegie Medal recipient and Printz Award winner, is told in two intersecting narratives from different time periods. Seventeen-year-old Jacob's third-person account is set in Amsterdam in the mid-1990s. He is visiting the country to honor his grandfather, a British soldier who died there during World War II, and to visit the

. . . OF HISTORICAL FICTION CATEGORIZED BY WAR

REVOLUTIONARY WAR

Give Me Liberty. L. M. Elliot, 2006. This novel addresses many issues surrounding the Revolutionary War. The Patriots want to leave the ways of England behind, and yet they follow the military customs of the British and continue a class system that allows abuse of servants, indentured servants, and slaves. Ages 10–14.

Midnight Rider. Joan Hiatt Harlow, 2005. Fourteen-year-old orphan Hanna is an indentured servant of the British colonial governor of Massachusetts. She joins the rebel cause and rides to Salem to warn villagers that the British are coming to confiscate arms. Ages 10–14.

Woods Runner. Gary Paulsen, 2010. Thirteen-year-old Samuel returns from a day in the woods to find his Western Pennsylvania settlement burned and the bodies of neighbors scalped. He must rescue his parents from their British captors. Excerpts about weaponry, civilian casualties, and the wilderness are interspersed with the chapters of this survival story set in the Revolutionary era. Ages 12 and up.

CIVIL WAR

Iron Thunder: The Battle between the Monitor and the Merrimac. Avi, 2007. This volume in the "I Witness" series weaves factual terms and historical events into the story of the USS *Monitor* from the pro-Union perspective of a 13-year-old boy who works and lives on the ship. Period photographs, engravings, newspaper headlines, and encounters with real people give a sense of authenticity to the account of the battle between the Union *Monitor* and the Confederate *Merrimac*. Ages 9–14.

Annie, between the States. L. M. Elliot, 2004. Annie, a Virginian girl, has two brothers. One fights for the Confederacy; the other is a vigilante. Annie is a loyal Southerner who puts herself in grave danger to support her side. A website (www.lmelliott.com/about_annie.php) links to sites about Civil War music and the importance of music during this era. Ages 12 and up.

WORLD WAR I

And in the Morning. John Wilson, 2003. Jim follows in his fallen father's footsteps and joins the army. He expects a quick victory so he can return home to his girlfriend. The Battle of the Somme in 1916, in which modern weapons caused horrific carnage, is a central focus in this book. The story is told through letters, newspaper clippings, and diaries, some based on actual diaries written by soldiers. Ages 14 and up.

Kipling's Choice. Geert Spillebeen, 2005. This fictionalized biography of 18-year-old John Kipling begins as he lies dying in France during World War I. As he awaits death, the memories of his privileged life before the war rush forth. His thoughts often focus on his father, Rudyard Kipling, who zealously championed the British war effort. The novel depicts vivid scenes of warfare, including the effects of chlorine gas and how British and German soldiers alike robbed the dead and dying. Ages 12 and up.

WORLD WAR II

A Boy at War: A Novel of Pearl Harbor, 2001; *A Boy No More,* 2004; *Heroes Don't Run: A Novel of the Pacific War,* 2005, all by Harry Mazer. This trilogy begins at Pearl Harbor where 14-year-old Adam Pelko witnesses the Japanese attack and is called into action. After the death of his father, he and his family move to Bakersfield, California, where he confronts racism in the form of Japanese internment camps. In the last book, Adam, now 17, enlists and experiences life as a soldier. The details of boot camp and the mind-numbing effect of battle told from Adam's first-person perspective are authentic and graphic. Ages 14 and up.

FILMS

Flag of Our Fathers. Directed by Clint Eastwood, 2006. The film focuses on the seven men who raised the American flag on Mount Suribachi on the Pacific island of Iwo Jima following the Allied victory in the crucial battle in early 1945. (R)

Judgment at Nuremberg. Directed by Stanley Kramer, 1961. This film is a fictionalized account of the military tribunal held after World War II. It focuses on the trials of four judges accused of crimes against humanity, including acts of genocide, during the Nazi regime. Actual historical footage is included. (NR)

Saving Private Ryan. Directed by Steven Spielberg, 1998. A 27-minute scene of the Omaha beachhead assault of 1944 establishes the brutal and realistic tone for this film. The story centers on a group of soldiers who are trying to stay alive as they search for Private James Francis Ryan, the last surviving brother of three fallen servicemen. (R)

VIETNAM WAR

Fallen Angels. Walter Dean Myers, 1988. This Coretta Scott King Award recipient may be the best known novel written for a young adult audience about combat during the Vietnam War. Richie Perry, an African American from Harlem, experiences horrifying situations that cause him to question the morality of the war and the reasons for American men, especially minorities, to be fighting in it. Ages 12 and up.

Search and Destroy. Dean Hughes, 2005. Rick, a recent high school graduate, joins the army to escape his life and is selected for the Special Forces serving in Vietnam. He is wounded and returns home, only to find that, like many veterans of that era, he is not welcome. Graphic battle scenes demonstrate how war profoundly changes a man. Ages 12 and up.

Dutch woman, Geertrui, who cared for him after he was wounded. Along with Jacob's story, Geertrui's story is told in first-person through her memoirs. It tells of her long-ago romantic relationship with Jacob's married grandfather. The past and present come together when the terminally ill Geertrui and young Jacob meet and she tells him of his grandfather's past. Jacob learns about the choices his grandfather made during the war, and he is confronted with several choices of his own.

All the Broken Pieces (2009), a novel in verse by Anne E. Burg, is about the collateral damage of war. Matt Pin is a boy adopted by an American family after he is airlifted out of Vietnam. He struggles with his memories of the atrocities of war, including leaving his mother behind and seeing his brother's arms and legs blown off. Matt encounters American soldiers, damaged both physically and mentally, who are struggling with their feelings of blame and retribution. Matt's first-person account is told in rapid-fire free verse that evokes a horrifying series of images.

These works focus on the price of war even for those who are not directly fighting. The literary selections in the accompanying box focus more directly on soldiers and warfare. The works are categorized by the war they portray, and the wars are listed chronologically. The films are selected for their authenticity. Ratings are included where applicable.

Strong Female Protagonists

Authors of historical fiction walk a fine line between providing inspiring role models for young adults and maintaining historical realism. The portrayal of young female characters is a case in point. Boreen (1999) examines how adolescent female readers respond to female protagonists as role models in historical fiction. The more realistic characters, those acting within the societal boundaries of their time periods, were not considered very exciting. The less realistic characters, who are portrayed as rebels or outcasts and often force change or take a stand against societal norms, were received more enthusiastically. In some of the books we describe, young female characters are portrayed as exceptionally talented, beautiful, intelligent, and courageous, or they may act with more free-dom than was typical in their time.

Louise Hawes' *The Vanishing Point* (2004) is based on the life of Lavinia Fon-tana, a 16th-century Italian painter. This work brings to light the restrictions placed on a woman during the Renaissance. In order to get her work appraised, Vini convinces one of her father's apprentices to pass it off as his own. Eventu-ally the truth is revealed, and Vini's father recognizes her advanced talent. He allows her to join the young men under his tutelage. A subplot focuses on her mother's mental collapse after the death of an infant son, illustrating the impor-tance of a woman producing a male heir. An interesting historical note states that Fontana married another artist who gave up his own career to support hers and to assist with their eleven children. The impact of this arrangement, extraordinary for the time, is speculative. Fontana did become, according to Hawes, the most famous female artist of her time.

Julie Hearn's *Ivy* (2008) explores the limited options open to the poor, espe-cially women, living in Paradise Row, London, during the mid-19th century. Ivy, like many others, is lured into thievery and becomes addicted to laudanum, a readily available drug at the time. Ivy's options differ from those of most girls. Her beautiful red hair and porcelain skin presents her with the opportunity to become an artist's model. The disdain between the classes creates the backdrop for the social mores of the time. Being beautiful, however, is advantageous, regard-less of social class. The people Ivy lives with do not care what the "painter man" does with her, as long as he pays. Ivy puts drugs behind her, cleverly escapes the past, and creates a new life for herself. The squalor of Victorian London, includ-ing the opium dens and quick-fingered thieves, are vividly portrayed.

In Kathleen Ernst's *Hearts of Stone* (2006), the father of 15-year-old Han-nah leaves East Tennessee to fight for the Union even though her mother pleads with him not to go. In a cold voice, her mother declares, "In the end, it's always the women who have to do what needs doing" (p. 4). Hannah's perspective of her responsibility for her younger siblings is shaped by this comment. After her mother dies, Hannah and the children set off to find their aunt in Nashville, only to find the aunt, too, has died. They end up in a refu-gee camp. Jobs are scarce, especially for females, and the streets are lined with homeless starving women and children trying to find their men or just trying to survive. Hannah's perseverance and commitment to her ideals are beyond what most adults could endure. Hannah and Ben, a former neighbor and love interest, return to the farm, not knowing what they will find but prepared to meet the challenge.

In *The Evolution of Calpurnia Tate* (2009) by Jacqueline Kelly, Callie Vee is the only girl in a family of nine in 1899 Texas. Callie does not like cooking or sewing, and she ponders what her future will be like if she chooses not to marry. Her naturalist granddaddy opens up his laboratory and library to her and offers her learning experiences she could never have had in school. She is drawn to Charles Darwin's *The Origin of the Species*. Working hand-in-hand, Cal-lie and her grandfather discover a new plant species. Callie's sense of self and her lack of convention, as well as her intelligence and perseverance, make her an endearing protagonist.

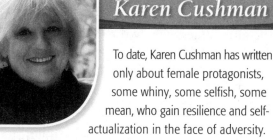

Karen Cushman

To date, Karen Cushman has written only about female protagonists, some whiny, some selfish, some mean, who gain resilience and self-actualization in the face of adversity. Cushman provided the reason for this pattern in her Newbery acceptance speech (1996):

> As children are what they eat and hear and experience, so too they are what they read. This is why I write what I do, about strong young women who in one way or another take responsibility for their own lives; about tolerance, thoughtfulness, and caring; about choosing what is life-affirming and generous, about the ways that people are all the same and the ways they are different and how rich that makes us all.

Cushman's first book, *Catherine Called Birdy* (1994) was set in medieval England and earned a Newbery Honor Award. Birdy is a 14-year-old girl who writes of her everyday concerns in her diary. She spends much of her energy avoiding her impending arranged marriage to an ugly old man she calls Shaggy Beard.

Published a year later, *The Midwife's Apprentice* (1995) was also set in medieval England and won the Newbery Medal. The protagonist, called Brat, Beetle, and finally Alyce, is a homeless girl who lives in a dung heap. A midwife hires her as a servant, and the girl slowly learns the trade of midwifery.

Cushman continues her focus on the 14th century with *Matilda Bone* (2000). Orphaned Matilda is educated by a priest and becomes an assistant to a bonesetter. She has no thoughts of her own; she echoes only what Father Leufredus has taught her about religion and piety. Matilda's initial sense of superiority gives way to understanding, and she gains a more realistic perspective of the lives of ordinary people. These three novels are a treasure trove of details about the lives of ordinary people in medieval times.

The filth and squalor of Elizabethan England provide the backdrop for *Alchemy and Meggy Swann* (2010). Unwanted, deformed Meggy Swann, whose favorite expression is "Ye toads and vipers," is sent to live with her alchemist father. Life is difficult for most people in Elizabethan England, but it is especially challenging for an unwanted, disabled girl. Her father is involved in nefarious dealings, and Meggy's increased understanding of alchemy helps her find the resources to save him.

Cushman's novels set in the United States include *The Ballad of Lucy Whipple* (1996), a young girl's story of survival during the California gold rush; *Rodzina* (2003), the story of a girl on the orphan train taking her west from Chicago for adoption; and *The Loud Silence of Francine Green* (2006). Set in 1949, this last story follows Francine's eighth-grade year at All Saints School for Girls in Los Angeles. The plot focuses on rising fear of communism and the blacklisting of people in the arts, especially Hollywood writers and actors identified, erroneously or not, as communists.

The language in Cushman's novels sounds authentic and evokes images of her settings. "Dang nab it, little sister, it's so cold in here, my britches is froze to my bum, pardon me altogether" (*The Ballad of Lucy Whipple*, p. 49), rings true as the voice of a gold miner. However, some of her work has been criticized as too modern in its perspective. For example, Catherine in *Catherine Called Birdy* acts in ways that are contrary to medieval thought and custom, such as resisting her father's dictates about her marriage (MacLeod, 1998).

Cushman, who did not begin her writing career until she was 50, compares herself to Jacqueline Woodson in her desire to leave her mark on literature. "I want to leave a sign of being here. I have ideas, opinions, things to say, and I want to say them before I go. I want to take sides, to argue from my own passions and values and beliefs" (Newbery Medal acceptance, 1996). For each novel, Cushman documents her research in author notes. Her explanations of the historical setting provide a context for the actions, behaviors, and thoughts of her characters. Her books appeal primarily to students between 10 and 15 years of age.

Tanita S. Davis' *Mare's War* (2009), a Coretta Scott King honor book, tells the story of an exceptional woman. Fifteen-year-old Octavia and 17-year-old Tali think their Grandmother Mare is a bit eccentric. She drives a red convertible, chain smokes, wears flashy wigs and stiletto heels, and refuses to be called "grandmother." Through alternating chapters of "Now" and "Then," the story of their grandmother as a young woman serving in the African American Women's Army Corps unfolds, and the girls come to know the struggles a poor black woman faced during the World War II era. It was their grandmother's individuality, her courage, and her ability to seek out new challenges and opportunities that made her unique, both then and now.

The restrictions on females sometimes resulted in women disguising themselves as males. Cross-dressing usually occurred when a girl or woman sought to "transgress the limitations of their sex roles and to access masculine privilege, to obtain education and pursue careers, to achieve wealth, social power, and independence, and to satisfy and conceal socially unaccepted sexual and gender orientation" (Riley, 2006, p. 2). Female-to-male cross-dressing is portrayed in a multitude of genres, including historical fiction for young adults.

Shelia Solomon Klass' *Soldier's Secret* (2009) is a fictionalized account of the life of Deborah Sampson, an indentured servant who, disguised as a man, joined the Colonial Militia during the Revolutionary War. Incredulous as it may be, she was able to maintain her disguise while surrounded by soldiers. Details explain how she disguised her body and concealed bodily functions. Her gender is not discovered until she is wounded. Robert Shurtliff (Sampson) was honorably discharged in October of 1783.

My Last Skirt: The Story of Jennie Hodgers, Union Soldier (2006) by Lynda Durrant is the fact-based account of Jennie Hodgers, a young Irish girl who realizes that a boy can make more money than a girl, even if the girl does the job better. While in Ireland, she begins dressing as a boy so that she can work as a shepherd. Jennie immigrates to the United States where she continues dressing and acting like a boy. As Albert Cashier, she joins the Union Army. She eventually receives a Civil War pension, the only woman to do so. She continues living as a man, and her biological sex remains hidden for fifty years. The novel raises questions regarding Jennie's ability to maintain her deception on the battlefield. Moreover, it questions how sexual identity is developed and how it frames expectations.

Sarah, the protagonist in Ann Rinaldi's *Girl in Blue* (2001), is a victim of abuse. Prompted both by her impending forced marriage and by her patriotism, she passes herself off as a man to fight for the Union. When she is betrayed and her identity revealed, she resumes her female identity, thinking she will be able to maintain her independence. Her talent at impersonations becomes more important than her deception, and she is asked to work for the Pinkerton espionage organization. She has a romantic relationship, but when she is not accepted as an equal, it ends. She returns home dressed as a male, but realizes that if she were to reveal her true self, she would lose her independence, and she leaves.

In *Samantha and the Cowboy* (2002), an Avon True Romance by Lorraine Heath, Samantha's older brother has lost an arm in the Civil War and is having trouble moving on with his life. Samantha takes on more responsibilities on the farm. She has a strong sense of herself as a girl and appreciates her appearance. When no other opportunity to make money presents itself, however, Samantha chooses to disguise herself as a male in order to join a cattle drive. Samantha misses being a girl and tells herself that the deception is only temporary. During the cattle drive her identity is discovered, however, and she is abandoned. As a result of joining the cattle drive, however, Samantha rescues the man she has fallen in love with, is paid well for her work, and returns home, happy to enjoy being a girl again.

"Historical Fiction Starring Girls" (www.mtpl.org/?q=node/100) provides a selective bibliography of novels with female protagonists for young adults. The website's intent is to introduce young women to the roles women and girls played in history.

CHRONOLOGICAL GROUPING OF HISTORICAL FICTION FOR YOUNG ADULTS

Categorizing literature by the historical time period it depicts allows teachers to make connections to the history curriculum, and it allows young adult readers to pursue their interest in a particular time and place. Websites that arrange literature in this chronological way include the following: Library Booklists (http://librarybooklists.org/fiction/ya/yahistorical.htm); Historical Fiction for Teens (http://teen-historical-fiction.suite101.com/article.cfm/historical_fiction_for_teens); and Logan Library Young Adult Booklists (http://library.loganutah.org/books/YA).

The box beginning below lists historical works categorized by time period, to help teachers match books to particular study units.

a sample

. . . OF **HISTORICAL FICTION** ACROSS TIME

ANCIENT TIMES

The Last Girls of Pompeii. Kathryn Lasky, 2007. Julia's parents intend to give her to the Temple of Damia to become a priestess and to sell her attendant as a concubine. The time frame (79 CE) is established through descriptions of slaves, gladiators, priests and priestesses, the lavish life of the wealthy, and, of course, the eruption of Mount Vesuvius. Ages 11–14.

Pharaoh's Daughter: A Novel of Ancient Egypt. Julius Lester, 2000. This story of Moses, known here as Mosis, provides a historical, not biblical, account from the perspectives of Mosis and his sister Almah. Both the Khemetian Egyptian and Habiru Hebrew people are portrayed. Lester includes a glossary and historical support for his interpretation. Ages 13 and up.

Rise of the Golden Cobra. Henry T. Aubin; Stephen Taylor, illustrator, 2007. Eighth-century Egypt is the setting for the fast-paced adventure of 14-year-old Nebamon, who must deliver a

critical message to the king. Descriptions of battles, weaponry, and military strategy provide a sense of authenticity. Ages 12–16.

THE MIDDLE AGES

The King's Arrow. Michael Cadnum, 2008. In 1100 after the Norman invasion, 18-year-old Simon, son of a Norman nobleman and an English lady, finds himself embroiled in the death of the King of England. The story presents the life of a young boy of noble birth during the time of Norman domination in England. Ages 12–16.

Blood Red Horse: Book One of the de Granville Trilogy. K. M. Grant, 2005. This tale of the bloody war to take back Jerusalem from Saladin, the real-life Sultan of Egypt and Syria, is set during the Third Crusade and the reign of King Richard I, known as Richard the Lionheart. The awe-inspiring chestnut stallion named Hosanna becomes a symbol for loyalty, honor, and perseverance in the tale that features both Muslim and Christian perspectives. Ages 11–15.

(continued)

Crispin: The Cross of Lead. Avi, 2002. Crispin, known only as "Asta's son," faces incredible struggles after the death of his mother in 1377 England. He is unjustly accused of murder and theft and declared a "wolf head," a criminal who can be killed on sight. The medieval world of the peasants comes alive through descriptions of disease, filth, poverty, and relentless hardship. The plot weaves around the Peasant Revolt of 1381, and Crispin questions the Holy Roman Church's teaching that the feudal system is ordained by God. Murder, clandestine acts of revolution, and the revelation of Crispin's real identity swiftly move this Newbery Medal winner to its climax. Ages 12–15.

Girl in a Cage. Jane Yolen and Robert J. Haris, 2002. The 11-year-old daughter of Robert Bruce, the new king of Scotland, is captured, locked in an iron cage, and put on display. Marjorie's first-person account alternates between her past and her present situation, in which she is tortured and starved. Ages 12–15.

THE RENAISSANCE

Duchessina: A Novel of Catherine de' Medici. Carolyn Meyer, 2007. Catherine de' Medici, often depicted as a cruel despot, was orphaned as a child, imprisoned in a convent, and married in a political union at the age of 14. The novel traces her life until she is crowned queen of France. Similar to the other novels in Meyer's "Young Royals" series, abundant details provide a strong sense of the time period. Ages 14–18.

The Smile. Donna Jo Napoli, 2008. Monna Elizabetta, a daughter of a nobleman, takes over the daily operations of their silkworm business after the unexpected death of her mother. She becomes a model for Leonardo da Vinci, who introduces her to a young heir of the Medici family. Monna falls in love with the young man, but is forced into an arranged marriage. This fictional account of da Vinci's model convincingly portrays the everyday aspects of life, politics, class differences, roles of women, and the art world of Renaissance Florence. Ages 12–17.

Leonardo's Shadow: Or, My Astonishing Life as Leonardo da Vinci's Servant. Christopher Grey, 2006. This detailed story set in 15th-century Milan is told from the first-person perspective of Giacomo, an orphaned boy who is taken in and trained as a servant in the da Vinci household. Ages 12–16.

1600s AND 1700s

The Brothers Story. Katherine Sturtevant, 2009. The bitter English winter of 1683–1684 is the setting for 15-year-old Kit's journey to London. Language, including sexual slang and ribald verse, lends authenticity to the lives of servants and peasants during this time. The countryside, the city streets, and especially the brothels of Covent Gardens are vividly portrayed as the author explores social mores, religion, and gender roles. Ages 13 and up.

The Minister's Daughter. Julie Hearn, 2005. The clashes between pagan and Puritan in 1645 England are seen from the perspectives of Grace and Patience, minister's daughters, and Nell, the granddaughter of the local healer. When Grace becomes pregnant, she blames Nell's witchcraft. Chapters set in 1645, written in third-person present tense, alternate with Patience's first-person, past-tense account in 1692. Ages 12 and up.

Blood on The River: Jamestown 1607. Elisa Carbone, 2006. Samuel Collier joins Captain John Smith as his page on his voyage to Virginia. Quotes from historical sources begin each chapter, and historical notes are included. Sam, the narrator of the story, lives with the natives and learns their customs and language. Ages 10–13.

Pocahontas. Joseph Bruchac, 2003. The narrative of this story alternates between 11-year-old Pocahontas and Captain John Smith. The Smith chapters begin with a short historical text. Pocahontas' narratives are supported with tales told in the native tradition. Bruchac paints a realistic picture of the differences between the White and Powhatan cultures. The "salvages" (sic) don't understand why the "coatmen" smell so bad and the settlers don't understand why the Powhatans take their children to the river every day. A lengthy author's note, sources, and glossary are appended. Ages 10 and up.

The Sacrifice. Kathleen Benner Duble, 2005. The Salem witch trials frame this story set in late 17th-century Andover, Massachusetts. Ten-year-old Abigail and her sister are denounced as witches and sent to prison. Mass hysteria, public punishment, horrible prison conditions, and women's limited choices thread through this story of Puritan times. Ages 10–15.

Fever, 1793. Laurie Halse Anderson, 2000. This novel is based on a yellow fever epidemic that wiped out a tenth of post-Revolutionary War Philadelphia. When the fever comes, Mattie's mother goes missing, her grandfather dies, and 14-year-old Mattie must take care of the ill and dying. Source notes are included, and each chapter begins with quotations from books and diaries of the time. Ages 10–15.

1800s

The Devil's Paintbox. Victoria McKernan, 2009. Sixteen-year-old Aiden and her young sister Maddy are orphans who face certain starvation unless they join a wagon train bound for the Pacific

Northwest. The siblings face obstacles as daunting as those left behind. The title refers to the smallpox virus, and the author comments on the controversy over whether or not Native Americans were intentionally infected. Ages 13 and up.

Black Storm Comin'. Diane Lee Wilson, 2005. On a wagon train headed to California, Colton Wescott, son of a black mother and a white father, is accidentally shot by his father who then promptly abandons the family. During the pre-Civil War era, mixed-race families faced harassment and worse. Colton, who can pass for white, joins the Pony Express. Ages 10–16.

1900s

Black Duck. Janet Taylor Lisle, 2006. Budding journalist David wants to know about elderly Ruben Hart's past. In 1929 Ruben and his friend found a body on the beach, which turned out to be a mob-related murder. This exciting story of Prohibition, murder, and criminal activity is told in alternating voices across time periods. Ages 12–16.

Ringside 1925. Views from the Scopes Trial. Jen Bryant, 2008. *Tennessee v. Scopes,* or "Scopes Monkey Trial" as it was often called, was one of the most controversial court cases in American history. On trial was science teacher John Scopes, who was accused of illegally teaching Charles Darwin's theory of evolution. In short sections of free verse, the voices of fictional and real people relate aspects of the trial. An epilogue explains what happened to the trial's key players: science teacher Scopes, prosecutor William Jennings Bryan, and the defense lawyer Clarence Darrow. Ages 12 and up.

Saving Grace. Priscilla Cummings, 2003. Grace and her family are suffering terribly from the effects of the Great Depression. Her father cannot find work and resorts to making beer illegally. Ultimately, Grace and her younger brothers are placed in a charity shelter, her older brother is dying from tuberculosis, and her mother is awaiting the birth of another child. Ages 10–14.

The Truth about Sparrows. Marian Hale, 2004. Twelve-year-old Sadie and her family have left the Dust Bowl of Missouri for coastal Texas, where her father who is disabled hopes to make a living in the fishing industry. While en route they scratch out a meager living and encounter several other families struggling with the upheaval caused by the Great Depression. Sadie, like many children of the time, must find work. Ages 10–14.

Ten Cents a Dance. Christine Fletcher, 2008. Teenager Ruby Jacinski works in the meatpacking district in 1940s Chicago, until a fast-talking guy urges her to become a taxi dancer at the Starlight Dance Academy. Ruby quickly learns that not only will men pay to dance with her, they will also buy her things and take her to fancy places. Elements of racism, jazz, and the criminal underbelly of Chicago create an authentic setting for this dark view of a seemingly glamorous life. Ages 14 and up.

White Sands, Red Menace. Ellen Klages, 2008. In this sequel to *The Green Glass Sea,* World War II is over, and Mr. Gordon is involved with the development of a rocket. His marriage reaches a crisis point when his wife, a chemist, discovers the truth about Hiroshima and begins working to stop nuclear proliferation. An author's note explains the impact of the first years of the Space Age and the beginning of the Cold War. Ages 11–15.

Yankee Girl. Mary Ann Rodman, 2004. In 1964, 11-year-old Valerie moves from Chicago to Mississippi because her FBI agent father is assigned to protect black people registering to vote. School integration, murdered civil rights workers, church bombings, and the violence of the Ku Klux Klan are interwoven with the story of a young girl desperately seeking friends. Chapter titles include newspaper headlines from this frightening time. Ages 9–12.

The Wednesday's Wars. Gary D. Schmidt, 2007. It is the 1960s, and seventh grader Holling likes baseball, contends with a bully, tries to impress a girl, and reads Shakespeare. Holling's older sister has left for California to "find herself." Holling is the only Protestant at his school, so each Wednesday, while the Jewish and Catholic students attend religious classes, Holling is left alone with the teacher, Mrs. Baker, whose husband is serving in Vietnam. When a young Vietnamese girl is brought over by the Catholic Relief Agency, she faces hatred and bigotry. Ages 10–14.

FILMS

Gangs of New York. Directed by Martin Scorsese, 2002. The film focuses on the conflict between the Irish immigrants and the natives, or people born in the United States. The Northern losses during Civil War have resulted in a draft. The hostilities between the immigrants, Blacks, established New Yorkers, and corrupt government officials collide. The climax is set during the New York Draft Riots of 1863. (R)

The Great Debaters. Directed by Denzel Washington, 2007. The film is based on the true story of Melvin B. Tolson, the debate coach at Wiley College in Texas, a small black college in the 1930s. The film is about how the debate team beat Harvard University. It depicts life for African Americans in Texas during the Great Depression, amid Jim Crow laws and the threat of lynching. PG-13.

HISTORICAL FICTION WITH METAFICTIVE CHARACTERISTICS

The dual nature of historical fiction means that it can be used both as a vehicle for exploring history and as an occasion to learn more about the elements of fiction. Some of the novels previously described in this chapter are told from multiple perspectives, feature nonlinear narratives, or have unusual formats such as verse or mixed genres. The following literature serves to emphasize the use of metafictive traits in historical fiction.

Multiple Narrators and A Nontraditional Format

Multiple narrators may emphasize multiple perspectives of the same event. Also, authors may use multiple narrators to reveal situations and thoughts that would not be evident from the viewpoint of a single narrator. A nontraditional format, which can mean any style other than a traditional narrative, may also present a particular aesthetic or emotional response.

Mudbound (2008) by Hillary Jordan won the Bellwether Prize for Fiction in Support of Social Change and an Alex Award. The hatred and bigotry are palpable in this post–World War II story set in rural Mississippi, where social mores reflect racist customs and the Klan, impervious to change, wields real power. Two soldiers, Jamie, who is white, and Ronsel, who is black, have returned to their families in rural Mississippi. Although terms such as "coon," "spade," "darky," and "nigger" resound in Ronsel's head, he and Jamie are bonded by their war experience and remain friends until a horrible tragedy unfolds. The story is told by six members of the two families and moves through the characters' lives in a nonlinear structure. It is Laura, the wife of Jamie's brother, who calls out for a different world.

Day of Tears: A Novel in Dialogue (2005; see the cover in Chapter 10, p. 302) by Julius Lester, won the Coretta Scott King Award. This book is based on real people and an actual slave auction in which more human beings were sold than at any other time in American history. The nonlinear story is told in dialogue and monologue and reaches across decades. The first-person voices are in present tense, and a multitude of voices are heard: slave, slave owner, slave seller, and abolitionist. The metafictive devices enable the author to believably portray the master's reasons for selling his slaves after promising he would not and to depict him as more than a one-dimensional, evil man. Slaves are presented as individuals, not as a single collective consciousness. The language reflects terminology of the time.

Crossing Stones (2009), a novel in verse by Helen Frost, is about four young adults from two interconnected Michigan families during World War 1. The narrative is told from three points of view in various poetic structures. (The author explains the poetic structure in an endnote.) Strong-willed Muriel's perspective is presented in sprawling free verse, resembling a flowing current. Ollie and Emma's voices are presented in "cupped hand sonnets" placed in a round shape that represents stones across the water. The first line rhymes with the last line, the second line with the second-to-last and so on. In Ollie's poems, the rhyme is in the beginning words of each line, and in Emma's poems the rhymes are the end words. Figure 5.2 demonstrates this form.

Frank, the first among them to go to war and the first to die, is seen only through the eyes of others and through his brief, censored letters. In addition to issues related to war, Frost also presents themes dealing with women's rights.

Written as a cinematic script, *Riot* (2009) by Walter Dean Myers begins with a list of characters followed by a fade-in to aerial shots that zoom in to New York City in the present day, 1954, 1900, and lastly, in 1863 to the Five Points neighborhood in Lower Manhattan. The casualties at Gettysburg have been heavy and a draft has been instituted. The Irish protest the draft because they do not want to fight on behalf of the blacks, who they see as a threat to their jobs. The protest sets the stage for the Draft Riots of 1863. The script format allows multiple voices—rich, poor, black, white, mixed race, soldier, policemen, looter, and innocent—to tell the story of an American city ripped apart by war, racism, classism, corruption, and violence.

Most readers will not immediately associate Vermont in the 1920s with the Ku Klux Klan, but that is the setting for Karen Hesse's *Witness* (2001). This series of narrative poems identified by character names presents a picture of fear, prejudice, hatred, and compliance in Vermont. Two of the 11 voices are a 12-year-old African American girl and a six-year-old Jewish girl. The allure of the Klan, its proclamations of patriotism, protection of women, and family values soon ring hollow as violence escalates. Pictures of the characters help readers visualize the person behind each voice. Historical events, such as prohibition, women's suffrage, and the Leopold and Loeb murder trial, establish a sense of the times.

Ollie's poem "The Scent of Soap" (Frost, 2009, p. 171).  *figure* **5.2**

Slings. Bandages. Red cross and white cap.
Smell of antiseptic. Squeaking wheel of the medic's cart.
Cold-sweat—I wake up. No, I'm not over there—then where am I?
I must be home. Yes, here in my childhood room. (I hope I didn't scream.)
Alone, dark night. But yes, home. I've been dreaming, remembering the war . . .
yet not only the war. Something new . . . like clean sheets, fresh off the clothesline,
sweet. Maybe the scent of soap? Lilac soap, And Emma's whisper. Oh! I remember.
Meet me at midnight in Grace's playhouse, Ollie. I was so sure I wouldn't fall asleep! I
get up (everyone else seems to be sleeping) and meet Emma as we planned. I take
a stone I've polished, and offer it. *It's beautiful,* she says. Then she mentions
my missing arm. She says, *Let me see it.* The stump of it? No! I say. I've
told her it is hideous. She touches it through my shirt. I'm adamant.
Tell me why not, Ollie. It's one part of—who I love. So I show her.
Wings of a butterfly could not be as gentle as Emma's touch.

classroom scenario

Thinking Aloud

AS YOU READ, consider why the teacher uses a think-aloud to model a strategy for reading a complex historical fiction novel. Also, think about how the teacher calls attention to the specific traits of nontraditional style, multiple genres, and multiple perspectives.

Ms. Casteletti has chosen *The Astonishing Life of Octavian Nothing, Traitor to the Nation, Volume I: The Pox Party* (2006), a National Book Award for Young People's Literature winner by M. T. Anderson, for a whole-class guided reading assignment for her eleventh grade American Literature class. The style of this novel approximates 18th-century language, and the format is challenging. It blends multiple genres told from multiple perspectives beginning with the first-person point of view of young Octavian, the son of a former African princess. Octavian lives in relative isolation on a large estate in Boston. He has received a classical education, reads Latin, and plays the violin. The Revolutionary War is brewing when Octavian learns of his real position, that of a slave and an object of research.

Ms. Casteletti knows that the complexity and uniqueness of this novel will challenge some of her students, so she plans to model metacognitive strategies. She knows that readers develop metacognitive knowledge—the ability to think about one's own thinking processes—slowly with time and experience (Unrau, 2004). She decides to use a think-aloud (Tierney & Readence, 2000) as a way to model the metacognitive strategies of previewing, planning, and self-monitoring. She begins at the point in the book where the initial narrative ends and multiple textual formats begin. She asks her students to turn to the section in the novel where Octavian's mother succumbs to smallpox and she describes the mother's appearance. Here is Ms. Casteletti's think-aloud for *The Astonishing Life of Octavian Nothing*.

> *Today I'm going to model some of the strategies that go on in my head while I'm reading. I don't typically think about my own thinking in such an obvious way, When the literature I'm reading is difficult or different from what I'm used to, I sometimes need to stop and consciously think about how to make sense of it. I'm going to read aloud and occasionally I'll stop and say out loud what I'm thinking about as I try to make sense of what is happening to Octavian.*
>
> *I'm starting with page 220, but I want to connect back to what I've already read and place this new chapter in that context. I remember that this section of the novel is called "The Pox Party" and that the very beginning of the book established that it was taken from the "Manuscript Testimony of Octavian Gitney." I remember that so far everything has been Octavian's first person account of his life. I know that Gitney is the name of the man who owns Octavian and his mother.*
>
> *With challenging material, it's often useful to look ahead for a preview of what's coming. When I look at the next few pages, I can't help but see that many of the words on this page and all of the text on the next two pages are crossed out. I've never seen this before in a novel, but I'm guessing that Octavian found these words so unbearable after writing them that he crossed them out.*

I'm going to skim over the next few pages before I go on because I want to see if there are more crossed out words. There are. I also notice that the next part shows a change in language to a form that is impersonal and scientific. It's the autopsy report of Octavian's mother. I notice that the chapter ends with an ellipsis, suggesting that the report provided more description of the procedure than included in the chapter. I'm thinking that Anderson made this choice in writing the book because by this point a reader will be emotionally drained, if not disgusted. I know I'm ready to move on.

After a few pages the format changes, and there is a letter. I notice that there are many more letters to follow. As I read this first letter I'm going to think about how to use these letters to piece the story together. At the top of the page it states who wrote the letter, so before I start the letter I want to think about the writer and receiver and what the letter's purpose might be. It's a letter about the autopsy, criticizing Gitney for caring about Octavian's mother. This makes me predict that Gitney will help Octavian because of the feelings he had for Octavian's mother.

I know now that this book is different, and I skim ahead again to get a sense of what to expect. I think this will help me make connections as I read, and I'm not worried about spoiling the ending. I can see more crossed out pages, more lists, letters, and other formats. I'm going to approach these pages by first thinking about what genre I am looking at and what type of information I expect. Will it be personal and subjective or impersonal and objective? I need to think about the perspective of each section, and I need to keep asking myself how each new page helps me make connections about what is happening to Octavian. I'm now feeling pretty confident about my strategy for reading the rest of the novel. I know that I need to be patient and not look for immediate conclusions about what is happening (Knickerbocker & Brueggeman, 2008).

In addition to modeling how she monitors, evaluates, and makes mental plans for proceeding, Ms. Casteletti also demonstrates her willingness to accept the ambiguity and uncertainty of interpretation that is often necessary with literature with metafictive traits. She plans to introduce the sequel *The Astonishing Life of Octavian Nothing, Traitor to the Nation, Volume II: The Kingdom on the Waves* (Anderson, 2008) and make it available for students who might want to read it for readers' workshop or for recreational reading.

Multiple Genres

Mixing genres, particularly adding nonfiction segments to historical fiction, allows the author to increase the amount of "history" included in the work without losing the narrative impact of the story. Gary Paulsen's *The Legend of Bass Reeves: Being the True and Fictional Account of the Most Valiant Marshal in the West* (2006) mixes fictional accounts of this former slave, who became the first African American marshal, with shorter factual sections. Paulsen informs the reader that the book moves back and forth among three factual sections about Bass's life and times and three fictional sections that cover his boyhood through old age. The imagined sections add drama and fill in the gap about Reeves' background, while the factual segments give credibility to Reeves' reputation. Although he killed 14 outlaws, Reeves never drew his gun first. In a foreword, Paulsen suggests that Reeves was the only true Western hero and debunks the heroism and honesty of many well-known western historical figures.

Countdown (2010) by Deborah Wiles is set in 1962 Maryland during the two weeks of the Cuban missile crisis. The story of 11-year-old Frannie, whose father is a pilot stationed at Andrews Air Force Base, is intermixed with black and white photographs and other artifacts from 1962. The threat of nuclear war is intense; scenes describe duck-and-cover practice at school, bomb shelters, and President Kennedy's address to the nation informing them of Russian missiles in Cuba. Frannie's first-person, present-tense narration is about what it is like to be a middle child, invisible at home and school. She is struggling with a friendship that is unraveling, liking a boy for the first time, an absent older sister, and an Uncle who has never recovered from World War I. Frannie's personal story will appeal to readers similar in age, but this work, taken as a whole, is fascinating for readers of all ages. The historical black and white photographs of Kennedy, Nikita Khrushchev, Dr. Martin Luther King Jr., Bob Dylan, the moon, mushroom clouds, drinking fountains labeled "colored" and "white," cartoons, song lyrics, and so much more give the novel a scrapbook feel.

Sometimes the mixing of genres functions as a stylistic device. Edward Bloor mixes elements of fantasy and historical fiction by using a World War II Philco radio as a mechanism for time travel in *London Calling* (2006). Martin shifts between present-day and war-torn London. While in 1940s London, Martin meets a boy who implores him to help find the truth about a murder. While in his own time, Martin immerses himself in research about the war and discovers that a local hero may not be a hero at all. Details of bombings and air raids during the blitz create a vividly integral setting. Language such as the term "conchie," for a "conscientious objector" adds authenticity. The use of the fantastical device to move through history fits well with the underlying question of how stories become history and how much of what we accept as the past has been manipulated in some way.

FINDING THE TRUTH IN HISTORY

Sometimes new evidence is found that dispels notions of history that have been taught for many years. Marc Aronson (2006) points out, for instance, that as far as historians are concerned, there never was a group who knew itself as Celts, but in all likelihood people will continue to envision the Celts as a group who danced in the moonlight during Druid rituals. Aronson suggests that history, and by extension historical fiction, should be thought of as an ongoing process and not static facts.

Facts sometimes change, but facts sometimes don't seem to matter. Alan Gratz points out in the author note of *The Brooklyn Nine: A Novel in Nine Innings* (2009) that some myths become so popular that the untrue story becomes embedded in history as fact. The story, for example, that Abner Doubleday invented the game of baseball in a field in Cooperstown, New York, was most likely started by Albert G. Spalding, a sporting goods manufacturer. The idea was presented as fact, and the Baseball Hall of Fame was built in Cooperstown, thus perpetuating this myth.

Sometimes credible authors make mistakes (Brown & St. Clair, 2006). Geoffrey Trease in *Mist over Athelney* (1958) describes his characters sitting down to a dinner of rabbit stew. There were no rabbits in England at the time his novel is set. A character in Kathryn Lasky's *Beyond the Burning Time* (1996) carries a kerosene lamp two centuries before they were invented.

Characters in historical fiction can be completely imaginary, but when they lack knowledge and experience that would be common to anyone during that time, readers may have a hard time accepting the novel as a whole. In *The Other Half* (2009) by Kim Ablon Whitney, 15-year-old Thomas is leaving Germany for Cuba. His Jewish father is in the Dachau concentration camp. His parents have been part of a resistance group and often held meetings at their apartment, and yet, Thomas does not know the specifics of keeping kosher (following Jewish dietary laws) or Shabbat (the Jewish Sabbath); he does not know there are different types of Judaism. He has seen Hasidic men, but never considered them beyond their funny clothing and hair. The explanation provided in the novel is that as a secular Jew he knew none of these things, but his ignorance still seems to strain credibility.

Accurate history, or what readers and viewers consider factual, may be based on "history created by a body of work" (Molin, 2005). Caroline B. Cooney's *The Ransom of Mercy Carter* (2001) is based on an actual abduction of Puritan children by Mohawks in 1704. Paulette F. Molin (2005) cautions that Cooney's novel is typical of what is referred to as "fictional captivity narratives" that perpetuate the Euro-American perspective of Indians as perpetrators of violence. Molin does not object to Cooney's novel outright, but she recommends balancing this type of literature with novels such as Joseph Bruchac's *The Winter People* (2002), which provides an alternative perspective. Bruchac's story is about a raid by the English against the Catholic Abenaki and their French allies and the abduction of women and children.

Teaching Ideas ▪ HISTORICAL FICTION

Historical fiction has not always been a popular genre for young people, but largely through the marketing of the American Girls series in 1986 this has changed (Campbell, 1996). The series features young female characters who live during important times in America's past. Publishers have since found historical fiction a profitable genre, and marketing campaigns focus on readers and teachers alike (Brown & St. Clair, 2006). Brown and St. Clair suggest that historical fiction has the psychological appeal of something familiar and comfortable because the outcome is known. The historical fiction of today is more complex, more thoughtful, and often better written than its antecedents in the 1980s.

Unlike historical accounts students typically read in their textbooks, historical fiction offers a synthesis rather than analysis. The focus is on human beings from a subjective perspective, which creates a stronger impression of place and time and potentially increases reader involvement. Historical fiction also provides a view of cause and effect that helps readers explore human problems and choices. Readers "see" the decisions characters make and their consequences and can evaluate those decisions. Through historical fiction, readers can explore the impact of the past on the present, which creates a sense of unity or connectedness (Nawrot, 1996).

A reader's experience with historical fiction can be more meaningful if the literature is approached critically. It may be necessary to read multiple works about a topic, theme, or event to determine the "representational truth" (Ozick, 1999). Questions that might encourage a critical perspective include those presented in Figure 5.3.

Instructional activities that encourage aesthetic responses, such as making personal connections in a journal and using creative and dramatic approaches to interpretation, are also helpful. The primary objective should be to enjoy the literary experience, not learn the history. The literature should not be turned into a textbook; however, readers will need to have adequate background prior to reading. They may also be excited to investigate events and people after completing the literary work.

Balancing the pleasure of reading historical fiction with teaching the history presented in the work can be a difficult act. An effective approach pairs fiction with nonfiction, print sources, the Internet, and films. The American Cultural History website and library guide (http://kclibrary.lonestar.edu/decades.html) is a helpful resource for quickly finding a wealth of information about a time period. It includes historical events, literature, and popular media.

 *figure* **5.3**   Questions encouraging a critical perspective in reading historical fiction.

- Does a literary work portray the norm of a situation or character or does it focus on the exception?
- What are the author's intent and perspective?
- Are characters' behaviors and decisions consistent with their time and place?
- What is the author saying about social, political, and cultural customs?
- If these customs and situations have changed, what brought about the change?
- What historical events and people play a central role in the story?
- How do historical events frame the narrative?
- Are the themes universal, or specific to a time and place?
- What people or events are not included in the narrative, and why?

A uthors of historical fiction can go where historians cannot. They add to a reader's understanding of complex people and events, partially through imagination and partially through fact (Marinucci, 2000). History and story should meld into a unified whole, with the story providing a window into the past and the history providing the foundation for the story.

In 2011 the Southern Poverty Law Center, publishers of *Teaching Tolerance* magazine, identified 1,018 active hate groups in the United States. Such groups promote beliefs or practices that attack or malign an entire class or group of people for an unalterable characteristic such as ethnic origin or skin color (www.splcenter.org/get-informed/hate-map). M. Lee Manning (2000) suggests that responsive multicultural education for adolescents should teach them to recognize, accept, and appreciate cultural, ethnic, social, class, religious, and gender differences. Well-written historical fiction balances historical accuracy with contemporary sensibilities and provides insights into the history that has contributed to people's beliefs, values, and behaviors.

Graham Salisbury, a Scott O'Dell Award winner, says that as a writer of historical fiction he must maintain a respect for the truth. Characters and situations can be imaginary, but when it comes to the actual events of the time being explored, the facts should be accurate. Salisbury views his responsibility as a writer of historical fiction as creating engaging entertainment and also as providing "a useful educational resource, another way to present the lessons of history" (Gill, 2007, p. 59). As Salisbury suggests, a work of historical fiction must be engaging for readers, but it must also be grounded in sound historical reasoning and documented fact. Adequate levels of factual accuracy are necessary to establish authenticity; however, the core of historical fiction remains the fiction. Characters must be interesting and they must do interesting things to capture the imagination of a young adult reader. Evaluation of the accuracy of the history and the quality of the literature must go hand in hand.

Richard Lee (n.d.), the founder of the Historical Novel Society, describes historical fiction by what it does: Historical fiction "makes us feel, as a protagonist, what otherwise would be dead and lost to us. It transports us into the past. And the very best historical fiction presents to us a TRUTH of the past that is NOT the truth of the history books, but a bigger truth, a more important truth—a truth of the HEART" (p. 5).

conclusion

BIBLIOGRAPHY OF LITERATURE FOR YOUNG ADULTS

Anderson, L. H. (2000). *Fever 1793.* New York: Simon & Schuster.

Anderson, L. H. (2008). *Chains.* New York: Simon & Schuster.

Anderson, M. T. (2006). *The astonishing life of Octavian Nothing, traitor to the nation, Volume I: The pox party.* Cambridge, MA: Candlewick Press.

Anderson, M. T. (2008). *The astonishing life of Octavian Nothing, traitor to the nation, Volume II: The kingdom on the waves.* Cambridge, MA: Candlewick Press.

Aubin, H. T. (2007). *Rise of the golden cobra.* (S. Taylor, Illus.). Toronto, ON: Annick Press.

Avi (2002). *Crispin: The cross of lead.* New York: Scholastic.

Avi (2007). *Iron thunder: The battle between the Monitor and the Merrimac.* New York: Hyperion.

Banks, L. R. (2005). *Tiger, tiger.* New York: Delacorte.

Barnes, J. (2009). *Tales of the madman underground.* New York: Viking.

Bartoletti, S. C. (2005). *Hitler youth: Growing up in Hitler's shadow.* New York: Scholastic.

Bartoletti, S. C. (2008). *The boy who dared*. New York: Scholastic.

Bloor, E. (2006). *London calling*. New York: Knopf.

Blume, L. M. M. (2008). *Tennyson*. New York: Knopf.

Blundell, J. (2008). *What I saw and how I lied*. New York: Scholastic.

Boyne, J. (2006). *The boy in the striped pajamas*. New York: David Fickling/Random House.

Bruchac, J. (2002). *The winter people*. New York: Dial.

Bruchac, J. (2003). *Pocahontas*. Orlando, FL: Silver Whistle Harcourt.

Bruchac, J. (2005). *Code talker: A novel about the Navajo marines of World War Two*. New York: Dial.

Bryant, J. (2008). *Ringside, 1925: Views from the Scopes Trial*. New York: Knopf.

Burg, A. E. (2009). *All the broken pieces*. New York: Scholastic.

Cadnum, M. (2008). *The king's arrow*. New York: Viking Juvenile.

Carbone. E. (2006). *Blood on the river: Jamestown, 1607*. New York: Viking Juvenile.

Chambers, A. (1999). *Postcards from no man's land*. New York: Speak, Penguin.

Collier, J. L., & Collier, C. (1974). *My brother Sam is dead*. New York: Four Winds Press.

Cooney, C. B. (2001). *The ransom of Mercy Carter*. New York: Delacorte.

Couloumbis, A., & Couloumbis, A. (2009). *War games*. New York: Random House.

Craig, C. (2008). *Afrika*. Toronto, ON: Tundra Books.

Cummings, P. (2003). *Saving Grace*. New York: Dutton.

Curtis, C. P. (1995). *The Watsons go to Birmingham—1963*. New York: Delacorte.

Curtis, C. P. (1999). *Bud, not Buddy*. New York: Delacorte.

Curtis, C. P. (2007). *Elijah of Buxton*. New York: Scholastic.

Cushman, K. (1994). *Catherine called Birdy*. New York: Clarion.

Cushman, K. (1995). *The midwife's apprentice*. New York: Clarion.

Cushman, K. (1996). *The ballad of Lucy Whipple*. New York: Clarion.

Cushman, K. (2000). *Matilda Bone*. New York: Clarion.

Cushman, K. (2003). *Rodzina*. New York: Clarion.

Cushman, K. (2006). *The loud silence of Francine Green*. New York: Clarion.

Cushman, K. (2010). *Alchemy and Meggy Swann*. New York: Clarion.

Dana, B. (2009). *A voice of her own: Becoming Emily Dickinson*. New York: HarperTeen.

Davis, T. S. (2009). *Mare's war*. New York: Knopf.

Draper, S. (2006). *Copper sun*. New York: Atheneum.

Draper, S. (2007). *Fire from the rock*. New York: Speak, Penguin.

Duble, K. B. (2005). *The sacrifice*. New York: Margaret K. McElderry.

Durrant, L. (2006). *My last skirt: The story of Jennie Hodgers, Union soldier*. New York: Clarion.

Eastwood, C. (Dir.). (2006). *Flags of our fathers*. USA: Malpaso Productions/Amblin Entertainment.

Elliot, L. M. (2004). *Annie between the states*. New York: HarperTeen.

Elliot, L. M. (2006). *Give me liberty*. New York: Katherine Tegen/HarperTrophy.

Ernst, K. (2006). *Hearts of stone*. New York: Dutton.

Fletcher, C. (2008). *Ten cents a dance*. London: Bloomsbury.

Forbes, E. (1943). *Johnny Tremain*. (L. Ward, Illus.). Boston, MA: Houghton Mifflin.

Frost, H. (2009). *Crossing stones*. New York: Francis Foster/Farrar, Straus & Giroux.

Grant, K. M. (2005). *Blood red horse*. New York: Walker Books.

Gratz, A. (2009). *The Brooklyn nine: A novel in nine innings*. New York: Dial.

Grey, C. (2006). *Leonardo's shadow: Or, my astonishing life as Leonardo da Vinci's servant*. New York: Simon Pulse.

Hale, M. (2004). *The truth about sparrows*. New York: Holt.

Harlow, J. H. (2005). *Midnight rider*. New York: McElderry, Simon & Schuster.

Hawes, L. (2004). *The vanishing point*. Boston, MA: Houghton Mifflin.

Hearn, J. (2005). *The minister's daughter*. New York: Atheneum.

Hearn, J. (2008). *Ivy*. New York: Atheneum.

Heath, L. (2002). *Samantha and the cowboy*. New York, NY: Avon.

Hemphill, H. (2008). *The adventurous deeds of Deadwood Jones*. Asheville, NC: Front Street.

Herman, M. (Dir.). (2008). *The boy in the striped pajamas*. UK: BBC Films.

Hesse, K. (2001). *Witness*. New York: Scholastic.

Hosseini, K. (2003). *The kite runner*. New York: Riverhead.

Hughes, D. (2005). *Search and destroy*. New York: Simon Pulse.

Jordan, H. (2008). *Mudbound*. Chapel Hill, SC: Algonquin Books.

Kadohata, C. (2004). *Kira-Kira*. New York: Atheneum.

Kadohata, C. (2006). *Weedflower*. New York: Atheneum.

Kelly, J. (2009). *The evolution of Calpurnia Tate*. New York: Holt.

Keneally, T. (1982). *Schindler's ark*. London, UK: Coronet.

Klages, E. (2006). *The green glass sea*. New York: Viking Penguin.

Klages, E. (2008). *White sands, red menace*. New York: Viking Penguin.

Klass, S. S. (2009). *Soldier's secret. The story of Deborah Sampson*. New York: Holt.

Klein, L. (2008). *Two girls of Gettysburg*. New York: Bloomsbury.

Kramer, S. (Dir.). (1961). *Judgment at Nuremberg*. USA: Roxlom Films.

Lasky, K. (1996). *Beyond the burning time*. New York: Scholastic.

Lasky, K. (2005). *Broken song*. New York: Viking.

Lasky, K. (2007). *The last girls of Pompeii*. New York: Viking.

Lasky, K. (2010). *Ashes*. New York: Viking.

Lester, J. (2000). *Pharaoh's daughter: A novel of ancient Egypt*. New York: Harcourt Children's Books.

Lester, J. (2005). *Day of tears: A novel in dialogue*. New York: Jump at the Sun Hyperion Books.

Lisle, J. T. (2006). *Black duck*. New York: Philomel.

Magoon, K. (2009). *The rock and the river*. New York: Aladdin.

Maltman, T. (2007). *The night birds*. New York: Soho Press.

Mazer, H. (2001). *A boy at war: A novel of Pearl Harbor*. New York: Simon & Schuster.

Mazer, H. (2004). *A boy no more*. New York: Simon & Schuster.

Mazer, H. (2005). *Heroes don't run*. New York: Simon & Schuster.

McKernan, V. (2009). *The devil's paint box*. New York: Knopf.

Meyer, C. (2007). *Duchessina: A novel of Catherine de' Medici*. New York: Harcourt.

Myers, W. D. (1988). *Fallen angels*. New York: Scholastic.

Myers, W. D. (2008). *Sunrise over Fallujah*. New York: Scholastic.

Myers, W. D. (2009). *Riot*. New York: Egmont.

Napoli, N. J. (2008). *The smile*. New York: Dutton.

Napoli, D. J. (2009). *Alligator Bayou*. New York: Wendy Lamb.

Park, L. S. (2002). *When my name was Keoko*. New York: Clarion.

Paulsen, G. (2006). *The legend of Bass Reeves. Being the true and fictional account of the most valiant marshal in the west*. New York: Wendy Lamb.

Paulsen, G. (2010). *Woods runner*. New York: Wendy Lamb.

Peck, R. N. (1976). *Hang for treason*. New York: Doubleday.

Peck, R. N. (2003). *The river between us*. New York: Dial.

Rinaldi, A. (2001). *Girl in blue*. New York: Scholastic.

Rodman, M. A. (2004). *Yankee girl*. New York: Farrar, Straus & Giroux.

Salisbury, G. (2000). *Eyes of the Emperor*. New York: Wendy Lamb.

Schmidt, G. D. (2007). *The Wednesday wars*. New York: Clarion.

Scorsese, M. (Dir.). (2002). *Gangs of New York*. USA: Miramax.

Sinclair, U. (1906). *The jungle*. Cambridge, MA: R. Bentley.

Smith, R. (2007). *Elephant run*. New York: Hyperion.

Smith, S. L. (2009). *Flygirl*. New York: Putnam.

Spielberg, S. (Dir.). (1998). *Saving Private Ryan*. USA: Amblin Entertainment.

Spielberg, S. (Dir.). (1993). *Schindler's list*. USA: Amblin Entertainment.

Spillebeen, G. (2005). *Kipling's choice*. (T. Edelstein, Trans.). New York: Houghton Mifflin.

Spinelli, J. (2003). *Milkweed*. New York: Knopf.

Sturtevant, K. (2009). *The brothers story*. New York: Farrar, Straus & Giroux.

Trease, G. (1958). *Mist over Atheley*. New York: Macmillan.

Venkatraman, P. (2008). *Climbing the stairs*. New York: Putnam.

Washington, D. (Dir.). (2007). *The great debaters*. USA: Harpo Productions.

Whitney, K. A. (2009). *The other half: A novel based on the true story of the MS St. Louis*. New York: Laurel Leaf Books.

Wiles, D. (2010). *Countdown*. New York: Scholastic.

Wilson, D. L. (2005). *Black storm comin'*. New York: Margaret K. McElderry.

Wilson, J. (2003). *And in the morning*. Toronto, ON: Kids Can Press.

Yolen, J., & Harris, R. (2002). *Girl in a cage*. New York: Philomel.

WEBSITES WITH ANNOTATIONS

American Cultural History • **http://kclibrary.lonestar.edu/decades.html**
Helpful resources for finding a wealth of information about a time period; includes historical events, literature, and popular media.

Elliott, L. M. • **http://lmelliott.com/index.php**
The author's official website, including summaries of works, author interviews, sample lesson plans, reading group guides, and other resources for educators.

Historial Fiction Starring Girl (Middletown Township Public Library) • **www.mtpl .org/?q=node/100**

Lists historical fiction starring girls.

Kushman, Karen • **www.karencushman.com/**

The author's official website, including summaries of works.

Lester, Julius • **www.juliuslester.net/**

The author's official website, including summaries of works and biographical information.

Library Booklists • **http://librarybooklists.org/ fiction/ya/yahistorical.htm**

Provides lists of literature for an adolescent audience arranged chronologically.

Logan Library Young Adult Booklists • **http://library. loganutah.org/books/YA/**

Provides lists of literature for an adolescent audience categorized by genre.

Uchronia • **http://uchronia.net/**

Provides a "bibliography of over 3100 novels, stories, essays and other printed material involving the 'what ifs' of history," or works referred to as "alternate history."

REFERENCES

Aronson, M. (July, 2006). Boy, were we wrong. *School Library Journal, 52*(7), 29.

Boreen, J. (1999). Images of women in historical young adult fiction: Seeking role models. *Alan Review, 26*(2), 14–21.

Brown, J., & St. Clair, N. (2006). *The distant mirror. Reflections on young adult historical fiction.* Lanham, MD: Scarecrow Press.

Campbell, P. (September/October, 1996). The sand in the oyster. *Horn Book, 72*(5), 636–639.

Cart, M. (April, 2009). Carte Blanche: Of headaches and history. *Booklist, 105*(16), 16.

Cory, M. E. (2005). Holocaust literature. In M. Keith Booker (Ed.), *Encyclopedia of literature and politics.* Westport, CT: Greenwood Press, p. 355.

Cushman, K. (July/August, 1996). Newbery Medal acceptance. *Horn Book, 72*(4), 413–419.

Gill, D. (February, 2007). A focused observer: An interview with Graham Salisbury. *Teacher Librarian, 34*(3), 58–59.

Johnson, S. (2002). What are the rules for historical fiction? Retrieved from http://www.historicalnovelsociety.org/ historyic.htm.

Knickerbocker, J. L., & Brueggeman, M. A. (2008). Making room on the shelf: The place of postmodern young adult novels in the classroom. *American Secondary Education, 37*(1), 65–79.

Kennedy, X. J., Gioia, D., & Bauerlein, M. (2006). *Longman dictionary of literary terms.* New York: Pearson Longman.

Lee, R. (n.d.). History is but a fable agreed upon: The problem of truth in history and fiction. Retrieved from http://www.historicalnovelsociety.org/historyis.htm.

MacLeod, A. S. (January/February, 1998). Writing backward: Modern models in historical fiction. *Horn Book, 74*(1). Retrieved from http://web.ebscohost.com.ehost/ detail?vid=4&hid=8&sid=90f3aa52-70a2-4fod-8930- 80a2.

Manning, M. L. (1999–2000). Developmentally responsive multicultural education for young adolescents. *Childhood Education, 76*(2) 82–87.

Marinucci, R. (January/February, 2000). Is historical fiction an oxymoron? *Book Report, 18*(4), 8–10.

McElmeel, S. (January/February, 2009). Getting it right: Historical fiction or not? *Library Media Connection, 27*(4), 40–41.

Molin, P. F. (2005). *American Indian themes in young adult literature.* Lanham, MD: Scarecrow Press.

Nawrot, K. (July/August, 1996). Making connections with historical fiction. *Clearing House, 69*(6), 343–345.

Ozick, C. (1999). The rights of history and the rights of imagination. Retrieved from http://www.commentary magazine.com/viewarticle.cfm/the-rights-of-history- and-the-rights.

Riley, E. A. (2006). *Female cross-dressing in young adult fiction: Protagonists' changing perceptions of women and femininity.* Master's paper submitted to University of North Carolina at Chapel Hill. Retrieved from http:// www.ils.unc.edu/MSpapers/3288.pdf.

Southern Poverty Law Center (2011). Hate map. Retrieved from http://www.splcenter.org/get-informed/hate-map.

Tierney, R. J., & Readence, J. E. (2000). *Reading strategies and practices: A Compendium* (5th ed.). Boston, MA: Allyn and Bacon.

Unrau, N. (2004). *Content area reading and writing: Fostering literacies in middle and high school cultures.* Upper Saddle River, NJ: Pearson Merrill Prentice Hall.

Wolk, S. (2009). Reading for a better world: Teaching for social responsibility with young adult literature. *Journal of Adolescent & Adult Literacy, 52*, 664–673.

CHAPTER SIX

Traditional Literature

RETELLING AND REINVENTING TALES

chapter overview

Every culture's literature is rooted in oral storytelling that is passed from generation to generation. In this chapter we explore how traditional tales such as myths, legends, and folktales are renewed for new audiences and adapted to new forms of storytelling. We also consider how traditional works can be reinvented in ways that question the assumptions and values represented in the original version. The literature and the classroom activities in this chapter will help readers who are approaching adulthood to appreciate both the tradition of storytelling and the continuous reinvention of traditional tales.

FOCUS QUESTIONS

1. How is the tradition of oral storytelling carried on in print and nonprint texts?
2. How can teachers guide students to appreciate the oral storytelling tradition?
3. How have authors retold and reinvented traditional tales for contemporary audiences?
4. How can reinventions of traditional tales support critical literacy for young adults?

introduction

I n the Canadian North American Indian story "Orphan Boy" (Clark, 1988), the "story rock" explains to the Seneca people that "You [the Seneca people] must keep these stories as long as the world lasts. . . . When you visit one another you must tell these things. You must remember them always" (p. 7). Literature began when storytellers shared tales and poetry that addressed their audiences' hopes, fears, and questions about life. Those stories became a way for a culture to celebrate its history and enduring values, even through changing times. Lechner (2004) notes that the term **traditional literature** is used interchangeably with *folk literature* and *oral literature*, to refer to "stories that have become the cultural heritage of a community or people, shaped and reshaped through continuous usage to fit the needs of tellers and audiences of a particular place or time" (p. 2).

In the questioning climate of a postmodern world, contemporary authors have sometimes turned traditional tales upside down and backward, often with a young adult audience in mind. They have turned heroes into villains, reversed gender roles, and changed points of view in order to explore new ideas and ways of storytelling. These reinventions challenge readers' assumptions about both their cultural heritage and the nature of the stories themselves. In this chapter, we explore ways teachers can help young adults experience and appreciate the connection between oral storytelling and other forms of literature. We identify the characteristics of various types of traditional literature and explore how traditional tales have been retold or reinvented for contemporary young adults.

THE STORYTELLING ROOTS OF TRADITIONAL LITERATURE

S ome works of traditional literature, such as legends, myths, and epic poems, were carried from place to place and passed to the next generation by troubadours, poets, priests, or shamans. Those stories celebrated great heroes and the accomplishments, beliefs, and values that were shared by an entire community or nation. The stories of the Trojan War told in the Greek epic of the *Iliad*, for instance, were memorized and repeated by professional storytellers.

Other types of traditional literature, such as folk tales, are told and retold, passed down through generations by common people. They have an immediate audience appeal because they deal with the issues and concerns of everyday life. "Goldilocks and the Three Bears" and "Little Red Riding Hood," for example, reflect the dangers faced by those who travel into the wild world alone. Even fairy tales, despite their elements of magic, are rooted in the real world. Couples without children, young men without property, and children who have lost a parent have always wished for magical solutions to problems that are beyond their power to solve.

Traditional literature's roots in oral storytelling have influenced its form as well as its content. When these tales were written down and even expanded into novels, writers often tried to maintain the diction and language structure of the oral version. They might, for example, have used a conversational tone, dialect expressions, and clichéd openings and closings such as "once upon a time" and "happily ever after" (de Vos & Altmann, 1999).

Traditional literature is structured to be easily remembered. Folk tales in the Western tradition are usually short with a highly predictable plot that is driven by a single problem or conflict. These tales often follow a "rule of three" in which characters make two unsuccessful attempts before they reach their goal. Goldilocks, for example, tries two bowls of porridge before finding the one that is "just right," and the three little pigs are forced to flee two houses before finding safety in a brick home. Longer forms of traditional literature, such as epics, are also highly structured. They often bring together a series of episodes, each of which is relatively simple. The *Iliad* and the *Odyssey* were both divided into 24 chapters and composed in verse. The structure of the verse helped the teller to remember the story and the listener to understand it.

Continuing the Storytelling Tradition: Urban Legends

Storytelling requires the teller to constantly monitor the audience's reaction. If interest seems to flag, the teller can throw in a few juicy details; if the audience shows disbelief, the teller can cite witnesses and convincing arguments. The audience's reaction is no less important in written stories even if it is harder to discern; thus, time spent exploring the oral tradition is not necessarily time that is taken away from print literature. One way to involve young adults in the tradition of oral storytelling is through urban legends.

Jan Harold Brunvand (2000), the leading authority on the topic, explains that an **urban legend** is typically told as fact, often as something that happened to, or was witnessed by, "a friend of a friend." Inglis (2007) adds that urban legends are remarkably long-lived and may be disseminated by the mass media as well as from person to person. Although they are told as true stories, they are usually about incredible or bizarre events, such as giant alligators lurking in sewers or funeral ashes mistakenly used as spices.

Most urban legends are probably created in the hothouse of a "bull session," where people are trying to outdo each other by relating shocking or frightening incidents. Some may have a factual basis, but even those are embellished over time, and ultimately local variations of the story emerge. Inglis (2007) identifies four types of urban legend storytellers:

1. *True believers* who are convinced that the story actually happened.
2. *Cynics* who convey to the audience that they know very well that the story did not happen.
3. *Entertainers* who add flourishes to make an audience respond enthusiastically.
4. *Experts* who enjoy sharing "information" that shows that they are "in the know."

The story of "The Vanishing Hitchhiker" as related by Brunvand (2000) is a typical urban legend. The essence of this story is simple: A driver picks up a young woman who is hitchhiking on a deserted road at night. The hitchhiker asks to be dropped off at her parents' house, and the driver agrees. At some point during the trip, the driver finds that the hitchhiker has vanished from the car. Hoping for some explanation, the baffled driver goes to the address the hitchhiker provided, only to be told by the parents that their daughter died years earlier.

Snopes.com, a comprehensive website dealing with all manner of hoaxes, rumors, and urban legends, points out that in some variations the hitchhiker leaves a book or scarf in the car, which the parents later identify as belonging to their deceased daughter. In other versions, the driver sees a family photograph in which the ghostly hitchhiker is wearing the same dress she had on when he picked her up, or the driver loans her a coat or scarf that is later found draped over the girl's tombstone. Mikkelson and Mikkelson (2007) point out that tellers usually add real details, such as the name of a local street where the driver picks up the hitchhiker.

Urban legends, like other traditional tales, often reappear in different places and different generations, suggesting they reflect concerns common to the human condition. "The Vanishing Hitchhiker" reflects both fear of the supernatural and the hope of life beyond death. Urban legends may also be cautionary tales that address the fears of a particular era or society (Mikkelson & Mikkelson, 2007). Stories of alligators in the sewers, for instance, may reflect concerns about the dire consequences of a throwaway society.

Keeping Storytelling Alive in the Classroom

Although our primary focus in this chapter is on written works, we agree with Zipes (1997) that "oral storytelling has never ceased, and it continues to play a significant role in our lives" (p. 1). Teachers can use the following suggestions to reawaken their students' appreciation of storytelling and to spark a discussion about why and how stories are told.

- Choose stories from a collection such as Brunvand's *Too Good to Be True: The Colossal Book of Urban Legends* (2000) to read aloud or, better yet, tell from memory.

- After they listen to a few legends, have students share variations of those stories or other urban legends they have heard. Remind them that literature began with this kind of group storytelling.

- Although too much analysis might ruin the fun, identifying which of Inglis' (2007) four types of narrators is relating each story can raise students' awareness of the craft of storytelling and complement discussions on point of view in other types of literature, such as tall tales.

- Explore organizations such as the American Folklore Society (www.afsnet.org) and the National Storytelling Association (www.storynet.org), which strive to keep traditional stories alive.

RETELLING AND REINVENTING

As a story passed from place to place and across generations, storytellers would update and adapt it to fit a new audience. Many of these changes were introduced when an oral story was transferred to a new medium, such as print, where it could be illustrated, or when adapted for television or film. We refer to these stories as **retellings,** and these changes are part of the natural evolution of traditional tales. Retellings may transform some elements of a story, but they generally preserve the overall plot, theme, and spirit of the original. Some contemporary versions of traditional tales, however, veer drastically from the basic form, plot, or meaning of the original. Altmann and de Vos (2001) refer to these versions as *reworkings*, but we prefer to use the term **reinventions** to emphasize the pervasive changes made to the story's original elements. Reinventions often include ideas that were entirely absent from the original or a deliberate twist to the original plot for comic purposes or to challenge traditional ideas and forms.

Altmann and de Vos (2001) identify specific techniques that authors use when reworking folk tales. We adapt their list to apply to all forms of traditional literature, and we include some metafictive techniques that are commonly used in reinvented stories for young adults. The distinction between retelling and reinventing traditional literature is more of a continuum than a hard and fast line, as shown in Figure 6.1. At one end of the continuum, writers, tellers, or filmmakers treat a traditional tale with great respect, even though they may change some elements. At the other end of the continuum, the writers, tellers, or filmmakers dismantle and reconfigure a traditional tale, sometimes for the purpose of incorporating metafictive devices or for making a thematic statement that was not part of the original story. This continuum between retelling and reinvention can be demonstrated with the fairy tale Rapunzel, as we show in the box on pages 170–171.

In the remainder of this chapter, we identify the content and forms that are characteristic of various types of traditional literature. We explore some of the ways in which these tales have been retold and reinvented, and we identify how both traditional and contemporary versions can be incorporated into a literature program for young adults.

figure **6.1**   A continuum for passing on traditional tales.

RETELLING ←		→ REINVENTING
Preserves essential personalities of main characters, but may change names or circumstances	May change gender or other traits of characters, or elaborate on characters' feelings or motivations	May invert characters, e.g., by making heroes into villains
May add minor characters or details	May add a major character or a subplot	May turn minor characters into protagonists
May update the setting and/or change locations	Setting may be updated and/or more integral to the plot	Setting is often chosen for commenting on social issues
Preserves central conflict, although it may be updated	May update conflicts to fit a contemporary setting and/or add backstory to explain the conflict	May be a prequel or sequel to the original story in order to explain events in that story
Preserves resolution, although it may be updated	Updates resolution and may add epilogue material	May significantly alter or reinterpret the resolution
Tends to reaffirm the themes, beliefs, and values of the original	May reaffirm or reinterpret themes and values that are most relevant for a contemporary audience	Often deliberately challenges traditional assumptions about gender, age, and class
May either echo or update the point of view, tone, or style of the original	May "play" with point of view, tone, or style	May shift point of view, adopt an ironic tone, or use multiple narrators and other metafictive devices

Retelling and Reinventing Rapunzel

In the versions of this story collected by the Brothers Grimm in the 19th century (Ashliman, 2007), a pregnant woman develops an intense craving for the greens in the garden of a neighboring witch. When her husband is caught stealing the greens, he promises their unborn child to the witch. When the baby, named Rapunzel, is born, the witch locks her in a tower. As Rapunzel grows up, the witch visits her by calling out for her to lower a braid of her very long hair. Eventually, a prince discovers the secret, calls out to Rapunzel, and scales the tower by climbing her hair like a rope. He begins

to visit her regularly, but when the witch finds out, she cuts off Rapunzel's hair and banishes her to the wilderness. The prince is blinded by thorns, and he wanders the wilderness until one day he happens on Rapunzel. When two of her tears fall into his eyes, his sight is restored, and he takes her to his kingdom.

Rapunzel was already an old story with many variations when the Brothers Grimm published it (Ashliman, 2007). Since then, many new versions have appeared in all forms of media that have ranged from faithful retellings to total reinventions with elements added, deleted, and changed. Paul Zelinsky's Caldecott Award-winning picture book *Rapunzel* (1997), for instance, is a clearly recognizable *retelling* of the traditional tale, although the conversion of the story from the oral tradition to picture book does provide additional information, such as illustrations that suggests a setting in Renaissance Italy.

Zelinsky's pictures also convey facial expressions and body language that provide insight into the characters' personalities and emotions. For example, he portrays Rapunzel as "innocent, passive, and repressed, as remote and unapproachable as the tower in which she is locked" (Hendrickson, 2000, p. 215). As the sorceress climbs the tower, Rapunzel stares straight ahead passively. She appears fearful when the prince first arrives, but by the end of the story, she gazes at him lovingly. The sorceress appears as more than a frightening witch. Her deep longing for a child is conveyed in a two-page spread in which she gazes at baby Rapunzel's face while carrying her away. Later, she fondly watches young Rapunzel playing in the orchard. When she discovers Rapunzel's betrayal, the sorceress looks more shocked than evil.

The Disney film *Tangled* (Greno & Howard, 2010) occupies a more extreme spot on the continuum than Zelinsky's book. The changes begin with the title, which was chosen to appeal to boys as well as girls (Corliss, 2010). In the film, Rapunzel is a princess who is kidnapped by the witch Gothel because her hair has magical powers that keep Gothel from aging. Rapunzel is imprisoned in the tower with no knowledge of her real family until she is almost 18, and by then her hair is 70 feet long. The male protagonist in this version is the bandit Flynn Rider. In the film's climax, Flynn is mortally wounded, and Rapunzel agrees to stay with the witch forever if she is allowed to heal him with her hair. Flynn sacrifices himself by cutting off Rapunzel's hair to erase its power. Gothel turns to dust, and Rapunzel's tears heal Flynn.

In the Brothers Grimm version, the Prince is drawn to Rapunzel's singing, so the music in the *Tangled* restores an element missing from Zelinsky's version. Nevertheless, the film demonstrates characteristics of reinvention. The language reflects a teenage vernacular, and characters have been added, including a group of criminals that Rapunzel charms and who eventually aid the young lovers. The most important change, however, is in the character of Rapunzel. In this version, she is the one with magical power. She has read extensively and is an accomplished singer and painter. She is naïve, but she is also bold, clever, and fiercely determined to explore the world.

Zel, Donna Jo Napoli's version of Rapunzel (1996), is set in Switzerland in the 1500s, which is very close to the setting of the Brothers Grimm version. In a significant departure from the traditional version, the story is told from three alternating perspectives. The first chapter is told from Zel's third-person point of view when she is still an innocent, content young girl living with her mother, far away from others. The witch tells her story in first person, except when she recounts the time when she was a barren woman who wanted a child so desperately that she would do anything to get one. Her third-person account of that part of her life creates a sense of detachment as she relates becoming a witch in order to steal a child. The story of Konrad, the prince figure, is told in third person and portrays an impetuous young man who is compelled to seek a girl he loves even though he has only seen her once. An intimate tower scene is told from his perspective and suggests the sexual relationship that was implied in the Brothers Grimm version (Ashliman, 2007), but that is absent from Zelinsky's and Disney's.

Like *Tangled, Rapunzel: A Groovy Fairytale,* written by Lynn Roberts (2003) and illustrated by David Roberts, replaces the passive, sheltered, and love-struck Rapunzel with a more modern and autonomous young woman; however, like *Zel,* it represents a much greater departure from tradition and falls even further on the continuum toward reinvention. The story is set in a 1970s apartment block, and the illustrations include film posters, products, clothes, and toys from that era. Rapunzel's Aunt Esme is the one who locks her in an apartment and climbs Rapunzel's hair because the building's elevator is broken. The handsome prince is played by Roger, who observes how Esme climbs Rapunzel's braids while he is fixing his bike.

Roger and Rapunzel meet, are separated, and eventually find each other when Roger and his band perform at the local school. In addition to the change in setting, the change in the main characters' "happily ever after" places this version on the reinvention end of the continuum. Roger and Rapunzel do not fall in love; they become good friends, and Rapunzel goes into business making wigs out of her red hair.

In the graphic novel *Rapunzel's Revenge* by Shannon Hale and Dean Hale (2008), Rapunzel has been raised by the witch, Gothel, and imprisoned in a kind of tower, the hollow of a tree. She still has long hair, which she uses to escape. But the story takes place in the Wild West. It is populated with cowboys, outlaws, creatures, and beasts, and words such as "skedaddale" and "giddyup." Rapunzel encounters a disguised Jack, who is escaping with the goose he stole from the top of the beanstalk. A determined and independent Rapunzel runs off with Jack to escape Gothel's control. After roaming the West for four years, they are caught and returned to Gothel, who cuts off Rapunzel's hair. In the end the witch is destroyed, and Rapunzel is reunited with her mother. The land, ravaged by Gothel, is restored to its natural splendor.

Although the location on the continuum from retelling to reinvention may be debatable for the versions of Rapunzel discussed above, *Letters from Rapunzel* by Sara Lewis Holmes (2007) is clearly at the far reinvention end. It uses a contemporary setting, replaces all the magical elements of the traditional tale with a realistic problem, and tells the story through a series of letters from a girl named Cadence. She is very close to her father, who is in the hospital for clinical depression,—or the Evil Spell as Cadence calls it. Cadence writes letters to an unidentified person and signs herself as Rapunzel because she feels as though she is stranded in a tower.

THE TELLING OF TALL TALES

lthough **tall tales** are not exclusive to the United States (Young, 2004), they are a fundamental element of our folk literature. Our tall tales reflect an era when Americans considered their country to be the biggest and best and celebrated individuals who were strongest, fastest, and boldest. The main character in a tall tale has superhuman attributes. Unlike other hero stories, however, tall tales are light in tone, and their events so exaggerated that they become humorously unbelievable. Rather than trying to convince an audience that the story is true, tellers of tall tales often relate them with a wink that acknowledges that they could not possibly be true. The image of Paul Bunyan's cooks greasing a giant flapjack griddle by skating across it on slabs of bacon is just one example (San Souci, 1991).

The story of John Henry is a traditional tale that has been passed on in ballad form as well as in story form. Although he is often depicted as African American, John has also been described as a white man and as both a womanizing trickster and a devoted family man (Stahl, Hanlon, & Keyser, 2007). The story has a more serious outcome than most tall tales, but it illustrates many of their other characteristics, beginning with John's superhuman strength and devotion to his work as a steel-driver, hammering steel and rock in the construction of railroads. In the version by Stahl, Hanlon, & Keyser (2007), he picked up his first hammer and steel when "he was a little baby, sitting on his papa's knee," (p. 345), and he actually wins his famous contest pitting his hammering strength against a steam-powered drill, even though the effort kills him.

John Henry's story, like many tall tales, is tied to the monumental task of settling the American West. In this case, the focus is on the workers who labored to extend the railroad across the country. In a similar way, tales about Paul Bunyan depict the enormous effort involved in clearing forests for settlement, and Pecos Bill exemplifies all the cowboys who blazed trails to open the West. Perhaps because tall tales generally grew out of pioneer settings and work crews where women were rare, tales featuring women are rare. Slue Foot Sue, the wife of Pecos Bill, is a notable exception. She rides a giant catfish that comes when she calls it, and she is not only pretty but can also do the work of ten men (San Souci, 1991). Polly Anne, the fictional wife of John Henry, also appears in some versions of his tale, taking over as a steel driver after her husband dies.

The ballad of John Henry illustrates one other important characteristic of tall tales. Even in printed versions, the story preserves the language used by its oral tellers. For example, the ballad describes how the contest challenge was delivered to John Henry:

> The captain said to John Henry
> I'm gonna bring that steam drill round
> I'm gonna bring that steam drill out on the job
> I'm gonna whup that steel on down (Stahl, Hanlon, & Keyser, 2007, p. 345)

The terms *gonna* and *whup* preserve colloquial language, the language of common people, as does the reference to *the captain*, which is a slang term for the boss. Brown (1987) points out that the informal, colorful, and regionally distinctive language of tall tales strongly influenced other forms of American literature: "The literature that brought tall tale humor into print . . . also helped to bring about significant changes in American prose style, for as the tall tale moved from the tributaries and backwaters of literature into the mainstream, it carried along with it the colloquial style" (p. 122).

This transition of colloquial language from tall tales to major works of American literature can most easily be seen in the work of Mark Twain. In stories like "The Notorious Jumping Frog of Calaveras County," Twain uses the tall tale elements of an untrustworthy narrator, a meandering style, and a lack of concern with traditional story structure. He also keeps the slang, regional expressions, and grammatical "errors" that would be found in an oral telling: "He was the curiousest man about always betting on anything that turned up you ever see" (Twain as quoted in Brown, 1987, p. 123).

Tall tales are probably an outgrowth of the bragging contests that were common in the Old West. Those verbal sparring matches were similar to the contemporary African American word game of "playing the dozens," as discussed in Christopher Myers' book *Lies and Other Tall Tales* (2005). Myers' work is based on tales collected by anthropologist Zora Neale Hurston from original sources such as a farmer named George Harris and a garage worker named Peter Noble. The classroom study below explores this aspect of tall tales.

THE ENDURING POWER OF MYTHS

*T*he word **myth** is derived from the Greek word "mythos," meaning *word* or *story*. Myths, which have endured anonymously throughout the centuries, attempt to explain the origins of the world, including human society and culture (Willis, 1993). For the people of ancient civilizations, myths were nonfiction. They were viewed either as true or as allegories in which metaphors or symbols conveyed cosmic truths. The power of a myth does not lie in its verisimilitude (its truthfulness) but rather in the insight it provides into the purpose of life and the hope and guidance it offers (Armstrong, 2005). The totality of a people's myths comprises a belief system, or mythology (Lechner, 2004). All mythologies include a belief in an invisible and powerful reality that exists alongside the human world (Armstrong, 2005).

Types of Myths

Mythologies may include three types of myth: creation myths, deity myths, and hero myths.

Creation myths

Creation myths explain how things began, so they provide a focus for studying themes that are universal to cultures both ancient and contemporary. Virginia Hamilton's book *In the Beginning: Creation Stories from Around the World* (1988),

classroom scenario

The Whoppers Club

Young adults are usually familiar with the type of the bragging, exaggerating, and "trash talking" that lie at the heart of tall tales. Teachers can build on this experience to create greater understanding of both the tall tale genre and the oral tradition. As you read this classroom study, consider how the teacher helps students appreciate the humorous tone and intent of tall tales.

Ms. Alverton has observed in past years that her sixth-grade students resist the unit on American tall tales. She decides to use picture books and oral storytelling to introduce the tales, assuming that the pictures will convey the wildly exaggerated spirit of the stories and that the length and language of

the books is well suited to oral telling. She obtains several copies of books that collect a number of tales, including *Big Men, Big Country* (Bearnard, 1993), which features both well-known and lesser-known characters and provides information about the origins of each tale. She also chooses *American Tall Tales* (Osborne, 1991), which gives an extensive introduction, notes on each story, and a list of primary sources for each tall tale character.

Ms. Alverton begins by showing the class two picture books, *Swamp Angel* (Isaacs, 1994), illustrated by Paul O. Zelinsky, and the tall tale collection *Cut from the Same Cloth* (San Souci, 1993) illustrated by Brian Pinkney. She asks what the cover illustrations suggest about the stories inside. Both feature pictures of very large women. One is holding up a cow, and the other has feet as big as an entire person. The students agree that both pictures look as if they are set in pioneer times, and they predict that the stories are not true, or even believable.

Ms. Alverton tells her students that the class will compete for a spot in the "Whoppers Club Hall of Fame" and will use similar picture books to prepare for the competition. Each student selects a different tall tale, and Ms. Alverton spends the next few days coaching them in storytelling techniques such as making eye contact, changing pace and volume, and using body language and gestures for emphasis. They decide whether they will act as if they believe the story, or if they will signal that they are only kidding. Students practice telling their stories, both in and outside of school. They are videotaped and work with partners to critique each other's performances.

Ms. Alverton invites a fourth grade class to the Whoppers Club performance, and the younger students vote for the best tall tale storyteller. Three students are inducted into the Whoppers Club Hall of Fame, but everyone experienced the fun of telling and hearing tales. At the same time, the class explored concepts about language and literature, such as the idea of an untrustworthy narrator and the differences between typical "book language" and the colloquial language of tall tales. Students also acquire a feel for a particular era in American history and the uniquely American attitude that went with it.

illustrated by Barry Moser, contains 25 creation myths that reveal both commonalities and differences across diverse cultures. Creation myths are often closely linked to deities. In the mythology of the Kono people of Guinea, for example, Death came first and made mud. Then the god Alatangana made the mud solid to create earth.

Students can compare creation myths and identify similarities and differences. They might, for instance, discover that the origin myth of the Maidu Indians of California and that of aborigines of Australia both begin in darkness. Students might also consider the connection between Iceland's geography and its creation myth, which begins with a world divided into two realms, one full of fire and blinding light, the other full of fog, ice, and snow, where the first living being was a frost giant.

Deity myths

Deity myths tell about the exploits of supernatural beings, usually gods. Willis (1993) explains how gods and their relationships with people provide insights into the beliefs of three ancient cultures: Egyptian, Greek, and Norse.

Egyptian deities. Osiris, the first Egyptian king, is killed by his brother Seth. Early versions of the myth have Seth throwing Osiris into a mythical river; in later renditions it becomes the Nile. In still later versions, Seth rips Osiris's body to pieces and buries the parts at sites all over Egypt. Osiris's wife, Isis, locates the pieces and summons Anubis, the jackal god. He embalms and bandages the pieces, thus creating the first mummy. After death, Osiris becomes the ruler of the underworld. Death and the afterlife play a central role in ancient Egyptian culture, so it is no coincidence that their mythology identifies the first king as both the first mummy and king of the underworld.

Greek deities. Ancient Greece, the cradle of democracy and the great military power of the ancient world, provides a second example of the connections between a civilization and its deity myths. The Greek goddess Athena springs from Zeus' head and so is associated with wisdom and intelligence. One of her symbols is the owl, the wisest of birds. Because she is born armed with helmet, shield, and spear, she is also the protector of heroes. Athena, therefore, symbolizes the balance between wisdom and military might that the ancient Greeks valued.

Norse deities. The prominence of the warrior in Viking mythology reflects the value the people placed on bravery and the willingness to die in battle. In ancient Norse myths, Odin, the All-Father, has a spear that gives him control of battles. Odin summons kings and heroes who have died in battle to Valhalla, an enormous feast hall located in the legendary kingdom of Asgard. The dead heroes enter Valhalla with great ceremony, escorted by warrior goddesses, the Valkyries. Like the other two examples, the actions and values of the Norse deities mirror the ideals of their people. At the same time, these gods exerted a powerful influence on people's imaginations and continue to do so today. This influence pervades the English language itself, as illustrated in the box on p. 176..

Hero myths

Hero myths are the most human, and so remain the most visible in contemporary literature (Leeming, 2002). The hero figures in myths "perform extraordinary

The Influence of Mythology on Modern Language

Tess awakes on a sunny Monday in June and quickly remembers that today she and her family are traveling to a natural history museum that features displays of flora and fauna and has a planetarium. She is hoping to see the constellation Cancer, because she has not been able to see it with her telescope. Tess looks at the atlas to figure out how many counties they have to travel through. As she eats her cereal, her brother starts yelling about how he is going to miss his martial arts competition on Thursday. Tess tells him to stop going berserk and not to panic, because they will be back by Wednesday. Her father declares, "It was a Herculean task, but the Mercury is finally loaded. Let's go." She ties up her Nikes and heads out.

The following words from the paragraph are directly related to deities in mythology:

Atlas	Atlas was a Greek god who was punished by having to hold the sky on his shoulders.	*June*	Juno was the queen of the gods in Roman mythology.
Berserk	The Berserkers were Norse warriors who fought with an uncontrollable rage.	*Martial*	Mars was the Roman god of war.
Cancer	Cancer was a crab sent by the goddess Hera to attack Hercules; he kicked it up to the sky where it became a constellation.	*Mercury*	Mercury was the Roman messenger god.
		Monday	Derived from Mani, the Norse god of the moon.
Cereal	Ceres was the Roman goddess of agriculture and grain.	*Museum*	A *mouseion* was a Greek temple devoted to the arts of the Muses.
Fauna	Fauna was the wife of Faunus, the Roman god of the forests, plains, and fields.	*Nike*	Nike was the Greek winged goddess of victory.
Flora	Flora was the Roman goddess of flowers and spring.	*Panic*	Derived from Pan, the Greek god of nature and shepherds, who loved to scream at goats and sheep to scare them.
Herculean	Hercules is the Roman name for Greek hero Herakles, the son of Zeus, who was tasked with completing 12 arduous labors to atone for killing his children.	*Thursday*	Derived from Thor, the Norse god of thunder.
		Wednesday	Derived from Odin, sometimes called Woden, the ruler of the Norse gods.

feats in the course of laying the foundations of human society" (Willis, p. 28). Mythical heroes are most often male and possess supernatural abilities. In some hero stories, a strong protector assists the hero. Athena, the goddess of wisdom, helps Perseus, the founder of the Greek kingdom of Mycenae, to slay the gorgon, Medusa. Poseidon, the god of the seas, aids Theseus, the King of Athens, in slaying the Minotaur. Mythic heroes may be the offspring of gods. They represent the heights to which humans can aspire, as well as the depths to which they can fall. Hero tales usually take place in the real world rather than in the mythical realm. Even when gods appear in the story, the focus is on humans. Hero stories are longer and more complex in structure than other myths (Helbig & Perkins, 1997).

Herakles, or Hercules, was the only human honored throughout Greece and the only human to be granted immortality among the gods. He is often considered the archetypal Greek hero, establishing the pattern for what a hero should be. Hercules is both good and evil. He fought monsters bravely and struggled with Death to save a friend. He also raped a woman, killed his own children, and destroyed cities. The story of Hercules is a good example of how stories change through retellings. In later Greek writing, he was willing to suffer to obtain virtue. Willis (1993) asserts that this reinvention brought the myth closer to Christian tradition. As shown in the film *Hercules* (Young, 2005), Hercules kills his six sons after being driven mad by the goddess Hera. He then performs 12 labors in penance, including capturing Cerberus, the three-headed dog that guarded the gates of the Underworld, and slaying a nine-headed hydra.

Retelling and Reinventing Myths

Richard Cavendish states that "when old myths are lost, new ones are needed. Myths flourish and fade and die, but new myths are born, old ones are resurrected, and hybrid forms combining new and old emerge when times change or cultures mingle" (1980, p. 9). Some contemporary authors have resurrected old myths by retelling them, and others have created hybrids that reinvent the traditional story. Michael Cadnum's *Starfall: Phaeton and the Chariot of the Sun* (2004) and *Nightsong: The Legend of Orpheus and Eurydice* (2006) retell the stories from the *Metamorphoses*, a collection of myths by Ovid, the Roman poet. Both stories retain a sense of the ancient Greek world. They refer frequently to the gods and goddesses, and the language and behaviors in both are consistent with ancient customs and beliefs.

The animated series *Greek Mythology for Students* (Schlessinger Media, 2005) retells the Greek stories in a way that captures their drama and illustrates the ancients' beliefs about the wonders of the universe. Each episode highlights mythological themes and shows students how the myth relates to life today.

Retellings of the Greek and Roman myths are the easiest to find, followed by Norse and Native American myths (Lechner, 2004). Teachers, however, can use several sources to identify collections of myths from other cultures. Some collections are limited to one culture, but others are multicultural (Helbig & Perkins, 1997; Sienkewicz, 1996). In *Changing Woman and Her Sisters: Stories of Goddesses from Around the World* (2006), Katrin Hyman Tchana retells the myths of ten goddesses from outside the familiar Greek, Roman, and Norse traditions. Each story maintains the rhythm of its original language and is accompanied by a paragraph about the goddess and her land of origin. Trina Schart Hyman's illustrations meld full-page ink and acrylic renderings with photographs and found materials.

Among the reinventions of Greek myths, one of the of the most popular is *The Lightening Thief* (2005), a Teen Choice Award winner and the first of Rick Riordan's novels about Percy Jackson, a modern-day son of Poseidon, the Greek god of the sea. When Percy first discovers that the gods and goddesses are alive and living in the United States, the centaur, Chiron, comments:

What you call "Western civilization." Do you think it's just an abstract concept? No, it's a living force. A collective consciousness that has burned bright for thousands of years. The gods are part of it. You might even say they are the source of it, or at least, they are tied so tightly to it that they couldn't possibly fade, not unless all of Western civilization were obliterated. (p. 72)

Chiron points out that for over 3,000 years the gods' influence has been immortalized in architecture and art. He reminds Percy that the symbol of the United States—the eagle—is the eagle of Zeus.

Like Riordan's Percy Jackson stories, Sarah Deming's *Iris, Messenger* (2007) retains the characteristics of the ancient gods even though it is set in the modern world and focuses on modern characters. Iris receives a copy of *Bulfinch's Mythology* (a well-known collection of Greek and Roman mythology) for her twelfth birthday. Mysterious messages keep popping up in her book, and she realizes that Greek gods and goddesses are living close to her home in suburban Pennsylvania. The deities' modern professions reflect their ancient identities. Aphrodite, goddess of love and beauty, runs a hair salon, and the god of the sea, Poseidon, runs a seaside oyster shack. The gods and goddesses tell Iris of their lives as Olympians in story and song. Their first-person stories are printed in italics and set off in separate chapters.

The intertextual connections to the ancient Greek gods in the Percy Jackson books and in *Iris, Messenger* introduce the ancient myths for readers in the middle grades in ways they can relate to. In contrast, *Psyche in a Dress* (Block, 2006) is a reinvention for mature readers that is more concerned with exposing realities of the modern world than with introducing the ancient myths to readers. In fact, one reviewer (Budin, 2006) suggests that *Psyche in a Dress* explains so little about the ancient myths that it will send readers hunting for *Bulfinch's Mythology*.

Set in Los Angeles, Block's free-verse novel depicts Greek deities who are as lustful, selfish, and power hungry as ever, but also thoroughly adapted to the modern world. The story is, moreover, told in an entirely modern manner. Psyche, a teen star in her father's violent movies, takes on several different personas, including Echo, Eurydice, and Persephone. Her affairs are graphically depicted as she falls in love with Eros in her father's movie, *Narcissus*, and with the musician Orpheus. Aphrodite, Hades, and Persephone's mother Demeter also appear.

See the box on the facing page for additional works that renew old myths by bringing modern teenagers together with Olympian gods or by adding elements of modern fiction, such as subplots and complex characterizations, to the traditional story. Others are reinventions that employ metafictive techniques or use mythic characters to raise questions about the ancient attitudes and beliefs that persist in modern culture, especially issues about gender roles.

ENCOUNTERING EPICS

Epics are connected to myths by the common thread of heroes. These long narrative poems tell the central events of a particular people and celebrate their ideas and values. Like other stories originating in oral tradition, including myths, epics are retold in multiple formats across many times and places. Some of the best-known myths and epics are described below,

Aphrodite's Blessings: Love Stories from the Greek Myths. Clemence McLaren, 2002. This trilogy of Greek love story myths is retold with a feminist slant. Atlanta, Andromeda, and Psyche each find a worthy mate. McLaren provides an insightful glimpse of women struggling in a male-dominated world. Ages 12 and older.

Cupid. Julius Lester, 2007. Lester retells the ancient tale of the ill-fated love of Cupid and Psyche. He reinvents the story by interspersing the story of two contemporary adolescents who are in love and facing their own trials. Ages 12 and older.

The Great God Pan. Donna Jo Napoli, 2003. Using first-person narration, Napoli tells the story of the god Pan, who is half man and half goat. Pan falls in love with Iphigenia, but the curse placed upon Pan at birth—that he will never be loved—seems to come true when Iphigenia disappears. In the end Pan sacrifices his own life to save his beloved. Ages 13 and up.

Oh.My.Gods. Tera Lynn Childs, 2008. Phoebe Castro moves to a remote island in the Aegean Sea with her mom and new stepfather. She attends an exclusive academy with students who are descendants of the Olympians. Ages 12 and up.

Pandora Gets Jealous. Carolyn Hennesy, 2008. Pandy needs something for school, so she borrows a mysterious box that her dad keeps hidden in a bunch of rolled up rugs. She accidentally opens the box and releases seven plagues. Zeus insists that Pandy track down the plagues and return them to the box. Ages 10–14.

The Shadow Thieves. Anne Ursu, 2006. This is the first book of the author's Cronus trilogy, although it can stand on its own. Thirteen-year-old Charlotte and her cousin, Zachary, called Zee, learn that the Greek god Hades really exists and so does the Underworld. An ambitious half-demon is planning to steal shadows from living children as part of a plot to overthrow Hades, and Charlotte and Zee must travel to the Underworld to save humanity. Ages 11–14.

---

along with a sampling of their contemporary retellings and reinventions. In epics, the hero is larger than life, and the settings have panoramic scope (Kennedy, Gioia, & Bauerlein, 2006). Unlike the mythic heroes, however, the epic hero is entirely human.

The epics that young adults are most likely to encounter are the *Odyssey* (Lombardo, Trans., 2000), the *Iliad* (Murray, Trans., 1999), *Beowulf* (Heaney, Trans., 2000), and, to a lesser extent, *Gilgamesh* (Kluger, Trans., 1991). The *Odyssey* and the *Iliad*, both poems about the Trojan War, are attributed to the Greek poet Homer. The stories were probably written down around 800 BCE to 600 BCE, many generations after they were first told. The *Iliad* focuses on the war between Troy and Greece, and the *Odyssey* is about Odysseus' journey home after the war. Odysseus is a human who endures long and perilous voyages and is called upon to fight supernatural beings. As translated by Fitzgerald (1963, p. 1) the Odyssey begins:

> Sing in me, Muse, and through me tell the story
> Of that man skilled in all ways of contending,
> The wanderer, harried for years on end, after he plundered the stronghold
> On the proud height of Troy

The poet calls upon his muse to provide inspiration to tell the story of Odysseus and gives a preview of its basic action. These opening lines suggest that the *Odyssey* reflects the Greeks' honor for both heroes and the poets who told their stories.

Beowulf, one of the oldest works in the English language, is known only from a single manuscript dating from the early eleventh century (Raven, 2007, p. x). No one knows who wrote this poem of more than 3,000 lines (Heaney, 2000). Unlike the Greek epics in which the gods take sides in a war, *Beowulf*, set in Denmark and Sweden, is about a brave warrior who slays monsters and is ultimately killed by a dragon. Beowulf's last battle occurs in his homeland after he has become king. Beowulf is not only an exciting story; it is also an excellent example of what written English looked like in its beginning stages. Comparing the original text with various translations may give students some insight into both the evolving nature of language and the process of translation.

Gilgamesh is the hero of a Sumerian epic even older than the *Iliad*. He is two-thirds god (as opposed to the Greek demigod, or half god), and his superhuman strength enables him to slay menacing beasts and to build a city wall to defend his people from enemies. Consistent with other hero tales, he embarks on a journey, must complete monumental tasks, and suffers intensely along the way (Kluger, 1991).

Retelling and Reinventing Epics

The first change that authors of reinvented epics generally make is to convert the story from poetry to prose or to a more visual medium, such as a film or graphic novel. They may also employ techniques of reinvention, such as shifting the story's point of view, as Adele Geras does in *Ithaka* (2006). This retelling of Odysseus' departure for the Trojan War and is told through Klymene, a kindly servant girl who attends to Odysseus' wife Penelope in her island castle while she waits for her husband's return.

Beowulf: The Graphic Novel by Gareth Hinds (2007) and *Beowulf: A Tale of Blood, Heat, and Ashes* by Nicky Raven, illustrated by John Howe, (2007) both reinvent the Old English epic but retain some of the cadence of the original language. Both include rather chilling illustrations of the monster Grendel and his mother. Raven's lengthy version tells the story from multiple perspectives, including that of a Norse storyteller and the beasts. Younger readers will find the 2008 Children's Choice Award finalist, *Beowulf: Monster Slayer, A British Legend* (Storrie, 2008), to be an accessible graphic version.

Retellings sometimes narrow the scope of an epic story. The film *Beowulf*, directed by Robert Zemeckis (2007), for instance, focuses on the epic's main episodes in which Beowulf kills the Grendel, who is terrorizing towns, and then defeats Grendel's mother, who begins killing to avenge her son. Geraldine McCaughrean's book *Gilgamesh the Hero* (2002) focuses on one quest Gilgamesh undertakes to seek immortality when his friend Enkidu dies. Both of these works add a new visual dimension for the modern reader in place of the poetic imagery of the traditional story. *Gilgamesh the Hero*, for example, adds illustrations, by David Parkins, that are inspired by Assyrian art and evoke the ancient world of the epic.

classroom scenario

Heroes Then and Now

AS YOU READ, consider how Mr. Anthony develops the concept of a hero and connects it to students' previous experiences.

Mr. Anthony's eighth-grade students are beginning a thematic unit called "Heroes Then and Now." He wants his students to make connections between the literature they read in class and the popular literature and media they are exposed to out of school. He begins by asking, "What is a hero?" Some respond that heroes are real-life people in dangerous professions, such as firefighters and soldiers; some say heroes are fictional characters such as Spiderman and Batman. Mr. Anthony tells the class that the word *hero* comes from Greek mythology, where heroes were often demigods, half human and half god, and that they are going to read novels about some of those ancient heroes.

Students are divided into groups of four, and each student in the group is assigned one of Geraldine McCaughrean's retellings of the Greek hero tales *Odysseus* (2004), *Theseus* (2005), *Perseus* (2005), and *Hercules* (2005). The books retain the essence of the characters, settings, and plots, but the stories are told in chapters chronicling major events, and they use modern dialogue and language conventions. For students who enjoy graphic novels, Mr. Anthony also shares books about the same heroes from the Graphic Universe series: *Odysseus* (Jolley, 2008), *Theseus* (Limke, 2008), *Perseus* (Storrie, 2008), and *Hercules* (Storrie, 2007). These graphic novels include a glossary of gods and goddesses, a summary of the story, websites, and other nonfiction sources.

Because he knows that ancient people listened to these stories orally for centuries before they were written down, Mr. Anthony makes audio versions of the stories available. He also provides the class with copies of *The Dictionary of Classical Mythology* (Grimal, 1996) and *The Encyclopedia of Ancient Deities* (Coulter & Turner, 2000). The students tell each other the basic plot of the hero myths they have read, and then each group composes a paragraph that summarizes the characteristics the heroes share.

The class compares and contrasts the characteristics of the ancient and modern superheroes. They agree that both are brave, extra strong, and sometimes also very smart. Both also have to face danger and powerful enemies. The students point out that the demigods were born powerful, but some superheroes get their powers from freak accidents, such as being bitten by a spider or getting caught in an experiment gone wrong. They note that none of the heroes in the ancient stories were women, but there are many female superheroes, like Hawk Girl and Wonder Woman in the Justice League, and Rogue and Storm in the X-Men.

Mr. Anthony reminds the class that Wonder Woman is an Amazon like the ones that Hercules fought. To encourage students to think a little more deeply, Mr. Anthony introduces Spiderman's slogan: "With great power comes great responsibility." He asks them to write an essay arguing whether the ancient heroes or the modern superheroes more fully live up to the slogan. He also asks them to include an example of an individual or group who lives up to it in real life.

Epics pose challenges for contemporary young adults because they are so different from modern literary forms. Showing a brief scene from the film *Troy* (Peterson, 2004), based on Homer's Iliad, or trailers from classic Hollywood epics such as *The Ten Commandments* (DeMille, 1956) might help them grasp the notion of an epic as a really big story, with a cast of thousands that spans many years and locations. A teacher might also do a read-aloud from a more modern narrative poem, especially a patriotic one such as Henry Longfellow's *Paul Revere's Ride* as adapted by T. Rand (1990).

Perhaps mythic and epic hero tales endure because they mirror the quest of young people to discover who they are, what they believe, and what matters to them. Leeming (2002) suggests thinking of hero tales as "metaphors for our personal and collective progress through life and history" (p. 7).

LEGENDS IN LITERATURE

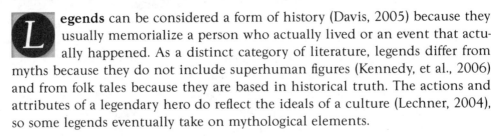

Legends can be considered a form of history (Davis, 2005) because they usually memorialize a person who actually lived or an event that actually happened. As a distinct category of literature, legends differ from myths because they do not include superhuman figures (Kennedy, et al., 2006) and from folk tales because they are based in historical truth. The actions and attributes of a legendary hero do reflect the ideals of a culture (Lechner, 2004), so some legends eventually take on mythological elements.

British Legends

Davis (2005) cites the story of St. George, the dragon slayer, to show how myth and legend merge. He points out that St. George's saintly reputation may have been enhanced by borrowing the story of the dragon slayer from ancient Egyptian or Mesopotamian mythology. Davis also cites King Arthur as another example of a legend that has gradually become more like a mythic hero. A historical Arthur is credited with defending Britain against Saxon invaders in the early sixth century, but Davis (2005) points out that tales about Arthur were first written down almost a thousand years after Arthur died and that parts of the legend seem to be drawn from stories that long predate his birth.

Later Christian influences may have added Queen Guinevere, as well as the knights' quest for the Holy Grail. Over the next several centuries the story became more like a medieval romance as Arthur and the Knights of the Round Table became proponents of chivalry, a code of conduct unknown in the more primitive time when the legend began. Eventually, the legend took on mythic elements such as the sword Excalibur, which sometimes is endowed with magical powers, and the notion that Arthur sleeps on the mystical Island of Avalon until he reawakens when Britain needs him most. Michael Cart (2006) suggests that the idea of Camelot "represents the perfect fantasy, the quintessential new realm into which we can escape" (p. 42).

Thomas Malory's 15th century *Le Morte d' Arthur* (1999) undoubtedly influenced most modern reinventions of Arthur, including T. H. White's story, "The

Sword and the Stone," which was part of *The Once and Future King* (1958) and adapted as an animated movie (Reitherman, 1963). More recently, White's tale about Merlin's tutelage of young Arthur became an audiobook read by Shakespearean actor Neville Jason (White, 2008). Many recent reinventions have shifted the spotlight from Arthur to Merlin, including Jane Yolen's Young Merlin Trilogy, beginning with *Passenger* (1996). T. A. Barron's series *The Lost Years of Merlin* (1996) introduces Merlin as a young boy who is washed up on a Welsh beach and told that his name is Emrys by a woman who claims to be his mother.

Next to King Arthur, Robin Hood is the most recognized legend to come from Great Britain. A Saxon commoner, he defended a conquered people against Norman injustice during the 12th century. Robin Hood first appeared in ballads written down sometime after 1450, but it was not until the 16th century that he became the chivalrous outlaw who robs the rich to help the poor. Leitch (2008) points out that it was even later, around 1595, when Maid Marian became a regular part of the story.

Robin Hood makes occasional appearances in a series of books by Nancy Springer that begins with *Rowan Hood: Outlaw Girl of Sherwood Forest* (2002). These books reinvent the legend by focusing on Rowan, who may be Robin's daughter. When her mother is killed as a suspected witch, Rowan enters Sherwood Forest hoping to find Robin. She gradually forms her own band of outcasts or fugitives, none of whom fits the mold of a traditional hero. Throughout the series, which includes *Lionclaw* (2004) and *Wild Boy* (2005), Rowan struggles with issues of identity and friendship as much as with the Sheriff of Nottingham.

Beginning with a silent film starring Douglas Fairbanks (Dwan, 1922) movies have played a major role in retelling his legend. The 1938 version (Curtiz & Keighley), starred Errol Flynn and won three Academy Awards. *Robin Hood, Prince of Thieves* (Reynolds, 1991), starring Kevin Costner, added the character of Azeem, a Moor who accompanies Robin back from the Crusades vowing to repay him for saving his life. *Robin Hood* (Scott, 2010) is the latest version. Robin Longstride, played by Russell Crowe, returns from the Crusades and takes the place of Robert Locksley, with the encouragement of Robert's father in order to preserve the Locksley estate. Robin, with the help of Locksley's wife, Marian, begins to organize opposition to royal corruption.

American Legends

Despite having a much shorter written history than Britain, the United States has begun to develop its own legends. Figures ranging from Pocahontas to Shoeless Joe Jackson have had their lives embellished to the point where it is difficult to tell where fact ends and fiction begins. Many of America's legends, like many of its tall tales, come from the settling of the West. These legendary Western figures, such as Annie Oakley, Buffalo Bill, and Billy the Kid, actually existed, but their frontier world valued colorful exaggeration over careful record keeping, and separating fact from fiction was difficult even in their own lifetimes.

Some towering personalities from sports and entertainment have also approached legendary status. The athletic feats of Babe Ruth are well documented, but facts about his reputed devotion to children and his prodigious eating and drinking are harder to come by. Shoeless Joe Jackson is another baseball hero whose tremendous abilities are partly overshadowed by legend because of the mystery that still surrounds his guilt over throwing the 1919 World Series. Harry Houdini is an entertainer who has acquired legendary status, partly because of his worldwide fame and unique role as the first escape artist, and partly because of the mysterious circumstances that surrounded his death.

An indication that a historical figure has become legendary is when he or she turns up in a work of fiction that is not primarily about him or her. Buffalo Bill Cody, for instance, plays a role in the plot of Richard Peck's book, *Fair Weather* (2001). Three farm children visit the 1893 Chicago World's Columbian Exposition, where they meet the legendary Buffalo Bill at a performance of his Wild West Show. An immortal version of Billy the Kid turns up working with Niccolo Machiavelli on the side of evil in Michael Scott's fantasy novel, *The Sorceress* (2009). In the movie *Field of Dreams* (Robinson, 1989), Iowa farmer Ray Kinsella meets the ghost of Shoeless Joe Jackson, and Harry Houdini becomes a detective in *Shots at Sea: A Houdini and Nate Mystery* (Lalicki, 2007). Houdini and his protégé young Nate Fuller try to stop the assassination of former president Teddy Roosevelt on board the RMS *Lusitania*.

In the classroom, students can research a legendary figure such as Shoeless Joe Jackson and debunk "facts" that are in doubt or definitely untrue even though they are widely believed. They could, for instance, investigate whether Jackson ever played without shoes. In the process, they can learn how to verify information by finding it in multiple sources and how to reconcile contradictory sources. The box on the facing page contains some additional examples of works that retell or reinvent British and American legends.

Teaching Ideas ▪ TALL TALES, MYTHS, EPICS, AND LEGENDS

Many of the tales described above preserve and retell traditional content in its traditional form. When students experience this literature, they are coming into direct contact with their cultural ancestors, or gaining at least an inkling of the ways that others see the world. Reading these stories also provides a foundation for better understanding how the stories have sprung from these cultural roots. Nevertheless, many contemporary young adults will need encouragement and guidance from their teachers to appreciate these stories. The following brief list of suggested classroom activities may foster such appreciation.

• Zipes (1997) states that "oral storytelling has never ceased, and it continues to play a significant role in our lives" (p. 1). As explored in the Classroom Scenario earlier, guide students in preparing a myth or tall tale for an oral performance. Organizations such as the American Folklore Society (www.afsnet.org/index.cfm) and the National Storytelling Network (www.storynet.org/) strive to keep the oral tradition, including folk tales, alive.

• Many American Indians feel that individuals own their stories. Have students explore a story's origin and ownership through research or by speaking

Parzival: The Quest of the Grail Knight. Katherine Paterson, 2000. This is a retelling of the story of Parzival based on Wolfram von Eschenbach's 13th century poem. Parzival was born of royal blood but was raised as a peasant. He leaves home to seek adventure and ends up winning the Red Knight's armor in a duel. Ages 9–12.

I Am Mordred: A Tale from Camelot. Nancy Springer, 2002. Unwittingly, young King Arthur sleeps with his half-sister Morgause, who conceives the child Mordred. The wizard Merlin predicts that Mordred is destined to destroy both Arthur and his kingdom. Ages 12 and up.

Robin Hood: Outlaw of Sherwood Forest. Paul D. Storrie. Illustrated by Thomas Yeates, 2007. This graphic novel includes several familiar adventures of the legend of Robin Hood. The novel is presented in a reader-friendly fashion. Ages 9–12.

Jackie and Me. Dan Gutman, 1999. This book is part of the Baseball Card Adventures series in which a boy named Joe Stoshach has the ability to visit the past through baseball cards. Joe gets a Jackie Robinson card and goes back to New York City in 1947, the year Robinson broke the color barrier in major league baseball. Ages 9–12.

Billy the Kid. Theodore Taylor, 2005. In this fictional account, Billy the Kid becomes a train robber and gunslinger, but he is portrayed as charming with a winning smile. An author's note gives a synopsis of the outlaw's real life. Ages 10–13.

The Collected Works of Billy the Kid. Michael Ondaatje, 1996. Ondaatje uses the metafictive technique of combining genres to create a collage that mixes poetry, narration, memoir, photography, and journalism. Billy is reinvented as a poet, lover, and observer, while maintaining his identity as a gunslinger. Adult.

Shoeless Joe and Me. Dan Gutman, 2003. In this Baseball Card Adventures series book, Joe Stoschack travels back to 1919 to try to save Shoeless Joe from being implicated in the conspiracy to throw the World Series. The book includes antique photographs, baseball cards, and news clippings. Ages 9–12.

The Floating Lady Murder: A Harry Houdini Mystery. Daniel Stashower, 2000. When a woman attempts to perform the "floating lady" illusion (suspending a body in mid-air), she falls 72 feet and dies. She is found, however, to have died from drowning, not the fall. Houdini, his wife, Bess, and his brother, Dash, and family are employed by Kellar, the dean of American magicians, to solve the crime. Adult.

My Lady Pocahontas. Kathleen V. Kudlinski, 2006. This history of Pocahontas combines legend and fact as Pocahontas falls in love with a white leader and ends up betraying her father. Later she moves to England where she is celebrated as an exotic Indian princess. Kudlinski explores the clash of two cultures while demonstrating the richness of each. Ages 12–15.

---

directly with American Indians. They might contact organizations such as the American Indian Studies Center in California (www.aisc.ucla.edu) and Oyate (www.oyate@oyate.org), an organization whose goal is to see that the lives and histories of American Indians are portrayed honestly. *A Broken Flute: The Native Experience in Books for Children* (Seale & Slapin, 2005) evaluates hundreds of Native American books published for children and teenagers.

• Because folk literature has strong roots in oral language, it also lends itself to choral reading and readers' theater. Add another dimension by staging a performance that is accompanied by music. The audio and video productions of Rabbit Ears Entertainment (www.rabbitears.com) can provide a model.

Although the company describes itself as a children's entertainment company, many of its productions include legends, tall tales, Native American tales, and folk and fairy tales. A production of John Henry, for example, features narration by Denzel Washington, illustrations by Barry Jackson, and music by B. B. King.

- Students can read about the debates concerning Robin Hood by searching the Worldwide Robin Hood Society at http://robinhood.info/robinhood/index.htm. They can watch a video of the Big Oak in Sherwood Forest at www.ignitecast.com. "Journey Through Time" at www.sherwoodforest.org.uk gives ideas for projects related to English history.

- Students can explore both the language and the spirit of traditional genres such as creation myths, tall tales, or epics by attempting to write their own. Often that process can be aided by providing a "pattern guide" that lays out slots for the particular elements that must be included. For example, a pattern guide for a group project for creating an epic might include the following points:

  - Hero (character of high stature and important to the culture or world)
  - Setting (vast in scope)
  - Deeds hero will achieve, requiring great courage
  - Supernatural forces that intervene in the action

- Similar to the activity shown in the earlier Classroom Scenario, have students work in groups to choose a hero myth collection and chart various characteristics that appear to determine a hero/heroine. Then have them choose those characteristics that they feel apply to contemporary life and write about a person who exemplifies those characteristics.

EXPLORING FOLK TALES AND FAIRY TALES

xperts often disagree on how to define or categorize traditional literature, particularly folk tales and fairy tales. According to Winters and Schmidt (2001), a **folk tale** is

> a narrative story that literally comes out of the folk; it is a tale with oral origins in a distinct culture, handed down year after year, generation after generation, refined and revised, always changing with the teller, always changing with the audience, always shifting in its detail, usually constant in its basic narrative form and plot situations, often constant in its basic meanings. (p. 101)

Folk tales are non-magical, even if they include talking animals such as the Three Little Pigs. Stories with strong elements of magic, such as Jack and the Beanstalk, are usually defined as **fairy tales.** Although folk tales and fairy tales are now associated with children, they did not necessarily start out that way. Early editions of Grimms' Fairy Tales were, in fact, considered too violent for children. In the original "Snow White," for example, the evil queen is forced to dance in red-hot iron shoes until she drops dead. Pressure from clergymen, educators, parents, and publishers influenced the Grimm Brothers to revise their 1819 edition to make it more suitable for children.

Bruno Bettelheim (1976) argued that fairy tales play a unique role in helping individuals work through some very important life issues. He pointed out that most fairy tales tell a story of a weak, forgotten, or oppressed character who eventually triumphs through a combination of personal worthiness and magical intervention. In Bettelheim's interpretation, rescuing a princess from a tower or passing a magical test is a symbol of achieving social and sexual maturity. The desire to achieve maturity, find true love, and prevail over enemies certainly resonates with young adults. This may explain why so many fairy tales have been reinvented for a young adult audience.

As we pointed out earlier in this chapter, folk tales and fairy tales were not created or performed by professional authors or storytellers. They were embellished by common people as they were passed from person to person and generation to generation. As we saw with urban legends, different versions of the same story are almost inevitable in the oral tradition because tellers tailor details for local audiences. Some of these **variants** of traditional stories may be the result of diffusion as travelers and traders carried stories across the world and they took root in different regions. It is also possible, however, that similar stories are found in different cultures simply because they reflect dreams and fears that are common to all people.

Folk tales often depict the traditional customs and cultural values of common people in a particular region. It is important to realize, however, that they are reflections of the time in which they developed, and they may not accurately depict people of today. Exploring the folk tales of other cultures may not give young adults more insight into the contemporary world, but it will give them a broader sense of human diversity and an understanding of stories outside the Western literary tradition. The plethora of traditional stories from around the world makes recommending a specific list difficult; we mention only a few noteworthy books that are good starting points for exploration. The two hefty volumes of *The Greenwood Encyclopedia of Folktales and Fairy Tales* (Haase, 2008), for instance, provide alphabetical entries on a wide range of topics that include themes, character types, and national traditions. Entries include further readings, and a bibliography includes both print and electronic sources.

Jane Yolen's book *Mightier than the Sword: World Folktales for Strong Boys,* illustrated by Raul Colon (2003), is unique because it contains 14 stories from around the world featuring male protagonists. Some of the stories are familiar, such as those based on Brothers Grimm tales, but some are less familiar, such as tales from Afghanistan, Israel, China, and Abenaki culture. Yolen includes thorough and interesting source notes.

Kathy Henderson, author of *Lugalbanda: The Boy Who Got Caught Up in a War* (2006), contends that this story is older than the Torah, the Bible, the Koran, and the Greek and Roman myths. The tale is based on clay tablets found 150 years ago whose translation was only recently completed. Lugalbanda is identified as the father of Gilgamesh. This 80-page version, illustrated by Jane Ray, tells this very old tale in a way that is accessible for a young adult audience.

Latin American Folktales: Stories from Hispanic and Indian Traditions (Bierhorst, 2002) is an impressive collection of 115 stories. "The stories represent the folktale traditions of Spanish-speaking America set within a frame of American Indian lore" (p. xi). The book includes folk tales, riddles, elements of prayer and song, and a glossary of native culture.

Virginia Hamilton's book *The People Could Fly: American Black Folktales,* illustrated by Leo and Diane Dillon (1985), is a collection of retold tales that captures the voices of African Americans in slavery. This much-honored book has received the Coretta Scott King Award, National Council of Teachers of English Choice Award, *School Library Journal* Best Book of the Year, and the *New York Times* Best Illustrated Book Award.

Retellings and Reinventions of Fairy Tales and Folk Tales

Novels based on traditional tales always go beyond simple retelling. The longer format allows authors to dispel stereotypes common in fairy tales and folk tales to create well-rounded characters with complex motivations and interior conflicts. Storylines in reinventions can include subplots and other expansions of detail, and settings can include historical and cultural details that add depth and color to the story. One of the most prolific authors of novels that reinvent traditional tales is Donna Jo Napoli, who is the featured author for this chapter.

As they are handed down over many generations, fairy tales and folk tales distill important cultural assumptions and values about social class, gender roles, and standards of honorable behavior that are being challenged in contemporary society. The idea that finding a prince is the same as finding happiness or that all dragons must be slain is woven into the stories that most young adults grew up with. From a critical literacy perspective, contemporary reinventions are a way to pull these cultural threads out of the cloth for closer inspection.

Critical literacy and contemporary reinventions

The cross-cultural twist that Napoli uses in *Beast* (2000) was also used by Patricia Santos Marcantonio in *Red Ridin' in the Hood and Other Cuentos* (2005), which infuses a Latino flavor to eleven classic European folk tales. Illustrated by Renato Alarcaeo, the collection presents middle grade readers with reversals of both class and gender. Like Napoli's *Spinners* (1999), Schmidt's *Straw into Gold* (2001), provides background information that explains, Rumpelstiltskin's motivations. Although he has his faults, as the protagonist of the story, Rumpelstiltskin is reinvented as a loving, loyal, and devoted father. Unlike the traditional version of this tale, he is not foiled by the Queen guessing his name. Instead, he is instrumental in helping the Queen to recover her lost son.

Francesca Lia Block's *The Rose and the Beast: Fairy Tales Retold* (2000) contains nine short adaptations for the mature reader. All the stories are told from a female perspective, and the one-word title of each story, such as Snow, Charm, Beast, and Wolf, connotes the original fairy tale. The modern settings for these tales are usually locations in California, such as Los Angeles, Laurel Canyon,

Donna Jo Napoli

Donna Jo Napoli, a professor of linguistics, published her first young adult novel, *The Magic Circle,* a twist on the Hansel and Gretel story, in 1993. The impetus for the story was a question by one of her children about why there are so many mean women in fairy tales (Notable Biographies, n.d.). Over the years, Napoli has revisited the notion of evil in many of her retold traditional tales. She says, "fairy tales deal with the evil that we know exists inside us and outside us" (Young Adult Books Central, n.d.). In her novels, characters often experience great suffering, sometimes as a result of uncontrollable evil forces, but often as a result of human faults and weaknesses.

The physical and psychological suffering experienced by the protagonist in *The Wager* (2010), a story based on an old Sicilian fairy tale, is difficult to imagine. The core of the tale remains intact: A once wealthy young man makes a pact with the devil; for three years, three months, and three days he will not wash. If Giovanni keeps this bargain he will have uncountable wealth for the rest of his life. The book explicitly describes his suffering, the decaying and putrefaction of his unwashed body, and the fragility of his mental state. He encounters a young boy, a portrait artist who is not repulsed by his odor and appearance. The artist is actually a young girl, disguised so that she can pursue her passion for a profession considered unacceptable for women. Mimi, the artist, and Don Giovanni achieve a fairy tale happy ending because of his transformation from a self-indulgent young adolescent to a caring, self-aware man.

Napoli's narratives often "give voice and perspective to those who have generally been considered as the Other in traditional fairy tales" (Crew, 2002, p. 78). Her witches are evil; they make poor and misguided choices, but they also solicit pity and understanding. She gives her characters a story of their own, stories that help explain their desperation, transformation and occasionally, forgiveness and acceptance.

The Magic Circle (1993) is a prequel to Hansel and Gretel. Napoli explores how the witch, the Ugly One, comes to live in the little cottage in the woods. The story begins with a hunchbacked midwife, content to bring babies into the world and care for her own daughter. She gladly lives this simple life until she desires more riches for her daughter. She makes a bargain with a devil to expand her healing powers, for which she will be well paid. For a while, she lives a pious life devoted to healing, but an evil trick transforms her from good sorceress into evil witch.

She knows that she must remove herself from evil temptations, for it is the nature of witches to eat children. The abandoned Hansel and Gretel find her cottage in the woods and she takes them in. She cannot stop the evil voices in her head. The witch sees death as the only way to end her suffering and reunite with God. She beckons Gretel to push her in the oven. The religious overtones fit well with the medieval time period, blurring the line between Christian and pagan traditions and softening the witchcraft theme, which makes the alternative ending plausible.

Spinners (1999), a retelling of Rumpelstiltskin by Napoli and Richard Tchen, explains the ugly little man's side of the story. *Spinners* has all the components of the familiar folk tale: the greedy king who demands that the miller's beautiful daughter spin straw into gold, and the repulsive deal maker who spins the gold for her in return for her first born. The unexpected twist is that the child Rumpelstiltskin wishes to steal is his own grandchild. This rendition of the tale provides the background of how a young man, passionately in love with a beautiful young woman, commits a wrong that destroys his body and her love. Napoli gives an identity to a man who has become, as his name indicates, a rumpled, deformed little man. *Spinners* also explores the choices made by desperate women trying to survive in a culture that does not value them.

Napoli occasionally places her stories in settings that necessitate cultural and historical explanations. She says, "I tried hard to give my readers other places—to let them experience via my stories cultures and lands that they might not be able to experience otherwise—to give them what I sought in books" (Notable Biographies, n.d). *Bound* (2004), for instance, preserves familiar aspects of the traditional Cinderella tale, but it is set in China during the Ming Dynasty. The story includes details of the era regarding medicine, ancestor worship, manifestation of spirits, foot binding, and the disposability of girls. Most importantly, the book explores the constraints, or bounds, of tradition and convention on women.

Most young adults will not be familiar with the Icelandic folk tale that inspired *Hush* (2007), a tale of a medieval Irish princess captured by slavers. The students' lack of intertextual connections will not matter in this detailed and descriptive story. A map provides context by tracing the route of the ship that takes Melkorka away. After she is captured, Melkorka realizes that her voice will reveal her highborn status so she chooses to remain silent. The story is told in first person, restricting the narration to what Melkorka experiences and thinks. The story shows how slavery was part of many cultures at the time including Irish, Viking, Russian, and Arabic. The antislavery theme verges on the didactic, but given the barbaric treatment of enslaved people at this time, Napoli's story recreates a plausible folk tale within the historical period.

Napoli states that she selects settings as "ways to tighten the screws" to intensify the situation (Reading Rocks, 2009). This is evident in *Beast* (2000), a Beauty and the Beast story set in Persia. Prince Orasmyn is turned into a lion after he fails to follow a Persian custom that protects animals that have suffered at the hand of man. Napoli deliberately chose a setting—a Muslim country where people do not eat bloody meat—to intensify the horror of Orasmyn being turned into a beast of prey (Reading Rocks, 2009).

Much of the story is about Orasmyn's psychological and physical journeys, told in first person as he travels from Persia to India and France. His human thoughts, in particular the tenets of Islam, conflict with the beastly acts of his lion body, which include eating raw meat and mating. In Southern France he finds an abandoned castle, replete with garden and roses. When he meets Belle, the possibility of an end to the curse surfaces. He speaks many languages, but his only means of communicating is to scratch words in the dirt. Gradually, he and Belle bond over ancient texts she reads to him. The curse is broken when she declares her love for Orasmyn. He vows his gratitude to the Merciful One, and their tears make a pool in his honor. This closure blends human and religious love and devotion.

These are only a few of the novels Napoli has based on traditional tales. The reading levels and conceptual difficulties of her works vary, but they work well for exploring the genre of traditional literature and the choices a writer makes when re-envisioning familiar tales. They also incorporate metafictive devices and other literary elements. Hillary S. Crew's *Donna Jo Napoli: Writing with Passion* (2010) is an excellent resource for examining Napoli's work.

and the San Fernando Valley, places that suggest wealth, beautiful people, and fast living. The characters often face the most negative aspects of contemporary society. For example, Red Riding Hood kills Wolf, a child molester and wife beater. Charm pricks herself with a heroin needle, and Snow is brought out of a coma by an inappropriate kiss from her stepfather.

Ella Enchanted (Levine, 1999) questions what it means to be a "good little girl" and how the unquestioning obedience of childhood must be left behind on the road to adulthood. At birth Ella is cursed by a well-meaning fairy who gives her the gift of obedience. Anything she is told to do, she must do. Her mother helped protect her against the spell, but when her mother dies and her father remarries, Ella is placed in a precarious situation. Before long her stepsisters find out about the spell and use it to their advantage. Rather than waiting for a fairy godmother, Ella embarks on a quest to free herself of the spell. She eventually finds her Prince Charming, but her "happily-ever-after" stems from taking control of her life and breaking the childhood curse herself.

Metafictive devices in reinventions

Many reinventions of traditional tales experiment with form as well as content by employing one or more metafictive devices, especially intertextuality. *Briar Rose* (Yolen, 1992) is a metafictive novel that breaks the conventions of storytelling in a complex narrative that blends fantasy, contemporary life, and history.

Initially written and published as an adult book in 1992, it was reissued as a novel for young adults in 2002 as part of a fairy tales series created by Terri Windling. In this story, Becca, a contemporary young woman, has grown up with her sisters listening to their grandmother's version of *Briar Rose*. The grandmother tells the story one last time on her deathbed, making Becca promise to learn all she can of the grandmother's past.

Becca travels to Poland and discovers her grandmother's connection to the horrors of World War II. Thought to be dead, Becca's grandmother was thrown into a pit of corpses. A group of refugees discovered her and gave her CPR, the "kiss of life." Becca comes to realize how her grandmother merged images from the traditional Sleeping Beauty story (the deep sleep, the awakening kiss, the wall of thorns, and the castle) with elements of her Holocaust experience (her near death, CPR, a barbed wire fence, the extermination camp) in order to tell her story in a way that was psychologically safe for herself and her family. She passed her history to her granddaughter to ensure that neither the family history nor the horrors of the Holocaust would be forgotten.

It is not too great an exaggeration to say that retelling and reinventing fairy tales has become a major trend in literature for young adults. The following box provides some additions to the many examples we have already presented.

a sample

. . . OF RETOLD AND REINVENTED **FAIRY TALES**

Beastly. Alex Flinn, 2007. Kyle Kingsbury is the big man on campus at his private Manhattan school, but he is also a cruel snob. He crosses Goth girl Kendra and finds himself turned into a beast. The curse is only reversed if someone loves and kisses Kyle. Ages 14 and up.

Fairest. Gail Carson Levine, 2006. Aza is awkward and homely, but she sings beautifully and can manipulate, or throw, her voice. Singing is prized in the kingdom, so the new queen forces Aza to throw her voice and make it look as if the queen were singing. The ruse is discovered and Aza flees. Through her adventures she discovers her own strength of character, learns about her true heritage, and decides that her physical appearance is not important. Ages 8–14.

Mira, Mirror. Mette Ivie Harrison, 2004. Mira is apprenticed to a witch and bonds with another beautiful young apprentice whom she thinks of as a sister. The girl, however, uses Mira to make herself beautiful, eventually turning Mira into a mirror. Ages 13 and up.

Spindle's End. Robin McKinley, 2000. In this version of the Sleeping Beauty tale, Rosie is taken into hiding by a peasant fairy who raises her and conceals her royal identity. On her fateful birthday, Rosie saves herself and her sleeping village, but not without a price. Ages 12 and up.

A Wolf at the Door: And Other Retold Fairy Tales. Ellen Datlow (Editor) & Terri Windling, (Author), 2001. This book revisits familiar and lesser known stories and includes diversity of content, style, and tone. These stories encourage readers to think a bit more about fairy tales and what they may be saying to and about people. Ages 11–15.

Teaching Ideas ■ FOLK TALES AND FAIRY TALES

At first glance, folk tales and fairy tales may not seem to have a place in a literature program for young adults, but many of these stories play a central role in the early literacy career of young adults and continue to resonate for students as they mature. Folk tales and their reinventions may be particularly valuable as points of comparison, either between traditional and contemporary life or between different modes and strategies for storytelling. In Chapter 3, we introduced the concept of bridging as a way to foster intertextual connections. The following classroom activities suggest ways to apply bridging to folk and fairy tales.

Bridging to more complex texts. In its classic form, bridging uses simple or conventional texts to prepare students to engage with works that are longer, more complex, or further from their previous experience. A progression of texts, such as the one using retellings and reinventions of Rapunzel that appeared earlier in this chapter, could be used to transition students from easy and familiar picture books and popular media toward works that incorporate sophisticated metafictive techniques and foster critical literacy discussions.

Bridging by author. The discussion of Napoli's works in this chapter can serve as a model for studying an author who reinvents traditional tales. The study can include highlighting particular techniques the author employs and drawing conclusions about the themes the author develops through the reinvention process. Possible authors include Jane Yolen, Nancy Springer, Gail Levine, and, for older students, Francesca Lia Block.

Bridging from media. The Walt Disney Studios were built in large part on animated features that retold traditional fairy tales. Comparing the version of a story published by the Brothers Grimm with the version produced by Disney provides an opportunity for students to engage in critical media literacy as they discuss what the animated version added, what it removed, and what might have motivated those changes. Even though Disney films were made primarily (but not exclusively) for children, they can still be used to address critical issues. Questions to guide this activity may include, "What assumptions does this film make about its audience?" and "What effect might this film have on the audience's values and beliefs about themselves and their society?"

Bridging between variants. Traditional tales may not be a source for understanding modern societies, but examining variants of a single tale can help students identify the elements that distinguish various cultures. Variants of Cinderella work well for this activity because they are particularly numerous and varied, *Mufaro's Beautiful Daughters* (Steptoe, 1987), for instance, allows students to make observations about the customs, work, and daily routines of village life in Africa, and *The Egyptian Cinderella* (Climo, 1989, illustrated by Ruth Heller) includes an appearance by the god Horus and the illustrations indicative of Egyptian art. It also highlights a little known aspect of Egyptian history by portraying the Cinderella character as a Greek girl who is a slave to the Egyptians. Variants from around the world are annotated on the American Library

Association website (www.ala.org/ala/aboutala/ofices/publishing/booklinks/resources/multicultural.cfm).

Students can work in groups to compare and contrast multiple variants with a focus on cultural elements, such as the roles of parents and stepparents, sibling relationships, courtship and marriage, and the differing responsibilities of male and female children. The "test" that Cinderella passes to establish that she should be the chosen bride, for instance, may indicate which characteristics of women were valued in a particular culture.

Bridging to writing. One of the surest ways to become more aware of the conventions of a genre is to create an original text in that genre. Students can learn a great deal about both the conventions of traditional folk tales and fairy tales and about modern reinventions by choosing a folk tale or fairy tale to reinvent. They can use a chart like the one in Figure 6.1 to consider the alterations they can make in form and content, although the chart may need to be simplified for younger writers. Or, students may learn just as much by creating a graphic novel, play, or short film. They might also create a parody of the traditional story along the lines of *The True Story of the Three Little Pigs* (Scieszka, 1989).

conclusion

Students' appreciation for all literature can be enhanced by reading, viewing, and telling tales that originate in the oral tradition. Revisiting traditional stories allows young adult readers to see how this literature reflects enduring human concerns and also to consider how the language and structure of literature changes over time. Reading reinvented tales, especially those created with a young adult audience in mind, allows readers to look more deeply at the cultural values and beliefs those stories convey and to consider the influence such stories have had on their own perception about the world.

In commenting on Block's reinvented stories, David Russell (2002) suggests that the appeal of her work lies in the way they become bridges between childhood and adulthood—just as adolescence itself is a bridge:

> Block's tales are tales of loss—the loss of parents, the loss of virginity, the loss of innocence—and of recovery. Because these losses most frequently occur during adolescence, Block's transformations become especially suited to the adolescent reader. They are tales of self-discovery and self-actualization, and this of course, is an abiding theme of adolescence. Block's stories are wrapped in surreal enchantment and, at times, luminous perplexity, which for better or worse captures the mystery and confusion so characteristic of the adolescent years. (p. 108)

BIBLIOGRAPHY OF LITERATURE FOR YOUNG ADULTS

Barron, T. A. (1996). *The lost years of Merlin epic: The lost years of Merlin.* New York: Philomel.

Bearnard, J. (1993). *Big men, big country.* New York: Harcourt.

Bierhost, J. (2002). *Latin American folktales: Stories from Hispanic and Indian traditions.* New York: Pantheon.

Block, F. L. (2000). *The rose and the beast: Fairy tales retold.* New York: HarperTeen.

Block, F. L. (2006). *Psyche in a dress.* New York: Joanna Colter Books, HarperCollins.

Cadnum, M. (2002). *Forbidden forest: The story of Little John and Robin Hood.* New York: Orchard Books.

Cadnum, M. (2004). *Starfall: Phaeton and the chariot of the sun.* New York: Scholastic Orchard.

Cadnum, M. (2006). *Nightsong: The legend of Orpheus and Eurydice.* New York: Orchard Books.

Childs, T. L. (2008). *Oh.my.gods.* New York: Penguin.

Clark, E. (1988). The origin of stories. In R. Hanna & S. Martin (Eds.), *The Canadian Children's Treasury.* Toronto, ON: Key Porter Books.

Climo, S. (1989). *The Egyptian Cinderella.* (R. Heller., Illus.). New York: Crowel.

Cooney, C. B. (2002). *Goddess of yesterday.* New York: Delacorte.

Curtiz, M., & Keighley, W. (Dirs.). (1938). *Robin Hood.* U.S.A.: Warner Brothers.

DeMille, C. B. (Dir.). (1956). *The ten commandments.* U.S.A.: Paramount.

Deming, S. (2007). *Iris, messenger.* New York: Harcourt.

Datlow, E., & Windling, T. (2001). *A wolf at the door and other retold fairy tales.* New York: Aladdin.

Dwan, A. (Dir.). (1922) *Robin Hood.* U.S.A.: Douglas Fairbanks Productions.

Flinn, A. (2007). *Beastly.* New York: HarperTeen.

Geras, A. (2006). *Ithaka.* New York: Harcourt.

Greno, N., & Howard, B. (Dirs.). (2010). *Tangled.* U.S.A.: Disney.

Gutman, D. (1999). *Jackie and me.* "Baseball card adventures" series. New York: HarperCollins.

Gutman, D. (2003). *Shoeless Joe & me.* "Baseball card adventures" series. New York: HarperCollins.

Hale, S., & Hale, N. (2008). *Rapunzel's revenge.* New York: Bloomsbury.

Hamilton, V. (1985). *The people could fly: American black folktales.* (L. Dillon & D. Dillon, Illus.). New York: Knopf.

Hamilton, V. (1988). *In the beginning: Creation stories from around the world.* (B. Moser, Illus.). New York: Harcourt, Brace.

Harrison, M. I. (2004). *Mira, mirror.* New York: Puffin.

Heaney, S. (2000). *Beowulf: A new verse translation.* New York: Farrar, Straus & Giroux.

Henderson, K. (2006). *Lugalbanda: The boy who got caught up in a war.* (J. Ray, Illus.). Cambridge, MA: Candlewick Press.

Hennesy, C. (2008). *Pandora gets jealous.* New York: Bloomsbury.

Hinds, G. (2007). *Beowulf: The graphic novel.* Cambridge, MA: Candlewick Press.

Holmes, S. L. (2007). *Letters from Rapunzel.* New York: HarperCollins.

Homer, (1963). *The Odyssey.* (R. Fitzgerald, Trans.). New York: Doubleday.

Homer, (1999). *Iliad.* (A. T. Murray, Trans.). Cambridge, MA: Harvard University Press.

Homer, (2000). *The Odyssey.* (S. Lombardo, Trans.). Indianapolis, IN: Hackett Publishing.

Isaacs, A. (1994). *Swamp angel.* (P. O. Zelinsky, Illus.). New York: Dutton Children's Books.

Jolley, D. (2008). *Odysseus: Escaping Poseidon's curse: A Greek legend.* (T. Yeates, Illus.). Minneapolis, MN: Graphic Universe.

Kudlinski, K. V. (2006). *My lady Pocahontas.* New York: Marshall Cavendish.

Lalicki, T. (2007). *Shots at sea: A Houdini and Nate mystery.* New York: Farrar, Straus & Giroux.

Lester, J. (2007). *Cupid.* New York: Harcourt.

Levine, G. C. (1999). *Ella enchanted.* New York: HarperCollins.

Levine, G. C. (2006). *Fairest.* New York: HarperCollins.

Limke, J. (2008). *Theseus: Battling the Minotaur.* (J. McCrea, Illus.). Minneapolis, MN: Graphic Universe.

Longfellow H. W. (1990). *Paul Revere's ride.* (T. Rand, Illus.). New York: Dutton Children's Books.

Malory, T. (1999). *Le Morte d' Arthur.* New York: Modern Library.

Marcantonio, P. S. (2005). *Red Ridin' in the hood and other cuentos.* New York: Farrar, Straus & Giroux.

McCaughrean, G. (2002). *Gilgamesh the hero.* Grand Rapids, MI: Eerdmans.

McCaughrean, G. (2004). *Odysseus.* Peru, IL: Cricket Books.

McCaughrean, G. (2005). *Hercules.* Peru, IL: Cricket Books.

McCaughrean, G. (2005). *Perseus.* Peru, IL: Cricket Books.

McCaughrean, G. (2005). *Theseus.* Peru, IL: Cricket Books.

McKinley, R. (2000). *Spindle's end.* New York: Puffin.

McLaren, C. (2000). *Waiting for Odysseus.* New York: Atheneum.

McLaren, C. (2002). *Aphrodite's blessings: Love stories from Greek myths.* New York: Simon & Schuster/Atheneum.

Myers, C. (2005). *Lies and other tall tales.* Adapted from Zora Neale Hurston. New York: HarperCollins.

Napoli, D. J. (1993). *The magic circle.* New York: Puffin.

Napoli, D. J. (1996). *Zel.* New York: Puffin.

Napoli, D. J. (2000). *Beast.* New York: Simon Pulse.

Napoli, D. J. (2003). *The great god Pan.* New York: Wendy Lamb.

Napoli, D. J. (2004). *Bound.* New York: Atheneum.

Napoli, D. J. (2007). *Hush.* New York: Simon Pulse.

Napoli, D. J. (2010). *The wager.* New York: Holt.

Napoli, D. J., & Tchen, R. (1999). *Spinners*. New York: Puffin.

Ondaatje, M. (1996). *The collected works of Billy the Kid*. New York: Random House.

Osborne, M. P. (1991). *American tall tales*. New York: Knopf.

Paterson, L. (2000). *Parzival: The quest of the grail knight*. New York: Penguin.

Peck, R. (2001). *Fair weather*. New York: Dial.

Peterson, W. (Dir.). (2004). *Troy*. U.S.A.: Warner Brothers.

Raven, N. (2007). *Beowulf: A tale of blood, heat, and ashes*. (J. Howe, Illus.). Cambridge, MA: Candlewick Press.

Reitherman, W. (Dir.) (1963). *The sword in the stone*. U.S.A.: Disney.

Reynolds, K. (Dir.). (1991). *Robin Hood, prince of thieves*. U.S.A.: Warner Brothers.

Riordan, R. (2005). *The lightning thief*. New York: Miramax Books.

Roberts, L. (2003). *Rapunzel: A groovy fairy tale*. (D. Roberts, Illus.). New York: Abrams.

Robinson, P. A. (Dir.). (1989). *Field of dreams*. U.S.A.: Universal.

San Souci, R. D. (1991). *Larger than life: The adventures of American legendary heroes*. (A. Glass, Illus.). New York: Doubleday.

San Souci, R. D. (1993). *Cut from the same cloth: American women of myth, legend, and tall tale*. (B. Pinkney, Illus.). New York: Philomel.

Schlesinger Media. (2005). *Greek mythology for students* [DVD]. Wynnewood, PA: Library Video.

Scieszka, J. (1989). *The true story of the three little pigs*. (L. Smith, Illus.). New York: Viking.

Schmidt, G. (2001). *Straw into gold*. New York: Clarion.

Scott, M. (2009). *The sorceress: Secrets of the immortal Nicholas Flamel*. New York: Random House.

Scott, R. (Dir.). (2010). *Robin Hood*. U.S.A.: Universal.

Springer, N. (2002). *I am Mordred: A tale from Camelot*. New York: Penguin.

Springer, N. (2002). *Rowan Hood: Outlaw girl of Sherwood Forest*. New York: Putnam.

Springer, N. (2004). *Lionclaw: A tale of Rowan Hood*. New York: Puffin.

Springer, N. (2005). *Wild boy, a tale of Rowan*. New York: Puffin.

Stashower, D. (2000). *The floating lady murder: A Harry Houdini mystery*. New York: Avon.

Steptoe, J. (1987). *Mufaro's beautiful daughters: An African tale*. New York: Lothrop, Lee & Shepard.

Storrie, P. D. (2007). *Hercules: The twelve labors*. (S. Kurth, Illus.). Minneapolis, MN: Graphic Universe.

Storrie, P. D. (2007). *Robin Hood: Outlaw of Sherwood Forest* [electronic graphic novel]. NetLibrary. Access: http://www.powells.com/biblio/9780822587934.

Storrie, P. D. (2008). *Perseus: The hunt for Medusa's Head*. (T. Yeates, Illus.). Minneapolis, MN: Graphic Universe.

Storrie, P. D. (2008). *Beowulf: Monster slayer, a British legend*. (R. Randall, Illus.). Minneapolis, MN: Lerner Publishing.

Taylor, T. (2005). *Billy the Kid*. New York: Harcourt.

Tchana, K. H. (2006). *Changing woman and her sisters: Stories of goddesses from around the world*. (T. Schart Hyman, Illus.). New York: Holiday House.

Ursu, A. (2006). *The shadow thieves*. New York: Atheneum.

White, T. H. (1958). *The once and future king*. New York: Putnam.

White, T. H. (Author), and Jason, N. (Narrator). (2008). *The sword in the stone* [audiobook]. London: Naxos AudioBooks.

Yolen, J. (1992). *Briar rose*. New York: Tor/Tom Doherty.

Yolen, J. (1996). *Passenger: The young Merlin trilogy*. New York: Harcourt, Brace.

Yolen, J. (2003). *Mightier than the sword: World folktales for strong boys*. (R. Colon, Illus.). Orlando, FL: Silver Whistle/Harcourt Brace.

Young, R. (Dir.). (2005). *Hercules*. [television miniseries]. U.S.A.: Hallmark Entertainment.

Zelinsky, P. O. (1997). *Rapunzel*. New York: Puffin.

Zemeckis, R. (Dir.). (2007). *Beowulf*. U.S.A.: Paramount.

WEBSITES WITH ANNOTATIONS

American Folklore Society • **www.afsnet.org/**
Resources for educators about oral storytelling and folklore tradition.

Journey Through Time • **www.sherwoodforest.org.uk**
Ideas for projects related to English history.

Napoli, Donna Jo • *www.donnajonapoli.com/*
The author's official website, including summaries of works and author interviews.

National Storytelling Network • **http://storynet.org/**
Resources for educators about oral storytelling and folklore tradition.

REFERENCES

Altmann, A. E., & de Vos, G. (2001). *Tales, then and now: More folktales as literary fictions for young adults.* Englewood, CO: Libraries Unlimited, Greenwood.

Armstrong, K. (2005). *Short history of myth.* Edinburgh, Scotland: Canongate.

Ashliman, D. L. (2007). Rapunzel by Jacob and Wilhelm Grimm: A comparison of the versions of 1812 and 1857. Retrieved from http://www.pitt.edu/~dash/grimm012a.html.

Bettelheim, B. (1976). *The uses of enchantment: The meaning and importance of fairy tales.* New York: Knopf.

Brown, C. S. (1987). *The tall tale in American folklore and literature.* Knoxville, TN: University of Tennessee Press.

Brunvand, J. H. (2000). *Too good to be true: The colossal book of urban legends.* New York: Norton.

Budin, M. L. (2006). Review of *Psyche in a dress. School Library Journal,* 52(8), 114–115.

Cart, M. (2006). The Camelot connection, *Booklist,* 102(18), 42.

Cavendish, R. (Ed.). (1980). *Mythology: An illustrated encyclopedia.* New York: Rizzoli.

Corliss, R. (2010, November 26). *Tangled:* Disney's Ripping Rapunzel. *Time.* Retrieved from http://www.time.com/time/arts/article/0,8599,2033166,00.html.

Coulter, C. R., & Turner, P. (2000). *Encyclopedia of ancient deities.* Jefferson, NC: McFarland & Company.

Crew, H. S. (2002). Spinning new tales from traditional texts: Donna Jo Napoli and the rewriting of fairy tale. *Children's Literature in Education,* 33(2), 77–95.

Crew, H. S. (2010). *Donna Jo Napoli: Writing with passion.* Lanham, MD: Scarecrow Press.

Davis, K. C. (2005). *Don't know much about mythology: Everything you need to know about the greatest stories in human history but never learned.* New York: HarperCollins.

de Vos, G., & Altmann, A. E. (1999). *New tales for old: Folktales as literary fictions for young adults.* Englewood, CO: Libraries Unlimited.

Grimal, P. (1996). *The dictionary of classical mythology.* Oxford, UK: Blackwell.

Haase, D. (Ed.). (2008). *The Greenwood encyclopedia of folktales and fairy tales.* Westport, CT: Greenwood Press, 2008.

Helbig, A. K., & Perkins, A. R. (1997). *Myths and hero tales: A cross-cultural guide to literature for children and young adults.* Westport, CT: Greenwood Press.

Hendrickson, L. (2000). The view from Rapunzel's tower. *Children's Literature in Education,* 31(4), 209–223.

Inglis, I. (2007). Sex and drugs and rock'n'roll: Urban legends and popular music. *Popular Music and Society,* 30(5), 591–603.

Kennedy, X. J., Gioia, D., & Bauerlein, M. (2006). *The Longman dictionary of literary terms.* New York: Pearson/Longman.

Kluger, R. S. (1991) *The archetypal significance of Gilgamesh: A modern ancient hero.* Einsiedeln, Switzerland, Daimon Verlag.

Lechner, J. V. (2004). *Allyn & Bacon anthology of traditional literature.* Boston, MA: Pearson.

Leeming, D. (2002). *Myth: A biography of belief.* New York: Oxford University Press.

Leitch, T. (2008). Adaptations without sources: The adventures of Robin Hood. *Literature Film Quarterly* 36(1), 21–30.

Mikkelson, D. P., and Mikkelson, B. (2007). The vanishing hitchhiker. *Urban Legends Reference Pages.* Retrieved from www.snopes.com/horrors/ghosts/vanish.asp.

Notable Biographies. (n.d.). Napoli, Donna Jo. Retrieved from www.notablebiographies.com/news/Li-Ou/Napoli-Donna-Jo.html.

Reading Rocks. (2009). An interview with author Donna Jo Napoli. Retrieved from www.readingrocks4me.com/2009/04/interview-with-author-donna-jo-napoli.html.

Russell, D. L. (2002). Young adult fairy tales for the new age: Francesca Lia Block's *The Rose and the Beast. Children's Literature in Education,* 33(2), 107–115.

Seale, D., & Slapin, B. (Eds.). (2005). *A broken flute: The native experience in books for children.* Lanham, MD: AltaMira Press.

Sienkewicz, T. J. (1996). *World mythology: An annotated guide to collections and anthologies.* Lanham, MD: Scarecrow Press, 1996.

Stahl, J. D., Hanlon, T. L., & Keyser, E. L. (2007). *Crosscurrents of children's literature: An anthology of texts and criticism.* New York: Oxford University Press.

Willis, R. (Ed.). (1993). *World mythology.* New York: Holt.

Winters, C. J., & Schmidt, G. D. (2001). *Edging the boundaries of children's literature.* Needham Heights, MA: Allyn & Bacon.

Young Adult Books Central (n.d.). Interviews: Donna Jo Napoli. Retrieved from www.yabookscentral.com.cfusion/index.cfm?fuseAction=authors.interview&interview.

Young, T. S. (Ed.). (2004). *Happily ever after: Sharing folk literature with elementary and middle school students.* Newark, DE: International Reading Association.

Zipes, J. (1997). *Happily ever after: Fairy tales, children, and the culture industry.* New York: Routledge.

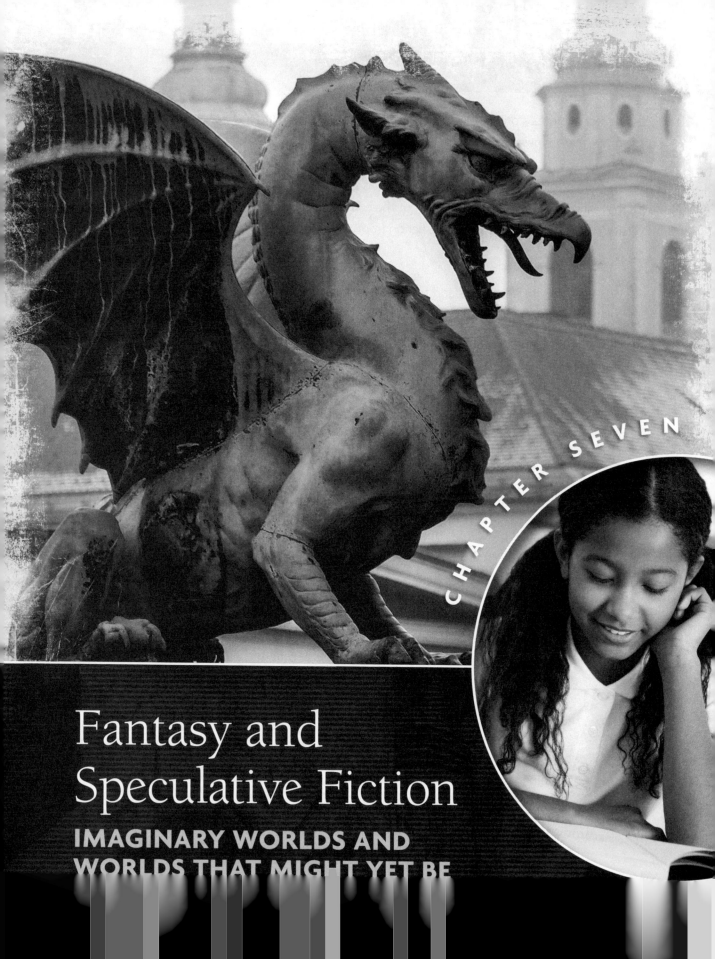

CHAPTER SEVEN

Fantasy and Speculative Fiction
IMAGINARY WORLDS AND WORLDS THAT MIGHT YET BE

chapter overview

This chapter explores stories set in imaginary worlds or peopled with imaginary beings. We identify some of the many types of fantasy literature that have emerged since the publication of J. R. R. Tolkien's *The Lord of the Rings* (1954a, 1954b, 1956) and discuss how fantasy stories can be used in the classroom. We also examine how science fiction, also known as speculative fiction, can help young adults engage with the real world by raising questions about the consequences of human actions. Finally, we explore diversity in both fantasy and speculative fiction from a critical literacy perspective.

FOCUS QUESTIONS

1. What are the characteristics and themes commonly found in fantasy literature?

2. Why is contemporary science fiction also known as speculative fiction?

3. How can teachers use fantasy and speculative fiction as part of a literature program for young adults?

introduction

The year 2001 was when Harry met Frodo—at least on movie screens—as both *Harry Potter and the Sorcerer's Stone* (Columbus, 2001) and *The Lord of the Rings: Fellowship of the Ring* (Jackson, 2001) premiered. The timing of the two films may have been coincidental, but it was also highly significant. *The Lord of the Rings*, first published in 1954, and J. K. Rowling's Harry Potter series, which concluded in 2007 with the publication of *The Deathly Hallows*, serve as bookends for an era in which fantasy literature, both in print and on screen, achieved unprecedented popularity, especially with young adults. Gilsdorf (2003) pointed out that Tolkien had sold at least 100 million books and the films of the *Lord of the Rings* trilogy were estimated in 2009 to have generated $6 billion in box office receipts, DVDs, and merchandise (Sims, 2009). Meanwhile, *Harry Potter and the Sorcerer's Stone* grossed $90 million on its opening weekend in the United States alone, and more than $900 million overall (Internet Movie Database, n.d.). J. K. Rowling was on her way to becoming the world's first billionaire author (Watson & Kellner, 2004).

The continuing appeal of science fiction is evident in the popularity of movies from *Frankenstein* (Whale, 1931) to *Avatar* (Cameron, 2009), which have entertained mass audiences while reflecting society's hopes and fears about science and technology. One of the most successful movie series of all time shows how fuzzy the dividing line between two genres can be. George Lucas's *Star Wars* (1977) combined the spaceships, futuristic weaponry, and interplanetary travel of science fiction with the fantasy genre's swords and sorcery in the form of light sabers and the mysterious Force.

Movies are, of course, only a small part of the huge body of fantasy and science fiction literature, but they provide the elements that make both genres attractive for young adults. As shown in Figure 7.1, both speculative fiction and fantasy allow a reader or viewer to explore other worlds. These imaginary landscapes are places into which young adults can escape while they are learning to see their own world more clearly and critically.

Exploring other worlds through fantasy and speculative fiction. *figure* **7.1**

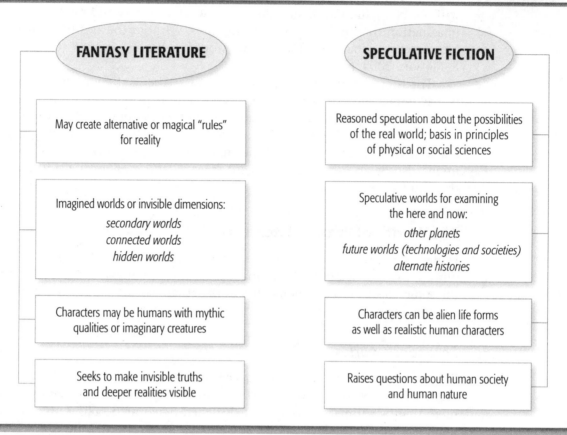

In this chapter we examine the different kinds of worlds created in classic and contemporary fantasy literature and identify some of the themes and motifs common to those genres. Then we discuss science fiction as one part of the broader category of speculative fiction, one that poses questions drawn from the social sciences as often as from astrophysics. Works of speculative fiction are grouped around the worlds they present as vantage points for examining the here and now. Throughout the chapter, we highlight diversity issues in fantasy and science fiction literature and suggest ways to use it in the classroom.

FANTASY: WORLDS THAT NEVER WERE

The simplest way to define **fantasy** literature is to say that it contains elements that are "nonexistent or unreal" and events that are influenced by "magic or the supernatural" (Lukens & Cline, 1995, p. 198), but the whole of a fantasy story is more than the sum of those elements. Gates, Steffel, and Molson (2003) note that the word *fantasy* comes from the Greek *phantasia*, which means "making visible" (p. 2), and they argue that the essential characteristic of fantasy as a genre is to create worlds that make truth and reality visible. "Fantasy is imaginative fiction that allows us to explore major life mysteries without being limited by size, time, or space. . . . Fantasy and myth nurture the imagination that fuels our creative impulses. Without the ability to 'make visible' something that does not exist, we would be limited indeed" (Gates, Steffel, & Molson, 2003, p. 2).

The literature included under the fantasy label is dizzying in its diversity. It may depict epic struggles between good and evil in an imaginary realm. It might also portray a teenager's awestruck exploration of a hidden world or the bond of friendship between a young adult and a dragon—or a vampire. The magic that influences fantasy stories may come from a ring or a wand, but it might also be an inborn talent, a gift from a god, or an arcane skill acquired through long years of study.

The Worlds of Fantasy Literature

Fantasy stories may create entirely new worlds, or they may highlight truths in our own world. We begin mapping the terrain of fantasy literature by grouping some classic and contemporary works of fantasy according to the kinds of imagined worlds they evoke.

Secondary worlds

While he was immersed in writing *The Lord of the Rings*, Tolkien described the process as one of "subcreation," and he argued that reading such stories required more than a willing suspension of disbelief. It required taking up temporary residence in a "secondary world," outside of space and time, and forgetting the existence of the primary world (Tolkien, 1966). The secondary world an author creates may be wildly fantastic, but it must be consistent and fully realized. No matter how vast their scope, these worlds are made believable in their small details, like a hobbit's furry feet or the owls swooping in to deliver the morning mail at Hogwarts. Although the works described below differ greatly, they all require multiple volumes to build their worlds.

The Chronicles of Narnia by C. S. Lewis has been many readers' introduction to fantasy literature. Like most secondary worlds, Narnia incorporates forests, mountains, and oceans that are much like those in the reader's primary world. Narnia is inhabited, however, by both humans and talking animals, the most notable of which is Aslan, an enormous and godlike talking lion. Narnia also includes creatures from other mythologies such as fauns and centaurs. Even Father Christmas makes an appearance.

In *The Lion, the Witch, and the Wardrobe* (1950), the first title in the series, the four children of the Pevensie family enter Narnia accidentally by passing through the back of an old wardrobe. They become kings and queens after helping to defeat the White Witch who wants to depose Aslan. In the following books, one or more of the Pevensie children must demonstrate loyalty and courage to protect Narnia. The stories also incorporate a great deal of the

Christian Bible, although not all readers notice. *The Lion, the Witch, and the Wardrobe* contains a close analogy to the death and resurrection of Jesus. *The Magician's Nephew* (1955) is a reworking of the creation story in Genesis, and *The Last Battle* (1956) echoes the Book of Revelation. Other books in the series are *Prince Caspian* (1951), *The Voyage of the Dawntreader* (1952), and *The Silver Chair* (1953).

The Wizard of Earthsea Trilogy by Ursula K. Le Guin, takes place in a world quite unlike Narnia, one without castles, princes, or mythological figures. Earthsea is a watery world; in fact, Dry Land is where Earthsea people go when they die. The center of this realm is a cluster of islands on the Inmost Sea. Four regions of scattered islands, known as Reaches, (North, South, East, and West) surround these central islands. The people of the Reaches are generally dark skinned, but the warlike inhabitants of the Karg Islands to the northeast are blond and fair skinned. Le Guin has stated (Martin, 2001) that she deliberately chose a Polynesian setting for her Earthsea series in order to counteract the prevailing tendency in fantasy literature to build imaginary worlds on a foundation of northern European myths.

Not surprisingly, boats and trade are a major part of life in this world of islands, so "weather mages," magicians who can calm storms or influence the wind, are always in demand. Magic in Earthsea is tied to nature but worked by words. Humans cannot lie in the Old Speech of Earthsea, so nature will conform to whatever a wizard states to be true in that language. If the wizard states that there is a wind from the southeast, a breeze will spring up in order to prevent the statement from becoming a falsehood. Language is power in another way as well. Speaking anyone's "true name" gives complete control over that person, so people reveal that name only to their closest friends and family. The true name of the trilogy's main character, for instance, is Ged, but his "use name" is Sparrowhawk.

In *A Wizard of Earthsea* (1968), the first book in the trilogy, Ged is a magical prodigy who becomes so arrogant that he carelessly lets an evil and destructive Shadow loose in Earthsea. After chasing the Shadow to the edge of the known world, Ged defeats it and goes on to become a legendary Archmage, chief among all of Earthsea's wizards. The second book in the series, *The Tombs of Atuan* (1970), won the Newbery Silver Medal, and the third book, *The Farthest Shore* (1972), won the National Book Award for Children's Books. In the climax of the latter book, Ged is able to cross over to the Dry Land and then return to the living. In doing so, however, he loses his magic forever.

His Dark Materials is a more recent trilogy by Philip Pullman that begins in an alternate version of Oxford, England, where people travel in zeppelins rather than airplanes and scientists understand particle physics. An even more striking difference from our world is that every human is bonded to a "daemon," a talking animal that embodies the person's soul. As Young (2008) points out: "Pullman excels at fleshing out his imagined universe with its unique technologies, its social rules (there is a strict taboo against touching another person's daemon), and its linguistic quirks (in Lyra's English chocolate is 'chocolatl' and electricity in 'anabaric power'" (unpaged).

In *The Golden Compass* (1996), the first book in the trilogy, 11-year-old Lyra Bellaqua embarks on a quest to the Arctic to rescue children who have been kidnapped on the orders of a powerful religious establishment called the Magisterium. They plan to preserve the children from sin by separating them from their daemons, a process that is agonizing and often fatal. Lyra is aided by nomadic

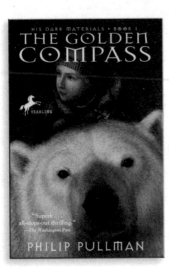

people known as "gyptians," as well as by flying witches and a talking armored bear named Iorek Byrnison, who becomes her champion. At the end of *The Golden Compass*, Lyra's estranged father, Lord Asriel, opens a rift to a parallel world by using the energy released when he separates one of Lyra's friends from his daemon.

The Subtle Knife (1997) expands Pullman's universe as Lyra and Will, a boy from our world, find a knife that can cut through anything, including the boundaries between universes. In *The Amber Spyglass* (Pullman, 2000), Lyra and Will lead the tormented souls of the dead out of the desolate Underworld and into the world of the living so they can dissolve and become one with the Universe. Eventually, Lyra and Will fulfill an ancient prophecy that says Lyra will be the new Eve and free humanity from the God-like "Authority" that the Magisterium serves.

Pullman has been called "the anti-Lewis" (Hitchens, 2002) for his atheism and his outspoken contempt of the Narnia stories. Chattaway (2007) notes that both Pullman's trilogy and the Narnia books include talking and protective animals and begin with a young girl hiding in a wardrobe. He points out, however, that Pullman's religious views directly oppose those of Lewis. The children in *The Chronicles of Narnia* willingly serve and obey Aslan, but Lyra and Will work with Lord Asriel to overthrow the Authority, an angel who claims to be the Creator. Despite their deep differences, however, Lewis and Pullman are tied together as creators of successfully realized imaginary worlds.

Connected worlds

The notion of another world that intersects with ours is a frequent motif in fantasy literature. Ordinary humans may find their way into these mysterious realms either by chance or by destiny. They may even find their way out. In *Coraline* by Neil Gaiman (2002), a literal doorway separates the safe but boring home of Coraline Jones from its evil clone. Coraline sees herself as an explorer, so despite several mysterious warnings from the other tenants in her rambling boardinghouse, she goes through the doorway. There she finds her "Other Mother," who tries to entice her to stay forever.

The Other Mother is revealed to be a powerful and sinister being called a "beldam." She has captured Coraline's parents and twisted the elements of her world into a grotesque alternate version in which the furniture looks the same but the people have black buttons for eyes. The beldam seeks to add Coraline to the three children whose souls she has already collected. In the end, Coraline leads her parents and the children down a horrible corridor that pulsates with evil and back through the door between worlds. The children are then able to move on into the afterlife.

The Graveyard Book (2008), another book by Neil Gaiman, also features a character who passes between two worlds. This Newbery Medal recipient is loosely based on *The Jungle Book* by Rudyard Kipling (1894). Instead of an orphan boy raised by animals in a jungle, though, the orphan Nobody Owens is raised in a graveyard by ghosts. He is protected by a guardian vampire until he grows old enough to identify his family's murderer and avenge their deaths. Nobody and his guardian both pass occasionally into the outside world where the inhabitants are unaware of the ghostly society in their midst.

The *Artemis Fowl* series by Eoin Colfer is notable for making fairies both contemporary and cool for a young adult audience. In the first book of the series, *Artemis Fowl* (2001), 12-year-old genius Artemis becomes convinced through extensive research that fairies are real, and he is determined to capture one as a means of extorting fairy gold. Artemis obtains a copy of "The Book," which contains the history of the fairies, sprites, and other creatures that have developed a technologically advanced civilization underground in order to avoid humans. It also contains all the rules by which fairies live.

Artemis and Butler, his massive bodyguard and valet, use the information in The Book to capture a fairy. Specifically, they capture Captain Holly Short, the first female fairy in the Lower Elements Police ever assigned to the Reconnaissance division, which makes her a member of "LEPrecon." As that pun suggests, the books do not take themselves too seriously, but they do show significant character development.

In books such as *The Arctic Incident* (2002) and *The Opal Deception* (2005), Artemis and Holly Short reluctantly team up to protect the Lower Elements while Artemis uses fairy magic and technology to locate his missing father and rebuild his family's fortunes. Artemis grows as a person as his unscrupulous genius is tempered by Holly's courage, skill, and devotion to duty. Colfer has also worked with author Andrew Donkin and illustrator Giovanni Rigano to create graphic novels of *Artemis Fowl* (2007) and *The Arctic Incident* (2009).

In the *Underland Chronicles*, Suzanne Collins creates a world that has existed beneath the streets of New York City since the 17th century. It was founded by a stonemason named Bartholomew Sandwich, who had a vision that told him life above ground would someday end. The Underland is markedly different from the Lower Elements of the Artemis Fowl books. It is a world inhabited both by the descendants of Bartholomew's 800 followers and by an array of giant sentient creatures ranging from "crawlers" (giant talking cockroaches) to "fliers" (giant bats that humans can ride). The humans can communicate telepathically with the bats, and the two sometimes form lifelong bonds.

The human city of Regalia is built of stone with a palace much like those found in other fantasy books, but it is a city where the sun never shines. In fact most of the Underland is in darkness and crisscrossed with tunnels. Many of the creatures have their own homelands, but there are also areas such as the volcanic Firelands, the deadly Jungle, and the desolate Deadlands that are virtually uninhabitable.

In *Gregor the Overlander* (2003), 11-year-old Gregor and his 2-year-old sister, Boots, fall through one of the five remaining gates into the Underworld, and he is identified as the warrior foretold in a prophecy. Gregor must learn the ways of this strange world while trying to protect Boots and find a way home. In the process, he unexpectedly finds his long-lost father, and the family is reunited. In subsequent books (Collins, 2004–2007), Gregor does, indeed, become a warrior with his own flier named Ares, and he and Luxa, the future queen of Regalia, fall in love. Gregor learns of additional prophecies as he and the other members of his family are repeatedly drawn into the problems of Underland, especially the humans' ongoing wars with the rats. In the last book, *Gregor and the Code of Claw* (2007), the rat leader, called The Bane, is overthrown, and peace is established.

One of the most notable fantasy series containing a permeable boundary between worlds is Cornelia Funke's *Inkheart* trilogy, which explores the line that separates reality and actual fiction. *Inkheart* (2003) begins with Meggie, who is 12 and has been living with her father, Mo, since her mother disappeared when she was three. Mo is a bookbinder who tells wonderful stories, but he will never read aloud to Meggie. She discovers this is because when Mo was reading aloud to her and her mother from a book called *Inkheart*, the beauty and power of his voice magically called the story's villains out of the book. Meggie's mother then vanished into the world of the book.

A fire-eater named Dustfinger was also called out of *Inkheart*, and he wants desperately for Mo to read him back into the book. Hounded by Dustfinger and the villains, Mo enlists the help of Fenoglio, the author of *Inkheart*. In the end Meggie's mother, Teresa, is restored to her family, Fenoglio is pulled into the world of his own book, and Dustfinger remains stranded in our world.

In the other two volumes of the story, *Inkspell* (2005) and *Inkdeath* (2008), Meggie, her family, and Dustfinger all find their way into the world of Fenoglio's book. There they marvel at the wonders of a realm inhabited by nymphs, brownies, and blue fairies, as well as tiny glassmen who serve as ink-stirrers and pen sharpeners for writers. Meggie and her family become allies of the Black Prince, a benign robber whose constant companion is a bear. They also learn firsthand the dangers and sorrows that lie beneath the surface of fantasy stories. Mo and Meggie fall into the clutches of the fearsome prince known as the Adder Head, and they are imprisoned in the Castle of Night. The way they manage their eventual release creates complications that ensnare every character living in the Inkworld.

The *Inkheart* series is a rich tale that raises fascinating questions about the nature of authorship and the power of stories to influence the real world, as Fenoglio struggles to maintain some control of the fantastic realm he has created. The story also explores the extent to which people can "write" their own destinies. In particular, the women in the story continually question how the male heroes of the story assign them the role of anxiously waiting at home. When Teresa finally rejects that role, her courage brings a resolution to the story.

Hidden worlds

In the Harry Potter books, wizards are aware of the Muggles, the non-magical people of the world, but only Muggles whose children have the gift of magic seem to be aware of witches and wizards. It is not until the fifth book of the series, *Harry Potter and the Order of the Phoenix* (Rowling, 2003), that readers discover the British prime minister is, in fact, in contact with the Minister of Magic. In addition to the Harry Potter series, many fantasy stories expose magical or monstrous beings that may live unnoticed among us. Some of these are discussed next.

The Dark Is Rising Sequence by Susan Cooper is anchored in the Thames Valley in the 20th century, but the action sometimes shifts backward in time or extends outside of ordinary time altogether. In Cooper's version of our world, the immortal Old Ones have been battling The Dark for thousands of years, and both sides sometimes draw ordinary mortals into their conflict. In *The Dark Is Rising* (1973), Will Stanton, while celebrating his 11th birthday, is beset by strange omens and confronted by a Dark Rider before he learns that he is actually the last of the Old Ones to come into the world.

Merriman Lyons, the first of the Old Ones, reveals to Will his newly awakened powers, including the ability to speak telepathically with other Old Ones and to snatch humans outside of time and hold them motionless. Will is given the task of traveling through time to seek six magical signs that will become weapons in the ultimate battle against the Dark. He is assisted by the other Old Ones and, occasionally, by other children. Merriman, who is strongly reminiscent of the wizard Merlin, is Will's constant guide.

The story becomes increasingly entwined with Celtic mythology and the legend of King Arthur. Merriman brings the Pendragon, Arthur's true son, forward in time, and he assumes the name Bran Davies. Will meets Bran in Wales, and the two work together to awaken ancient knights from Arthur's time to help them fight The Dark. When they win the battle, however, neither Bran nor any of the other children who were involved in the struggle clearly remember their part in it. *The Dark Is Rising* (1973) was a Newbery Honor book, and *The Grey King* (1975) was the winner of the Newbery Medal. The other books in the series are *The Greenwitch* (1974), *Over Sea, Under Stone* (1976), and *Silver On The Tree* (1977).

The Spiderwick Chronicles by Tony DiTerlizi and Holly Black, are all about hidden creatures in our world. In fact, the cover of the boxed set of the series (DiTerlizi & Black, 2004) warns "Their world is closer than you think." In the first book of the series, called *The Field Guide* (DiTerlizi & Black, 2003), 13-year-old Mallory Grace and her twin brothers, Jared and Simon, move into the rundown mansion owned by their Great Aunt Lucinda. In an old trunk, they find a field guide to fabulous creatures written by a Victorian gentleman named Arthur Spiderwick. Immediately, they become the targets of every goblin, troll, and ogre for miles around who all want to take the book and keep their existence a secret.

In the remaining books of the series (DiTerlizi & Black, 2004), the children acquire "The Sight," which allows them to see "faeries," and they discover, along with the reader, a whole menagerie of fabulous creatures. They rescue a griffin while fighting goblins. Jared is captured by elves and Mallory by dwarves. In the last two books, the children defeat Mulgareth, a horrible ogre who wants to rule the world. Because each novel in the series is approximately 100 pages long and contains an illustration every few pages, the series is appropriate for readers ages 9–12. Older readers might read all five books together as if they were a single work.

A secret war between powerful beings is raging in Jenny Nimmo's *Children of the Red King* series. In the first book in the saga, *Midnight for Charlie Bone* (2002), Charlie's father has disappeared, and he and his mother are living with his dreadful Grandma Bone and his reclusive Uncle Paton. Charlie seems perfectly ordinary until his 12th birthday, when he discovers that he has the ability to enter into photographs and talk with the people portrayed. He learns that he is one of the magical Red King's descendants, who all have unusual "endowments" but who have divided into two warring camps. Once his endowment appears, Charlie is sent to a weekday boarding school called Bloor's Academy, where many of the students have similar gifts, such as the ability to control the weather or to transform into a bird.

As the *Children of the Red King* series progresses (Nimmo, 2003–2006), Charlie acquires both friends and enemies at school. He and his friends investigate a series of mysteries concerning missing students and adults, including Charlie's father. They repeatedly hinder the schemes of a cruel group of students led by Manfred Bloor, who has the power to hypnotize anyone who looks into his eyes. Those students often follow the orders of Manfred's evil grandfather, Ezekiel Bloor. The endowed members of Charlie's family are as divided as his school. His Grandma Bone and her sisters are allied with the Bloor family, but his Uncle Paton, after years of seclusion in his room, begins to take an active role in opposing them.

The peculiar powers of the Red King's descendants are not confined to Bloor's Academy. Uncle Paton, for instance, is a "power booster" who often blows out the bulbs on streetlights when he passes by them. When necessary, Charlie's friend Tancrid, and his father brew up violent and highly noticeable storms. Still, most of the city's inhabitants find ways to explain away strange occurrences. They remain unaware of the small war that occasionally spills over into their streets.

Themes in Modern Fantasy

Examining imaginary worlds is one way to think about the rich and diverse genre of fantasy literature available to young adults. Another way is to identify plot elements and themes that occur repeatedly in the genre. Some of those themes are reviewed below.

Echoes of ancient epics

In the previous chapter, we described books for young adults that retold or reinvented ancient myths and epics, but modern fantasy includes works that echo the spirit and tone of ancient hero tales but create entirely new characters and often entirely new worlds. Shearin (2011) identifies these stories as "high fantasy" and describes their characteristics: "This subgenre is what the general population thinks of as fantasy. At its core is the battle between good and evil, and the stakes are high with specific races, civilization, or even the entire world at risk. High fantasy usually takes place in a quasi-medieval or Renaissance world. Quests and magic are an integral part of the plot" (p. 13).

Shearin (2011) notes that such stories could also be called **epic fantasy.** We prefer that label because it emphasizes both the broad scope of such stories and the conscious connection their authors often make to ancient hero stories. Between *The Lord of the Rings* (1954–1956) and *Harry Potter and the Sorcerer's Stone* (1998), a number of notable works fed readers' appetites for epic fantasy. *The Sword of Shannara* by Terry Brooks (1977), for instance, is set in a world 2,000 years after a nuclear war and incorporates many of the epic elements and plot devices of Tolkien's story (Attebery, 1980). In fact, Brooks' Shannara trilogy (1977, 1982, 1985) was both welcomed (Herbert, 1977) and criticized (Carter, 1978) for its similarity to *The Lord of the Rings.*

Another epic fantasy series is Lloyd Alexander's *Prydain Chronicles*. In *The Book of Three* (1964), the first book of the series, an orphan named Taran is a lowly assistant pig keeper for a wizard named Dalben. When Dalben's "oracular pig" inexplicably runs away, Taran goes in search of her. He soon finds himself fighting alongside his idol, Prince Gwydion, against Arawn, the Death-Lord who conjures undead armies out of a magical black cauldron. Despite his humble origins, Taran also establishes a friendship with Princess Eilonwy, a young sorceress, and he eventually falls in love with her.

By the end of the *Prydain Chronicles*, Taran has wielded the magical sword Dyrnwyn to vanquish the cauldron-born armies and to slay Arawn. As in *The Lord of the Rings*, victory signals the departure of all Prydain's magical people, including Prince Gwydion. A prophecy reveals Taran to be the rightful High King, and Eilonwy chooses to renounce magic and stay behind as his queen. *The Black Cauldron* (1965) was a Newbery Honor book, and *The High King* (1968) was the winner of the Newbery Medal. The other books in the series are *The Castle of Llyr* (1968) and *Taran Wanderer* (1967).

Like Taran, the hero of *The Blue Sword* (McKinley, 1982) is an orphan who is unexpectedly called to become warrior and is given a magical sword. The difference is that this hero is a young woman. This Newbery Honor book tells the story of Angharad Crewe, usually called Harry. Following the promptings of a mystical force, Harry learns the ways of the native people who are ignored or despised by her countrymen and becomes a member of the King's Guard. In the end she is the key to saving both the country where she grew up and the country she adopts.

Eragon (2003), the first book of Christopher Paolini's *Inheritance Cycle*, begins when a 15-year-old boy finds a mysterious stone that is eventually revealed to be a dragon's egg. Finding the egg is a sign of Eragon's destiny to become a Dragon Rider. Spring (2004) notes how well *Eragon* fits in with other works in the epic tradition:

[Paolini's] influences include myths, folk tales, medieval stories, Beowulf, Tolkien, and E. R. Eddison. He deliberately set out to include the archetypal ingredients—a quest, a journey of experience, revenge, romance, betrayal and a special sword—and he is unperturbed by charges of being derivative, pointing out the difference between 'drawing on' traditional stories and 'plagiarism.' (p. 20)

Taran, Harry Crewe, and Eragon all fit the pattern that Joseph Campbell (2008) identifies as the "monomyth," the story that is lived out by every human being. In that story, the hero leaves home, ventures into the unknown, and returns home with a new self-awareness and a new understanding of the world.

Apprentices to magic

The coming-of-age of a young magician is a theme in many fantasy works for young adults. Harry Potter, of course, learns his craft at Hogwarts School of Witchcraft and Wizardry. Perhaps, more importantly, he is gradually prepared for his confrontation with the evil Voldemort by the school's headmaster, Professor Dumbledore. In contrast, Ged, in A *Wizard of Earthsea* (Le Guin, 1968), is sent to the wizard's school on the Island of Roke, but he fails to learn its lessons about the limits and dangers of magical power. In the following stories, talented young people are apprenticed in the properties and proper use of magic.

In *Magyk* (2005), the first book of Angie Sage's *Septimus Heap* series, strange events surround the birth of Septimus. The midwife declares him dead and spirits him away. On that same day, Septimus' father finds a baby girl abandoned in the snow and brings her home. Later, the Heaps learn that the Extraordinary Wizard, Alther Mella, and the Queen have both been assassinated, and the Queen's baby daughter has disappeared. Eventually, Septimus is discovered alive, and the Heap's adopted daughter is revealed to be the missing Princess Jenna.

Septimus is the seventh son of a seventh son, and he shows unusual magical promise. He becomes apprentice to Marcia Overstrand, the new Extraordinary Wizard. She is genuinely fond of Septimus, although she generally hides it in order to be an effective taskmaster. Septimus is also mentored by the ghost of Alther Mella. In each book of the series (Sage, 2005–2007), Septimus develops new magical skills, such as the power of flight or the healing science of "physik." All the while, he and Jenna work to preserve the shattered traditions of Jenna's ancestors and to protect the ordinary people who live near the castle.

Circle of Magic is a series by Tamora Pierce that tells of four magically talented young people who are brought to a community by a powerful mage where they can develop their skills. Each is given a mentor. Briar, who was formerly a "street rat" named Roach, develops his talents with plants under the guidance of a stern teacher named Rosethorn. Sandry learns about "thread magic" from a gentle weaver named Lark, and Daja is taught all the properties of metals by a smith mage named Frostpine. Triss, who has the power to affect the weather, is mentored by the powerful mage Niklaren Goldeneye, who brought the group together. Although they often combine their magical skills to protect the community, each of the young mages is featured in one book of the series, beginning with *Sandry's Book* (Pierce, 1997, 1998a, 1998b, 1999).

Pierce gives each of her major characters a distinctive ethnic, social, and cultural identity. Sandry is from an aristocratic family in a country that is reminiscent of India, and Briar's home suggests the Middle East. Daja is dark-skinned and comes from a family of seagoing merchants. Triss has a less distinct ethnic background, but she is identified by her social class. The four students learn from a group of teachers that is similarly diverse, and their school resembles a

Buddhist temple rather than the quasi-medieval European monastery common in other works.

Older readers may appreciate *The Secrets of the Immortal Nicholas Flamel* by Michael Scott. The series could be described as a war of the mentors in which three immortals struggle for influence over young Josh and Sophie Newman, the long-awaited "Twins of Legend" who are expected to develop unprecedented magical powers (Scott, 2007–2010). The twins are first identified by the immortal 14th century alchemist Nicholas Flamel and his wife Perenelle. They begin the twins' education by bringing them to a succession of mythic and legendary figures, beginning with the goddess Hecate, who awakens Sophie's powers. The demigod Prometheus teaches Josh the magic of fire, and his sister, the Witch of Endor, teaches Sophie the magic of air. Both twins learn the magic of water from Gilgamesh the King, who is the oldest of human immortals.

The Flamels and the twins are constantly dogged by the necromancer John Dee, who was court magician to Queen Elizabeth I. Dee is Flamel's former student, but he now works in the service of the Dark Elders, who are seeking to destroy humankind and reclaim the Earth for themselves. Dee brings Josh to be awakened by the god Mars, and he gradually gains influence over him. Throughout the series, a succession of famous historical figures, such as Joan of Arc and William Shakespeare, are revealed to be immortal and they teach and protect the twins while legendary villains, including Niccolo Machiavelli, the Egyptian cat goddess Bastet, and a trio of Valkyries, seek to destroy them.

Creatures of fantasy

In general, stories that feature talking animals as main characters are for very young children, not young adults. One notable exception is *Watership Down* (Adams, 1972). It is the story of a clairvoyant rabbit named Fiver who alerts his warren of its imminent destruction by humans. Fiver's brother Hazel leads those rabbits that believe the warning on a long trek to find a new home. *Watership Down* not only describes the rabbits' actions, it also weaves their social structure, language, and folklore throughout the story.

For slightly younger readers, another animal society is found in the Redwall series by Brian Jacques (1986, 1988, 1989). The stories are set in and around Redwall Abbey, which resembles a secular version of a medieval monastery. The abbey's animals all have assigned roles and tasks, and they share a history centered around the legendary mouse Martin the Warrior (1993). One final example of animals living in a human-like society is found in a series by Kenneth Oppel (1997, 2000). *Silverwing* (1997) tells the story of Shade, an undersized bat who defies the law of the silverwing bats that forbids them from ever seeing the sun. The bats have a social structure and history that revolves around their long struggle against the owls. They also have a religion and a prophecy that Shade seems destined to fulfill.

Unlike the previous works that focus on animal-to-animal interactions, stories about dragons almost always focus on their interactions with humans. Ancient storytellers and modern authors have characterized dragons as both the incarnation of evil and the noblest of beings, and they have endowed dragons with a wide array of physical features, magical powers, and character traits. Anne McCaffrey's stories about dragon riders of the planet Pern are probably the most comprehensive picture of humans and dragons working together (McCaffrey, 1968, 1970). They show how dragon riders "impress" hatchling dragons and establish telepathic communication with them. The two then take to the skies to fight "Thread," a kind of spore that is fatal if it falls on living creatures.

McCaffrey's books should, perhaps, be classified as science fiction because settlers from Earth genetically engineered the dragons from the fire lizards they found on Pern (McCaffrey, 1988). For much of the series, however, neither the residents of Pern nor the reader know that history, so they see the dragons as remarkable, but natural to the planet. Most of the Pern books were intended for adults, but the *Harper Hall Trilogy* (McCaffrey 1976, 1977, 1979) focuses on younger characters, especially Menolly, a gifted singer and composer who becomes the first female harper of Pern. She also rediscovers fire lizards and actually teaches them to sing. Not all fictional dragons are bonded closely to humans, of course, as seen in the works contained in the box below.

Metafictive "Mashups" in Fantasy Literature

As we noted in Chapter 1, blurring the lines between genres to create new hybrids is one of the metafictive devices that is often used in contemporary literature for young adults. As fantasy literature for young adults has become increasingly popular, authors have combined fantasy elements with those of many other genres. Rabey (2010) contends that combining historical fiction and fantasy broadened the appeal of both genres, and she called such a genre combination a "mashup," a term borrowed from popular music that describes how elements of two or more songs are electronically combined into a unique remix. Besides historical fiction, elements of fantasy have been combined with many other genres, including horror and romance. Authors have also blurred the line between fantasy and science fiction. The following discussion provides just a few examples of **metafictive mashups.**

Fantasy and historical fiction

Rabey (2010) cites *Sorcery and Cecilia* (Wrede & Stevermer, 2003) as a particularly successful example of a mashup between fantasy and historical fiction. Its subtitle, "being the correspondence of two young ladies of quality regarding various magical scandals in London and the country," reveals its hybrid nature. The story follows the experiences of two cousins, Cecilia in the country and Kate in London, as they experience the social life of England in the early 1800s—an England that has a Royal College of Wizards.

Elizabeth Wein (2009) calls her novels "sort of historical fantasy" and explains that they feel like fantasy, "but they are purposely set in a historical place and time, in this world and in this world's past" (p. 38). Wein notes that her novel *The Sunbird*, which is set in what is now Ethiopia and Eritrea during the sixth century, won awards as both "Outstanding Historical Fiction" and "Best Fantasy." *The Sunbird*, which features the half British, half Ethiopian character

City of Fire. Lawrence Yep, 2009. This novel combines elements of Japanese, Chinese, Norse, and Hawaiian mythology. Set in 1941, magical creatures disguised as humans inhabit our world. 12-year-old Scirye travels to the newly formed Hawaiian island of Houlani to stop an evil dragon from destroying the world. Ages 12 and up.

Dragon Rider. Cornelia Funke, 2004. Actor Brendan Frazier reads the audiobook version of this novel. It tells how a young dragon named Firedrake goes in search of other dragons at the legendary Rim of Heaven. He is accompanied by a young orphan boy and a Brownie named Sorrel. In order to reach his goal, Firedrake must ultimately defeat Nettlebrand, a dragon with impregnable golden scales who long ago decimated the population of real dragons. Ages 9–12.

The Last Dragon. Silvana Mari, 2006. This offbeat and often humorous story begins with the adventures of a naïve elf-child named Yorsh who is the last of his kind. He becomes friends with a woman named Sajra and her husband Monser. Although Yorsh's ignorance about the world and childlike adherence to elfish values sometimes infuriates his human friends, they find his magical powers useful. Yorsh eventually finds himself raising the newly hatched last dragon in the world, and together they save Sajra and Monser's daughter and fulfill a prophecy by setting right the wretched world in which she lives. Ages 9–12.

The Last Dragon. Jane Yolen and Rebecca Guay (Illustrator), 2011. This graphic novel is an updated version of Yolen's previously published story "Dragonfield" (1985). It tells of a dragon hatchling that terrorizes an island village. The villagers dispatch three boys to find a dragonslayer, but they return with Lancot, a kite maker and storyteller who has no idea how to fight a dragon. Fortunately, Tansy, the talented and courageous daughter of the local healer, steps in to guide and encourage Lancot. After defeating the dragon, Tansy and Lancot fall in love and get married. Ages 12 and up.

FILMS

Dragonheart. Rob Cohen (Director), 1996. This film presents a fearsome but wise and world-weary dragon. An ordinary man named Bowen enlists Draco, the last of the dragons, in a quest to defeat an evil king who has become immortal. Together they inspire the people of the kingdom to fight for their own freedom. Sean Connery supplies the voice of the dragon. Rated PG-13.

Dragonslayer. Matthew Robins (Director), 1981. This movie tells of a kingdom where young virgins are sacrificed to appease a dragon and buy safety for the kingdom. When the king's own daughter is selected in a lottery as the next victim, an old wizard prepares his young apprentice to hunt down and kill the dragon. Rated PG-13.

How to Train Your Dragon. Dean DuBlois & Christopher Sanders (Directors), 2010. This animated feature by Dreamworks tells of a young prospective dragon hunter who learns that everything his Viking-like people believe about the vicious nature of dragons is wrong. He befriends and trains a young dragon who becomes a powerful fire-breathing ally in a crucial battle for his people's survival. Rated PG.

Telemakos Meder, is the final book of a trilogy that is connected to the Arthur legend. The first book of the trilogy, *The Winter Prince* (Wein, 1993), focuses on Arthur's illegitimate son Mordred and is set in sixth-century Britain. *A Coalition of Lions* (2003) follows Arthur's daughter to the Horn of Africa.

In *The Book Without Words* (2005), Avi mixes fantasy with history in a setting that is much like the gritty medieval world that he portrayed in *Crispin, Cross of Lead* (Avi, 2002). The fantastic element comes from a nasty alchemist who will stop at nothing to acquire the ingredients for the potion that keeps him alive and young. Those ingredients include the life's breath stolen from a young girl.

Fantasy and romance

An obvious example of supernatural fantasy blended with teen romance is Stephenie Meyer's *Twilight* (2005). Adams (2010) notes that Meyer's teenage heroine, Bella, compares her relationship with the vampire Edward to the doomed love between Cathy and Heathcliff in *Wuthering Heights* (Bronte, 1847). Adams then draws some conclusions about the series' appeal: "In YA literature, the vampire romance is a powerful metaphor for coming of age: entry into the heady, grown-up world of sex alongside a creeping new awareness of human mortality. Innocence lost, but knowledge—and new pleasures gained" (p. 64).

The tremendous popularity of vampires may be waning, but stories that combine fantastic creatures with romance are still plentiful. *Pride and Prejudice and Zombies* (Austen & Grahame-Smith, 2009) combines romance and the undead, but with a touch of humor. The book is a parody that is close to the plot and the style of Jane Austen's novel. Mrs. Bennet is still trying to marry off her daughters to wealthy suitors, but Mr. Bennet is teaching them martial arts and musketry in order to turn them into a fearsome zombie fighting force. In the end, Elizabeth marries D'Arcy, and they then engage in the first zombie fight of their married life.

Fantasy and speculative fiction

The distinction between fantasy and speculative fiction is easy to state in general but sometimes hard to apply to a particular book. Madeline L'Engle's Newbery Award winner *A Wrinkle in Time* (1962), for instance, is considered a classic fantasy for young adults, but L'Engle describes it and the other works that make up her Time Quartet as "science fantasy" (L'Engle, 1993). The books do mix science and mythology along with elements of religion. The "wrinkle in time" is called a tesseract in the book, but is now known as a wormhole in popular culture and has become part of accepted scientific theory.

Most time travel books are categorized as science fiction, and traveling through time and outside of time is also an element of all books of the series (L'Engle 1973, 1978, 1986). On the other hand, the main characters, Meg Murry, her youngest brother Charles Wallace, and her friend (and eventual husband) Calvin O'Keefe, cross the universe to confront evil, often face-to-face. In *A Wrinkle in Time*, 12-year-old Meg uses a combination of love and logic to battle IT, a malevolent force that has captured her father and is about to absorb Charles Wallace. The three heroes are guided by teachers who evoke both mythology and religion, including three witches, a singular cherubim, and a seraph, and they are threatened by evil angels called Ecthroi.

The *Witch and Wizard* series (Patterson & Charbonnet, 2009; Patterson & Rust, 2010) contains elements that are common to the fantasy genre, including an evil overlord who is attempting to stamp out all art and original thought and a prophecy that his New Order will be overthrown by two young liberators. The world, however, is more contemporary and urban than the typical fantasy; for example, multiple dimensions are connected by portals, famous musicians include the Irish band B4 and rapper Lay-Z, and young adults read the classic coming-of-age novel *The Pitcher in the Wheat* and the popular fantasy story *Gary Blotter and the Guild of Rejects.*

Teaching Ideas ▪ FANTASY LITERATURE

Students can learn a great deal about the conventions of a genre by attempting to create their own stories. The following activities are appropriate for guiding students to plan, create, and share their own fantasy stories.

Le Guin states that drawing a map of Earthsea was a necessary first step for her to create the imaginary landscape for her books (Martin, 2001). Give students samples of maps of imaginary lands and have them chart the major features of a setting where a fantasy story could take place.

Shearin (2011) endorses map-making as a way to create a world, but she suggests going further by choosing an actual location as a model for the imaginary world. Students might draw inspiration, for instance, from an unusual place near their home such as an old amusement park, or they might use photos of exotic landscapes or ancient cities collected from the Internet.

Another way of planning a fantasy story is to decide how to limit the power of magic so the characters cannot just wave a wand to solve all their problems. Davis (2005) notes that "it may seem paradoxical that fantasy is not really about magic, but about a character consumed by a strong emotional issue to which magic is not the answer" (p. 23). Davis suggests that magic should be a last resort and that some kind of consequence or "bounce back" should result from magical acts so there is a cost to the character who uses it. The magic also might be somewhat unpredictable so that it only works, for example, when a character is truly desperate.

After students have read a fantasy story as a class, they might be encouraged to create a further adventure for the same characters, either in the same setting or a different one, and incorporate one or more of these consequences of magic.

Hays (2010) suggests that students check out the fan fiction site at www.fanfiction.net/book. It contains fan fiction about many of the books described in this chapter, including the *Artemis Fowl* series, *Twilight*, and the *Children of the Red King* (Charlie Bone) series. Rather than a conventional story, students might create some other type of media, such as a trailer for a movie that is set in their imagined world or an opening scene represented in a comic strip format. Fisher (2010) suggests a free website for creating comics at www.make-beliefscomix.com.

SPECULATIVE FICTION: WORLDS THAT MIGHT YET BE

Some experts suggest that both science fiction and fantasy be placed under the umbrella term "speculative fiction." We acknowledge that both fantasy and science fiction convey imaginary worlds in order to make readers consider their own world, but we have chosen to apply the term **speculative fiction** a little more narrowly, defining it as fiction that is based in established principles of physical or social science.

Robert Heinlein, one of the most influential authors in the science fiction genre, wrote that science fiction should be thought of as only one segment of a larger field called "speculative fiction" (Heinlein, 1953). He distinguished science fiction not only from fantasy but also from "adventure stories with exotic and non-existent locales," such as Flash Gordon movies, and from "sociological speculation." Although he doubted that he could influence people to use the term more precisely, Heinlein proposed the following definition for science fiction:

> Science fiction is speculative fiction in which the author takes as his first postulate the real world as we know it, including all established facts and natural laws. The result can be extremely fantastic in content, but it is not fantasy; it is a legitimate—and often very tightly reasoned—speculation about the possibilities of the real world. This category excludes rocket ships that make U-turns, serpent men from Neptune who lust after human maidens, and stories by authors who flunked their Boy Scout merit badge tests in descriptive astronomy. (p. 1)

Heinlein's best-known work of speculative fiction is *Stranger in a Strange Land* (1961), which tells the story of Valentine Michael Smith, the orphaned son of two members of a human expedition to Mars. After 20 years of absorbing Martian culture, Smith is "rescued" and returned to Earth, but his adjustment to his home planet is difficult, and his Martian perspective makes him uncomfortable with the values and customs of his new home planet.

Stranger shares a number of characteristics with *The Martian Chronicles*, Ray Bradbury's 1950 collection of short stories. Besides the shared setting, the two books both contrast real humans with fictional Martians in order to comment on human society and human nature. Heinlein admired *The Martian Chronicles*, although he classified them as pseudoscientific fantasy rather than science fiction.

Like Robert Heinlein, Zigo and Moore (2004) prefer the term *speculative fiction* (SF) in place of science fiction. They promote high quality SF in the literature classroom and draw a sharp distinction between that literature and "the formulaic and outdated characterization of SF as 'space operas' centered on plucky action heroes zapping bug-eyed monsters with ray guns" (p. 84). Zigo and Moore, however, are less concerned with tightly reasoned applications of physical science than with the sociological speculations Heinlein dismissed. They argue that SF is particularly well-suited "for social and cultural introspection and for inspiring multiple interpretive possibilities" (p. 85).

The Worlds of Speculative Fiction

Good speculative fiction, like good fantasy, should help readers achieve a new perspective on the familiar through its contrast with "the other." This may involve encountering other planets and their inhabitants, using current scientific knowledge to speculate about future technology, or extending current trends to picture the pitfalls that may await future societies. It may even involve rethinking the past to imagine how things might have been different. The works described below represent each of these approaches in turn.

Other planets and their inhabitants

With or without bug-eyed monsters, alien life forms and other planets have been a recurring theme in speculative fiction for over a hundred years. In *The War of the Worlds* (1898), H. G. Wells envisioned Mars as having civilizations so much older than Earth that the Martians had evolved into creatures more advanced than humans. His concept may have been influenced by an Italian astronomer's discovery of lines on the surface of Mars that he called "channels." The word was widely translated as "canals," which led to the notion that intelligent creatures must have constructed them (Brians, 1995). Wells speculated that once their irrigation canals failed, the Martians abandoned their dry and desolate planet for another one.

The War of the Worlds examines many of the attitudes and beliefs that were common in Great Britain at the time. The Martians' arrogant seizure of a planet inhabited by a "lesser" species was not very different from the behavior of "civilized" 19th-century imperialists toward the undeveloped world. Flynn (2005) suggests that Wells might also have been influenced by the widespread idea that some sort of apocalypse would occur at midnight of the last day of 1899.

In contrast to the genocidal invasion of Martians depicted by Wells, speculative fiction sometimes suggests that human evolution has involved contact with extraterrestrials. In Arthur C. Clark's novel *2001: A Space Odyssey* (1968) and the film version (Kubrick, 1968), advanced aliens planted giant slab-like monoliths on other planets. The objects gave off mysterious rays that triggered the potential of the planet's inhabitants to evolve. Steven Spielberg's films *Close Encounters of the Third Kind* (1977) and *ET: The Extraterrestrial* (1982) provide contradictory views of whether scientists are capable of dealing with extraterrestrial life, but they both suggest that alien contact could cause ordinary individuals to grow wiser.

The Host by Stephenie Meyer (2008) is a novel about a young woman who falls in love with the wrong kind of guy, but it is very different from *Twilight* (Meyer, 2005). The female protagonist is an alien called the Wanderer, and she is occupying the body of a young woman named Melanie Stryder in an attempt to discover where Melanie's brother Jamie, and her lover, Jared, are hiding. Wanderer has lived eight full lives on other planets in host bodies that included a flower and a bear. This time, however, something has gone wrong. She cannot entirely displace Mel's consciousness, and she finds herself loving Jamie and Jared rather than wanting to turn them in.

The action and suspense in *The Host* come from the human characters' struggles to evade being assimilated by the aliens. The book also raises questions about the role of mind and body in forming an identity and about the ethical blindness of "superior" creatures. The "souls," as the Wanderer's people call themselves, believe they have greatly improved Earth by eliminating all of its violence, selfishness, and disease.

Only when she finds herself in an ongoing dialogue with Melanie does the Wanderer consider what her people have taken away from their hosts. Melanie's remarkable Uncle Jeb decides to give Wanderer (renamed Wanda) the chance to become a member of a human community that is hiding in a cave, even if he has to do it at gunpoint. Gradually, Wanda's gentleness and humility win over her "hosts" in the cave, but she comes to a decision to sacrifice herself to free Melanie.

The title character in *I Am Number Four*, by Pittacus Lore (2010) is neither a visitor nor an invader. "John Smith" as he calls himself, is a refugee from the planet Lorien, which was attacked and devastated by an army from the planet Mogadore. John arrived on Earth with nine other children who were chosen because they would each develop "legacies," powers that would make them formidable warriors. Once those powers develop, they are expected to reclaim and repopulate their planet.

The action of the story centers on John's efforts to keep his existence secret from the Mogadoreans, who have also infiltrated Earth. The book's title refers to the number John was assigned when he fled Lorien. Numbers 1, 2, and 3 have already been killed. John also faces the challenge of trying to fit in at the various high schools he attends, and he is falling in love with an Earth girl named Sarah who is endangered by being near him. At the end of the book, John parts from Sarah and leaves with Number 6, a girl from Lorien, to fight the Mogadoreans.

Novels set on other planets sometimes provide a new perspective on our own. In Kurt Vonnegut's complex novel *The Sirens of Titan* (1959), an Earth man named Malachi Constant is exiled to one of the moons of Saturn. There he is humbled to learn that all of human history has been manipulated by an alien race in order for him to bring a needed spare part for a spaceship that is stranded there.

Frank Herbert's novel *Dune* (1965) imagines a time 10,000 years in the future when the human race has spread to many planets throughout the universe. Powerful families, somewhat like the Medici and Borgia families of Renaissance Italy, struggle to control the distribution of "spice," a substance that expands consciousness and allows navigators to plot courses for instantaneous interplanetary travel.

Dune won both the Hugo Award for science fiction and the Nebula Award for best novel. It suggests that even in the far distant future, humans who travel to other planets bring their human nature with them. The film *Avatar* (Cameron, 2009) examines similar themes. It shows how an insatiable need for natural resources, coupled with ignorance about other people, leads to violence and genocide on the planet Pandora. The film's protagonist comes to understand and appreciate the culture of Pandora and rejects its wholesale destruction by his own people.

Ender's Game by Orson Scott Card (1985) is the first of a series of novels about Andrew Ender Wiggin (Card, 1986, 1991). Ender is a 22nd-century child prodigy with a genius for tactical thinking. During the Formic Wars, Earth's desperate battle for survival with a race of ant-like creatures, Ender is taken to Battle School and engages in a constant stream of simulated battles. In the last of these simulations, he totally destroys the ant's home planet, as well as many of his own pilots. Only after the battle is Ender told that the simulations were real.

As in many works where humans confront aliens, Ender's life reflects a tension between a human need for dominance and a desire to make contact with the unknown. Ender eventually finds and rescues the last living queen ant, and they establish telepathic communication. For the rest of his life, however, he struggles between guilt and the satisfaction he finds in using his abilities.

Future world technologies

Some of the earliest and best-known works of science fiction established a pattern of examining new developments in technology and extending them to speculate about the future. *The Time Machine* by H. G. Wells (1895) begins with the Time Traveler, the book's protagonist, explaining to colleagues that time travel is theoretically possible based on the notion of time as a fourth dimension. The Traveler then reveals that he has already built a time machine, and he embarks on a journey through time to demonstrate that his theories are correct.

In the last part of the story, the Traveler arrives thousands of years in the future to explore the concept of evolution. The world he finds is inhabited by two types of creatures, the brutish Morlocks and fragile Eloi. Theories about time travel and other scientific speculations fade into the background as the Traveler marvels at this new world, falls in love with one of the Eloi, and fights to protect her from the Morlocks.

I, Robot (1968) by Isaac Asimov is a collection of stories that play with the possibilities and implications of technology. Ames (2004) notes that these stories introduced Asimov's Three Laws of Robotics: (1) A robot may not injure a human or allow a human being to come to harm; (2) a robot must obey orders given by a human, unless the order would conflict with the First Law; and (3) a robot must protect its own existence unless that conflicts with the First or Second Law. Ames (2004) notes that the laws seem simple and obvious, but they are actually ambiguous enough to generate plots in which humans or robots misunderstand the laws, willfully manipulate them, or find themselves caught in a dilemma in which two of the laws contradict each other.

The three laws assume that humans, as the creators of a "mechanical man," have a claim on the robots' loyalty and service without bearing any equal responsibility to their creations in return. In the movie *AI: Artificial Intelligence* (Spielberg, 2001), David is an experimental childlike robot capable of feeling love and inspiring love in return. David is given to Monica, whose natural son has slipped into a coma. When Monica's son revives, he resents David and plots to make him appear dangerous. David is sent back to the factory where he will be destroyed as a failed experiment. He escapes and becomes a fugitive roaming the seedier side of the human world. The movie is rated PG-13 partly because David ends up traveling in the company of a former robot gigolo that has also been rejected.

Speculative fiction has often focused on biomedical technology. *Jurassic Park* (Crichton, 1990) and the film version (Spielberg, 1993) speculates about how far genetic science can and should go. Could scientists, for instance, recreate dinosaurs from some petrified DNA? The story answers that question with a "yes," but also points out emphatically that just because scientists *can* do something, that does not mean they *should* do it. *Maximum Ride: The Angel*

Experiment by James Patterson (2005) tells the story of a group of winged "bird kids," who are the result of genetic experimentation and who escape from the "school" where they are being studied. Maximum Ride, usually called Max, is the teenage girl who becomes the unofficial leader of this "flock" by virtue of her quick thinking, her fierce concern for the other kids, and her genetically enhanced fighting abilities. The flock's struggle to stay free and together stretches across four more books (Patterson 2006–2009).

The House of the Scorpion (2002) by Nancy Farmer explores the implications of human cloning. Farmer also envisions a world where the United States is in decline, and a lawless region called Opium exists between its border and that of Aztlan, formerly Mexico. Although he does not know it, the book's main character, Matt, is a clone of 140-year-old El Patron, the drug lord who rules Opium. For most of his childhood he is shunned for being less than human. Eventually, Matt learns that he was created so that El Patron could harvest his organs when they were needed, although he vainly hopes that his "father" will spare him.

Matt falls in love with Maria, the daughter of a U.S. senator. When the crucial time comes for Matt to be harvested, he attempts unsuccessfully to flee with Maria. He is saved, however, by his foster mother who has made his organs poisonous by feeding him low doses of arsenic. Matt escapes to Aztlan only to find himself virtually enslaved, along with orphans called Lost Boys, in a plankton farm run by a group of men known as Keepers.

Matt organizes a rebellion and flees. He finds Maria's mother, who has the political connections to save him and prosecute the Keepers. He returns to Opium and, ironically, learns that as El Patron's genetic heir, he is the new ruler of Opium. *The House of the Scorpion* was a Newbery Honor Book for 2003, winner of the National Book Award for Young People's Literature in 2002, and winner of the Michael L. Printz Award.

Future world societies: Dystopian worlds

Many of the works that Heinlein (1953) called "sociological speculation" can be described as **dystopian fiction,** a label meant to contrast with the notion of a vision of Utopia as a perfect society. Cart (2010) describes a dystopian novel as "a literary form that imagines (sometimes satirically, sometimes somberly) a future world made even worse than the present one" (p. 1). He explains that dystopian stories often extend disturbing current trends to show how disaster, misery, and injustice may be looming in the future—often the near future.

Brave New World (1932) by Aldous Huxley, *Nineteen Eighty Four* by George Orwell (1949), and *Fahrenheit 451* by Ray Bradbury (1953) all provide visions of social disaster based on aspects of society the authors found alarming. Huxley, writing in the early years of the Great Depression, worried about the consequences of trusting the future to governments and large corporations, and he was concerned that scientific and social change (such as the acceptance of birth control) would undermine families and traditional values.

Following the rise of totalitarian states in Germany and Russia and the horrors of World War II, Orwell was understandably concerned about governments' power to use media to manipulate citizens, and governments' ability to plunge a country into war. Those concerns are reflected in *Nineteen Eighty Four* by the constant presence of "Big Brother" and by the use of perpetual war as a device to make citizens support a strong leader. *Fahrenheit 451* is the temperature at which paper burns, and Bradbury's novel (1953) tells the story of a "fireman" whose job is to carry out government policy by burning books. Book burning had been a common practice in the Nazi era, and Bradbury may have seen anticommunist measures like Senator Joseph McCarthy's blacklist as the postwar American equivalent that allowed the government to suppress unpopular ideas.

Cart (2010) notes the increasing popularity of dystopian works for young adults and cites the series by Scott Westerfeld that begins with *Uglies* (2005) as an example. Cart identifies the "evergreen adolescent obsession with appearance and celebrity" (p. 34) as the current folly that is exposed by Westerfeld's fictional world, in which radical cosmetic surgery turns everyone "pretty" at the age of 16. Reeve (2011) suggests several reasons for the appeal of dystopian fiction among contemporary young adults:

> Stuck in those awkward years between childhood and full adulthood, bridling against the authority of parents and high school teachers, [young adults] can draw a bleak satisfaction from imagining adult society reduced to smoking rubble. They are also, perhaps, becoming aware of the deep injustices in the wider world which dystopian fiction often reflects. (p. 2)

Reeve worries that there is no counterbalance for the grim view of the future portrayed in these novels, but he does see some relief in the way the young heroes of those books resist oppression by using their intelligence, resourcefulness, and courage. One of the examples Reeve cites is Katniss Everdeen, the hero of the trilogy that begins with *The Hunger Games*, our Focus Novel (see p. 220).

Future world societies: The post-apocalyptic world

Dystopian stories often show dysfunctional societies heading for disaster, but some stories explore how the survivors pick up the pieces after a catastrophe occurs. Such stories bear the weighty name **post-apocalyptic,** which means that they take place after total destruction. *The Last Book in the Universe* (Philbrick, 2000) is one example. After a catastrophic earthquake referred to as the "Big Shake," Spazz, who has epilepsy, is on a quest to rejoin his dying sister. On his journey he is accompanied by Ryter, the old man who is the author of what may be the last book ever written.

Ryter personifies wisdom and the power of words in a world where young people are addicted to electronic fantasy games and gangs of adolescent thugs rule the streets. The only people who prosper in this hellscape are the "proovs," genetically improved residents of a prosperous world called Eden that is entirely closed off from contact with "normals." When Spazz and Ryter enlist one of the proovs to aid them in their quest, the book raises issues about economic and social justice and explores how diversity, and even weakness, can be strength.

The Hunger Games (Collins, 2008) is the first book of a trilogy set in Panem, a post-apocalyptic future society that includes much of the current United States. The despotic rulers in the Capitol have cruelly subjugated Panem's twelve districts and obliterated the thirteenth. While the people of the conquered districts live in constant deprivation and hunger, the Capitol is a sophisticated and modern city where people live in luxury. The Hunger Games are an annual event staged by the Capitol to remind the districts of their powerlessness. A boy and a girl between the ages of 12 and 18 are chosen from each district to participate in a gruesome national reality show in which the 24 Tributes fight to the death until only one remains.

The story focuses on 16-year-old Katniss Everdeen, who comes from a poor family in the poor, coal-mining District 12. Before her father died in a mine explosion, he taught Katniss to hunt and forage in the woods surrounding the District, although doing so was forbidden. As a result, Katniss is a deadly shot with a bow and arrow, and she is accustomed to defying the Capitol's rules in small ways to make sure her family does not starve to death.

Katniss's mother had a breakdown after her husband died, leaving Katniss responsible for taking care of herself and her gentle younger sister, 12-year-old Prim. Katniss's best friend Gale is 18 and responsible for supporting his seven siblings. He and Katniss regularly hunt together and sell whatever they can in the local black market. Katniss suspects he has feelings for her, but she has no interest in marrying or having children.

The story begins on the day of the annual Reaping, when representatives from the Capitol come to the District to conduct the nationally televised lottery that will choose the Tributes. Because children can earn extra food rations for their families by entering their names into the lottery more than once, both Katniss and Gale have submitted their names dozens of times. They are both mentally prepared to be chosen for likely death, but instead it is Prim's name that is chosen. Katniss volunteers to fight in her sister's place, and the people of the District show their respect for Katniss's courage by remaining silent instead of appearing jubilant as they are supposed to.

The boy Tribute from District 12 is Peeta Mellark, a baker whose mother once beat him for giving Katniss a loaf of burnt bread when the girl was starving. The two are whisked away to the Capitol, where they are treated as celebrities for the brief period before they are taken out into the wilderness to kill or be killed.

In an interview that appeared in the *Journal of Adolescent and Adult Literacy* (Blasingame, 2009), Collins discussed the roots of the Hunger Games in both ancient history and modern media. The games in the book were inspired by the story of King Minos of Crete, who defeated Athens in a war and then required a regular tribute to remind the Athenians of their subjugation to Crete. Every nine years, seven Athenian boys and seven Athenian girls were sent to Crete to be devoured by the Minotaur, a monster with the body of a man and the head of a bull.

Theseus, the young prince of Athens, volunteered to take the place of one of the children. He found his way through the maze called the Labyrinth and killed the Minotaur. Collins notes that, like the Athenian children, the 24 boys and girls who fight to the death in her book are called "Tributes," and Katniss takes the place of her sister, Prim, who would surely have died. Katniss is not able to end the Games, but she manages to defy the Capitol.

The games in the book are strikingly similar to the games sponsored by the ancient Roman emperors, in which gladiators from conquered lands fought wild animals or each other. Collins acknowledges that another source of inspiration was the story of the gladiator Spartacus who led a slave rebellion against the Roman Empire. When Collins researched Spartacus she "found three things always present in the gladiator paradigm: (1) a ruthless government that (2) forces people to fight to the death and (3) uses these fights to the death as a form of popular entertainment" (Blasingame, 2009, p. 727).

Echoes of ancient Rome are found throughout the Hunger Games, especially in the names of characters who control the games, Seneca Crane and Plutarch Heavensbee, and Katniss's stylist, Cinna, and his assistants Octavia, Venia, and Flavius.

Despite its roots in the ancient world, however, Collins acknowledges that her story challenges the cruelty and control ingrained in modern as well as ancient governments (Blasingame, 2009).

> The sociopolitical overtones of *The Hunger Games* were very intentionally created to characterize current and past world events, including the use of hunger as a weapon to control populations. Tyrannical governments have also used the techniques of geographical containment of certain populations, as well as the nearly complete elimination of the rights of the individual. (p. 726)

The third element that clearly influenced *The Hunger Games* is pervasive media, particularly reality TV shows like *Survivor.* Everywhere the Tributes go, they are on camera, and if there is a lull in the action, the Gamemakers will send a fire or a flood to force them into the open to kill each another. Collins also connects the story to the graphic television news reports she saw as a child when her father was serving in the Vietnam War (Blasingame, 2009). She describes how these two elements of media came together in *The Hunger Games* (Margolis, 2008):

> One night when I was lying in bed, and I was channel surfing between reality TV programs and actual war coverage. On one channel, there's a group of young people competing for I don't even know what, and on the next, there's a group of young people fighting in an actual war. I was really tired, and the lines between these stories started to blur in a very unsettling way. That's the moment when Katniss's story came to me. (p. 30)

One final aspect of *The Hunger Games* is worthy of comment. It is part of a trend that breaks down distinctions between "boy's books" and "girl's books." The main character is a girl who fights ruthlessly when she must, but who is also unexpectedly pleased by the makeover she receives from her design team. Katniss and Peeta also find themselves working as a team through much of the competition, with both assuming the hero role at times.

In the televised interview at the start of the games, Peeta confesses that he is in love with Katniss. She plays along in hopes that they will gain the support of the viewers, which can translate into gifts sent to them in the field. Katniss is not really sure, however, whether Peeta is sincere or if he is playing her. Peeta warns Katniss about the danger of losing her soul in the effort to survive while she slips easily into the traditionally male role of blocking out feelings to focus on the task at hand. In the other books of the *Hunger Games* trilogy, *Catching Fire* (Collins, 2009) and *Mockingjay* (2010), Katniss does, in fact, struggle to keep her identity, a struggle that is complicated by her feelings about both Peeta and Gale.

Cormac McCarthy's post-apocalyptic novel *The Road* (2006) details the harrowing journey of a man and his son as they trudge grimly through an American landscape that has been devastated by an unexplained catastrophe. They scavenge for food and necessities in abandoned houses that have already been picked clean by others, and they avoid the few other humans they encounter, some of whom have gathered into roving bands of cannibals. The father and son are on a journey to reach the sea, which becomes a symbol of safety and hope. *The Road* was the winner of the 2007 Pulitzer Prize for literature.

Alternate History and Steampunk

Dystopian and post-apocalyptic fiction are set in an imagined future, but sometimes speculative fiction explores an imaginary past, a version of our world that might have existed if circumstances had been slightly different. One early example of such an **alternate history** is *The Man in the High Castle* by Philip K.

classroom scenario

After the Apocalypse

A catastrophe reveals the best and worst of human nature and gives individuals opportunities to learn and grow. AS YOU READ the following, consider how Ms. Mulligan encourages her students to explore these issues through post-apocalyptic fiction and relate them to their own experiences.

Ms. Mulligan and a team of seventh grade teachers are planning a unit called "E pluribus unum" that will explore how diverse groups of people learn to live or work together. The teachers believe the unit is appropriate for their students, who have just arrived from different elementary schools and are struggling to fit in. Ms. Mulligan has decided to pursue the themes of the unit in her language arts class by reading the novel *The People of Sparks* (DuPrau, 2003), the sequel to *The City of Ember* (DuPrau, 2003). Both novels, as well as *The Diamonds of Darkhold* (DuPrau, 2008), are set in a post-apocalyptic world where only small pockets of humanity have survived a world war.

Ms. Mulligan shows selected scenes from the movie adaptation of *The City of Ember* (Kenan, 2008) in order to introduce Ember and its residents. They have been living in an underground city for so many generations that they no longer realize that their ancestors lived above ground. Two young people, Doon Harrow and Lina Mayfleet, find the way out of Ember and into the outside world just as the

generators that make life possible in the city begin to fail. Ms. Mulligan draws students' attention to the reasons why people emigrate, including a sudden failure of the food and water supply, such as the people of Ember experience. They also discuss how people might feel as they leave behind the only home they have ever known to enter a new world.

Ms. Mulligan introduces *The People of Sparks* by distributing anonymous letters written by her school's current eighth graders. Some letters welcome the seventh graders and give them advice for succeeding; others complain about the newcomers invading their school and warn them to avoid acting "like typical seventh graders." In small groups, students discuss what they would like to say back to the older students. Ms. Mulligan reveals that the letters are fictional but points out that they express attitudes common when people are confronted with newcomers. Furthermore, their own feelings of uncertainty are common to new arrivals. She explains that they are going to read a book that explores similar emotions as immigrants from Ember cross the wasteland left by a great war and arrive in Sparks, one of the few livable settlements left in the world.

The plot is organized around four meetings of the three-person council that governs Sparks. At first the council worries about their ability to provide for the newcomers, but generosity wins out over caution. They decide to let the Emberites stay for six months while they learn the skills to survive on their own. By the second meeting some months later, tensions have developed between the people from Ember, who believe they are overworked and underfed, and the people of Sparks, who believe the Emberites are depleting the town's stores of food while contributing few useful skills. The council votes to reduce food rations and reaffirms that the Emberites will leave at the end of six months even though that will be the beginning of winter.

In the following weeks, misunderstandings and deliberate deceptions bring the people of Sparks to the brink of armed conflict. A local boy falsely accuses Doon Harrow of vandalism, and the Emberites are victims of insulting anonymous messages as well as a prank that leaves them all suffering from poison oak. A charismatic young Emberite named Tick urges them to protest their treatment, and he eventually organizes a group of "warriors" armed with makeshift weapons. At the third meeting of the council, Ben, who has never wanted the Emberites to stay, prevails when the decision is made to expel them from the town and to use a powerful ancient weapon against them if they threaten violence. Meanwhile, Tick is preparing his army to resist. After reading each passage in which the council meets, the students meet in small groups to discuss four questions:

1. What do the people of Ember want at this point? What do they fear?
2. What do the people of Sparks want, and what do they fear?
3. Would your group vote for or against the council's decisions?
4. What other plan(s) might meet the needs and calm the fears of both groups?

In the novel's climax, the people of Ember, led by Tick and his warriors, confront the leaders of Sparks. Ben attempts to use the town weapon, a sort of Gatling gun, but it explodes, setting fire to the town hall. Doon rescues the same boy who had falsely accused him, and Lina leads the people of Ember to join in fighting the fire. The next day, at a final town meeting, everyone learns that Tick faked attacks on the Emberites to provoke a conflict that would make him a leader.

The last town meeting concludes with the leader of the council attempting to unite the two groups by declaring that they would no longer use the term "people of Ember" because, from then on, they would all be "People of Sparks." Ms. Mulligan raises the question of whether it was wise to erase the identity of the people of Ember. She explains the melting pot and salad bowl metaphors for describing the assimilation of immigrants in the United States and asks the class to consider the advantages and disadvantages of each approach. Then she divides the class into an Emberite half and a Sparks half. She asks the Emberite half to write letters explaining why they do or do not appreciate the leader's melting pot decision and asks the Sparks half to write letters in reply.

Dick (1962). It speculates about what the world might have been like if the attempted assassination of Franklin Roosevelt in 1933 had succeeded. Having won World War II, Germany and Japan each occupy a region of the United States and are engaged in a cold war with each other. The title character of this complex story is the author of a novel within Dick's novel that explores what would have happened if Germany and Japan had *lost* the war.

Alternate history is a major ingredient in the hybrid genre known as **steampunk.** Jean Rabe says that steampunk shows what the future would look like if it had come along during the Victorian era. He also notes one of the genre's most distinctive characteristics, a fondness for Victorian "high tech" such as steam power, clockwork, airships, and goggles (Rabe and Greenberg, 2010). Like early science fiction classics such as *The Time Machine* (Wells, 1895), and *Twenty Thousand Leagues Under the Sea* (Verne, 1870), steampunk is inspired by the technological advancements made in the 19th century as well by the pulp fiction of the 1920s, 1930s, and 1940s (Sondericker, 2010).

The film *The League of Extraordinary Gentlemen* (Norrington, 2003) is based on a series of graphic novels that were influential in launching steampunk. In addition to the basic steampunk elements, the story uses the metafictive device of combining characters drawn from other works of fiction. In effect, it creates an alternate history for fictional worlds. Among the members of the league are Captain Nemo, Dorian Gray, Dr Jekyll (accompanied, of course, by Mr. Hyde), and Tom Sawyer. The deliberate disregard for whether these characters could plausibly come together is the attitude that puts the "punk" in steampunk.

Two novels by Cherie Priest are set in an alternate version of the American Civil War, in which the fighting has continued to rage for over 20 years. In *Boneshaker* (2009), the war explains why the people of Seattle cannot easily flee when a deadly blight escapes from the ground and turns citizens into zombies. In addition to several airships and plenty of goggles, *Boneshaker* provides a detailed alternate history of Seattle in the 1880s. At the end of the book, Priest explains that she distorts the city's true chronology but adds, "I realize that the story is a bit of a twisted stretch, but honestly—isn't that what steampunk is for?" (p. 416).

In *Dreadnought* (Priest, 2010), Mercy Lynch is a nurse in a Confederate hospital when she learns that her husband, a Union soldier, has died in the Andersonville prison camp. When she finds out that her father is also dying, Mercy sets out for the Washington Territories to be with him. She travels by both dirigible and riverboat then finds herself on the Union's famous steam engine, the *Dreadnought*. The cross-country trip allows Priest to develop her alternative American history as Mercy encounters hostile Indians, Confederate soldiers, and (of course) a Mexican legion of zombies.

The Death Collector (Richards, 2006) is another work that brings together many of the elements of steampunk, including a giant steam-powered robotic dinosaur that terrorizes London. The novel is set in the late Victorian era, and it includes a budding love affair between a proper but spirited young girl and an expert in clockwork devices. They team up with a Victorian street urchin to oppose a mad industrialist who is building steam-powered robotic exoskeletons that will equip an army of (of course) zombies. *The Death Collector* exemplifies the lighter side of steampunk that is all about action, adventure, and mystery, but not necessarily plausibility.

In *Leviathan* (2009), Scott Westerfeld invents two completely different technologies for the opponents in his alternate World War I. The Germans and their allies (The Clankers) favor huge diesel-powered "stormwalkers," while the British and their allies (The Darwinists) use fabricated animals as weapons. The *Leviathan*, in fact, is an airship fabricated from a whale. *Leviathan* alternates between two characters. Prince Aleksander is fleeing Austria after the murder of his parents, the Grand Duke Franz Ferdinand and Princess Sophie. Deryn Sharpe is a British girl who disguises herself as a boy in order to join the British Air Service. Deryn is on the *Leviathan* when it crashes on the mountain where Aleks and a few supporters are hiding. Aleks and Deryn and their friends eventually join forces to repair the *Leviathan* and capture by German soldiers. In an afterword, Westerfeld notes that "blending future and past" is the nature of steampunk, and he sorts the real history from the alternate history contained in the book.

Teaching Ideas ▪ SPECULATIVE FICTION

Zigo and Moore (2004) recommend bridging as an approach for using specula-tive fiction in the high school English class. They suggest, for instance pairing *The Martian Chronicles* (Bradbury, 1950) with *Heart of Darkness* (Conrad, 1902) as a way of exploring colonialism, or using *The House of the Scorpion* (Farmer, 2002) as a bridge to *Great Expectations* (Dickens, 1861) because they are both coming-of-age stories. A second suggestion they make is to give students only a few pages of a work of speculative fiction and then ask them to become "discourse detectives" and infer characteristics of the society that would use such language.

For younger students, Fink (ReadWriteThink, n.d.) suggests a unit in which students read a work of speculative fiction with an eye toward its scientific accuracy by carefully noting its technical terminology and its concepts of engi-neering, mathematics, and other disciplines. Students then conduct research to find ten facts that either confirm or dispute the science portrayed in the book. The unit would culminate with students completing a project such as creating a glossary of science words and phrases from the novel or writing a persuasive essay concerning an ethical decision or action in the plot. Fink also suggests an extension to the unit in which students read a second work of speculative fiction and create a Venn diagram comparing the two works.

conclusion

In this chapter we argue that the imaginary worlds created by authors of fantasy and speculative fiction are places where young adults can find a new perspective on the world they will someday inherit. Fan-tasy helps a reader to create and refine an identity free from the physical and social limitations imposed by the "real world." Speculative fiction invites a reader to view our world more critically from a vantage point in space or in an imaginary past or future. The potential usefulness of an imaginary world is enhanced, however, when it is truly different from our own and when its inhabitants are diverse.

Belton (2009) pointedly wonders why the "post-racial" future portrayed in science fiction movies looks so white, and Baker (2007) raises similar issues about the lack of diversity in fantasy literature (though citing Ursula LeGuin and Tamora Pierce as exceptions). Pierce's website (http://www.tamora-pierce.com) includes a "So Not-White Medieval Europe" booklist, and she highlights fantasy literature of interest to female readers with a page called "Pumpkin? We Don't Need No *Stinkin'* Pumpkin!"

Lea (2006) uses Lois Lowry's dystopian novel *The Giver* (1993) as a metaphor to criticize the supposed color-blindness of much speculative fiction. She notes that the community in *The Giver* gave up the ability to see in color as the price of a smoothly functioning society. But Lea warns that eliminating the racial and cultural identities of characters in speculative fiction might create readers who have little awareness of their own history and the richness of its diversity.

We certainly do not suggest choosing literature by some quota system. Teachers can plan activities that address the lack of diversity in an otherwise good book. On the other hand, teachers may want to seek out authors whose imaginary worlds help young adults contemplate issues of gender, class, and culture that are part of their own world.

BIBLIOGRAPHY OF LITERATURE FOR YOUNG ADULTS

Adams, R. (1972). *Watership down.* London: Rex Collings.

Alexander, L. (1964). *The book of three.* New York: Holt.

Alexander, L. (1965). *The black cauldron.* New York: Holt.

Alexander, L. (1967). *Taran wanderer.* New York: Holt.

Alexander, L. (1968). *The high king.* New York: Holt.

Alexander, L. (1968). *The castle of Llyr.* New York: Holt.

Austen, J., & Grahame-Smith, S. (2009). *Pride and prejudice and zombies.* Philadelphia, PA: Quirk Books.

Avi. (2005). *The book without words.* New York: Hyperion.

Avi. (2002). *Crispin: Cross of lead.* New York: Hyperion.

Asimov, A. (1968). *I, robot.* London: Grafton Books.

Bradbury, R. (1953). *Fahrenheit 451.* New York: Random House.

Bradbury, R. (1950). *The Martian chronicles.* Garden City, NY: Doubleday.

Bronte, E. (1847/2007). *Wuthering Heights.* [Facsimile ed.], Washington, DC: Orchises.

Brooks, T. (1977). *The sword of Shannara.* New York: Random House.

Brooks, T. (1982). *The elfstones of Shannara.* New York: Random House.

Brooks, T. (1985). *The wishsong of Shannara.* New York: Random House.

Cameron, J. (Dir.). (2009). *Avatar.* U.S.A.: 20th Century Fox.

Card, O. S. (1985). *Ender's game.* New York: Tor Books.

Card, O. S. (1986). *Speaker for the dead.* New York: Tor Books.

Card, O. S. (1991). *Xenocide.* New York: Tor Books.

Clark, A.C. (1968). *2001: A space odyssey.* New York: New American Library.

Cohen, R. (Dir.). (1996). *Dragonheart.* U.S.A.: Universal.

Colfer, E. (2001). *Artemis Fowl: Book 1.* New York: Disney–Hyperion.

Colfer, E. (2002). *Artemis Fowl: The arctic incident.* New York: Disney–Hyperion.

Colfer, E. (2005). *Artemis Fowl: The opal deception.* New York: Disney–Hyperion.

Colfer, E., & Donkin, A. (2007). *Artemis Fowl: Book 1* (G. Rigano, Illus.), [graphic novel]. New York: Disney–Hyperion.

Colfer, E., & Donkin, A. (2009). *Artemis Fowl: The arctic incident,* (G. Rigano, Illus.), [graphic novel]. New York: Disney–Hyperion.

Collins, S. (2003). *Gregor the Overlander.* New York: Scholastic.

Collins, S. (2004). *Gregor and the prophecy of Bane.* New York: Scholastic.

Collins, S. (2005). *Gregor and the curse of the warmbloods.* New York: Scholastic.

Collins, S. (2006). *Gregor and the marks of secret.* New York: Scholastic.

Collins, S. (2007). *Gregor and the code of claw.* New York: Scholastic.

Collins, S. (2008). *The hunger games.* New York: Scholastic.

Collins, S. (2009). *Catching fire.* New York: Scholastic.

Collins, S. (2010). *Mockingjay.* New York: Scholastic.

Columbus, C. (Dir.). (2001). *Harry Potter and the sorcerer's stone.* U.S.A.: Warner Brothers.

Conrad, J. (1902). *Heart of darkness.* Retrieved from University of Virginia Electronic Text Center, http://etext.lib.virginia.edu.

Cooper, S. (1973). *The dark is rising.* New York: Simon & Schuster.

Cooper, S. (1974). *The greenwitch.* New York: Simon & Schuster.

Cooper, S. (1975). *The grey king.* New York: Simon & Schuster.

Cooper, S. (1976). *Over sea, under stone.* New York: Simon & Schuster.

Cooper, S. (1977). *Silver on the tree.* New York: Simon & Schuster.

Crichton, M. (1990). *Jurassic park.* New York: Random House.

Dick, P. K. (1962). *The man in the high castle.* New York: Putnam.

Dickens, C. (1861). *Great expectations.* Retrieved from www.gutenberg.org/ebooks/1400.

DiTerlizi, T., & Black, H. (2003). *The field guide* (Spiderwick Chronicles, Book 1). New York: Simon & Schuster.

DiTerlizi, T., & Black, H. (2004). *The Spiderwick chronicles* [boxed set]. New York: Simon & Schuster.

DuBlois, D., & Sanders, C. (Dirs.). (1981). *How to train your dragon.* U.S.A.: Dreamworks.

DuPrau, J. (2003). *The city of Ember.* New York: Random House/Yearling.

DuPrau, J. (2003). *The people of Sparks.* New York: Random House/Yearling.

DuPrau, J. (2008). *The diamonds of Darkhold.* New York: Random House/Yearling.

Farmer, N. (2002). *The house of the scorpion.* New York: Simon & Schuster.

Funke, C. (2003). *Inkheart.* New York: Scholastic.

Funke, C. (2004). *Dragon Rider.* [Audiobook]. New York: Listening Library.

Funke, C. (2005). *Inkspell.* New York: Scholastic.

Funke, C. (2008). *Inkdeath.* New York: Scholastic.

Gaiman, N. (2002). *Coraline.* New York: HarperCollins.

Gaiman, N. (2008). *The graveyard book.* New York: HarperCollins.

Heinlein, R. A. (1961). *Stranger in a strange land.* New York: Ace/Putnam.

Herbert, F. (1965). *Dune.* Chilton Books.

Huxley, A. (1932). *Brave new world.* Garden City, NY: Doubleday.

Jackson, P. (Dir.). (2001). *The lord of the rings: The fellowship of the ring.* U.S.A.: New Line.

Jacques, B. (1993). *Martin the warrior.* New York: Penguin Putnam.

Jacques, B. (1989). *Mattimeo.* New York: Penguin Putnam.

Jacques, B. (1988). *Mossflower.* New York: Penguin Putnam.

Jacques, B. (1986). *Redwall.* New York: Penguin Putnam.

Kenan, G. (Dir.). (2008). *The city of Ember.* U.S.A.: Playtone/Walden Media.

Kubrick, S. (Dir.). (1968) *2001: A space odyssey.* U.S.A.: MGM.

LeGuin, U. K. (1968). *A wizard of Earthsea.* New York: Random House.

LeGuin, U. K. (1970). *The tombs of Atuan.* New York: Simon & Schuster.

LeGuin, U. K. (1972). *The farthest shore.* New York: Simon & Schuster.

L'Engle, M. (1962). *A wrinkle in time.* New York: Bantam Doubleday.

L'Engle, M. (1973). *A wind in the door.* New York: Crosswicks.

L'Engle, M. (1978). *A swiftly tilting planet.* New York: Holtzbrinck Publishers.

L'Engle, M. (1986). *Many waters.* New York: Macmillan.

Lewis, C. S. (1950). *The lion, the witch, and the wardrobe.* New York: HarperCollins.

Lewis, C. S. (1951). *Prince Caspian.* New York: HarperCollins.

Lewis, C. S. (1952). *The voyage of the Dawntreader.* New York: HarperCollins.

Lewis, C. S. (1953). *The silver chair.* New York: HarperCollins.

Lewis, C. S. (1955). *The magician's nephew.* New York: HarperCollins.

Lewis, C. S. (1956). *The last battle.* New York: HarperCollins.

Lore, P. (2010). *I am number four.* New York: HarperCollins.

Lowery, L. (1993). *The giver.* Boston, MA: Houghton Mifflin.

Lucas, G. (Dir.). (1977). *Star wars episode IV: A new hope.* U.S.A.: Lucasfilm, 20th Century Fox.

Mari, S. (2006). *The last dragon.* U.S.A.: Miramax.

McCaffrey, A. (1968). *Dragonflight.* New York: Del Rey/Random House.

McCaffrey, A. (1970). *Dragonquest.* New York: Del Rey/Random House.

McCaffrey, A. (1976). *Dragonsong.* New York: Simon & Schuster.

McCaffrey, A. (1977). *Dragonsinger.* New York: Simon & Schuster.

McCaffrey, A. (1979). *Dragondrums.* New York: Simon & Schuster.

McCaffrey, A. (1988). *Dragonsdawn.* New York: Del Rey/Random House.

McCarthy, C. (2006). *The road.* New York: Knopf.

McKinley, R. (1982). *The blue sword.* New York: Greenwillow Books.

Meyer, S. (2005). *Twilight.* New York: Little, Brown.

Meyer, S. (2008). *The host.* New York: Little, Brown.

Nimmo, J. (2002). *Midnight for Charlie Bone.* New York: Scholastic.

Nimmo, J. (2003). *Charlie Bone and the time twister.* New York: Scholastic.

Nimmo, J. (2004). *Charlie Bone and the invisible boy.* New York: Scholastic.

Nimmo, J. (2005). *Charlie Bone and the castle of mirrors.* New York: Scholastic.

Nimmo, J. (2006). *Charlie Bone and the hidden king.* New York: Scholastic.

Norrington, S. (Dir.). (2003). *The league of extraordinary gentlemen.* U.S.A.: 20th Century Fox.

Oppel, K. (1997). *Silverwing.* New York: Simon & Schuster.

Oppel, K. (2000). *Sunwing.* New York: Simon & Schuster.

Paolini, C. (2003). *Eragon.* New York: Knopf.

Patterson, J. (2005). *Maximum ride: The angel experiment.* New York: Little, Brown.

Patterson, J. (2006). *Maximum ride: School's out—forever.* New York: Little, Brown.

Patterson, J. (2007). *Maximum ride: Saving the world and other extreme sports.* New York: Little, Brown.

Patterson, J. (2007). *Maximum ride: The final warning.* New York: Little, Brown.

Patterson, J. (2009). *Maximum ride: Max.* New York: Little, Brown.

Patterson, J., & Charbonnet, J. (2009). *Witch and Wizard, Volume 1.* New York: Little, Brown.

Patterson, J., & Rust, N. (2010). *Witch and wizard: The gift.* New York: Little, Brown.

Philbrick, R. (2000). *The last book in the universe.* New York: Scholastic.

Pierce, T. (1997). *Magic circle: Sandry's book.* New York: Scholastic.

Pierce, T. (1998). *Magic circle: Tris's book.* New York: Scholastic.

Pierce, T. (1998). *Magic circle: Daja's book.* New York: Scholastic.

Pierce, T. (1999). *Magic circle: Briar's book.* New York: Scholastic.

Priest, C. (2009). *Boneshaker.* New York: Tor Books.

Priest, C. (2010). *Dreadnought.* New York: Tor Books.

Pullman, P. (1996). *The golden compass.* New York: Knopf.

Pullman, P. (1997). *The subtle knife.* New York: Knopf.

Pullman, P. (2000). *The amber spyglass.* New York: Knopf.

Richards, J. (2006). *The death collector.* New York: Bloomsbury U.S.A.

Robins, M. (Dir.). (1981). *Dragonslayer.* U.S.A.: Walt Disney/Paramount.

Rowling, J. K. (1998). *Harry Potter and the sorcerer's stone.* New York: Scholastic.

Rowling, J. K. (2003). *Harry Potter and the order of the phoenix.* New York: Scholastic.

Rowling, J. K. (2007). *Harry Potter and the deathly hallows.* New York: Scholastic.

Sage, A. (2005). *Magyk.* New York: Katherine Tegen.

Sage, A. (2006). *Flyte.* New York: Katherine Tegen.

Sage, A. (2007). *Physik.* New York: Katherine Tegen.

Scott, M. (2007). *The alchemyst: The secrets of the immortal Nicholas Flamel.* New York: Delacorte.

Scott, M. (2008). *The magician: The secrets of the immortal Nicholas Flamel.* New York: Delacorte.

Scott, M. (2009). *The sorceress: The secrets of the immortal Nicholas Flamel.* New York: New York: Delacorte Press.

Scott, M. (2010). *The necromancer: The secrets of the immortal Nicholas Flamel.* New York: Delacorte.

Spielberg, S. (Dir.). (1977). *Close encounters of the third kind.* U.S.A.: Columbia Pictures.

Spielberg, S. (Dir.). (1982). *ET: The extraterrestrial.* U.S.A.: Universal/Amblin Entertainment.

Spielberg, S. (Dir.). (1993). *Jurassic park.* U.S.A.: Universal/Amblin Entertainment.

Spielberg, S. (Dir.). (2001). *AI: Artificial intelligence.* U.S.A.: Warner Brothers/DreamWorks.

Tolkien, J. (1954a). *The fellowship of the ring.* Boston, MA: Houghton Mifflin.

Tolkien, J. (1954b). *The two towers.* Boston, MA: Houghton Mifflin.

Tolkien, J. (1956). *The return of the king.* Boston, MA: Houghton Mifflin.

Verne, J. (1870). *Twenty thousand leagues under the sea.* Retrieved from www.gutenberg.org/ebooks/2488.

Vonnegut, K. (1959). *The sirens of Titan.* New York: Dell.

Wein, E. (1993). *The winter prince.* New York: Penguin Putnam.

Wein, E. (2003). *A coalition of lions.* New York: Penguin Putnam.

Wein, E. (2004). *The sunbird.* New York: Penguin Putnam.

Wells, H. G. (1895). *The time machine.* London: Heinemann.

Wells, H. G. (1898). *The war of the worlds.* London: Heinemann.

Westerfeld, S. (2005). *Uglies.* New York: Simon Pulse.

Westerfeld, S. (2009). *Leviathan.* New York: Simon Pulse.

Whale, J. (Dir.). (1931). *Frankenstein.* U.S.A.: Universal Pictures.

Wrede, P. C., & Stevermer, C. (2003). *Sorcery and Cecilia.* New York: Harper.

Yep, L. (2009). *City of fire.* New York: Starscape.

Yolen, J., & Guay, R. (2011). *The last dragon.* [Graphic novel]. Milwaukie, OR: Dark Horse.

WEBSITES WITH ANNOTATIONS

Collins, Suzanne • **www.suzannecollinsbooks.com/**
Author's official website, including summaries of works, biographical information, and author interviews.

FanFiction • **www.fanfiction.net/book**
An "archive and forum where fanfic writers and readers around the globe gather to share their passion."

Make Beliefs Comix • **www.makebeliefscomix.com**
Allows students to create their own comic strips.

Pierce, Tamora • **http://tamora-pierce.com/**
Author's official website, including summaries of works and biographical information as well as lists of fantasy books that feature strong non-European and female characters.

REFERENCES

Adams, L. (2010, January/February). Bitten. *Horn Book*, 86(1), 58–64.

Ames, M. R. (2004). *Asimov's deliberate failures*. Retrieved from www.azimovlaws.com/articles/archives/2004/07/robot_opressio.html.

Attebery, B. (1980). *The fantasy tradition in American literature: From Irving to Le Guin*. Bloomington, IN: Indiana University Press.

Baker, D. F. (2007, January/February). Reader at large: Musings on diverse worlds. *Horn Book*, 83(1), 41–47. Retrieved from http://70.42.48.98/magazine/articles/2007/jan07_baker.asp.

Belton, D. C. (2009). Blacks in space. *American Prospect*, 20(5), 47–50.

Brians, P. (1995). *Study guide for H. G. Wells: The war of the worlds*. Retrieved from http://public.wsu/`brians/science_fiction/worofworlds.html.

Blasingame, J. (2009). Books for adolescents, review of *The Hunger Games*. *Journal of Adolescent and Adult Literacy*, 52(8), 724–739.

Campbell, J. (2008). *The hero with a thousand faces* (2nd ed.). Berkeley, CA: Publishers Group West.

Carpenter, S. (2010, Sept. 5). *Mockingjay* closes trilogy: Tale twists and turns through brutal and confusing world. *Los Angeles Times*.

Cart, M. (2010, May). Carte blanche: Dateline darkness. *Booklist*, 106(18), 34. Retrieved from http://booklist online.com/ProductInfo.aspx?pid=4196564&Aspx AutoDetectCookieSupport=1.

Carter, L. (1978). *The year's best fantasy stories: 4*. New York: DAW Books.

Chattaway, P. T. (2007). The chronicles of atheism. *Christianity Today*. Retrieved from http://www.christianitytoday.com/ct/2007/december/12.36.html.

Davis, C. (2005, March). Hocus pocus! Make your fantasy spellbinding by using just the right amount of magic. *Writer*, 118(3), 23–25.

Fink, L. S. (n.d.). Finding the science behind science fiction through paired readings. ReadWriteThink. Retrieved from http://readwritethink.org/classroom-resources/lessonplans/finding-science-behind-science-927.html.

Fisher, D. (2010). Side trip: Sites for creating your own comics and graphic novels. *Voices from the Middle*, 17(4), 16.

Flynn, J. L. (2005). *War of the worlds: From Wells to Spielberg*. Owings Mills, MD: Galactic Books.

Gates, P. S., Steffel, S. B., & Molson, F. J. (2003). *Fantasy literature for children and young adults*. Lanham, MD: Scarecrow Press.

Gilsdorf, E. (2003, November 16). Lord of the gold ring. *Boston Globe*.

Hays, S. (2010). Making the shift: YA lit 2.0. *Voices from the Middle*, 17(4), 50–52.

Heinlein, R. (1953). Ray guns and rocket ships. *Library Journal*, 78, 1188.

Herbert, F. (1977, April 10). Some author. Some Tolkien. *New York Times Book Review*, p. 15.

Hitchens, P. (2002, January). This is the most dangerous author in Britain. *Mail on Sunday*, p. 63. Retrieved from http://home.wlv.ac.uk/~bu1895/hitchens.htm.

Internet Movie Database (n.d.). *Harry Potter and the sorcerer's stone*. Retrieved from http://www.imdb.com/title/tt0241527/.

L'Engle, M. (1993). *The rock that is higher: Story as truth*. Colorado Springs, CO: Waterbrook Press.

Lea, S. G. (2006). Seeing beyond sameness: Using *The Giver* to challenge colorblind ideology. *Children's Literature in Education*, 37(1), 51–67.

Lukens, R. J., & Cline, R. K. J. (1995). *A critical handbook of literature for young adults*. New York: HarperCollins.

Margolis, R. (2008, September). A killer story: Suzanne Collins's *The hunger games* has plenty of blood, guts, and heart. *School Library Journal*, 54(9), 30.

Martin, P. (2001, November). 10 secrets to writing fantasy stories. *Writer*, 114(11), 34–40.

Martin, P. (2001, November). Ursula K. LeGuin. *Writer*, 114(11), 38–39.

Rabe, J., & Greenberg, M. H. (Eds.) (2010). *Steampunk'd*. New York: DAW Books/Penguin Group.

Rabey, M. (2010, Fall). Historical fiction mash-ups: Broadening appeal by mixing genres. *Young Adult Library Services*, 9(1), 38–41.

Reeve, P. (2011). The worst is yet to come. *School Library Journal*, 57(8). Retrieved from http://www.school libraryjournal.com/slj/home/891276-312/the_worst_is_yet_to.html.csp.

Shearin, L. (2011). 6 fantasy subgenres to inspire you. *Writer*, 124(7), 13.

Shearin, L. (2011). 4 keys to world-building in fantasy. *Writer*, 124(8), 13.

Sims, B. (2009). J.R.R. Tolkien estate and New Line settle lawsuit over films. Retrieved from http://blog.al.com/scenesource/2009/09/jrr_tolkien_estate_new_line_se.html.

Sondericker, J. H. (2010). Foreword: A word from the publisher. In G. D. Falkson (Ed.), Steampunk tales: An unfortunate engagement. Retrieved from www.steampunktales.com.

Spring, K. (2004, Jan.). Elf and efficiency. *Observer.* Retrieved from guardian.co.uk.

Tolkien, J. R. R. (1966). On fairy-stories. In *The Tolkien reader.* New York: Ballantine (pp. 2–83).

Watson, J., & Kellner, T. (2004, Feb. 26). J. K. Rowling and the billion-dollar empire. *Forbes.* Retrieved from http://www.forbes.com/maserati/billionaires2004/cx_jw_0226rowlingbill04.html.

Wein, E. (2009, March/April). The art of the possible. *Horn Book, 85*(2), 163–167.

Young, C. (2008, March). A secular fantasy: The flawed but fascinating fiction of Philip Pullman. *Reason.* Retrieved from http://reason.com/archives/2008/02/26/a-secular-fantasy.

Zigo, D., & Moore, M. T. (2004). Science fiction: Serious reading, critical reading. *English Journal, 94*(2), 85–90.

CHAPTER EIGHT

Nonfiction
ARTISTRY AND INFORMATION

chapter overview

Nonfiction literature does more than convey information. It can communicate both fact and feeling and be both useful and inspiring. This chapter begins with a general introduction to contemporary nonfiction. Next, we focus on literary nonfiction that displays significant artistry and information. Then we describe many kinds of nonfiction available for young adults and recent changes in the genre. A case study and instructional suggestions illustrate the place of nonfiction in the English language arts classroom. Finally, we explore the place of nonfiction in young adults' personal reading and as support for the content area curriculum.

FOCUS QUESTIONS

1. What are the characteristics of contemporary nonfiction?
2. What distinguishes literary nonfiction from informational nonfiction?
3. What are the categories or subgenres of literary nonfiction?
4. What is the role of informational nonfiction in the content area curriculum and in the development of young adult readers?

introduction

Nonfiction celebrated a banner year in 2010. Phillip Hoose's *Claudette Colvin: Twice Toward Justice* (2009), a collection of interviews related to an unsung but important civil rights figure, beat out the fiction competition to win the prestigious National Book Award for Young People's Literature. *Claudette Colvin* was also chosen as the ALA Best Book for Young Adults and as a Newbery Honor Book. It was, however, just one of the nonfiction books recognized for its quality during the year.

Stitches (2009), a graphic autobiography by David Small, received one of the 10 Alex Awards that recognizes adult books with a special appeal for readers ages 10 to 18, and it was also a finalist for the National Book Award. *Charles and Emma: The Darwins' Leap of Faith* (Heiligman, 2009), a biography of the author of *The Origin of the Species by Means of Natural Selection* (1859) and his wife, centers on the conflict his writings presented in their religious and social lives. *Charles and Emma* received the first-ever YALSA Excellence in Nonfiction Award and a Michael L. Printz Honor Book Award, and it was a finalist for the National Book Award for Young People's Literature. Finally, nonfiction author Jim Murphy was honored with the Margaret A. Edwards Award for lifetime achievement in writing for young adults. Taken together, these awards announced the arrival of nonfiction literature. Even though nonfiction is being recognized for its literary qualities, questions remain about its place in the language arts classroom.

Teachers may view nonfiction only as a source of content rather than as a genre of literature with its own unique conventions. Sullivan (2001) notes that "because nonfiction is usually regarded in purely utilitarian terms, it does not seem to occur to some educators that a nonfiction work can simply be a 'good read'—something entertaining, fun, enjoyable, or just plain interesting" (p. 43). Due to this perception, many middle-grade classrooms contain few nonfiction books (Moss & Hendershot, 2002), even though many students at that age actually prefer nonfiction (Livingston, Kurkjian, Young, & Pringle, 2004).

Perhaps, as Jocelyn Bartkevicius (2010) suggests, part of the dilemma may be that the term *nonfiction* defines the genre in relation to what it is not: it is not fiction. Fiction is considered art. It is created out of someone's imagination; it is made up. **Nonfiction** is not made up, therefore, it is perceived not as art, but rather a gathering of facts presented through reason and logic.

This view of nonfiction as nonliterary and not creative may have been exacerbated by the use of the widely accepted terms "informational books" or "information books" in place of nonfiction. These terms became section labels in libraries and may have contributed to narrowing views about the richness and variety of works categorized as nonfiction (Colman, 2007).

In Chapter 1, we defined literature as writing that encourages both understanding and appreciation. That definition raises questions about which nonfiction is actually literature, which nonfiction works should be read in the English language arts classroom, and what kind of instruction young adults need to support their reading of nonfiction. The Common Core State Standards (National Governors Association Center for Best Practices/Council of Chief State School Officers, 2010) indicate that through fifth grade, instruction should emphasize informational texts, including history/social studies, science, and technical texts. Starting with sixth grade, the emphasis should shift to literary nonfiction and qualities of "literariness." In this chapter, we acknowledge the importance of nonfiction trade books, both for enriching young adults' understanding of academic subjects and for helping them negotiate the developmental tasks of adolescence. We are particularly focused, however, on literary or creative nonfiction—those works that allow young adults to develop an appreciation for the artistry of nonfiction that parallels their appreciation for fiction.

THE ARTISTRY: LITERARY NONFICTION

 work of **literary nonfiction** is more than a well-written informational book. Literary nonfiction "recognizes both the inherent power of the real and the deep resonance of the literary. It is a form that allows a writer both to narrate facts and to search for truth, blending the empirical eye of the reporter with the moral vision the—I—of the novelist" (University of Oregon, n.d., p. 1). Literary nonfiction is sometimes called creative nonfiction, narrative nonfiction, or literature of reality. It has also been labeled the "fourth genre" to elevate it to the status of literature, while distinguishing it from poetry, fiction, and drama (Root & Steinberg, 2010).

Literary or creative nonfiction is a hybrid that blends the power of fact with techniques such as theme, setting, characterization, dialogue, and tone, as well as stylistic devices such as metaphors and similes. It is broad enough to include travel writing, nature writing, science writing, biography, autobiography, memoir, interview, and various types of essay (Nordquist, n.d.). Literary nonfiction includes information; however, it may be the insights about that information that predominate. "Sometimes the subject of the literary nonfiction may not at the onset be of great interest to the reader, but the character of the writing may lure the reader into that subject" (Nordquist, n.d). Creative nonfiction "has the range to sweep inward, follow the path of the mind, add layers of contemporaneous imagination, memory, and dream to the observable events of the present moment" (Bartkevicius, 2010, p. 322). This is the artistry in literary nonfiction.

THE CHARACTERISTICS OF LITERARY NONFICTION

We use the terms *literary* and *creative nonfiction* interchangeably to denote a subjective "literariness" of a work of nonfiction and not a specific genre of nonfiction. Root and Steinberg suggest that works of nonfiction exist on a continuum stretching from the most informative to the most literary. It is the nonfiction that "brings artistry to information and actuality to imagination" (2010, xxxiii) that we contend should be part of the literature taught and appreciated in English class.

The criteria for the YALSA Award for Nonfiction for Young Adults include excellence in writing, research, presentation, and readability. The audience designated by the publisher must be between 12 and 18 years old. Although this criterion may seem a bit broad, this broadness is necessary to encompass the wide range of nonfiction being written for young adults.

Root and Steinberg (2010) suggest that the most significant common elements of creative nonfiction are personal presence, self-discovery and self-exploration, flexibility of form, veracity, and literary techniques. Although not always present in uniform proportions, these characteristics do distinguish creative nonfiction from more informational types of nonfiction.

Personal Presence

In creative nonfiction an *author's voice is identifiable*. This is evident in personal essays or memoirs, but it is also true in more objective genres such as literary journalism and academic writing. The author may reveal himself or herself through first-person recollection, contemplation, opinion, perspective, or tone. Tanya Lee Stone, author of *Almost Astronauts: 13 Women who Dared to Dream* (2009), stresses that everything written or spoken, from books to newspaper articles to the evening news, is colored by the perspective of the person who wrote it (2011, p. 86).

Self-Discovery and Self-Exploration

Writers may have a personal motive, a sense of *self-discovery and self-exploration* that propels them to investigate a topic. "Writers who seem most at home with this genre are those who like to delve, to inquire, to question, to explore, probe, mediate, analyze, turn things over, brood, worry—all of which creative nonfiction allows, even encourages" (Root & Steinberg, 2010, p. xxv). Self-discovery and self-exploration need not be limited to an intensely personal level; authors can also explore connections in the broader world. Marc Aronson and Marina Budhos' personal family histories shape their inquiry in *Sugar Changed the World: A Story of Magic, Spice, Slavery, Freedom, and Science* (2010). Aronson's ancestors came from Russia, Budho's from the Caribbean, two parts of the world with long histories of economic, political, and social deprivation, and two parts of the world where sugar played a significant role in the advancement of human equality. As the title indicates, the scope of the book is expansive, and yet each section offers a mingling of personal stories and factual information, accompanied by images that compel a reader to discover all the authors have to say.

Flexibility of Form

By definition, creative nonfiction employs characteristics of fiction and nonfiction. It also *extends the boundaries of content and format.* Root and Steinberg note that the writers of creative nonfiction, more than any type of literature, experiment with structure (p. xxvi).

Claudette Colvin: Twice Toward Justice is an example of an effective mix of biography, interviews, informational inserts, and visuals, including photographs, newspaper clippings, and police reports. As a teenager, Colvin greatly influenced the landmark anti-segregation case, *Browder vs. Gayle.* This work provides new perspectives and insights into the story of the civil rights struggle and the girl who refused to give up her seat on a bus nine months before Rosa Parks did.

They Called Themselves the K.K.K.: The Birth of an American Terrorist Group by Susan Campbell Bartoletti (2010) traces the origins of the Ku Klux Klan from a social club established in 1866 to its status as one of 926 hate groups recognized in the United States as of 2008. This winner of multiple awards integrates newspaper articles and illustrations, historical documents, photographs, first-person accounts, sketches, maps, political cartoons, and interviews, with Bartoletti's analysis. What might be considered auxiliary text becomes an integral component in relating this history. The author's extensive documentation serves to elicit an emotional response from readers in this astounding work.

Russell Martin and Lydia Nibley explain how they crafted *The Mysteries of Beethoven's Hair* (2009) from a combination of historical research and new investigation. Chapters alternate between the biography of Beethoven and a modern scientific investigation of a lock of his hair. They describe their style as narrative nonfiction or creative nonfiction. They explain that "this form requires a writer to stick to well-researched facts while using the tools of fiction. . . . In this form the writer can't ever make up something and pass it off as being true. And, the writer owes it to readers to make it very clear when they are leaving the verifiable and imaging some possibility" (p. 113). The authors point out that they use language such as "it is easy to imagine" when they are speculating. This distinction may not always be clear to the young adult reader, however, raising issues of the author's responsibility of clarity and veracity.

Veracity

Veracity is a foundational component of creative nonfiction. "Creative nonfiction is reliably factual, firmly anchored in real experience, whether the author has lived it or observed and recorded it" (Root & Steinberg, 2010, p. xxvi); however, this is not the same type of verifiable factuality found in a science report. Creative nonfiction often includes feelings, interpretations, and personal memories, which may never be corroborated or confirmed in an empirical manner or by an objective investigator.

In his frequently reprinted essay "The Creative Nonfiction Police" (2005, p. 349), Lee Gutkind, the founder of the literary magazine *Creative Nonfiction*, suggests that creative nonfiction writers should strive for the truth and should write as accurately and honestly as possible; however, not everyone has the same truth nor can it always be verified. Combining that which is true with the techniques of fiction poses unique problems.

Gutkind cites several examples of authors who strayed from the truth in varying ways, some that seemed to matter and others that did not. Henry David Thoreau compressed two years of living on Walden Pond into one in his essay on nature. Does it matter to someone reading this now, or for that matter, in Thoreau's time? Truman Capote took no notes, so the absolute accuracy of *In Cold Blood* (1967), often considered one of the first and most notable works of creative nonfiction, may be questionable.

John Berendt, author of *Midnight in the Garden of Good and Evil* (1997), another account of a murder, made up transitions in order to move the book from scene to scene. Although initially selected as a finalist for the Pulitzer Prize in general nonfiction, it was eliminated after the extent of Berendt's fictionalizing was determined (Colman, 2007).

Michael Chabon wrote about real people in *Wonder Boys* (1995) but presented them as fictional and was criticized by readers who recognized the actual people and incidents. Janet Cooke, a former reporter for the *Washington Post*, was awarded the Pulitzer Prize for a depiction of a young drug dealer who, it turned out, did not exist. In actuality, he was a composite of several youths she had encountered. Cooke lost her job, and her reputation as a journalist was permanently damaged (Gutkind, 2005).

Root and Steinberg (2010) contend that all writers of creative nonfiction must decide on what to include and what to exclude; therefore, they are all guilty of acts of omission. All writing is also guilty of acts of commission—deliberately altering experiences and events to focus on those elements the writer most wants to emphasize. Some minor alterations, such as changing details to disguise a person, have become routine in creative nonfiction. Root and Steinberg recognize that conflation of time (representing something as taking less time than it did) and creating a composite character are significant alterations that readers may find more difficult to accept (p. xxix).

Tanya Lee Stone states that writers of narrative nonfiction "balance the role of historian and storyteller by making sure we don't interject tension or emotion or events without thorough knowledge. We do it by employing fiction techniques without ever making a single thing up" (2011, p. 85).

In contrast, Mark Salzman states in the author's note to *True Notebooks* (2003) that a combination of a memoir of his time as a writing teacher in a correctional facility, content from his notebooks and collections of writings by his incarcerated students, is nonfiction; however, it is not journalism. He took no notes and recorded no classes or conversations. He readily declares that the dialogues have been re-created from memory, and to those who object he responds, "pshaw."

Although creative nonfiction may spur disagreements over the interpretation of truth and the balance between the aesthetic and information, the facts should be as accurate as possible. To this end, some writers of creative nonfiction, especially when writing about historical and scientific events, include notes documenting their research process and sources.

Susan Campbell Bartoletti drew from a variety of sources, including charity records, newspaper accounts, workhouse records, diaries, letters, parish and tax records, and personal accounts for the Sibert Award-winning *Black Potatoes: The Story of the Great Irish Potato Famine, 1845–1850* (2001). She comments on the challenge of dealing with multiple opinions as to whose fault the famine was, opinions that were often influenced by nationalism and politics. She also notes the difficulty of accurately depicting a historical account from the oral histories of a largely illiterate population. She includes a timeline and sources.

Literary Techniques

Creative nonfiction incorporates the same literary techniques as fiction, such as imagery, figurative language, tone, and point of view, all of which are described in Chapter 3. The effective use of literary techniques can be seen in the rich imagery and parallel construction of the following paragraph from Rick Bowers' *Spies of Mississippi: The True Story of the Spy Network that Tried to Destroy the Civil Rights Movement* (2010):

> The Mississippi River Delta is a study in contrast. The vast stretches of green and white cotton fields are interspersed with eerie, moss-draped cypress swamps. The white-pillared mansions of the plantation elite stand near the huts of the poor dirt farmer. The Delta is home to debutante balls and backroom gambling dens, ramble shackle houseboats and majestic paddle wheelers. This sweltering, insect-ridden, and amazingly fertile stretch of bottomland forms, in the words of author James C. Cobb, "the most southern place on earth." (p. 23)

These contrasting images reflect the social, political, and economic chasm between whites and blacks in Mississippi during the civil rights movement of the 1950s and 1960s.

TYPES OF LITERARY NONFICTION

Categories or genres of nonfiction include literary journalism, biography, autobiography, memoir, diaries, journals, and essays. These types of nonfiction are most likely to be literary and most likely to fulfill the Common Core State Standards for the English Language Arts (National Governors Association, 2010) objective for creative nonfiction; namely that students are able to determine how an author's choices of "style and content contribute to the power, persuasiveness or beauty of a text."

Literary Journalism

Literary or **creative journalism** was referred to as New Journalism in the 1960s when authors such as Joan Didion, Gay Talese, and Tom Wolfe challenged the traditional view of objective reporting. Their work incorporated dialogue, dramatic action, and other elements of fiction (Nguyen & Shreve, 2005, p. 3). Wolfe's name became synonymous with this movement when he edited *The New Journalism* in 1973.

Wolfe's *The Right Stuff* (1979), an account of U. S. test pilots and early astronauts, is an example of well researched journalism presented from a limited omniscient perspective. The first chapter focuses on the wives of the pilots as they wait to learn which of their husbands' bodies "lies incinerated in the swamps or the pines or the palmetto grass, burned beyond recognition, which anyone who had been around an air base for very long realized was quite an artful euphemism to describe a human body that now looked like an enormous fowl that has burned up in a stove, burned a blackish brown all over, greasy and blistered, fried." (p. 5).

Wolfe's account combines the drama of fiction with the force of the facts about a highly dangerous profession and the fiercely competitive, loyal, and brave men who chose it. The film of the same name (1983), directed by Philip Kaufman, portrays the individuals who had "the right stuff" to make the space program work. *Contemporary Creative Nonfiction: I & Eye* (2005), edited by Nguyen and Shreve, contains several short selections of literary journalism appropriate for young adults, including an excerpt from *The Right Stuff*.

Biography

A **biography** is the history of a person's life written by someone else. Biographies can be about a person's entire life, or they can focus on only a portion of that person's life. As the title indicates, *The Life and Death of Adolf Hitler* (2002) by James Cross Giblin includes information about all phases of Hitler's life, from childhood to adulthood, and continues through his death. Giblin posed three questions: "What sort of man could plan and carry out such horrendous schemes? How was he able to win support for his deadly ventures? And why did no one try to stop him until it was almost too late?" (p. 3). Responding to these questions requires a vast amount of information. A final, brief chapter called "Hitler Lives" looks at contemporary neo-Nazis, as a reminder of Hitler's legacy of hatred and fear.

In contrast, partial biographies focus on a particular segment of a person's life, often their early years or the time period for which the person is well known or remembered. Sid Fleishman's *The Trouble Begins At 8: A Life of Mark Twain in the Wild, Wild West* (Fleischman, 2008) covers Samuel Clemens' life from his early years until he published his first book. During this time he experienced life as a steamboat pilot, gold miner, newspaper man, typesetter, lecturer, and humorist. An "afterstory" and timeline fill in some of the important events that occurred during the remainder of his life, such as his marriage, the birth and death of his children, and the publication of his various works. The title refers to a poster advertising one of his speeches which proclaimed, "The Trouble to begin at 8 o'clock."

Jack: The Early Years of John F. Kennedy (Cooper, 2003) is, as the title indicates, a biography of Kennedy's life from birth to his graduation from prep school. Included are numerous pictures of his home and family and samples of his early writing and his report cards. Young Kennedy was constantly compared to his siblings and under a great deal of pressure to succeed at everything he did. An afterword briefly describes his adult years. The book poignantly ends with the statement: "John Fitzgerald Kennedy had been president two years and ten months, about one thousand days" (p. 153).

In addition to being categorized as complete or partial, a biography can also be classified by whether it focuses on a single subject or is a collection of individual biographies. Albert Marrin's *The Great Adventure: Theodore Roosevelt and the Rise of Modern America* (2007) is a single subject biography that focuses on both the man and the vast changes that occurred in the United States during Roosevelt's lifetime. Roosevelt, the youngest president, was also a conservationist, scholar, soldier, and explorer and the first American to receive a Nobel Prize.

Diane Stanley, recipient of numerous awards, has written several single subject, illustrated biographies geared toward younger adolescents that present insights into people and places unfamiliar to most of them. *Saladin: Noble Prince of Islam* (2002) provides the Muslim perspective of the crusades. A map, author's note, and postscript provide background of the time period, location, and perspective of this biography of Saladin, a Muslim knight who fought the invading Crusaders. Illustrations are inspired by Islamic artwork of the time.

Stanley's *Charles Dickens: The Man Who Had Great Expectations* (1993), written with Peter Vennema, includes facts that describe Dickens as a man shaped by his economical and historical circumstances. An early romance was ended by the girl's parents, due to Dickens' lack of money and social standing. Poverty and social status were prominent themes in his work, and obtaining wealth was a major goal in his life. Although his wife bore ten children, he considered his marriage misguided; he thought she did not do enough to help him. Thus, he directed his passion to his wife's sister. She died young and his idolized vision of her became the model for several characters in his work. Stanley includes a list of works by Dickens as additional sources for this biography.

Janis Joplin: Rise Up Singing (2010) by Ann Angel is a recent recipient of the YALSA Award for Excellence in Nonfiction. Dozens of photographs augment the story of Joplin's rise as a rock icon of the 1960s, her ongoing struggle with low self-esteem and her feelings of being unaccepted. She died of an overdose of drugs and alcohol alone in a hotel room in 1970 at the age of 27. Television host Dick Cavett described her life: "I think there were two Janises: there was the high school girl who desperately wanted acceptance and that character she created which was the tough talking, tough-drugging, drinking rock and roll star" (p. 99). The biography reveals both.

Collective biographies are a collection of individual biographies usually connected by a common theme or topic. The collective biography, *Let It Shine:*

Russell Freedman

Russell Freedman's career as a biographer, historian, creative nonfiction writer, and photo essayist spans more than 50 years and almost as many books. He has been awarded the Newbery Medal, three Newbery Honor Awards, the *Washington Post*/Children's Book Guild Nonfiction Award, the Laura Ingalls Wilder Award, and the National Humanities Medal.

Freedman's success is due, in part, to his grasp of the possibilities of nonfiction. He explains, "I've always been a history buff. I believe that a book of history or biography can carry within its pages a certain magical power; it can convey all the life and immediacy of great fiction while retaining the authenticity, the additional power of truth" (1998, p. 2).

In his view, the historian strives for objectivity, does the best he or she can, but the result inevitably reflects the life experience and values of the person writing the book. Freedman says that "there are today as many different strategies employed in the writing of history and biography as there are authors, who in many cases combine original research, an independent point of view, and adherence to the documented historical record" (2011, p. 4).

"When I sit down to write," he says, explaining his creative process, "I simply want to capture the reader's attention and tell a story about a person, an event or a series of events that for some reason happen to interest me. I want to lose myself in the world where those events took place and through the transformative power of language, make that world, that person, those events live again for my readers" (2006, p. 21).

Lincoln: A Photobiography (1987), the first nonfiction work to earn a Newbery Medal, covers the entirety of Lincoln's life from his backwoods beginnings to his assassination, in approximately 130 pages of texts and pictures. This effort obviously required a lot of "distilling." Nonetheless, Freedman presents Lincoln as a multifaceted man, a man who was at times plagued with depression, emotionally distant, lacking in military acumen, and superstitious. He was also brilliant, ambitious, and determined to keep the country intact.

Since the Lincoln book, Freedman has written many biographies for young adult readers, choosing subjects who, he feels, have something to tell a reader about how to live. Freedman explains that "a biography for young people calls for the demanding art of distillation, the art of storytelling, and your responsibility is to stick as closely as possible to the documented record" (Sutton, 2010, p. 205). The difficulty comes in deciding what to include and what to exclude. It is this selection process that Freedman considers most speculative about writing nonfiction.

This selection process applies to visuals in his books as well as to text. He might consider over 1,000 photographs before selecting 140 or so to be included in one book. Photographs and text are carefully coordinated, and information from a photo caption is not repeated in the text. He says that "photos make the past come alive; scenes show the subjects are time bound; expressions are timeless" (*Children's Literature,* 2006, p. 1).

Some of his biographies that include numerous and powerful images are *Franklin Delano Roosevelt* (1990); *The Wright Brothers: How They Invented the Airplane* (1991); *The Life and Death of Crazy Horse,* with drawings by Amos Bad Heart Bull (1996); *Eleanor Roosevelt: A Life of Discovery* (1997); *Martha Graham: A Dancer's Life* (1998); *Confucius: The Golden Rule* (2002); *Washington at Valley Forge* (2008); and *Lafayette and the American Revolution* (2010).

Freedman created several historical works that focus on the lives of young people. *Immigrant Kids* (1980) was inspired by an art exhibit commemorating the 125th anniversary of the Children's Aid Society. *Children of the Wild West* (1990a) describes the duties, clothes, equipment, and day-to-day lives of cowboys from the 1860s to the 1890s. *Kids at Work: Lewis Hine and the Crusade Against Child Labor* (1998) portrays the story of children in early 1900s America in a photo essay that documents child labor. *Children of the Great Depression* (2005) includes memoirs, diaries, letters, and other firsthand accounts that cut across economic and social boundaries to depict the effects of the depression on children of the 1930s.

As part of his effort to make history more accessible and to counteract the "historical amnesia" suffered by many adolescents (Freedman, 2006, p. 23), he has written books based on U. S. documents, such as *In Defense of Liberty: The Story of America's Bill of Rights* (2003) and *Give Me Liberty! The Story of the Declaration of Independence* (2000).

Freedman grew up hearing his father's nostalgic stories of World War I, initially called the Great War because of its massive scale, both in the number of countries involved and the number of people who died. In *The War to End all Wars: World War I* (2010), Freedman synthesized voluminous scholarly work to create a readable and well-researched account of many aspects of this horrific war.

In his acceptance speech for the Flora Stieglitz Straus Award for *Freedom Walkers: The Story of the Montgomery Bus Boycott* (2006a), Freedman reflected on how he approaches writing history: "I've learned that one of the most effective ways to write history is to focus on a single dramatic event, a self-contained story, so to speak, that in itself illuminates a larger historical era or theme" (Bank Street, 2007, p. 3). The idea for writing about the Montgomery boycott came from an experience he had as a young man recently back from the Korean War. He was traveling across the country in a Greyhound bus when he witnessed legal racial segregation for the first time. At the end of his trip in New York, the news was full of events that he later realized were the beginnings of the modern civil rights movement.

Freedman explains why he writes history: "What finally matters most to me about the reading and writing of history is the way it deepens us, allows us to glimpse worlds different from our own—the way an understanding of history extends our own feelings and compassion, enlarges our ability to recognize someone's humanity" (2006, p. 28). His most important goal is that his work becomes "a piece of literature, a compelling read" that helps the reader to discover the joy of reading (Sutton, 2010, p. 208).

Stories of Black Women Freedom Fighters (Pinkney, 2000), is a grouping of beautifully illustrated short biographies of women who changed history, including Harriet Tubman, Rosa Parks, and Shirley Chisholm. Pinkney comments that these individual lives woven together become the story of the challenges and triumphs of civil rights as the movement spanned American history (p. xi).

Bolden's *Wake Up Our Souls: A Celebration of Black American Arts* (2004) looks at the lives, creations, and artistic movements of African American artists of the 20th century. The book was produced in conjunction with the Smithsonian's American Art Museum, and reproductions of the art, paintings, sculptures, and photographs are from the Smithsonian collection. A glossary of art terms and source notes for quotations are included. *Wake Up Our Souls* presents obstacles faced and triumphs achieved by African American artists.

The Dark Game: True Spy Stories (2010) by Paul B. Janeczko, a finalist for the YALSA Nonfiction Award, examines the history of spying by weaving together biographies of famous spies such as Mata Hari and Benedict Arnold and people not usually thought of as spies, including as Harriet Tubman and Benjamin Franklin. Information about invisible ink, codes, cyber spying, and spy satellites creates a chronology of the ever-developing world of espionage.

Another type of collective biography is about a people defined by some aspect of their culture. Such a biography may describe individuals, but the life story of the group is at the center of the work. *Skywalkers: Mohawk Ironworkers Build the City* (2010) by David Weitzman recounts the history of the Mohawk tribe's move to large urban areas and how they became the steelworkers who built the skyscrapers of America. From the title *American Patriots: The Story of Blacks in the Military from the Revolution to Desert Storm* (2003), it is apparent that Gail Buckley is focusing on a specific group of people, African Americans, and their experiences in many wars throughout many eras. Short descriptions of many individuals' participation in various military efforts are included; however, the expansive time frame precludes in-depth biographies. The cohesiveness of this biographical history is the sum of parts, the life stories of so many people adding up to the life story of a group.

Sue Barancik's *Guide to Collective Biographies for Children and Young Adults* (2004) is a helpful resource for finding biographies of both well-known and unknown people—5,760 in all—who are mentioned in 721 collective biographies published from 1988 to 2002. Individuals are listed alphabetically and also by topic and theme.

Autobiographies and Memoirs

Autobiographies and **memoirs** are accounts of a person's life written by that person. The expectation is that these personal histories will be read by someone else. Memoirs often focus on specific events in the writer's life or encounters with certain people. Memoirs typically are written as a commentary or reflection about these selected moments (Shaw, 1972, p. 234).

William Zinsser (1987) explains the difference between memoir and autobiography: "The writer of a memoir takes us back to a corner of his or her life that was unusually vivid or intense—childhood, for instance—or that was framed by unique events. By narrowing the lens, the writer achieves a focus that isn't possible in autobiography, a memoir is a window into life" (p. 21).

One of the most profound types of historical memoir is the **slave narrative.** *Growing Up in Slavery: Stories of Young Slaves as Told by Themselves* (2005), edited by Yuval Taylor, is composed of the first-person accounts of ten slaves excerpted from their original works. These slave narratives provide insight into both slavery and personal narrative as autobiography and memoir. Taylor explains:

> [The slaves] transformed themselves from victims into agents of resistance just by telling their stories and protesting the vast injustices that were done to them. Along with other writers who had been slaves, they established a popular literary genre, sold hundreds of thousands of books, and advanced the antislavery cause. While they wrote mainly for their contemporaries, they produced works of lasting literary and historical value. In doing so, they performed an act of liberation. (p. ix)

Taylor points out that many 19th and 20th century authors were influenced by slave narratives. Included in this list are works often read in whole or part in English classes: Zora Neale Hurston's *Their Eyes Were Watching God* (1937), Richard Wright's *Black Boy* (1945), Ralph Ellison's *Invisible Man* (1952), James Baldwin's *Go Tell It on the Mountain* (1953), *The Autobiography of Malcolm X* (1965), Maya Angelou's *I Know Why the Caged Bird Sings* (1969), Ernest Gaines' *The Autobiography of Miss Jane Pitman* (1971), and Toni Morrison's *Beloved* (1987). Taylor suggests that most, if not all, post-Civil War African American prose works are descended from the slave narrative: "Not only because it was the first distinctive African American literary genre, but because of its powerful mix of storytelling, racial awareness, social critique, and self-reflection—elements of the greatest black literary achievements" (p. xvi).

With few exceptions, the slave narratives were written or dictated by former slaves. The dictated works were sometimes edited or expanded by editors and publishers. Taylor retains the words of the slaves, but emends spellings and edits content for ease of reading. He also provides explanations of words with which readers may not be familiar. For example, Olaudah Equiano, identified by Taylor as the "father of Afro-American autobiography," describes his initial experience on a slave ship:

> I was not long suffered [allowed] to indulge my grief; I was soon put down under the decks, and there I received such a salutation [welcome] in my nostrils as I had never experienced in my life: so that, with the loathsomeness of the stench, and crying together, I became so sick and low that I was not able to eat, nor had I the least desire to taste anything. I now wished for the last friend, death, to relieve me. (p. 5)

The narratives are written by individuals all under 19 years of age. A brief biographical introduction, publication history, interpretation, and information about what happened to the writer after the publication of the narrative provide a context for the adolescent reader. Black and white illustrations by Kathleen Judge add a layer of intensity.

Memoirs that express the emotions, experiences, and fears shared by young adults can be personally satisfying reading experiences and developmentally appropriate even when language is mature and circumstances stark and depressing, perhaps even because of this. The memoirs adolescents read usually present individuals who have succeeded or triumphed over difficult circumstances.

Liz Murray's *Breaking Night: A Memoir of Forgiveness, Survival, and My Journey from Homeless to Harvard* (2010) contains one picture, that of the author's mother when she was a teenager. This Alex Award-winning memoir begins with Murray's mother visiting her father in prison and dramatically showing him her belly, pregnant with Murray. Her mother explains later that life was not supposed to turn out the way it did. Nonetheless, Murray, the child of drug-addicted parents, found herself homeless and on her own at age 15. Through incredible forbearance she returns to school, wins a *New York Times* scholarship and is accepted at Harvard University, where she graduates in 2009. Her memoir ends with the realization that "life takes on the meaning that you give it" (p. 329).

Nic Sheff's *We All Fall Down: Living with Addiction* (2011) continues the story of his struggle with addiction presented in *Tweak: Growing up on Methamphetamines* (2008). Sheff identifies his work as a memoir and clarifies that it is based on recollections and dialogue. Events have been recreated. He also indicates in a note to readers that names have, in some incidences, been changed and events have been compressed "to convey the substance of what was said or what occurred" (unpaginated). He began drinking at age 11 and stumbled through addiction for years. He ends his second memoir with the statement that he has been sober a year and six months, providing a sense of hope after his long journey of despair.

War often provides the setting for both deeply disturbing memories as well as remembrances of triumph and survival. Ibtisam Barakat's *Tasting the Sky: A Palestinian Childhood* (2007) is a memoir of the author's life during the Six-Day War and as a postwar refugee. She begins and ends with her thoughts in 1981 while living on the West Bank. The core of her story covers 1967 to 1971,

The Abracadabra Kid: A Writer's Life. Sid Fleishman, 1996. Fleishman's witty, insightful autobiography explains how he made his way from boy magician to sailor, Hollywood script writer to award-winning writer. He offers advice for becoming a writer. Black and white photographs are included. Ages 12 and up.

Bad Boy: A Memoir. Walter Dean Myers, 2001. Myer's autobiography covers his childhood growing up in Harlem in the 1940s and 1950s. He faced gangs, a speech impediment, and problems at school. Ages 13 and up.

Bowman's Store: A Journey to Myself. Joseph Bruchac, 1997. Bruchac's childhood story of living with his beloved maternal grandparents, even though his parents lived close by, is woven with Abenaki tales and his discovery of his Abenaki Indian heritage that had been kept secret from him. Ages 12 and up.

A Hole in My Life. Jack Gantos, 2004. Gantos tells about the last of his teenage years, his involvement with selling drugs, his arrest, and his prison sentence. He states that mistakes are far more interesting to read about than redemption, so he "start[s] with where I think I went around the bend" (p. 8). Age 13 and up.

King of the Mild Frontier: An Ill-Advised Autobiography. Chris Crutcher, 2004. Crutcher's raucously funny descriptions of his childhood growing up in Idaho with a stern father and an alcoholic mother and the importance of athletics provide insights into his characters, plots, and themes. He also discusses censorship and writing. Ages 13 and up.

Knots in My Yo-Yo String: The Autobiography of a Kid. Jerry Spinelli, 1998. Spinelli's story of growing up during the 1950s in Pennsylvania has hilarious vignettes of his preadolescent and adolescent angst and nostalgic memories. Ages 10–14.

Looking Back. Lois Lowry, 1998. This memoir spans part of her mother's life, Lowry's childhood, and her adulthood up to the time of this publication. Black and white photographs tell of her past in a style that jumps from one story to the next. Excerpts from her work are included. Ages 10–13.

Weeds in Bloom: Autobiography of an Ordinary Man. Robert Newton Peck, 2005. Peck's life is revealed through character sketches of the "weeds," the simple, often poor people that Peck has encountered throughout his life. His humor is revealed in his descriptions of ordinary things; for instance, the suit he bought for college became his "going away suit" not because he was leaving, but because everyone who saw him in it told him to go away. Ages 14 and up.

beginning when she is three and a half years old and "the war came to us at sundown" (p. 19). It ends with her thinking that "I am midway from forgetting to remembering. I do not know how long it will take before I return to all of myself" (p. 169). This memoir is about war, but Barakat also reveals much about her family, friends, and her developing love for writing.

Autobiographies and memoirs of authors of literature for young adults may be of particular interest to adolescents. These personal stories may motivate students to read additional works by an author or to revisit novels they have already read with a better understanding of the author's motivations for writing them.

Diaries/Journals/Notebooks

Diaries usually have a day-to-day or week-to-week format and tend to be chronological (Shaw, 1972, p. 39). Perhaps the most well-known diary read by young adults is *Anne Frank: The Diary of a Young Girl*, written by Frank from June 12,

1942, until August 1, 1944, while hiding with her family during the German occupation of Amsterdam. When the family was discovered by the Nazis, they were taken to a concentration camp, where Anne later died. The diary was found by her father and first published in 1947.

Thura's Diary: My Life in Wartime Iraq (2004) by Thura Al-Windawi is the diary of another young woman living through a war. Nineteen-year-old Al-Windawi began her diary a few days before the bombing of Bagdad, her hometown, began in March, 2003, and continued through December, 2003. The book is written in a simple, straightforward style that captures the impact of the war on all aspects of her family's existence, such as her disrupted education, inadequate food, and her father's inability to find employment. She also points out the irony that in post-Saddam Hussein Iraq, interpretations of customs, in particular restrictions placed on women, were stricter than they were before the war. A map, list of people and places, and a timeline provide a context for readers unfamiliar with locations and events. Al-Windawi later pursued a college career in the United States.

Notebooks and **journals** often focus on a specific experience or event and may include observations, dialogue, and the private thoughts of the author. Middle-grade students will readily understand the journal format in Jennifer Owings Dewey's *Antarctic Journal: Four Months at the Bottom of the World* (2000). This chronological account of Dewey's expedition contains excerpts from her journal, letters sent to her family, and a wide variety of photographs of landscapes and wildlife. Her color pencil sketches of the indigenous animals add interest and information.

David Carroll's (2009) *Following the Water: A Hydromancer's Notebook*, a National Book Award nominee, chronicles the life of the inhabitants of a New Hampshire wetland through his pen and ink drawings and observations of turtle life. His love for the wetlands began as a child, and he weaves these early memories with his account of the changing wetland landscape.

In *The Burn Journals* (2004), Brent Runyon relates his year of recovery after attempting suicide by dosing himself with gasoline and lighting himself on fire. The journal has only a few dates: February 4, 1991, the day he attempts to kill himself; February 5, when he enters Children's National Medical Center in Washington, D. C.; June 12, when he moves to a rehab center; September 13, when he goes home; and January 26, 1992, when he returns to school. He describes the days and nights in between, sometimes through a drug-induced veil and sometimes in excruciating detail, the procedures he undergoes in the hospital and later at a rehabilitation center. His recovery, both physical and mental, was long and difficult and far from complete at the end of this journal.

Essays

Writers and critics have argued about the characteristics of an **essay** since around 1600. Over the centuries the definition of the essay has remained difficult to pin down, partially because of its ability to change in accordance with the social, political, and literary climate of the times. Thus, the essay may be labeled familiar, personal, autobiographical, literary, creative nonfiction, or academic; or it may be named for its chief subject, such as the nature essay or philosophical essay. Essays are usually short; the word *essay* comes from a French word meaning *trial* or *attempt*. Essays can be written in several formats including letters, as a periodical serial, a political tract, or a newspaper or magazine column (*The Oxford Encyclopedia of American Literature*, 2005).

The Best American Essays, published annually by Houghton Mifflin Harcourt as part of the "Best American" series, is an excellent source of contemporary essays. Susan Orlean, editor of *The Best American Essays: 2005* spoke of the appeal of the essay:

> That they continue to be written and read is enduring proof that, all indications to the contrary, our voices matter to each other; that we do wonder what goes on inside each other's heads; that we want to know each other, and we want to be known. Nothing is more meaningful—more human, really—than our efforts to tell each other the stories of ourselves, of what it's like to be who we are, to think the things we think, to live the lives we live. (Orlean, 2005, p. xviii, cited in Campbell, 2010, p. 54).

Iris Jacob's collection of poetry and essays in *My Sister's Voices: Teenage Girls of Color Speak Out* (2002) addresses racism, sexism, body image, family heritage, identity, and personal loss. The authors, all young women of color, speak of their childhoods and adolescence, frankly and often eloquently. Jacob sought submissions through teachers and youth organizations. She introduces each piece and explains why it was chosen for the collection and how she personally relates to it.

In *Father Water, Mother Wood: Essays on Fishing and Hunting in the North Woods* (1994) Gary Paulsen recounts his experiences in the north woods of Minnesota. The book is divided into three sections: Fishing, Camping, and Hunting, with the majority of the book about fishing. The seasons are determined by the type of fishing or hunting legal at that time. Paulsen writes of his adventures, but his essays also reflect the challenges of growing up in a dysfunctional family. For Paulsen, the power of the woods and the comfort of fishing helped assuage the pain of life.

If a letter can reveal aspects of its author's life, then collections of letters can reveal the history of a nation. *Women's Letters: America from the Revolutionary War to the Present* (2005) edited by Lisa Grunwald and Stephen J. Adler, presents the experiences by hundreds of women, many of whom had no public outlet for their opinions and others who did. The editors explain that they chose each letter not because of a certain agenda or historical perspective, but rather because they could "imagine telling a friend about a letter in a normal course of conversation" (p. 6).

The over 700-page book begins with a letter written in 1776 by a wife telling her cowardly husband that she will gladly exchange places with him on the battlefield. It ends with an e-mail from *Wall Street Journal* correspondent Farnaz Fassihi, posted from Bagdad in September 2004. She writes of the dangerous situation for journalists (not to mention civilians) and the constant threat of bombings. Assassinations, kidnappings, and beheadings are commonplace, and nearly a hundred American forces come under attack daily by insurgents. She concludes that it may be impossible to "salvage [Iraq] from its violent downward spiral" (p. 760–761).

The letters are written by women from all walks of life, including author Louisa May Alcott; first ladies Martha Washington, Mary Todd Lincoln, and Eleanor Roosevelt; suffragette Elizabeth Cady Stanton; and actresses Judy Garland

and Marilyn Monroe. Letters from friends and family members are published along with letters written to newspapers, magazines, and influential people. Some letters are about everyday affairs, such as a mother's disappointment that her daughter intends to live with a man before marriage. Some personal correspondence did not seem important when it was written but took on significance after later events. Nicole Brown wrote to O. J. Simpson decrying their marriage as a mistake, and Julie Nixon Eisenhower told her father, then President Nixon, to take time before deciding whether or not to resign. The book is divided by time periods, each with an introduction that provides historical background.

Many adolescents may think that letters are an artifact of the past. However, letters remain an effective approach for presenting a position or opinion. *Letters to a Young Brother: MANifest Your Destiny* (2006) by Hill Harper, an actor and Harvard Law School graduate, provides advice and words of encouragement to young African Americans through letters and e-mails. In *Letters to a Young Brother* he responds to questions he has received from young men. The letters are arranged by chapter topics such as single parenthood, sexually transmitted diseases, and the allure of wealth. He followed this ALA award-winning book with a companion piece for young women, *Letters to a Young Sister: DeFINE Your Destiny* (2008). Topics include health, service and faith, the differences between need and purpose, money, education and careers, self-respect, and the expectations of how a boy should treat a girl.

EXPANDING BOUNDARIES OF CONTEMPORARY NONFICTION

 e mentioned earlier that literary or creative nonfiction writers often experiment with format, structure, and style. This style of nonfiction writing is similar to the metafictive characteristics described throughout this book.

Mixing Genres

No Choirboy: Murder, Violence, and Teenagers on Death Row (Kuklin, 2008), for example, mixes several genres, including interviews, dialogues, poetry, personal memoir, self-portrait, and photograph. Voices of the incarcerated young men and of family members of the people they murdered are both heard. Kuklin's commentary about the death penalty is interspersed throughout the book.

In *The Lincolns: A Scrapbook Look at Abraham and Mary* (2008), Candace Fleming weaves together a wide variety of artifacts from Mary Lincoln's white cake recipe to Abraham Lincoln's draft of the Emancipation Proclamation. The book begins with separate chapters for Abraham and Mary, representing their separate, early lives and then shifts to the Lincolns' shared personal and political lives. Extensive notes, acknowledgements, and a section addressing the author's method of research are included in this 2009 *Boston Globe* Award-winning book.

Anne Frank: Her Life in Words and Pictures from the Archives of The Anne Frank House (2009) by Menno Metselaar and Ruud van der Rol begins with a timeline printed on the left side page, across from the table of contents. The first visual is a photograph of the checkered cover of Frank's diary. Throughout, chronologi-

classroom scenario

The Voices of War

This classroom study demonstrates an approach for helping readers to analyze how an author or editor's point of view alters the content of a work of nonfiction and how the perspective from which a writer presents the content influences the choice of genre. The students in the following scenario are familiar with the genres previously described. They will be reading books representing a variety of nonfiction genres related to the topic of war. AS YOU READ, consider how students learn about the characteristics of nonfiction genres within an inquiry approach. Also, consider how the work selected, both by the teacher and the students, fits with the purposes of this inquiry.

Mrs. Bee is preparing her eleventh grade students to engage in self-directed inquiries about war experiences as depicted in nonfiction. Her goal is for her students to investigate voice and perspective in the authoring and editing of stories of war. The class is reading *War Is . . . soldiers, survivors, and storytellers talk about war* (2008) edited by Marc Aronson and Patty Campbell. The book contains various forms of writing, including newspaper columns and interviews, letters, essays, memoirs, blogs, a one-act play, and song lyrics.

The editors indicate their individual positions at the onset of this collection of both historical and contemporary works of fiction and nonfiction. Campbell states that "as a first step, young people considering the military as an option need to have the realities of war clearly revealed to them in many different voices so that they can make a decision based on truth. I have gathered pieces for this anthology with that essential goal in mind, and I make no secret of the fact that they reflect my passionate revulsion toward war" (p. 6).

Aronson states that "There is no YA section on war. . . . And yet it is teenagers who make up the next generation of soldiers and civilians. Both fighters and those at home need to know what they are

in for" (pp. 8–9). He sought out works written by military personnel, journalists, and people who grew up in military families. The book is divided into three sections: "Deciding about War," "Experiencing War," and "The Aftermath of War."

Foreign war correspondent Chris Hedges' essay "The Moment of Combat" answers questions such as "How can I avoid being shot?" and "Is there a chance I will enjoy killing?" The lyrics for "Masters of War" by Bob Dylan challenge the economic motives of war. "In the Front Lines," drawn from columns by Pulitzer Prize-winning war correspondent Ernie Pyle, provides an on-the-scene perspective of the common soldier serving in Europe during World War II.

The essay the class is reading today, "Women at War: What It Is Like to Be a Female Soldier in Iraq" by Helen Benedict, was selected for the book by Campbell. Mrs. Bee asks students what their expectations are for the content and tone of the piece given Campbell's stated perspective. She also asks students what their views are on women serving in the military, especially combat. Next, the class looks at the website Experiencing War: Women at War, developed as part of the Veterans History Project (2008) (www.loc.gov/vets/stories/ex-war-womenatwar.html). This site links to numerous audio and video inter-views of female veterans of four wars. After viewing this site for about 30 minutes, Mrs. Bee asks the students to read the essay and to discuss the following questions in their discussion groups:

1. Why did Campbell include this piece in the collection? Does it present a biased or unbiased ac-count of women serving in the military?

2. How did Helen Benedict obtain the information for this nonfiction piece? What does she want readers to think? Do you agree or disagree with her?

3. How did Montoya's, Garcia's, Naylor's, Tascon's, and Sanchez's military experiences differ? How are they the same?

4. Do their experiences and reasons for joining the military influence your original viewpoint about women in war?

Next, students respond to the journal prompt: Did other people's ideas or insights during the group discussion or from the Women at War website cause you to reconsider your perspective about war and women in war?

Completing the book over the course of a week, students further investigate the voices of those who write about war. They may select any topic related to war, contemporary or historical, and they may choose the nonfiction texts they will read. In particular, they are to consider the perspective of the author or editor and the genre.

Mrs. Bee works with the school librarian to make resources available to the students. They start by locating the books excerpted in the Aronson and Campbell work. Multiple copies of Hedges' *War Is a Force that Gives Us Meaning* (2003) and *What Every Person Should Know About War* (2003), Benedicts' *The Lonely Soldier: The Private War of Women Serving in Iraq* (2010) and *Brave Men* by Ernie Pyle and G. Kurt Piehler (2001) are set out for the students.

Knowing that her students are very involved in music, Mrs. Bee obtains books about how music is used to voice opinions about war: *The Songs that Fought the War: Popular Music and the Home Front, 1939–1945* by John Bush Jones (2006) and *Battle Notes: Music of the Vietnam War* by Lee Andresen (2003). She directs the students to the website JW'S Rock Garden, Vietnam Era Anti War Music (www.jwsrock garden.com/jw02vvaw.htm) as another possible resource.

Mrs. Bee also chooses Andrew Carroll's collections of war letters across time and around the world captured in *War Letters: Extraordinary Correspondence from American Wars* (2002) and *Behind the Lines: Powerful and Revealing American and Foreign War Letters—and One Man's Search to Find Them* (2006). *The Greatest Generation* (1998) by Tom Brokaw serves as an example of how dozens of individual profiles were used to create a collective voice for the World War II generation. Mrs. Bee directs students to the Goodreads.com's list of best nonfiction war books (www.goodreads.com/list/show/824.Best_Non_fiction_War_Books), which lists over 300 titles. Students are encouraged to seek out works they personally want to read. One student asks to read *I Am a Soldier Too* (Bragg, 2003), which is publicized as the authorized biography of Private First Class Jessica Lynch, who served in the Iraq war and was the first American female P.O.W. In March of 2003, Lynch was captured follow-ing an ambush and held captive in an Iraqi hospital until April, when she was rescued by U. S. Special Operations Forces. The accuracy of the media coverage at the time and the ensuing biography have been challenged.

Another student asks to read *The Good Soldiers* (2009). This account by Pulitzer Prize–winning re-porter David Finkel chronicles the lives of a battalion of soldiers, known as the 2-16, from April 6, 2007,

(continued)

until April 10, 2008. It focuses on their involvement in "the surge" of U. S. troops in Iraq. The book ends with the pictures of those who died serving their country.

Students also request to read Ryan Smithson's *Ghosts of War: The True Story of a 19-Year-Old GI* (2009), a memoir of a young man who was deployed to Iraq in 2003. In a letter to readers Smithson states that his time in Iraq solidified his belief that everyone is responsible for changing the world. After his tour of duty he became involved in organizations serving veterans, a camp for children and teenagers dealing with a seriously ill or dying family member, and also Big Brothers Big Sisters of America. He asks readers to be responsible and help others.

Mrs. Bee explains the students will be expected to present a 10-minute overview of what they have read and to critique the effectiveness of the genre, for example, autobiography, letter, essay, or newspaper column as it relates to the intent and perspective of the author or editor. They are asked to agree or disagree with the author's position. They are to use Glogster (www.eduglogster.com) a free online resource for creating a visual, virtual, and interactive poster. This format allows students to use text, image, video, and music. She directs them to an interactive tutorial on how to use the site (http://glogstered.eduglogster.co,/glog-edu/).

Mrs. Bee soon discovers that the presentations take much longer than she anticipated. The students eagerly ask questions after each presentation, especially if the content or perspective of a classmate's presentation differs from their own. Mrs. Bee intends to use Glogster to provide feedback (*School Library Monthly*, 2010).

cally organized captioned family pictures, news photographs, and photographs from the museum are interspersed with background information and short excerpts from her diary, written in both her own hand and translated. This small book, less than seven inches in length and width, feels like a diary both in terms of its size and in maintaining Anne's voice.

Shifting Point of View and Narrative Order

Point of view and narrative order shift in *Strength in What Remains* (2009) by Pulitzer Prize-winning author Tracy Kidder. The first part recounts from a third-person omniscient perspective the story of Deogratis, a young man fleeing his war-ravaged homeland of Burundi. The chapters alternate between Deo's life in Burundi and his struggles as an immigrant and medical student in New York City. The second part of the book is Kidder's first-person account of their meeting, subsequent friendship, and trip together to Burundi and Rwanda. An epilogue describes Deo, who becomes an American citizen, as he struggles to establish a medical center in his homeland. Extensive notes and sources support the credibility of the historical events.

Visually Oriented Nonfiction Works

Nonfiction graphic novels are gaining popularity and increasing in number. We describe many graphic works in Chapter 10 and add an additional few nonfiction works here. *Gettysburg: The Graphic Novel* (Butzer, 2008) begins with a map, cast of characters, and a summary of events up to late June, 1863, when the action starts. The black, white, and blue illustrations of buzzards flying overhead, doctors, saw in hand ready to amputate, and bodies strewn across the battlefield capture the horrific toll of the Battle of Gettysburg. Lincoln's Gettysburg Address is spread over 16 pages. Illustrations of people throughout American history, fighting for their rights, are interspersed with phrases from Lincoln's speech.

Rich Geary, known for his nonfiction books about Victorian murder cases, investigates another famous murder in the graphic work *The Lindberg Child: America's Hero and the Crime of the Century* (2008). There is a lot of text and as many as nine panels on a page, but the information fully explains the complex events, evidence, and multitude of people surrounding the kidnapping and death of the infant son of the famous aviator Charles Lindberg. Although Bruno Richard Hauptmann was executed for the crime, he never admitted guilt, and speculation about the kidnapping and death of the child remains. Readers interested in crime scene investigation and forensic science will find the detailed evidence interesting. The starkness of the pen and ink illustrations matches the images and the topic.

The award-winning *Stitches* (Small, 2009), mentioned in this chapter's introduction, is an example of the powerful blending of illustration and text. The illustrations of Small's parents show the depth of his hatred for them. His father, a radiologist, used unnecessary x-rays on David, causing him to develop cancer. After a mass in his neck was detected, surgery was delayed because his parents wanted a new car and furniture. The surgery resulted in significant damage to his vocal cords, leaving him mute for a time.

King: A Comics Biography, Special Edition (2010) by Ho Che Anderson mixes realistic drawings with expressionistic paintings and photo collage. A few color pages break the predominately black and white palette. Martin Luther King Jr., is presented as both a historical icon and as a man with considerable flaws. The content is mature and the text extensive, a repackaging of three volumes printed over a decade. Anderson also includes a description of the effort, time, and frustrations involved in bringing his work to print.

Syncopated: An Anthology of Nonfiction Picto-Essays edited by Brendan Burford (2009) is a unique collection of graphic nonfiction including first-person reportage, memoir, profiles, historical essay, and visual portfolio essay. Greg Cook's powerful entry "What We So Quietly Saw" is about interrogations of prisoners at Guantanamo Bay. Rina Piccolo's "Penny Sentiments" combines the history of postcards with written messages.

Teaching Ideas ▪ LITERARY NONFICTION

Consider pairing nonfiction with fiction to help develop awareness of the differences and similarities of the genres. *Shutting Out the Sky: Life in the Tenements of New York 1880–1924* (Hopkinson, 2003) provides a factual account of urban life for many poor immigrants. *Ashes of Roses* (Auch, 2002) tells the story of an Irish immigrant, Rose Nolan, who is looking for the land of opportunity, but finds only the hard life of tenements and factory work.

You may likely select works to coordinate with content area units of study. For example, a unit for middle-grade students on children in U. S. history might include *We Were There, Too! Young People in U. S. History* (Hoose, 2001); *Alone in* the World: Orphans and Orphanages in America (Reef, 2005); Children of the Dust Bowl (Stanley, 1992); When Johnny Went Marching: Young Americans Fight in the Civil War (Wisler, 2001); and Russell Freedman's works about children described earlier in this chapter.

Include instruction on evaluating a work's credibility and accuracy within a larger theme unit. For a "mini lesson," call attention to bibliographies, source notes, photography sources, auxiliary information, author notes explaining the research process, and so on without detracting from the focus on theme. For example, Albert Marrin's Years of Dust: The Story of the Dust Bowl (2009) includes, in addition to a bibliography for each chapter, a timeline, a glossary, maps, related nonfiction, and an additional bibliography of books, articles, music, films, and websites.

As students read specific genres, have them explore how individual works differ, even when the topic and genre are the same, such as with these memoirs: Hands of My Father: A Hearing Boy, His Deaf Parents and the Language of Love (Uhlberg, 2009); My Sense of Silence: Memoirs of a Childhood with Deafness (Davis, 1999); and Deaf Hearing Boy: A Memoir (Miller, 2004).

You may need to directly teach the characteristics of literary nonfiction, especially for readers who associate nonfiction with textbooks. After students are comfortable with what distinguishes literary nonfiction from informational texts, have them create fun labels to explore these characteristics, either in their journals or in their literature circles. For example, the "Voice Detective" is responsible for finding the purpose and perspective of the author. "The Discoverer" looks for evidence of personal revelations that might be aspects the author has discovered about him or herself through the writing. "The Structure Strategist" notes any blending of genres or unusual structure or format. "The Literary Looker" searches for literary techniques and the artistic qualities of the piece. "The Verifier" considers the truthfulness of the work and possible compression or omission of facts and events. The bestselling Three Cups of Tea: One Man's Mission to Promote Peace (Mortenson & Relin, 2006), the story of mountain climber and humanitarian Greg Mortenson works well with older students. The author faced several allegations of falsehoods and fabrication that will be of interest to readers during their evaluation of the book.

Reading literary magazines written by young adults and writing literary nonfiction will help students both understand and appreciate the genre. Encourage your students to enter writing contests. The Newpages site (www.newpages.com/npguides/young_authors_guide.html) lists numerous magazines and links to nonfiction writing opportunities and contests, such as a Teen Ink (www.teenink.com/Contests) and the John F. Kennedy Profile in Courage Essay Contest (www.jfklibrary.org/Education/Profile-in-Courage-Essay-Contest/Contest-Information-and-Topic-Guidelines.aspx), both for students in grades nine through twelve.

THE INFORMATION: NONFICTION TRADE BOOKS

Informational nonfiction, or practical nonfiction, "is designed to communicate information in circumstances where the quality of the writing is not considered as important as the content" (Nordquist, n.d., p. 1). This does not mean such a book is not well crafted or interesting to read.

Well-written informational texts utilize careful source notation. They may include forewords, afterwords, acknowledgments, bibliography notes, annotated glossaries, a geographical dictionary called a gazetteer and detailed indexes to support the authenticity of the material. *Tracking Trash: Flotsam, Jetsam, and the Science of Ocean Motion* by Loree Griffin Burns (2007) contains several annotated illustrations taken from primary sources, maps, photographs, charts, and diagrams. The author includes many resources, such as websites, for readers interested in learning more about the pollution of the earth's water resources and how to become an advocate for cleaning up the world's oceans and rivers.

Over the years informational books have become more flexible in form and structure and more visually orientated (Gill, 2010; Kerper, 2001). They are less sequential than they used to be, make extensive use of sidebars and boxed information, and include pictures, maps, and diagrams. Captions and sidebars introduce concepts integral to comprehending the information. Unlike the captions and short statements that previously accompanied illustrations, these text features may introduce concepts that are vital for comprehension (Carter, 2000). The effect is to encourage readers to explore the printed text as they might a digital text, jumping around rather than proceeding page by page.

DK Publishing, publisher of the Eyewitness series, is a pioneer in creating informative and visually orientated texts. DK's website (http://us.dk.com/) offers a lengthy listing of their publications, which cover dozens of academic topics (history, science, literature, geography, art, religion) and general interest subjects (robots, computers, dance, cars, travel). Some titles are directly related to literature, for example, books on Shakespeare and mythology, while many others provide background information on wars and famous people that could be helpful when reading historical fiction and biographies. The Eyewitness books often come with a large attractive poster and a DVD of clip art related to the content. The books usually are divided into topics presented across a two-page spread. The introduction to each topic is short. Graphics are accompanied by paragraph-length captions in a diagram-like fashion.

Nonfiction Trade Books for Personal Reading

Much of what young adults choose to read for personal reasons may not be literary; however, informational texts can provide the gateway to more artistically written nonfiction. "For many young adult readers nonfiction serves the same purposes as fiction does for other readers: it entertains, provides escape, sparks imagination, and indulges curiosity" (Sullivan, 2001, p. 44). If reading informational books provides a satisfying experience, students may be receptive to reading increasingly more challenging literary nonfiction.

Hughes-Hassell and Rodge's (2007) study of adolescent leisure reading habits revealed that urban teens prefer to read about celebrities, sports figures, and people like themselves. Sports ranked high on their list. Sports nonfiction can be about a sport, its history and traditions, or about the athletes. The following list is a brief sampling of nonfiction sports books that will appeal to adolescents, regardless of age, who are fans of the sport in question.

Don't Let the Lipstick Fool You. Lisa Leslie & Larry Burnett, 2009. Leslie is a three-time Olympic gold medal winner and the first woman to dunk in a professional game. She relates her story from her childhood in South Central Los Angles through her successful adulthood career.

Far From Home: Latino Baseball Players in America. Tim Wendel & Jose Luis Villegas. 2008. This book provides a personal look at the Latino baseball players who make it to the major leagues as well as those who don't. The authors describe the pressures of illegal immigration, cut-throat big league competition, and the pain of dashed dreams.

Fearless: One Woman, One Kayak, One Continent. Joe Glickman, 2012. Freya Hoffmeister circumnavigated Australia in a kayak by herself. The book is the story of a remarkable kayak feat as well as the determination of a competitive athlete.

Heroes of Baseball: The Men Who Made It America's Favorite Game. Robert Lipsyte, 2006. The history of baseball is told through the biographies of numerous baseball players, including the controversial figures Mark McGwire and Sammy Sosa.

Hockey: A People's History. Michael McKinley, 2009. This history of hockey was originally published as a companion to a Canadian Broadcast Company series. This illustrated book provides an overview of ice hockey at all levels of competition.

Lebron James: The Making of an MVP. Terry Pluto & Brain Windhorst, 2009. These *Cleveland Plain Dealer* sports writers chronicle James' childhood, his teenage years, and his rise to fame as a player in the NBA starting with the Cleveland Cavaliers.

The Soccer Book: The Sport, The Teams, The Tactics, The Cups. David Goldblatt. 2010. This is a comprehensive guide to soccer rules, skills, moves, and suggestions for succeeding with the game. The World Cup 2010 is covered.

Sweet Thunder: The Life and Times of Sugar Ray Robinson. Wil Haygood, 2009. Sugar Ray Robinson is considered to be one of the greatest—if not the greatest—American boxer. His life as a youngster in Harlem in the years following the Harlem Renaissance, his rise as a fighter, and his post-career celebrity and problems are chronicled in this biography.

When March Went Mad: The Game that Transformed Basketball. Seth Davis, 2010. This is the story of Magic Johnson's and Larry Bird's college basketball careers, which culminated in their only game against each together—the 1979 NCAA finals. Some attribute to this event the renewed interest in college basketball and the surging popularity of the NBA in subsequent years.

Women Who Win: Female Athletes on Being the Best. Lisa Taggart, 2007. Ten champion female athletes share their views about competing, training, and accepting the challenges that go with becoming the best. Athletes include surfer Jamilah Star, soccer player Julie Foudy, gymnast Wendy Hillard, and basketball player Tamika Catching. The book includes black and white photographs of each athlete.

Young adults seek information about themselves, their immediate situations, and broader concerns and issues. They are interested in a wide range of topics and enjoy learning obscure facts. YALSA's "Quick Picks for Reluctant Young Adult Readers" (www.ala.org/yalsa/booklists/quickpicks) includes several nonfiction titles that provide advice and information about typical adolescent concerns:

- *This Is Why You're Fat: Where Dreams Become Heart Attacks* (Amason & Blakely, 2009).
- *Sex: A Book for Teens: An Uncensored Guide to Your Body, Sex and Safety* (Hasler, 2010).
- *Rare: Portraits of America's Endangered Species* (Sartore, 2010).

- *NatGeo Amazing!: 100 People, Places and Things That Will Wow You* (Bellows, 2010).
- *Ripley's Believe it or Not!: Enter if You Dare* (Tibballs, 2010).

Informational books written for young adults also present serious issues they may be struggling with. *Teen Cyberbullying Investigated: Where Do Your Rights End and Consequences Begin* (2010), by Judge Tom Jacobs, speaks directly to a teen audience. He presents court cases about teenagers, first asking the reader to consider his or her position and then revealing the court's decision. He explains state and federal laws and encourages students to continue researching issues covered.

Strong at the Heart: How It Feels to Heal from Sexual Abuse by Carolyn Lehman (2005) includes the personal narratives of nine young men and women who experienced horrific personal trauma as children and teenagers. Photographs, sources for finding professional help, a bibliography, and opportunities for activism enrich this already powerful account of courage and perseverance.

What the World Eats (D'Aluisio, 2008) is a photo essay that highlights issues related to the global marketplace and food intake around the world. The weekly food consumption of 25 families from 21 countries is profiled in photographs and written text. This commentary on the availability of food discusses fast food, safe water, life expectancy, and literacy rates.

Chew on This: Everything You Don't Want to Know About Fast Food (2006) by Eric Schlosser and Charles Wilson is a young adult adaptation of the Schlosser's influential *Fast Food Nation*.

It's Your World—If You Don't Like It, Change It (Halpin, 2004) speaks to the young adult's desire not only to complain about issues, but also to be proactive. Following information about each topic, including helping animals, saving the environment, stopping school violence and bullying, activities are provided for the home activist, campus activist, community activist, and five-minute activist resources.

Nonfiction Trade Books for Instruction

You can take simple steps to add nonfiction titles for recreational reading as well as for extending the curriculum. In Chapter 2 we suggested using surveys to determine the types of texts students read out of school and what they want to read in school. Students may be more inclined to read in school if the choices resemble their out-of-school reading. Add nonfiction to your book talks and popular nonfiction titles to the classroom library. A helpful resource for locating informational books students will likely find interesting is YALSA's "Quick Picks," mentioned earlier, which is published annually. Nonfiction titles are listed separately. Elizabeth Fraser's *Reality Rules! A Guide to Teen Nonfiction Reading Interests* (2008) contains 500 titles arranged by genre and topic. The book gives reading levels for each title and fiction selections to match each one.

Content area teachers often seek out English language arts teachers for nonfiction recommendations relating to a unit. Ink Think Tank: Nonfiction Authors in Your Classroom (www.inkthinktank.com) is a helpful resource for grades up through eighth. It aligns books with grade levels, topics, and content area standards, and provides numerous links to nonfiction author blogs, audio interviews, and video conferences. This book's companion website, Literature and Literacy for Young Adults (www.hhpcommunities.com/youngadultlit), offers "book talks" searchable by subject area (as well as by genre, author, title, and format). Content-area teachers can use this site as a resource when seeking fiction and non-fiction titles for a particular unit or class. The ALA (www.ala.org/ala//mgrps/divs/yalsa/teenreading/trw/trw2005/nonfiction.cfm) provides a list of nonfiction culled from their YALSA's award lists. Although works are not categorized by topic, the books are annotated. The quickest approach to locating nonfiction works by topic is most likely an online search.

conclusion

In an essay exploring readers' resistance to nonfiction, writer, editor, and publisher Marc Aronson states:

> A book is a path an author has taken in search of knowledge. It is the journal, the record, of that search, as well as the reward for undertaking the journey. If we approach nonfiction for younger readers in this way it will have the excitement of the adventure story, the inspiration of the quest, the drama of the pathway into the unknown, and the unique satisfaction of offering those readers nuggets of insight that allow them to understand the world around them. This is a high calling and as long as we keep it in mind, nonfiction, instead of being the step child of our literature, will take its rightful place as its glory. (2003, p. 115)

The informational nonfiction and creative nonfiction described in this chapter indicates that Aronson's plea for high quality and appealing nonfiction written for young adults is being fulfilled by authors. The challenge is to get this nonfiction into the hands of young adults.

The Common Core State Standards for the English Language Arts (National Governors Association, 2010) have repositioned the place of nonfiction in the curriculum. Literary nonfiction receives greater emphasis than it has in the past. Students are expected to "grapple with works of exceptional craft and thought whose range extends across genres, cultures and centuries" (p. 35).

Perhaps the availability of well-written, interesting, and thoughtful nonfiction supported by the desire to have students read a variety of texts will create the "perfect storm" for bringing young adults and nonfiction together.

BIBLIOGRAPHY OF LITERATURE FOR YOUNG ADULTS

Al-Windawi, T. (2004). *Thura's diary: My life in wartime Iraq.* (R. Bray, Trans.). New York: Viking.

Amason, J., & Blakeley, R. (2009). *This is why you're fat: Where dreams become heart attacks.* New York: HarperCollins.

Anderson, J. W. (2006). Vietnam era anti-war music. JW's Rock Garden. Retrieved from www.jwsrockgarden.com/jw02vvaw.htm.

Anderson, H. C. (2010). *King: A comics biography. The special edition.* Seattle, WA: Fantagraphics.

Andresen, L. (2003). *Battle notes: Music of the Vietnam war* (2nd ed.). Superior, WI: Savage Press.

Angel, A. (2010). *Janis Joplin: Rise up singing.* New York: Amulet.

Angelou, M. (1969). *I know why the caged bird sings.* New York: Random House.

Aronson, M., & Budhos, M. (2010). *Sugar changed the world: A story of magic, spice, slavery, freedom and science.* New York: Clarion.

Aronson, M., & Campbell, P. (Ed.) (2008). *War is . . . : soldiers, survivors, and storytellers talk about war.* Cambridge, MA: Candlewick Press.

Auch, M. J. (2002). *Ashes of roses.* New York: Dell Laurel Leaf.

Baldwin, J. (1953). *Go tell it on the mountain.* New York: Dial.

Barakat, I. (2007). *Tasting the sky: A Palestinian childhood.* New York: Farrar, Straus & Giroux.

Bartoletti, S. C. (2001). *Black potatoes.* Boston: Houghton Mifflin.

Bartoletti, S. C. (2010). *They called themselves the K.K.K.: The birth of an American terrorist group.* New York: Houghton Mifflin.

Bellows, M. G. (2010). *NatGeo amazing: 100 people, places, and things that will wow you.* Washington, DC: National Geographic.

Benedict, H. (2008). Women at war: What it is like to be a female soldier in Iraq. In M. Aronson & P. Campbell (Eds.), *War is . . . : soldiers, survivors, and storytellers talk about war* (101–117). Cambridge, MA: Candlewick Press.

Benedict, H. (2010). *The lonely soldier: The private war of women serving in Iraq.* Boston: Beacon Press.

Berendt, J. (1997). *Midnight in the garden of good and evil.* New York: Random House.

Bolden, T. (2004). *Wake up our souls: A celebration of Black American arts.* New York: Harry N. Abrams.

Bowers, R. (2010). *Spies of Mississippi: The true story of the spy network that tried to destroy the civil rights movement.* Washington, DC: National Geographic.

Bragg, R. (2003). *I am a soldier too.* New York: Knopf.

Brokaw, T. (1998). *The greatest generation.* New York: Random House.

Bruchac, J. (1997). *Bowman's store: A journey to myself.* New York: Dial.

Buckley, G. (2003). *American patriots: The story of Blacks in the military from the Revolution to Desert Storm.* (T. Bolden, Adapt.). New York: Crown.

Burford, B. (Ed.) (2009). *Syncopated: An anthology of nonfiction picto-essays.* New York: Villard.

Burns, L. G. (2007). *Tracking trash: Flotsam, jetsam, and the science of ocean motion.* Boston: Houghton Mifflin.

Butzer, C. M. (2008). *Gettysburg: The graphic novel.* New York: HarperCollins.

Capote, T. (1967). *In cold blood.* New York: Random House.

Carroll, A. (2006). *Behind the lines: Powerful and revealing American and foreign war letters—and one man's search to find them.* New York: Scribner.

Carroll. A. (2002). *War letters: Extraordinary correspondence from American wars.* New York: Scribner.

Carroll, D. M. (2009). *Following the water: A hydromancer's notebook.* New York: Houghton Mifflin Harcourt.

Chabon, M. (1995). *Wonder Boys.* New York: Villard.

Cook, G. (2009). What we so quietly saw. In B. Burford, (Ed.), *Syncopated: An anthology of nonfiction picto-essays* (53–70). New York: Villard.

Cooper, I. (2003). *Jack: The early years of John F. Kennedy.* New York: Dutton Children's Books.

Crutcher, C. (2004). *King of the mild frontier: An ill-advised autobiography.* New York: Greenwillow.

D'Aluisio, F. (2008). *What the world eats.* (P. Menzel, Photographer). Toronto, ON: Tricycle Press.

Darwin, C. (1859). *The origin of the species by means of natural selection.* London: John Murray.

Davis, L. J. (1999). *My sense of silence: Memoirs of a childhood with deafness.* Urbana, IL: University of Illinois Press.

Davis, S. (2010). *When March went mad: The game that transformed basketball.* New York: Holt.

Dewey, J. O. (2000). *Antarctic journal: Four months at the bottom of the world.* New York: HarperCollins.

DK Publishing. (n.d.) "Eyewitness" series. Retrieved from http://us.dk.com/nf/Browse/BrowseStdPage/ 0,,231463,00.html.

Dylan, B. (2008). Masters of war. In M. Aronson & P. Campbell (Eds.), *War is . . . : soldiers, survivors, and storytellers talk about war* (50–52). Cambridge, MA: Candlewick Press.

Ellison, R. (1952). *Invisible man.* New York: Modern Library.

Finkel, D. (2009). *The good soldier.* New York: Picador.

Fleischman, S. (2008). *The trouble begins at 8: A life of Mark Twain in the wild, wild west.* New York: Greenwillow Books.

Fleischman, S. (1996). *The abracadabra kid.* New York: Greenwillow Books.

Fleming, C. (2008). *The Lincolns: A scrapbook look at Abraham and Mary.* New York: Schwartz & Wade Books.

Freedman, R. (1980). *Immigrant kids.* New York: Puffin.

Freedman, R. (1987). *Lincoln: A photobiography.* New York: Clarion.

Freedman, R. (1990a). *Children of the wild west.* Boston, MA: Sandpiper.

Freedman, R. (1990). *Franklin Delano Roosevelt.* New York: Clarion.

Freedman, R. (1991). *The Wright Brothers: How they invented the airplane.* New York: Holiday House.

Freedman, R. (1996). *The life and death of Crazy Horse.* (A. Bull, Illus.). New York: Holiday House.

Freedman, R. (1997). *Eleanor Roosevelt: A life of discovery.* Boston, MA: Sandpiper.

Freedman, R. (1998). *Kids at work: Lewis Hine and the crusade against child labor.* Boston, MA: Sandpiper.

Freedman, R. (1998). *Martha Graham: A dancer's life.* New York: Clarion.

Freedman, R. (2000). *Give me liberty: The story of the Declaration of Independence.* New York: Holiday House.

Freedman, R. (2002). *Confucius: The golden rule.* (F. Clement, Illus.). New York: Arthur A. Levine.

Freedman, R. (2003). *In defense of liberty: The story of America's Bill of Rights.* New York: Holiday House.

Freedman, R. (2005). *Children of the Great Depression.* New York: Clarion.

Freedman, R. (2006a). *Freedom walkers: The story of the Montgomery Bus Boycott.* New York: Holiday House.

Freedman, R. (2008). *Washington at Valley Forge.* New York: Holiday House.

Freedman. R. (2010). *Lafayette and the American Revolution.* New York: Holiday House.

Freedman. R. (2010). *The War to end all wars: World War I.* New York: Clarion.

Gaines, E. (1971). *The autobiography of Miss Jane Pitman.* New York: Dial.

Gantos, J. (2004). *A hole in my life.* New York: Farrar, Straus & Giroux.

Geary, R. (2008). *The Lindberg child.* New York: Nantier.

Giblin, J. C. (2002). *The life and death of Adolf Hitler.* New York: Clarion.

Glickman, J. (2012). *Fearless: One woman, one kayak, one continent.* Guilford, CT: FalconGuides.

Goldblatt, D. (2010). *The soccer book: The sport. The teams. The tactics. The cups.* New York: DK Publishers.

Grunwald, L., & Adler, S. J. (Eds.). (2005). *Women's letters: America from the Revolutionary War to the present.* New York: Dial.

Halpin, M. (2004). *It's your world—if you don't like it, change it: Activism for teenagers.* New York: Simon Pulse.

Harper, H. (2006). *Letters to a young brother: MANifest your destiny.* New York: Gotham Books/ Penguin.

Harper, H. (2008). *Letters to a young sister: DeFINE your destiny.* New York: Gotham Books.

Hasler, N. (2010). *Sex: A book for teens: An uncensored guide to your body, sex, and safety.* San Francisco: Zest Books.

Haygood, W. (2009). *Sweet thunder: The life and times of Sugar Ray Robinson.* New York: Knopf.

Hedges, C. (2003). *War is a force that gives us meaning.* New York: Anchor Books/Random House.

Hedges, C. (2003). *What every person should know about war.* New York: Simon & Schuster.

Hedges, C. (2008). The moment of combat. In M. Aronson & P. Campbell (Eds.), *War is . . . : soldiers, survivors, and storytellers talk about war* (27–39). Cambridge, MA: Candlewick Press.

Heiligman, D. (2009). *Charles and Emma.* New York: Holt.

Hoose, P. (2009). *Claudette Colvin: Twice toward justice.* New York: Farrar, Straus & Giroux.

Hoose, P. (2001). *We were there, too! Young people in U.S. history.* New York: Farrar, Straus & Giroux.

Hopkinson, D. (2003). *Shutting out the sky: Life in the tenements of New York 1880–1924,* New York: Orchard Books.

Hurston, Z. N. (1937). *Their eyes were watching God.* Urbana, IL: University of Illinois Press.

Jacob, I. (2002). *My sisters' voices: Teenage girls of color speak out.* New York: Holt Paperbacks.

Jacobs, T. (2010). *Teen cyberbullying investigated.* Minneapolis, MN: Free Spirit Publishing.

Jones, J. B. (2006). *The songs that fought the war: Popular music and the home front, 1939–1945.* Waltham, MA: Brandeis University Press.

Janeczko, P. B. (2010). *The dark game: True spy stories.* Cambridge, MA: Candlewick Press.

Kaufman, P. (Dir.). (1983). *The right stuff.* U.S.A.: Warner Brothers.

Kidder, T. (2009). *Strength in what remains.* New York: Random House.

Kuklin, S. (2008). *No choirboy: Murder, violence, and teenagers on death row.* New York: Holt.

Lehman, C. (2005). *Strong at the heart: How it feels to heal from sexual abuse.* New York: Farrar, Straus & Giroux.

Leslie, L., & Burnett, L. (2009). *Don't let the lipstick fool you.* New York: Dafina Books.

Lipsyte, R. (2006). *Heroes of baseball: The men who made it America's favorite game.* New York: Atheneum.

Lowry, L. (1998). *Looking back.* Boston, MA: Houghton Mifflin.

Marrin. A. (2007). *The great adventure: Theodore Roosevelt and the rise of modern America.* New York: Dutton.

Marrin, A. (2009). *Years of dust: The story of the dust bowl.* New York: Dutton Children's Books.

Martin, R., & Nibley, L. (2009). *The mysteries of Beethoven's hair.* Watertown, MA: Charlesbridge.

McKinley, M. (2009). *Hockey: A people's history.* Toronto, ON: McClelland & Stewart.

Metselaar, M., & van der Rol, R. (2009). *Anne Frank: Her life in words and pictures from the archives of the Anne Frank House.* (A. J. Pomerans, Illus.). New York: Roaring Brook Press.

Miller, R. H. (2004). *Deaf hearing boy: A memoir.* Washington, DC: Gallaudet University Press.

Morrsion, T. (1987). *Beloved.* New York: Knopf.

Mortenson, G., & Relin, D. O. (2006). *Three cups of tea: One man's mission to promote peace . . . one school at a time.* New York: Viking/Penguin Group.

Murray, L. (2010). *Breaking night: A memoir of forgiveness, survival, and my journey from homeless to Harvard.* New York: Hyperion.

Myers, W. D. (2001). *Bad boy: A memoir.* New York: HarperCollins.

Paulsen G. (1994). *Father water, mother woods: Essays on fishing and hunting in the north woods.* (R. Wright Paulsen, Illus.). New York: Bantam Doubleday.

Peck, R. N. (2005). *Weeds in bloom: Autobiography of an ordinary man.* New York: Random House.

Piccolo, P. (2009). Penny sentiments. In B. Burford, (Ed.), *Syncopated: An anthology of nonfiction picto-essays* (pp. 1–18). New York: Villard.

Pinkney, A. (2000). *Let it shine: Stories of black women freedom fighters.* New York: Harcourt.

Pluto, T., & Windhorst, B. (2009). *Lebron James: The making of an MVP.* Cleveland, OH: Gray & Co.

Pyle, E., & Piehler, G. K. (2001). *Brave men.* Lincoln, NE: Bison Books, University of Nebraska Press.

Pyle, E. (2008). In the front lines. In M. Aronson & P. Campbell (Eds.), *War is . . . : soldiers, survivors, and storytellers talk about war* (pp. 63–75). Cambridge, MA: Candlewick Press.

Reef, C. (2005). *Alone in the world: Orphans and orphanages.* New York: Clarion.

Runyon, B. (2004). *The burn journals.* New York: Knopf.

Salzman, M. (2003). *True notebooks.* New York: Knopf.

Sartore, J. (2010). *Rare: Portraits of America's endangered species.* Washington, DC: National Geographic.

Schlosser, E., & Wilson, C. (2006). *Chew on this: Everything you don't want to know about fast food.* Boston, MA: Houghton Mifflin.

Sheff, N. (2008). *Tweak: Growing up on methamphetamines.* New York: Ginee Seo, Simon & Schuster.

Sheff, N. (2011). *We all fall down: Living with addiction.* New York: Little, Brown.

Small, D. (2009). *Stitches: A memoir.* New York: Norton.

Smithson, R. (2009). *Ghosts of War: The true story of a 19-year-old GI.* New York: HarperTeen.

Spinelli, J. (1998). *Knots in my yo-yo string.* New York: Knopf Books for Young Readers.

Stanley, D. (2002). *Saladin: Noble prince of Islam.* New York: HarperCollins.

Stanley, D., & Vennema, P. (1993). *Charles Dickens: The man who had great expectations.* New York: William Morrow.

Stanley, J. (1992). *Children of the dust bowl.* New York: Crown.

Stone, T. L. (2009). *Almost astronauts: 13 women who dared to dream.* Cambridge, MA: Candlewick Press.

Taggart, L. (2007). *Women who win: Female athletes on being the best.* New York: Perseus Books.

Taylor, Y. (Ed.). (2005). *Growing up in slavery.* (K. Judge, Illus.). Chicago: Lawrence Hill Books.

Tibballs, G. (2010). *Ripley's believe it or not! Enter if you dare.* Versailles, IN: Ripley Publishing.

Uhlberg, M. (2009). *Hands of my father: A hearing boy, his deaf parents, and the language of love.* New York: Bantam.

Wendel, T., & Villegas, J. L. (2008). *Far from home: Latino baseball players in America.* New York: National Geographic.

Weitzman, D. (2010). *Skywalkers: Mohawk ironworkers build the city.* New York: Roaring Brook Press.

Wisler, G. C. (2001). *When Johnny went marching: Young Americans fight the Civil War.* New York: HarperCollins.

Wolfe, T. (1973). *The new journalism.* New York: HarperCollins.

Wolfe, T. (1979). *The right stuff.* New York: Farrar, Straus & Giroux.

Wright, R. (1945). *Black boy.* New York: Harper.

X., M. (1965). *The autobiography of Malcolm X.* New York: Grove Press.

WEBSITES WITH ANNOTATIONS

Eduglogster • **www.eduglogster.com/**
Resource for creating a visual, virtual, and interactive poster. Allows students to use text, images, video, and music.

Ink Think Tank • **http://inkthinktank.com/**
Database of nonfiction works that aligns books with grade levels, topics, and content area standards. Includes numerous links to nonfiction authors.

Literature and Literacy for Young Adults • **www.hhp communities.com/youngadultlit**
This book's companion site; offers "book talks" searchable by subject area as well as by genre, author, title, and format.

Newpages: Young Authors Guide • **www.newpages.com/ npguides/young_authors_guide.htm**
Lists numerous magazines and links to nonfiction writing contests.

Women at War • **www.loc.gov/vets/stories/ex-war-womenatwar.html.**
Developed as part of the Veterans History Project; links to numerous audio and video interviews of female veterans of four wars.

Young Adult Library Services Association • **www.ala.org/ yalsa/**
Provides resources for educators including booklists, handouts, and titles for reluctant young adult readers.

REFERENCES

Aronson, M. (2003). *Beyond the pale: New essays for a new era.* (pp. 105–115). Lanham, MD: Scarecrow Press.

Bank Street. (2007). *Award ceremony acceptance speeches: Speech by Russell Freedman.* Bank Street College of Education. Retrieved from www.bankstret.edu/bookcom/speeches07.html.

Barancik, S. (2004). *Guide to collective biographies for children and young adults.* Lanham, MD: Scarecrow Press.

Bartkevicius, J. (2010). The landscape of nonfiction. In R. L. Root, Jr., & M. Steinberg (Eds.), *The fourth genre: Contemporary writers of/on creative nonfiction* (5th ed.). (pp. 317–323). New York: Longman.

Campbell, K. H. (2010). Eavesdropping on contemporary minds: Why we need more essays in our high school classrooms. *English Journal, 99*(4), 50–54.

Carter, B. (2000). A universe of information: The future of nonfiction. *Horn Book, 76*(6), 697–707.

Children's Literature (2006). *Meet Russell Freedman.* Retrieved from www.childrenslit.com/com/childrenslit/mai_freedman_russell.html.

Colman, P. (2007). A new way to look at literature: A visual model for analyzing fiction and nonfiction texts. *Language Arts, 84*(3), 257–268.

Frank, A. (1947, 1993). *Anne Frank: The diary of a young girl.* (B. M. Moovaart, Trans.). New York: Bantam.

Fraser, E. (2008). *Reality rules! A guide to teen nonfiction reading interests.* Westport, CT: Libraries Unlimited.

Freedman, R. (1998, July/August). Wilder medal acceptance. *Horn Book, 74*(4), 450–454. Retrieved from http://web.ebscohost.com/ehost/detail?vid=5&hid=25&sid=31f0fb40-7c36-490badc1-adf.

Freedman, R. (2006). May Hill Arbuthnot honor lecture: The past isn't past: How history speaks and what it says to the next generation. *Children & Libraries, 4*(2), 21–28.

Freedman, R. (2011, May/June). Letter to the editor. *Horn Book, 87*(3), 4.

Gill, S. R. (2010). What teachers need to know about the "new" nonfiction. *Reading Teacher, 63*(4), 260–267.

GoodReads. (2008). Nonfiction war books. Retrieved from www.goodreads.com/list/show/824.Best_Non_fiction_War_Books.

Gutkind, L. (2005). The creative nonfiction police. In B. M. Nguyen & P. Shreve (Eds.), *Contemporary creative nonfiction: I & Eye* (pp. 349–354). New York: Pearson Longman.

Hughes-Hassell, S., & Rodge, P. (2007). The leisure reading habits of urban adolescents. *Journal of Adolescent and Adult Literacy, 51*(1), 22–33.

Kerper, R. M. (2001). Nonfiction book design in a digital age. In M. Zarnowski, R. M. Kerper, & J. M. Jensen (Eds.), *The best of children's nonfiction: Reading, writing & teaching Orbis Pictus award books* (pp. 22–31). Urbana, IL: National Council of Teachers of English.

Livingston, N., Kurkjian, C., Young, T., & Pringle, L. (2004). Nonfiction literature: An untapped goldmine. *Reading Teacher, 57*(6), 582–591.

Moss, B., & Hendershot, J. (2002). Exploring sixth graders' selections of nonfiction trade books. *Reading Teacher, 58*(5), 426–434.

National Governors Association Center for Best Practices, Council of Chief State School Officers. (2010). *Common core state standards for English language arts & literacy in history/social studies, science, and technical subjects.* Washington DC: Author.

Nordquist, R. (n.d.). *Creative nonfiction.* Retrieved from http://grammar.about.com/od/c/g/creatnonfiction.htm.

Nguyen, B. M., & Shreve, P. (Eds.). (2005). *Contemporary creative nonfiction: I & eye.* New York: Pearson Longman.

Orlean, S. (Ed.). (2005). *The best American essays: 2005.* Boston: Houghton Mifflin.

Oxford Encyclopedia of American Literature. (2005). The American Essay. New York: Oxford University Press. Retrieved from http://ebooks.ohiolink.edu/xtf-ebc/view?docId=tei/drs/t197/t197.xml&chunk.id=E&toc.id=E&brand=default;query=essay%20definition.

Root, R., & Steinberg, M. (Eds.). (2010). *The fourth genre: Contemporary writers of/on creative nonfiction* (5th ed.). New York: Longman.

School Library Monthly. (2010, April). Going beyond Loch Ness monster. *School Library Monthly, XXVI*(8), 6–7.

Shaw, H. (1972). *Dictionary of literary terms.* New York: McGraw-Hill.

Stone, T. L. (2011, March/April). A fine, fine line: Truth in nonfiction. *Horn Book, 87*(2), 84–87.

Sullivan, E. (2001). Some teens prefer the real thing: The case for young adult nonfiction. *English Journal, 90*(3), 43–47.

Sutton, R. (2010). An interview with Russell Freedman. In Roger Sutton & Martha V. Parravano (Eds.), *A family of readers. The book lover's guide to children's and young adult literature* (pp. 204–208). Cambridge, MA: Candlewick Press.

University of Oregon School of Journalism and Communication (n.d.). What is literary nonfiction? Retrieved from http://www.inf.uoregon.edu/whatis.

Veterans History Project (2008). Experiencing war: Women at war. Retrieved from www.loc.giv/vets/stories/ex-war-womenatwar.html.

Zinsser, W. (Ed.). (1987). *Inventing the truth: The art and craft of memoir.* Boston: Houghton Mifflin.

THERE IS
NO DARKNESS
BUT
IGNORANCE

CHAPTER NINE

Poetry, Short Stories, and Drama

THE OTHER LITERATURE

chapter overview

Novels have long been the best-selling form of literature for both adults and young adults. Nevertheless, poetry, short stories, and drama also present themes that are important in the lives of young people, and each of these forms provides unique opportunities for teaching and learning about literature. This chapter begins with a discussion of poetry in the classroom and the wide range of contemporary poetry available for young adults. Next we examine short stories and the many collections that have been published for young adult readers. Finally, we explore ways to use drama both in and out of the classroom. Throughout the chapter, we identify resources that help teachers locate and use poetry, short fiction, and drama in new and better ways.

FOCUS QUESTIONS

1. How can teachers build an understanding and appreciation for the unique qualities found in poetry?

2. What advantages do short stories offer the young adult literature class?

3. What plays and drama activities are appropriate for young adults, both inside and outside of the classroom?

Short stories, poetry, and plays are unique literary forms, but they share characteristics with all the genres of fiction and nonfiction. A narrative poem such as "The Charge of the Light Brigade" (Tennyson, 1854), for instance, shares characters, events, and themes with both nonfiction history and historical fiction. Science fiction, mysteries, and romance have all flourished in short story form, and biographies, autobiographies, and personal memoirs have been adapted into plays such as *The Diary of Anne Frank* (Goodrich & Hackett, 1956) and *The Night Thoreau Spent in Jail* (Lee, 1970). Many metafictive devices we have previously highlighted also appear in these forms. Poems for two voices, such as those in Paul Fleischman's *Joyful Noise* (1988) for instance, use the device of multiple perspectives, as does Harry Mazer's short story collection, *Twelve Shots* (1997), which provides twelve different views of gun use.

We refer to poetry, short stories, and drama as "the other literature" because all three are likely to be overshadowed by the popularity of novels and book-length nonfiction. Perhaps because of their relatively short length, these "other" forms of literature are often relegated to anthologies and studied as if they were historical artifacts rather than living forms of literature. Students—even teachers—may be unaware of the contemporary poems, stories, and plays currently being produced for young adults or the range of adult works that are appropriate for a young adult audience.

In Chapter 2, we explained how literary appreciation develops gradually through repeated successful experiences with literature. Many young readers develop an appreciation of novels through hearing and reading hundreds of storybooks and beginning chapter books. Their experience with poetry and drama, however, may be much more sporadic, and their experience with literary short stories may not have progressed beyond fairy tales. In this chapter, we propose classroom activities that allow students to experience and analyze these other forms of literature. We also suggest ways to help students connect with poems, short stories, and plays beyond the classroom.

POETRY: FUNCTION AND FORM

 ost writers who try to define **poetry** soon give up the attempt. In a highly entertaining online article, Mark Flanagan (n.d.) includes a number of definitions from poets that are more metaphorical than analytical. He then concludes:

> To borrow a phrase, poetry is a riddle wrapped in an enigma swathed in a cardigan sweater or something like that. It doesn't like your definitions and will shirk them at every turn. If you really want to know what poetry is, read it. Read it carefully. Pay attention. Read it out loud. Now read it again. There's your definition of poetry. Because defining poetry is like grasping at the wind—once you catch it, it's no longer wind. (http://contemporarylit.about.com/od/poetry/a/poetry.htm)

One of the most widely quoted definitions of poetry is William Wordsworth's explanation that it is "the spontaneous overflow of strong emotion reflected in tranquility" (Wordsworth, cited in Lukens & Cline, 1995, p. 154). This definition captures the notion that poems should communicate real feelings about things that matter, and it also conveys that poems require thought. Tranquility is necessary for the careful crafting that is the work of a poet. Rather than describing poetry itself, Hirsh (1999) cites a metaphor describing the relationship between poet and reader in which a poem is a message in a bottle that a poet tosses into the sea with a faint hope that it will be found and understood.

These attempts to define poetry do not list its genres, its devices, or the rules that govern its forms. They focus instead on its function, what it does for the poet and, possibly, for the reader. Lukens and Cline (1995) explore the difference between form and function by drawing a distinction between poetry and verse. They see meter, rhyme, and other elements of form as characteristics of verse, but they also emphasize that not all verse is poetry. They are concerned that students, especially in the middle grades, might be experiencing verse rather than true poetry.

Clearly, both function and form are elements that identify poetry. Every poetic genre has both a characteristic content and a characteristic form. In this chapter, however, we emphasize function because we believe that students will not appreciate poetry until they understand what it is for. We also emphasize that poetry is both visual and auditory; it creates vivid mental pictures through a musical use of language. The approaches to poetry in the classroom that we highlight, therefore, are those that allow students to experience both its visual and its auditory qualities through performance and the visual arts.

The Purposes of Poetry

Heard suggests that "we read poetry from the deep hunger to know ourselves and the world" (2009, p. 10). Self-knowledge and broader understanding of the world are just two of poetry's purposes. Poems may be used, for instance, to inspire. "High Flight" (Magee, 1941) describes the exhilaration of pilots when they "slip the surly bonds of earth." This poem is memorized by cadets at the United States Air Force Academy and was quoted in President Reagan's speech honoring the astronauts who died in the Space Shuttle *Challenger* disaster (Noonan, 1986). Poems are also used to mark important ceremonial occasions; for instance, Maya Angelou wrote and read "On the Pulse of Morning" (1993) for President Clinton's inauguration.

Poetry collections can make the purposes of poetry clearer to young adults by showing variations on a theme, expressing common feelings, or highlighting shared experiences. In Liz Rosenberg's collection *Light-Gathering Poems* (2000), for instance, bringing the individual poems together illuminates their theme. Rosenberg arranges the poems alphabetically by author. She explains that "this emphasizes the notion that each poet is a 'shard' of light forming a greater whole. There is something mysterious about the way a series of small brilliants light up an entire night sky, and these poems, too, form remarkable constellations" (p. xiv).

Many adolescents probably think of love poems as a type of literature only girls read, but *More than Friends: Poems from His and Her* (Holbrooke & Wolf, 2008) is for both boys and girls. Told in alternating perspectives, the poems explore the feelings an adolescent boy and girl experience as their relationship changes from friendship to affection, to disenchantment, and once again to friendship. The authors explain the different poetic formats, such as sonnet, free verse, and quatrains. They also provide examples of famous poems that use these forms.

The 59 love poems and letters found in *Blushing: Expressions of Love in Poems and Letters*, collected by Paul Janeczko (2004), are organized around the cycle of love starting with the passionate beginnings of a new love to the remnants of love found in memories. Classic works such as Elizabeth Barrett Browning's well-known "How Do I Love Thee? Let Me Count the Ways" are interspersed with poems written by more contemporary poets such as Nikki Giovanni, Maya Angelou, and Naomi Shihab Nye.

Naomi Shihab Nye illuminates another common experience in *What Have You Lost?* (1999). This collection of 140 poems centers on a multitude of losses, such as the petty loss of a misplaced glove, as well as the life-altering losses of a loved one and of innocence and youth. Notes on the contributors include quotes from the poets about their lives and work. Michael Nye's black-and-white photographs add a visual dimension for interpreting loss.

Patrice Vecchione's *Revenge and Forgiveness: An Anthology of Poems* (2004) was inspired by the events of September 11, 2001. Some of the poems explore the hatred that leads to war, including "The Minefield" by Diane Thiel and "To a Terrorist" by Stephen Dunn. In contrast, Walt Whitman's "Stronger Lessons" and Derek Walcott's "Love After Love" address the importance of forgiveness.

Biographical information about the poets and the ideas or events that prompted each poem are included.

Greenberg (2001) invited distinguished American poets such as Angela Johnson, David Mura, and X. J. Kennedy to write poems about specific works of modern art for *Heart to Heart: New Poems Inspired by Twentieth-Century American Art*. Artists included Thomas Hart Benton, Romare Bearden, Jacob Lawrence, Grandma Moses, Faith Ringgold, Man Ray, Georgia O'Keeffe, and many others. The poems are loosely grouped in categories determined by the content of each poem: "Stories," "Voices," "Expressions," and "Impressions."

Greenberg's *Side by Side: New Poems Inspired by Art from Around the World* (2008) also explores the relationship of art and poetry, but in this collection the work is from 33 countries on six continents, and it features classical, folk, and contemporary art. Each two-page spread includes the poem in its original language, the translation, and a work of art, usually from the same country or culture as the poem. Biographical information about the artists, poets, and translators and a world map identifying the countries represented in the collection add information that highlights the appreciation for artwork shared by people from around the world.

Similarly, Nye (1998) pairs poetry and art from 19 Middle Eastern countries for *The Space Between Our Footsteps: Poems and Paintings from the Middle East*. A variety of artistic styles such as abstract art, folk art, and collage are included. This translated collection highlights both the differences between cultures and the commonalities among adolescents in diverse parts of the world.

Poetry "Caught" Not Taught

Billy Collins, the former poet laureate of the United States, addresses the way poetry is typically taught in his poem "Introduction to Poetry" (1996), which includes these lines:

> I want them to waterski
> across the surface of a poem
> waving at the author's name on the shore.
> But all they want to do
> is tie the poem to a chair
> and torture a confession out of it.
> They begin beating it with a hose
> to find out what it really means.

During his time as poet laureate, Collins launched a project called "Poetry 180" with a website (www.loc.gov/poetry/180/) that provides a poem for each school day of the year and does not require young adult readers to beat the meaning out of it.

Collins also provides an example for both approaches to including poetry in the classroom that we advocate in this chapter: having students experience poetry through both the visual and performing arts. He has often performed on radio and television, in a highly recognizable deadpan style that is especially effective for his humorous poems, and he has released a recording of one of his concerts (2005). Many short videos of Collins reading his poems are available on YouTube. Even better, some videos animate his poems to emphasize their imagery. These videos can easily inspire students to produce their own visuals, either short films or still images, to accompany recordings of Collins and other poets.

Poetry and the visual arts: Images to imagery

Images can be evoked though all five senses; however, most image-laden words appeal to sight (Abriza, n.d., p. 1). Langston Hughes is one of the most accessible of American poets, partly because of his use of strong visual imagery. In his poem "Dreams" (1932/1994), for instance, he describes a life without dreams with the unforgettable image of "a broken-winged bird that cannot fly," and in "Harlem" (1951/1994), he pictures a dream deferred as drying up "like a raisin in the sun." Twenty-six of Hughes' poems are illustrated by artist Benny Andrews in the collection *Poetry for Young People: Langston Hughes*, edited by David Roessel and Arnold Rampersad (2006).

Hughes wrote poems about ordinary people and the struggles confronted by African Americans. He infused his work with African American musical traditions, urban language, and his feelings about civil rights. Andrews includes all of these elements in his illustrations. He draws on African art traditions in his use of elongated torsos and limbs, his vivid colors, and the patterns in clothing. The collage and watercolor illustrations fit the language of each poem, often depicting a sense of movement and rhythm.

Although picture books that illustrate poems are generally intended for younger audiences, a skillful visual interpretation may contribute to a young adult reader's experience. The illustrated books in the accompanying box contain one or more poems appropriate for middle-school and high-school students.

Poetry and the performing arts

"Poetry is the music of our language and can be appreciated more fully when it is both heard and read" (Lown & Steinbergh, 1996, p. xi). Nikki Giovanni's *Hip Hop Speaks to Children: A Celebration of Poetry with a Beat* (2008) is a good initial source for teaching oral interpretation of poetry. This anthology has a wide range of authors and is accompanied by a CD of selections from the book performed by actual authors and children. Giovanni is also the editor of *The 100 Best African American Poems* (2010), suitable for older readers. It includes a CD that features actress Ruby Dee, poets Sonia Sanchez and Robert Hayden, and Giovanni herself reading classic and contemporary poems on a wide range of subjects.

Active engagement with poetry through listening, writing, and performing is featured in *Let's Poem: The Essential Guide to Teaching Poetry in a High-Stakes, Multimodal World (Middle through High School)* (2010). Author Mark Dressman describes the instructional activities he has found successful: "They do not require students simply to read or write or talk abstractly about poetry but rather to do something active and concrete with poems—mark them for a choral read-

Festival in My Heart: Poems by Japanese Children. Translated by Bruno Navasky, 1993. This collection of poems written by Japanese elementary students was originally published in a Japanese newspaper. Seventy-seven works of art collected from the 13th through the 20th centuries are included. Each illustration is dated, labeled and described, and its location (usually a museum) identified. The art alone could stand as an overview of Japan's artistic history. In conjunction with the poems, some by children only in kindergarten, a reader develops an understanding and appreciation for an ancient culture and the culture's modern love for poetry.

The Highwayman. Alfred Noyes, 1990. Illustrated by Neil Waldman. Noyes' famous story of a young woman who shoots herself to warn her lover that King George's men are waiting to capture him is exciting and romantic, yet tragic, since both the lovers die. Noyes' description of the highwayman lends plausibility to Bess' action. He is wearing a French cocked-hat, skin-tight leather breeches, thigh-high boots, and a red velvet jacket. Waldman's illustrations, however, suggest rather than show. The highwayman is seen only in shadow and silhouette, high on a rearing horse with his sword raised. Bess' death is conveyed in the muted tones of a blood-stained ground, the blood seeping through the black border of the illustration. The final refrain, a testament to their unending love, is written in cursive against a muted barren landscape.

Poetry for Young People: Edgar Allan Poe. Edited by Brod Bagert, 1995. Illustrated by Carolynn Cobleigh. This collection includes 13 of Poe's poems and eight prose selections reworked into verse. The editor's intent is "to give the full range of Poe's poetic voice, so children can feel the full power of his poetry" (p. 7). Opinions may differ as to the success of this endeavor. Illustrations are often chilling and include a skull on a stairway, a skeleton ringing a bell, ghosts floating above a lake, a large raven perched on a statue, and sunken-cheeked judges about to render a sentence of death. Other illustrations, such as Annabel staring into the sea and Poe lying ill, watched over by a female friend, seem sad. The illustrations may draw readers to Poe's work.

Stopping by Woods on a Snowy Evening. Robert Frost, 1978. Illustrated by Susan Jeffers. One or two lines of Frost's famous poem are printed on each two-page spread. Jeffers' pencil and pen drawings have small splashes of light orange, green, and blue, most often confined to an old man's clothing and the blankets on his sleigh and horse. In one illustration, the old man lies down to make a snow angel. The illustration for the line "but I have promises to keep" is of the old man hugging a woman in front of a house as children feed his horse. The double page illustration for the final line "And miles to go before I sleep" shows the man on his laden sleigh, moving slowly through a snowy night. Some see this rendition of the poem as a Christmas Eve story, which raises questions about how illustrations can distort rather than guide the interpretation of a poem.

The Tyger. William Blake, 1993. Illustrated by Neil Waldman. The eye-catching cover presents a glimpse of a vividly colored tiger amid a black background. The endpapers are bright orange. Each illustration is set up as a two-page spread in grey and black with white cursive lettering on the left and a brightly colored boxed image on the right. The final grey illustration of the tiger opens into a four-page, full-color pull-out that contains all the images presented throughout the book. Waldman's illustrations may create interest as well as foster interpretation of this frequently anthologized poem about the creation of something that is both beautiful and destructive.

Twelve Rounds to Glory: The Story of Muhammad Ali. Charles R. Smith Jr., 2007. Illustrated by Bryan Collier. Collier's bold and powerful watercolor and collage-style images fit the content of the poem and the spirit of its subject. Large, bold headings count off each round in a boxing match, but sometimes the adversary is not another boxer; it is the U. S. government, poverty, and later, Parkinson's syndrome. Numerous direct quotations capture Ali's personality. The rhythm of his fighting style is conveyed in lines such as "slipping and sliding and bobbing, and hiding." Words scattered throughout the poem evoke the sounds Ali heard in the ring: "Boooooo," "ding-ding," "crack," "thwack," and "splat." The interplay of text and images conveys a strong emotional response that would be unlikely if either were presented alone. This title was recognized as a Coretta Scott King Honor Book.

classroom scenario

Visualizing Poetry

Even when an illustrator's work does not resonate with students, it may still serve a purpose. The teacher can ask students to find or create more appropriate images. Similarly, if several different illustrated versions of the same poem exist, students can decide which one best captures the poem's essence. AS YOU READ this classroom scenario, consider how the students' interpretations of a poem change as they read different illustrated versions.

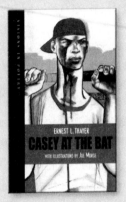

Mrs. O'Reilly tells her students they will be reading about a popular baseball player and describes the following scene:

The player's team is down by two runs. There are two outs with a runner on second and another on third, both in scoring position. The player eases up to home plate and takes his batting stance. As the first pitch whizzes by, he doesn't move. It is a strike. The second pitch, the same. On the third pitch, he swings and misses. The game is over; his team has lost.

The class discusses the images Mrs. O'Reilly's words created in their minds. She then asks her students to draw this scene. They share their pictures and discuss the similarities and differences. She explains to them that an artist's interpretation of a story can influence a reader's understanding.

Next, she shows them *Casey at the Bat* written by Ernest Thayer with drawings by LeRoy Neiman (2000). She has covered the words, so as she pages through the book they see only the pictures. She asks them for their impressions. They mention that the charcoal drawings look as if they were drawn quickly and this drew their attention to the shapes. The players look tough and professional, and the drawings show movement and action. She asks them when the story takes place, and they respond that it looks modern.

Mrs. O'Reilly then shares with her students a 2006 rendition of Thayer's poem illustrated by Joe Morse. Some of the students recognize the poem and say they think maybe it is really old. They note that the teams pictured are multiracial and the setting seems like an inner city. People are watching from their apartments and on television. The book seems like a graphic novel, and certain words are printed in bold for emphasis, such as "yell," "rumbled," "rattled," and "pounded." The bodies are elongated and outlined in black. People look really angry. The hitter falls to his knees when he misses the last pitch. In the first book, his face was partly obscured, giving a sense of, "oh well, tomorrow's another game." With this book, they feel sorry for Casey. The students liked the modern quality of the illustrations.

The next day Mrs. O'Reilly tells the class the complete title of the poem: *Casey at the Bat: A Ballad of the Republic Sung in the Year 1888,* and she explains that it was originally published in a newspaper. She then shows them the Caldecott Honor Book version illustrated by Christopher Bing (Thayer, 2000), and they discuss that illustrator's choice to recreate the 1888 setting. The poem is presented within a faux scrapbook that contains illustrations that look like newspaper clippings, game tickets, baseball cards, and score sheets. Players wear uniforms representing the era, and articles discuss changes in rules and equipment at the time. The terms "Cake" and "Lulu" are explained as derogatory references to players using a glove, a recently allowed addition to the list of accepted protective gear.

Casey is the only figure in Bing's final double page illustration; he is seen from behind, his posture and head slumped in defeat. The students think the pen and ink drawings look as if they are from old newspapers. They conclude that the author wanted to tell about baseball in the late 1800s as much as he wanted to retell the poem. Even the endpapers had more information, including Thayer's obituary.

The last book Mrs. O'Reilly presents is a 2003 version illustrated by C. F. Payne. The class laughs at the exaggerated cartoonish pictures of people dressed in the clothing of the period. They note that Casey looks very cocky, and the illustration showing him bored and looking at his fingernails made them like him a lot less. They also comment that the close-up picture of his grimacing face matches the words "the sneer is gone from Casey's lip, his teeth are clenched in hate." They notice that there is no picture of Casey after he has struck out and that the final illustration of the "Welcome to Mudville" city sign with a baseball in a puddle does not have the same sense of dejection as Morse's interpretation.

The students return to their original drawings and discuss how they might redraw them given the full text of the poem and their experiences looking at the different artistic interpretations of the same text.

ing, write and play with them on paper, sing them as the blues, write them for reading and performance, or remix them multimodally" (p. 144).

Dressman elaborates on each of these activities. In Chapter 1 of his book, "Choral Reading: Studying Rhythm, Inflection, and Meaning," he describes how students "score" poems, by learning how to focus attention on certain words to emphasize meaning and to control the sound and rhythm of the poem. They then group themselves and perform for an audience.

In the chapter "Digital Performance," Dressman describes ways of applying digital tools such as video editing to classic texts as well as the students' own writing. He describes step-by-step how students can interpret poems by creating a PowerPoint presentation with animated text and images accompanied by a soundtrack. Music also features in a project where students listen to or watch YouTube videos of classic blues performances and write their own songs to "sing the blues" about some aspect of their school, such as the cafeteria. Visit the Let's Poem Resources website (http://letspoemresources.ning.com/) for more information and support for teaching poetry.

Poetry Beyond the Classroom

Many projects promote poetry among the general population and provide an audience for contemporary student work. "Poetry in Motion," which began in New York City and London, England, regularly places poetry on the walls of subways, trains, and buses along with ads for products and opening plays. This project is organized by the Poetry Society of America, and participating cities include Atlanta, Chicago, Dallas, Los Angeles, and Portland.

The University of Virginia created the "Kinetics: UV Art and Poetry in Motion" project, which resulted in a series of posters featuring both art and poetry.

Gary Soto

Gary Soto, a writer from Fresno, California, is an accomplished poet, short story writer, novelist, essayist, and playwright whose works frequently concern Chicano culture. Soto began his career writing poetry for adults. The impetus for expanding his audience to include children and young adults came from letters from Mexican American adolescents. He wrote his first short story collection for young adults, *Baseball in Spring and Other Stories,* in 1990. It was recognized as the ALA's Best Book for Young Adults (Lee, 2010). Since that time Soto has become the author most frequently read by Latino youth (Amen, 2002).

The numerous awards and prizes Soto has received reflect his versatility as a writer. The list includes the Andrew Carnegie Medal for Film Excellence, the United States Award of the International Poetry Forum, the Bess Hokin Prize, and the Levinson Award from *Poetry* magazine. He was awarded the PEN Center West Book Award for a young adult short story collection, the Literature Award from the Hispanic Heritage Foundation, the Author-Illustrator Civil Rights Award from the National Education Association, and the Tomas Rivera Mexican American Children's Book Award. His work also has been recognized as a Pura Pelpre Award Honor book (Poets.org, n.d.; Soto, 2008a).

Poetry is at the heart of Soto's work. He states that "poetry writing is a life order, a serious artistic calling. I started in 1973 as a student poet at Fresno State College and have been at it ever since" (Coughlan, 2007, p. 3). Soto identifies his approach to poetry as that of an Imagist. "I try to appeal to the sense of seeing—and sometimes hearing, as in the cadence of a poem—as I believe that poems should convey a realism, even if that realism is a fiction" (TeachingBooks.net, 2007, p. 2). For Soto, "poetry means—language that surprises and keeps us on our toes" (TeachingBooks.net, 2007, p. 1).

In the introduction to *Fire in My Hands* (2006a), a collection of over 30 poems, Soto says that he likes to think of his poems as a "working life." He wants them to be about the ordinary everyday things in life. "The poems keep alive the small moments that add up to a large moment: life itself" (pp. xiii–xiv). He demonstrates the economy of words used to create an image familiar to most young adults in "All My Luck" (p. 18):

I was in love with the homecoming queen
And she with some muscle in a letterman's jacket,
Medals dangling like fishing lures on his mountainous chest.

Another example of Soto's mastery for describing simple things is "Oranges" from the same collection. In this poem a young boy is on his first date. He brings along two oranges for them to share. They end up at a drugstore, and the boy attempts to impress Margarita by suggesting she choose a chocolate. However, the candy costs a dime. The young man only has a nickel, so he places one of his precious oranges on the counter to complete the payment. The salesperson understands. The last few lines describe their walk home as Margarita enjoys her chocolate while the young man pulls out his second orange:

I peeled my orange
That was so bright against
The gray of December
That, from some distance,
Someone might have thought
I was making a fire in my hands. (p. 11)

Soto's *Neighborhood Odes* (1992a) celebrates everyday items such as sprinklers, tennis shoes, weightlifting and fireworks. *New and Selected Poems* (1995) was chosen as a finalist for both the *Los Angeles Times* Book Award and the National Book Award. More recently Soto has authored *Partly Cloudy: Poems of Love and Laughing* (2009) that deals with young love from the perspectives of both boys and girls. The book is divided into two sections, "A Girl's Tears, Her Songs" and "A Boy's Body, His Words." *Fearless Fernie: Hanging Out with Fernie and Me* (2002) and *Worlds Apart: Traveling with Fernie and Me* (2005) are poems about two best friends, beginning when they are babies and continuing through adolescence.

Soto found a new freedom writing prose: "I felt I could be louder, more direct, also sloppier, whereas with poetry, I believed you had to control your statement, not be so obvious" (Lee, 2010, p. 2). Although Soto does not consider his fiction autobiographical, he recognizes the tremendous influence living in Fresno has had on his writing. Nonetheless, he sees his work as transcending the Chicano experience: "I hope that my writing shows how universal issues are shared by Latino characters—though their settings and names are not the standard literary fare" (Coughlan, 2007, p. 2). Soto writes in English but adds Spanish expressions and phrases in order to capture the voice of his characters (Teaching Books.net, 2007). Many of his works include a glossary of Spanish terms.

A few of Soto's more recent short story collections are *Facts of Life* (2008b), about the trials and tribulations of growing up; *Help Wanted* (2005), which includes ten funny and occasionally sad stories of kids almost messing up when small events turn out to be huge problems; and *Petty Crimes* (2006b), about the complicated relationships among family and friends. It is also about getting in and out of trouble.

Soto considers novels more accessible than poetry or short stories because the reader does not have to work as hard to find meaning (TeachingBooks.net, 2007). His novels for older teens include *Jesse* (1994), set during the Vietnam War and the beginning of the United Farm Workers movement; *Buried Onions* (1997), the story of a Mexican American boy facing the limited choices of his environment; and *The Afterlife* (2003), a story told from the perspective of a teenager knifed to death, reflect the conflicts faced by many young Mexican Americans from both within and outside their culture. *Mercy on these*

Teenage Chimps (2007), a short novel for middle grade readers, looks at puberty from a humorous perspective.

Soto's plays include *Nerdlandia* (1999) set in Fresno, where a Chicano nerd, replete with pocket calculator and hiked up pants, falls in love with Ceci, the most beautiful girl on campus. *Novio Boy: A Play* (1997) is a lighthearted story about the awkwardness and excitement of a ninth-grade boy going out with an older girl. Both plays include performance notes and a glossary. Non-Spanish-speaking readers may find the lack of a pronunciation guide limiting. His film *The Pool Party* (Independent Television Service, 1992b) based on his book with the same title, received the 1993 Andrew Carnegie Medal for Film Excellence. The book and film reflect the everyday life of a working-class Mexican American family when Rudy is invited to a pool party given by a wealthy classmate.

Although most of his characters and situations are about Chicanos and reflect his own cultural heritage, Soto does not see himself as a cheerleader for Mexican Americans (Soto, 2008a, p. 2), nor does he purposely exploit an issue (Coughlan, 2007, p. 3). His goal is to provide "portraits of people in the rush of life" (Soto, 2008a, p. 2) that have a universal appeal. The many accolades he has received attest to his success creating work that attracts a wide audience including children, young adults, and adults.

The art does not merely illustrate the poem, but juxtaposes illuminating connections to foster conversation. Poetry and photos of artwork are submitted by members of the student body.

"Poet's House" in New York City is a national poetry library and literary center founded by former poet laureate Stanley Kuntz. It promotes the living tradition of poetry through "Poetry at Large" events such as "Poem in Your Pocket Day." That program distributes poems written by New York teachers and students for community members to carry and read. Teachers can easily adapt these outreach ideas to their own schools and communities. For more information, consult www.poetshouse.org/programs-and-events/poetry-in-the-world.

The WritersCorps program sponsors Youth Poetry Slam, which connects young adults in disadvantaged neighborhoods with professional writers and poets. The writers help the students learn to read and write poems for contests called "slams." Students from across the nation compete in the National Youth Poetry Slam League held annually in Washington, D. C. The objective of the program is to get young adults excited about the written and spoken word. Middle schools, in particular, are the focus of this project.

SHORT STORIES: CONCENTRATED FICTION

Washington Irving's "Rip Van Winkle" (1819), a story about a man who slept for twenty years, is usually considered the first American short story. However, another twenty years passed before much attention was given to the short story as a form of literature. It was not until Edgar Allan Poe wrote a review in 1842 of Nathaniel Hawthorne's *Twice-told Tales* (1837) that the short story began to be viewed as a unique type of writing.

Poe described a **short story** as a narrative that could be read in one sitting (Boyd, 2006). The brevity of the writing does not means it is less complex or less developed than a longer piece; quite the contrary. Poe stated that "in an artful story every incident in the story should contribute to a single effect and in the whole composition there should be no word written, of which the tendency, direct or indirect, is not to the one pre-established design" (Poe, 1842 cited in Feddersen, 2001, p. xix). In other words, every aspect of a short story should function toward a particular effect. Poe recognized that this type of writing would require the reader to be attentive to each word and detail and to look beneath the surface of a story (Feddersen, 2001).

Apparently, readers accepted this, and the short story genre flourished during the early to mid-20th century. Popular magazines and periodicals of the day provided writers with opportunities for publishing shorter works. As distinctions between commercial and literary short fiction developed, magazines such as *The New Yorker* and *Story* became known for their literary short stories. The O. Henry Memorial Award was created to recognize short stories of literary distinction (*Oxford Encyclopedia of American Literature*, 2005). Literature instruction in secondary schools and colleges at this time focused on the form and structure of literature. Short stories worked well for this purpose, and they became a popular part of the English curriculum (Dobie, 2012).

Although short stories were widely used in the upper grades throughout most of the 20th century, editor and author Don Gallo notes that in 1980 there were only five single-author collections of short fiction written for young adults. Of note was *8 plus 1* (1991), by Robert Cormier, the well-known author of *The Chocolate War* (1974). Gallo also notes that in the early 1980s there were no anthologies of short stories by a variety of authors written for adolescents. Gallo wanted to change that. He sought out established authors of literature for young adults to contribute stories to a single collection. The only criteria were that the stories could not be previously published and they must be about teenagers and of interest to them. The result was *Sixteen: Short Stories by Outstanding Writers for Young Adults* (1984). Contributors included Robert Lipsyte, Richard Peck, Norma Fox Mazer, Rosa Guy, Joan Aiken, Robert Cormier, and Bette Greene (Lesesne, 2002).

Gallo, a recipient of the ALAN Award for outstanding contributions to the field of adolescent literature, has been labeled the "Godfather of YA Short Stories." He is attributed with establishing the short story for young adults as a genre and creating a market for the short story anthology. When asked why short stories have become popular with young adults, he responded that the reason is that there are now so many good stories to read (Crowe, 1997).

Richard Peck's description of the unique characteristics of the short story in the introduction to his collection *Past, Perfect, Present Tense* (2004) provides additional insights into the popularity of short stories:

> In fiction writing, the epiphany is a sudden breakthrough of understanding, of self-awareness. It's the moment of change that changes every moment after. It's the light bulb switched suddenly on over somebody's head. Novels tell of epiphanies acted upon. A short story tends to turn upon a single epiphany, sometimes in the last line. The change to come is to play out in the reader's mind. (p. 2)

Perhaps it is this notion of a quickly encountered change that adolescents, in the midst of their own change and growth, relate to in a short story. Anthologies of short stories, both by a single author and as edited collections, have remained popular with young adults.

Short Story Thematic Collections

Short story collections are usually composed of works that are thematically related or of the same literary genre. Short stories can accommodate individual needs and tastes, and a collection enables a teacher to have large group instruction about a theme or genre while matching stories to readers. Typically, the stories in an edited collection vary in style and tone. Often male and female writers are chosen from diverse backgrounds. For example, *Necessary Noise: Stories About Our Families as They Really Are* (2003), edited by Michael Cart, has stories by Joan Bauer, Norma Howe, Emma Donoghue, Nikki Grimes, Walter Dean Myers, Joyce Carol Thomas, Michael Cart, Lois Lowry, Sonya Sones, and Rita Williams-Garcia. Some of the stories are lighthearted and humorous, other serious and dark.

Most of the selections are written in prose, but the collection also includes stories told in verse and conversation. Sones' "Dr. Jekyll and Sister Hyde" captures the dysfunctional relationship between two sisters from the younger sister's point of view. The story, written in verse, is divided into very short titled segments. The titles provide a context for each memory or event. In "A Family Illness: A Mom–Son Conversation," by Joyce Carol Thomas, conversation alternates between the perspective of a mother and that of her mentally ill son. The text is sparse, the images intense.

Themes prominent in longer fiction also appear in short stories, and many of these themes are related to the changes that occur during adolescence. The next section describes several collections that have to do with accepting and knowing oneself.

Gender roles and sexual identity

Figuring out gender roles and societal expectations is a significant part of growing up. *Every Man for Himself: Ten Short Stories About Being A Guy* (2005), edited by Nancy Mercado, features 10 male authors including Walter Dean Myers, David Levithan, Rene Saldana Jr., David Lubar, Terry Trueman, and Mo Willems. This collection is written for older adolescent males, but it will appeal to girls as well.

The humorous stories written for a younger audience in *Guys Read: Funny Business* (2010), edited by Jon Scieszka, approach some of the same themes. Marilyn Singer's first anthology, *Stay True: Short Stories for Strong Girls* (1998), includes 11 stories by female writers such as M. E. Kerr, Andrea Davis Pinkney, and Norma Fox Mazer. The stories take place in a variety of cultures in which girls discover their inner strength and ability to persevere. Similar in purpose is *On Her Way: Stories and Poems About Growing Up Girl* (2004), compiled by Sandy Asher, which has stories by outstanding female writers geared toward middle-grade readers.

Am I Blue? Coming Out of the Silence (1994), edited by Marion Bauer, is the first short story collection dealing with being gay. Authors include M. E. Kerr, Jacqueline Woodson, Jane Yolen, William Sleater, James Cross Giblin, and Lois Lowry. Bauer notes that some of the contributors are gay and others are not. A second edition of *Not the Only One: Lesbian and Gay Fiction for Teens*, edited by Jane Summer, was published in 2004. About half of the stories in the second edition are new. Nancy Garden's *Hear Us Out! Lesbian and Gay Stories of Struggle, Progress, and Hope, 1950 to the Present* (2007) combines essays describing the progress of gay rights, decade by decade, with short stories by Garden.

David Levithan's *How They Met and Other Stories* (2008) is a collection of stories, some dating from his high school and college days, about love. The stories are about defining and finding love of all kinds, including love that encompasses different sexual orientations. "Andrew Chang" provides a happy ending for a Chinese American girl whose parents arrange her date for prom. Years later she is still happy with a boy she met and laughed with at prom, who was not the boy her parents picked. In "The Number of People Who Meet on Airplanes," the protagonist finds out that meeting his wife on an airplane was not the lucky coincidence he thought it was. In "Miss Lucy Had a Steamboat," Ashley, the new girl in school, and the narrator whom Ashley calls "Miss Lucy" embark on a doomed relationship. In the end Miss Lucy realizes that she wants more than Ashley can give her.

Love & Sex: Ten Stories of Truth (2001), edited by Michael Cart, is another collection that examines adolescent love from many perspectives. Included are stories about virginity, romantic obsession, being gay or transsexual, the consequences of unwanted pregnancy, and interracial relationships.

Cultural and ethnic diversity

One of the early collections dealing with cultural diversity was *American Dragons: Twenty-five Asian American Voices* (1993), edited by Laurence Yep. Yep's collection of stories, essays, and poems relates to Asian Americans struggling to reconcile the values and customs of diverse cultures. Yep's afterword reveals his purpose was to portray Asian American culture as bearing "the stamp not only of a common humanity, but also of its own uniqueness" (p. 236).

Marilyn Singer's edited collection *Face Relations: Eleven Stories About Seeing Beyond Color* (2004) explores stereotypes and prejudice within and across cultural groups. In "Mr. Ruben" by Rita Williams-Garcia, Myra refuses to have a crush on her teacher until she can confirm that he is the same race as she, and she cannot tell from his shaved head and physical appearance. In "Negress," Marilyn Singer's exploration of race and color, Beth's best friend Vonny now wants to be called

Negress. The story is based on historical events describing the sexual exploitation of an African woman. Joseph Bruchac's "Skins" raises issues of ethnic identity, particularly for Native Americans, based on physical appearance and aptitude. In "Hum" by Naomi Shihab Nye, Sami and his parents have recently arrived in Texas from Bethlehem in Palestine. After the terrorist attacks on September 11, 2001, Sami deals with violence and hatred directed at him and his family, considering that no one he knew—or any Palestinians, for that matter—were involved.

Walter Dean Myers provides a glimpse into an African American neighborhood in his *Boston Globe–Horn Book* Honor Book, *145th Street: Short Stories* (2000). Together, the individual stories of people living and working in this Harlem area become the story of a community.

Additional collections that focus on race and ethnicity include *Moccasin Thunder: American Indian Stories for Today* (Carlson, 2005), an edited collection focusing on Native Americans, and Graham Salisbury's *Island Boyz* (2002), a collection of ten of his stories set in both historical and contemporary Hawaii. *First Crossing* (2004), an anthology edited by Don Gallo, consists of ten stories about contemporary teen immigrants. Characters come from countries as diverse as Venezuela, Romania, Sweden, Haiti, and Cambodia. The young adults in the stories have come to the United States for a variety of reasons, including escaping political oppression, seeking a better life, and of course, because of their parents.

Soul Searching: Thirteen Stories About Faith and Belief (Fraustino, 2002) is an edited collection about young adults from diverse religious backgrounds, including Amish and Voodoo, who are struggling with issues of faith, beliefs, and customs. *I Believe in Water: Twelve Brushes with Religion* (Springer et al., 2000) also centers on adolescents' spiritual inquiries. Authors include Kyoko Mori, Joyce Carol Thomas, Jess Mowry, Margaret Peterson Haddix, Jacqueline Woodson, and Marilyn Singer.

Coping with differences and difficulties

Being different can be difficult for adolescents, but it is a lot easier when there is a group of like-minded people to hang out with. Holly Black and Cecil Castellucci wrote and collected stories from their "geekiest friends" (who happen to be best-selling and award-winning authors) for *Geektastic: Stories from the Nerd Herd* (2009). Some of the contributing geeks include Scott Westerfeld, M. T. Anderson, David Levithan, Garth Nix, Lisa Yee, John Green, Barry Lyga, and Libba Bray. The geeks in this collection include Trekkies, Buffy fans, role-playing gamers, and science nerds. Each story is accompanied by a comic book style illustration.

Owning It: Stories about Teens with Disabilities (Gallo, 2008) is a collection about physical and psychological differences. Living with paraplegia, asthma, learning disabilities, cancer, alcoholism, and Tourette syndrome are some of the situations encountered. Each story is followed with information about the author and the story, providing additional insight and sources for information and assistance. *What Are You Afraid Of? Stories About Phobias* (Gallo, 2006) is a collection about teens dealing with their own—or someone else's—phobia. Some of the phobias are familiar, such as fear of public speaking or open spaces, others, such as fear of knives or string, may seem a bit bizarre.

Growing up

Several short story collections address the joys and challenges young adults may experience as they mature. *Destination Unexpected*, edited by Don Gallo (2003), celebrates the transition from adolescence to adulthood. The adolescents in these 10 stories embark on a journey of one form or another; for example, across town on a bus, to a small town in Ohio, to a racetrack, and on a hunting trip. During their journey they gain insights about life, people, and themselves.

In "Bad Blood" by Will Weaver, Jared introduces himself to an old lady as Jared Righetti, the alias his father has chosen. Jared wonders if being a thief is in his genes, as he comes from a long line of con artists. He begins doing odd jobs for an old woman, helping her take care of her house. As a result, he persuades her to give him an old Corvette. At the end of the story he contemplates where his next journey will take him and if he can forge a path different from that of his father and grandfather. Graham Salisbury's "Mosquito" is set in the wilds of Hawaii where Ricky has to decide if shooting something makes him a man. At the end of the story Ricky has become Rick. In "Tourist Trapped" by Ellen Wittlinger, Helene expects her summer vacation with relatives in Cape Cod to be the reward she deserves for working at her minimum wage job. She ends up taking care of her nephew and doing housework when her pregnant aunt becomes bedridden. The loss of the baby turns everything upside down. Richard Peck's "The Kiss in the Carry-on Bag" is about socially inept Seb and his chance encounter with a girl from Indiana. Seb has no money, he does not know where the bus stop is, and he wears sunglasses inside at night. It turns out that Seb is a future king who rarely gets to meet girls. This humorous story pokes fun at the awkwardness of adolescent encounters and the insular life of royalty. Seb describes his grandmother, the Queen Mother, as being "like a grenade going off in an ostrich farm" (p. 159). He comments that his younger brother "went to a special Swiss school for Gifted Royalty who were reading on grade level" (p. 158).

For many adolescents, participating in sports or supporting a team is a central part of school-based social activities. *Love, Football, and other Contact Sports* (2008) by Alden Carter is a *Booklist* Top Sports Book of the Year. Set in a Wisconsin high school, the stories include the perspectives of football players, the girls who date them, and other students. The roles of the protagonists are listed at the beginning of each selection. Some characters appear in several stories, creating a strong sense of interconnectedness.

Chris Crutcher's *Angry Management* (2009) is a collection of three stories thematically linked to an anger management counseling group. The high school students attending the therapy sessions have experienced physical abuse, prejudice, and hate crimes. They have legitimate reasons for being angry, but they need to learn to cope with their anger or eliminate the cause. Crutcher's fans will recognize many characters from his earlier works, such as *Athletic Shorts: Six Short Stories* (1989), which itself has characters from even earlier stories. Readers may appreciate this deliberate, decades-spanning intertextuality.

Jealousy is another emotion often experienced by young adults. In *Not Like I'm Jealous or Anything: The Jealousy Book* (2007), edited by Marissa Walsh, short stories are combined with essays and poetry. The selections explore all types of jealousy: sibling rivalry; compulsive behavior leading to abuse; desire for wealth and materials goods; and jealousy of someone's abilities, talent, or beauty.

Beauty is the central focus of *Such a Pretty Face: Short Stories about Beauty* (2007) edited by Ann Angel. These stories consider the privileges and challenges of being pretty, finding beauty in unexpected places or people, and cultural expectations associated with of physical attractiveness. In "Farang" by Mary Ann Rodman, Lauren, a newcomer to Thailand, is surprised to discover that foreigners, or farangs, such as herself, are expected to wear a certain type of clothing and look a certain way. Thai women will not work for Americans who they consider fat for fear of losing face with their peers. Everyone is trying to look like someone else. In Chris Lynch's "Red Rover, Red Rover" the narrator declares his love for a night nurse he has never seen. He feels beauty in her hands as she gently soothes his broken back, hears beauty in her voice, and fantasizes about her beauty in his morphine-induced dreams.

Make Me Over: 11 Original Stories about Transforming Ourselves (2005), edited by Marilyn Singer, includes stories of teenagers who embark on some type of makeover. The changes are physical, geographical, emotional, and spiritual. Self-discovery, independence, and the transformations of young adulthood are recurring themes.

Fearing and imagining the unknown

The number of collections categorized as fantasy, science fiction, and horror reflect the enduring popularity of being scared, imaging all sorts of "what ifs" and contemplating the future. Editor Deborah Noyes introduces *Gothic! Ten Original Dark Tales* (2004) by inviting teens "to seek uneasy refuge in these pages. As the child in you knows, it's sweet to be scared, no matter who you are . . . so catch your breath. Come in" (p. xi). This collection includes short Gothic-style stories told by 10 well-known authors. Ghosts, witches, and vampires are among the creatures encountered.

Noyes' *The Restless Dead: Ten Original Stories of the Supernatural* (2007) is, as the title indicates, a collection of scary stories about dead people who do not want to be dead. *M is for Magic* (2007), written by Neil Gaiman and illustrated by Teddy Kristiansen, is primarily a collection of previously published stories. A strange mix of characters, such as ghosts, aliens, trolls, Little Jack Horner, Sir Galahad, and Humpty Dumpty's sister Jill, inhabit these fantasies.

"Screaming at the Night," "Soul Survivor," and "Alexander's Skull" declare the nature of Neil Shusterman's *Darkness Creeping: Twenty Twisted Tales* (2007). In this collection, seemingly normal situations are anything but normal. All the stories in Vivian Vande Velde's *All Hallows' Eve: 13 Stories* (2006) occur on Halloween and, as one might expect, are about scary or gruesome happenings.

Older students who like this genre may also enjoy adult writers such as the perennial favorite Stephen King. His *Just After Sunset* (2008) and *Full Dark, No Stars* (2010) are short story collections. At the end of each collection he provides background on the origins of each story.

The Firebird series edited by Sharon November offers a wide range of fantasy and science fiction stories. The series includes *Firebirds: An Anthology of Original Fantasy and Science Fiction* (2003), *Firebirds Rising: An Original Anthology of Science Fiction and Fantasy* (2006), and *Firebirds Soaring: An Anthology of Speculative Fiction* (2009). Stories for this collection are written by well-known fantasy writers such as Garth Nix, Nancy Farmer, Lloyd Alexander, Jane Yolen, and Michael Cadnum.

Life on Mars: Tales from the New Frontier (2011) edited by Jonathan Strahan is, as the title suggests, a collection of stories about Mars. Strahan challenged science fiction writers, including Nancy Kress, Ellen Klages, Kim Stanley Robinson, and Ian McDonald "to imagine stories set in a world where the mission was a success, and humanity gained a permanent foothold on a new world" (pp. 3–4). Strahan promises readers that these 12 stories are nothing like the Mars stories of the past.

Classic Short Stories

Many short stories originally written for adults demonstrate Douglas Angus's dictum that "the distinctive power and beauty of the short story are involved in its very brevity, the discipline of its strict limits challenging the writer to ever more brilliant inventiveness in such areas as symbolism, suggestiveness and plotting" (1962, p. vii). The unexpected and twisted endings in the following short stories have undoubtedly contributed to their ongoing popularity.

A second reading may be needed to find clues to the unexpected and surprise endings in many classic short stories. In "The Lady or the Tiger?" (1882) by Frank R. Stockton, the princess' lover must stand trial for their affair. His guilt or innocence will be determined in the public arena. Behind one door is a tiger; behind the other a beautiful woman who would become his wife. The princess has given him a message telling him which door to choose. The story ends with the question, "Which came out of the opened door—the lady, or the tiger?"

The open ending forces the reader to determine the choice the princess made. Careful attention to details does reveal the answer. The princess is jealous of the woman waiting behind the door because she believes her lover flirted with her. The man is far below the station of the princess, and the semibarbaric king will not allow the relationship to continue. The commoners will be equally entertained by a slaughter or a wedding. The shortness of the story encourages students to take a second look before answering the question. Students may begin to see rereading as purposeful and often necessary.

The box on the facing page offers a few additional suggestions of classic short stories.

Teaching Ideas ■ SHORT STORIES

The primary objective for reading short stories, as with all literature, is to gain pleasure and understanding through the experience. When teaching, strive to avoid the "short story unit" that confines stories to a concentrated but small cor-

"Charles." Shirley Jackson, 1948. The stories Laurie tells his mom about his misbehaving classmate, Charles, are shocking. Laurie's mom can't wait to meet Charles' mom at a PTA meeting. She is perplexed when the kindergarten teacher tells her there is nobody named Charles in the class.

"The Gift of the Magi." O. Henry (William Sydney Porter), 1906. This Christmas love story is about a young wife and husband who sell their most precious belongings to buy each other a gift. The story has a typical O. Henry surprise ending. An illustrated edition by John Hollander (2005) includes seven stories by O. Henry. Unfamiliar words are defined in the margins.

"The Lottery." Shirley Jackson, 1948. The residents of a small town have an annual lottery to determine who will be stoned to death. The story has been adapted numerous times for radio, television, and film. Many contemporary works, such as *The Hunger Games* (2008) by Suzanne Collins, have created stories based on the outcome of a lottery.

"The Monkey's Paw." W. W. Jacobs, 1902. A family comes into possession of a magical monkey paw. They are warned of the evil nature of the paw and told to throw it in the fire, but the temptation is too great and they keep it. Their first wish, to have money, begins a series of horrifying events.

"The Necklace." Guy de Maupassant, 1884. Vanity costs the young Madame Mathilde Loisel and her husband a decade of poverty and labor when a necklace borrowed and lost must be replaced. How were they to know the gems were not real?

"The Most Dangerous Game." Richard Connell, 1924. The hunter becomes the prey when a big-game hunter is washed ashore on an island inhabited by a Russian general. The general has been waiting for a quarry that will test his abilities.

"The Tell-Tale Heart." Edgar Allan Poe, 1843. A murderer is driven insane over his guilt in this psychological thriller, considered one of Poe's most famous stories.

---

ner of the curriculum. Students will develop a sense of story through multiple experiences with the form.

Short stories work well for direct instruction in literary elements and devices of style. For example, Joyce Sweeney's "Something Old, Something New" from *Destination Unexpected* (2003) references many common customs, people, places, and pop culture. Darius is wearing "something old, something new, something borrowed and something blue" (p. 2). He is a young black man on a city bus headed for the wealthy part of town. While considering where he should sit on the bus he thinks, "Rosa Parks, I'm not" (p. 3). He assumes the fancy library where he is going to accept an award for his writing looks likes the Taj Mahal (p. 2). He imagines the entire cast of the television show "90210" walking around at a mall (p. 3). His tie feels like some kind of *The Silence of the Lambs* caterpillar trying to crawl up his throat (p. 15). Readers will probably require help understanding some of the allusions in the story. They may also need guidance to understand that the author chose specific words and phrases to create an image, tone, or feeling. Each reference adds to the meaning of the story.

Short stories may be used to introduce students to authors whose novels will be read, either as recreational reading or as assigned reading. Most of the short story authors mentioned previously in this chapter also have written novels for young adults. Short stories can also be used to introduce classical or canonical authors whose works are often included in the secondary curriculum. You may focus on general differences in writing style, or on particular literary elements they may encounter later when studying the novels. Recommended titles include "The Chrysanthemums" (1938) by John Steinbeck, "The Snows of Kilimanjaro" (1936) by Ernest Hemingway, and "A Rose for Emily" (1931) by William Faulkner. These complete stories are available on the websites for classical short stories mentioned below.

Besides guided literature study, teachers can include short stories as read alouds, for recreational reading and literature circles, or for workshop. Choosing and reading a significant number of stories in a workshop may provide confidence and a sense of accomplishment that cannot be gained by analyzing a single story.

Theme-based collections work well for literature circles. Students in the same group can select a particular story to read for circle. The individual group discussions can be followed by a whole class discussion about the theme(s) common to all the stories. *Shattered: Stories of Children and War* (2002), edited by Jennifer Armstrong, includes stories of the Civil War, World War II, the Vietnam War, the Cold War of the 1950s, the Six-Day War between Israel and neighboring Arab countries, the Soviet invasion of Afghanistan, and several other wars and conflicts. The stories look beyond the battlefields to the wars' children, refugees, detainees, survivors, and conscientious objectors. A single line of text running across the bottom of each page provides background information. Each selection describes a story of a child or young adult impacted by war. Collectively, the stories create an exploration of the theme from multiple perspectives that will help students see beyond a simplistic idea that war is bad.

Students should have opportunities to read both classics written for adults and stories written for adolescents. A good source for classic short stories is "Twenty Great American Short Stories" (www.americanliterature.com/ss/ssindx.html). The website includes the full text for 20 classic stories. The site links to dozens of author sites, which in turn list additional works, including more short stories. Each day a different story is highlighted, which viewers can forward to friends via email. The Classic Short Stories website (www. classicshorts.com.) is another excellent source for author information and free full-text stories.

DRAMA: COLLABORATIVE LITERATURE

Although play scripts can be read alone, real drama is collaborative and requires both actor and audience to bring it to life. Drama is also multimodal. In the 4th century BCE Aristotle characterized the six elements of tragic plays as plot, character, thought, music, and spectacle (Hatlen, 1987). **Drama** differs from other forms of literature because its "raw materials" include human voices, facial expressions, and movement, and may include art, music, props, and costumes as well.

Brockett (2007) states that drama always includes three essential elements: "What is performed (script, scenario, or plan); the performance (including all of the processes involved in the creation and presentation of a production); and the audience (the perceivers)" (pp. 5–6). Regardless of whether the class will undertake a fully realized production of a play, students must be involved in bringing a story to life and in witnessing the performance. Rutsky (2001) clearly describes the unique qualities of drama:

> When a student reads a novel, the characters speak through the voice of a narrator, and the action is recollected, recounted—in the past. Drama allows the teacher to bring the students into the action rather than merely discussing it. Plays can be walked through, interpreted, and manipulated far more easily than novels, and that gives us the opportunity to engage students with the text in new and exciting ways. (p. xii)

Diversity in Plays

Because walking in another person's shoes is the essence of drama, students should have opportunities to explore plays from many cultures and eras. Drama has often provided a creative outlet for the voices of minority groups such as African Americans, Latinos, and Asian Americans, as well as for women and the LGBT community. Learning about these diverse groups through these plays will help students understand the world around them. It will also reinforce the belief that every minority group may find and celebrate its voice through theatrical expression.

Young adults should also experience plays reflecting diverse traditions and eras. Across the centuries, different regions have influenced the theatrical world and made unique contributions to drama. Students in the United States may require background information in order to comprehend theatrical traditions such as Greek or Kabuki theater, but they should have opportunities to explore the vast canon of dramatic literature.

The ancient Greeks gave birth to the drama of the Western world. Greek playwrights produced hundreds of plays, but only 44 of them have survived: 32 tragedies by Sophocles, Aeschylus, and Euripides, and a dozen comedies by Aristophanes. The surviving plays continue to be studied and performed as vehicles for exploring ancient mythology. **Greek theater** is also the source for one of the most important ideas in theater history: Aristotle's explanation that the three "unities" of time, place, and action are the keys to an effective plot.

Hatlen (1987) explains the effect of the unities in Greek tragedy: "A tragedy is complete; it has a beginning, middle, and end—and according to Aristotle, each of these parts is a well-articulated structure without extraneous material" (p. 72). Since Aristotle's time, every major theatrical movement around the globe has been defined according to whether it accepts or rejects the unities. Shakespeare, for instance, was remarkable not only for his poetry, but also for his exploratory rejection of the unities. The Ancient Greek Theatre website (www.greektheatre.gr) not only presents great Greek playwrights, but it also provides information related to areas such as costumes, masks, and plans for staging ancient theater in a school environment.

One of the most influential Italian theatrical traditions is the **Commedia dell'Arte.** These plays do observe the three unities, but they are very different from Greek tragedies. In lieu of a script, actors receive just an outline of the main events of each scene. Actors play highly recognizable stereotypes such as lovers, servants, and masters. They then enrich the simple plots with improvisation and *lazzi*, practiced bits of clowning they have developed over many years (Brockett, 2007). Commedia particularly influenced the plays of Renaissance England, France, and Spain. **Renaissance theater** often combined Greek source material and commedia stereotypes, and some of the plays in this tradition are the most famous in Western theatrical history. They include the works of Shakespeare, Moliere, and Lope de Vega (Brockett, 2007).

Japan offers colorful Kabuki, Noh, and Bunraku. **Kabuki** is a type of dance drama with elaborate costumes, stylized acting, elaborate makeup, song, and exaggerated movement. **Noh** are stately, classical musical productions based on themes about heroes. Often the actors wear masks, and the performance includes a chorus. **Bunraku** is an intricate form of puppet theater that requires puppeteers to train for years to handle the puppets, which can be up to four feet high. The Kabuki for Everyone website (http://park.org/Japan/Kabuki/Kabuki.html) includes an online theater as well as information on kabuki sounds and make-up. China and Indonesia also have a theatrical history involving puppets, but their primary interest is shadow puppetry (Brockett, 2007). Eastern traditions, with their focus on folk stories and emphasis on puppetry, provide an excellent means of introducing diverse drama texts in all classrooms, but particularly those with younger students.

By the 20th century, Aristotle's unities were dismissed completely. Western theater responded to the tragedies of two world wars with drama that reflected a pessimistic worldview, such as Samuel Beckett's absurdist play *Waiting for Godot* (1949) and the realistic drama *Death of a Salesman* (Miller, 1949), which showed ordinary individuals beaten down by modern life. During the same time period, however, producers in the United States were combining melodrama with the skits and songs of vaudeville to create the musical, the greatest American contribution to theater (Brockett, 2007).

Given the wide range of eras, traditions, and subject matter available, teachers may find choosing plays to be a challenge. They need to balance the play's historical or literary significance with its appeal for a young adult audience and its potential for helping students to explore the elements of theater.

Choosing Plays for the Classroom

Drama reflects society, providing either a clarifying or distorting mirror of the current political landscape and social milieu. The majority of plays, particularly those with classic or historic significance, address issues such as gender and sexuality, the virtues and vices of different political systems, or the value of human life. Teachers should not reject *Romeo and Juliet* to avoid the topic of

The Complete Works of William Shakespeare (Abridged). Adam Long, Daniel Singer, and Jess Winfield, 2011 (Rev. ed.). This play covers all of Shakespeare's plays, some more thoroughly than others, in a humorous, often slapstick, way that is sure to spark student interest.

Metamorphoses. Mary Zimmerman, 2002. A sharp, contemporary retelling of Ovid's poem and, therefore, of many prominent Greek myths.

Actor's Nightmare. Christopher Durang, 1981. This one-act comedy follows an unwitting and unwilling actor through several famous plays from major periods of theatrical history.

Buried Child. Sam Shepard, 1977. A surrealistic, symbolic work that offers a postmodern interpretation of the American farming family during an economic slowdown.

A Raisin in the Sun. Lorraine Hansberry, 1959. This play, based on true events, details the experience of an African American family in postwar Chicago trying to thrive despite racial and economic hardships.

The Laramie Project. Moises Kaufman and the Tectonic Theatre Project, 2001. This documentary-style play details the events surrounding the 1998 murder of University of Wyoming student Matthew Shepard, who was gay, and the reactions of people in and around Laramie, Wyoming, where the crime occurred. Teacher discretion advised.

Spoon River Anthology. Edgar Lee Masters, adapted by Charles Aidman (1966). Masters's classic poems provide students with rich characters to inhabit and distinctive voices to explore.

teenage sexuality or ban *Oedipus* because incest plays a role in the plot, but they should adequately prepare for students' questions on these topics.

Joshua Rutsky's book *Beyond the Bard: Fifty Plays for Use in the English Classroom* (2001) is particularly valuable in helping teachers choose the right play for their classes. Each listing contains a brief synopsis, an overview of important themes, and ideas on how to connect the play to other texts or ideas that can be explored through classroom activities. Each entry notes the play's appropriate grade level and any red flags teachers need to be aware of that might offend students or their parents. Finally, it supplies sources of critical commentary on the play. Rutsky's book combines classic and more contemporary plays. The box above lists additional plays from the last 50 years, including some retellings of classic plays, that would be appropriate for young adults.

Teaching Ideas ▪ DRAMA

Drama in a classroom presents a valuable differentiation tool. Plays and scenes offer students a choice of characters, and some students welcome actions and dialogue as a respite from exposition and explanation. Some students may appreciate the freedom of an improvisation, while others may desire the familiarity of plays with extensive expository stage directions. Without some hands-on activities that explore the performance of drama, however, it is impossible for any student to fully appreciate this type of literature. Drama as a vehicle for focusing on social issues and its wide range of subject matter make it a useful supplement for any subject. One-act plays that are intended for middle and high school competitions present succinct, entertaining enactments of everything from famous novels to mathematical theorems. Whatever the lesson, any classroom benefits with drama.

As Brockett (2007) suggests, understanding drama requires students to participate in all the processes involved in the creation and presentation of a play, and those processes are highly collaborative. A dramatic activity is not complete without someone to witness, critique, or appreciate it. Kutz and Roskelly (1991) explain drama's power to transform classrooms by fostering new ways for students to work together:

> [Drama] is created as a collaborative effort among actors, writer, director, stage designer, and audience. In fact, one of the real problems in interpreting drama—envisioning its performance—is circumvented by group work where group members can take on those roles. . . . In doing this work, the group recreates the play: the relationship between actor and character, between audience and writer, between production and interpretation. (p. 261)

Collaborative drama activities can be undertaken with the full script of a classic play or with a "text" that is improvised by the actors from nothing more than the suggestion of two characters and a situation. Next, we discuss informal activities that develop the tools of dramatic interpretation and activities that can be scaffolds to complete plays. The section concludes with suggestions about bridging plays to films.

Informal classroom drama

The National Council of Teachers of English (NCTE) has long endorsed informal or improvisational drama, which they define as an activity in which participants compose and enact their parts as the drama progresses (1982). The NCTE's guidelines note that informal drama, also known as creative dramatics, can range from simple sensory exercises to acting fairly complex scenes. Informal drama activities allow students to develop three basic dramatic tools: movement, voice, and dramatic imagination. The National Council of Teachers of English and the International Reading Association provide a detailed plan for involving high school students in process drama and a variety of other lesson plans for drama in the classroom at www.ReadWriteThink.org.

Activities for movement. Dramatic movement may be easier for self-conscious adolescents when they can do it in a group. Such group activities also help students to understand the collaborative "we're all in this together" attitude that characterizes theater. Swados (2006) suggests various directing exercises that are much like the game Simon Says. As the teacher gives commands for the whole group to follow, students become less self-conscious and more responsive to moving along with the group. These commands can be as simple as "turn toward the window and wave."

Activities for voice. Swados (2006) suggests exercises that help students develop the use of their voices. By repeating words or phrases louder, softer, faster, slower, or with various emotions, students learn to fine tune their "instrument." As a next step, they can practice using their voices to interpret short written texts. Poetry is a prime genre for oral interpretation, especially when accompanied by background sounds, music, or visuals. Readers' theater is also an excellent activity for developing voice. In this activity, a cast of characters and a narrator enact a story relying only on their voices. They may use published scripts such as those created by Barchers and Kroll (2002), or they can create their own scripts by choosing scenes from young adult novels.

Activity for dramatic imagination. Students can develop their dramatic imaginations through improvisations in which they must simultaneously create and act a scene. Rutsky (2001) suggests a game called "Freeze Chain" (p. xv), in which two students start acting out a situation. When a member of the audience calls out "freeze," the actors become motionless. The person who froze them takes the place of one of the actors. When they "unfreeze," the new person can take the scene in a totally new direction, while the original partner must play along.

Activities with formal scripts

Students may explore the themes of a full-length play by creating a dramaturgy project. **Dramaturgy** is the term used for information that helps the actors create their roles and the audience to appreciate the play. Student projects might range from traditional research to artistic inspiration; from academic papers analyzing a theme or character to an imaginary soundtrack meant to motivate actors during different events of the play. The list below suggests some collaborative activities to support students' understanding of a play.

Character interviews. These interviews are part of the method acting technique. Students examine the play closely and use their imaginations to answer questions from the point of view of the characters in the play.

Living verse. This activity is useful for Shakespeare and verse plays. Each student represents a single syllable in a line of verse. Students representing stressed or accented syllables stand and shout their syllables, while those representing unstressed syllables kneel or remain seated and whisper. For greater clarity, try having the students stress the wrong syllables and whisper the accented syllables.

In your own words. This activity requires students to paraphrase a monologue or scene. It can be a written project or you can have students read or reenact their versions in front of the class.

Production grid. Have students chart the scenery, lighting, sound, costume, props, and special effect needs for a play. This activity highlights information that often appears in the exposition of a novel or story, yet is easily lost when reading a play.

Jigsaw groups. This activity involves assigning student groups different scenes or acts from the same play. Each group may create a presentation or act out part of the play for the rest of the class.

classroom scenario

Story of the Play in Snapshots

AS YOU READ the following, consider how it illustrates the notion of drama as collaborative litera-ture. Also consider how the teacher's use of photography and the students' performance contribute to their understanding and appreciation of the play.

Miss Landis tells her class that today they will act out one of the funniest fairy tales of all time. She hands out large nametags to her students. Some students receive character names such as "Theseus" and "Hippolyta," while others have names and pictures of places such as "Forest" and "Athens"; a few students receive tags that say such things as "Magic Flower" and "Donkey Head." The back of each nametag con-tains several lines and phrases from Shakespeare's play *A Midsummer Night's Dream.* Miss Landis explains

that the nametags are also scripts, and when she points to a stu-dent, he or she will read the line on his or her paper.

Miss Landis has a synopsis of the play on her nametag, which says "Narrator." She proceeds to narrate the simplified story of *A Midsummer Night's Dream,* pausing frequently and pointing to students. She does not, however, reveal the title of the play or the author. As the story progresses, students playing charac-ters move between students playing places and interact with students playing items. The students laugh when Puck enchants Bottom by covering him with a picture of the donkey head, and Miss Landis encourages them to find a way to move together in tandem. Occasionally, she repeats part of the story more em-phatically, encouraging the students to use gestures or repeat their lines with more emotion.

When the class finishes the story, Miss Landis lets the students ask questions and express their opinions about the plot and characters. Next, she asks them to identify the most important moments in the play and which lines best exemplify that moment. She writes these lines on an interactive white board in separate text boxes. After the class feels satisfied that they have identified the most important moments and correlating lines, Miss Landis places the text boxes in chronological order and discusses how the moments represent major events in the story.

Miss Landis then has the students perform their roles to recreate a picture of each important mo-ment, with the students freezing immediately after they say the line that epitomizes the moment. She encourages the students to make bigger facial expressions and gestures, then takes their picture. That night Miss Landis uploads the photos to her computer and pastes them into her file of "Important Moments" and adds character names and major events to provide a visual scaffold of the play as the students move toward reading it independently.

The next day, Miss Landis reveals that the fairy tale the class enacted yesterday was actually Shake-speare's *A Midsummer Night's Dream.* Some students admit that they already knew, but one student claims "it wasn't boring enough to be Shakespeare." Miss Landis acknowledges that silently reading a play by Shakespeare is not nearly as exciting as seeing, speaking, and hearing it. Finally, Miss Landis assigns roles and the students begin reading the play aloud. She occasionally interrupts them to confirm their understanding or to review an archaic word or phrase. She introduces Alexander Schmidt's *Shakespeare Lexicon and Quo-tation Dictionary,* so students can investigate unfamiliar terms on their own. Over several days, as the class progresses through the play, she refers students to the interactive white board so they can make stronger connections between the text of the play and their previous enactment of it.

Finally, the class examines video clips and production stills from professional productions of *A Midsummer Night's Dream* that match the moments they identified as the most important. Students compare their photos with the professional ones, identifying the strengths of each and evaluating which one provides the best portrayal of each particular event. The class decides to film a digital short of Act IV Scene I in which the Queen of the Fairies, Titania, is under a spell and falls in love with the uncouth Bottom, who now has the head of a donkey. Miss Landis posts the video in the interactive white board file renamed "Our Midsummer's Night Dream." The class now has visual documentation of their learning and a new-found respect for the power of drama to inspire them.

Bridging with film

Miss Landis empowered students to build a play out of their background knowledge and their collaborative imagination. When working with a well-known or historic drama such as a play by Shakespeare, a teacher may also choose to build a bridge to the play by showing part of a film version or a recorded live performance of the play, as Miss Landis did. Many libraries carry recordings of classic plays, or they may be purchased online. Major retailers carry more commercial film versions, while niche retailers such as Lear Media can supply more obscure titles. We provide three of the dozens of examples of films and videos that could be used as a bridge to one of Shakespeare's plays.

Macbeth (1979), directed by Philip Casson, is a television version of a Royal Shakespeare Company production that stars Ian McKellen (*Lord of the Rings, The X-men*) and Judi Dench (M in several James Bond films). In the famous first scene, a trio of witches tells Macbeth that he shall be king. Macbeth and his equally power hungry wife help the prophecy along by killing everyone who stands between them and the throne. Macbeth is one of Shakespeare's shortest tragedies, and this is a fast-moving production that is faithful to the original text.

Romeo + Juliet (1996) is a film adaptation directed by Baz Luhrmann. The setting has been changed from Renaissance Italy to the suburb of Verona Beach in the contemporary United States, but this film, which stars Leonardo DiCaprio and Claire Danes, is otherwise faithful to the original text. The addition of a giant fireball and several gun battles give it a Hollywood feel, but the violence surrounding the two lovers is consistent with the original; it is part of what makes them "star-crossed."

Sometimes a less direct adaptation of a play can act as a bridge for students by grounding them in the basic action or themes of a play; *10 Things I Hate About You* (1999), directed by Gil Junger, is an example. This loose adaptation of *The Taming of the Shrew* retains none of Shakespeare's language, but it does keep the key elements of the original plot. High school sophomore Bianca is not allowed to date until her older sister Katerina, does, but Kat is independent and hot-headed, and she has no interest in either popularity or boys. Bianca's would-be boyfriend, Cameron, bribes a mysterious outcast senior named Patrick Verona to date Kat, and, after some emotional fireworks, the two develop a genuine relationship. The film avoids the outdated and heavy-handed parts of the original play's "battle of the sexes," in favor of a surprisingly successful exploration of the play's themes of balancing independence against love and belonging.

Beyond the Classroom

Many high schools, and even some middle schools, support co-curricular drama clubs. These clubs prepare and present theatrical performances, allowing students to experience all the artistic and technical elements that come together in dramatic productions. A drama club may prepare a one-act play or an abridged play for regional or national competition. Leagues and organizations such as the International Thespian Society (ITS) set strict rules, production standards, and time limits for competition plays, so selections must be made accordingly.

Schools more commonly stage a larger scale production, typically a musical. These productions tend to play to the tastes of the community, and they involve a greater number of students and community members than plays intended for competition. Both of these experiences allow students to connect with the world of professional theater beyond the walls of a classroom, and both allow students to learn the dynamics of this versatile multidimensional art form. The musicals performed at high schools are generally chosen from a short list of classics that are familiar to the local audience. The following list of contemporary plays for drama clubs focus on works from the past 50 years that provide a variety of performance opportunities for students. These plays work equally well for schools with limited resources as well as those with extensive resources.

Plays and resources for drama club use are as varied as theater itself. Teachers wishing to produce a play or musical or to access the plays most commonly used as competition and performance pieces can contact Playscripts, Inc. (www.playscripts.com/guthrie). They feature the most comprehensively cross-indexed catalog of plays available, with up to 90 percent of the script freely accessible online. Furthermore, their production fees are among the most competitive. They also offer a production history and reviews, so teachers may easily evaluate which plays are suitable for their classrooms.

Although it does not offer the same amount of online accessibility, the Pioneer Drama website (www.Pioneerdrama.com) has an extensive catalog of plays available online, many of which address serious social and ethical issues at a middle or high school level. They also offer 10-minute plays for teens. The companies that feature the most prestigious playwrights and recognized musicals (Samuel French and Music Theatre International, respectively) do not offer much online, but are the primary sources for any professional, amateur, or educational productions of popular plays such as Arthur Miller's *The Crucible* (1953), or musicals such as Rodgers and Hammerstein's *Oklahoma!* (1943). Other sources of dramatic material are listed in the box on the facing page.

Teachers and students who want to learn more about the world of theater can visit a number of websites representing national and regional organizations. The ArtsEdge program of the Kennedy Center for the Performing Arts, for instance, provides theater standards and lessons at www.Artsedge.kennedy-center.org. The young playwrights festival in Chicago is described at www.pegasusplayers.

Hard Candy. Jonathan Rand, 2000. This one-act play, performed by hundreds of U. S. high schools over the past decade, delights students while providing a clever demonstration of storytelling methods, characterization, and business practices.

Pride and Prejudice. Jane Austen, adapted by Jon Jory, 2006. Classic novels are often adapted for the stage, but few share this play's finesse.

Class Action/Second Class. Brad Slaight, 1996/1998. These companion plays consist of scenes and monologues that address the social issues high school students face every day.

30 Reasons Not To Be in a Play. Alan Haehnal, 2007. This versatile play with an army of characters allows extensive student participation while, despite its title, educating students on all of the reasons they will want to be in a play.

The Art of Rejection. Christian Kiley, 2008. This flexible one-act play addresses rejection and bullying with wit and humor and is perfect for imaginative students.

War at Home. Nicole Quinn & Nina Shengold, 2003. This one-act piece presents the responses to the events of September 11, 2001, of students in a New York State high school. It was created from journal writings of students, teachers, and community members in the weeks immediately following the attacks. All royalties from the play are donated to charity.

---

org/cms/?q=node/61, and information about a summer program for young people interested in acting Shakespeare is available from the American Shakespeare Center at www.americanshakespearecenter.com.

conclusion

In this chapter we have placed a special emphasis on connecting young adults with poetry, short stories, and plays outside as well as inside the classroom. That emphasis comes from understanding that all three of these literary forms were once popular as well as artistically successful. Even small towns had active community theaters; poems and short stories were published in monthly magazines and even in daily newspapers. Now all three struggle to remain viable. The marketplace lacks mechanisms to sustain new works in these "other" literary forms the way that novels and nonfiction are supported. Books have the *New York Times* Best Sellers Lists, movie tie-ins, and talk shows where authors can be interviewed. The only close parallel for marketing is Broadway theater, but generally only musicals are heavily promoted.

To bolster the role poetry, short stories, and drama play in students' lives, both inside and outside the classroom, take three steps. First, adopt instructional approaches that balance in-depth study with engaging activities and a wide range of experiences, such as an emphasis on performing poetry and drama and reading workshops that focus on short stories. Second, instruct young adults how to find and choose short stories and poems and alert them to local theater productions. Guide students to use the Internet and social media to find and share stories and poems.

Finally, encourage students to produce as well as enjoy these literary forms. School drama clubs are the classic example of such efforts. Performing in even one school play gives students an understanding of drama that is hard to achieve in the classroom. Too often, however, budget and time constraints mean that the number of productions and students involved is far too small. One-act play festivals, poetry slams, media productions, and online publishing can all empower young adults to participate in literature rather than just study it.

We have provided only a small sample of the contemporary poetry, short stories, and drama available to young adults. We encourage you to explore this literature for yourself, find works you like, and then share them with your students.

BIBLIOGRAPHY OF LITERATURE FOR YOUNG ADULTS

Angelou, M. (1993). On the pulse of morning. Oral presentation; text retrieved from http://gos.sbc.edu/a/angelou.html.

Angel, A. (2007). *Such a pretty face: Short stories about beauty.* New York: Amulet Books.

Armstrong, J. (Ed.). (2002). *Shattered: Stories of children and war.* New York: Knopf.

Asher, S. (Ed.). (2004). *On her way: Stories and poems about growing up girl.* (H. Larson & B. L. O'Malley, Illus.). New York: Dutton Children's Books.

Austen, J., & Jory, J. (2006). *Pride and prejudice: A romantic comedy.* New York: Playscripts.

Barchers, S. L., & Kroll, J. L. (2002). *Classic readers theater for young adults.* Greenwood, CO: Greenwood Publishing Village.

Bauer, M. (Ed.). (1994). *Am I blue? Coming out of the silence.* New York: HarperCollins.

Beckett, S. (1954). *Waiting for Godot.* New York: Grove Press.

Black, H., & Castellucci, C. (Eds.). (2009). *Geektastic: Stories from the nerd herd.* New York: Little, Brown.

Blake, W. (1794, 1993). *The Tyger.* (N. Waldman, Illus.). San Diego, CA: Harcourt Brace.

Bruchac, J. (2004). Skins. In M. Singer (Ed.), *Face relations: 11 stories about seeing beyond color* (pp. 18–42). New York: Simon & Schuster.

Carlson, L. M. (Ed.). (2005). *Moccasin thunder: American Indian stories for today.* New York: HarperCollins.

Cart, M. (Ed.). (2001). *Love & sex: Ten stories of truth.* New York: Simon & Schuster.

Cart, M. (2003). *Necessary noise: Stories about our families as they really are.* New York: HarperCollins.

Carter, A. (2008). *Love, football and other contact sports.* New York: Holiday House.

Casson, P. (Dir.). (1979). A *performance of Macbeth* [televised performance] UK: Thames Television and the Royal Shakespeare Company.

Collins, B. (1996). Introduction to poetry [poem]. Retrieved from http://www.loc.gov/poetry/180/001.html.

Collins, B. (2005). *Billy Collins live* [audio recording]. New York: Random House Audio.

Collins, S. (2008). *The hunger games.* New York: Scholastic.

Connell, R. (1924). The most dangerous game. Retrieved from http://en.wikipedia.org/wiki/The_Most_Dangerous_Game.

Cormier, R. (1974). *The chocolate war.* New York: Pantheon.

Cormier, R. (1991). *8 plus 1.* New York: Laurel Leaf.

Crutcher, C. (1989). *Athletic shorts.* New York: Bantam Doubleday.

Crutcher, C. (2009). *Angry management.* New York: Greenwillow Books.

de Maupassant, G. (1884). The necklace. Retrieved from www.eastoftheweb.com/short-stories/UBooks/Neck.shtml.

Demme, J. (Dir.). (1991). *The silence of the lambs.* U.S.A.: Orion Pictures.

Durang, C. (1981). *Sister Mary Ignatius explains it all for you* [and] *The actor's nightmare: Two one-act plays.* Garden City, NY: Nelson Doubleday.

Faulkner, W. (1931). A rose for Emily. Retrieved from http://flightline.highline.edu/tkim/Files/Lit100_SS2.pdf.

Fleischman, P. (1988). *Joyful noise: Poems for two voices.* New York: Scholastic.

Fraustino, L. R. (Ed.). (2002). *Soul searching: Thirteen stories about faith and belief.* New York: Simon & Schuster.

Frost, R. (1923, 1978). *Stopping by woods on a snowy evening.* (S. Jeffers, Illus.). New York: Dutton.

Gaiman, N. (2007). *M is for magic.* New York: HarperCollins.

Gallo, D. (Ed.). (1984). *Sixteen short stories by outstanding writers for young adults.* New York: Delacorte.

Gallo, D. (Ed.). (2003). *Destination unexpected.* Cambridge, MA: Candlewick Press.

Gallo, D. (Ed.). (2004). *First crossing: Stories about teen immigrants.* Cambridge, MA: Candlewick Press.

Gallo, D. (Ed.). (2006). *What are you afraid of? Stories about phobias.* Cambridge, MA: Candlewick Press.

Gallo, D. (Ed.). (2008). *Owning it: Stories about teens with disabilities.* Cambridge, MA: Candlewick Press.

Garden, N. (2007). *Hear us out! Lesbian and gay stories of struggle, progress and hope, 1950 to the present.* New York: Farrar, Straus & Giroux.

Giovanni, N. (Ed.). (2008). *Hip hop speaks to children: A celebration of poetry with a beat.* Naperville, IL: Sourcebooks.

Giovanni, N. (Ed.). (2010). *The 100 best African American poems.* Naperville, IL: Sourcebooks.

Goodrich, F., & Hackett, C. (1956). *The diary of Ann Frank.* [Acting Edition]. New York: Samuel French.

Greenberg, J. (Ed.). (2001). *Heart to heart: New poems inspired by twentieth-century American art.* New York: Harry N. Abrams.

Greenberg, J. (Ed.). (2008). *Side by side: New poems inspired by art from around the world.* New York: Abrams Books for Young Readers.

Haehnal, A. (2007). *30 reasons not to be in a play.* New York: Playscripts.

Hansberry, L. (1959). *A raisin in the sun.* New York: Random House.

Hawthorne, N. (1837). *Twice-told tales.* Retrieved from http://www2.hn.psu.edu/faculty/jmanis/hawthorn/2-Told-Tales.pdf.

Hemingway, E. (1938). The snows of Kilimanjaro. Retrieved from http://xroads.virginia.edu/~drbr/heming.html.

Henry, O. (1906, 2005). The gift of the Magi. In *Stories for young people: O. Henry.* John Hollander (Ed.), (M. Hyman Illus.), (pp. 8–17). New York: Sterling Publishing.

Holbrooke, S., & Wolf, A. (2008). *More than friends: Poems from him and her.* Honesdale, PA: Front Street/Boyds Mills Press.

Hughes, L. (Author), Roessel, D., & Rampersad, A. (Eds.). (2006). *Poetry for young people: Langston Hughes.* (B. Andrews, Illus.). New York: Sterling Publishing.

Hughes, L. (Author), Rampersad, A., & Roessel, D. (Eds.). (1994). *The collected poems of Langston Hughes.* New York: Knopf.

Irving, W. (1819). Rip Van Winkle. Retrieved from http://www.bartleby.com/195/4.html.

Jackson, S. (1948). The lottery. Retrieved from www.classicshorts.com.stories/lotry.html.

Jackson, S. (1949). Charles. Retrieved from http://storyoftheweek.loa.org/2010/06/charles-html.

Jacobs, W. W. (1902). The monkey's paw. Retrieved from www.englishclub.com/reading/story-monkeys-paw.htm.

Janeczko, P. (Ed.). (2004). *Blushing: Expressions of love in poems.* London: Orchard Books; New York: Abrams Books for Young Readers.

Junger, G. (Dir.). (1999). *Ten things I hate about you.* U.S.A.: Touchstone Pictures.

Kaufman, M., Fondakowski, L., & Tectonic Theatre Project. (2001). *The Laramie Project.* New York: Dramatists Play Service.

Kiley, C. (2008). *The art of rejection.* Crystal Beach, ON: Theatrefolk.

King, S. (2008). *Just After Sunset.* New York: Scribner.

King, S. (2010). *Full dark, no stars.* New York: Scribner.

Lee, R. E. (1970). *The night Thoreau spent in jail.* (theatrical production). Washington, DC: Arena Stage.

Levithan, D. (2008). *How they met and other stories.* New York: Knopf.

Long, A., Singer, D., & Winfield, J. (1994/2001). *The complete works of William Shakespeare (Abridged).* New York: Broadway Play Publishing.

Luhrmann, B. (Dir.). (1996). *Romeo + Juliet.* U.S.A.: 20th Century Fox.

Lynch, C. (2007). Red Rover. Red Rover. In A. Angel (Ed.), *Such a pretty face* (pp. 37–65). New York: Amulet Books.

Magee, J. G. (1941). High flight. Retrieved from http://www.woodiescciclub.com/high-flight.htm.

Masters, E. L., & Aidman, C. (1966). *Spoon River anthology.* Los Angeles, CA: Samuel French.

Mazer, H. (Ed.). (1997). *Twelve shots.* New York: Delacorte.

Mercado, N. E. (Ed.). (2005). *Every man for himself: Ten original stories about being a guy.* New York: Dial.

Miller, A. (1949). *Death of a salesman.* New York: Viking Penguin.

Miller, A. (1953). *The crucible: A play in four acts.* New York: Viking.

Myers, W. D. (2000). *145th Street: Short stories.* New York: Delacorte.

Navasky, B. (Trans.). (1993). *Festival in my heart: Poems by Japanese children.* New York: Harry N. Abrams.

November, S. (Ed.). (2003). *Firebirds: An anthology of original fantasy and science fiction.* New York: Firebird/Penguin.

November, S. (Ed.). (2006). *Firebirds rising: An original anthology of science fiction and fantasy.* New York: Firebird/Penguin.

November, S. (Ed.). (2009). *Firebirds soaring: an anthology of speculative fiction.* New York: Firebird/Penguin.

Noyes, A. (1906, 1990). *The highwayman.* (N. Waldman, Illus.). New York: Harcourt Brace.

Noyes, D. (Ed.). (2004). *Gothic! Ten original dark tales.* Cambridge, MA: Candlewick Press.

Noyes, D. (Ed.). (2007). *The restless dead: Ten original stories of the supernatural.* (T. Kristiansen, Illus.). Cambridge, MA: Candlewick Press.

Nye, N. S. (Ed.). (1998). *The space between our footsteps: Poems and paintings from the Middle East.* New York: Simon & Schuster.

Nye, N. S. (1999). *What have you lost?* New York: Greenwillow Books.

Nye, N. S. (2004). Hum. In M. Singer (Ed.), *Face relations: 11 stories about seeing beyond color* (pp. 68–88). New York: Simon & Schuster.

Peck, R. (2003). The kiss in the carry-on bag. In D. Gallo (Ed.), *Destination unexpected* (pp. 147–162). Cambridge, MA: Candlewick Press.

Peck, R. (2004). *Past, perfect, present tense: New and collected stories.* New York: Dial.

Poe, E. A. (1843). *The tell-tale heart.* Retrieved from www.literature.org/authors/poe-edgar-allan/tell-tale.

Poe, E. A. (Author), & Bagert, B. (Ed.). (1995). *Poetry for young people: Edgar Allan Poe.* (C. Cobleigh, Illus.). New York: Sterling Publishing.

Rand, J. (1994). *Hard candy.* New York: Playscripts.

Rodman, M. A. (2007). Farang. In A. Angel (Ed.), *Such a pretty face* (pp. 21–36). New York: Amulet Books.

Rodgers, R., & Hammerstein, O. (1943). *Oklahoma!* New York: Random House.

Rosenberg, L. (Ed.). (2000). *Light-gathering poems.* New York: Holt.

Quinn, N., & Shengold, N. (2003). *War at home.* New York: Playscripts.

Salisbury, G. (2002). *Island boyz.* New York: Wendy Lamb.

Salisbury, G. (2003). Mosquito. In D. Gallo (Ed.), *Destination unexpected* (pp. 164–191). Cambridge, MA: Candlewick Press.

Scieszka, J. (Ed.). (2010). *Guys read: Funny business.* New York: HarperCollins.

Shepard, S. (1977). *Buried child, a play in three acts.* New York: Dramatists Play Service.

Shusterman, N. (2007). *Darkness creeping: Twenty twisted tales.* New York: Puffin.

Singer, M. (Ed.). (2004). *Face relations: 11 stories about seeing beyond color.* New York: Simon & Schuster.

Singer, M. (Ed.). (1998). *Stay true: Short stories for strong girls.* New York: Scholastic.

Singer, M. (Ed.). (2005). *Make me over: 11 original stories about transforming ourselves.* New York: Penguin.

Singer, M. (2004). Negress. In M. Singer (Ed.), *Face relations: 11 stories about seeing beyond color* (pp. 189–207). New York: Simon & Schuster.

Slaight, B. (1996). *Class action.* Quincy, MA: Walter H. Baker Co.

Slaight, B. (1998). *Second class.* Quincy, MA: Walter H. Baker Co.

Smith, C. R., Jr. (2007). *Twelve rounds to glory: The story of Muhammad Ali.* Cambridge, MA: Candlewick Press.

Sones, S. (2003). Dr. Jekyll and sister Hyde. In Michael Cart (Ed.), *Necessary noise* (pp. 173–216). New York: HarperCollins.

Soto, G. (1990). *Baseball in April and other stories.* New York: Harcourt Brace.

Soto, G. (1992a). *Neighborhood odes.* (D. Diaz, Illus.). New York: Harcourt Brace.

Soto, G. (also Producer). (1992b). *The pool party* [film]. U.S.A.: ITVS.

Soto, G. (1994). *Jesse: A novel.* New York: Harcourt Brace.

Soto, G. (1995). *Gary Soto: New and selected poems.* San Francisco: Chronicle Books.

Soto, G. (1997a). *Buried onions.* New York: Harcourt Children's Book.

Soto, G. (1997b). *Novio boy: A play.* New York: Harcourt Brace.

Soto, G. (1999). *Nerdlandia: A play.* New York: Putnam.

Soto, G. (2002). *Fearless Fernie.* (R. Dunuick, Illus.). New York: Putnam.

Soto, G. (2003). *The afterlife.* New York: Harcourt Children's Books.

Soto, G. (2005). *Worlds apart: Traveling with Fernie and me.* (G. Clarke, Illus.). New York: Penguin.

Soto, G. (2005). *Help wanted.* New York: Harcourt.

Soto, G. (2006a). *A fire in my hands.* Orlando, FL: Harcourt.

Soto, G. (2006a). All the luck. In G. Soto, *A fire in my hands* (pp. 18–19). Orlando, FL: Harcourt.

Soto, G. (2006a). Oranges. In G. Soto, *A fire in my hands* (pp. 9–11). Orlando, FL: Harcourt.

Soto, G. (2006b) *Petty crimes.* Boston: Sandpiper.

Soto, G. (2007). *Mercy on these teenage chimps.* New York: Harcourt.

Soto, G. (2008b). *Facts of life.* New York: Harcourt.

Soto, G. (2009). *Partly cloudy: Poems of love and longing.* Boston: Houghton Mifflin.

Springer, N., (Ed.). (2000). *I believe in water: Twelve brushes with religion.* New York: HarperCollins.

Steinbeck, J. (1938). The chrysanthemums. Retrieved from http://nbu.bg/webs/amb/american/4/steinbeck/chrysanthemums.htm.

Stockton, F. (1882). The lady or the tiger? Retrieved from http://www.eastoftheweb.com/short-stories/UBooks/Ladytige.shtml.

Strahan, J. (Ed.). (2011). *Life on Mars: Tales from the new frontier.* New York: Viking/Penguin.

Summer, J. (Ed.). (2004). *Not the only one: Lesbian and gay fiction for teens.* New York: Alyson Books.

Sweeney, J. (2003). Something old, something new. In D. Gallo (Ed.), *Destination unexpected* (pp. 1–19). Cambridge, MA: Candlewick Press.

Tennyson, A. (1854). The charge of the light brigade. Retrieved from http://poetry.eserver.org/light-brigade.html.

Thayer, E. L. (2000). *Casey at the bat.* (L. Neiman, Illus.). New York: HarperCollins.

Thayer, E. L. (2000). *Casey at the bat: A ballad of the republic sung in the year 1888.* (C. Bing, Illus.). San Francisco, CA: Chronicle Books.

Thayer, E. L. (2003). *Casey at the bat: A ballad of the republic sung in the year 1888* (C. F. Payne, Illus.). New York: Simon & Schuster.

Thayer, E. L. (2006). *Casey at the bat* (J. Morse, Illus.). Tonawanda, NY: Kids Can Press.

Thomas, J. C. (2003). A family illness: A mom–son conversation. In Michael Cart (Ed.), *Necessary noise* (pp. 97–128). New York: HarperCollins.

Vecchione, P. (Ed.). (2004). *Revenge and forgiveness: An anthology of poems.* New York: Holt.

Velde, V. V. (2006). *All Hallows' Eve: 13 stories.* New York: Harcourt Children's Books.

Walsh, M. (Ed.). (2007). *Not like I'm jealous or anything: The jealousy book.* New York: Delacorte.

Weaver, W. (2003). Bad blood. In D. Gallo (Ed.), *Destination unexpected* (pp. 84–104). Cambridge, MA: Candlewick Press.

Williams-Garcia, R. (2004). Mr. Ruben. In M. Singer (Ed.), *Face relations: 11 stories about seeing beyond color* (pp. 174–188). New York: Simon & Schuster Books for Young Readers.

Wittlinger, E. (2003). Tourist trapped. In D. Gallo (Ed.), *Destination unexpected.* Cambridge, MA: Candlewick Press.

Yep, L. (1993). *American dragons: Twenty-five Asian American voices.* New York: Harper Trophy.

Zimmerman, M. (2002). *Metamorphoses: A play.* Chicago, IL: Northwestern University Press.

WEBSITES WITH ANNOTATIONS

American Literature Short Stories • http://americanliterature.com/ss/ssindx.html

Provides full text for 20 classic short stories written specifically for young adults. A different story is highlighted each day.

American Shakespeare Center • www.americanshakespearecenter.com

Offers information about a summer program for young people interested in acting Shakespeare.

Ancient Greek Theatre • http://greektheatre.gr/

Presents Greek playwrights and provides general information for staging ancient theatre in a school environment.

ArtsEdge • http://artsedge.kennedy-center.org/educators.aspx

Provides theatre standards and lessons for educators.

Brigham Young University Theatre Education • http://tedb.byu.edu/standards

Provides theatre lessons based on grade level.

Classic Short Stories • http://classicshorts.com/

This site encourages readers to read short stories. Full story texts available, as well as message boards.

Dramatic Publishing • http://dramaticpublishing.com/

Offers musicals, full-length and one-act plays, and high-quality theatrical books suitable for high-school theatre, children's theatre, professional theatre, and community theatre.

Pegasus Players • www.pegasusplayers.org/cms/?q=node/61

The site of Chicago's young playwrights festival, offering information and resources.

Pioneer Drama Service • www.pioneerdrama.com/Default.asp

Provides extensive list of plays available online. Also offers 10-minute plays for teens.

Playscripts, Inc. • http://playscripts.com/guthrie

Features comprehensive cross-indexed catalog of plays, with most scripts accessible online. Also offers production history and reviews.

Poetry 180 • www.loc.gov/poetry/180/

Project designed to expose young adult readers to one poem on each of the 180 days of the typical school year.

Poet's House • www.poetshouse.org/programs-and-events/poetry-in-the-world

Site for a national poetry library and literary center founded by former poet laureate Stanley Kuntz; provides information about their programs such as Poetry at Large events and Poem in Your Pocket Day.

Kabuki for Everyone • http://park.org/Japan/Kabuki/Kabuki.html

Includes an online theatre as well as information on kabuki sounds and make-up.

ReadWriteThink • **www.ReadWriteThink.org**
Sponsored by the NCTE and the IRA; provides a detailed plan for involving high school students in process drama and a variety of other lesson plans for drama in the classroom.

Soto, Gary • **www.garysoto.com/**
The author's official website, including summaries of works, biographical information, and information on classroom visits.

REFERENCES

Abriza, C. (n.d.). Imagery. Retrieved from http://litera1 no.4tripod.com/imagery_frame.html.

Amen, J. (2002, June/August). Gary Soto featured writer: Interview with Gary Soto. *Pedestal*, 10. Retrieved from www.thepedestalmagazine.com/gallery.php/item=507.

Angus, D. (Ed.). (1962). *The best short stories of the modern age*. Greenwich, CT: Fawcett Publications.

Boyd, W. (2006, Summer). A short history of the short story. *The Quarter*, 5–9.

Brockett, O. G., & Ball, R. J. (2007). *The essential theatre* (9th ed.). Stamford, CT: Wadsworth.

Coughlan, M. (2007). *Interview with Gary Soto*. Retrieved from www.papertigers.org/interviews/archived_interviews/gsoto.html.

Crowe, C. (1997). Don Gallo: The godfather of YA short stories. *English Journal*, 86(3), 73–77.

Dobie, A. B. (2012). *Theory into practice: An introduction to literary criticism* (3rd ed.). Stamford, CT: Wadsworth Cengage Learning.

Dressman, M. (2010). *Let's poem: The essential guide to teaching poetry in a high-stakes, multimodal world (middle through high school)*. New York: Teachers College Press.

Feddersen, R. C. (2001). Introduction: A glance at the history of the short story in English. In E. Fallon, R. C. Feddersen, J. Kurtzleben, M. A. Lee, & S. Rochette-Crawley (Eds.), *A reader's companion to the short story in English* (pp. xv–xxiv). Westport, CT: Greenwood Press.

Flanagan, M. (n.d.). *What is poetry? Grasping at the indefinable*. Retrieved from http://contemporarylit.about.com/od/poetry/a/poetry.htmhttp://contemporarylit.about.com/od/poetry/a/poetry.htm.

Hatlen, T. W. (1987). *Orientation to the theater* (4th ed.). Englewood Cliffs, NJ: Prentice Hall.

Heard, G. (2009). Celestino: A tribute to the healing power of poetry. *Voices in the Middle*, 16(3), 9–14.

Hirsch, E. (1999). *How to read a poem and fall in love with poetry*. San Diego, CA: Harvest Books/Harcourt.

Kutz, E., & Roskelly, E. (1991). *An unquiet pedagogy: Transforming practice in the English classroom*. Portsmouth, NH: Boynton/Cook.

Lee, D. (2010). About Gary Soto: A profile. *Ploughshares*. Retrieved from www.pshares.org/read/article-detail.cfm?intArticleID=3863.

Lesesne, T. (2002). The long and the short of it: An interview with Don Gallo. *Teacher Librarian*, 30(2), 48–52.

Lown, F., & Steinbergh, J. W. (1996). *Reading and writing poetry with teenagers*. Portland, OR: Walch Education.

Lukens, R. J., & Cline, R. K. J. (1995). *A critical handbook of literature for young adults*. New York: HarperCollins.

National Council of Teachers of English. (1982). *Guideline on informal classroom drama*. Retrieved from http://www.ncte.org/positions/statements/informalclassdrama.

Noonan, P. (1986). President Ronald Reagan's speech on the *Challenger* disaster. Retrieved from http://www.historyplace.com/speeches/reagan-challenger.htm.

Oxford Encyclopedia of American Literature. (2005). The short story in America. Retrieved from http://ebooks.ohiolink.edu/xtf-ebc/view?docId=tei/drs/t197/t97.xml&doc.view=content&.

Poe, E. A. (1842, May). Review of Hawthorne, *Twice-told tales*, *Graham's Magazine*, pp. 298–300.

Poets.org. (n.d.). Gary Soto. Retrieved from www.poets.org/poet.php/prmPID/230.

Rutsky, J. (2001). *Beyond the bard: Fifty plays for use in the English classroom*. Boston: Allyn & Bacon.

Soto, G. (2008a). Gary Soto. www.garysoto.com/bio.html.

Swados, E. (2006). *At play: Teaching teenagers theater*. New York: Faber & Faber.

Teaching Books.net (2007). Gary Soto: Original in-depth author interview. Retrieved from http://www.teachingbooks.net/content/interviews/Soto_qu.pdf.

Wordsworth, W. (1798). Lyric poems. In R. J. Lukens & R. K. J. Cline, (1995), *A critical handbook of literature for young adults*. New York: HarperCollins.

CHAPTER TEN

The Art of Literature

COVER ART, PICTURE BOOKS, ILLUSTRATED LITERATURE, AND GRAPHIC NOVELS

chapter overview

We begin this chapter by describing how cover art has evolved to reflect a changing marketplace and how young adults can use that art as a tool for selecting and interpreting books. Next, we explore works that use illustrations to integrate visual design with storytelling. We examine the characteristics of graphic novels and evaluate their role in the literature classroom. The chapter concludes with a discussion of the newest form of visually oriented texts, interactive ebooks. Throughout the chapter we offer instructional strategies.

FOCUS QUESTIONS

1. How do book covers influence a reader's selection and how can they add to the reader's interpretation?

2. How do art and text work together in picture books and illustrated literature?

3. What are the elements that are important for interpreting and appreciating graphic novels?

4. How can graphic novels and other illustrated texts be incorporated into the curriculum?

introduction

Marjane Satrapi, author and illustrator of *Persepolis: the Story of a Childhood* (2003), a graphic novel about growing up in an increasingly conservative Iran, says that "images are a way of writing. When you have the talent to be able to write and to draw it seems a shame to choose one. I think it's better to do both" (Satrapi, n.d.). The combination of words and pictures can create a literary experience that is richer, denser, or more readily understood than what is provided by text alone. We owe the image of Sherlock Holmes wearing a deerstalker cap, for instance, to the artist Sidney Paget, who illustrated many of the original stories in *Strand* magazine. The deerstalker cap is barely mentioned in the text of the stories, but Paget seized on every opportunity to depict Holmes wearing it (Klinefelter, 1975). That iconic image endures because it artfully represents both Holmes's eccentricity and his bloodhound instincts for hunting down criminals.

Although illustrations are less common now than they were in the heyday of Sir Arthur Conan Doyle, images and visual design continue to enrich literature. This chapter helps teachers take full advantage of the power of visuals. By understanding the elements of art and design, teachers can help their students appreciate visuals as an art form and as an aid to interpreting and engaging with narratives. Although most people associate pictures with books for beginning readers, visual artistry continues to have an impact on young adult readers. Illustrations and graphic design influence how those readers choose, interpret, and appreciate literature. Moreover, young adult readers are increasingly embracing literary forms that combine images and text, especially graphic novels. Anecdotal evidence, research, and expert opinion all indicate that graphic novels have the potential to enhance motivation and learning in powerful ways (Downey, 2009), so we will explore their potential for engaging reluctant readers and for examining social and cultural themes.

JUDGING A BOOK BY ITS COVER: COVER ART

Understanding and interpreting the visual elements of book covers may assist young adults in selecting literature that will resonate with them. The look of a book does matter to the young adult reader. Seventy-six percent of middle school students responding to an online survey indicated that covers usually influence their selection of fiction (Jones, 2007). Research by *Publisher's Weekly* (Fitzgerald, 2009) revealed similar results. Seventy-nine percent of teens in that study indicated they chose a book by its cover. Covers and dust jackets are designed to draw a reader's attention to the book, and good marketing is based on this "grabability" factor (Yampbell, 2005).

Andrew Palmer (2008) suggests that the overall design of a book cover can be judged using the criteria established by the Washington Book Publishers for their Book Design and Effectiveness Award:

1. An effective book cover appeals to the book's intended audience, while allowing for potential expansion of that audience.
2. It should represent the book's contents, including the subject matter, as well as its tone.
3. The cover should draw readers in through its aesthetic appeal.

Book design has become especially important because many books are now first encountered on the Internet, where the image is smaller than actual size. The title, subtitle, and author of the book need to be discernible at a glance, and the image should not detract from those textual components of the cover. In a library or bookstore the spine of the book is often seen first, so that element should be integrated into the overall design of the front and back covers (Palmer, 2008).

Changing Styles, Changing Covers

Styles of book art change just as fashion and hairstyles change. In the 1970s and 1980s, covers of books for young adults were primarily watercolors of teenagers in a scene from the book. In the late 1980s and early 1990s, photography became the most popular medium, although contemplative teenagers remained the focus. The trend in the 2000s was away from realistic covers and toward more abstract images. Innovative computer graphics and printing improvements allowed for the use of holograms, foil, and matte lamination. Colors mirrored those in trendy clothing (Yampbell, 2005). Today's young adults prefer simpler covers, and photography is again more popular than illustrations. Black with bold colors and a central image are effective, but overly cute covers do not sell (Jones, 2009).

Some book covers have remained popular for many years. Gary Paulsen's *Hatchet* (1987) has featured the original Bradbury Press cover for nearly twenty years (Lohmiller, 2008). That image depicts a two-toned sketch of a young adult male with a muted forest as the background, with images of an airplane, a wolf, and a hatchet superimposed on the boy's profile. The hatchet remained the focus of the cover for the 2006 Aladdin edition and the 2007 anniversary edition by Simon & Schuster. The cover for Harry Mazer's *The Last Mission* (1981) shows a fighter jet on fire. It has not changed since its initial publication (Lohmiller, 2008).

Repackaging and Redesigning Book Covers

It is not unusual for publishers to redesign or repackage books. In fact, about 75 percent of books published by Viking get redesigned at some point. These makeovers, or "botox for books" (Jones, 2009), can be used to reintroduce a book to the young adult market. Covers may be redesigned if the original seems dated or has not drawn new readers. Covers based on a film adaptation of a book, for example, quickly become dated. When books are added to a series, the entire series may be redesigned with similar covers.

Sometimes, multiple versions of a book are available simultaneously. The 1975 Bradbury hardcover and paperback editions of Judy Blume's *Forever* featured a locket and key against a pink background. The same year, Pocket Books featured a cover with a face in a locket. A 2007 cover by Simon Pulse depicts two people laying side by side on a bed, only their legs visible. The girl is wearing shorts, the boy is wearing jeans. In contrast, the Pocket's 2007 edition was less explicit, showing only a picture of an envelope emblazoned with a lipstick kiss.

Problems develop when a book's cover does not accurately reflect what is inside. For example, a misleading cover may have contributed to *The Leaving and Other Stories* (Wilson, 1992) quickly going out of print. The cover of this collection of realistic coming-of-age stories showed a terrified teenage girl looking back toward a forest, where she sees a figure carrying a suitcase. The intended audience of realistic fiction readers may have avoided the book because the cover suggested terror and mystery, and mystery lovers might have been disappointed when they realized the stories were neither terrifying nor mysterious (Yampbell, 2005).

As another example, the initial American cover for *Liar* (Larbalestier, 2009a), showed a picture of a long-haired girl who appears to be white, although the author describes Micah, the protagonist, as having nappy hair, worn short and natural. Larbalestier (2009b) was concerned that if the cover misled readers, they might then question everything about the character. After the motives for the cover were explored (Springen, 2009), it was eventually changed.

Book covers create expectations that may influence whether readers will choose a particular book and, to some extent, whether they will be satisfied with it. Publishers and book designers strive to create covers that combine elements to create positive expectations; they may, perhaps, even deliberately misrepresent the content of the book. Literature teachers should remember that the cover sells one book over another only when the reader is not look-ing for a specific title, author, or genre (Yampbell, 2005). Nevertheless, teachers can increase the probability of their students choosing books they will enjoy by making them more aware of the information provided by both the text and graphic elements of book covers.

Choosing Books by Their Covers

Although young adults may be already inclined to choose books on the basis of their covers, you as a teacher can develop their ability to do so effectively. For instance, use book talks to draw students' attention to visuals and model how to make use of both text and visuals to make a choice. Ask students to make predictions on the content of a book solely on the basis of the cover design. Guide students to reflect on which elements in a book cover have influenced their previous book choices. Finally, explore with students how cover art can help them determine whether they will identify with the book's characters, enjoy its content, tone, and genre, and be able to connect it to other texts they have read.

Inviting a connection with the characters

The images, colors, and design of a book cover can all signal potential read-ers whether or not they are the book's intended audience. A cover can create an instant identification between a reader and a book, particularly when it depicts the main characters. With one glance at either the front dust jacket or the spine of *Wild Roses* by Deb Caletti (2005), for instance, a reader knows the age, gender, and ethnicity of the protagonist. The cover photograph by Soren Hold shows a white high school girl dressed in a winter coat, red scarf, and knit hat. Her enigmatic expression indicates that she has something on her mind. The cover suggests that high school girls are the expected audience, especially girls who enjoy realistic stories that are more focused on character than action.

The jacket illustration by Leo Espinosa, designed by Elizabeth B. Parisi, for Walter Dean Myers' *The Cruisers* (2010) shows four adolescents in different colored silhouettes. Their clothing and hair give the impression that the kids are from an urban setting. The cover may entice African American readers, espe-cially if they recognize the author's name, but it might also attract readers from other ethnic backgrounds if they relate to the realities of life in a contempo-rary city. The cover of *Crunch* (2010) by Leslie Connor suggests a very different intended audience. Illustrator Greg Swearingen used a retro, whimsical illustra-tion that shows a young boy with a backpack full of tools peddling hard on a red bike while being chased by a friendly dog. The illustration conveys the book's humorous tone as well as its younger intended audience.

Ethnicity and gender are characteristics that can create identification with a book. The photograph on the cover and spine of *Joseph* by Shelia P. Moses (2008) shows an African American teenage boy clad in an orange short-sleeved shirt. He appears sad, or perhaps disappointed, as he glances to the side. The title looks like the signature a young person might use to sign a letter or a school paper. The cover art suggests that the intended reader for the book is male and/or African American rather than white and/or female. Although showing gender and ethnicity as on the cover of *Joseph* may create identification with a book, it may also unintentionally exclude other potential readers. In some cases, in fact, publishers may choose not to include people on book covers to ensure appeal to readers of both genders and many cultures (Yampbell, 2005).

Providing a preview of content, tone, and genre

Besides inviting the reader to connect with the main character, a book cover can also provide potential readers with a "sneak peak" that suggests a book's content, genre, or tone without giving away too much. For instance, a removable yellow strip of paper with large black print "POLICE LINE DO NOT CROSS" surrounds the cover designed by Robert Hult for Walter Dean Myers' *Shooter* (2004). The only image (by artist Robert Beck) seen under the yellow strip is that of a bullet hole. On both the cover and the spine, the red title is covered in scratches. A reader immediately knows the book is serious in tone; someone has been shot. The right reader will wonder who it is.

The dust jacket for Sarah Aronson's *Head Case* (2007) is another example of a cover that provides visual clues about the content. Laurent Lynn's design features a photographic close-up of a horribly smashed car. Tire tracks begin on the spine and continue across the silver-colored back. The red, silver, and black color scheme, the tire tracks, and the stark image of a smashed car are eye-catching, but a careful reader will also notice the line drawing of a wheelchair behind the "h" in the title. Even before reading a single word, the reader knows the plot involves a terrible accident.

The dust jacket design for *I Am Number Four* (Lore, 2010) effectively combines text and visual elements to signal the book's genre but only hints at the essence of its plot. The jacket design by Ray Shappell and art by Scott Meadows catch the reader's attention with bright red-orange letters printed over raised concentric circles of yellow on a white background that appear to form some type of emblem or symbol. The reader has an immediate clue about the dilemma faced by the title character, because the title, *I Am Number Four*, appears directly under the words "Three Are Dead."

The back cover jacket of *I Am Number Four* creates a further mystery. The photograph of the author, taken by Howard Huang, is a black, rippling reflection in water; the face unidentifiable. The brief author biography states that the author is Lorien's ruling Elder, who is awaiting the battle that will determine the fate of Earth. The title and emblem design, together with the pen name, picture, and biography of the fictitious author all signal to the potential reader that the novel is science fiction, but their full meaning can only be understood by reading the book.

Genre is also clearly signaled in the art by Oliver Burston and graphic design by Phil Falco for the cover of Rebecca Promitzer's *The Pickle King* (2010). It features a full cover illustration of a pickle jar against a glowing chartreuse background. Inside the jar, in addition to pickles, is an eyeball. Crawling on the outside of the jar is a large bug. The pickle jar is expected, given the title, but the eyeball pulls the reader into the story by suggesting a murder mystery.

Occasionally, cover artists embed images within a book's typography to offer a hint about the story. The "i" in the word "king" in *The Pickle King* is dotted with a crown. A lizard-like red eye ominously peers out from the center of the first "O" in *Eon, Dragoneye Reborn* (Goodman, 2008), accentuating the frightening nature of the fantastical beast, whose sharp talons are wrapped around an amulet. On *Thirteen Reasons Why* (2007) by Jay Asher, the jacket design by Christian Funfhaussen displays the title in white letters, except the "i" is replaced by a red numeral 1 and the "e" is a red "3." The number 13, a symbol of misfortune, cues readers to the misfortune of the plot.

Making intertextual connections

Book covers make intertextual connections to other works, just as their text does. The most obvious example is how books in a series have similar designs, such as the mockingjay symbol that appears in slightly different form on all three volumes in the *Hunger Games* trilogy (Collins 2008, 2009, 2010). *Fairest of All: A Tale of the Wicked Queen* (2009), by Serena Valentino, makes an intertextual connection to the Walt Disney animated movie *Snow White and The Seven Dwarfs*. The book jacket by Adrienne Brown and Caroline Egan shows the familiar Disney image of the wickedly beautiful queen. The illustration on the hardcover book shows the evil queen transformed into the ugly witch. For any reader familiar with the movie, the covers indicate the novel is a retelling of the Snow White story.

Cover Art as an Aid to Interpreting Literature

Usually, "reading" the cover art on some books is similar to reading text at a literal level. The picture explicitly depicts what the book is about. Some book covers, however, are more subtle or enigmatic. The artist's interpretation may not be fully understood or appreciated until after one reads part or all of the book. Sometimes, a cover may be purposefully confusing. The cover photograph (credited to Peist/zefa/Corbis) of *Shark Girl* by Kelly Bingham (2007) shows the left side of a bikini-clad girl, standing thigh deep in water, her back to the camera. A set of smaller photographs (by Rommil Santiago) is inset along the left side of the cover, like frames of a film, showing a turbulent ocean moving from the surface to darker depths. Together, the photographs signal that this novel is about more than a pretty girl romping in the ocean, but the true meaning of the cover is not immediately clear. The "ah ha" moment comes when the reader discovers that only the left side of the girl is visible on the cover because her right arm has been amputated after it was nearly ripped off by a shark.

The dramatic lack of color in the jacket illustration by Ellice M. Lee for Julius Lester's *Day of Tears* (2005) contributes to the theme of slavery. A boy's head and cupped hands are shown in close-up profile in a black silhouette against a white background. His hands catch a falling tear. No facial features are discernible. A white tear and the author's name printed in white are positioned where his eye would be. The black silhouette continues across the spine, and the back cover

is completely black. Engaging students in a discussion about how these visual elements represent the content of the book should help students to think more deeply about both the author's slavery theme and about artistic expression and interpretation.

Linda McCarthy's jacket design for John Green's *Looking for Alaska* (2005) incorporates a photograph of smoke rising from a recently extinguished candle. The image evokes thoughts of "out, out brief candle" from *Macbeth*. For the young adult who does not make the connection between the image of a snuffed flame and death, the flameless candle and spreading smoke against a black background still elicit a sense of foreboding. The significance of the image emerges early in the novel when Alaska, an exciting and vibrant teenager, is killed in an automobile crash that may or may not have been accidental.

Although not evident at a glance, the cover art and design of Amy Achaibou's dust jacket for *Blue Plate Special* (Kwasney, 2009) does not match the image on the hardcover. The hardcover of the book shows an image of a white plate that wraps around to the back cover. The dust jacket also shows a white plate, but this one is broken. Three pieces are visible on the front, two more on the back. Most young adults will be unfamiliar with the term *blue plate special*, a daily special at a casual restaurant, usually consisting of a meat and vegetables. The significance of the title and the accompanying image becomes apparent only after reading the novel, and teachers can engage their students in a spirited discussion about the reasons for the artist's different renderings on the jacket and hardcover. Students who have read this particular book can discuss the cover with others who have not. This helps students understand the dual purposes of a cover as an attention getter and as an artist's interpretation of the book's content and theme.

Teaching Ideas ▪ "COVERING" COVER ART

Teachers can use the visual elements of book covers for guiding book selection, for raising questions before reading, and for encouraging appreciation of both the author's theme and the designer's artistic interpretation. We have incorporated advice by librarian Leigh Ann Jones (2007, 2009) into the following suggestions.

Use book awards for guidance. "Quick Picks for Reluctant Young Adult Readers" is the only national list of books that considers the entire book, beginning with the cover. Young adults influence the nominations, and the chosen books have been "field tested" by young adults (Watson et al., 2006).

Set up book displays. Arrange books to resemble a bookstore display. Place eye-catching, colorful books with covers facing out so students can see them and pick them up. Change the displays often.

Survey your students. Gather information about students' opinions about what they are reading or would like to read. Use an online survey such as Survey

Monkey (www.surveymonkey.com), a free online survey program, your classroom blog, or a comment box by the book display.

Have students create their own covers. The ReadWriteThink site (www.readwritethink.org/files/resources/interactives/bookcover) provides a template for creating colorful book covers. Also, several YouTube videos describe how to make a book cover (with varying levels of complexity); these include the following:

- How to make a brown paper book cover (simple), www.youtube.com/watch?v=IevGAai8CrE.
- How to make a book cover in Microsoft Word (requires basic computer skills), www.youtube.com/watch?v=5r6VhQZ4ARY.
- How to make a book cover in Photoshop (requires specific software and skills), www.youtube.com/watch?v=dYqgZmwYpRc.

Have students visit the websites and blogs of cover artists and designers. Students interested in art may enjoy learning more about the art and artist. For example, David Small, the illustrator of both the cover and the illustrations for Kathi Appelt's *The Underneath* (2008) and the graphic memoir *Stiches*, discussed in Chapter 8, has a website at http://davidsmallbooks.com/.

In the next section of this chapter, we consider the elements of art and design that can influence readers' interpretation and appreciation of picture books and illustrated books. We also expand on the discussion we began in Chapter 1 about the place of those works in literature classes for young adult readers, particularly the role they can play in extending students' understanding of the aesthetic connection between literary and visual art.

PICTURE BOOKS AND ILLUSTRATED NOVELS: ART AND TEXT WORKING TOGETHER

The elements of art are line, shape and form, space, color, and texture (Education at the Getty, n.d.). Shelley Esaak (n.d.) compares these elements to atoms. Without atoms, there are no molecules, and a molecule is what makes something what it is. Similarly, in every work of art an artist has combined at least two of the basic elements to create a composition that directs a viewer's attention and brings out specific impressions and feelings. Teachers can foster students' understanding and appreciation of illustrated texts by making them more aware of the choices that artists make when creating illustrations. One way to do so is to use and explain the basic terminology found on the following page.

Outside of the classroom, multimodal texts that combine print with strong graphics, illustrations, and visual design are proliferating. Comics, websites, print ads, and television commercials may have very different purposes, but they all use the same visual vocabulary. Bringing illustrated literature such as picture books, illustrated novels, and graphic novels into the classroom allows teachers to build students' ability to understand and produce visual language at the same time they are gaining experience with all the other aspects of literature.

Basic Elements of Art

Medium is the material used to create art, such as watercolor, acrylics, pencil, or print. The choice of medium impacts on the mood of the story and the overall feeling that is conveyed by the illustrations. Commonly used media for illustrated books include pen and ink, watercolors, computer-generated images, and collages.

Line is an identifiable path of a point moving in space that can vary in width, direction, and length. Line has great expressive potential and is one of the most important elements in picture books. Lines can be straight or curved, thick or thin, and horizontal, vertical, or diagonal. Each choice an artist makes regarding line conveys something different. For example, thin lines might suggest fragility, thicker lines strength or weight (Kiefer, 1995, p. 121).

Shape and **form** define objects in space. Shapes are two-dimensional, having height and width, and forms are three-dimensional because they also have depth. **Space** is an element of art that refers to the areas around, between, or within the different elements in a work, serving to create illusion of depth or of being three-dimensional.

Texture is the surface quality of an object that a viewer senses through touch. Artists try to portray how something would feel in real life. An illustrator might choose a medium such as collage or create a hatch work of lines to give the illusion of texture.

Color can be described in terms of **value**—how light or dark it is—and its **intensity**—how bright or dull it is. A particular **hue**, or gradations of color, often suggests a symbolic interpretation. Pink may symbolize love and romance while red may symbolize passion and white purity or innocence. Yellow may suggest happiness and hope or, conversely, cowardice and jealously (Incredible Art Department, n.d.).

Style refers to the artist's manner of expression (Kiefer, 1995, pp. 118–123). Put simply, style can be thought of along a continuum. At one end is realistic art in which the picture faithfully presents the world as seen by the naked eye; at the other end is abstract art, in which the picture is intentionally nonrepresentational and does not attempt to be true to life (Boddy-Evans, n.d.). Impressionist and expressionist styles lie somewhere in between. They depict identifiable people or objects, but the artist adds personal perceptions or feelings using various artistic techniques that go beyond photographic accuracy.

The Art of Picture Books

At a basic level, a **picture book** is a profusely illustrated book that communicates through both written and visual elements. Picture books are distinguished from illustrated novels in that the illustrations are intertwined with the text, rather than simply supplementing the written text. Moreover, the pictures in picture books are so pervasively intertwined with the text that the story cannot be understood without them. In the previous chapter, we described how picture books could help middle and high school readers understand the use of imagery in poetry, and in earlier chapters, we examined their use for a variety of other purposes including:

1. Providing scaffolds for learning the terminology of traditional literary analysis (Whitehurst & Snyder, 2000) or for understanding metafictive characteristics.

2. Retelling traditional stories, or reinventing them to question societal norms with a safe and familiar form (O'Neil, 2010).

3. Vividly depicting social issues, as author Eve Bunting does with homelessness in *Fly Away Home* (1991) and for race relations in *Smoky Nights* (1994).

classroom scenario

Pictures and Stories

This Classroom Scenario explores how to use picture books to teach characterization. AS YOU READ, consider the effect of the specific artistic elements and techniques used by the artist. Also think about how the illustrations impact the story; in particular, how they show character development.

Ms. Stanich wants to reinforce her sixth graders' understanding of the elements of fiction, especially characterization, and she picks an illustrated text that fits the bill perfectly, Joan Blos' *Old Henry* (1987), illustrated by Caldecott-winning artist Stephen Gammell. The book tells a simple story of a nonconforming man who upsets his neighbors because he does not keep up his house or yard. She is pleased that her students will also be able to apply some basic concepts they have learned in art class. She begins the unit by modeling the process of connecting the visual elements of a picture book and the literary content of the story.

Ms. Stanich reads the story aloud using a document projector to present the text and illustrations together. She begins by drawing the class's attention to the cover, which shows Henry wearing a red flower print shirt and a blue cap. He leans on a dilapidated fence, smiling and gazing at a brightly colored bird. A large shopping bag full of miscellaneous objects sits on the ground next to him. Ms. Stanich opens the book and draws the students' attention to the end papers, front and back, which are turquoise. She displays the title page, which shows Henry wearing the same blue cap and surrounded by household objects on the ground, including two bird cages. He carries a stuffed dog under his arm, and a pale green balloon on a string floats above him.

The dedication, a simple "For Margery and Ray," is written on a splash of rainbow colors in the left top corner of the first page. The page also includes a single rhyming sentence: "The story begins when a stranger appears and moves into a house that was vacant for years." Ms. Stanich invites the students to make predictions about Henry's character traits based on the illustrations and what it might be like to live next door to him. She also asks them whether they expect the tone of the story to be humorous or serious based on style and colors of the artwork.

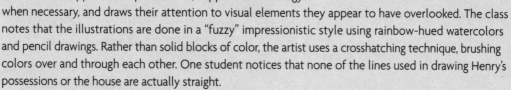

Ms. Stanich encourages students to refer to specific visual elements to support their predictions, supplies terminology when necessary, and draws their attention to visual elements they appear to have overlooked. The class notes that the illustrations are done in a "fuzzy" impressionistic style using rainbow-hued watercolors and pencil drawings. Rather than solid blocks of color, the artist uses a crosshatching technique, brushing colors over and through each other. One student notices that none of the lines used in drawing Henry's possessions or the house are actually straight.

The students generally agree that the multicolored drawings suggest that the story will not be too serious, and they conclude that Henry is probably eccentric but harmless. They predict that Henry will "pile lots of junk into the house," and that he and the house seem to match because they both seem to be "kind of run-down" and untidy. They are split on the question of whether they would want Henry as a neighbor. Some are concerned about whether he is strange, "like a cat lady" or a hoarder. Others conclude from his smile, the balloon, and the birdcages that he would be fun to be around.

As the story goes on, some pages contain no words and some pages have no images. Ms. Stanich points out how illustrations provide information about Henry that is not contained in the text. He has

(continued)

unkempt hair, wears mismatched socks, and most often wears his blue cap, even when standing on his porch in his underwear or sitting on his bed in his pajamas. He keeps to himself and the company of his birds. He paints pictures and he enjoys reading; piles of books turn up in almost every picture.

When winter arrives, the colors in the illustrations shift from pastel greens to darker blues and the conflict in the story emerges. The neighbors nag Henry about repairing and cleaning up his property. They become increasingly annoyed, and Henry eventually tires of their disapproval and moves away. His neighbors miss him greatly, and he them. The last page of text contains the image of lined paper, on which Henry writes a letter, asking the Mayor what the conditions might be for him to return. The final illustration repeats the rainbow colors of the early pages and shows Henry sitting next to a pile of his belongings, apparently waiting patiently for the reply.

Ms. Stanich leads a discussion about how many of the students' predictions were confirmed and how the illustrations matched or added to the text, which is written in rhyming couplets. She draws their attention to a small illustration in the center of the back cover. It shows a window with one cracked pane, but still awash with color. The class decides that the window symbolizes that Henry may be a little bit "broken," but he can still fit in.

The students in Ms. Stanich's class can see that Henry's personality and the unencumbered way he lives his life are developed through every image and word from cover to cover. They go on to select another fiction picture book to analyze in a similar way. Although the books are easy to read, they find that a simple story told in relatively few words can acquire a depth of meaning with the right type of illustrations.

4. Providing a rich context for exploring historical events, as Tsuchiya does for World War II in *Faithful Elephants: A True Story of Animals, People and War* (1988) and Maruki does in *Hiroshima No Pika* (1980), which shows the aftermath of the atomic bombings of Japan.

In all these examples, adolescents are guided to use picture books primarily to explore or analyze content, the information and perspective presented. In this chapter, we suggest that picture books are a useful vehicle for exploring the conventions of telling stories with visuals. Perry Nodelman, a noted expert on picture books, suggests that "children who come to understand their [picture books] conventions and structures can enjoy them with great vitality and conscious appreciation, discovering how pictures and texts work together," (as cited in Lukens, 2003, p. 41).

Illustrated Novels

The term **illustrated books** is most often used when the narrative is composed predominately of text and the illustrations take on a supportive or subordinated role (Nikolajeva & Scott, 2000). Illustrated books are not a new type of literature. Illuminated religious texts written by hand more than a thousand years ago intertwined illustration and text in a way that encouraged more contemplative reading (Howard, 2010). The work of 19th century novelists such as Charles Dickens often appeared originally in serial form in illustrated magazines, and the eventual book versions were sold as illustrated volumes.

Perhaps because of the expense involved, illustrations, other than cover photos, have largely disappeared from the paperbacks marketed to adults, but illustrations survive in books for children and young adults. *The Tale of Despereaux* by Kate DiCamillo (2003), for instance, is a throwback to the stories of previous centuries not only in its use of such conventions as directly addressing the "dear reader," but also in its illustrations, which are in a style that seems to come from a bygone era. The opening of each "book" in this Newbery winner has a border that resembles the illuminated pages of religious texts of the Middle Ages. Some pages have incorporated borders with ornate details that tell a story about the text. The paper ends are ragged, as they would be in an era before paper cutters. The artwork in the original edition is softly applied and printed in values of gray, which emphasize the light/dark metaphor central to this story of a mouse, a princess, a servant girl, and a rat. Candlewick Press has, however, reissued the novel (2008) with color illustrations.

In *Winter Town*, author and illustrator Stephen Emond (2011) uses realistic black and white illustrations to tell the story of Evan and Lucy. Childhood friends, they now see each other only at winter break when Lucy visits her divorced dad. Lucy has changed; she is moody and sarcastic. Her appearance has changed as well. She wears only black, her hair is chopped and dyed black, and she has many piercings. Evan would like to pursue his art work, but instead he dutifully prepares for the Ivy League college his parents expect him to attend. Chapters begin with a double-page spread of black and white illustrations. Some illustrations are close-ups of the characters and reveal their attitudes and feelings. Others show items such as a teddy bear and a graduation cap that are significant to them. Many depict settings such as the mall shopping scene shown in Figure 10.1. Also interspersed throughout the novel is a fantasy comic strip created by Evan.

Author and illustrator Grace Lin suggests that illustrations in novels "give a glimpse of visualization into the world you are reading, but not so much that you aren't left with anything to imagine" (Baker, 2009). Many illustrated books can be understood without the illustrations, but then the story loses its richness and the reader's interpretation is less layered. The box on page 310 shows some additional examples of books for young adults that are enriched by their illustrations.

An illustration from *Winter Town*: Shopping at the mall.

Lips Touch: Three Times by Laini Taylor

In some books, illustrations and words weave together to create a literary experience with unusual depth and feeling. Laini Taylor's *Lips Touch: Three Times* (2009) is such a book. This National Book Award for Young People's Literature finalist contains three short stories set in different times and places, each connected by the theme of a fateful first kiss. For each story, Jim Di Bartolo, Taylor's husband, created a series of illustrations that form wordless prequels, stories that are separate from, yet connected to, each novella. A reader can predict the meaning of these images and then adjust that interpretation only after reading the story. Each story begins on the right side of the opened book. On the left, a single illustration stands alone to move the reader into the time and place of that story. Also, a single illustration containing a bird is placed at the end of each story, which provides both continuity and symbolic closure.

Color in the illustrations is used sparingly yet effectively. Red, the color of passion, predominates throughout. Red fruit, red lips, red blood, red hair, and hell itself, are shown in varying degrees of intensity. Ice blue is another significant color. It is the color of the eyes of those who are not human. The cream colored paper is the color that distinguishes human skin from the demons and shape shifters. The lush and lurid pen and ink drawings are outlined in frames of red and black, suggesting a purposeful containment of the exotic, sensual, and frightening images. Each chapter number is written in bold uppercase red letters, as is the first letter of the initial word. That letter is printed over a swirling design that is also found on the end papers and the back of the dust jacket.

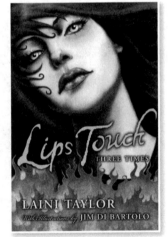

The wordless backstory that introduces the first of the book's three stories, "Goblin Fruit," depicts two girls from a time gone by who encounter a parade of goblins. The hideous creatures carry bowls of red fruit as they march through the forest. One of the girls runs away; the other remains. She becomes sickly and gaunt, apparently tainted by the fruit. The girl who escaped—presumably the sick girl's sister—eventually returns, knife in hand, to confront the goblins. The final two-page spread of illustrations consists of four panels. The first three depict the sister running through the woods and arriving home exhausted. In the last panel, the ill girl sits up in bed, reaching toward her sister's outstretched hand.

A turn of a page reveals an illustration showing a framed picture of the bedridden girl. On the opposite page, the story title "Goblin Fruit" appears in red, above a brief introduction that establishes how the story's main character, Kizzy, yearns for romance and fervently wishes to be as pretty as other girls. However, such girls attract goblins. Her strange and backward family believes in demons and ghosts, and her grandmother reveals that she (the grandmother) was the courageous sister in the prequel story. Kizzy's grandmother warns her about eating fruit out of season. Kizzy meets a new student, a handsome and compelling boy.

She recalls her grandmother's warnings about the goblins and that a local girl has recently died from anorexia, but she cannot seem to resist this boy. After a restless night, Kizzy awakes to see swan feathers sifting down into her room. The knife that was buried with her grandmother lies on the pillow. She ignores these omens and meets the boy for a picnic.

The boy offers her a peach; she refuses it so he eats it instead. Then she finds the urge to kiss him irresistible. The final words say, "It was Kizzy's first kiss and maybe it was her last, and it was delicious." The illustration following the story explains Kizzy's fate. She lies with her head at the bottom of the picture, her red lips visible. Her hands folded in repose around a knife and her chest covered by swan feathers, Kizzy lies in a coffin.

The second story, "Spicy Little Curses Such as These," is set in India around World War I. The backstory revealed through the illustrations is that of a young man and woman in love. He dies. She travels to hell, lantern in hand, and encounters a red flaming demon. She receives a small vial, contents unknown. She is pictured in hell, still young and beautiful, with a baby in her arms. The last panels show her middle-aged and then very old. Both panels show her with a baby in her arms and several children following behind her.

The illustration opposite the title page of this story depicts a teapot, two cups, and the vial with flames in the background. The first page mentions a curse and a kiss and states that the story begins in hell. Estella is taking tea with Vasudev, a demon. For 40 years she has been bargaining with Vasudev for the souls of children. Estella gathers the souls of evil men and women and offers them in exchange for the lives of the children. Vasudev changes his tactics and presents Estella with a very different bargain. He will allow Estella to save the lives of 22 children killed in an earthquake if she will deliver a curse at the christening of the baby daughter of a local politician.

If the child ever speaks, everyone around her will die. When the child, Anamique, is grown she falls in love with a handsome suitor, James. He knows of the curse, so when he asks her to marry him, he kisses her fast and hard in an attempt to prevent her from answering. But it does not stop her. She opens her mouth, and "her voice at last burst from its cage." The curse is fulfilled, and everyone within hearing distance dies. Anamique searches hell for her beloved. Estella offers herself in exchange for James, but Vasudev demands more. Anamique must take Estella's place as the Ambassador to Hell. She agrees, and there-after her voice, enchanting and hypnotic, is heard only in hell.

Thirteen pages of illustrations establish the context for "Hatchling," the third and longest story. The sequence begins with a dark-haired woman holding a red-haired baby. The child is next seen sitting among flowers and butterflies, and then locked in a cage suspended from a bridge in an unearthly place. In a two-page illustration, the dark-haired woman is in a sleigh pulled by grotesque animals. A series of three panels shows the red-haired baby, now a teenager, with attendants painting her body in swirls of blue. Then she stands naked before a naked red-haired boy who looks very much like her. The dark-haired woman stands behind her, and a dark-haired man stands behind the boy. Both the adults have piercing blue eyes. The introductory picture for "Hatchling" is a beautiful dark-haired girl with the same blue eyes and with cobwebs attached to her eyelashes.

The story is set in modern times, although this is easy to forget as most of it takes place in a world of immortal demons and shape shifters. One morning, 14-year-old red-haired Esme discovers that one of her eyes has turned blue, and she is having memories of an experience, a kiss, she never had. Her mother, Mab, also red headed, has feared this moment since her daughter's birth. She tells her daughter that they have been found by the Druj, creatures who never grow old but cannot love. The queen, the dark-haired beauty in the illustrations, violently enters young girls' bodies when they are forced to mate with another human. Esme is the result of such a union, and Mab stole her for her own.

Esme is forcibly brought to the land of the Drujs, where souls are shared, taken, and sometimes destroyed, and the price for immortality is the loss of humanity. There, the ritual that created Esme is repeated. After Esme is pregnant, she is rescued by Mihai, a Druj who remembers what it is like to be human, to care, and to have a family. A love story from across centuries ends as the queen, finally willing to trust another, comes to Mihai in the form of an eagle, hoping he will return her to her human form.

Reality and fantasy meld in each of these stories, as do human and demon, good and evil. Through words and illustrations in each novella, the book raises the questions, "What is the price of love?" and "Does love save or destroy souls?" Especially for some teenage girls, these questions will linger long after finishing the book.

GRAPHIC NOVELS

Michele Gorman's definition of a **graphic novel** as "an original book length story, either fiction or nonfiction, published in comic book style, or a collection of stories that have been published as individual comic books" seems inclusive (2003 p. xii). Steven Weiner calls them simply, "book length comics that are meant to be read as one story" (2003, p. x). Shaun Tan, author and illustrator of the wordless *The Arrival* (2006), a heavily symbolic story about the immigrant experience, states that he is not really sure what

Creepers. Joanne Dahme, 2008. Illustrated by Frances Soo Ping Chow. Color is used as a unifying element throughout the novel. Beginning with the cover, green is used in chapter titles and for the tint of the pages. Very light green ivy leaves are sporadically added in such a way that the text appears to be superimposed on the ivy. Authentic documents such as news clippings, diary pages, and photographs introduce each chapter and provide clues to the haunted adventure. The artwork is beautiful, but also mysterious, which fits the book's mood. Ages 12–14.

The Last Apprentice: Wrath of the Bloodeye. Joseph Delaney, 2008. Illustrated by Patrick Arrasmith. In this fifth book of the Last Apprentice series, apprentice Thomas Ward faces an ancient, evil water witch. Black and white scratchboard illustrations provide images with strong contrasts. Light sources help define objects and figures; sometimes the light source vaguely suggests the forms. Each chapter illustration of a frightening image has text placed above, below, or on the image. The illustration is placed on the right page across from a black page containing only the chapter number and the chapter title. The menacing images, often demonic and very scary, foreshadow the events in the chapter. Ages 10–14.

Leviathan. Scott Westerfeld, 2009. Illustrated by Keith Thompson. This book is an example of a steampunk alternate history. Set in an alternate version of World War I, the Clanks' technology is pitted against the Darwinists' fabricated species. The muted black and white drawings, sometimes full-paged, captioned, and extending past the margin, capture intricate details of machine, beast, and men at war. A double-page map appears before the title page and displays the 1914 versions of Austria-Hungry, the Ottoman Empire, and Great Britain. Created with shapes and images of creatures and monstrous weapons, the map can be quite useful if carefully studied before beginning the story. Ages 13 and up.

Riding Invisible. Sandra Alonzo, 2010. Illustrated by Nathan Huang. Yancy is a runaway who tells his story of persecution and abuse at the hands of his mentally disturbed brother. The diary, printed in a font that suggests it was handwritten, also has cartoonlike drawings. Some reflect Yancy's experiences, others his imagination. The cartoons balance the difficult situation and mature language. Ages 13–16.

The Underneath. Kathi Appelt, 2008. Illustrated by David Small. The sketch-like illustrations are done with neutral colors of white, gray, and black. Three illustrations are located at the bottom of double pages, perhaps reinforcing the sense of "the underneath," the place under cruel Gar Face's porch that is the only safe place for abandoned cats in the bayou. There are an additional 14 full-page illustrations and a final small silhouette of a hound and two cats. The illustrations illuminate character and help explain the action of the three intersecting stories. Ages 9–12.

Why We Broke Up. Daniel Handler, 2011. Illustrations by Maira Kalman. Quirky Min Green has broken up with her basketball star boyfriend. She dumps on his doorstep a box of mementos, including a movie ticket from a vintage theater, an umbrella, and a sugar container along with a written account of their short-lived relationship. Each chapter begins with an intriguing full-color painting of a memento. The final words in the novel are "Love, Min." Love is crossed out. The final painting is a pen. Ages 15 and up.

---

constitutes the line between picture book and graphic novel. "There is not a great difference between the two, but in a graphic novel there is perhaps more emphasis on continuity between multiple frames, actually closer in many ways to film-making than book illustration" (Tan, n.d. par. 11).

There are many different types of graphic novels, including superhero tales, science fiction and fantasy, realistic and historical stories, adapted and retold classics, satire, nonfiction, and Japanese-influenced manga. It may seem incongruous to use the term with nonfiction, but it is the form, not the content, that defines a work as a graphic novel (Bucher & Manning, 2004). The 9/11 Commission established by President Bush and the U. S. Congress actually enlisted well-known DC and Marvel comic book artists to create a graphic novel version of the Commission's 9/11 report that the general public could read and understand. Sid Jacobson and Ernie Colon's *The 9/11 Report: A Graphic Adaptation* (2006) contains 144 pages, versus over 600 in the original document. It conveys the stories of the four tragic flights in foldout pages so that the simultaneous events that overwhelmed defense and information systems can be seen at the same time. Colon tells about creating *The 9/11 Report: A Graphic Adaptation* in an interview found on the Teaching Books website (http://teachingbooks.net/ecolon).

Literature teachers unfamiliar with graphic novels may be reluctant to use them because of misconceptions about their content and quality. As Stephen Tabachnick points out, however, graphic novels have "plots and themes with the depth and subtlety that we have come to expect of traditional novels and extended nonfiction texts" (2009, p. 2). Knowing a bit of the history of graphic novels as a literary/art form may help teachers reconsider their place in the curriculum.

Graphic Novels: Then and Now

Young adults in the World War II era were the first generation to grow up with comic books. Superheroes such as Superman, who first appeared in 1938, and Captain Marvel, who followed in 1940, coexisted with non-hero comic book characters such as Archie and his teenage friends. Although often thought of as a more recent addition to the curriculum, *The Classic Comics*, later marketed as *Classics Illustrated*, emerged during the 1940s (Gorman, 2003, p. 1–2). These graphic adaptations typically reproduced the classical works that were frequently read in high school.

The 1950s were controversial times for comic books as new guidelines, called the Comics Code, were established to prevent violent and sexual comics being produced (Gorman, 2003; Weiner, 2003). In the late 1950s and 1960s, many of the superheroes who are still prominent today, Spider-Man, the Fantastic Four, and the X-Men, became popular. Comic fandom developed, and adults gathered at conventions and magazines about comics were published. By the late 1960s an underground "commix" movement developed, with counterculture artists creating comics for their peers (Weiner, 2003, pp. 9–12).

The first modern graphic novel was written and illustrated by Will Eisner. He is credited with coining the term *graphic novel* as a means of distinguishing his book, *A Contract with God and other Tenement Stories* (1978), from collections of newspaper comic strips. He described graphic novels as "sequential art," a series of illustrations which, when viewed in order, tell a story (Graphix, n.d., p. 3). Illustrations conveyed most of the narrative in Eisner's book, which consists of four thematically related short stories about Jewish working class life in New York during the Great Depression.

When Pantheon Books published the first volume of Art Spiegelman's graphic novel, *Maus: A Survivor's Tale* (1986), a biographical family memoir of the Holocaust, the status of graphic novels as literature was forever changed. Following the publication of the second volume in 1992, the work won a special Pulitzer Prize and soon became required reading in many high schools (Gorman, 2003, p. 3). The many literary graphic novels that followed *Maus* created a genre for readers who were not interested in typical comics (Weiner, 2005).

Watchmen (1987), written by Alan Moore and illustrated by Dave Gibbons, won the Hugo Award and later appeared in *Time* magazine's 2005 "The 100 Best English Language Novels from 1923 to the Present." The success of Jeff Smith's *Bone*, first self-published as a comic series and later reissued as a graphic novel (2004), and Neil Gaiman's *Sandman* (1989–1996) demonstrated that there was readership for comics beyond superhero stories. These original literary fantasies had well developed narration, engaging characters, and appealed to a wide audience (Weiner, 2003, pp. 45–46).

In the late 1990s, Japanese-style film animation, **anime,** and comics, **manga,** which means comics in Japanese, were introduced in the United States and quickly became popular (Gorman, 2003, p. 3). Manga maintains the Japanese format of reading right-to-left and back to front. Stylistically, most manga characters have "exaggerated eyes, simplified features, and straight spiked hair" (Frey & Fisher, 2008, p. 30).

In Japan manga is divided into genres with a sharp division between genders. **Shonen** is for boys and **shojo** for girls. Manga frequently contains gay characters and characters who switch gender. Goldstein and Phelan (2009) speculate that manga might influence how young people view gender roles (p. 32).

Schwartz and Rubinstein-Avila (2006) suggest that shojo manga provides a mirror into the paradox of female power and submission presented in Western media. Kurhee Choo's extensive analysis of the gender concepts in shojo manga (2008) provides a good starting point for examining how manga influences gender perceptions. Readers may find it interesting to examine the assumptions shojo authors make about their readers and societal expectations for females. A few popular shojo romances are *Fruits Basket* (2004) by Natsuki Takaya, *Paradise Kiss* (2002) by Ai Yazawa, and *Beast Master* (2010) by Motomi Kyousuke.

Examples of shonen, action stories for boys, are *Pandora Hearts* (2000) by Jun Mochizuki, *Soul Eater* (2003) by Atsushi Okubo, and *Tegami Bachi* (2006) by Hiroyuki Asada. Boys' shonen manga often stress values such as friendship and competition. Athletic prowess as a corollary to masculinity is often a core value (Schwartz & Rubinstein-Avila, 2006). Cultural influences can be analyzed and comparisons made between gender roles depicted in Japanese and American literature.

Although the popularity of manga has dropped in recent years, it remains a significant part of the American comics market (Cha, 2010, p. 6). Manga accounts for two-thirds of the graphic novel market in the United States, and girls make up 75 percent of the readership (Goldstein & Phelan, 2009, p. 32).

Graphic novels first appeared on the *USA Today*'s Best-Selling Books List in 2002 (McTaggart, 2008, p. 29). *American Born Chinese* (Yang, 2006), a Printz Award winner, was the first graphic novel nominated for a National Book Award. The ALA initiated awards for graphic novels in 2007, an indicator of the increased acceptance of graphic novels and their place in the English language arts curriculum. Major review sources such as *School Library Journal*, *Booklist*, and *Publishers Weekly* regularly review graphic novels (Graphix, n.d., p. 3).

Contemporary advances in print technology have enabled low-cost, high-resolution, and full-color production of graphic novels (Drucker, 2008), contributing both to their quality and availability. Publishers as diverse as Marvel, Tokyopop, Yen Press, and Del Rey Books publish graphic novels based on original popular novels, as well as teaming up prose writers with illustrators to create new graphic works. The marketing for graphic adaptations is designed to build on the existing fan base of both comics and the original prose and to expand the audience for both. The bridge between comics and traditional prose is seen as originating from either side (Price, 2010).

Reading Graphic Novels

Thinking of graphic novels as books in which "images and text arrive together, work together, and should be read together" (Gravett, 2005, p. 11) may help teachers and readers realize that reading them differs from reading word-only texts, but there is no single rule on how to do so. In addition to elements of art previously described, graphic novels have some unique features that are essential to interpreting the genre.

A **panel** is a block of content with a visual or implied boundary. Individual panels vary in size, shape, and position. A panel can contain only words, only images, or both. Panels can also be categorized by the story element they reveal, such as setting or conflict (Monnin, 2010). Inside a panel, **balloons** may contain dialogue spoken by the characters, words that represent their thoughts, or mental images. Balloons can also be used for plot exposition or for sound effects. Some graphic artists do not use any type of internal boundary to separate the words from the graphics in a panel (Monnin, 2010).

The **gutter,** the space between panels, is considered by Scott McCloud (1993) to be the most fundamental element in understanding graphic novels. A reader has to infer the relationship between one panel and the next. For example, the space may indicate a transition when action jumps across place and time. It might also mark a change in subject or even a purposeful disconnect (Monnin, 2010).

Words in graphic novels are sometimes written in boldface or italics for emphasis or to convey a sense of sound (Monin, 2010). For example, *Calamity Jack* (Hale & Hale, 2010), a fast-moving follow up to *Rapunzel's Revenge* (Hale & Hale, 2008) discussed in Chapter 6, frequently incorporates sound effects. An illustration of Jack falling has the letters "A A A A" descending, with the word *WHUMP* at the bottom of the frame. The repeated word/sound pattern "thrum-thrum-thrum" serves as background noise that, in effect, increases tension as people are seen running from attacking ants. The size of print and change in typography signal a change in the significance of a sound. One frame shows slight movement of the magic beanstalk with the sound effects text *r-r-r-r* and *creeee* in white small letters. On the next panel, a large purple *KARUMP* indicates that the whole beanstalk and building have collapsed. Sound effects also move the story forward. A character's guns go "click, click," showing that they are out of bullets. Sounds also can foreshadow events. For example, "coo coo" appears before a flock of giant pigeons arrives.

Selecting Graphic Novels

Graphic novels, like all literature, are intended for a variety of audiences and purposes. Criteria for selecting a graphic novel for recreational reading should probably differ from those used to select a graphic novel selected for literary analysis. Fiction graphic novels should be evaluated with the same criteria as print novels: Characters should be multidimensional, and conflict should be developmentally appropriate. The action should keep a reader involved, ending with a climax and resolution that creates a satisfying end. Themes and ethical issues relevant to the reader are a must.

The illustrations in a graphic novel should be evaluated with many of the same criteria that apply to book covers or picture books. The color palette should fit with the mood and tone, and character development should be enhanced by the illustrations. Objects and the space between them should create a visually pleasing effect. Illustrations should provide adequate context and action. Another consideration for evaluating graphic novels is the format, the external and interior elements such as font and font size, word placement and appearance, and the arrangement of the frames (Griffith, 2010). The following sources offer guidance for selecting and teaching graphic novels:

- *Diamond Bookshelf*, www.diamondbookshelf.com/Home/1/1/20/163. Graphic novels are categorized by age groups. Reviews from *School Library Journal* and *Publishers Weekly* are included, as are a menu of lesson plans, new releases, and articles.
- *Comic Books: Internet Resources—University at Buffalo Libraries*, http://library.buffalo.edu/libraries/asl/guides/comics.htm. This website serves as a clearinghouse of Internet resources for comic book and graphic novel distributors, reviews, author and illustrator interviews, and commentary.
- *No Flying No Tights*, www.noflyingnotights.com. This website reviews graphic novels for teens. Starred titles indicate novels for younger teens.
- *The Readers' Advisory Guide to Graphic Novels* (2010), by Francisca Goldsmith. Published by the American Library Association. This work includes annotated bibliographies by genre, rationales for using graphic novels, and instructional suggestions.
- *The 101 Best Graphic Novels* (2005), by Stephen Weiner. This book, by a well-known expert on graphic novels, contains an alphabetical annotated list of graphic novels. Recommended age levels are included.

Connecting Readers with Complex Issues and Critical Literacy through Graphic Novels

Jonathan Seyfried suggests that graphic novels have not only saved the day for recreational reading, but they also have "turned out to be a heavyweight in the teaching of advanced themes in literature and visual literacy" (2008, p. 45). Many graphic novels have rich themes, multifaceted characters, and well developed stories that may appeal to a variety of adolescents (Gorman, 2008). James Bucky

Carter (2007a; 2007b) argues that graphic novels "have great transformative potential." By that he means that many graphic novels focus on subject matter relevant to adolescents, including social issues, alternative personal points of view, and "hot button topics." The graphic novel provides a reader-friendly point of entry into discussions of these important topics.

Heart Transplant (2010), written by Andrew Vachss and illustrated by Frank Carusco, is a powerful work about bullying that forces young adults to consider the social practices and norms that perpetuate bullying in and out of school. The story is about a young boy who is neglected and bullied. After the murder of his mother and her boyfriend, he is taken in by the boyfriend's father. This older man is presented as a dark figure, and there is a momentary expectation that he too will abuse the boy. Unexpectedly, he becomes a source of love and protection and teaches the boy to stand up for himself and others. The novel also includes a lengthy informational piece about bullying by Zak Mucha, a licensed clinical social worker.

The format of the book is large, 10 by 13 inches, and has a variety of illustration and text combinations. Some pages are wordless pages, and some have continuous text. The illustrations are dark and evocative; colors are most often subdued. The story, illustrations, and information combine to present a powerful perspective on what bullying does to people and how it must be stopped.

Graphic novels cross all genre categories and focus on the same themes and issues as prose literature for young adults. The highly regarded *Maus*, mentioned earlier, is a central text for Holocaust studies and an excellent choice for engaging in critical literacy. Spiegelman's memoir "raises issues such as the politicization of ethnic identity and nationalist sentiment." (Barr, 2009, p. 76). It also raises questions about who survived the concentration camps and why. Spiegelman confronts issues not usually considered when examining the Holocaust, such as wealthy Jews being able to buy their safety while poorer people suffered. Blame is not singularly focused on the Nazis. He raises the question of the culpability of fellow inmates in the horrible treatment of the victims of concentration camps (Vizzini, 2009, p. 243). Vizzini suggests that Spiegelman's choice to have Jews depicted as mice, Nazis as cats, Poles as pigs, and Americans as dogs provided a way for readers to understand the complex concepts involved because they were able to think of the characters as enemies in the way mice, cats, pigs, and dogs would be natural enemies.

Will Eisner's *Fagin the Jew* (2003) focuses on the infamous character from Charles Dickens' *Oliver Twist*. This graphic rendering of a classic miscreant by the creator of *A Contract with God* (1978), the first modern graphic novel as mentioned earlier, speculates about Fagin's childhood and background, which are portrayed as the cause of Fagin's situation and his behavior. The book explains Fagin's difficult history as a Middle European Jew trying to assimilate into British culture. *Fagin the Jew* can also be a vehicle for critically examining Jewish stereotypes and the perpetuation of these stereotypes through classical literature that has been part of the English curriculum for generations. Norman Lebrecht commented on Dickens' depiction of Fagin by saying, "a more vicious stigmatization of an ethnic community could hardly be imagined and it was not by any means unintended" (2005, p. 1.) The intertextuality is obvious and may prompt readers to reread Dickens' work from a very different perspective as they examine the bias and intent of this author.

Martha Cornog (2009) briefly describes several graphic novels that may appeal to a gay audience. We select three titles from her list that are also recommended by Devon Greyson (2007) as appropriate for library collections for young adults: *Young Avengers* (Heinberg, 2008); *The Authority* (Ellis & Hitch, 2000); and *Stuck Rubber Baby* (Cruse, 2000). The first two titles are about superheroes; the third is set in the Southern United States in the 1960s and includes a lynching of the main character's gay friend.

Pedro and Me: Friendship, Loss, and What I Learned (2000) is a graphic work by Judd Winick written as a tribute to Pedro Zamora, a Cuban American Winick met on the reality show *The Real World*. The novel chronicles their experiences on the show, in particular, their friendship. Zamora's main purpose in life is to educate people about HIV. This memoir includes Zamora's relationship with another HIV-positive man, their commitment ceremony, and his developing and dying from AIDS.

Superhero comics and numerous subgenres lend themselves to critical analysis. African American superheroes, super heroines, vigilantes and antiheroes, postmodern heroes, and parodies of super heroes have the potential to create discussion of heroism, power, and racial and gender stereotypes across the decades. Daiman Duffy and John Jennings' *The Black Comix: African American Independent Comics, Art & Culture* (2010), *The Marvel Encyclopedia* (DeFalco, Sanderson, Brevoort, & Teitelbaum 2009), and *The DC Encyclopedia, Updated and Expanded Edition* (Teitelbaum, Beatty, Greenburger, & Wallace (2008), are helpful resources for teachers unfamiliar with the history and content of the superhero genre.

Graphic novels can also help readers investigate major historical events from the perspective of other countries. *Barefoot Gen, Volume 1: A Cartoon Story of Hiroshima* (Nakazawa, 2004) introduces the reader to the suffering of innocent Japanese people during World War II. The story is told through the eyes of the artist as a young boy growing up in Japan. Gen's father questions Japan's war efforts and the need for civilians to go to the "trainings." This belief labels him a traitor, and his whole family suffers. The horrors of the atom bomb begin at the end of Volume 1 and the aftermath continues in Volume 2 (2004). Apart from the nuclear disaster, the people also endure the selfishness of their fellow Japanese.

Graphic novels can easily be included in thematic units, especially when a critical stance is being used. Michael Boatright (2010) recommends *The Arrival* (Tan, 2007); *The Four Immigrants Manga: A Japanese Experience in San Francisco, 1904–1924* (Kiyama, 1931/1999), and *American Born Chinese* (Yang, 2006) for providing differing perspectives and biases that relate to current issues of immigration in the United States.

Nonfiction graphic works can also provide readers with opportunities to critically consider decisions by those in power. In *A.D: New Orleans after the Deluge* (2009), John Neufeld tells the stories of survivors of Hurricane Katrina. The decisions of people in power, such as the police and politicians, as well as the actions of ordinary people are examined. The events themselves are true, and dialogue has been adapted from interviews or entries from blogs as discussed in the book's afterword.

Metafictive Characteristics in Graphic Novels

Graphic novels incorporate the same metafictive characteristics as text-only literature (see Chapter 3). The blurring of genres, nonlinearity, and intertextuality are popular conventions in graphic novels, and the combination of visual and text components may actually make it easier for students to understand these stylistic devices.

Blurring of genres

Monnin uses the term **creative nonfiction graphic novel** to indicate "a nonfiction graphic novel that focuses on factually accurate events, people, places and/or times and the author's use of creative license (storytelling)" (2010, p. 67). An example of this mixing of nonfiction and fiction is *The Stuff of Life: A Graphic Guide to Genetics and DNA* (Schultz, 2009). It is a fact-based introduction to the history and complex science of genetics, but the information is embedded in the story of an interplanetary biologist, Bloort 183, who lives on a planet experiencing a genetic crisis. Bloort is transmitted to Earth to study its inhabitants. He writes and draws his report concerning the regenerative and reproductive strategies of species on Earth. A middle-school audience would enjoy Jay Hosler's biological fiction, *Clan Apis* (2000), which presents the life cycle of bees from a bee's perspective, beginning when the bee is a larva. Although the bees in the book are anthropomorphic, they present factual information about themselves and other plants and animals.

The Storm in the Barn (2009) by Matt Phelan, a recipient of the Scott O'Dell Award for Historical Fiction, blends fantasy with history. The first chapter, "Kansas, 1937," shows a family packing the car, surrounded by whirling dust; the father utters, "The dust can have it." After being bullied, Jack runs to his family and finds his sister Dorothy is suffering from a lung disease caused by the excessive dust in the air. Dorothy is reading *The Wizard of Oz*, a story about another Dorothy in Kansas. The local storekeeper, who knows about the bullies, creates another intertextual connection by telling Jack different "Jack tales" in which the hero is always named Jack.

Phelan uses pencil, ink, and watercolor to create dusty images that provide a glimpse into the devastation caused by the dust bowl. A great deal of the story is rendered in muted browns, tans, and grays. However, when Jack's mother reflects on her childhood in Kansas, the pictures slice across the page in fertile green. The local men gather to kill some rabbits. The deed is conveyed in a single panel of red. Later, a less vibrant red is used to show Jack's memory of the hunt. Many pages are wordless, and text is contained within the panels. The author does not use speech balloons. The words of the Storm King appear in a different typeface. Sound effects look as if they are hand printed.

Realistic fiction is paired with fantasy in *Foiled* (2010), written by Jane Yolen and illustrated by Mike Cavallaro. Aliera feels invisible in her high school, even though she is a star fencer. Then her life changes when handsome Avery Castle becomes her lab partner. Realism gives way to fantasy while Aliera waits for Avery at Grand Central Station. Illustrator Mike Cavallaro skillfully uses tones of green and black when the setting is realistic and switches to bright colors for fantasy. A sword with a bright-colored jewel appears to be the key to this and future adventures.

Nonlinearity

Speigelman uses techniques in *Maus* that help the reader follow the present episodes about his interactions with his father, which are interspersed with stories of his father's experiences in World War II. In many cases, action that takes place in the past is surrounded by frames with black borders, while the present-day frames are borderless (see Figure 10.2). Darker tones in the drawings indicate the setting has returned to Europe. Stories are interrupted by questions shown by speech bubbles. These visual cues identify shifts in time and setting.

Deogratias: A Tale of Rwanda by Jean-Philippe Stassen (2006) is a graphic novel meant for a mature audience. Although Deogratias, the young adult protagonist, is fictional, the setting is all too real. Translator Alexis Siegel informs the reader in a prologue about the Rwandan genocide that occurred in the early 1990s. Deogratias, a Hutu, becomes caught up in the Hutu massacre of the Tutsi, the minority group who spent decades in power. The author skillfully alternates between before and after the massacre. As the novel progresses, the past moves closer and closer to the present. This non-sequential movement is depicted, in part, by depicting Deogratias wearing a battered, stained shirt after the rebellion. Prior to mass killings, the teen is wearing a clean white shirt. As the conflicts become more and more violent, the teenager loses his grip on reality and begins to think he is a dog.

Intertextuality

The Tale of One Bad Rat (1994, 2010) by Bryan Talbot has won numerous awards, including the Will Eisner Comic Industry Award. Talbot explains that the basic premise of the story is "a homeless girl [Helen] with a synchronistic link with Beatrix Potter [who] follows Potter's escape into her new life in the Lakes" (afterword, 2010). Even Talbot's cover pays homage to Potter; it has a typeface and a white cover with a softly colored illustration reminiscent of Potter's original *The Tale of Peter Rabbit* (1902). Potter, whose first name was actually Helen, created *The Tale of Peter Rabbit*, *The Tale of Two Bad Mice* (1904), and many other miniature

figure 10.2 A page from *Maus I* using differing frame styles.

Differing styles show present day (no frames) vs. past episodes (black frames).

books. She was dominated by her father well into adulthood, but eventually broke free and lived independently.

Helen Potter, the girl in the graphic novel, is abused by her father. She runs away from home, taking her pet rat and her favorite childhood books by Beatrix Potter. She eventually confronts her father and is able to establish a life independent of him. The story ends with Helen no longer needing to copy Potter's work; she is now able to create her own. Talbot's goal was to make the graphic novel "easily readable by those without an acquired knowledge of comics grammar." In part, this meant the characters had to be based on real people, and the scenes on real places. The reader without knowledge of Beatrix Potter and her work would still understand the basic plot and theme of *The Tale of One Bad Rat*, but having that knowledge adds another level to the story.

Fables: 1001 Nights of Snowfall (Willingham, 2006) provides the backstory for the *Fables* series in which fairy tale and folk tale characters have been thrown out of Fairyland and live as refugees in contemporary New York. Although the characters in *Fables* are childhood favorites, the book is written for a mature audience and contains mature themes and situations.

Snow White, for example, has been sent as an ambassador to the lands of the Arabian Fables. To amuse the sultan and save her life, she takes on the role of Scheherazade and tells him a series of stories. The tales are illustrated by different artists with varying styles that complement each tale. For example, James Jean renders "A Frog's Eye View" in shades of green and tan, which reflects not only the green of the frog but also the general mood of the story. In contrast, Jill Thompson uses multiple colors and much detail for the variety of nursery rhyme and fairy tales found in "Fair Division."

Teaching Ideas ▪ GRAPHIC NOVELS

For some time graphic novels have been recognized as literature that reluctant readers may find more accessible than traditional novels (Schneider, 2005; Snowball, 2005). Struggling readers are often unable to visualize pictures in their heads, which can affect their comprehension. The graphic format provides visual clues that help with interpretation (Lyga & Lyga, 2004). The visuals can provide scaffolding for the written text, and the rapidly moving action keeps readers interested. The typically shorter format also adds to the appeal for the reluctant reader. English language learners gravitate to graphic novels because the syntax is usually simpler than in more traditional formats (Gorman, 2003).

Teachers can capitalize on the popularity of graphic works by including them in school-based reading programs. The widely used Accelerated Reader Program, which provides interest and reading levels (AR Book Finder, n.d.), includes a wide range of graphic novels. Graphic novels for middle-level readers include *The Secret Science Alliance and the Copycat Crook* (Davis, 2009), a humorous story about conformity and self-acceptance, and *The Plain Janes* (2007) by Cecil Castellucci and Jim Rugg. This latter book is about being a transfer student and fitting in, beginning with an escape from the reject table in the lunchroom. The program also includes highly acclaimed works appropriate for high school students,

Bram Stoker's Dracula: The Graphic Novel. Adapted by Gary Reed, 2006. Illustrated by Becky Cloonan. This classic rendering of the horror tale includes a discussion of the visuals and a short biography of Stoker. The story is told through black and white illustrations as well as dialogue. Ages 9–12.

Call of the Wild. Adapted by Neil Kleid, 2006. Illustrated by Alex Nino. This adaptation of the Jack London story captures the harshness of the Yukon during the gold rush from the perspective of Buck, a kidnapped dog. The action-packed story contains some of London's original language. Adapter and illustrator notes and biographical information provide insight on the process of adapting a classic. Illustrations are black and white. Ages 12–15.

Fahrenheit 451: The Authorized Adaptation. Tim Hamilton, 2009. This adaptation of Ray Bradbury's 1953 story about book burning and censorship remains set in a futuristic dystopia where firemen do not put out fires, they start them. Illustrations, often two-toned with well-chosen but minimal detail, reflect a 1950s feel. Recognizable classic books are engulfed in flames. Bradbury provides the introduction. Ages 13 and up.

The Hobbit: An Illustrated Edition of the Fantasy Classic. Adapted by Charles Dixon, 2001. Illustrated by David Wenzel. This abridged adaptation of Tolkien's work has beautiful illustrations that retain a magical quality. Additional explanatory information about the novel is included. Ages 12 and up.

The Merchant of Venice. Gareth Hinds, 2008. This modern retelling of Shakespeare's story of greed, hatred, and mercy mixes 21st-century language with dialogue closer to that of the original. Colors of slate blue and pale grey create a sense of antiquity. Page headings, for example, Act 1 Scene 1, refer to the original play. Ages 13 and up.

Macbeth: Original Text: The Graphic Novel. Adapted by John McDonald, 2008. This full-color unabridged adaptation of the play provides vivid illustrations to support interpreting the play as Shakespeare wrote it. Ages 14 and up.

Metamorphosis. Peter Kuper, 2003. This adaptation of Franz Kafka's dark comedy of an ordinary man who inexplicably turns into an insect is illustrated in black and white scratchboard, a technique in which drawings are created using a sharp instrument to etch into layers of clay. The heavily detailed background fills in much of the story. Ages 14 and up.

Outlaw: The Legend of Robin Hood. Tony Lee, 2009. *Outlaw* begins with an incident from Robin Hood's boyhood, covers his experience in the Crusades, and finally presents the more familiar struggle with the Sheriff of Nottingham and Prince John. Bold colors vary as the story changes from one setting to another. Age 12 and up.

The Wonderful Wizard of Oz. Eric Shanower, 2009. Illustrated by Skottie Young. This adaptation of L. Frank Baum's text keeps the original story intact. Details excluded in the 1939 MGM film version are maintained in this graphic version. Illustrations are whimsical and stylish and maintain the flavor of the original. Ages 9–12.

---

such as *Persepolis* (Satrapi, 2003), mentioned earlier, and *Palestine* (Sacco, 2002), which is based on the Israeli-Palestinian conflict in the early 1990s.

McTaggart (2008) suggests that graphic novels serve as an equalizer between academically achieving and struggling readers. The students develop a sense of unity and togetherness over their common interest (p. 33). Students can work together to create an original graphic novel. Peter David's *Writing for Comics & Graphic Novels* (2009) or online resources such as the ComicLife website (http://comiclife.com) can be used as a guide. As part of the Comic Book Project, students can submit their work for publication by Dark Horse. Teacher training is included on their website at www.comicbookproject.org/participate.

Stories told in both graphic novel format and text-only format can be compared and contrasted. Take *Artemis Fowl, Book 1* by Eoin Colfer, for example. Colfer and Andrew Donkin adapted the series into graphic novels. The popular *Twilight* series by Stephenie Meyer has also been written as a graphic novel, illustrated by Young Kim.

Graphic novels can be used to motivate reluctant readers, scaffold literary elements, and expose readers to texts they might not have otherwise experienced. The books listed in the box on the facing page are novels that have often been required in classrooms but can be read independently in these graphic novel renditions.

Finally, graphic novels and picture books can be used as writing prompts. Frey and Fisher (2007) recommend using a text as a shared reading (see Chapter 2) and think-aloud (see Chapter 5) for strategy instruction, and vocabulary and words choice discussion as preparation for writing. They also suggest examining how visual stories convey mood through images and how a writer does this with words.

VISUALLY ORIENTED TEXTS AND INTERACTIVITY

Picture books, illustrated novels, and graphic novels can be a welcome addition to both an adolescent's recreational reading and classroom instruction. Questions about visually oriented texts no longer focus on whether young adults should read this literature (they are), or if it should be used in the curriculum (it is). The question now seems to be, "what's next?"

Interactive ebooks (also referred to as enhanced ebooks) will continue to gain popularity. "An interactive eBook is a complete multimedia experience, typically read on a tablet computer, which allows the reader/user to interact with the storyline in sound, sight and touch" (Interactive eBook, n.d.). The initial primary markets for interactive or multimodal books are books for younger children and the information and textbook market. However, it is likely that markets will continue to broaden. Readers are exposed to the connections between text, images, and the virtual world at an early age and they quickly adapt to interactive works with online links and video (Stine, 2010). In 2011 the National Book Foundation began accepting submissions of interactive books for the National Book Award (Dilworth, 2011), providing interactive works with the same opportunity as written texts to gain prestigious literary recognition.

Added features may be "mission-critical or merely cause distraction" (Uhlmann, 2011, p. 80). Here is one example, for an idea of the types of possible "actions" in such books. The interactive ebook *Dracula: The Official Stoker Family Edition* (Stoker, 2010) includes many user-driven features. Eye-catching visuals, music, and sound effects, such scratching out a signature, a wolf howling, pages turning, flies buzzing, are constant. The pages turn as if flipping a page of a journal. One page incinerates, leaving the journal scorched. Features include touching the word *letter*, which opens an envelope, a clock that dongs when touched, and a knife that opens to display a bloody blade. Tap the word *spyglass* and one appears and opens to reveal a ship in the distance. Touch *translated* and a letter is typed on an old typewriter. The variety of genres and formats includes diaries, letters, telegrams, and newspaper articles, and visuals appear to move as if changing the distance of a camera. Links to music and other websites are included. Despite the numerous interactive features, several of the 285 pages are text-only. Credits at the end of the book are similar to those following a movie.

The evolution of visual texts will continue in response to the marketplace and improving technology. Readers will ultimately decide if interactive features enhance or impede their understanding of literature.

conclusion

Book covers catch a reader's attention and influence whether or not a book is opened. An artist's interpretation of a text influences a reader's interpretation, and readers should understand how visual images evoke particular responses to a literary work. Understanding the basic elements of art enhances an appreciation of book illustration, and taking pleasure in these aesthetic qualities adds to a reader's experience. Older readers who have been steered away from illustrations as meaningful components of literature may need to be taught the value and interpretation of book art.

Graphic novel expert James Bucky Carter has declared that graphic novels are now experiencing a golden age in education. Graphic novels benefit a wide range of students, cover numerous subject areas, and develop multiple types of literacy, especially visual and critical literacies (2007b). They motivate reluctant readers and challenge capable readers. Graphic novels connect to pop culture and react to social and cultural changes in ways that are more immediate than most other media, thus creating a timely connection between school and the world (Lyga & Lyga, 2004). At this point in time, graphic novels are "one of the most popular and fastest growing types of young adult literature" (Bucher & Manning, 2006, p. 285). It seems apparent that graphic novels belong in libraries, the English language arts classroom, and most of all in the hands of young adults. It remains to be seen whether interactive ebooks find a permanent place in the literature for young adults.

BIBLIOGRAPHY OF LITERATURE FOR YOUNG ADULTS

Alonzo, S. (2010). *Riding invisible.* (N. Huang, Illus.). New York: Hyperion.

Appelt, K. (2008). *The underneath.* (D. Small, Illus.). New York: Atheneum.

Aronson, S. (2007). *Head case.* New York: Roaring Brook Press.

Asher, J. (2007). *Thirteen reasons why.* New York: Razorbill Penguin.

Asada, H. (2006). *Tegami Bachi.* San Francisco, CA: VIZ Media.

Bingham, K. (2007). *Shark girl.* Cambridge, MA: Candlewick Press.

Blos, J. (1987). *Old Henry.* (S. Gammell, Illus.). New York: William Morrow.

Blume, J. (1975). *Forever.* New York: Pocket Books.

Blume, J. (1975). *Forever.* New York: Bradbury Press.

Blume, J. (2007). *Forever.* New York: Pocket Books.

Blume, J. (2007). *Forever.* New York: Simon Pulse.

Bradbury, R. (1953). *Fahrenheit 451.* New York: Random House.

Bunting, E. (1994). *Smoky nights.* (D. Diaz, Illus.). New York: Harcourt.

Bunting, E. (1991). *Fly away home.* (R. Himler, Illus.). New York: Clarion.

Caletti, D. (2005). *Wild roses.* New York: Simon & Schuster.

Castellucci, C., & Rugg, J. (2007). *The plain Janes.* New York: Mix Imprint, DC Comics.

Connor, L. (2010). *Crunch.* New York: Katherine Tegen/ HarperCollins.

Colfer, E. (2002). *Artemis Fowl, Book 1.* New York: Disney/ Hyperion.

Collins, S. (2008). *The hunger games.* New York: Scholastic.

Collins, S. (2009). *Catching fire.* New York: Scholastic.

Collins, S. (2010). *Mockingjay.* New York: Scholastic.

Cruse, H. (2000). *Stuck rubber baby.* New York: DC Comics.

David, P. (2009) *Writing for comics and graphic novels.* Manassas Park, VA: Impact.

Davis, E. (2009). *The secret science alliance and the copycat crook.* New York: Bloomsbury U.S.A.

Dahme, J. (2008). *Creepers.* (F. S. P. Chow, Illus.). Philadelphia, PA: Running Press Kids.

Delaney, J. (2008). *The last apprentice: Wrath of the blood-eye.* (P. Arrasmith, Illus.). New York: Greenwillow Books/HarperCollins.

DiCamillo, K. (2003). *The tale of Despereaux.* (T. Ering, Illus.). Cambridge, MA: Candlewick Press.

DiCamillo, K. (2008). *The tale of Despereaux: Special signed edition: Being the story of a mouse, a princess, some soup and a spool of thread.* (T. Ering, Illus.). Cambridge, MA: Candlewick Press.

Dixon. C. (Adapter). (2001). *The Hobbit: An illustrated edition of the fantasy classic.* (J. R. R. Tolkien, Author; D. Wenzel, Illus.). St. Louis, MO: Turtleback Books.

Ellis, W., & Hitch, B. (2000). *The authority.* La Jolla, CA: Wildstorm.

Eisner, W. (1978). *A contract with God and other tenement stories.* New York: Baronet Books.

Eisner, W. (2003). *Fagin the Jew.* New York: Doubleday.

Emond, S. (2011). *Winter town.* New York: Little, Brown.

Gaiman, N. (1989–1996). *Sandman.* New York: DC Comics.

Goodman, A. (2008). *Eon: Dragoneye reborn.* New York: Viking Juvenile.

Green, J. (2005). *Looking for Alaska.* New York: Dutton.

Hale, D., & Hale, S. (2008). *Rapunzel's revenge.* (N. Hale, Illus.). New York: Bloomsbury U.S.A.

Hale, S., & Hale, D. (2010). *Calamity Jack.* (N. Hale, Illus.). New York: Bloomsbury USA Children's Books.

Hamilton, T. (Adapter). (2009). *Ray Bradbury's Fahrenheit 451: The authorized adaptation.* New York: Hill & Wang.

Hand, D. (Dir.). (1938). *Snow White and the seven dwarfs.* U.S.A.: Disney.

Handler, D. (2011). *Why we broke up.* (M. Kalman, Illus.). New York: Little, Brown.

Heinberg, A. (2008). *Young avengers.* (J. Cheng, A. Divito, M. Gaydos, N. Adams, G. Ha, J. Lee, B. Sienkiewicz, & P. Ferry, Illus.). New York: Marvel Comics.

Hinds, G. (2008). *The merchant of Venice.* Cambridge, MA: Candlewick Press.

Hosler, J. (2000). *Clan Apis.* Columbus, OH: Active Synase.

Jacobson, S., & Colon, E. (2006). *The 9/11 report.* New York: Hill and Wang.

Kiyama, H. Y. (1999). *The four immigrant manga: A Japanese experience in San Francisco, 1904–1924.* (F. L. Schodt, Trans.). Berkeley, CA: Stone Bridge.

Kleid, N. (Adapter). (2006). *Call of the wild.* (Jack London, Author; A. Nino, Illus.). New York: Puffin.

Kuper, P. (Adaptor). (2003). *Metamorphosis.* (Franz Kafka, Author). New York: Crown.

Kwasney, M. (2009). *Blue plate special.* San Francisco, CA: Chronicle Books.

Kyousuke, M. (2010). *Beast master.* San Francisco: VIZ.

Larbalestier, J. (2009a). *Liar.* New York: Bloomsbury U.S.A.

Lee, T. (2009). *Outlaw: The legend of Robin Hood.* (S. Hart, Illus.). Cambridge, MA: Candlewick Press.

Lester, J. (2005). *Day of tears.* New York: Jump at the Sun/Hyperion.

Lore, P. (2010). *I am number four.* New York: Harper.

Maruki, T. (1980). *Hiroshima no pika.* New York: Lothrop, Lee & Shepard.

Mazer, H. (1981). *The last mission.* New York: Laurel Leaf.

McDonald, J. (Adapter). (2008). *Macbeth: Original text: The Graphic Novel.* (J. Howard & G. Erskine, Illus.). Towcester, UK: Classic Comics Limited.

Meyer, S. (2010). *Twilight: The graphic novel. Vol. 1.* (Y. Kim, Illus.). New York: Yen Press.

Mochizuki, J. (2000). *Pandora hearts.* New York: Yen Press.

Moore, A. (1986–1987). *Watchmen.* (D. Gibbons, Illus.). New York: DC Comics.

Moses, S. P. (2008). *Joseph.* New York: Margaret K. McElderry.

Myers, W. D. (2004). *Shooter.* New York: Amistad/HarperCollins.

Myers, W. D. (2010). *The cruisers.* New York: Scholastic.

Nakazawa, K. (2004). *Barefoot Gen, Volume 1: A cartoon history of Hiroshima.* San Francisco: Last Gap of San Francisco.

Nakazawa, K. (2004). *Barefoot Gen, Volume 2: The day after.* San Francisco: Last Gap of San Francisco.

Neufeld, J. (2009). *A.D: New Orleans after the deluge.* New York: Pantheon.

Okubo, A. (2003). *Soul eater.* New York: Yen Press.

Paulson, G. (1987). *Hatchet.* New York: Bradbury Press.

Paulson, G. (2006). *Hatchet.* New York: Aladdin.

Paulson, G. (2007). *Hatchet: 20th anniversary edition.* New York: Simon & Schuster.

Phelan, M. (2009). *The storm in the barn.* Cambridge, MA: Candlewick Press.

Potter, B. (1902). *The tale of Peter Rabbit.* London: F. Warne & Co.

Potter, B. (1904). *The tale of two bad mice.* London: F. Warne & Co.

Promitzer, R. (2010). *The pickle king.* New York: Scholastic.

Reed, G. (Adapter). (2006). *Bram Stoker's Dracula: The graphic novel.* (B. Cloonan, Illus.). New York: Puffin.

Sacco, J. (2002). *Palestine.* Seattle, WA: Fantagraphics.

Schultz, M. (2009). *The stuff of life: A graphic guide to genetics and DNA.* (Z. Cannon & K. Cannon, Illus.). New York: Farrar, Straus & Giroux.

Shanower, E. (2009). *The wonderful wizard of Oz.* (S. Young, Illus.). New York: Marvel.

Smith, J. (2004). *Bone: The complete cartoon epic in one volume.* Columbus, OH: Cartoon Books.

Spiegelman, A. (1986). *Maus I: A survivor's tale: My father bleeds history.* New York: Pantheon.

Spiegelman, A. (1992). *Maus II: A survivor's tale: And here my troubles began.* New York: Pantheon.

Satrapi, M. (2003). *Persepolis: The story of a childhood.* New York: Pantheon.

Small, D. (2009). *Stitches: A memoir.* New York: Norton.

Stassen, J. P. (2006). *Deogratias, a tale of Rwanda.* (A. Siegel, Trans.). New York: First Second.

Stoker, B. (2010). *Dracula: The official Stoker family edition.* Los Angeles, CA: PadWorx Digital Media.

Talbot, B. (1994, 2010). *Tale of one bad rat.* Milwaukie, OR: Dark Horse Books.

Takaya, N. (2004). *Fruits basket.* Los Angeles, CA: TokyoPop.

Tan, S. (2007). *The arrival.* New York: Arthur A. Levine.

Taylor, L. (2009). *Lips touch: Three times.* (J. Di Bartolo, Illus.). New York: Arthur A. Levine.

Tsuchiya, Y. (1988). *Faithful elephants: A true story of animals, people and war.* (T. Lewin, Illus.; T. T. Dykes, Trans.). Boston: Houghton Mifflin.

Vachss, A., & Caruso, F. (2010). *Heart transplant.* (Z. Mucha, Illus.). Milwaukie, OR: Dark Horse Books.

Valentino, S. (2009). *Fairest of all.* New York: Disney Press.

Westerfeld, S. (2009). *Leviathan.* (K. Thompson, Illus.). New York: Simon Pulse.

Willingham, B. (2006). *Fables: 1001 nights of snowfall.* (E. Andrews et. al, Illus.). New York: DC Comics.

Wilson, B. (1992). *The leaving and other stories.* New York: Scholastic.

Winick, J. (2000). *Pedro and me: Friendship, loss and what I learned.* New York: Holt.

Yang, G. (2006). *American born Chinese.* New York: First Second.

Yazawa, A. (2002). *Paradise kiss.* Los Angeles: TokyoPop.

Yolen, J. (2010). *Foiled.* (M. Cavallaro, Illus.). New York: First Second.

WEBSITES WITH ANNOTATIONS

Comic Book Project • **http://comicbookproject.org/participate/**
Students may submit their work for publication by Dark Horse; educator training available.

Comic Life • **http://comiclife.com/**
Website with resources to assist those wishing to create their own comic. Includes resources for educators to integrate comics in classrooms.

Diamond Comics Bookshelf • **www.diamondbookshelf.com/Home/1/1/20/163**
Graphic novels categorized by age groups. Includes lesson plans, new releases, and articles.

Lester, Julius • **www.juliuslester.net/**
The author's official website, including summaries of works and biographical information.

Taylor, Laini • **www.lainitaylor.com/**
The author's official website, including summaries of works, biographical information, and personal blog.

No Flying No Tights • **http://noflyingnotights.com/**
Reviews of graphic novels for teens. Titles are grouped by genre and common graphic topics and include complete synopses.

ReadWriteThink • **www.readwritethink.org/files/resources/interactives/bookcover/**
Provides a template for creating book covers, including how-to videos.

Recommended Graphic Novels for Public Libraries • **http://my.voyager.net/~sraiteri/graphicnovels.htm**
Graphic novels reviewed by librarian Steve Raiteri; superhero genre categorized by hero.

Survey Monkey • **http://surveymonkey.com/**
A free online survey program providing polls, blogs, and comment boxes to for teachers to use in classrooms.

TeachingBooks • **www.teachingbooks.net/**
Resources for K–12 educators. Provides online instructional materials, video and audio interviews, and lesson plans.

REFERENCES

AR Book Finder (n.d.). Retrieved from www.arbookfind. com.

Baker, K. C. (2009). Grace Lin interview: Where the mountain meets the moon. Retrieved from http:// waggingtales.wordpress.com/2009/09/16/grace-lin-Interview-where-the-mountain-meets-the-moon.

Barr, T. (2009). Teaching *Maus* to a Holocaust class. In Stephen Tabachnick (Ed.), *Teaching the graphic novel* (pp. 76–83). New York: Modern Language Association.

Boatright, M. D. (2010). Graphic journeys: Graphic novels' representations of immigrant experiences. *Journal of Adolescent and Adult Literacy, 53,* 468–476.

Boddy-Evans, A. (n.d.). Art styles explained: From realism to abstract. About.com: Painting. Retrieved from http://painting.about.com/od/oldmastertechniques/ tp/art-styles.htm.

Bucher, K. T., & Manning, M. L. (2004). Bringing graphic novels into a school's curriculum. *Clearing House, 78*(2), 67–71.

Carter, J. B. (2007a). Transforming English with graphic novels: Moving toward our "Optimus Prime." *English Journal, 97*(2), 49–53.

Carter, J. B. (2007b). Introduction: Carving a niche: Graphic novels in the English language arts classroom. In James Bucky Carter (Ed.), *Building literacy connections with graphic novels: Page by page, panel by panel* (pp. 1–25). Urbana, IL: National Council of Teachers of English.

Cha, K. M. (2010). Down, but not out: Manga holds on in a tough market. *Publishers Weekly, 257*(3), 6–7.

Choo, K. (2008). Girls return home: Portrayal of femininity in popular Japanese girls' manga and anime texts during the 1990s in Hana Yori Dango and *Fruits basket. Women: A Cultural Review, 19*(3), 275–296.

Cornog, M. (2009). The library don't have a closet: 19 graphic novels for gay & lesbian pride month. *Library Journal OneClickdigital.* Retrieved from http://www. libraryjournal.com/article/CA6660740.html.

DeFalco, T., Sanderson, P., Brevoort, T., & Teitelbaum, M. (2009). *Marvel encyclopedia.* New York: DK Publishing.

Dilworth, D. (2011, August 11). National Book Awards accepted interactive book. *Galleycat.* Retrieved from http://www.mediabistro.com/galleycat/national-book-awards-accepts-its-first-interactive-ebook_b36039.

Downey, E. (2009). Graphic novels in curriculum and instruction collections. *Reference & User Services Quarterly, 49*(2), 181–188.

Drucker, J. (2008). What is graphic about graphic novels? *English Language Notes, 46*(20), 39–55.

Duffy, D., & Jennings, J. (2010). *The black commix: African American independent comics, art & culture.* New York: Mark Batty.

Education at the Getty (n.d.). *The elements of art.* Retrieved from www.getty.edu/education/teachers/building_ lessons/elements.html.

Esaak, S. (n.d.). What are the elements of art? Why are they important? *About.com: Art History.* Retrieved from http://arthistory.about.com/cs/reference/f/ elements.htm.

Fitzgerald, C. (October 26, 2009). What do teens want? *Publishers Weekly, 256*(43), 22–26.

Frey, N., & Fisher, D. (2007). Using graphic novels, anime, and the Internet in an urban high school. In James Bucky Carter (Ed.), *Building literacy connections with graphic novels: Page by page, panel by panel* (pp. 132–144). Urbana, IL: National Council of Teachers of English.

Goldsmith, F. (2010). *The readers' advisory guide to graphic novels.* Chicago, IL: American Library Association.

Goldstein, L., & Phelan, M. (2009). Are you there God? It's me manga. *Young Adult Library Services, 7*(4), 32–38.

Gorman, M. (2003). *Getting graphic: Using graphic novels to promote literacy with preteens and teens.* Worthington, OH: Linworth.

Gorman, M. (2008, March). Getting graphic: A new generation of graphic novels: Expect the unexpected. *Library Media Connection, 26*(6), p. 38.

Graphix (n.d.). Using graphic novels with children and teens: A guide for teachers and librarians. Retrieved from www.scholastic.com/graphix/.

Gravett, P. (2005). *Graphic novels: Everything you need to know.* New York: HarperCollins.

Greyson, D. (2007). GLBTQ content in comics/graphic novels for teens. *Collection Building, 26*(4), 130–134.

Howard, J. (2010, December 10). 21st century imaging helps scholars reveal rare 8th century manuscript. *Chronicle of Higher Education,* p. 1.

Incredible Art Department. (n.d.). Color symbolism and culture. Retrieved from http://www.princetonol. com/groups/iad/lessons/middle/color2.htmwww. princetonol.com.

Interactive ebook (n.d.). What is an interactive ebook. Retrieved from http://interactiveebook.wordpress. com/what-is-an-interactive-ebook/.

Jones, L. A. (June, 2007). The great cover-up. *School Library Journal, 53*(6), 44–47.

Jones, L. A. (September, 2009). Operation facelift. *School Library Journal, 55*(9), 44–46.

Kiefer, B. Z. (1995). *The potential of picturebooks: From visual literacy to aesthetic understanding.* Englewood Cliffs, NJ: Merrill, Prentice Hall.

Klinefelter, W. (1975). *Sherlock Holmes in portrait and profile.* New York: Schocken Books.

Larbalestier, J. (2009b). Ain't that a shame. Retrieved from http://justinelarbalestier.com/blog/2009/07/23/aint-that-a-shame/.

Lebrecht, N. (2005, September 29). How racist is Oliver Twist? *The Lebrecht Report.* Retrieved from www.scena.org/columns/lebrecht/050929-NL-twist.html.

Lohmiller, D. (2008, Spring). Go ahead: Judge a book by its cover. *Young Adult Library Services, 6*(3), 13–15.

Lukens, R. (2003). *A critical handbook of children's literature* (7th ed.). Boston, MA: Allyn & Bacon.

Lyga, A. A. W., & Lyga, B. (2004). *Graphic novels in your media center: A definitive guide.* Westport, CT: Libraries Unlimited.

McCloud, S. (1993). *Understanding comics.* New York: HarperCollins.

McTaggart, J. (2008). Graphic novels: The good, the bad and the ugly. In Nancy Frey & Douglas Fisher (Eds.), *Teaching visual literacy using comic books, graphic novels, anime, cartoons, and more to develop comprehension skills* (pp. 27–46). Thousand Oaks, CA. Corwin Press.

Monnin, K. (2010). *Teaching graphic novels: Practical strategies for the secondary ELA classroom.* Gainesville, FL: Maupin House.

Nikolajeva, M., & Scott, C. (2000). The dynamics of picture book communications. *Children's Literature in Education, 31,* 225–239.

Nodelman, P. (1988). *Words about pictures: The narrative art of children's picture books.* Athens, GA: University of Georgia.

O'Neil, K. (2010). Once upon today: Teaching for social justice with postmodern picture books. *Children's Literature in Education, 41,* 40–51.

Palmer, A. W. (2008). How to design an award-winning book cover. *Magnificent Publications.* Retrieved from http://magpub.com/246/.

Price, A. (2010, April). Novel to graphic novel: Turning popular prose into comics. *Publishers Weekly, 257*(14), 23–26.

Satrapi, M. (n.d.). On writing *Persepolis.* Retrieved from www.randomhouse.com/pantheon/graphicnovels/ssatrapi2.html.

Schneider. R. (2005, September, 6). Graphic novels boost interest in reading among students with disabilities. Retrieved from http://www.iupui.edu/news/releases/050906_graphic_novels.

Schwartz, A., & Rubinstein-Avila, E. (2006). Understanding the manga hype: Uncovering the multimodality of comic-book literacies. *Journal of Adolescent and Adult Literacy, 50,* 40–49.

Seyfried, J. (2008). Reinventing the book club: Graphic novels as educational heavyweights. *Knowledge Quest, 36*(3), 44-48.

Snowball, C. (2005, Summer). Teenager reluctant readers and graphics novels. *Young Adult Library Services, 3*(4), 43–45.

Springen, K. (2009, July 23). Justine Larbalestier's cover girl: Controversy over a YA book jacket. *Publishers Weekly.* Retrieved from http://www.publishersweekly.com/pw/by-topic/childrens/childrens-book-news/article/16014-justine-larbalestier—s-cover-girl.html.

Stine, C. (2010, October 25). *Illustrated novels and interactive eBooks—new trends in young adult literature.* Retrieved from http://redroom.com/member/catherine-stine/blog/illustrated-novels-and.

Tabachnick, S. E. (2009). Introduction. In Stephen E. Tabachnick (Ed.), *Teaching the graphic novel* (pp. 1–15). New York: Modern Language Association.

Tan, S. (n.d.). Comments on *The Arrival.* Retrieved from www.shauntan.net/books/the-arrival.html.

Teitelbaum, M., Beatty, S., Greenburger, R., & Wallace, D. (2008). *The DC comics encyclopedia, updated and expanded edition.* New York: DK Publishing.

Uhlmann, D. (2011). Pick Me! Pick me! *School Library Journal, 57*(4), 80–83.

Vizzini, B. E. (2009). Hero and holocaust: Graphic novels in the undergraduate history classroom. In Stephen E. Tabachnick (Ed.), *Teaching the graphic novel* (pp. 238–244). New York: Modern Language Association.

Watson, J., et al. (2006, Winter). Picking the quick picks. *Young Adult Library Services, 4*(2), 7–9.

Weiner, S. (2003). *Faster than a speeding bullet: The rise of the graphic novel.* New York: Nantier, Beall, Minoustchine Publishing.

Weiner, S. (2005). *The 101 best graphic novels.* New York: Nantier, Beall, Minoustchine Publishing.

Whitehurst, L. S., & Snyder, W. J. (2000, October) Middle grade picture books: A look at the ways to use picture books in language arts classes, *School Library Journal, 46*(10), 38–39.

Yampbell, C. (2005). Judging a book by its cover: Publishing trends in young adult literature. *Lion and the Unicorn, 29*(3), 348–372.

CHAPTER ELEVEN

Film

**EXPANDING THE
LITERATURE CURRICULUM**

chapter overview

Films can be used in the classroom as a complement to print literature, but they should also be studied and enjoyed as a literary form in their own right. As a form of popular media, films are especially useful as a reflection of contemporary society, including youth culture. Because they are aggressively marketed, they make apparent the simple truth that all literary works are shaped by the need to appeal to a paying audience. This chapter explores the role of film in the literature classroom. First, we explain concepts that students need to understand to analyze and discuss films. Then we identify specific ways to compare films with print literature to understand elements and themes that are common to all literary forms. Finally, the chapter explores films from a critical literacy perspective that acknowledges both the cultural impact of films and the social and economic forces that influence filmmaking.

FOCUS QUESTIONS

1. What are the important characteristics of film as an art form?
2. How can film and literature complement each other?
3. How does film shape and reflect culture?
4. How does the film business influence filmmaking and viewing?

introduction

William Costanzo called movies "the premier literature of our time" (2004, p. x). That may be an overstatement, but films have been part of people's everyday experiences for over one hundred years, and they play a prominent role in the lives of young adults. Costanzo estimates that his young adult students see approximately 20 films each month at local theaters, on broadcast television, on cable networks, on DVD, and online (2004, p. xv).

Films are closely related to other forms of literature. Around 50 percent of all major film releases today are sequels, remakes, or adaptations from other sources such as books, television programs, comic books, and plays. Films based on existing works consistently rate among the highest grossing films (Wasko, 2008, p. 44), probably because they come equipped with a ready-made audience—viewers who are already familiar with the story and/or characters. Adaptations are not only more profitable than films based on original scripts but are also frequently judged to be better films. Approximately 85 percent of Academy Awards for Best Picture have gone to adaptations (Phillips, 2007).

Films entertain, but they have also profoundly influenced American culture. Understanding the ways in which films both reflect and shape the values and beliefs of society is part of developing a critical perspective of film. Developing this viewpoint requires that young adults become aware of how films can influence the ideas and the identities of the people who view them. Another aspect of a critical viewpoint is an understanding that making films is a business as well as an art. The desire to make a profit affects what movies are made and how they are marketed.

Young adults are targeted by advertisers and inundated with enticements to see particular films. They need to be aware of the marketing tactics used to persuade them to choose one movie over another, and they need to analyze a film's underlying messages as they consider their willingness to be part of the audience.

An art form as pervasive and influential as film deserves a prominent place in the curriculum. The Common Core State Standards for English Language Arts (National Governors Association Center for Best Practices, 2010) include a focus on comparing print and nonprint renditions of a work of literature, in particular the degree to which a film or live production veers from the original written text. This type of comparison requires students to understand the techniques unique to each medium. Films should be selected for the classroom by using criteria very similar to those we outlined in Chapter 2 for print literature: (1) The film should provide students with a viewing experience to which they can personally connect; (2) The film should provide a window to the social, cultural, or ethical issues facing young adults and society today; (3) The film should merit analysis, either in part or as a whole, whether the focus is on literary elements that are shared with written texts or on aspects of film that are unique to the medium. These criteria allow students to analyze both content and form.

This chapter identifies some of the characteristics of film as a literary art form and explores how and why film study should be part of the general literature program. Part of the enjoyment of watching a film is getting lost in the story, but many people find that understanding the unique aspects of film adds to the experience (Belton, 2005, p. 352). In the same way that understanding how a novel is written can add to a reader's appreciation, understanding how film works as an art form can add a layer of pleasure.

STUDYING FILM: CONTENT AND FORM

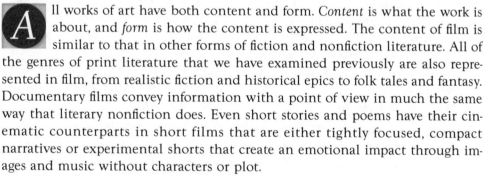

All works of art have both content and form. *Content* is what the work is about, and *form* is how the content is expressed. The content of film is similar to that in other forms of fiction and nonfiction literature. All of the genres of print literature that we have examined previously are also represented in film, from realistic fiction and historical epics to folk tales and fantasy. Documentary films convey information with a point of view in much the same way that literary nonfiction does. Even short stories and poems have their cinematic counterparts in short films that are either tightly focused, compact narratives or experimental shorts that create an emotional impact through images and music without characters or plot.

In the broadest sense, form includes all the artistic choices involved in making the film. It is how the content is put together. Form refers to the elements that make a film uniquely a film. Each part can be analyzed individually and in terms of how it affects the film as a whole, as well as how it affects a viewer.

The Language of Film Study

Because of the similarities between film and print genres, young adults and their teachers usually have the tools they need in order to discuss the content of films. Both teachers and students may, however, lack the basic concepts they need to analyze and discuss the form of films, the combination of elements that make films unique and distinct from other kinds of art such as novels, paintings, or theatrical productions (Benshoff & Griffin, 2009).

Several authors have developed frameworks and terminology for analyzing and evaluating films (e.g., Bordwell & Thompson, 2010; Costanzo, 2004; Krueger & Christel, 2001). We have selected Benshoff & Griffin's (2009) framework because it provides a succinct overview that combines content and form. The framework shows how film works as art and how it is both similar to and different from other media. It does so by focusing on the following five specific components (pp. 4–5):

1. *Literary design.* This refers to the elements of a film that come from the script and story ideas. These include story, setting, action, characters and their names, a film's title, and thematic meanings. Films contain many literary devices, such as metaphor or allegory, and they can also be categorized by genre. As is true with oral or print texts, film genres help viewers to know what to expect. They know that a slapstick comedy has different elements than a science fiction movie, and they use that knowledge to interpret what they are seeing.

2. *Visual design.* This component includes the sets, costumes, makeup, lighting, and color, as well as the arrangement of those elements.

3. *Cinematography or cinematic design.* This refers to how the camera records the visual elements that have been dictated by the literary design. This includes framing, camera lenses, camera angles, camera movement, what is in focus and what is not. The combination of visual and cinematic design—what goes into a shot—is called mise-en-scene (pronounced "meez-ahn-sen"), a French term roughly translated as "what is put in the scene."

4. *Editing.* This element of filmmaking refers to how the individual shots recorded by the camera are put together. Longer shots are usually more contemplative, while shorter shots suggest action and movement. Movies comprise hundreds of shots, which must then be put together in a meaningful way. Often, a director records multiple takes of the same scene, deciding which shots to use and in what order only after all the filming is completed. All of this is part of the editing process.

5. *Sound.* An audience both sees and hears a film. Sound affects mood, contributes to establishing a time period, and sometimes foreshadows future events or a character's intent. Point of view and characterization are influenced by what the audience hears and what it does not hear.

In Chapter 3, we showed how literary and metafictive terms facilitate conversations about young adult novels and other fiction. In the same way, understanding basic film terms helps viewers to analyze and discuss films. The glossary of film terms in the box at right is drawn from four excellent sources: John Golden's *Reading in the Dark: Using Film as a Tool in the English Classroom* (2001); William Costanzo's *Great Films and How to Teach Them* (2004); Timothy Corrigan's *A Short Guide to Writing About Film* (2010); and John Belton's *American Cinema/American Culture* (2005).

Glossary of Film Terms

Acting. An actor's interpretation of character. The acting may be controlled by factors beyond an actor's own interpretation, such as direction and style.

Arrangement. The physical relationship or position of people, objects, and background in a single shot.

Camera angle. The angle at or from which the camera looks at the action.

High angle: the camera looks down at what is being photographed.

Eye level: the camera looks at the action head-on from a position that is chest or head high.

Low angle: the camera looks up at what is being photographed.

Camera distance. The relative distance between the camera and the action being filmed, usually in relation to the actors.

Extreme close-up: the frame is filled with a part of a face or a small object.

Close-up: the frame consists of a shot of one face or object.

Medium shot: the camera pulls back far enough to show two full figures or several people from the waist up.

Long shot: the frame shows people in the distance, a landscape scene, or a large crowd.

Camera movement. The physical movement of the camera.

Pan: a stationary camera moves left or right.

Tilt: a stationary camera moves up or down.

Zoom: the camera is stationary but the lens moves, making the objects appear to grow larger or smaller giving the impression that the camera is getting closer.

Dolly: the camera moves along with the action, either on a track or manually.

Color. Colors often have symbolism. White may represent coldness or innocence, and grey may convey dullness or sadness. Color saturation refers to the intensity of a specific color.

Costumes. Clothes the characters wear, ranging from realistic contemporary attire to stylized costumes. Clothes may suggest important aspects about characters or setting.

Editing or transitions. The selection of images and sounds for inclusion in the film and how those shots are put together.

Cut: the simplest transition, in which one scene ends and another begins abruptly.

Fade in/fade out: the end of one scene gradually goes dark and the new one gradually emerges.

Dissolve: a gradual transition in which the end of one scene is superimposed over the beginning of a new one. Both images are briefly visible at the same time.

Montage: an assembly of shots intended to condense time or to develop a theme.

Wipe: a scene ends by fading from one side of the screen to the other as if being wiped away.

Flashback: a shot or sequence that shows events that take place at an earlier time than the present time in the film.

Focus. The clarity and detail of an image, produced by the type of lens used and the distance between the camera and the object being filmed.

Soft focus: blurs images slightly. Sometimes used on a close-up.

Rack focus: changing focus within a shot so a clear image becomes out of focus and something not in clear focus becomes clear. Used to highlight objects or people in a different focal plane without interrupting the shot.

Deep focus: all objects in both the foreground and background remain in focus.

Framing. What is included and what is left out of a shot. It is the "picture frame" for the shot.

Lighting. Lighting can be natural or artificial; it can direct a viewer's attention toward people or objects; and it contributes to the mood of the scene. Lighting styles are called *keys*.

High key: the scene is brightly lit, creating a lively mood and a sense of openness.

Low key: less illumination creates contrasts and can create an ominous feeling. Patches of light are set against darkness and shadows.

(continued)

Glossary of Film Terms, continued

Neutral key: lighting is even and balanced.

Front lighting: light is even across a character's face, creating a flattering effect of innocence or openness.

Bottom lighting: lighting is from below the face, which can produce distortions and a feeling of terror.

Sets and setting. The location in which the action takes place and the props contained therein.

Shot. The basic unit of film construction. A shot is a consecutive series of film frames that shows continuous action. It is the image that remains on screen until it is replaced by another. Shots of the same general

action, time, and location are arranged into scenes. A scene is a segment of a narrative film that most often takes place in a single time and place and is comprised of a series of shots.

Sound. Sound and music create a mood, give a sense of pace, create realism, develop plot and character, and create symbolism.

Diegetic: sound that can be heard by the characters.

Nondiegetic: sound that cannot be heard by the characters. Often this includes the musical score and voice-over narration.

This specialized vocabulary should not be regarded as a list of terms to be memorized. Rather, these concepts are tools to help teachers and students think about film. Just as the tools of construction are mastered by a carpenter, film terminology will be learned effectively if it is introduced when relevant for analyzing and discussing films. Film concepts can be taught in ways similar to literary elements, throughout the K–12 curriculum with a variety of increasingly complex texts. Viewers develop cinematic literacy over time by viewing, talking, and writing about movies.

Film Study Scope and Sequence

Alan Teasley and Ann Wilder (1997) recommend a sequence of film study that fits well with a traditional English language arts curriculum. They suggest that students in grades six through eight learn basic film terms and learn to write film reviews within a thematic unit. By ninth grade, film reviews should be expanded to include an analysis of cinematic elements. Studying film genres fits well with the curriculum at this level.

Following the introduction to film study in grades six through nine, students will be prepared to engage in complex analyses of films. Teasley and Wilder (1997) suggest adding international films in tenth grade; the unfamiliarity of these films will force close viewing. American film classics easily fit in with the study of American literature, the mainstay of many eleventh-grade literature classes. British films or films from countries historically influenced by Britain are a good choice for twelfth grade. Films of canonical works, especially Shakespeare, are readily available.

Just as an author study helps to develop students' appreciation for the craft of written literature, a director study can develop students' appreciation for the craft of filmmaking. In a director study, students view selected scenes, discuss films in their entirety, and even read about the films of a single master of the art form.

Alfred Hitchcock

The filmmaking career of Alfred Hitchcock (1899–1980) spanned more than 50 years, beginning in the silent film era and transitioning to television in the mid-1950s. Hitchcock's films are a rare mix of critical and commercial success. His work is considered all the more remarkable because he was able to make "exceptionally personal films entirely within the genre factory system" (Monaco, 2009, p. 348). The popularity and quality of his films, along with their availability (all of his post–silent era films are available through commercial sites), make Hitchcock's films a good choice for classroom viewing.

In the 1950s French critics began to include Hitchcock in a small group of directors they referred to as auteur, meaning author. An **auteur director** develops a personal vision for a film by controlling all aspects of filmmaking. As an auteur, one of Hitchcock's proclivities was making cameo appearances in his films as a way of "signing his work" (Carter, 2008). Hitchcock made no attempt to maintain fidelity to literary source materials; in fact, he stated, "What I do is to read a story only once, and if I like the basic idea, I just forget all about the book and start to create cinema" (Truffaut, 1966, cited in Camp, 1978, p. 232). Hitchcock explained:

> A film cannot be compared to a play or a novel. It is close to a short story, which, as a rule sustains one idea that culminates when the action has reached the highest point of the dramatic curve. As you know, a short story is rarely put down in the middle, and in this sense it resembles a film. And it is because of this peculiarity that there must be a steady development of the plot and the creation of gripping situations which must be presented, above all, with visual skill.

The films of an auteur director can be recognized by their cohesive themes, perspectives, and stylistic traits and techniques (Corrigan, 2010, p. 94). As an auteur Hitchcock is closely associated with the suspense genre (Carter, 2008), although he considered his earliest films thrillers (Bordwell & Thompson, 2010). Just as calling a book "reminiscent of Stephen King" leads a reader to expect a certain kind of horror fiction, the label "Hitchcock film" leads a viewer to expect a suspense, mystery, and a twist ending.

"Part of the allure of thrillers comes from not only what their stories are about, but also how they are told. High stakes, nonstop action, plot twists that both surprise and excite, settings that are both vibrant and exotic, and an intense pace that never lets up until the adrenaline packed climax" (Find Me an Author, n.d.). Hitchcock's protagonist was usually an ordinary person who becomes embroiled in a dangerous situation that pits the main character against some person or political force (Costanzo, 2004).

Hitchcock's films serve as exemplars of specific literary and film devices. *Rear Window* (1954) is an excellent film for analyzing point of view. A photojournalist, incapacitated with a broken leg, becomes enthralled with watching the people who live in the apartment building across his back courtyard. The shots of each apartment reveal intimate details of the apartment dwellers' lives. Through a series of shots, each character's story unfolds. A point-of-view sequence shows a close-up of the photographer's face, followed by a shot of what he is looking at, and then a shot back at him for his reaction. He becomes convinced that one of the neighbors has murdered his wife. The photographer sends his girlfriend into the murderer's apartment and watches helplessly when the murderer returns home unexpectedly and she is trapped in the bedroom. Witnessing events from the point of view of the photographer, the audience is figuring out the clues the same time he is.

North by Northwest (1959) is a good choice for teaching viewers to construct meaning by combining events seen and heard with inferred information. The difference between what is seen and what is "known" is central to the film's story (Bordwell & Thompson, 2010). This film is also a good option for illustrating filmmaking techniques. The movie's trailer is available on YouTube, with Hitchcock introducing the film and its famous cornfield scene (www.youtube.com/watch?vHRfmTpmIUow).

In this scene the protagonist, Roger Thornhill (an innocent man caught up in the intrigue), gets off a bus in the middle of cornfields. Camera angles, camera movements, and the soundtrack cleverly create a sense of impending danger. An extreme high-angle shot shows Thornhill getting off the bus, followed by eye-line shots that reinforce that he is in the middle of an isolated rural area. Suspense builds: Why was this man

(continued)

dropped off on the empty road? The absence of nondiegetic sounds reinforces this isolation; diegetic sounds remain faint until a car passes. Then a car comes along and a man gets out. A long shot shows this man and Thornhill standing across the road, alone, in the middle of nowhere. The suspense builds; Thornhill's face shows his concern. However, the unknown man turns out to be one of Hitchcock's trademark misdirections. He is simply waiting for the bus. The tension drops. The sound of an airplane, at first just a low, distant rumble in the background, gradually becomes louder. The stranger comments that the crop duster is dusting where there are no crops. The plane flies closer and Thornhill starts running. The plane dives for Thornhill, and he is viewed running toward the camera with the airplane looming over him. A close shot of the plane coming toward him intensifies the danger. When the plane crashes into a truck, nondiegetic music signals that Thornhill has survived. Thornhill backs away from the burning truck and literally backs out of the scene.

The Birds (1963) can be used to teach literary elements such as motifs and symbolism as well as techniques of filmmaking. The bird motif is introduced early in the film when the main characters, Melanie and Mitch, meet at a pet shop. A mid-close-up shot shows them on either side of a birdcage. Later, another interesting shot frames Mitch beneath a large portrait of his father. The portrait represents the looming presence of the dead patriarch, whose role Mitch is expected to fill. His mother sits back to the right, stiff and austere. She has berated him for not being the man his father was.

The birds attack children on more than one occasion, representing how even the innocent are not safe. The birds also target people's eyes, perhaps commenting on people's voyeuristic nature. The final shot in the movie shows the birds in the foreground as Mitch and Melanie's car recedes in the background. The open ending offers no resolution or answer as to why the birds attacked, and what the birds symbolize is never fully revealed. Nevertheless, the image of the attacking birds is indelibly etched into many viewers' minds.

Most of the film was made on location in Bodega Bay, California, but some of the scenes were filmed in a studio. The effect of the setting on the film, described on the Film in America website (www.filminamerica.com/Movies/TheBirds/), as well as the effects of the filmmaking on the actual location, as described on Bodega Bay official website (www.bodegabay.com/features/birds.html), illustrates how setting, both real and constructed, blend together in filmmaking.

These films, or any of Hitchcock's other American films, can be used to teach the characteristics of the suspense genre. Another example is The Man Who Knew Too Much (1956). The suspense created by Hitchcock's basic story of "everyman caught in a terrible situation beyond his control" takes on a particularly ominous note because the innocent bystander in this case is a young boy. The child is kidnapped in a foreign country in an attempt to keep his parents from revealing what they have learned about a plot to assassinate a foreign dignitary.

Nine and a half minutes of what is known as the "Symphony Scene," available on YouTube (http://www.youtube.com/watch?v=rRyrDahMLOM), demonstrates how various filmmaking techniques are used to masterfully create tension that builds to a breaking point. Shot after shot of a huge concert hall is intercut with shots of the boy's mother, the killer, the intended victim, and the musicians and their instruments. Shots vary between long shots and close-ups. The music becomes louder and louder, building toward the anticipated clashing of cymbals that will signal the assassination. The mother screams as the killer takes aim, causing him to flinch. As a result he wounds—but does not kill—his target.

Music also plays a part in the boy's rescue when the mother sings very loudly and the boy, held captive in the same building, calls out when he hears the familiar voice. Shots cut back and forth between the mother singing loudly, people staring at her, the father searching for the boy, and the kidnappers trying to escape with the boy. The suspense finally breaks when the father rescues his son.

CONNECTING FILMS AND BOOKS IN THE CLASSROOM

*J*ames Monaco (2009) notes that the narrative potential of film binds it closer to the novel than to any other art form. Although Hitchcock compares the film to the short story, films, like novels, have the capacity to tell long stories in rich detail. Both are popular arts that depend on consumers. The novel and film evolved through stages of invention and change, each at one point dominating the arts and each developing multiple genres appealing to a wide range of audiences. Both have been challenged by an emerging medium—novels by films, and film by television, to a point where the novel, movies, and television are now closely intertwined.

Comparing a novel, short story, picture book, or drama to the film adaptation usually raises the issue of fidelity. Is the film true to its source material? Being faithful to the overall spirit of the original may be admirable, but William Costanzo cautions that the story in a fiction film must be refashioned using the tools of cinema.

> A movie adaptation is not so much an illustrated copy of a book but a new rendering of the story, to be appreciated on its own terms. The narrative terrain, with its significant settings, characters, and action, is redrawn on to a different kind of map by a different sort of cartographer. . . . By paying close attention to what is unique about each medium . . . students become aware of what it means to represent reality through fiction. By attending to the similarities between a movie and a book they can come to recognize what is universal in all narrative, the motives, and rewards of storytelling that transcend all media. (2004, p. 15)

Golden (2007) suggests that an initial step for understanding how the words on a page become images on a screen is to determine if an excerpt in a novel is directly filmable or requires a lot of interpretation on the part of the director or screenwriter, the person who writes the adaptation. In directly filmable excerpts, the words require little interpretation.

Consider this excerpt from *Jake Reinvented* (Korman, 2003). "I wet a wash cloth and started sponging at the front of my shirt. I looked down and noticed that Jennifer was doing the same—only her sweater was spread out on the bathmat." Actors could easily duplicate these actions, but the next paragraph cannot be adapted with the same ease. "I dropped the cloth. At that moment, I wouldn't have noticed if my shirt was soaked with sulfuric acid that was eating my flesh down to the bone. The cleanup operation, for all intents and purposes, was over" (p. 159). Jake's feelings are clear to a reader, but his thoughts cannot be shown directly. This part of the novel will require interpretation in the film adaptation.

Students can speculate about the choices a filmmaker might make. Can an expression on an actor's face adequately convey the character's feelings? Will the director use a voiceover to convey Jake's thoughts? What are other possibilities? Students can also select excerpts from well-known literary works that have been made into films and speculate on how a scene will be adapted. They can then view that scene in the film to see how closely their speculation matches the director's vision (Golden, 2007).

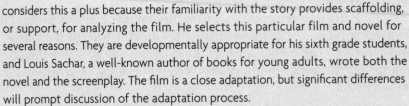

classroom scenario

Pairing a Film with a Novel

AS YOU READ, consider how the film and the book differ. In particular, think about the choices that are unique to each medium. Also, think about why Mr. Caser begins with the film instead of the novel. What knowledge of filmmaking do students need to have prior to comparing and contrasting a novel with a film adaptation?

Mr. Caser has selected the film *Holes* (Davis, 2003), based on the Newbery Medal novel by Louis Sachar (1998), for whole class study. Mr. Caser knows that many of his students have seen the film, and he

considers this a plus because their familiarity with the story provides scaffolding, or support, for analyzing the film. He selects this particular film and novel for several reasons. They are developmentally appropriate for his sixth grade students, and Louis Sachar, a well-known author of books for young adults, wrote both the novel and the screenplay. The film is a close adaptation, but significant differences will prompt discussion of the adaptation process.

The Disney DVD includes several features useful for learning about how film works, including a running commentary by Sachar and the director, Andrew Davis. The DVD also includes a short segment on making the film and a table of contents allowing scenes to be accessed individually. The Spanish and French audio tracks, Spanish subtitles, and English captions give all of Mr. Caser's students access to the film.

Mr. Caser's students are familiar with basic literary elements such as plot, setting, and character from their previous literature study; therefore, the lessons in the two-week study will focus on learning about film and considering how and why film and book versions are alike and different. He plans to begin and end the study of *Holes* with the film.

Holes is the story of teenager Stanley Yelnats. Stanley is wrongly convicted of stealing a pair of shoes and sent to Camp Green Lake. Stanley quickly learns that going to camp is not what he thought it would be. The daily routine at this detention center consists of digging holes in the desert. Stanley figures out that digging holes is more than a character building experience when he determines that the Warden is looking for something.

Mr. Caser gives students a viewing guide (see Figure 11.1) organized around the Benshoff and Griffin framework. Analyzing a film is a new experience for many of his students; therefore the questions are limited to those he considers essential for understanding the movie. He will start and stop the video whenever appropriate for discussion and writing.

After reading the novel, students return to their notes on the actors' portrayals and evaluate the performances in light of textual evidence or inferences they have made. They also examine other changes, including the addition of the Grandfather, who is not in the novel, the placement of Barf Bag's story at the beginning of the film instead of later as it was in the novel, and the added scene of Hector's mother getting off the bus. They will discuss the similarities between the abrupt transitions between present and past events. In the book, everything in present time is told from Stanley's point of view, but this is altered in the movie. The class discusses why the point of view was changed and what additional scenes became possible because of the change.

Mr. Caser's viewing guide.    *figure* 11.1

Viewing Guide

LITERARY DESIGN

1. Describe Stanley, Zero, Mr. Sir, and the Warden as they are portrayed by the actors. Consider their physical appearance, mannerisms, and how they talk.

2. Did your feelings or impressions about these characters change by the end of the movie? Why?

3. *Holes* has stories within the story. Describe the three historical flashbacks. How do the flashbacks contribute to the overall meaning of the story?

4. What is the climax, or turning point of the story?

VISUAL DESIGN

1. Once at the camp, the boys are seen in the same costume. How does this attire add to the setting?

2. When Zero returns to Camp Green Lake to get a shovel it is dark. How is this scene lit? Does this seem authentic?

3. Most of the film is in color, but some of it has a sepia or brownish tone. It also includes black and white footage from old movies. How does use of these color formats influence the Kissing Kate story?

4. What details are included in the set of the Warden's house that provide connections to the Kate Barlow story?

5. The peaches and onions are an ongoing motif. What is the importance of the peaches and onions in the outcome of the story?

CINEMATOGRAPHY

1. At the end of the movie the Warden, Mr. Sir, and Dr. Pendanski are sitting on a bench. A police officer on either side of them serves as a frame around the shot. How does this arrangement affect the resolution of the story?

2. There are many aerial and long shots of the holes and the landscape. What impression of the camp does this create?

3. When Kissing Kate Barlow is found sitting in the desert by the boat, Onion Sam is seen in an out-of-focus long shot. How does the lack of focus fit with what is happening?

4. When Zero and Stanley are climbing the mountain, shots alternate between those from below the boys and those from above them. How does this camera movement show their progress?

EDITING

1. The cuts between scenes and the flashbacks are rapid and frequent. How does this affect the viewer's understanding of the plot structure?

(continued)

2. The first encounter of the Warden is a shot of her boots. The camera slowly moves from her boots, tilts up her body, and stops at her face. What effect does this tilt movement have on the viewer's impression of her?

3. Water plays a part in transitioning, or moving, from one scene to another. Describe a scene in the story where water is used this way.

4. The montage, the succession of shots of the boys during free time, reveals a lot about the camp and the boys. Describe some of these shots. What new information is learned about the characters and setting from this scene?

5. The counseling session includes several close-ups of faces. How do these shots influence your understanding of the relationships between the characters?

SOUND DESIGN

1. Stanley's voiceover helps introduce the story. Select another place in the film with a voiceover and explain how the voiceover helps a viewer understand the story.

2. Music is used as background in many of the scenes. Pick two musical selections and describe how those songs contribute to the film. Consider music that creates a mood or is used to set up a flashback.

3. The sound of the rattlesnake adds to the suspense of Barf Bag approaching the snake. What are some other diegetic sounds—sounds the characters would hear—that add a sense of realism to the story?

Finally, the class views the film while listening to the director and author's commentary. Davis and Sachar discuss topics that should be of interest to students, such as special effects, digitally created images, their concern over the ratings of the fight scenes, and the mechanics of filmmaking, such as using a rain-making machine. They address their reasons for adding characters and scenes and changing the placement of events. They also discuss how budget costs restricted the sets they could use. Their discussion about the out-of-order way in which scenes were shot brings to light the art of filmmaking and the realization that a creative work, whether print or nonprint, is the result of a long process of development that is usually invisible to the audience. Sachar comments that Stanley had to be part of the group without being like the group. Discussion of this comment closes the film/novel study.

Choosing Books and Films to Pair

Numerous film adaptations of both contemporary and classical literature work well for a film and novel study similar to the approach modeled with *Holes*. Various film adaptations are discussed throughout this book, so we will mention just a few book-to-film adaptations that have not been discussed elsewhere. The annotated list of films supplied on the *Teenreads* site (www.teenreads.com/features/books2movies.asp) includes the film's rating and the original print source.

Bridging with Films

In Chapter 3, we described bridging as an approach in which literary works are paired or grouped for the purpose of creating intertextual connections. By comparing literary works that have literary elements, themes, or other aspects in common, you can create scaffolds in which each work supports the understanding of another. Several bridging approaches to help develop an understanding of the intertextual connections between film and literature are discussed in the following sections.

Combining books and films in an author study

An author study can effectively bridge print texts and films. Multiple film adaptations of Jane Austen's classic novels can be used in such a study, including *Emma* (1996), directed by Douglas McGrath; *Sense and Sensibility* (1995), directed by Ang Lee; and *Pride and Prejudice* (2005), directed by Joe Wright. Any one of these films could be paired with a different Austen novel. This approach should help to reveal insights into Austen's work and her world that would not likely emerge from even an in-depth study of a single novel.

By noticing recurring motifs in Austen's work, students might, for instance, acquire a new understanding of women's roles during the early 1800s, or the social conventions of dances or letter writing. *Becoming Jane* (2007) directed by Julian Jarrold, chronicles the early years of Austen's writing career. Comparing Austen's life as portrayed in this film with her life as depicted in the biography, *Jane Austen: A Life Revealed* (2011) by Catherine Reef is another possibility. This biography, written for the young adult reader, includes situations and events in Austen's life that provided the background for her novels, creating the opportunity to compare and contrast her life with the lives of her heroines.

Some film adaptations alter the setting or genre of a classic work. *Clueless* (1995), directed by Amy Heckerling, is a reimaging of Austen's *Emma*. Cher (Emma) is a good-hearted, but ditzy Beverly Hills high school student who considers herself a matchmaker. Many characterizations, events, and conflicts in the film closely parallel the novel. *Bride and Prejudice* (2004), directed by Gurinder Chadha, obviously an adaptation of *Pride and Prejudice*, is a romantic musical. Some of the dialogue remains intact from the novel, and the characters are very close to the original depictions in temperament and role. The film is set in India, England, and California; this cross-cultural setting emphasizes Austen's theme of the social barriers created by nationality, class, and economic status.

Combining books and films to demonstrate a literary element

Another approach to bridging is to examine a single literary element as it appears in two different works. The technique of multiple narrators, for example, can be explored by viewing *Reversal of Fortune* (Schroeder, 1990) in preparation for reading the complex classic *The Sound and the Fury* (Faulkner, 1929). Both works are told from multiple points of view. Mary T. Christel (2001) recommends stopping the film after each character presents his or her account of the

a sample

. . . OF **FILMS** BASED ON LITERATURE

The Adventures of Huck Finn. Directed by Stephen Sommers, 1993. Based on *The Adventures of Huckleberry Finn* by Mark Twain (1885). Huck runs away from his drunken father. He floats down the Mississippi River with Jim, an escaped slave. PG.

The Color Purple. Directed by Steven Spielberg, 1985. Based on the Pulitzer Prize-winning *The Color Purple* (1982) by Alice Walker. The film chronicles the life and oppressive marriage of a poor Southern black woman during the early to mid-1900s. PG-13.

The Count of Monte Cristo. Directed by Kevin Reynolds, 2002. Based on *The Count of Monte Cristo* (1844) by Alexandre Dumas. Edmond Dantes is wrongfully imprisoned. He escapes after 14 years, finds a treasure, and becomes the fabulously rich Count of Monte Cristo. He seeks revenge on those responsible for his imprisonment. PG-13.

December Boys. Directed by Rod Hardy, 2007. Based on *December Boys* (1994) by Michael Noonan. A group of four adolescent orphans, all with the same birth mother, compete to be the most adoptable. PG-13.

The Diary of Anne Frank. Directed by George Stevens, 1959. Based on a screenplay by Frances Goodrich and Albert Hackett (1956). This is the story of Anne Frank's life during World War II.

Flipped. Directed by Rob Reiner, 2010. Based on *Flipped* (2001) by Wendelin Van Draanen. The changing relationship of neighbors Bryce and Juli is chronicled from second grade through junior high. PG.

The Gift of the Magi. Directed by Scott Mansfield, 2002. Based on a short story of the same name by O. Henry (1906). A young husband and wife both sell what they hold most dear to buy the other a special gift, only to find out the gift they bought was for the item they each sold. PG.

Great Expectations. Directed by David Lean, 1946. Based on *Great Expectations* (1876) by Charles Dickens. Orphaned Pip grows up under the patronage of an unknown benefactor. He later discovers that he is being helped by a convict he once befriended. Pip's expectations for himself change as he comes to realize that wealth and social class are not as important as he once thought. In the end Pip is reunited with his love interest, Estella.

Lord of the Flies. Directed by Peter Brook, 1963. Based on *Lord of Flies* (1954) by William Golding. A plane-load of schoolboys is stranded on a tropical island during war time. The boys revert to their most basic instincts in their quest to stay alive. Issues of the nature of mankind and civilization are explored. PG.

The Lovely Bones. Directed by Peter Jackson, 2009. Based on *The Lovely Bones* (2002) by Alice Sebold. A teenage girl murdered by a neighbor watches over her family, her killer, and a detective trying to solve the case. PG-13.

My Sister's Keeper. Directed by Nick Cassavetes, 2009. Based on *My Sister's Keeper* (2004) by Jodi Picoult. Anna was conceived to keep her ill older sister alive, but she takes her parents to court to stop an impending organ transplant. PG-13.

The Remains of the Day. Directed by James Ivory, 1993. Based on *The Remains of the Day* (1989) by Kazuo Ishiguro. The narrator for this novel is a loyal butler who, through a series of flashbacks, considers his relationship with Lord Darlington, his own father, and a female servant. PG.

Whip It. Directed by Drew Barrymore, 2009. Based on *Whip It* (2009) by Shauna Cross. Bliss' mother wants her to compete in beauty pageants. Bliss, played by Ellen Page, wants to be the queen of the roller derby. PG-13.

events to discuss how each perspective alters students' interpretation of what has happened.

Films need not be viewed in their entirety to provide purposeful links to literary elements that also appear in written texts. John Golden's (2001) description of a few scenes from *Jaws* (Spielberg, 1975) is sufficient for demonstrating point of view. Golden points out that after several shots of people in the water and men in boats with rifles, the camera switches to a water-level shot, which is a signal to the audience of an imminent attack. This is followed by several underwater shots, which could represent the shark's point of view or an authorial point of view similar to third-person omniscient. Next, a dorsal fin emerges above the surface of the water. The audience sees the swimmers panic but cannot see where the shark is. The viewers then learn that the fin was a hoax and there is no shark. The different shots in the scene illustrate how point of view can be used to create suspense. They also provide an example of how the rapidly shifting viewpoints in films differ from the fairly consistent point of view used in many print works of fiction (p. 79).

Centering a literacy unit on films and books

Bridges between multiple films and literary works can be created within a unit-centered literacy routine. If a unit focuses on a topic or theme, then student engagement with that topic or theme will be intensified by analyzing multiple works (Christel, 2001). In a unit to help build understanding of living with a disability, for example, the teacher may begin by showing the highly acclaimed film *My Left Foot* (1989), directed by Jim Sheridan. The movie is based on Christy Brown's autobiography (1954). Brown was a 20th-century Irish painter born with cerebral palsy. He held the paintbrush in his left foot, the only part of his body that he could control. This film pairs well with *Stuck in Neutral* (Trueman, 2000), a novel about a very intelligent boy named Shawn who also has cerebral palsy. Shawn is totally aware of his surroundings, and he can remember everything he has ever heard. He considers his life fulfilling, but he fears his father is going to kill him because his father sees him as severely retarded and assumes he must be suffering greatly. Other books about teenagers with cerebral palsy include *Stoner & Spaz* by Ron Koertge (2002) and *Accidents of Nature* by Harriet McBryde Johnson (2006).

The study of cerebral palsy could continue by viewing selected scenes from *Door to Door* (2002) directed by Steven Schachter. It is about a man with cerebral palsy who creates a successful life for himself as a door-to-door salesman.

Most commercial feature films either create or adapt a fictional story, so they can be easily connected with the content and even many of the techniques of novels and other fiction. Documentary films provide similar connections to the content and form of nonfiction print literature.

DOCUMENTARY FILMS: CINEMATIC NONFICTION

Like literary nonfiction, **documentary films** combine information and artistry in order to elicit both understanding and appreciation from an audience. Although documentary films have sometimes been used in content area classrooms, little attention has been given to exploring the broad range of documentary films or to examining the techniques used to create effective nonfiction on film.

Types of Documentaries

Documentary films may be categorized or grouped in different ways. Bordwell and Thompson (2010) classify documentaries by genre, including the following:

- The **compilation film** is produced by combining images from archival sources.
- The **interview,** or "talking heads," **film** is a compilation of people's testimony about something.
- The **portrait documentary** centers on someone's life.
- The **nature documentary,** as its name implies, records some aspect of nature; these films may be seen in IMAX format.
- The **direct cinema documentary** records an ongoing event as it happens with minimal interference from the filmmaker. This type of documentary became possible following the development of portable cameras and sound equipment in the 1950s and 1960s. These films may also be called *cinema verite*, a French term for "truthful cinema." An example of cinema verite is *Hoop Dreams* (James, 1994), a documentary about two aspiring basketball players.
- A **synthetic documentary** combines several genres. This kind of film may combine archival footage with interviews and cinema verite–type filming.

Bordwell and Thompson (2010) also make a distinction between films intended to provide information in an analytical way, which they call **categorical documentaries,** and documentaries intended to make an argument and present a particular point of view, which they label **rhetorical documentaries.**

The focus of categorical documentaries is on informing the viewer about the subject, and they usually progress from a narrow focus to a broader view on the topic. The introduction of the topic is usually followed by interviews or narration grouped by subtopics related to the main subject. *Gap-toothed Women* (1987) directed by Les Blank is an example (www.lesblank.com/more/gap.html). The film is segmented into clearly defined sections such as genetic and cultural explanations for gaps—the space between the front teeth—and its relation to self-esteem, careers, and creativity of women with this facial feature (Bordwell and Thompson (2010). It is a good film for young adults because of its positive portrayal of individuals with unique traits in a society that narrowly defines attractiveness. A categorical documentary does not preclude a message or point of view, but its primary intent is to inform, not persuade.

The purpose of a rhetorical documentary is to persuade an audience to adopt a particular opinion and sometimes to take action in support of that opinion. By its nature, a rhetorical documentary is not about scientific truth but rather viewpoints that are frequently ideological. The filmmakers often provide an emotional context for their argument in an attempt to influence a viewer's behavior (Bordwell & Thompson, 2010, p. 359).

Arguably, Michael Moore is the best-known documentary filmmaker in the rhetorical category. His films *Bowling for Columbine* (2002), about the 1999 tragedy at Columbine High School in Colorado and the U.S. penchant for guns and violence; *Fahrenheit 9/11* (2004), about President Bush and the War in Iraq; and *Sicko* (2007), an analysis of health care in the United States, are among the five top-grossing nonfiction films of all time as of 2009. Moore is the narrator and central figure in all of his "essay" films and makes no pretense of objectivity (Monaco, 2009, pp. 315–316).

Another well-known nonfiction film that profoundly impacted public opinion was *An Inconvenient Truth* (2006), a documentary of former Vice President Al Gore's lectures on global warming directed by Davis Guggenheim. The film won two Academy Awards and resulted in Gore sharing in a Nobel Peace Prize with the UN Intergovernmental Panel on Climate Change (Monaco, 2009, pp. 315–316).

Analyzing Documentary Films

A different approach to understanding documentaries is to consider how information is presented. Golden (2006) proposed a useful framework for analyzing a nonfiction film by examining each of its tracks—visual, audio, and text or graphics. The visual track includes all the images presented on screen. This can include primary footage shot by the documentarian and archival or found footage shot by someone else. Visual images can also be still images such as photographs. The audio track is comprised of the film's sounds, including voices in dialogue or narration, music, or sound effects. The text or graphic track is made up of all the writing and graphics. This includes charts, drawings, and captions that identify a person or place or provide language translations.

The Endurance: Shackleton's Legendary Antarctic Expedition (2000) directed by George Butler is an example of a documentary that successfully blends audio, visual, and graphic elements to present a factually based biography. In 1914, British explorer Sir Ernest Shackleton set out on an ill-fated expedition to Antarctica. The ship became trapped in ice, and the crew tried to escape in the lifeboats.

The 2000 documentary is an excellent choice for directing students to consider how the audio, visual, and graphic elements work together to create a cohesive film. The film includes some original black and white footage taken by the expedition's photographer, Frank Hurley. Interspersed with the original film is contemporary footage of the original sites in Antarctica. Still photos and original negatives are shown. The film, narrated by actor Liam Neeson, includes interviews with the surviving relatives of key crew members. Subtitles augment speech that is difficult to understand. Parts of letters and diaries are read aloud. Sound effects (wind, breaking ice) and background music flesh out the audio track. A map of Antarctica illustrates the location of the *Endurance*.

Documentaries in the Classroom

Documentaries can develop the context, the underlying values and beliefs, for a particular theme, situation, or genre. For example, the Shackleton film illustrates the state of mind of an explorer struggling to survive. Viewing this film as a preface to reading novels about survival and adventures may help students better understand a character's motivation and determination.

Historical documentaries can provide factual background in preparation for reading historical fiction about a particular place, person, or event. *Hiroshima-Nagasaki, August 1945* by Eric Barnouw (1970) is fashioned around actual footage taken by a Japanese cameraman following the dropping of the atomic bomb (www.youtube.com/watch?v=Ob76d6B1AuI). *Triumph of the Will* (1935) by Leni Riefenstahl records the 1934 Nazi Party Congress at Nuremburg, a massive propaganda rally designed to spread the party's beliefs to the German people. These two films could be grouped thematically with other war documentaries, such as the Academy Award–winning film about the Vietnam War, *Hearts and Minds* (1974) by Peter Davis. These and other historical documentaries could provide a prelude to many of the novels described in Chapter 5.

Documentaries can help young adults understand that history is complex and that a historical event can be interpreted in different ways. Documentaries also can help students consider important current issues from various perspectives. For example, Marshall Curry's *If a Tree Falls: A Story of the Earth Liberation Front*, a 2012 Academy Award-nominated film, examines when and how environmental activism becomes terrorism. The film focuses on Daniel McGowan, an environmental activist who participated in two acts of arson in 2001. He was arrested years later and sent to prison. No one was killed during in the arson; nonetheless, the crime was declared an act of terrorism and resulted in a severe sentence. The film asks whether or not McGowan was guilty of terrorism, if the severity of his punishment is appropriate, and what constitutes legitimate acts of protest.

The list of documentaries on page 345 about topics relevant to today's youth should solicit questions about the different perspectives presented in the films.

Resources for using documentaries in the classroom

The Media Education Foundation (www.mediaed.org) provides outstanding resources for teaching, viewing, and buying documentaries. Their available documentaries cover a wide range of topics and issues categorized into four critical media literacy categories: media, gender & diversity; media & health; media, race & representation; and commercialism, politics & media. Each title links to a video clip of the documentary, a print summary, free teaching guides, and purchase information. The documentaries must be purchased from this site, but the auxiliary resources are free and extensive. Several minutes of the films can be viewed, providing a good sense of the content and form. Print materials include synopses, supporting data, instructional suggestions, and links to related websites. Also available are techniques for active listening.

"Documentaries Searching for the Truth" (Young Minds Inspired/Academy of Motion Picture Arts and Sciences, n.d.) available at www.oscars.org/education-outreach/teachersguide/documentaries/index.html provides excellent background information on viewing and making documentaries. This guide is designed for students in high school English language arts, visual arts, and communications classes. Lorraine Grula's *Making a Video: Where to Start* (n.d.) at http://videoproductiontips.com/making-a-documentary-where-to-start/ includes specific information on equipment, video production, and the journalism skills necessary to create quality documentaries.

America the Beautiful. Directed by Darryl Roberts, 2010. This film examines our beauty-obsessed culture, especially the role of media in forming and perpetuating standards of beauty. Roberts explores issues such as plastic surgery, harmful ingredients in beauty products, and eating disorders.

As Real as Your Life. Directed by Michael Highland, 2006. Highland exposes his 10-hour per day addiction to video games. He also addresses the role video games have in our society and the impact on people's lives when the virtual world becomes all-consuming. The original version of the film was presented at the Princeton Student Film and Video Festival.

Billy the Kid. Directed by Jennifer Venditti, 2007. Billy is a teenager who is dealing with issues familiar to most teens, like first love and struggling to fit into the small town where he lives. Billy's behavior, however, signals that he is unlike other kids. It is not until after the completion of the film that Billy is diagnosed with Asperger's syndrome.

Bigger, Stronger, Faster. Directed by Chris Bell, 2008. Winning at all costs is explored in this film about the personal use of steroids by Bell and his brothers. He interviews athletes, trainers, medical experts, members of a fitness center, and a congressional representative. The concept of which drugs society finds acceptable and unacceptable is explored.

Devil's Playground. Directed by Lucy Walker, 2002. This film tells the stories of four teens' undergoing the Amish tradition of *rumspringa,* a time during adolescence when they are allowed to experience the "English" world so that they can decide whether or not they will remain Amish. Most do. If they do not, the consequences can be severe. One of the issues that emerges is whether or not adolescents should be expected to make life-altering decisions.

Frontline: Juvenile Justice. Directed by Laura Rabhan Bar-On and Janet Tobias, 2001. This film focuses on four juvenile offenders and the issue of whether teens should be tried as adults or juveniles. Defenders of the juvenile system stress the youths' dysfunctional families, their possibility of being rehabilitated, and the fact that the juvenile system is less harsh. Prosecutors stress the severity of the teens' crimes and the failure of past rehabilitation attempts.

Gunnin' for that #1 Spot. Directed by Adam Yauch, 2008. Eight of the nation's top-ranked high school basketball players are documented as they work toward playing in the first Boost Mobile Elite 24 Hoops Classic game. Includes footage of games and interviews with players, coaches, trainers, and family.

Monica & David. Directed by Alexandra Codina, 2009. Two individuals with Down syndrome marry. The film focuses on the days before the wedding and the months after as they and their families adjust to their married life.

Supersize Me. Directed by Morgan Spurlock, 2004. Spurlock examines the impact of fast food on the health of Americans. As part of his study he ate all his meals at McDonalds for one month. His physical and psychological well-being was dramatically damaged, illustrating that a unhealthy diet can have a very negative effect in a short amount of time. The documentary was nominated for an Academy Award.

Waiting for "Superman." Directed by Davis Guggenheim, 2010. This exposé of the failures of the American educational system focuses on specific students and how their schools are not adequately educating them.

Anita Jetnikoff's two-part series "Making a Micro-documentary on a Shoe-string Budget" (2008) and Andrea Hayes' "Cut to the Chase: A Guide to Teaching Documentary Film as Text" (2007), provide step-by-step directions for developing and making student documentaries. These sources were used for the following Classroom Scenario.

classroom scenario

Making a Documentary

AS YOU READ, consider the steps the teacher follows to guide the students as they make a documentary.

Mr. Novitsky's class has been viewing, discussing, and evaluating documentaries. They are familiar with the different types and purposes of documentaries and with basic filmmaking techniques. He is ready to introduce them to another stage in their critical media literacy development. The class is going to make documentaries.

This is a new experience for his class, so he limits the types of documentaries to interview, portrait, nature, or direct (described earlier) and the length from five to seven minutes. Students brainstorm ideas, including interviewing the principal, a teacher, or a coach; portraying particular students such as the editor of the school paper or the lead in the spring play; filming the animals that live in a nearby park; and documenting the basketball team as they prepare for a game or the school choir as it performs during a district competition.

Each team of five students identifies the central problem or issue they want to examine. They write a single focus sentence about the topic, asking themselves if it is a topic that someone would care about and what they want the audience to think or feel. They write a detailed summary that includes considerations of their subjects and audience, filmmaking techniques, the action sequence, and the points of tension. Then they determine each person's primary role, such as videographer, interviewer, and editor.

Mr. Novitsky goes over the equipment, digital cameras, tripod, USB drives, and external microphones that they will use. Their technology lab has computers with editing software and a video capture facility. They develop a shooting schedule. After shooting, they edit the film and prepare it for viewing. They add elements such as music, a title, and credits. The final product is viewed only by the class. Students analyze each film in terms of the filmmakers' intent. They also consider if it changed how they felt about the topic or issue. Mr. Novitsky directs the discussion from the specific to the general, and the filmmakers draw some conclusions about the influence of media based on their classmates' responses to their films.

CRITICAL MEDIA LITERACY: FILM AS A CULTURAL AND ECONOMIC FORCE

Most of the readers of this book have never known a time when television did not exist or a movie theater did not show several new releases each week. Television programs advertise films, and the theater's coming attractions advertise more films. Bookstores display books paired with DVDs of the film adaptation, and book covers feature actors from the film version of the novel. Audiences have an endless array of films to choose from, and they are inundated with these choices.

Media permeates young adults' lives, so teachers may assume that constant exposure has made them more astute about interpreting the meaning and intentions of various forms of mass media. In fact, secondary students who have no instruction in critical media literacy tend to cite films over text sources when asked to consider historical events (Butler, Zaromb, Lyle & Roediger, 2009, as cited in Stoddard & Marcus, 2010). Students also tend to consider the events depicted in historical motion pictures as fact, even when they recognize inaccuracies (Marcus, 2005, as cited in Stoddard & Marcus, 2010). It appears that young adult viewers are likely to benefit from explicit instruction in critical media literacy.

Critical media literacy recognizes that media images are constructed and that the media makers are influenced by their own culture and experiences. Likewise, consumers construct meaning based on their own cultural background and life experience (Tisdell & Thompson, 2007). **Critical media literacy** focuses on analyzing media and related components. For many educators, critical media literacy also includes the production of media texts, especially media texts that challenge messages in the dominant discourse (Kellner & Share, 2007).

Film: Reflecting and Shaping Culture

Culture is shaped by many forces, including family, church, school, and mass media. A culture emerges when a group or class of people has a shared ideology, or a set of beliefs considered true and acceptable. Ideology is spread by example (Benshoff & Griffin, 2009). "Film has become a major component in the way individuals and groups view the world and consequently how they operate in it" (Monaco, 2009, p. 291). "This is especially significant in regard to current social issues, and to how media affects people's beliefs and ideas about groups both similar to and very different from themselves based on race, class, gender religion, marital status and sexual orientation" (Tisdell & Thompson, 2007, p. 654).

A critical media approach to film includes understanding how film, like every other art form, is a product of a particular culture and a reflection of a particular time. Culture contributes, for instance, to the fluctuating popularity of film genres. What was happening during a particular time period and how people reacted to those historical events influenced the kinds of movies they watched. The science fiction films of the 1950s, replete with monsters and mutants created by hydrogen bombs, reflect society's anxieties about the rapidly developing technology of that decade. Bordwell and Thompson (2010, pp. 336–337) suggest that genre conventions work by arousing emotions while remaining within socially approved attitudes. For example, gangster or bad guy films are popular because film audiences enjoy the tough, antisocial view of the world, but at the same time they want order and justice. The bad guy usually is caught or dies.

Consider for a moment, the first epic feature-length motion picture movie ever made, D. W. Griffith's *Birth of a Nation* (1915). The technology used to make this three-hour silent movie was highly praised, and it was the highest grossing film of the silent film era. This film depicts the Reconstruction of the South after the Civil War, using vicious stereotypes of African Americans. It promotes the superiority of the Aryan race and praises the Ku Klux Klan (Berkhofer, 2008, p. 176). It may be conjecture to say that there was a causal relationship between this movie and resurgence in Klan membership that escalated violence toward blacks; however, it definitely contributed to the way Reconstruction was viewed in the early decades of the 20th century (Lavender, 2001). "*The Birth* illustrated the enormous power of the motion picture medium to communicate ideological arguments" (Belton, 2005, p. 16).

An image of a group of people does not have to be malicious or overtly negative to have a deleterious effect if the portrayal perpetuates a cultural stereotype. The authors of this book watched "The Lone Ranger" on television in the 1950s, with Clayton Moore as the Lone Ranger and Jay Silverheels as Tonto, the "good Indian." As the faithful sidekick, Tonto spoke little, perhaps suggesting his limited English. He followed the Lone Ranger without question, and most viewers now would see him as subservient. When we were children, however, the faithful Tonto seemed a positive image, especially compared to the more common depiction of American Indians as savage warriors in many westerns of the day. In either case we unquestioningly absorbed the dominant ideology of the time, one that saw white expansion as natural and American Indian assimilation as inevitable.

Films that have been instrumental in shaping attitudes toward American Indians over the years (Benshoff & Griffin, 2009; Costanzo, 2004) include John Ford's early Westerns such as *Stagecoach* (1939); *Billy Jack* (Laughlin, 1971); *Little Big Man* (Penn, 1970); *A Man Called Horse* (Silverstein, 1970); *Windwalker* (Merrill, 1981); *Dances with Wolves* (Costner, 1990); *The Last of the Mohicans* (Mann, 1992); the animated *Pocahontas* (Gabriel & Goldberg, 1995); *Smoke Signals* (Eyre, 1998); *Windtalkers* (Woo, 2002); and *Bury My Heart at Wounded Knee* (Simoneau, 2007). Viewing these films in chronological order may help students identify how attitudes toward American Indians and the settling of the West have shifted throughout the years. A similar list could be made for most cultural and minority groups.

Questions for viewing these films could include:

- Does the film perpetuate stereotypes; for example, portraying individuals as primitive savages or as noble, tragic figures, or are they portrayed as multifaceted human beings?
- Is the diversity within the American Indian culture portrayed?
- From whose point of view is the story told?
- Are the American Indians, especially in the lead roles, played by white or American Indian actors?
- How does the choice of lead actors impact the portrayal of American Indians?
- How is the relationship between whites and American Indians depicted?

Oppositional viewing

An **oppositional viewing** or **reading** actively questions the ideological assumptions in the film or text (Benshoff & Griffin, 2009). A dominant reading means that the filmmaker and viewer share the same cultural position. Critical media literacy encourages individuals to "interrogate" texts that may reproduce prejudices (Gainer, 2010).

We have selected a few points from Harry Benshoff and Sean Griffin's summary of an alternative or oppositional reading of *The Lion King* (Allers & Minkoff, 1994), a highly profitable animated Walt Disney feature, to demonstrate how a film might be interrogated. They suggest that people who enjoy the film most likely cheer for Simba and his acceptance of his role as future king. Those with an oppositional perspective view the film as perpetuating the belief of white patriarchal privilege. Simba inherits his right to be a ruler because he is the son. The powerless female lions are delegated to the role of love interests, when in reality female lions are hunters. Other oppositional observations are that this film, which is set in Africa, depicts no African culture and that the African-influenced music was written by white musicians. Simba and his love interest are voiced by white actors. African Americans voice only characters who behave foolishly, thus perpetuating old racial stereotypes.

Benshoff and Griffin do not suggest that the Walt Disney Company purposely made a racist or sexist film, nor do they posit a particular reading as more valid than another. In fact, they point out that there is no single definitive reading of any text. If a reader can provide examples from a text to support a reading, then that interpretation becomes valid. They do, however, explain that when a particular oppositional perspective becomes accepted by a culture and consumers' ideological assumptions change, films will change. For example, overtly racist images are no longer acceptable to most audiences (p. 17).

Critical viewing of documentaries

Some of the stereotyping and oversimplifying that may characterize Westerns and other popular movie genres can be explained by the audience's expectations of a gripping story with plenty of action in a short time. Documentaries, on the other hand, promise audiences true stories. With that in mind, it is important to help students view documentaries critically. Persuasive documentaries, in particular, are likely to manipulate elements in order to promote a point of view or message. The classic *Nanook of the North* by Robert Flaherty (1922), considered to be the first important documentary, combined genuine footage of the Canadian Inuit with staged events of traditional customs that were no longer practiced (Berkhofer, 2008, p. 181). Documentaries often focus on cultural conventions and the ideologies of various groups or individuals. As John Golden states, "Ostensibly, documentaries are true stories starring real people, produced to inform an audience about an issue" (2006, p. 3). Even though documentaries claim to describe "real" events or tell the truth, they do "straddle the categories of fact and fiction, art and document, entertainment and knowledge" (Godmilow & Sharpiro, 1997, p. 80).

The Business of Films

Making a commercial film involves a succession of decisions. Some decisions have to do with artistic choices, others with financial concerns. All art forms have some economic ties. Financial support may come in the form of selling a novel to a publisher, a painting to a museum, or a movie to a distributor. Some artists support their projects through a grant or private patronage (Bordwell & Thompson, 2010).

The public is probably more aware of the economics of film than any other art form. Several daily television shows report how much money newly released movies make and remind people about the opulent lifestyles of some movie stars. However, most young adults probably do not consider the economic structure of the film industry from a critical media perspective. But doing just that will help them understand how the desire for profit shapes their filmgoing experiences (Kellner & Share, 2005).

Filmmaking is a business that involves many, many people, all presumably trying to make a living. Most films, however, lose money (Moore, 2007). This basic economic fact influences what films get made and where they are shown. Only the big Hollywood studios, most of which are international media conglomerates (McDonald & Wasko, 2008), have the capital to cover the losses from a film. They support their many money-losing films with the profits made from their few blockbusters (Moore, 2007).

In addition to production costs, a company must consider the amount needed for marketing and distributing the completed movie. To put this into perspective, the conglomerate-owned film companies produce one third to one half of all theatrical releases, but this accounts for 74 to 85 percent of all box office revenues. In 2005, the top five major studio releases earned more domestically than all of the 345 independent releases combined (Schatz, 2008). Most independent production companies do not stay in business long; they simply lack the money to support their efforts (Moore, 2007).

The genre and star systems

In order to minimize their risk, filmmakers rely on both the genre and star systems. When a genre of film is financially successful, many films of the same ilk follow as producers try to duplicate a box office winner. The challenge for a film producer is that a film must be similar to commercially successful genre films, while offering something different (Belton, 2005). The Hitchcock films mentioned earlier are good examples of films that balanced the audience's expectations for a thriller with unique settings, characters, and circumstances.

Any commercial magazine rack, television programming guide, or online search quickly reveals the amount of print and nonprint media devoted to movie stars. Their private lives are anything but private, and film producers view them as a form of capital.

> Since stars sell things—films, magazines, tabloid papers, etc.—stardom is a form of resource or capital used by Hollywood. The value of stardom partly relies on its rarity, for only a few lead performers achieve star status, and the star system also manages the deployment of stardom, determining who will be recognized as a star and controlling the contexts in which stardom will be used. The small cluster of companies that form the contemporary star system therefore make, manage, and control the capital of stardom in Hollywood cinema. (McDonald, 2008, p. 180)

We agree with film studies experts Bordwell and Thompson (2010) and Corrigan (2010) that money considerations do not make an artist any less creative or a project less worthwhile. We also agree with Corrigan's recommendation that viewers adjust their expectations depending on the type of film. An independent film shown in a local art house cannot fairly be judged by the same criteria as a multimillion dollar movie shown in a showcase theater. Simply put, viewers should adjust their expectations in light of a film's budget. This does not mean they lower them but rather that they consider the relationship of economics, aesthetics, and the politics of filmmaking when viewing various types of films (Monaco, 2009, p. 255).

The marketing of films

Students can investigate how films are sold to an audience and how specific marketing tactics are used to influence people, particularly themselves, to see a film. The all-encompassing marketing strategy for the popular Twilight Saga movies is a good example. Many students have seen the films *Twilight* (Hardwicke, 2008), *New Moon* (Weitz, 2009), *Eclipse* (Slade, 2010), *Breaking Dawn, Part 1* (Condon, 2011), and *Breaking Dawn, Part 2* (Condon, 2012), and many will have read the books. The first film in the series, *Twilight*, was an independent film that cost $37 million to make, which is about half of the average cost of making a major studio film. An additional $30 million was spent on domestic theatrical marketing. That is comparable to the average amount spent for a major studio release. The film was an outstanding commercial success. *Twilight* made $700 million in box office and DVD revenues worldwide (Fry, 2010).

The buzz about the movie increased through social media and Internet websites such as MySpace. CNN did a segment on the book. The books' author and the films' stars appeared on national talk shows and were featured on numerous magazine covers (Marich, 2008). Chop Shop/Atlantic Records released the film's soundtrack in 2008. The midnight release of the DVD of the first film coincided with contests, sales of autographed merchandise, and surprise appearances by the actors at selected locations (Meyer, 2009).

The Twilight franchise expanded, partially because of the faithful audience of the forthcoming books and partially because of the large amount of money that was made. Students may find it interesting that product placement added to the film's financial success. The vampire Edward drives a Volvo in the film as he does in the book. Volvo featured the novels in their advertisements. Burger King invested $10 to $15 million in *Eclipse*. Their campaign included not only items at the restaurant but also games on Facebook.

The connections among the novels, the films, and other media were magnified with the publication of *Twilight: The Complete Illustrated Movie Companion* (Vaz, 2008), a behind-the-scenes guide that includes interviews, details of special effects, and photographs of the cast and scenes. Another strand linking film to print was *Twilight: Director's Notebook: The Story of How We Made the Movie Based on the Novel by Stephenie Meyer* by Catherine Hardwicke (2009).

Films are marketed in many ways. The marketing strategy for *Twilight* included targeting young and technologically astute viewers, making connections to the popular books and their author, and creating a general media blitz about the young actors. An awareness of the economic and commercial influences behind a movie can add to students' understanding of how the film industry manipulates an audience. Students can discuss how they heard about the movie. Did they hear about it online, on television, or from friends? Will they see all the films in the franchise? Why?

Selecting and Viewing Films

There is nothing inherently wrong with enjoying popular media, but teachers can help young adults become more than passive consumers who accept whatever is most vigorously marketed at them. Students can learn to make their own choices and develop their own tastes. Film festivals and reviews provide two avenues for doing so (Marich, 2009).

Film festivals

Attending film festivals provides students with opportunities to discuss film with a committed and interested young adult and adult audience. There are an estimated 800 annual multi-day film festivals in the United States (Marich, 2009, p. 285). The Toronto International Film Festival, the world's largest public festival, encourages student attendance, as does the Athens (Ohio) International Film Festival, which is free to students of Ohio. The New York International Children's Film Festival and the Chicago International Children's Film Festival are very large film fests for children and youth. Those who cannot go to festivals can take advantage of the films from the Sundance Film Festival that are shown on the Sundance Television Channel.

Some festivals are specifically for young adult filmmakers. For example, the Princeton Student Film & Video Festival's mission is to encourage and support the work of youth filmmakers and to provide a venue for showing their work to a broad audience (http://pplwebserver.princetonlibrary.org/find/teens/student-film-festival). The Student Horror Film Festival in Pennsylvania (www.emmausarts.org/when_it_happens/2011_student_horror_film_festival) is a contest open to high school and college students. The Director in the Classroom (www.thedirectorintheclassroom.com/festivals4.php) lists student film festivals by region. Each listing provides contact information, guidelines, and links to the festival's web page.

Several film festivals focus on cultural groups, thematic issues, or genres. Examples include the Cine Las Americas International Festival, showcasing Latin American, Latino, and indigenous films; the New Jersey Independent South Asian Cine Fest, dedicated to South Asian independent films; the Native American Film and Video Festival held at the Smithsonian National Museum of the American Indian; and Reel Pride Michigan, films about the LGBTI (lesbian, gay bisexual, transsexual, and intersexual) experience. The Sun Valley Spiritual Film Festival celebrates the human spirit through film. The L.A. Comedy Shorts Film Festival supports comedy shorts and includes a screenplay competition. DocUtah is dedicated to documentaries. The Maelstrom International Fantastic Film Festival is for action, animation, cult, fantasy, horror, and science fiction films.

Film criticism

Publicity campaigns rely on media outlets such as magazines, television, radio, newspaper, and websites to cover and help promote a film with stories, gossip, column items, reviews, and posted content. If consumers do not hear the buzz about a film, they are far less likely to see it (Marich, 2009). Print reviews in publications with established and respected critics, particularly the *New York Times*, influence viewers who attend more sophisticated films and art films. More than one-third of Americans actively seek the advice of film critics, and approximately one of every three filmgoers indicates he or she chooses films because of favorable reviews (Basuroy, Chatterjee & Ravid, 2003). It may be that critics influence consumers or it may be that consumers seek out the critics or review publications that they believe accurately reflect their taste. As a rule, negative reviews have less impact on big budget films with special effects and big stars. Youth and audiences of action adventure and horror films are more influenced by television coverage, especially those showing film clips (Marich, 2009, pp. 151–153).

The purpose of a film review is to persuade someone to either see or skip a film (Golden, 2007). It expresses an opinion, includes a plot summary, and provides some context for the viewer, such as the genre of the film, the name of the director or the actors, and other information that helps a filmgoer understand what the film is about. Reading professional reviews may help young adult viewers consider a film in new ways. A review sometimes opens up questions about a film that students were unable to articulate or pin down. The *New York Times* film review archives (www.nytimes.com/ref/movies/archive_a.html) is an easily accessed comprehensive index of film reviews.

Films are designed to make viewers feel a certain way and to provide an experience that no other media can provide. Writing a review is a good beginning point for students to articulate how they feel about a movie, but they also should reflect on aspects of the film that produced their feelings, expectations, and reactions. They need to relate their feelings to more objective factors concerning the film, such as its historical context, cultural background, and artistic style (Corrigan, 2010, p. 17). When reviewing a film, students should consider not only why a sequence in the film made them feel a certain way but also how the filmmaker made them feel that way (Masterpiece Theatre Learning Resources, n.d.).

"How to Write A Movie Review for Aspiring Movie Critics" on the MovieFilmReview website (www.moviefilmreview.com) provides simple guidelines for writing a five paragraph review.

- **Paragraph one.** The review should begin with bibliographic information including the title of the film, names of actors, when and where the story is set, and the genre.
- **Paragraph two.** The next paragraph is a general plot summary. Writers are cautioned not to reveal the ending.
- **Paragraphs three and four.** The third and fourth paragraphs focus on aspects of filmmaking such as acting, editing, set design, and so on. Specific examples from the film should be included.

- **Paragraph five.** The last paragraph is the reviewer's overall reaction to the film and opinion as to the quality of the film. The reviewer ends with a recommendation for potential reviewers.

Students can submit their reviews for publication to MovieFilmReview. com and *Reel Show Film Student Film Reviews* at ReelshowInt Mag, http://mag. reelshowint.com/2012/02/05/reelshow-film-student-film-reviews/ (2012).

conclusion

The rationale for including film in the English language arts curriculum, as presented by Alan Teasley and Ann Wilder in their seminal work *Reel Conversation: Reading Films with Young Adults* (1997), remains relevant today. They believe that films are already being viewed in the classroom, but often in ways that do them a disservice. Teachers may spend weeks analyzing a novel, followed by a single viewing of the film. Too frequently, film is used to entertain, fill time, or provide a reward. Teasley and Wilder propose that film is an art form that ought to have its own place in the curriculum.

Teasley and Wilder also suggest that film allows both proficient and reluctant readers to share a literary experience. Objectives for the English language arts curriculum include learning to discuss, analyze, make interpretations, and argue a position. Based on their own experiences, they found students enjoy learning about "film technique, genre conventions or the psychological and social nature of interpretation" (p. 5), all of which can encourage discussion and writing.

Lastly, Teasley and Wilder highlight the growing interest in the role of nonprint texts and the need for students to be "discerning consumers and competent producers of a variety of media" (p. 7). All media influence people's beliefs, values, and attitudes. Viewing films from a critical perspective encourages young adults to consider how films have influenced what they think about a particular group, event, or idea. Critically analyzing a creative endeavor, no matter what form it takes, requires considering the motives behind its production and the means by which people are persuaded to share in the experience.

Language arts teachers who did not experience film study in their own schooling may need some guidance in locating and selecting films. The National Film Registry (www.filmsite.org/filmreg.html) is an excellent source for this. James H. Billington, Librarian of Congress, explains that films selected and preserved by the Library of Congress must be at least ten years old and culturally, historically, or aesthetically significant. Films selected for preservation include feature films, documentaries, avant-garde and amateur productions, regional interest films, animated and short film subjects. Students may enjoy debating about whether or not they agree with selections (Library of Congress, 2009) such as Michael Jackson's *Thriller* (Landis, 1983), *The Muppet Movie* (Frawley, 1979), created by Jim Henson and Frank Oz, and *The Jungle* (Davis, 1967), a hybrid docudrama credited with changing the lives of gang members.

Print texts and visual texts can be quite literally side by side on the classroom bookshelf and in the English language arts curriculum. Young adults may view a lot of movies, but that does not guarantee that they fully appreciate how film works or why a particular film is judged to be better or worse than another. Students need direct instruction in the elements that make film a unique and distinct medium. Film and print literature have many differences, but they share many similarities as well. Films, in part, or in their entirety, provide learning opportunities for expanding students' understanding of literature. All media influence people's beliefs, values, and attitudes. Viewing films from a critical perspective encourages young adults to consider how films have influenced what they think about a particular group, event or idea. Films should be taught purposefully and directly as a component of literature study.

BIBLIOGRAPHY OF LITERATURE AND FILM FOR YOUNG ADULTS

Allers, R., & Minkoff, R. (Dirs.). (1994). *The lion king.* U.S.A.: Walt Disney Pictures.

Barnouw, E. (Dir.). (1970). *Hiroshima-Nagasaki: August 1945.* Retrieved from www.you.tube.com/watch?v+61NsljMow4.

Bar-On, L. R., (Dir.), & Tobias, J. (Dir./Writer) (2001). *Frontline: Juvenile justice.* U.S.A.: Frontline/PBS.

Barrymore, D. (Dir.). (2009). *Whip it.* U.S.A.: Mandate Pictures.

Bell, C. (Dir./Writer). (2008). *Bigger stronger faster.* U.S.A.: BSF Films.

Blank, L. (Dir.). (1987). *Gap-toothed women.* U.S.A.: Flower Films.

Brook, P. (Dir.), & Allen, L. M. (Producer). (1963). *Lord of the flies.* United Kingdom: British Lion.

Brown, C. (1954). *My left foot.* London: Secker & Warburg.

Butler, G. (Dir.). (2000). *The Endurance: Shackleton's legendary Antarctic expedition.* U.S.A.: Discovery Channel Pictures.

Cassavetes, N. (Dir.). (2009). *My sister's keeper.* U.S.A.: Curmudgeon Films.

Chadha, G. (Dir./Producer). (2004). *Bride and prejudice.* United Kingdom/U.S.A.: Pathe Pictures/Miramax films.

Codina, A. (Dir.). (2009). *Monica & David.* U.S.A.: CineMia.

Condon, B. (Dir.). (2011). *Twilight: Breaking dawn, part 1.* U.S.A.: Summit Entertainment.

Condon, B. (Dir.). (2012). *Twilight: Breaking dawn, part 2.* U.S.A.: Summit Entertainment.

Costner, K. (Dir.). (1990). *Dances with wolves.* U.S.A.: Orion Pictures.

Cross, S. (2009). *Whip it.* New York: Square Fish.

Curry, M. (2011). *If a tree falls: A story of the Earth Liberation Front.* U.S.A.: Oscilloscope Laboratories.

Davis, A. (Dir.). (2003). *Holes.* U.S.A.: Walt Disney Pictures.

Davis, C. B. (Dir.). (1967). *The jungle.* U.S.A.: 12th Oxford.

Davis, P. (Dir./Producer), & Schneider, B. (Producer). (1974). *Hearts and minds.* U.S.A.: Rialto Pictures.

Dickens, C. (1876). *Great expectations.* (F. A. Fraser, Illus.). New York: Harper.

Dumas, A. (1844). *The Count of Monte Cristo.* London: Chapman & Hall.

Eyre, C. (Dir.), & Alexie, S. (Dir./Writer). (1998). *Smoke signals.* U.S.A.: Miramax.

Faulkner, W. (1929). *The sound and the fury.* New York: J. Cape & H. Smith.

Flaherty, R. (Dir.). (1922). *Nanook of the north.* U.S.A.: Robert J. Flaherty.

Ford, J. (Dir.). (1939). *Stagecoach.* U.S.A.: Walter Wagner Productions.

Frawley, J. (Dir.). (1979). *The muppet movie.* U.S.A.: Henson Associates.

Gabriel, M., & Goldberg, E. (Dirs.). (1995). *Pocahontas.* U.S.A.: Walt Disney Pictures.

Golding, W. (1954). *Lord of the flies.* London: Faber & Faber.

Griffith, D. W. (Dir./Producer). (1915). *Birth of a nation.* U.S.A.: Epoch Film Co.

Guggenheim, D. (Dir.), & Bender, L. (Producer). (2006). *An inconvenient truth.* U.S.A.: Lawrence Bender Productions.

Guggenheim, D. (Dir.). (2010). *Waiting for "Superman."* U.S.A.: Electric Kinney Films.

Hardy, R. (Dir.). (2007). *December boys.* Australia: Australia Film Finance Corporation.

Hardwicke, C. (Dir.). (2008). *Twilight.* U.S.A.: Summit Entertainment.

Hardwicke, C. (2009). *Twilight: Director's notebook: The story of how we made the movie based on the novel by Stephenie Meyer.* New York: Little, Brown.

Heckerling, A. (Dir.), & Rudin, S. (Producer). (1995). *Clueless*. U.S.A.: Paramount Pictures.

Henry, O. (1906). The gift of the Magi. Retrieved from http://www.auburn.edu/~vestmon/Gift_of_the_Magi.html.

Highland, M. (Dir.). (2006). *As real as your life*. All Games Productions. Retrieved from http://www.michaelhighland.com/asrealasyourlife/.

Hitchcock, A. (Dir./Producer). (1954). *Rear window*. U.S.A.: Paramount.

Hitchcock, A. (Dir./Producer). (1956). *The man who knew too much*. U.S.A.: Paramount.

Hitchcock, A. (Dir./Producer). (1956). Symphony scene from *The man who knew too much*. Retrieved from www.youtube.com/watch?v+NM-SKOBfy6U.

Hitchcock, A. (Dir./Producer). (1959). *North by northwest*. U.S.A.: Metro-Goldwyn-Mayer.

Hitchcock, A. (Dir./Producer). (1959). Cornfield scene from *North by northwest*. Retrieved from www.youtube.com/watch?vHRfmTpmIUow.

Hitchcock, A. (Dir./Producer). (1963.). *The birds*. U.S.A.: Universal.

Hollander, J. (Ed.). (2005). *Stories for young people: O. Henry*. (M. Hyman, Illus.). New York: Sterling Publishing.

Ishiguro, K. (1989). *The remains of the day*. London: Faber & Faber.

Ivory, J. (Dir.). (1993). *The remains of the day*. United Kingdom/U.S.A.: Merchant Ivory Productions.

Jackson, P. (Dir./Producer), & Spielberg, S. (Producer). (2009). *The lovely bones*. New Zealand/U.S.A./United Kingdom: DreamWorks.

James, S. (Dir.) (1994). *Hoop dreams*. U.S.A.: Fine Line Features.

Jarrold, J. (Dir.) (2007). *Becoming Jane*. United Kingdom: Ardmore Studios.

Johnson, H. M. (2006). *Accidents of nature*. New York: Holt.

Koertge, R. (2002). *Stoner & Spaz*. Cambridge, MA: Candlewick Press.

Korman, G. (2003). *Jake reinvented*. New York: Hyperion.

Landis, J. (Dir./Writer), & Folsey, G. (Producer). (1983). *Thriller*. U.S.A.: Vestron Music Video.

Laughlin, T. (Dir.). (1971). *Billy Jack*. U.S.A.: Warner Brothers.

Lean, D. (Dir.). (1946). *Great expectations*. United Kingdom: General Film Distributors.

Lee, A. (Dir.). (1995). *Sense and sensibility*. U.S.A.: Columbia Pictures.

Mann, M. (Dir.). (1992). *The last of the Mohicans*. U.S.A.: 20th Century Fox.

Mansfield, S. (Dir.). (2002). *The gift of the magi*. U.S.A.: Monterey Video.

Merrill, K. (Dir.). (1981). *Windwalker*. U.S.A.: Pacific International.

McGrath, D. (Dir.). (1996). *Emma*. U.S.A.: Miramax.

Moore, M. (Dir./Writer). (2002). *Bowling for Columbine*. U.S.A.: Alliance Atlantis Communications.

Moore, M. (Dir./Writer). (2004). *Fahrenheit 9/11*. U.S.A.: Fellowship Adventure Group.

Moore, M. (Dir./Writer). (2007). *Sicko*. U.S.A.: Dog Eat Dog Films.

Noonan, M. (1994). *December boys*. Australia: University of Queensland Press.

Penn, A. (Dir.). (1970). *Little big man*. U.S.A.: Cinema Center Films.

Picoult, J. (2004). *My sister's keeper*. New York: Atria Books.

Reef, C. (2011). *Jane Austen: A life revealed*. New York: Clarion.

Reiner, R. (Dir.). (2010). *Flipped*. U.S.A.: Warner Brothers.

Reynolds, K. (Dir.). (2002). *The Count of Monte Cristo*. United Kingdom/U.S.A.: Touchstone Pictures.

Riefenstahl, L. (Dir./Producer). (1935). *Triumph of the will*. Germany: Reichsparteitag Film.

Roberts, D. (Dir./Writer). (2010). *America the beautiful*. U.S.A.: First Independent Pictures.

Sachar, L. (1998). *Holes*. New York: Farrar, Straus & Giroux.

Schachter, S. (Dir./Writer). (2002). *Door to door*. U.S.A.: Turner Home Entertainment.

Schroeder, B. (Dir.). (1990). *Reversal of fortune*. U.S.A.: Warner Brothers.

Sebold, A. (2002). *The lovely bones*. New York: Little, Brown.

Sheridan, J. (Dir.), & Pearson, N. (Producer). (1989). *My left foot*. Ireland/United Kingdom: Ferndale Films.

Silverstein, E. (Dir.). (1970). *A man called horse*. U.S.A.: National General Pictures.

Simoneau, Y. (Dir.). (2007). *Bury my heart at Wounded Knee*. U.S.A.: HBO Films.

Slade, D. (Dir.). (2010). *Twilight Saga: Eclipse*. U.S.A.: Summit Entertainment.

Sommers, S. (Dir.). (1993). *The adventures of Huck Finn*. U.S.A.: Walt Disney Pictures.

Spielberg, S. (Dir./Producer), & Kennedy, K. (Producer). (1985). *The color purple*. U.S.A.: Amblin Entertainment.

Spielberg, S. (Dir./Producer). (1975). *Jaws*. U.S.A.: Zanuck/Brown Productions.

Spurlock, M. (Dir./Producer). (2004). *Supersize me*. U.S.A.: Samuel Goldwyn Films/Roadside Attractions.

Stevens, G. (Dir.), Goodrich, F., & Hackett, A. (Writers). (1959). *The diary of Anne Frank*. U.S.A.: 20th Century Fox.

Trueman, T. (2000). *Stuck in neutral*. New York: HarperCollins.

Twain, M. (1885, 1962). *The adventures of Huckleberry Finn*. (J. Falter, Illus.). New York: Macmillan.

Van Draanen, W. (2001). *Flipped*. New York: Random House.

Venditti, J. (Dir.). (2007). *Billy the kid*. U.S.A.: Zeitgeist Films.

Walker, A. (1982). *The color purple*. New York: Harcourt Brace.

Walker, L. (Dir.) (2002). *Devil's playground*. U.S.A.: Stick Figure Productions/Columbia Pictures.

Weitz, C. (2009). *The Twilight saga: New moon*. U.S.A.: Summit Entertainment.

Woo, J. (Dir. & Producer). (2002). *Windtalkers*. U.S.A.: MGM.

Wright, J. (Dir.). (2005). *Pride and prejudice*. France/United Kingdom: Studio Canal/Working Title Films.

Yauch, A. (Dir./Producer). (2008). *Gunnin' for that #1 spot*. U.S.A.: Oscilloscope Laboratories.

WEBSITES WITH ANNOTATIONS

Director in the Classroom • **www.thedirectorinthe classroom.com/profile4.php**

Resources for educators to incorporate filmmaking in the classroom. Includes listing of student film festivals by region.

Documentaries: Searching for Truth • **www.oscars.org/ education-outreach/teachersguide/documentaries/ index.html**

Provides excellent background information on critically viewing and making documentaries.

How to Write A Movie Review for Aspiring Movie Critics • **www.moviefilmreview.com/ht**

Offers simple guidelines for writing a five paragraph review.

Making a Video: Where to Start • **http://video productiontips.com/making-a-documentary-where-to-start/**

Lorraine Grula's site; includes specific information on equipment, video production, and the journalism skills necessary to create quality documentaries.

Media Education Foundation • **www.mediaed.org/**

Resources for teaching, viewing, and buying documentaries. Each title links to a videoclip of the documentary, a print summary, free teaching guides, and purchase information.

New York Times Film Review Archives • **www.nytimes. com/ref/movies/archive_a.html**

Allows access to reviews of previously published film reviews, from the 1990s on; films are listed alphabetically.

Princeton Student Film & Video Festival • **http://ppl webserver.princetonlibrary.org/find/teens/student-film-festival**

Encourages and supports the work of youth filmmakers and provides a venue for showing their work to a broad audience.

Student Horror Film Festival • **www.emmausarts.org/ when_it_happens/2011_student_horror_film_festival**

Gives information about a contest open to high school and college students.

Teenreads • **www.teenreads.com/**

Book reviews, writing contests, author interviews, and synopses of teen fiction.

ReelshowInt Mag • **http://mag.reelshowint.com/ 2012/02/05/reelshow-film-student-film-reviews/**

Allows students to submit reviews for possible publication to MovieFilmReview.com and *Reel Show Film Student Film Reviews*.

REFERENCES

Basuroy, S., Chatterjee, S., & Ravid, S. A. (2003). How critical are critical reviews? The box office effects of film critics, star power, and budgets. *Journal of Marketing, 67*, 103–117.

Belton, J. (2005). *American cinema/American culture* (2nd ed.). New York: McGraw-Hill.

Benshoff, J. M., & Griffin, S. (2009). *America on film: Representing race, class, gender, and sexuality at the movies*. West Sussex, UK: Wiley-Blackwell.

Berkhofer, R. (2008). *Fashion history: Current practices and principles*. New York: Palgrave Macmillan.

Bodegabay.com (n.d.). *The Birds* and Bodega Bay. Retrieved from www.bodegabay.com/features/ birds.html.

Bordwell, D., & Thompson, K. (2010). *Film art: An introduction* (9th ed.). New York: McGraw Hill.

Butler, A., Zaromb, F., Lyle, K., & Roediger, H. (2009). Using popular films to enhance classroom learning:

The good, the bad, and the interesting. *Psychological Science*, 20(9), 1161–1168.

Camp, J. (1978). John Buchan and Alfred Hitchcock. *Literature Film Quarterly*, 6(3), 230–240.

Carter, R. (2008, July-August). The great Alfred Hitchcock's memorable movie cameos. *New York Amsterdam News*, p. 11.

Christel, M. T. (2001). Film in the literature class: Not just dessert anymore. In Ellen Krueger & Mary T. Christel (Eds.), *Seeing and believing: How to teach media literacy in the English classroom* (pp. 68–88). Portsmouth, NH: Boynton/Cook Heinemann.

Corrigan, T. (2010). *A short guide to writing about film* (7th ed.). New York: Longman.

Costanzo, W. V. (2004). *Great films and how to teach them.* Urbana, IL: National Council of Teachers of English.

Director in the Classroom (n.d.). Film festivals. Retrieved from www.thedirectorintheclassroom.com/festivals4.php.

Film in America (n.d.). *The birds.* Retrieved from www.filminamerica.com/Movies/The Birds/.

Find Me an Author (n.d.). Thriller fiction genre definition. Retrieved from www.findmeanauthor.com/thriller_fiction_genre.htm.

Fry, A. (2010, July 28). Movie series: *Twilight:* Marketing industries paying attention now. *Economic Times.* Retrieved from http://economictimes.indiatimes.com/features/brand-equity/Movie-series-Twilight-Marketing.

Gainer, J. (2010). Critical media literacy in middle school; Exploring the politics of representation. *Journal of Adolescent & Adult Literacy*, 53, 364–373.

Godmilow, J., & Shapiro, A. (1997). How real is the reality in documentary film? *History and Theory*, 36(4), 80–101.

Golden, J. (2001). *Reading in the dark: Using film as a tool in the English classroom.* Urbana, IL: National Council of Teachers of English.

Golden, J. (2006). *Reading in the real world: Teaching documentaries and other nonfiction texts.* Urbana, IL: National Council of Teachers of English.

Golden, J. (2007). Literature into film (and back again): Another look at an old dog. *English Journal*, 97(1), 24–30.

Hayes, A. (2007). Cut to the chase: A guide to teaching documentary film as text. *Screen Education*, 46, 96–100.

Jetnikoff, A. (2008, Spring). Making a micro-documentary on a shoestring budget. Preproduction. *Screen Education*, 5, 98–104.

Jetnikoff, A. (2008, Summer). Making a micro-documentary on a shoestring budget. Production. & post production. *Screen Education*, 52, 62–71.

Kellner, D., & Share, J. (2005). Toward critical media literacy: Core concepts, debates, organizations, and policy.

Discourse: Studies in the cultural politics of education, 26(3), 369–386.

Kellner, D., & Share, J. (2007). Critical media literacy is not an option. *Learning Strategy*, 1(10), 59–69.

Krueger, E., & Christel, M. T. (2001). *Seeing and believing: How to teach media literacy in the English classroom.* Portsmouth, NH: Heinemann.

Lavender, C. (2001). D. W. Griffith, *The Birth of a Nation* (1915). Retrieved from www.library.csi.cuny.edu/dept/history/lavender/birth/html.

Library of Congress (2009). News from the Library of Congress. Retrieved from www.loc.gov/today/pr/2009/09-250.html.

Marcus, A. S. (2005). "It is as it was": Feature film in the history classroom. *Social Studies*, 96(2), 61–67.

Marich, R. (2008). Kudos Pile Up for "Twilight" marketing. Retrieved from www.marketingmovies.net/news/kudos-pile-up-for-twilight-marketing.

Marich, R. (2009). *Marketing to moviegoers: A handbook of strategies and tactics* (2nd ed.). Carbondale, IL: Southern Illinois University Press.

Masterpiece Theatre Learning Resources. (n. d.). *Film in the classroom.* Retrieved from www.pbs.org.wgbh/masterpiece/learningresources/fic_language.html.

McDonald, P. (2008). The star system. In P. McDonald & Janet Wasko (Eds.), *The contemporary Hollywood film industry* (pp. 167–181). Oxford, UK: Blackwell Publishing.

McDonald, P., & Wasko, J. (2008). Introduction: the new contours of the Hollywood film industry. In P. McDonald & Janet Wasko (Eds.), *The contemporary Hollywood film industry* (pp. 1–9). Oxford, UK: Blackwell Publishing.

Media Education Foundation (n.d.). Documentary films; challenging media. Retrieved from www.mediated.org.

Meyer, S. (2009). *Twilight.* Retrieved from www.stepheniemeyer.com/twilight_movie.html.

Monaco, J. (2009). *How to read a film: Movies media and beyond* (4th ed.). New York: Oxford University Press.

Moore, S. (2007). *The biz: The basic business, legal and financial aspects of the film industry* (3rd ed.). Beverly Hills, CA: Silman James Press.

MovieFilmReview.com (2012). *How to write a movie review for aspiring movie critics.* Retrieved from http://www.moviefilmreview.com/ht.

National Film Registry (n.d.). National Film Registry Titles of the Library of Congress. Retrieved from www.filmsite.org/filmreg.html.

National Governors Association Center for Best Practices, Council of Chief State School Officers. (2010). *Common core state standards for English language arts & literacy in history/social studies, science, and technical subjects.* Washington, DC: Author.

New York Times. (n.d.). Film reviews. Retrieved from http://www.nytimes.com/ref/movies/archive_a.html.

Phillips, N. C. (2007). *Beyond fidelity: Teaching film adaptations in secondary schools.* Master of Arts Thesis Brigham Young University Department of English.

ReelshowInt Mag. (2012). Reelshow film student film reviews. Retrieved from http://mag.reelshowint.com/2012/02/05/reelshow-film-student-film-reviews/.

Schatz, T. (2008). The studio system and conglomerate Hollywood. In P. McDonald & J. Wasko (Eds.), *The contemporary Hollywood film industry* (pp. 13–42). Oxford, UK: Blackwell Publishing.

Stoddard, J. D., & Marcus, A. S. (2010). More than "showing what happened": Exploring the potential of teaching history with film. *High School Journal, 93*(2), 83–90.

Teasley, A. B., & Wilder, A. (1997). *Reel conversations: Reading films with young adults.* Portsmouth, NH: Heinemann.

Teenreads (n.d.). Books into movies. Retrieved from www.teenreads.com/features/books2movies.asp.

Tisdell, E., & Thompson, P. (2007). Seeing from a different angle: The role of pop culture in teaching for diversity and critical media literacy in adult education. *International Journal of Lifelong Education, 26*(6), 651–673.

Truffaut, F. (1966). *Hitchcock.* New York: Simon & Schuster.

Vaz, M. C. (2008). *Twilight: The complete illustrated movie companion.* New York: Little, Brown.

Wasko, J. (2008). Financing and production: Creating the Hollywood film commodity. In P. McDonald & J. Wasko (Eds.)., *The contemporary Hollywood film industry* (pp. 43–62). Oxford: UK: Blackwell Publishing.

Young Minds Inspired/Academy of Motion Picture Arts and Sciences, (n.d.). *Documentaries searching for the truth.* Retrieved from www.oscars.org/educationoutreach/teachersguide/documentaries/activity3.html.

CHAPTER TWELVE

Literary Criticism in the Classroom

THEORY INTO PRACTICE

chapter overview

In this chapter we define literary theory and explain the relationship between literary theory and literary criticism. We highlight three literary theories: New Criticism, reader response, and critical literacy. In our discussions, we align these theories with the criteria for literature selection (literary significance, developmental significance, and social significance) described in Chapter 2. We offer instructional approaches and methods supported by these theories. Following the discussion of the three theories, we give examples of how theories can be remixed and re-envisioned, including a discussion of instructional frameworks for combining theories. Last, a classroom scenario demonstrates how multiple theoretical perspectives can be incorporated in literature study.

FOCUS QUESTIONS

1. How does literary theory influence literary criticism?

2. How might the theories of New Criticism, reader response, and critical literacy influence the selection of literature read in school?

3. How might New Criticism, reader response, and critical literacy influence the instructional methods used to teach literature?

4. What are the benefits of teaching from multiple theoretical perspectives?

When a reader analyzes and evaluates a literary work, he or she is engaged in literary criticism. The reader's opinion regarding what is important about the work and what adds or subtracts from its value is influenced by literary theory. The word *theory* is derived from the Greek word *theorein*, which means "to look at" (Moore, 1997, p. 9). It is theory that "provides a rationale for what constitutes the subject matter of criticism, 'the literary' and the specific aims of critical practice—the act of interpretation itself" (Brewton, 2005, para. 2). In practice, criticism and theory cannot be separated. A **literary theory** frames how a reader investigates assumptions, principles, and concepts about literature, and **literary criticism** results in an opinion or a judgment about the value or worth of a literary work that is based on what a particular theory directs a reader to consider.

Readers may or may not be conscious of it, but a theory often influences their decisions. Tracey and Morrow (2006) note that "when individuals are conscious of their theories, or belief systems, they are able to label them, think about them, talk about them with others, and compare their own theories with alternatives ones" (p. 3). An understanding of literary theory can help teachers reflect on their reasons for selecting particular literary works and also on their rationale for choosing particular instructional approaches.

Teachers are not the sole decision makers regarding the curriculum they are expected to teach. Sometimes committees make these decisions, and often state or national standards influence their choices. The ability to discuss the driving forces behind curricular decisions can perhaps prevent discord between teachers, administrators, community members, and even students.

Over the past few decades, literary theories have grown in number, complexity, and contentiousness. New theories typically emerge in opposition to prevailing traditions or customs that are perceived to be limited or exclusionary. They may also develop as part of a larger shift in beliefs that may come from anthropology, sociology, psychology, or other areas of study. Opposing theories often exert influence simultaneously, until one emerges as the dominant framework for studying literature, while others fade in popularity (Dobie, 2012).

Out of numerous theories, we discuss the few that we believe are most applicable to the study of literature in middle and secondary classrooms: New Criticism, reader response, and critical literacy. We match specific works of literature as categorized by their types of significance: literary, developmental, and social significance (as described in Chapter 2) with these theories. We also discuss how theories evolve and how they can be remixed and re-envisioned. Generally, any print or nonprint literary work can be viewed through multiple theoretical lenses. It is important to note, however, that excellent instruction often reflects the influence of multiple theories, and excellent literature frequently has multiple types of significance.

Many educators believe not only that teachers should understand how literary theory influences their instructional choices, but also that young adult readers should have opportunities to consider different ways of analyzing and responding to literature (Appleman, 2009; Eckert, 2006, 2008; Moore, 1997). With this in mind, we also include suggestions for teaching theoretical terminology and for showing students how to apply literary theories to their own reading experiences.

Figure 12.1 provides an overview of the major literary theories discussed in this chapter.

A comparison of literary theories. *figure* **12.1**

NEW CRITICISM	READER RESPONSE	CRITICAL LITERACY
Literature is an object of art to be studied objectively.	Literature portrays and enlivens the human experience.	All texts are constructed and read in social, political, and historical contexts.
Literature is selected for its literary merit (literary significance).	Literature is selected to match readers' past experiences and emotional maturity (developmental significance).	Literature is selected to encourage readers to examine beliefs about language and society (critical significance).
Literature can be understood only by close reading, a step by step analysis of form and content.	A literary work and a reader mutually evoke an experience in a moment in time.	Readers examine the social, political, and historical factors influencing their response.
Literacy routines include guided literature study and read alouds.	Literacy routines include literature circles, book clubs, and readers workshop.	Literacy routines include inquiry, comparing multiple texts and perspectives, and social action.

NEW CRITICISM/FORMALISM LITERARY THEORY

New Criticism began in the United States in the 1930s as a type of formalism. The terms **New Criticism** and *formalism* are sometimes used interchangeably, as both refer to an objective theory of literary criticism. From a formalist perspective literature is considered a discrete form of expression whose significance lies in its form as much as in its content.

New Criticism emerged in direct response to popular literary theories of the time, which emphasized an author's life or historical time period (Carey-Webb, 2001, p. 21). The theorists adhering to formalist criticism argued that literary texts were complete works of art that should be studied without consideration of external influences. From this perspective, literary texts are viewed as objects of study separate from readers, authors, or historical or cultural contexts.

To reinforce these beliefs, the "new critics" called any consideration of a reader's personal interpretation of literature an **affective fallacy.** They suggested that any shift away from the text itself resulted in the loss of standards. They also disregarded an author's intention as having anything to do with interpreting a work. The new critics labeled this **intentional fallacy.** Why an author wrote something might never be known, and even if it were, it did not matter. Only the result itself was of concern to the new critics (Dobie, 2012).

The new critics wanted to bring a greater intellectual rigor to the study of literature. They endorsed multifaceted and dense literary texts and a close, deliberate, step-by-step analysis of those texts. Their genre of choice was poetry because it fostered a "language laboratory" for studying concepts such as irony, tone, paradox, tension, and symbolism. Partially because the followers of New Criticism believed that literature could be studied objectively, and partially because of their exacting methodology, New Criticism developed a reputation of being "quasi scientific," aligning it with the sciences as an academic discipline (Showalter, 2003, p. 23).

John Noell Moore refers to formalism as *normal criticism* because its strategies dominated the practices of literary criticism in both universities and secondary schools. He described the goal of New Criticism: "We trace the weave of images, plot, characters, and theme, and our close reading reveals patterns that produce order, harmony, and unity in the structure, the forms, of the work. If we are properly trained . . . we can arrive at one 'correct' reading of a text" (1997, p. 11). Underlying this assertion is the belief that only the most competent scholars can truly understand a text, and these scholarly interpretations become the basis on which readers' interpretations are to be measured (Probst, 1992).

The belief that scholars know best led to their collecting the "best" literature and assembling it into anthologies, along with notes, interpretations, and instructions for reading. Works were chosen for artistic excellence, and a literature textbook might feature only well-established authors such as Poe, Hawthorne, Emerson, Melville, Whitman, Thoreau, Dickinson, Twain, and James. In an attempt to diminish the influence of historicism on literary study, the anthologies developed by the new critics were not divided into historical periods. They were organized instead around intellectual and artistic movements, such as **transcendentalism** (belief that spirituality was gained through individual intuition), **naturalism** (a belief that natural laws, not supernatural laws, governed the world), and **modernism** (a preference for the new and the avant-garde over the traditional) (Csicsila, 2004, cited in Vollaro, 2008).

Insisting that literary theory must be isolated from external social forces meant that new critics ignored literature that might reflect a changing world or potentially influence society. Works that were already considered worthy, however, remained in the mainstream of literature study, and thus the status quo was maintained (Showalter, 2003, p. 23). The canon was accepted as it existed, and works were considered "good" if they were amenable to formalist methods (Krupat, 1987).

Widely read books such as *The Closing of the American Mind* (1987) by Alan Bloom and *Cultural Literacy* (1987) by E. D. Hirsch Jr. supported a curriculum centered on classical literature. Classical works were seen as a means to preserve the American culture and to pass on to future generations the great thinking of the past. Literary classics were thought of as the works that all literate individuals should be familiar with (Milner & Milner, 1999, p. 177). An often-cited study by Arthur N. Applebee (1993) revealed that the classics held a dominant position in education in the late 1980s. Works by Shakespeare were read most often, in both public and private high schools, distantly followed by Steinbeck, Dickens, and Twain. No authors from a minority culture made the list, and Harper Lee was the only female author listed in the top ten.

New Criticism continues to exert influence over works selected for literature study. The suggested texts recommended by the Common Core State Standards for English language arts (National Governors Association Center for Best Practices, 2010) reflect a strong formalist influence. Many are classical texts written for an adult audience. For example, recommended literature titles for ninth and tenth grades include the *Odyssey* by Homer, *The Tragedy of Macbeth* (1606) by Shakespeare, "Ozymandias" (1818) by Percy Bysshe Shelley, "The Raven" (1845) by Edgar Allan Poe, *The Grapes of Wrath* (1939) by John Steinbeck, *Candide* (1759) by Voltaire, and *A Doll's House* (1879) by Henrik Ibsen.

Even though these "text exemplars" are provided with the caveat that they are intended to be representative of a range of topics and genres and not dictate a curriculum, the list may function explicitly or implicitly to do just that as well as advocate a linear approach for teaching literature. Once a book is studied in a designated grade, students will typically not read it again (Lynch, 2008). Books become part of the curriculum for a particular grade regardless of reader interest or needs.

Another significant aspect of formalism carried into contemporary classrooms is the practice of close reading and rigorous attention to the words on a page. The basic vocabulary of close reading begins with literary terminology described in Chapter 3: plot, character, theme, setting, point of view, conflict, and style. Moore suggests that a detailed close reading "allows us to trace the interconnections of these literary elements and to discover how they interpenetrate each other to create a harmonious and unified structure, a work of art" (1997, p. 15).

Showalter (2003) suggests the process of close reading be separated from all of the "baggage of the New Criticism or political labels" (p. 56). Close reading can occur before or along with attention to other factors outside of the text, but as a neutral first step it requires a reader to understand the verbal, formal, and structural elements of the words themselves.

Teaching Ideas ▪ NEW CRITICISM/FORMALISM

Close reading is not an approach most young adult readers adopt intuitively, so explicit instruction is required. Michael Lockett likens close reading to understanding the rules of a competitive game. Such games are not fun unless the player understands its fundamental principles (2010, p. 404). Within this approach, literary appreciation emerges from an increased understanding of the craft of the writing.

Guided literature study, discussed in Chapter 2 and in a classroom scenario in Chapter 3, is an appropriate literacy routine for developing an understanding of literary terminology, the tools of literary analysis, and the ways that literary elements work together as a unified work of art. In a guided literature study, the teacher selects challenging, but not frustrating, classical or contemporary works, and provides the necessary instruction and support to enable the students to accomplish the goals set forth by the teacher (Rycik & Irvin, 2005). Guided literature study and teacher read-alouds, especially the mediated listening–thinking activity, all described in Chapter 2, provide a framework for study of stylistic devices, specific language choice, and other literary elements.

Arda Arikan (2008) developed an inductive model of instruction of formalist criticism that includes visual art, particularly film, as a scaffold. Consistent with formalism, challenging canonical and classical texts are selected; however, excerpts are used instead of entire texts, and students are guided to examine descriptions of a single action or object. They consider the language used and how other wording might change the meaning. After sharing opinions about the construction of a text, its setting, characters, plot, and language choice, students use the examples as models for their own writing. Then the students write their own pieces. Following a discussion of their work, the teacher provides more explicit instruction about the literary techniques they emulated and others they might have used.

Next, students apply the concepts of formalism with visual art or by viewing films. The teacher guides them to observe how the ordinary becomes extraordinary through artistic use of language and images. This process of **defamiliarization** helps students understand that the purpose of art is the process. Their goal is not to get to find out how the story ends, but rather to understand how the work was constructed and to form a well-considered opinion about the effectiveness of the author's choices following a formalist approach to literary criticism (Arikan, 2008). Chapter 11 outlines several approaches for using film to teach literary concepts.

Robert Probst (1984) reminds teachers that although literature can be studied in scholarly ways, secondary school students are not scholars, and literary history and scholarship must be secondary to the direct experience of reading and reflecting. We believe the following contemporary literary works for young adults, as well as many other mentioned throughout this book, can provide satisfying reading experiences for many students and sufficient literary significance to warrant guided study.

Frozen Fire. Tim Bowler, 2008. A phone call from a stranger who knows too much about Dusty and her missing brother initiates this eerie and unresolved fantastical mystery. Rape, the frigid English terrain, and otherworldly and unstable characters heighten the tension. What is real and what might be supernatural remain unanswered. The limited closure encourages a close rereading to support alternative interpretations. Ages 14 and up.

Going Bovine. Libba Bray, 2009. This nearly 500-page book tells the story of Cameron, a disinterested high school student who is diagnosed with Creutzfeldt-Jakob, or "mad cow," disease, which destroys the brain. He encounters strange characters such as a punk rock angel, a dwarf, and a lawn gnome who is a Norse god. They set out to find Dr. X, who can cure Cameron and save the world. Whether hallucinatory or real, his trip is littered with numerous disjointed references to pop culture and connections to his real life. Elements from *Don Quixote,* the book Cameron was reading in English class, add a layer of intertextuality. Ages 15 and up.

Heart of a Samurai. Margi Preus, 2010. Set in 1841, this Newbery Honor book incorporates whaling terminology and Japanese words throughout. A shipwrecked 14-year-old Japanese fisherman is rescued by Americans who take him to New England. He confronts strange customs from people he initially thinks of as barbarians. Ten years later, after numerous adventures, he returns to Japan an educated and accomplished man. The novel is based on a true story and warrants a close reading of how the author mingles fact with fiction. A glossary, extensive notes, and illustrations are included. Rhonda Blumberg's nonfiction *Shipwrecked! The True Adventure of a Japanese Boy* (2001) provides a resource for verifying facts. Ages 11–15.

The Monstrumologist. Rick Yancey, 2009. This Printz Honor Book contains a wealth of horror elements. A monstrumologist, a scientist who studies monsters, and his apprentice encounter grave robbers, monster hunters, and ship captains. The well-crafted imagery creates terrifying descriptions of cemeteries, laboratories, insane asylums, and the lairs of the Anthropophagi, a race of cannibals. Language is reminiscent of the late 1800s; for example, "countenance," "recompense," and "the appalling issuance of his loins." This first book in the series is presented as the apprentice's diary and reflects the typical elements of this genre. Ages 14 and up.

Moon over Manifest. Clare Vanderpool, 2010. This Newbery Award winner shifts between the Great Depression in 1936 Missouri and the Great War of 1918. Twelve-year-old Abilene, whose father left her with strangers in what she thinks must be his home town, searches for her father's past and discovers the town's history. Abilene's first-person narration is intertwined with newspaper columns, letters from World War I soldiers, and stories told by an old Gypsy woman. The language and dialect is consistent with the time, place, and characters, and the multiple narrative devices that require close reading create an interesting tale. Ages 10–13.

Revolver. Marcus Sedgwick, 2009. The novel's opening line, "Even the dead tell stories," foreshadows both content and structure in this Printz Award finalist. Sig is alone in the Arctic wilderness with his father's corpse. Through a nonlinear plot, his father's part in the theft of gold years earlier is revealed. Sig is confronted by his father's brutal partner, who has killed before and has no hesitations to do so again. The history of the Alaskan gold rush deftly frames a chilling survival story. Ages 13 and up.

Ship Breaker. Paolo Bacigalupi, 2010. The appealing 17-year-old protagonist in this Printz Award winner and National Book Award for Young People's Literature finalist fights to survive from enemies known and unknown, human and subhuman, in this fast-paced action novel. Set in a Gulf Coast depleted of natural resources and ruined by climate change, the story depicts a future of extreme economic deprivation and division between the scavengers and "swanks." The characters are complex and the backstory is revealed a bit at a time. The descriptions of horrific acts and unexpected events and bizarre characters create an intensity that continues to build throughout the story. Age 13 and up.

The White Darkness. Geraldine McCaughrean, 2005. Fourteen-year old Sym, who is hearing impaired, is taken to Antarctic under false premises by her uncle, who is searching for access to the center of the earth. Following the death of her father, Sym handles the stress by developing an imaginary friend, an incarnation of a famous Arctic explorer Titus Oates, with whom she carries on an inner dialogue. Sym's desire for her fantasy to become her reality, characters who are not what they seem, and the symbolism of the title in this Printz Award winner provide a reason for close reading. Age 13 and up.

READER RESPONSE LITERARY THEORY

The reader response theories were a movement that turned away from both the biographical–historical perspective, which the New Critics so thoroughly rejected, and the notion that texts should be studied in isolation, which was the New Critics' core belief. Adherents of the reader response perspective resisted the way both approaches predisposed readers to one specific interpretation. They believed that a central goal of literature is to portray and enliven the human experience. A narrow focus on either information about the literature or its content and form diminished the capacity of literature to fulfill this purpose (Karolides, 1992, pp. 28–29). Robert Probst (1984) argues that literature is not the private domain of the intellectual elite. It is written for readers, not for professional literature students to analyze. Readers read because through their reading they come to better understand themselves.

The label **reader response theory** applies to a range of theoretical perspectives that focus on what literature *does*, not what it *is*. The most influential of the subjective theories for middle and secondary pedagogy was Louise Rosenblatt's transactional theory of literature. Rosenblatt first presented her perspective on reader response in 1938 in *Literature as Exploration*. Rosenblatt adopted the term *transaction* from John Dewey, an American philosopher and educational reformer. The pragmatic philosophy developed by Dewey argues that meaning is not an objective entity waiting to be found; rather meaning comes from human experience (Connell, 2008, p. 104). The term **transaction** suggests that when the reader and the text come together they mutually affect each other to evoke an experience. It is during this transaction that a reader finds meaning from the words and images on a page.

Rosenblatt asserted that a literary work exists only in the moment that a reader transforms the symbols on the page into something meaningful. If a reader were to read the same text at another time and place or under different circumstances, the transaction—the experience of creating meaning—would likely differ. She explained that "the literary work exists in the live circuit set up between reader and text; the reader infuses intellectual and emotional meanings into the pattern of verbal symbols, and those symbols channel his thoughts and feelings. Out of this complex process emerges a more or less organized imaginative experience" (1938/1968, p. 25).

A reader's transaction is influenced by the stance taken. A **stance** is the way a reader approaches a text based on the purpose for reading the text. Rosenblatt labeled the kind of reading done to extract information as **efferent** and reading done for pleasure in a "lived through moment" as **aesthetic.** It may be tempting to think about stance in relationship to the type of text, to presume that novels are read aesthetically and informational texts efferently; however, this assumes that a reader is neutral and passive. Instead, a reader consciously or unconsciously selects a stance that is aesthetic, efferent, or somewhere in between. The choice is based on many factors, such as the particular reading occasion, present needs, or personal concerns. The reader decides what matters and what results to expect or desire (Karolides, 1992, p. 26). Rosenblatt explained:

Confusion about the matter of stance results from the entrenched habit of thinking of the text as efferent or aesthetic, expository or poetic, literary or nonliterary, and so on. Those who apply these terms to texts should realize that they actually are reporting their interpretation of the writer's intention as to what kind of reading the text should be given. The reader is free, however to adopt either predominant stance toward any text. Efferent and aesthetic apply, then, to the writer's and the reader's selective attitude toward their own stream of consciousness during their respective linguistic events. (2005, pp. 11–12)

Without the opportunity to read aesthetically, the prospect of readers experiencing literature as a way to think about themselves and others is diminished. If an evocation—the lived-through experience—is the goal, fiction and poetry must be read from an aesthetic stance (Galda, & Liang, 2003). Nonfiction offers opportunities to read efferently, to learn about the world, but nonfiction, especially creative nonfiction, might also provide readers with opportunities to respond aesthetically.

Rosenblatt noted that writers in the natural and social sciences have been increasingly aware of the semantic and syntactic practices thought of as literary and have been using narrative and metaphor in their writing to the point that the efferent, aesthetic distinction may be erased (2005, p. 24). For many young adult readers, a personal connection to a work of nonfiction can be a powerful link to understanding and appreciating its concepts. It also can result in personal insights about oneself, others, and the world.

Teaching Ideas ▪ READER RESPONSE

A class of students will most likely respond to the same literary work in a variety of ways. This does not mean that all responses are equally valid and that a student's opinion of a literary work is in itself sufficient. Responses should be evaluated in relation to text features, language, and the construction of a coherent interpretation. In other words, reader response theory recognizes that while there is no single correct interpretation, it is not an "anything goes" interpretation of literature (Karolides, 1992, p. 27). Teachers can make the intended purpose of a reading clear. They also need to communicate the criteria for evaluating whatever meanings are evoked. Students need guidance in developing the ability to adopt an appropriate critical stance in response to the situation at hand (Rosenblatt, 2005, p. 95).

Probst suggests that certain conditions are required for a reader response perspective to thrive in a classroom (1984). Students must respect their teacher's and their peers' differing points of views. Students accustomed to responding quickly with correct answers may find it challenging to accept peer responses they think should be dismissed. Students need to learn to cooperate and work together and to assume, at varying times, both an assertive role in directing the conversation and a passive role in accepting viewpoints with which they disagree.

Students need to be willing to change their minds and to deal with uncertainty and ambiguity. They need to analyze why they made certain assumptions about a literary work. Each student creates an individual reading, but it is possible to have a foolish or incorrect reading. The challenge for the teacher is to accept individual responses while encouraging readers to reconsider incorrect readings by exploring what in the text or what in their personal experiences influenced their interpretations and response. Readers must accept responsibility for their responses.

Rosenblatt considered the teacher's role to be that of a guide who helps students improve their capacity to evoke meaning from literature though self-critical reflection and thereby to discover the satisfaction of literature (1938/1968, p. 26). She adamantly opposed using any predetermined format or structure that would constrain response when reading aesthetically. She believed "to set up some stereotyped form will probably focus the student's attention on what is to be required of him after he has read the book, rather than on the work itself as he evokes it from the text" (1938/1968, p. 67).

As a teacher, your primary responsibility is to encourage aesthetic reading and not get in the way with exercises or tasks that redirect the experience. This does not mean that literary concepts are not important, but they should come from the reading experience, and literary terminology should be taught when needed (Rosenblatt, 2005, p. 85). This applies to social and historical understandings as well. They should not "lead away from the work of art, but feed back into the reader's heightened awareness of how it fits into the context he himself provides" (2005, p. 69).

Stanley Fish (1976) pointed out that the interpretive strategies students use to engage in conversations about texts are not natural or universal, they are learned. Readers come to construct knowledge and to accept certain values and beliefs that have been supported and reinforced during their past shared reading experiences. Fish saw reading activities not as leading to meaning, but as having meaning.

Rosenblatt recognized the complexity of establishing instructional approaches within a reader response perspective. She cautioned that response modes, verbal or nonverbal, should not become ends in themselves (2005, p. 84). Protocols, such as student writing, creative interpretations, and dramatic interpretations at best "provide indirect evidence about the students' evocation, the work as experienced, and reactions to it" (Rosenblatt, 2005 p. 32).

The literacy routines that are most likely to support a response perspective are those that develop interpretive communities and encourage peer-led discussions such as literature circles and reading workshop (Rycik & Irvin, 2005). By listening to diverse responses, readers are able to consider a variety of possible interpretations. Give students numerous opportunities to respond, for example, through journaling and letter writing, and to share their responses through creative endeavors such as readers' theater, art, or music.

Reader response has been criticized for failing to assist teachers in the selection of literature (Carey-Webb, 2001). Although no specific list of recommended titles has emerged from reader response theory, Rosenblatt did suggest that the literature students are asked to read "reflect a sense of the possible links between these materials and the student's past experience and present level of emotional maturity" (1968, p. 42). She included classics in this mix as long as the classical work was not being used for teaching literary concepts, literacy skills, or history through a formalist methodology. Whatever the literature, it must be "relevant to the nourishment of a personal sense of literature as a mode of experience" (2005, p. 69).

Use caution when matching a literary work with a student based on a presumed association, for example assigning a book about divorce to a student whose parents are divorcing. This might elicit a reaction from the reader, but not a response. A response requires the ability to take a "spectator stance" and set aside initial feelings (the reaction) in order to reflect on characteristics of the text that resulted in the reaction (the response) (Galda, 1990).

Furthermore, connections might be found in an underlying emotional structure that is not fully realized until after the actual transaction of reader and text. For example, a young female student relates that *A Step from Heaven* (Na, 2001), a story about a Korean immigrant family, made her angry. She was from a small town, had no experience with people from cultures other than her own, and had never even travelled. She did not relate to the young girl protagonist. After reflecting on what characteristic about herself influenced her reaction, she realized that it was the young girl's angry, bitter father with whom she emotionally connected. The scene where the father battled government bureaucracy to obtain a green card reminded her of when she was about eight years old, standing in line with her mother as she applied for public assistance. The student remembered how alone and embarrassed she felt and how rude the government employees were to her mother. She said the father in the story must have felt these same emotions as her mother, only more intensely. Upon further reflection, she realized that it was not her mother who was angry; it was she. Prompted by this personal revelation, she reread the novel focusing on the father's character and how he dealt with his anger.

The literature selected for classroom reading must be worthy of reflection, and it must have adequate substance to warrant the time and energy to respond. It must also have the potential to interest readers. The ultimate goal of literature study is for students to develop a personal statement that says "I, because of who I am, conclude this about the work, myself, and the other students in the class" (Probst, 1984, p. 25). The contemporary fiction and nonfiction titles for young adults listed in the box on page 372 have developmental significance and the potential of helping young adults discover the "I" in literature.

Rosenblatt first proposed reader response theory in part as an alternative to the predominate theory of formalism in the late 1930s; however, it was not until the late 1960s that social, political, and cultural factors created an educational climate that enabled reader response to become the theory behind the restructuring of literature study in many middle and secondary schools.

As described in Chapter 1, postmodern influences resulted in a move away from absolutes. The role of literary experts as the arbiters of interpretation and "keepers of the canon" was challenged on many fronts. In the mid-1960s, theorists who were labeled "deconstructionists" challenged the literary purity of canonical works. According to Milner and Milner (1999), the deconstructionists suggested that historical or political motives drive the canonization of particular

. . . OF CONTEMPORARY LITERATURE FOR YOUNG ADULTS WITH **DEVELOPMENTAL SIGNIFICANCE**

Half Brother. Kenneth Oppel, 2010. What it means to communicate and what it means to be a member of a family are two of the underlying questions in this novel. Ben's scientist parents want to determine if a chimpanzee can learn American Sign Language. Ben's resentment against the newest member of his family, Zan, wanes as he comes to care about the chimp. Popularity, sexual awakening, bad grades, parental discord, and a dangerous rescue frame the animal rights issue. Ages 12–15.

Hate List. Jennifer Brown, 2009. Valerie and Nick keep a hate list of the people they feel have bullied them, called them names, or generally created an unpleasant school environment. Nick goes on a shooting rampage and kills six students and a teacher and wounds several other students, including Valerie. She is cleared of conspiracy charges, but must deal with her part in his actions. Most of the story focuses on the aftermath of the shooting, but flashbacks provide insights into her relationship with Nick, her family, and high school in general. Ages 13 and up.

The Rules of Survival. Nancy Werlin, 2006. This book's dedication says that "this book is for all survivors. Always remember: The survivor gets to tell the story." Survival is the theme of this National Book Award for Young People's Literature finalist. Matthew is writing to his little sister about their family's past so that Emmy will know what happened to their mother. Through his writing Matthew hopes to come to understand why their mother abused her children, her sister, and everyone else who was close to her. Ages 13 and up.

The Season. Sarah MacLean, 2009. This novel set in Regency England is about wealthy girls, their hair, dresses, and social customs as they experience their "first season." This series of parties and balls is arranged specifically for young woman of social breeding to find husbands and secure their place in soci-

ety. Alexandra balks at the idea of being displayed in this way. She discovers romance, based on her own terms, in the midst of a murder mystery and political intrigue. Ages 12–16.

Split. Swati Avasthi, 2010. Jace must come to terms with the effect of long-term physical abuse by a parent. His agony is intensified by his continued love for his father. Jace and his older brother, who ran away from the abuse six years earlier, expect their mother to join them. She does not come, choosing instead to remain their father's most available and regularly scheduled target. The abuse is graphically depicted, and the long term effects are devastating. Ages 14 and up.

Tattoos on the Heart: The Power of Boundless Compassion. Gregory Boyle, 2010. Boyle, a Jesuit priest who spent more than two decades with the gangs of Los Angeles, recounts in this memoir his sometimes frightening but always life-affirming experiences working with the poor. The stories of gang members, the challenges they face, and their successes and failures are presented in short thematically organized vignettes. His humor and compassion evoke a sense of connectedness to life experiences not familiar to most young adults. Ages 14 and up.

Where She Went. Gayle Forman, 2011. This sequel to the bestseller *If I Stay* (2009) is told from Adam's point of view. He stuck with Mia through her recovery after a car accident killed the rest of her family, but ultimately she ended their relationship. Three years later he becomes disillusioned with his life as a rock star, while Mia seems to be progressing well with her classical music. Adam's emotional suffering is reflected in his music. An encounter in New York forces them to deal with their feelings about each other. The life of a musician, especially a rocker, and the grieving process for family and lost young love, are strong components of this novel. Ages 14 and up.

works. For example, they argued that the commercialization of Shakespeare was the real force behind the continued inclusion of his work in the curriculum. They attributed the inclusion of Nathaniel Hawthorne's work in the canon to his political affiliations and the persistent lobbying efforts of his children (Milner & Milner, 1999, p. 179). Women and people of color challenged the notion of the universality of the literature that was selected for study and demanded the expansion of the curriculum to include more non-Eurocentric texts and more works written by women. Well-crafted literature for young adults began to be plentiful as did popular fiction, vying for a place in the curriculum (Milner & Milner, 1999, pp. 182–202).

Reader response theory was very much at the center of these changes, and yet it was criticized for maintaining an exclusively personal view of reading that was acultural. Reader response was thought to "overlook the power differentials and social inequities that can ensure when some readings have greater cachet than others in a particular setting" (Smagorinsky, 2001, p. 163).

Proponents of Rosenblatt's work countered that the notion that reader response theory failed to embrace critical literacy was a misinterpretation. Although Rosenblatt's transactional theory did not promulgate a particular set of critical questions, it did *not* exclude critical perspectives as long as they derived from an initial aesthetic approach. A reader's evocation is based on a multitude of factors, including a personal belief system and external social and political influences (Cai, 2008). Nonetheless, a greater emphasis on interpretations as culturally mediated and on readers and texts as conditioned by their cultural history supported the emergence of critical literacy.

CRITICAL LITERACY LITERARY THEORY

Although definitions of this literary theory vary (Green, 2001), at the heart of **critical literacy** is the idea that beliefs about the social practices involved in literacy use should be questioned. Critical literacy theory focuses on sociopolitical and ideological components considered from cultural and multicultural perspectives. Most often multicultural studies have focused on African American culture, but, as described in Chapter 4, questions of authority, authenticity, and accuracy apply to literature of and about all types of diversity.

Feminist theory, a complex and multifaceted theory, focuses on how women are portrayed in literature, female authors, and sexual politics. **Gender criticism** broadens the underlying issues related to gender and includes questions regarding both femininity and masculinity. **Gay/lesbian studies** and queer studies explore issues relating to sexual orientation and gender identity, usually focusing on LGBTQ people and cultures. **Marxist theory,** which first became an established part of literary criticism during the Great Depression, remains relevant. Marxist literary theory focuses on social and economic class, economic inequities and the relationship of wealth and power (Dobie, 2012; Murfin & Ray, 1998).

The literary theories described above have been applied individually to literary criticism, but they also can be categorized collectively within a critical literacy perspective: "A critical literacy perspective focuses on the ways texts are constructed in social, political and historical contexts, and the ways in which these contexts position readers and texts and endorse particular interpretations" (Serafini, 2004, p. 3). A **critical stance** encourages students to consider the choices made in creating texts. It also helps them become aware of how a text is influencing them (Bean & Moni, 2003).

Within a critical literacy theoretical perspective, readers consider how their own gender, culture, class, and race position their response to a text. Readers ask themselves whether the views portrayed in a text should be accepted, rejected, or reconstructed to better fit with their own experiences of the world. They recognize that response is not neutral, but rather conditioned by the reader's own experiences (Cervetti, Pardales & Damico, 2001). When reading from a critical perspective, readers question whose voice is represented, whose voice is silenced, and who gains and who loses by the reading of a text (McLaughlin & DeVoogd, 2004).

Based on the work of Paulo Freire (1987), some believe that reading texts critically is only a part of critical literacy theory. From his perspective, critical literacy must bring individuals to social action. Doug Morris (2011) succinctly captures Freire's view of critical literacy:

> Critical literacy is committed to projects that enhance and expand our abilities to read the world in order to read the word and read the word in order to read the world (where read carries with it the demands to critique in order to deepen and extend our understanding of our place, options and the role in the world); write the word in order to write the world; write the world in order to write the word (where write carries with it the need to engage and transform a strong sense of human agency); right the world in order to right the word; and, right the word in order to right the world; (where right is tied to the ways in which we examine, analyze and explore the interpenetrations between power, language, ideology, culture and institutions in learning and teaching in order to undertake activities directed toward righting the wrongs of the world)." (pp. 291–292)

In this view, critical literacy cannot be separated from civic competencies, and literacy is positioned as a set of social practices designed to disrupt the commonplace, interrogate multiple viewpoints, focus on sociopolitical issues, and take action to promote social justice (Lewison, Flint, & Van Sluys, 2002). Critical literacy is intended to help students become "critically competent and caring citizens" (Ciardiello, 2004, p. 138), "to function fully and authentically as a citizen of a democracy" (Kraver, 2007, p. 68), and to move beyond being "social actors" to become "social transformers" of their world (Wood, Soares, & Watson, 2006, p. 59).

Teaching Ideas ▪ CRITICAL LITERACY

Edward Behrman (2006) outlines six classroom practices that support a critical perspective:

1. *Reading supplementary texts.* Reading additional texts, whether considered supplemental or primary, including fiction, film, nonfiction, fiction, and music, increases the students' opportunities to experience differing treatments of the same topic or theme.

2. *Reading multiple texts.* Reading multiple versions of the same work, or conflicting criticisms of that work, also demonstrates that text is a rendering as portrayed by an author, and not true in an absolute sense.

3. *Reading from a resistant perspective.* Resistant reading has several applications, but usually includes looking at the motives and ideologies of both the writer and the reader. Teachers help students gain social consciousness by having them adopt a resistant perspective by questioning their world, asking who has power and who benefits from power, and by analyzing why their world is the way it is.

4. *Producing counter texts.* When students produce texts from a nonmainstream perspective they often are writing from the voice of a marginalized subgroup. This can be in the form of a personal response in a journal, a personal narrative or a conscious effort to write from another's point of view.

   Making films, writing music, performing, and creating artistic renderings also are avenues for producing countertexts. Through their own words and images students can examine the critical issues underlying the construction of a text. Then they can explicitly consider the underlying values inherent in their own products. For example, did they perpetuate a familiar social or cultural position, or did they challenge their definition of the status quo? How did their choices of language and style impact meaning?

5. *Conducting student-choice research projects.* Inquiries about social and cultural issues are most effective when the concerns are directly experienced by the students. Researching and presenting information on these issues in oral, written, and/or visual form may in turn lead to taking social action within the community.

6. *Taking social action.* Whatever the outcome, "taking social action allows students to recognize literacy as a sociocultural process and to engage literacy as a vehicle for social change" (p. 495).

Selecting literature that explicitly addresses social, cultural, and economic inequities also facilitates learning to read through a critical literacy lens. *Trash* (2010) by Andy Mulligan is such a book. (See the Focus Novel on the following page.)

The contemporary literary works listed in the box on page 377 address many significant social, cultural, and political issues. These works are ideal for reading from a critical literacy perspective. They will also appeal to many young adults.

LITERARY THEORIES REMIXED AND RE-ENVISIONED

As previously discussed, new theories develop in response to existing theories, societal and cultural changes, and influences from nonliterary fields. As these theories evolve, bits and pieces are forgotten, remixed, or re-envisioned.

Trash by Andy Mulligan

Trash is set in a nameless underdeveloped country, most likely in Latin America, where three young boys, Raphael, Gardo, and Rat, survive by picking through huge heaps of trash. One day they find a small leather bag containing a key, wallet, an ID, a map, and money. Their guess that these items are important is confirmed when the police come looking for them. In trying to outwit the authorities, the boys encounter political corruption and abuse, deception, and mysterious codes. The boys embark on a quest to seek justice for a houseboy and to find a better life for themselves. *Trash* portrays the pervasive poverty in this place and the futility felt by the people who work to change it. A young volunteer from the United States, who has become wrapped up in the boys' plot to discover the treasure, comments:

PICK IT UP—AND KEEP IT HIDDEN

TRASH

andy mulligan

> I learned perhaps more than any university could ever teach me. I learned that the world revolves around money. There are values and virtues and morals; there are relationships and trust and love—and all of that is important. Money, however, is more important, and it is dripping all the time, like precious water. Some drink deep; others thirst. Without money, you shrivel and die. The absence of money is drought in which nothing can grow. Nobody knows the value of water until they've lived in a dry, dry place—like Behala. So many people, waiting for the rain. (p. 149)

Trash, a fast-paced, action-filled story, can readily be analyzed through a critical lens, in particular a Marxist perspective. The powerful and the powerless are easily recognized, as is the source of power, corruption. The various characters make decisions heavily influenced by the economic system in which they live.

The novel focuses on the plight of the boys, but another interesting aspect is the role of money provided by American nonprofit organizations. What prompts someone to donate funds or volunteer to help the poor in another country? Are their motives socially, culturally, or politically constructed? Students might be encouraged to investigate agencies that solicit funds for international causes and to consider what acts of social justice are available to them. For example, they might collect funds for UNICEF, an organization of the United Nations dedicated to children or join the Coalition Against Trafficking in Women, a nongovernmental organization dedicated to an issue presented in Patricia McCormick's *Sold* (2006) discussed in Chapter 4.

Archetypal Literary Criticism

Archetypal literary criticism grew out of Jungian psychology popular in the 1950s and 1960s. William G. Brozo (2002) revisits literary archetypes to address a contemporary issue—the lack of interest in reading by many male adolescents.

Jung believed that certain generalized models, or **archetypes,** are present in the psyche, the mind or soul, of all people. Archetypes that evoke strong emotional responses eventually recur so frequently in literature that they become a part of the literary experience (Kennedy, Giora, & Bauerlein, 2006, pp. 10–11, 102). In this way, archetypes, which are seen as models or patterns of characters, situations or actions, influence a reader's expectations and interpretations.

For example, male heroes are expected to rescue females, protect kings, or perhaps even defend entire communities. A reader is not surprised when a protagonist in a work with a coming-of-age theme embarks on a journey or quest

Angry Young Man. Chris Lynch, 2011. Chapter titles such as "The Good Causes," "Mission Creep," "Collateral Damage," and "Terror Eyes" reflect the plot of this story about two brothers and the choices they make to right social injustices. Questions of moral and social responsibility and individual rights versus a "greater good" frame this story. Ages 14 and up.

Between Shades of Gray. Ruta Sepetys, 2011. This first-person narrative of the deportation and decade-long forced encampment of Lithuanians in Siberia by the Russians gives voice to the oppressed and raises questions about the role of the United States in this deplorable act by one of its World War II allies. The descriptions of inhumanity are gruesome, and the strong factual foundation accentuates the depth of cruelty perpetrated on the powerless Lithuania people by the powerful. Ages 13 and up.

Dark Water. Laura McNeal, 2010. This National Book Award for Young People's Literature finalist tells the story of 15-year-old Pearl, who becomes infatuated with an undocumented worker employed on her uncle's Southern California ranch. They become engulfed by a raging fast-moving forest fire and must decide whether to evade the flames or follow the evacuation plan that would most certainly result in Amiel being caught by the police and deported. Age 13 and up.

Shine. Lauren Myracle, 2011. The horrific beating of a popular and well-liked openly gay young man propels Cat, a former close friend of his, to search for the perpetrator when the sheriff of this rural county fails to investigate. Cat fears her brother and his "redneck posse" may have something to do with it. Cat places herself in danger as she questions many old friends and townspeople. Issues related to rural poverty, religion, and lack of educational opportunities frame people's homophobic responses. Ages 14 and up.

Touching Snow. M. Sindy Felin, 2007. Seventh-grader Karina, a first-generation American born to Haitian immigrants, tells a chilling story of unrelenting physical abuse by "the daddy," her stepfather. She ultimately retaliates. Differences between American and Haitian culture, especially attitudes about discipline and the roles of children and adults and the power held by those with money and those without, undergird this National Book Award for Young People's Literature finalist. Ages 14 and up.

What They Always Tell Us. Martin Wilson, 2008. This book is told in alternating third-person voices of brothers James and Alex, a senior and junior respectively. A comparison between their sexual identities and how those identities are beginning to shape who they will be frames the story. James and his friends regularly have sex with girls they don't care about. Alex, who previously tried to poison himself, realizes he is gay and revels in his new found sense of self. The open-ended novel forces the reader to consider the brothers' future relationship and their respective sexual choices. A secondary plot about a young neighbor boy also highlights the theme of sexual relationships. Ages 14 and up.

FILMS

Billy Elliot. Stephen Daldry, director, 2000. Billy is the son of a working class British mine worker. He secretly takes ballet lessons from a supportive teacher who helps him get an important audition. Billy's father and brother are coal miners enmeshed in a violent strike. Already struggling with their own issues of gender expectations and loss of economic power, they must also confront their opinions about male dancers, which are based on sexual stereotypes. PG-13.

Rabbit Proof Fence. Phillip Noyce, director, 2002. This Australian film based on a true story follows three Aboriginal girls who ran away from the Moore River Native Settlement in 1931. In accordance with government policy, they, and hundreds of other children at the settlement, were separated from their families to be trained as domestics for white families. The girls endure weeks of walking through the desert, along a fence constructed by the government to keep rabbits away from vegetation. They are tracked by both a white government official and an Aboriginal tracker. PG.

(Brozo, 2002). Similarly, "everyone knows" that the outcome of selling one's soul to the devil can only be thwarted through acts of redemption and sacrifice.

Brozo recommends using archetypes as a structure for studying literature because of the inherent and potentially powerful connection male readers have with male archetypes. Literature for or about young adult males will intentionally or unintentionally contain traditional archetypes and will therefore not be difficult to select. Brozo asserts that literature for young adults with positive male archetypes has the potential to counter the negative and often destructive images of men in popular culture.

Brozo focuses on 10 positive male archetypes that he believes will draw young men into reading literature (see Figure 12.2). He believes that these positive male archetypes "may be thought of as signposts along a boy's psychic journey to claim or reclaim an honorable masculine identity" (p. 25).

Even though Brozo focuses on males, both males and females need to engage in critical explorations of masculinity and femininity as depicted in literature, popular culture, and the media to consider what it means to be a man or a woman in contemporary society. His mix of archetypal theory with contemporary gender studies encourages readers to consider how an author perpetuates or unravels an archetype—an ancient belief—in relation to gender attributes perceived as positive or negative in contemporary literature for young adults.

 **figure 12.2**   Positive male archetypes to draw young men into literature (Brozo, 2002).

1. The *pilgrim* is a wanderer who leaves the familiar behind and searches for spiritual freedom.

2. The *patriarch* is the male who cares for others and is willing to make personal sacrifices for them.

3. The *king* embodies male greatness and serves as a role model.

4. The *warrior,* brave and honorable, opposes evil and wrongdoers.

5. The *magician* evokes amazement through intuition and cleverness.

6. The *wildman,* unpredictable and independent, challenges the status quo and conformity.

7. The *healer,* mystical and spiritual, brings wholeness to people and societies who are incomplete.

8. The *prophet* fights falsehoods and insists on telling the truth.

9. The *trickster* is irreverent and funny, and through his pranks he keeps the pompous and self-righteous humble.

10. The *lover* is a caring and giving male who takes care of others.

Multiple Perspectives

Brozo's contemporary twist on archetypal theory suggests that theories need not be relegated to a particular time period, scholar, or academic setting. Literary theories such as New Criticism, reader response, and critical literacy have influenced significantly the study of literature because elements of each of these theories contributed positively to the understanding of how readers analyze and value literature; in other words, how they engage in literary criticism. These theories continue to inform our understanding of literature and ourselves.

Lisa Shade Eckert states that "teaching students to use literary theory as a strategy to construct meaning is teaching reading. Learning [literary] theory gives them a purpose in approaching a reading task" (2006, p. 8). Teaching literature from multiple perspectives will help students understand that there is no single way to think about literature. Deborah Appleman believes that anything less becomes "dogmatic or propagandistic" (Appleman, 2009, p. 9).

Classroom experiences with theory can be implicit as students discover the factors that influence their responses, and interpretations or instruction can be made explicit by labeling theories and identifying their basic tenets. The Critical Response Frame, described next, encourages exploration of underlying theoretical perspectives without directly teaching a theory. It builds on aesthetic response as a means to explore a more critical stance.

The Critical Response Frame

The Critical Response Frame (CRF) (Knickerbocker & Rycik, 2006) is a scaffold that blends multiple theoretical perspectives to guide students as they consider the many factors that influence how they respond to and interpret a literary work. The CRF expands on the response record developed by Carol Cox (2002) as a planning tool for keeping student response at the center of literature study. Cox focuses on the personal connections readers make to the text and encourages them to be more accepting of their peers' responses.

The CRF, as shown in Figure 12.3, guides students to consider the contextual, textual, authorial, and cultural factors that influence their response to a work. The function of the frame is to encourage readers to become aware of how their "situatedness" affects the meaning they construct. The framework is not intended to be used in a linear fashion; students should be encouraged to revisit the various components throughout their literature experience. Next, we discuss each of the framework elements in more detail.

Reading context

The first component of the CRF is for the reader to examine his or her own *reading context*—or situation or circumstances—while reading the literature. Students are asked to consider when, where, why, and how the novel was read and to consider how these circumstances affect their reading stance as aesthetic or efferent, or somewhere between the two on a continuum. Students often comment that they began reading to complete a particular assignment but became lost in the story and read for pleasure.

figure **12.3**   Critical Response Frame.

Name:	Date:
Novel:	Author:
Discussion Group Members:	
Reading Context:	
Author's Presumed Intent:	
Authorial Audience:	
Reader's Self:	

Meaning/Interpretation:
Text Support:
Post-Reading Group Discussion:
Post-Discussion Writing:
Post-Reading Reflections/Actions:

Author's presumed intent

This component suggests that authors have a purpose for writing and that their purpose influences their choices. In particular, readers should consider whether or not an author is promoting or attacking any social practices. Usually an author's intent is inferred from the literary text, but sometimes an author directly states his or her intent in articles, interviews, or even on the book jacket. Young adults often search out information about an author or work prior to reading. They may be familiar with the author from previous author studies or past reading. Examining authorial intent prior to reading establishes the author's ideology or beliefs as part of the process of constructing the text.

Authorial audience

Because authors cannot know each of their potential readers, they must make some general assumptions regarding their audience. Rabinowitz and Smith (1998) call this hypothetical audience the **authorial audience** and suggest that a critical reading requires readers to consider the characteristics of this audience.

Readers speculate on the author's assumptions about their social, political, or cultural characteristics and values. Readers can also consider the assumptions the author makes about their past experiences and background knowledge. If young adult readers lack knowledge the author assumes they will have, the teacher should guide them to consider how this mismatch affects their feelings about the book. Finally, teachers can guide readers to examine the assumptions an author makes about their understanding of artistic conventions and language. Slang, dialect, or esoteric vocabulary and stylistic devices such as metaphors and symbolism can leave some readers feeling as if the book were written for someone else.

Reader's self

This section guides readers to think about a multitude of factors that determine whether a reader responds to a text enthusiastically, neutrally, or with open resistance by aiding them in examining their own characteristics and past experiences that contribute to how they respond. One student wrote with open hostility about *Like Sisters on the Homefront* (Williams-Garcia, 1995). The student identified herself as conservative, middle-class, white, and Christian. She related that the language, sexuality, and focus on teen promiscuity bothered her to the point that she wanted to burn the book. She considered her resistance to the book an indication of her own moral superiority.

Meaning/interpretation

The meaning/interpretation section focuses on the reader articulating the theme or significance of the novel. This process of interpretation answers the questions, "What is this novel trying to say?" and "What does it say to me?" Initial interpretations often focus on the personal connections readers find to the text, either through their own life experiences or through other literary works they have read. The teacher can guide students' interpretations from a more critical perspective to include social and cultural factors such as gender, ethnicity, and peer group.

The goal isn't to highlight differences. It is to help readers see how literary texts might have multiple meanings that may not emerge unless viewed from multiple perspectives. Students might be asked to consider an interpretation from someone else's perspective. For instance, an older adolescent European American female might be asked to consider how the text might be interpreted differently by a younger Mexican American male.

Text support

The text support section of the CRF may be considered an extension of the meaning/interpretation section. Linking their interpretations to specific passages from the text helps students examine how much of their interpretation stems from the text and how much from their own social and cultural identity. The student who resisted *Like Sisters on the Homefront* was asked to provide examples of the language and situations that caused her resistance and examples that supported her interpretation of the theme. When she reread passages and considered the changes in the protagonist's values and beliefs, she was willing to acknowledge the merits of the novel, but only as they applied to an African American young adult audience.

Post-reading group discussion

A *post-reading group discussion* involves a small group of readers either after finishing the novel or at designated points during the reading of the novel. This discussion should remain unfettered by teacher questions or control as much as possible. Students jot down salient comments to help them with recall. Students learn that it is all right to have different interpretations at various times as well as interpretations different from other readers. New meanings, whether gained through insights from others or rereading, do not cancel each other out.

Post-discussion writing

Each student writes an additional paragraph or two to sum up the discussion experience. Final writing can describe what aspects of the novel were discussed and areas of agreement and disagreement about response and interpretation. Students consider aspects of the novel mentioned by group members that they had not thought about, as well as ideas they may have shared that were not brought up by the others. They are requested to consider how influence worked within the group: how they were influenced by other students' ideas, and how they may have influenced others. This component of the CRF helps students develop awareness of how their own interpretations may have been shaped by their interpretive community.

Post-reading reflection/actions

The CRF guides each student to consider what post-reading reflection/actions will be taken. This could be to reread sections of the text in order to confirm or reject an idea shared during group discussions. This might encourage a biographical perspective, which prompts the student to seek out more information on the author. The critical literacy perspective encourages students to consider what kinds of actions they might take based on social and political issues raised in the literature. Figure 12.4 shows a completed student example of the CRF.

The CRF doesn't directly solicit theoretical terminology; it does however, engage students with components of reader response theory, close reading as developed from New Criticism, and a consideration of social and cultural aspects of both author and reader as supported by critical literacy theory.

The Classroom Scenario on pages 386–388 demonstrates a more explicit, direct approach for teaching literary theory.

Students' Critical Response Frame.

Name: **Becca**   Date: **October 24**

Novel: **My Name Is Not Easy (2011)**   Author: **Debby Dahl Edwardson**

Discussion Group Members: **P. J., Emma, Katie, Jake, Jarell**

Reading Context:

Mrs. Brown gave a book talk on three books and this one sounded the most interesting so I picked it. She said it was a finalist for The National Book Award for Young People's Literature so it should be good. Mrs. Brown gives some time in class to read every day and I have last period study hall so I read then, too. I have volleyball after school so I try to get all my school work done in class. I did think about it as school work because I knew I would have to write about it and I already have my own book that I am reading for fun at home.

Author's Presumed Intent:

The book is set up in parts and it has a Table of Contents. I noticed the "Author's Note" so I read that. She says the book is fiction but that it is based on stories people told her and many of the stories were true. She started talking about things that happened in Alaska to Eskimos. She calls them Native Alaskans and I didn't want to wreck the book so I stopped reading her "Note" because I figured it would be in the book. But some of the things mentioned were children being taken away from their families and sent to boarding schools and there was something about the government doing experiments on the students. She seems to be making the point that Native Alaskans were treated badly. She also seems to be pretty negative about the Catholics who ran the school.

Authorial Audience:

She said she wrote it for the children and grandchildren of these people so that they would know about what their relatives endured. She doesn't mean that she doesn't want other people to read it. It says on the book cover for ages 12 and up so I guess that is who she thinks will read it. I think the author is assuming the people who read her book, at least those who finish it, are pretty good readers. She switches narrators in the book starting with Luke whose name is really Aamaugak and next Chickie, who is a white girl. There are five characters listed as narrators, but there are other characters who are described well, too. Sometimes there is more than one narrator at the same time. This is when more than one character is equally important. Toward the end, when the section is called "Our Story," there aren't any names to indicate whose story it is

(continued)

figure **12.4**   Students' Critical Response Frame, *continued.*

because it is everyone's story now that all the students have decided to work together against the wrong things that have been done to them. Each section has a date so the reader can figure out when each character is talking. The book starts in 1960 and ends in 1964. There is an epilogue so I expect that to provide some closure. I think the author knows that teenagers like stories that don't leave you hanging. At least, I do.

I don't think the author is assuming that the reader needs to have background on the history of Alaska because the school and where the students lived is described well, and when the soldiers come, it explains why, even though it is a really lame excuse to give the students radiation so they can see how come they can survive in the cold. Sometimes italics are used to show a character is emphasizing a particular word, or thinking about something. Eskimo words are included, but they are always explained so there isn't a glossary or anything. I think it would help to know something about Catholic schools and priests and nuns and how kids are supposed to do whatever they say.

Reader's Self:

I think the fact that I am a typical teenager made me pay more attention to the relationships between the students than the mean priest and what the soldiers did. Sure, I knew that was unjust and bad, but I thought more about how Luke felt when they took his little brother, Isaac, away and then his other brother Brunna died. I also thought about Donna and Amiq's relationship, and they were both lonely and wanted to be with someone who made them feel they mattered. I didn't like Amiq drinking, especially because of what it did to his dad, and I was worried what he would do to Donna.

Meaning/Interpretation:

I think the theme was about the act of civil disobedience the students did and the way that they got over their differences and came together. In the first chapter Luke's mom tells him to take care of his brothers. As they fly away he sees all the families wishing goodbye get smaller and smaller. The Eskimos and Indians and white people had to be loyal to each other, which was not the case in the beginning of the story when they even sat at separate lunch tables. They had to care about what was right for all of them and not just themselves. They had to think about justice for all of them and to think about themselves as a family and to think about everyone as the great human family.

Students' Critical Response Frame, *continued.*   *figure* **12.4**

Text Support:

The setting, the boarding school in Alaska, was the reason the kids were brought together and that is where they learned that they are all part of the human family. Using the different narrators for most of the book emphasized their differences and personal backgrounds, but at the end the author didn't identify a narrator and the story was about everyone sticking together, now. When Amiq asked Junior about the duck hunters and their act of civil disobedience, Junior said they were only trying to feed their family. Then he realizes he meant families. But when he thought about it more he said it was family, the human family. Chickie talks about love (p. 160) and says it is holding on and "letting go, holding on and letting go." I think this is about all kinds of love and not just how she feels about Brunna. I think the author was also talking about her respect for the Inupiaq people when Luke's mom told him they are Eskimos and Eskimos survive.

Post-Reading Group Discussion:

We talked about what we thought the climax was. I was surprised when P.J. said the climax was when the earthquake struck on Good Friday and both Sister Sarah and Father Mullen died. He said this was God telling them that their way of "doing God's work" was wrong. People shouldn't make people give up their culture and language and become Christians just because that is what the people in charge believe. Jarell said this is what Mrs. Brown does when she corrects the way he talks. We talked about that a little bit. I said that I thought the climax was when the kids all stuck together and got an affidavit notarized to say they all sent the letter to the newspaper that exposed how the school gave away Eskimo children.

Post-Discussion Writing:

I thought about what P.J. said, and especially in the book when Luke said "the earth is always trying to right itself" (p. 239). I think he was talking about how to balance being true to yourself, and still be thinking about others. I don't think the author is saying God purposefully kills people for being bad. Edwardson explained in the Author's Note that there really was an earthquake on Good Friday in 1964 and 115 people in Alaska were killed. I did think it was interesting that the nun was always talking about "providence." So, I'm wondering if God's will and providence is the same thing.

Post-Reading Reflections/Actions:

It said on the book cover that the author had written a book called Blessing's Bead (2009) and it won an award for historical fiction so I figured I would check it out because I liked My Name Is Not Easy.

classroom scenario

Explicit Instruction in Literary Theories

AS YOU READ this classroom scenario, consider why Mr. Petrie presented each theory individually, before asking students to apply multiple theories with a single novel. Also, consider the concepts or information solicited by each question and the match between the questions and the theory.

Mr. Petrie's twelfth-grade class has been analyzing literature from different theoretical perspectives throughout the semester. He has been matching a single theory with a specific novel, explicitly explain-

ing each theory as they analyze and critique the novel. He chose three sophisticated novels with challenging content and structure.

The class read *The Astonishing Life of Octavian Nothing* (Anderson, 2006; see Chapter 5), from a critical perspective, in particular, multicultural and Marxist perspectives. Students discussed how politics and economics were intertwined and the effect of external events on Octavian's developing racial identity. *Postcards from No Man's Land* (Chambers, 2002; see Chapter 5) was read from a formalist perspective with attention to the metafictive characteristics of intertwining two narratives across time. *Blue Plate Special* (Kwasney, 2009; see Chapter 2) was read from a reader response perspective, emphasizing personal con-

nections readers had with the characters, the way the characters dealt with family relationships, and the consequences of decisions made in adolescence.

Now that the students have read the three novels from the three theoretical perspectives, Mr. Petrie wants them to experience reading a book from multiple theoretical perspectives. He considers the background information that will be needed to facilitate understanding the novel students will read next, *Revolution* (2010) by Jennifer Donnelly. Mr. Petrie has chosen the book because it lends itself to analysis from multiple theoretical perspectives. *Revolution* has a complex structure and challenging

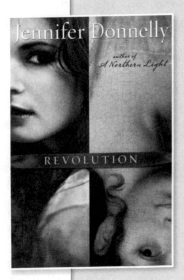

content; it focuses on human problems across time, including love, family, finding one's identity, and personal growth. It brings to bear the historical and personal consequences of economic and gender disparity. The audio version, an Odyssey Award winner, is available for students who wish to listen as they read.

The novel is organized in sections labeled Hell, Purgatory, and Paradise, paralleling Dante's 14th-century work *The Divine Comedy*. The young French man who befriends Andi, one of the protagonists, is named Virgil in homage to the Roman poet who guided Dante through hell. Earlier in the year students read part of the Dante's poem and watched part of an animated video adaptation (2010) directed by Mike Disa. Therefore, Mr. Petrie feels confident his students will have the background to make important intertextual connections.

Revolution is told from the alternating perspectives of a troubled contemporary adolescent girl, Andi, and the recollections, told in non-sequential diary entries, of a young woman, Alexandrine (Alex), living during the French Revolution. The characters are well developed and the plots have several parallel components, including the death of young boys, the powerlessness felt by both protagonists, and the importance of music. Numerous allusions to modern and classical music and real and imagined composers add depth to the critical role of music in Andi's personal revolution.

Mr. Petrie knows that the sections on the French revolution will prompt many students to read independently about that time period, but he also realizes that some students will not do so. He consults with the history teacher, who assures him that students have a general knowledge about this event and the important historical figures of the time. Mr. Petrie also makes available the documentary film *The French Revolution* (Shultz, 2005) for students who might want a review.

Mr. Petrie sets up a discussion board on his school's website and posts sets of questions designed to solicit various theoretical perspectives (see Figure 12.5). Mr. Petrie has developed his questions based in part on the work of Ann Dobie (2012). Students are expected to post comments in response to five questions listed under each theory as well as respond to three classmates' entries under each theory.

To assess the students' understanding of literary theory and its influence on literary criticism, they will select a novel, either contemporary or classic, and analyze it from the theoretical perspective of their choice. After completing this analysis, they will reconsider the work from a different theoretical perspective. The final component of the assessment is for them to reflect on how each theory altered the criteria for judging the literature.

Theoretical perspective questions for exploring the novel *Revolution*.  *figure* **12.5**

FORMALIST

1. How does the nonlinear structure of the diaries affect the historical fiction part of the novel? How does the sequential structure of the contemporary story line affect that part of the novel? The diaries interrupt the contemporary plot line. How does this affect the narrative?

2. What are some of the parallels between the contemporary and historical stories? Consider characters, plot elements, and stylistic devices.

3. What is the denouement and does it provide closure?

4. What is the effect of telling the story from two points of view and through two different genres?

5. What is the effect of the recurring musical allusions?

6. How does the choice of language affect the authenticity of the contemporary and historical settings?

7. What does a plot chart of this novel look like?

8. How does the intertextual connection to Dante's poem impact the story? Why is most of *Revolution* devoted to hell?

9. What images or words are used to foreshadow later events?

10. What is ambiguous in the novel?

11. What narrative device does the author use to bring the two stories together?

(continued)

READER RESPONSE

1. What does the author intend for you to feel while reading this novel, and did you feel this way?

2. How did your previous experiences with the first genre you encountered in the novel affect the way you expected to feel? How did the switch to Alexandrine's diary change your feelings?

3. What images and events in the novel have you already been conditioned to approve and disapprove?

4. What kind of a reader is implied in this novel?

5. How did your responses change as you progressed through the novel?

6. What are the most vivid images in the text? How did you construct them from the text?

7. What did you know about contemporary New York and Paris and France during the French Revolution before you read? How has this changed?

8. What bothered you about the text? Why?

9. What is one comment you would make about this book?

10. What else would you like to know about Andi and Alex?

11. Identify a line in the novel or an image that immediately caught your attention or that you remember clearly. Why is this important to you?

CRITICAL LITERACY

1. Who are the powerful people in Andi's story? In Alex's? Which groups have limited or no power in the contemporary settings and the French Revolution?

2. How did the powerful people come to have their power?

3. What class struggle exists in both the contemporary and the historical parts of the novel?

4. How do the beliefs and expectation of the characters differ? Are cultural, gender, historical, or economic considerations a factor?

5. How does Virgil being Tunisian and French affect the story?

6. Vijay Gupta is portrayed in a stereotypical manner. How does this add or detract from his character's role as Andi's friend?

7. Alex takes on male characteristics when she pretends to be a man. Why does she do this, and does she accomplish her goal?

8. Do female characters rely on male characters for aid or approval? In addition to Andi and Alex, consider Andi's mother, Alex's mother and sister, and G's wife. How does gender relate to mental instability and infirmity?

9. How do G and Lewis Alpers, Andi's father, differ in their opinions about what constitutes history? How do these different perspectives influence what people believe as historical truth?

10. How do the sexual mores of the characters affect their lives? Are sexual behaviors portrayed within or beyond traditional expectations?

T heories can seem daunting and may seem superfluous because there are so many of them and their popularity keeps shifting. However, if theories are considered beyond each "ism," they can provide a way of thinking that enhances—not hinders—the study of literature (Showalter, 2003). Literature study isn't the study of history, psychology, pedagogy, philosophy, science, linguistics, culture, authors' motives, moral dilemmas, finding an identity, or being a citizen of the world. In varying combinations, however, these elements come together to inform literary theories, which in turn, influence the value given to a literary work, how a reader interprets it, and the effect it has on the reader.

Literary theories continue to emerge and evolve. A case in point is ecocriticism, the study of literature according to ecological concepts or the relationship between literature and the physical environment (Dobie, 2012, p. 238). Only time will tell if this theory joins the ranks of the mainstream theories of literary criticism or fades away. In either case, this theory, as with others, provides a unique perspective for analyzing and judging literature. And it may, as other theories have done, alter the literature studied in school.

Knowledge of theory helps teachers strike a balance between activities designed to develop students' understanding of texts, activities designed to help readers learn about themselves, and activities to help them investigate the world they live in. Knowledge of theory helps students understand and appreciate the complexities of texts and the multiple ways of experiencing the world through literature.

conclusion

BIBLIOGRAPHY OF LITERATURE FOR YOUNG ADULTS

Anderson, M. T. (2006). *The astonishing life of Octavian Nothing: Traitor to the nation. Volume I: The pox party.* Cambridge, MA: Candlewick Press.

Avasthi, S. (2010). *Split.* New York: Knopf.

Bacigalupi, P. (2010). *Ship breaker.* New York: Little, Brown.

Blumberg, R. (2001). *Shipwrecked! The true adventure of a Japanese boy.* New York: HarperCollins.

Bowler, T. (2008). *Frozen fire.* New York: Philomel.

Boyle, G. (2010). *Tattoos on the heart: The power of boundless compassion.* New York: Free Press.

Bray, L. (2009). *Going bovine.* New York: Delacorte.

Brown, J. (2009). *Hate list.* New York: Little, Brown.

Chambers, A. (2002). *Postcards from no man's land.* New York: Dutton.

Daldry S. (Dir.). (2000). *Billy Elliot.* UK: Universal Focus.

Disa, M. (Dir.). (2010). *Dante's inferno.* U.S.A.: Starz/Anchor Bay.

Donnelly, J. (2010). *Revolution.* New York: Delacorte.

Edwardson, D. D. (2009). *Blessing's bead.* New York: Farrar, Straus & Giroux.

Edwardson, D. D. (2011). *My name is not easy.* Tarrytown, NY: Marshall Cavendish.

Felin, M. S. (2007). *Touching snow.* New York: Atheneum.

Forman, G. (2011). *Where she went.* New York: Dutton.

Forman, G. (2009). *If I stay.* New York: Dutton.

Homer, (2000). *The odyssey.* (S. Lombardo, Trans.). Indianapolis, IN: Hackett.

Ibsen, H. (1897). *A doll's house.* Retrieved from http://www.gutenberg.org/ebooks/2542.

Kwasney, M. (2009). *Blue plate special.* San Francisco: Chronicle Books.

Lee, H. (1960). *To kill a mockingbird.* Philadelphia, PA: Lippincott.

Lynch, C. (2011). *Angry young man.* New York: Simon & Schuster.

MacLean, S. (2009). *The season.* New York: Orchard Books.

McCaughrean, G. (2005). *The white darkness.* New York: HarperTempest.

McCormick, P. (2006). *Sold.* New York: Hyperion.

McNeal, L. (2010). *Dark water.* New York: Knopf.

Mulligan, A. (2010). *Trash*. New York: David Fickling Books.

Myracle, L. (2011). *Shine*. New York: Amulet Books.

Na, A. (2001). *A step from heaven*. Asheville, NC: Front Street.

Noyce, P. (Dir. and Prod.). (2002). *Rabbit proof fence*. Australia: Miramax.

Oppel, K. (2010). *Half brother*. New York: Scholastic.

Poe, E. A. (1845). The raven. Retrieved from http://www.houseofusher.net/raven.html.

Preus, M. (2010). *Heart of a samurai*. New York: Amulet Books.

Sedgwick, M. (2009). *Revolver*. New York: Roaring Brook Press.

Sepetys, R. (2011). *Between shades of gray*. New York: Philomel.

Shakespeare, W. (1606, 1936). *The tragedy of Macbeth*. In G. L. Kittredge (Ed.), *The complete works of Shakespeare* (pp. 1113–1144). Boston, MA: Ginn.

Shelley, P. B. (1818). Ozymandias. Retrieved from http://www.online-literature.com/shelley_percy/672/.

Shultz, D. (Dir.). (2005). *The French Revolution*. U.S.A.: History Channel/A&E Home Video.

Steinbeck, J. (1939). *The grapes of wrath*. New York: Viking.

Vanderpool, C. (2010). *Moon over Manifest*. New York: Delacorte Press.

Voltaire. (1759). *Candide*. Retrieved from http://www.literature.org/authors/voltaire/candide/.

Werlin, N. (2006). *The rules of survival*. New York: Dial.

Williams-Garcia, R. (1995). *Like sisters on the homefront*. New York: Puffin.

Wilson, M. (2008). *What they always tell us*. New York: Delacorte.

Yancey, R. (2009). *The monstrumologist*. New York: Simon & Schuster.

REFERENCES

Applebee, A. (1993). *Literature in the secondary school: Studies of curriculum and instruction in the United States*. Urbana, IL: National Council of Teachers of English.

Appleman, D. (2009). *Critical encounters in high school English: Teaching literary theory to adolescents* (2nd ed.). New York: Teachers College Press; Urbana, IL: National Council of Teachers of English.

Arikan, A. (2008). Formalist linguistic criticism in an English language teacher education program: The reward approach. *Iranian Journal of Language Studies*, 2(4), 417–430.

Bean, T. W., & Moni, K. (2003). Developing student's critical literacy: Exploring identity construction in young adult fiction. *Journal of Adolescent & Adult Literacy*, 46, 638–648.

Behrman, E. (2006). Teaching about language, power, and text: A review of classroom practices that support critical literacy. *Journal of Adolescent & Adult Literacy*, 49, 490–498.

Bloom, H. (1987). *The closing of the American mind*. New York: Simon & Schuster.

Brewton, V. (2005). Literary theory. *Internet Encyclopedia of Philosophy*. Retrieved from http://www.iep.utm.edu/literary.

Brozo, W. G. (2002). *To be a boy, to be a reader: Engaging teen and preteen boys in active literacy*. Newark, DE: International Reading Association.

Cai, M. (2008). Transactional theory and the study of multicultural literature. *Language Arts*, 85(3), 212–220.

Carey-Webb, A. (2001). *Literature & lives: A response-based, cultural studies approach to teaching English*. Urbana, IL: National Council of Teachers of English.

Cervetti, G., Pardales, M. J., & Damico, J. S. (2001, April). A tale of differences: Comparing the traditions, perspectives, and educational goals of critical reading and critical literacy. *Reading Online*, 4(9). Retrieved from http//www.readingonline.org/articles/cervetti/index.html.

Ciardiello, V. (2004). Democracy's young heroes: An instrumental model of critical literacy practices. *Reading Teacher*, 2, 138–147.

Connell, J. M. (2008). The emergence of pragmatic philosophy's influence on literary theory: Making meaning with texts from a transactional perspective. *Educational Theory*, 58(1), 103–122.

Cox, C. (2002). Resistance to reading in school. In M. Hunsberger & G. Labercane (Eds.), *Making meaning in the response-based classroom* (pp. 141–153). Boston: Allyn & Bacon.

Csicsila, J. (2004). *Canons by consensus: Critical trends and American literature anthologies*. Tuscaloosa, AL: University of Alabama Press.

Dobie, A. B. (2012). *Theory into practice: An introduction to literary criticism* (3rd ed.). Boston: Wadsworth Cengage Learning.

Eckert, L. S. (2008). Bridging the pedagogical gap: Intersections between literacy and reading theories in secondary and postsecondary literacy instruction. *Journal of Adolescent and Adult Literacy*, 52, 110–118.

Eckert, L. S. (2006). *How does it mean: Engaging reluctant readers through literacy theory.* Portsmouth, NH: Heinemann.

Fish, S. (1976). Interpreting the "variorium." *Critical Inquiry, 2*(3), 465–485.

Freire, P. (1987). *Literacy: Reading the word and the world.* Westport: CT: Bergin & Garvey.

Galda, L. (1990). A longitudinal study of the spectator stance as a function of age and genre. *Research in the Teaching of English, 24*(3), 261–278.

Galda, L., & Liang, L. A. (2003). Literature as experience or looking for fact: Stance in the classroom. *Reading Research Quarterly, 38*(2), 268–275.

Green, P. (2001). Critical literacy revisited. In H. Fehring, & P. Green (Eds.), *Critical literacy: A collection of articles from the Australian Literacy Educators' Association* [Electronic version]. Newark, DE: International Reading Association.

Hirsh, E. D., Jr. (1987). *Cultural literacy: What every American needs to know.* New York: Vintage.

Karolides, N. (1992). The transactional theory of literature. In Nicholas J. Karolides (Ed.), *Reader response in the classroom: Evoking and interpreting meaning in literature* (pp. 21–32). New York: Longman.

Kennedy, X. J., Gioia, D., & Bauerlein, M. (2006). *The Longman dictionary of literary terms: Vocabulary for the informed reader.* New York: Pearson Longman.

Knickerbocker, J. L., & Rycik, J. A. (2006). Reexamining literature study in the middle grades: A critical response framework. *American Secondary Education, 34*(3), 43–56.

Kraver, J. (2007). Engendering gender equity: Using literature to teach and learn democracy. *English Journal, 96*(6), 67–73.

Krupat, A. (1987, Summer). Criticism and the canon: Cross-relations. *Diacritics,* 3–20.

Lewison, M., Flint, A. S., & Sluys, K. V. (2002). Taking on critical literacy: The journey of newcomers and novices. *Language Arts, 79*(5), 382–392.

Lockett, M. (2010). Close reading; A synergistic approach to the (post)modern divide. *Changing English, 17*(4), 399–409.

Lynch, T. L. (2008). Rereading and literacy: How students' second readings might open third spaces. *Journal of Adolescent and Adult Learning, 52,* 334–341.

McLaughlin, M., & DeVoogd, G. (2004). Critical literacy as comprehension: Expanding reader response. *Journal of Adolescent & Adult Literacy, 1,* 52–62.

Milner, J. O., & Milner, L. M. (1999). *Bridging English* (2nd ed.). Upper Saddle River, NJ: Merrill, Prentice Hall.

Moore, J. N. (1997). *Interpreting young adult literature: Literary theory in the secondary classroom.* Portsmouth, NH: Heinemann.

Morris, D. (2011). Critical literacy: Crises and choices in the current arrangement. In J. B. Cobb & M. K. Kallus (Eds.), *Historical, theoretical, and sociological foundations of reading in the United States* (pp. 286–315). Boston: Pearson.

Murfin, R., & Ray, S. M. (1998). Critical approaches. *The Bedford glossary of critical and literary terms.* Retrieved from http://bcs.bedfordstmartins.com/virtualit/poetry/critical_define/crit_struct.html.

National Governors Association Center for Best Practices, Council of Chief State School Officers (2010). *Common core state standards for English language arts & literacy in history/social studies, science, and technical subjects.* Washington, DC: Author.

Probst, R. E. (1984). *Adolescent literature: Response and analysis.* Columbus, OH: Charles E. Merrill.

Probst, R. E. (1992). Five kinds of literary knowing. In J. Langer (Ed.), *Literature instruction: A focus on student response.* Urbana, IL: National Council of Teachers of English.

Rabinowitz, P. J., & Smith, M. W. (1998). *Authoring readers: Resistance and respect in the teaching of literature.* New York: Teachers College Press and Urbana, IL: National Council of Teachers of English.

Rosenblatt, L. M. (2005). *Making meaning with texts: Selected essays.* Portsmouth, NH: Heinemann.

Rosenblatt, L. M. (1938/1968). *Literature as exploration* (Revised ed.). New York: Noble & Noble.

Rycik, J. A., & Irvin, J. L. (2005). *Teaching reading in the middle grades: Understanding and supporting literacy development.* Boston: Pearson.

Serafini, F. (2004). *Informing our practice: Modernist, transactional and critical perspectives on children's literature and reading instruction.* Reading Online. Retrieved from www.readingonline.org/articles/serafini.

Showalter, E. (2003). *Teaching literature.* Maiden, MA: Blackwell.

Smagorinsky, P. (2001). If meaning is constructed, what is it made from? Toward a cultural theory of reading. *Review of Educational Research, 71*(1), 133–169.

Tracey, D. H., & Morrow, L. M. (2006). *Lenses on reading.* New York: Guilford Press.

Vollaro, D. R. (2008). *Origins and orthodoxy: Anthologies of American literature and American history.* English Dissertations, Paper 36. Retrieved from http://digitalarchive.gsu.edu/english_diss/36.

Wood, K. D., Soares, L., & Watson, P. A. (2006). Empowering adolescents through critical literacy. *Middle School Journal, 37*(3), 55–59.

Appendix A

For each award, we have not attempted to provide a full list of award winners over the years. Rather, we have provided a brief description of the intent of the award and a brief representative list of winning titles and authors. Also included are the website URLs for each award.

Alex Award

www.ala.org/yalsa/booklists/alex

Each year this award is "given to ten books written for adults that have special appeal to young adults ages 12 to 18." It is sponsored by the Margaret A. Edwards Trust through the American Library Association's Young Adult Library Services Association (YALSA). The Alex Award began in 1998 and became an official American Library Association (ALA) award in 2002.

2012 Award

Big Girl Small by Rachel DeWoskin

In Zanesville by Jo Ann Beard

The Lover's Dictionary by David Levithan

The New Kids: Big Dreams and Brave Journeys at a High School for Immigrant Teens by Brooke Hauser

The Night Circus by Erin Morgenstern

Ready Player One by Ernest Cline

Robopocalypse: A Novel by Daniel H. Wilson

Salvage the Bones by Jesmyn Ward

The Scrapbook of Frankie Pratt: A Novel in Pictures by Caroline Preston

The Talk-Funny Girl by Roland Merullo

2011 Award

The Boy Who Couldn't Sleep and Never Had To by D.C. Pierson

Breaking Night: A Memoir of Forgiveness, Survival, and My Journey from Homeless to Harvard by Liz Murray

Girl in Translation by Jean Kwok

The House of Tomorrow by Peter Bognanni

The Lock Artist by Steve Hamilton

The Particular Sadness of Lemon Cake: A Novel by Aimee Bender

The Radleys by Matt Haig

The Reapers Are the Angels: A Novel by Alden Bell

Room by Emma Donoghue

The Vanishing of Katharina Linden: A Novel by Helen Grant

2010 Award

Everything Matters! by Ron Currie, Jr.

My Abandonment by Peter Rock

Soulless: An Alexia Tarabotti Novel by Gail Carriger

Stitches: A Memoir by David Small

The Boy Who Harnessed the Wind: Creating Currents of Electricity and Hope by William Kamkwamba and Bryan Mealer

The Bride's Farewell by Meg Rosoff

The Good Soldiers by David Finkel

The Kids Are All Right: A Memoir by Diana Welch and Liz Welch with Amanda Welch and Dan Welch

The Magicians by Lev Grossman

Tunneling to the Center of the Earth by Kevin Wilson

Fabulous Films and Amazing Audio Books for Young Adults

www.ala.org/yalsa/fabfilms
www.ala.org/yalsa/audiobooks

These related lists are created by the YALSA division of the ALA. The Fabulous Films are "films relating to a specific theme that will appeal to young adults ages 12–18"; the films can be from any year. The Amazing Audiobooks are chosen from items released during the previous two years. The titles represent a wide variety of genres and styles.

Films Selected in 2012

Theme: "Song and Dance," including fiction and nonfiction films "that showcase varying genres of music and dance from around the world."

A few examples from the list of 25 winners include *Almost Famous* (Dreamworks, 2000); *Bride and Prejudice* (Miramax Home Video, 2004); *Drumline* (Fox, 2002); *Hairspray* (New Line Home Video, 2007); *Foo Fighters: Back and Forth* (RCA, 2011); and *Mao's Last Dancer* (20th Century Fox, 2009).

Films Selected in 2011

Theme: "Other Times/Other Places," including a variety of genres that "show teens reacting to society and how they develop as individuals."

A few examples from the list of 40 winners include *Alice in Wonderland* (Walt Disney, 2010); *American Graffiti* (Universal, 1973); *Back to the* *Future* (Universal, 1985); *Becoming Jane* (Miramax, 2007); *Empires: The Medici, Godfathers of the Renaissance* (PBS Paramount, 2004); and The *Untold Story of Emmett Louis Till* (ThinkFilm, 2005).

2012 Ten Top Amazing Audiobooks

Are These My Basoomas I See Before Me? by Louise Rennison, read by Stina Nielson

Beauty Queens by Libba Bray, read by Libba Bray

Carter's Big Break by Brent Crawford, read by Nick Podehl

Chime by Franny Billingsley, read by Susan Duerden

Curse of the Wendigo by Rick Yancey, read by Steven Boyer

Fever Crumb by Philip Reeve, read by Philip Reeve

How They Croaked by Georgia Bragg, read by L. J. Ganser

Marbury Lens by Andrew Smith, read by Mark Boyett

Ring of Solomon by Jonathan Stroud, read by Simon Jones

The Best Bad Luck I Ever Had by Kristine Levine, read by Kirby Heyborne

Wake of the Lorelei Lee by L. A. Meyer, read by Katherine Kellgren

2011 Ten Top Amazing Audiobooks

Dreamdark Silksinger by Lani Taylor, read by Cassandra Campbell

Finnikin of the Rock by Melina Marchetta, read by Jeffrey Cummings

The Knife of Never Letting Go by Patrick Ness, read by Nick Podehl

Muchacho by Louanne Johnson, read by Ozzie Rodriguez

One Crazy Summer by Rita Williams-Garcia, read by Sisi Aisha Johnson

Precious by Sapphire, read by Bahni Turpin

Rapture of the Deep by L. A. Meyer, read by Katherine Kellgren

The Rock and the River by Kekla Magoon, read by Dion Graham

Will Grayson, Will Grayson by John Green and David Levithan, read by MacLeod Andrews and Nick Prodehl

American Indian Youth Services Literature Award

www.ailanet.org/activities/youthlitaward.htm

The American Indian Library Association (AILA), an affiliate of the ALA, established its American Indian Youth Services Literature Award in 2006. This award focuses on literature written about and by American Indians, and "books selected to receive the award will present Native Americans in the fullness of their humanity in the present and the past contexts."

2012 Award

Picture Book: *The Christmas Coat: Memories of My Sioux Childhood* by Virginia Driving Hawk Sneve

Middle School: *Free Throw by Jacqueline Guest and Triple Threat* by Jacqueline Guest

Young Adult: *Pipestone: My Life in an Indian Boarding School* by Adam Fortunate Eagle

2010 Award

Picture Book: *A Coyote Solstice Tale* by Thomas King, illustrated by Gary Clement

Middle School: *Meet Christopher: An Osage Indian Boy from Oklahoma* by Genevieve Simermeyer, photographs by Katherine Fogden

Young Adult: *Between the Deep Blue Sea and Me: A Novel* by Lurline Wailana McGregor

2008 Award

Picture Book: *Crossing Bok Chitto: A Choctaw Tale of Friendship and Freedom* by Tim Tingle, illustrated by Jeannie Rorex Bridges

Middle School: *Counting Coup: Becoming a Crow Chief on the Reservation and Beyond* by Joseph Medicine Crow and Herman Viola

Young Adult: *The Absolutely True Diary of a Part-Time Indian* by Sherman Alexie, illlustrated by Ellen Forney

Américas Award for Children's and Young Adult Literature

www.uwm.edu/clacs/aa/index.cfm

This annual award is sponsored by the Consortium of Latin American Studies Program (CLASP). The award is given "in recognition of U.S. works of fiction, poetry, folklore, or selected non-fiction published in the previous year in English or Spanish that authentically and engagingly portray Latin American, the Caribbean, or Latinos in the United States." Titles range from picture to young adult books.

2011

Clemente! by Willie Perdomo, illustrated by Bryan Collier

The Dreamer by Pam Muñoz Ryan, illustrated by Peter Sis

2010

Return to Sender by Julia Alvarez

What Can You Do with a Paleta? by Carmen Tafolla

Arab American Book Award

www.arabamericanmuseum.org/bookaward

This award was established in 2006 by the Arab American National Museum to celebrate and support the research and written work of Arab Americans and their culture. The Arab American Book Award "encourages the publication and excellence of books that preserve and advance the understanding, knowledge, and resources of the

Arab American community by celebrating the thoughts and lives of Arab Americans."

2011 Award

Adult Fiction: *Loom* by Thérése Soukar Chehade

Nonfiction: *Arab Americans in Toledo: Cultural Assimilation and Community Involvement* edited by Samir Abu-Absi

Poetry: *Tocqueville* by Khaled Mattawa

Children/Young Adult: *Saving Sky* by Diane Stanley

2010 Award

Adult Fiction: *Master of the Eclipse* by Etel Adnan

Adult Nonfiction: *Angeleno Days: An Arab American Writer on Family, Place, and Politics* by Gregory Orfalea

Poetry: *Diary of a Wave Outside the Sea: Poetry and Stories from Iraq* by Danya Mikail

Best Books for Young Adults

www.ala.org/yalsa/booklists/bbya

YALSA's Best Books for Young Adults committee selects and prepares an annual, annotated list of significant adult and young adult books and publishes the top ten "Best Books" from the full list. Best Books include both fiction and nonfiction titles that are chosen "for their proven or potential appeal to personal reading tastes of the young adult." (In 2011, this award became the Best Fiction for Young Adults Award, discussed next.)

2010 Top Ten Best Books

Demon's Lexicon by Sara Rees Brennan

The Orange Houses by Paul Griffin

The Great Wide Sea by M. H. Herlong

The Reformed Vampire Support Group by Catherine Jinks

Alligator Bayou by Donna Jo Napoli

Stitches: A Memoir by David Small

When You Reach Me by Rebecca Stead

Marcelo in the Real World by Francisco X. Stork

Lips Touch: Three Times by Laini Taylor

Written in Bone: Buried Lives of Jamestown and Colonial Maryland by Sally M. Walker

Best Fiction for Young Adults

www.ala.org/yalsa/bfya

Best Books for Young Adults (BBYA) became the Best Fiction for Young Adults after the 2010 BBYA list was published.

2012 Top Ten Best Fiction Books

The Girl of Fire and Thorns by Rae Carson

Leverage by Joshua C. Cohen

Everybody Sees the Ants by A. S. King

Under the Mesquite by Guadalupe Garcia McCall

Shine by Lauren Myracle

A Monster Calls by Patrick Ness

Between the Shades of Gray by Ruta Sepetys

The Scorpio Races by Maggie Stiefvater

Daughter of Smoke and Bone by Laini Taylor

How to Save a Life by Sara Zarr

2011 Top Ten Best Fiction Books

Ship Breaker by Paolo Bacigalupi

Revolution by Jennifer Donnelly

Finnikin of the Rock by Melina Marchetta

Amy & Roger's Epic Detour by Morgan Matson

Hold Me Closer, Necromancer by Lish McBride

Trash by Andy Mulligan

Bamboo People by Mitali Perkins

The Things a Brother Knows by Dana Reinhardt

Last Night I Sang to the Monster by Benjamin Saenz

Revolver by Marcus Sedgwick

Boston Globe–Horn Book Awards

www.hbook.com/bghb

The Boston Globe–Horn Book Awards are "among the most prestigious honors in the field of children's literature and young adult literature." The editor of the *Horn Book* magazine chooses a panel of judges, and awards are given in the categories of picture book, fiction, poetry, and nonfiction. Selections must be published in the United States, but they may be written or illustrated by citizens of any country. Publishers submit nominations. The *Boston Globe* and the children's literature magazine *Horn Book* have collaborated since 1967 to offer this award.

2011

Picture Book: *Pocketful of Posies: A Treasury of Nursery Rhymes* by Salley Mavor

Nonfiction: *The Notorious Benedict Arnold: A True Story of Adventure, Heroism, & Treachery* by Steve Sheinkin

Fiction: *Blink & Caution* by Tim Wynne-Jones

2010

Picture Book: *I Know Here* by Laurel Croza, illustrated by Matt James

Nonfiction: *Marching for Freedom: Walk Together, Children, and Don't You Grow Weary* by Elizabeth Partridge

Fiction: *When You Reach Me* by Rebecca Stead

Caldecott Medal

www.ala.org/alsc/awardsgrants/bookmedia/caldecottmedal/caldecottmedal

This annual award is presented by the Association of Library Service to children (ALSC), a division of the ALA. The medal is given to the illustrator of a selection that is considered the "most distinguished American picture book for children" published in the previous year. The artist must be a citizen or resident of the United States. This medal has been given annually since 1937.

2012 Medal: *A Ball for Daisy* by Chris Raschka

2011 Medal: *A Sick Day for Amos McGee* by Philip C. Stead, illustrated by Erin E. Stead

2010 Medal: *The Lion & the Mouse* by Jerry Pinkney

Carnegie Medal in Literature

www.carnegiegreenaway.org.uk/livingarchive

The Carnegie Medal, established in 1936, is "given annually to an outstanding book for children and young adults." The Chartered Institute of Library and Information Professionals (CILIP) sponsors the award. Selections must be written in English and first published in the United Kingdom during the previous year. Nominated books are read by students, who send feedback to the judging panel, which consists of 13 children's librarians from the Youth Libraries Group of CILIP.

2011: *Monster of Men* by Patrick Ness

2010: *The Graveyard Book* by Neil Gaiman

Carter G. Woodson Award

www.ncss.org/awards/woodson

Since 1973, the Carter G. Woodson Award has been sponsored by the National Council for the Social Studies (NCSS) to honor the "most distinguished social science books appropriate for young readers that depict ethnicity in the United States." Books nominated for the award must accurately reflect the experience of one or more racial or ethnic minority groups in the United States.

2011

Elementary: *Sit-In: How Four Friends Stood Up by Sitting Down* by Andrea Davis Pinkney, illustrated by Brian Pinkney

Secondary: *An Unspeakable Crime: The Prosecution and Persecution of Leo Frank* by Elaine Marie Alphin

2010

Elementary: *Shining Star: The Anna May Wong Story* by Paul Wo, illustrated by Lin Wang

Middle School: *Claudette Colvin: Twice Toward Justice* by Phillip Hoose

Secondary School: *Denied, Detained, Deported: Stories from the Dark Side of American Immigration* by Ann Bausum

Coretta Scott King Award

www.ala.org/csk

The Coretta Scott King Award, sponsored by the ALA, is presented to "African American authors and illustrators for outstanding inspirational and educational contributions . . . [that] promote understanding and appreciation of the culture of all peoples and their contribution to the realization of the American dream of a pluralistic society." The award celebrates the work of both Dr. Martin Luther King, Jr. and his wife Coretta Scott King.

2012 Award: *Heart and Soul: The Story of America and African Americans* by Kadir Nelson

2011 Award: *One Crazy Summer* by Rita Williams-Garcia

2010 Award: *Bad News for Outlaws: The Remarkable Life of Bass Reeves, Deputy U.S. Marshal,* by Vaunda Micheaux Nelson, illustrated by R. Gregory Christie

Edgar® Awards

www.theedgars.com

The Edgar® Awards, named for the 19th-century author Edgar Allan Poe, are presented every year by the Mystery Writers of America. They honor the best in mystery fiction, nonfiction, television, film, and theater published or produced in the previous year.

2011 Awards

Best Juvenile: *The Buddy Files: The Case of the Lost Boy* by Dori Hillestad Butler, illustrated by Jeremy Tugeau

Best Young Adult: *Interrogation of Gabriel James* by Charlie Price

2010 Awards

Best Juvenile: *Closed for the Season* by Mary Downing Hahn

Best Young Adult: *Reality Check* by Peter Abrahams

Excellence in Poetry for Children

www.ncte.org/awards/poetry

This award was established in 1977 by the National Council of Teachers of English (NCTE) to "honor a living American poet for his or her aggregate work for children ages 3–13." The award was given annually until 1982 and every three years until 2009. In 2008 the Poetry Committee updated the criteria and changed the time frame to every other year.

2011 Award Winner: J. Patrick Lewis
2009 Award Winner: Lee Bennett Hopkins
2006 Award Winner: Nikki Grimes

Golden Kite Awards

www.scbwi.org

The Golden Kite Award, instituted in 1973, is presented annually by the Society of Children's Book Writers & Illustrators "to recognize excellence in children's literature." It is the only children's literary award judged by a jury of peers. Categories include fiction, nonfiction, picture book text, and picture book illustration.

2011 Award

Fiction: *Turtle in Paradise* by Jennifer Holm

Nonfiction: *The Good, the Bad, and the Barbie* by Tanya Lee Stone

Picture Book Text: *Big Red Lollipop* by Rukhsana Khan

Picture Book Illustration: *A Pocketful of Posies: A Treasury of Nursery Rhymes* by Salley Mavor

2010 Award

Fiction: *Sea of the Dead* by Julia Durango

Nonfiction: *Ashley Bryan: Words to My Life's Song* by Ashley Bryan

Picture Book Text: *The Longest Night* by Marion Dane Bauer

Picture Book Illustration: *Gracias/Thanks* illustrated by John Parra, written by Pat Mora

Great Graphic Novels for Teens

www.ala.org/yalsa/ggnt

This annotated list is prepared annually by a committee of YALSA members that includes a mix of public and school librarians. Works include recommended graphic novels, both fiction and nonfiction, that appeal to teens, ages 12 to 18. Works are to be in a sequential art format and represent literary and artistic quality.

Top Ten 2012

Zahra's Paradise by Amir and Khalil

Scarlet by Brian Bendis and Alex Maleev

Anya's Ghost by Vera Brosgal

The Influencing Machine: Brooke Gladstone on the Media by Brooke Gladstone, Josh Neufeld and others

Thor: The Mighty Avenger Vol. 1 and *Thor: The Mighty Avenger Vol. 2* by Roger Langridge, Christ Samnee, and others

Infinite Kung Fu by Kagan McLeod

A Bride's Story Vol. 1 by Kaoru Mori

Axe Cop Vol. 1 by Malachai Nicolle and Ethan Nicolle

Daybreak by Brian Ralph

Wandering Son Vol. 1 by Shimura Takako

Top Ten 2011

The Zabime Sisters by Aristophane, translated by Matt Madden

Green Monk by Brandon Dayton

Saturn Apartments Vol. 1 by Hisae Iwaoka

Brain Camp by Susan Kim, et. al.

Chew Vol. 1: Taster's Choice by John Layman and Rob Guillory

Yummy: The Last Days of a Southside Shorty by G. Neri and Randy Duburke

Meanwhile: Pick Any Path: 3,856 Story Possibilities by Jason Shiga

Smile by Raina Telemeier

Ghostopolis by Doug TenNapel

Set to Sea by Drew Weing

Top Ten 2010

The Helm, Vol. 1 by Jim Hardison and Bart Sears

Children of the Sea, Vol. 1 by Daisuke Igarashi

Pinocchio: Vampire Slayer by Van Jensen and Dusty Higgins

I Kill Giants by Joe Kelly and J. M. Ken Nimura

Omega the Unknown by Jonathan Lethem and Farel Dalrymple

Bayou, Vol. 1 by Jeremy Love

A.D.: New Orleans after the Deluge by Josh Neufeld

Gunnerkrigg Court, Vol. 1: Orientation by Tom Siddell

Pluto by Naoki Urasawa and Takashi Nagasaki

Ooku: The Inner Chambers, Vol. 1 by Fumi Yoshinaga

Hugo Award for Science Fiction

www.thehugoawards.org

The Hugo Awards are sponsored every year by the World Science Fiction Society (WSFS) and voted on at the World Science Fiction Convention to honor the best science fiction or fantasy works of the previous year. The award is named after Hugo Gernsback, the founder of the pioneering science fiction magazine *Amazing Stories* and is considered science fiction's most prestigious award. Hugo Awards have been presented every year since 1955. Of the 16 award categories, we selected only the short story and graphic novel.

2011 Awards

Short Story: "For Want of a Nail" by Mary Robinette Kowal

Graphic Novel: *Girl Genius Vol. 10: Agatha Heterodyne and the Guardian Muse* by Phil and Kaja Foglio, art by Phil Foglio, color by Cheyenne Wright

2010 Awards

Short Story: "Bridesicle" by Will McIntosh

Graphic Novel: *Girl Genius, Volume 9: Agatha Heterodyne & the Heirs of the Storm* by Kaja & Phil Foglio, art by Phil Foglio, color by Cheyenne Wright

Jane Addams Children's Book Award

www.janeaddamspeace.org/jacba/index_jacba.shtml

The Women's International League for Peace and Freedom (WILPF) and the Jane Addams Peace Association annually sponsor the Jane Addams Children's Book Awards. Award winners "effectively promote the cause of peace, social justice, world community, and the equality of the sexes and all races." This award has been presented since 1953, with the picture book category added in 1993.

2011

Emma's Poem: The Voice of the Statue of Liberty by Linda Glaser with paintings by Claire A. Nivola.

A Long Walk to Water: Based on a True Story by Linda Sue Park

2010

Nasreen's Secret School: A True Story from Afghanistan by Jeanette Winter

Marching for Freedom: Walk Together, Children, and Don't You Grow Weary by Elizabeth Partridge

Lambda Award

www.lambdaliterary.org/awards

The Lambda Literary Awards, presented since 1989 by the Lambda Literary Foundation (LLF), are "based primarily on literary merit and on significant content relevant to LGBT lives." The award consists of 22 categories. One of the categories is LGBT Children's/Young Adult.

2011 Children's/Young Adult Award: *Wildthorn* by Jane Eagland

2010 Children's/Young Adult Award: *Sprout* by Dale Peck

Michael L. Printz Award for Excellence in Young Adult Literature

www.ala.org/yalsa/printz

The Printz Award is presented annually by the YALSA division of the ALA to honor the best book written for teens based on literary merit. Books may be fiction, nonfiction, poetry, or an anthology and must be identified by the publisher as intended for young adults or those between the ages of 12 and 18.

2012 Award: *Where Things Come Back* by John Corey Whaley

2011 Award: *Ship Breaker* by Paolo Bacigalupi

2010 Award: *Going Bovine* by Libba Bray.

Mildred L. Batchelder Award

www.ala.org/alsc/awardsgrants/bookmedia/batchelderaward

The ALA's Batchelder Award is given to an American publisher for a children's book that has been translated into English and published in the United States. The book is considered to be the "most outstanding of those books originally published in a language other than English in a country other than the United States."

2012 Award: *Soldier Bear* by Bibi Dumon Tak, illustrated by Philip Hopman, translated by

Laura Watkinson, and published by Eerdmans Books for Young Readers

2011 Award: *A Time of Miracles* by Anne-Laure Bondoux, translated by Y. Maudet, and published by Delacorte Press

2010 Award: *A Faraway Island* by Annika Thor, translated by Linda Schenck, and published by Delacorte Press

National Book Award for Young People's Literature

www.nationalbook.org

The National Book Award, an American literary prize established in 1950 and sponsored by the independent National Book Foundation, is given to books in various categories, including books for young adults or older middle grades. The award is given to writers by writers, with the purpose of "raising cultural appreciation of great writing in the United States."

2011 Award: *Inside Out & Back Again* by Thanhha Lai

2010 Award: *Mockingbird* by Kathryn Erskine

2009 Award: *Claudette Colvin: Twice Toward Justice* by Phillip Hoose

Newbery Medal

www.ala.org/alsc/awardsgrants/bookmedia/newberymedal/newberymedal

The Newbery Medal is awarded annually (beginning in 1922) by the Association for Library Service to Children (ALSC), a division of the ALA, to the author of the "most distinguished contribution to American literature for children" for a book published by an American publisher in the United States in English during the preceding year. The only limitation on the character of the book is that it is to be original work. All forms of writing are considered, and the audience is children up to and including age 14.

2012 Medal: *Dead End in Norvelt* by Jack Gantos

2011 Medal: *Moon Over Manifest* by Clare Vanderpool

2010 Medal: *When You Reach Me* by Rebecca Stead

Notable Books for a Global Society

www.csulb.edu/org/childrens-lit/proj/nbgs/intro-nbgs.html

Twenty-five books are selected each year by the International Reading Association's (IRA) Children's Literature and Reading Special Interest Group (CL/R SIG) committee to form the list of books honored as Notable Books for a Global Society. These trade books are chosen for increasing student "understanding of people and cultures throughout the world." Titles span a variety of genres and are written for students in grades K–12. Books must have been published for the first time in the United States. The following are a few titles honored in 2006: *The Story of My Life: An Afghan Girl on the Other Side of the Sky* by Farah Ahmedi and Tamim Ansary; *Hitler Youth: Growing Up in Hitler's Shadow* by Susan Campbell Bartoletti; *Sawdust Carpets* by Amelia Lau Carling; *Sweetgrass Basket* by Marlene Carvell; and *Mama Panya's Pancakes: A Village Tale from Kenya* by Mary Chamberlin and Rich Chamberlin, illustrated by Julia Cairns.

Orbis Pictus Award

www.ncte.org/awards/orbispictus

The Orbis Pictus Award is presented by the NCTE for "promoting and recognizing excellence in non-fiction." The literary criteria for the Orbis Pictus is accuracy, organization, design, and style. Nonfiction or informational literature, including biography, whose main purpose is sharing information are considered for the award.

2012 Award: *Balloons over Broadway: The True Story of the Puppeteer of Macy's Parade* by Melissa Sweet

2011 Award: *Ballet for Martha: Making Appalachian Spring* by Jan Greenberg and Sandra Jordan, illustrated by Brian Floca

2010 Award: *The Secret World of Walter Anderson* by Hester Bass, illustrated by E. B. Lewis.

Popular Paperbacks for Young Adults

www.ala.org/yalsa/booklists/poppaper

A YALSA committee creates these annual lists of books "to encourage young adults to read for pleasure." The selected books represent a wide variety of themes and genres.

2012 Themes

Adventure Seekers

Forbidden Romance

Get Your Geek On

Sticks and Stones

TOP TEN LIST

Geektastic: Stories from the Nerd Herd by Holly Black and Cecil Castellucci (Eds.)

Super Human by Michael Carroll

Brain Jack by Brian Falkner

Shattering Glass by Gail Giles

Here Lies Bridget by Paige Harbison

Jane by April Lindner

Sidescrollers by Matthew Loux

Hero by Perry Moore

My Boyfriend Was a Monster 1: I Love You to Pieces by Evonne Tsang

Tripping by Heather Waldorf

2011 Themes

Thrillers & Killers

What's Cooking?

What If

Zombies, Werewolves, and Things with Wings

TOP TEN LIST

Burger Wuss by M. T. Anderson

The Manga Cookbook: Dust Off Your Chopstick Skills and Chow Down on Manga-Inspired Japanese Cuisine by Yoko Ishihara

Other by Karen Kincy

Zombie Haiku: Good Poetry for Your . . . Brains by Ryan Mecum

Shadoweyes by Campbell Ross

Unwind by Neal Shusterman

Tantalize by Cynthia Leitich Smith

Wherever Nina Lies by Lynn Weingarten

Leviathan by Scott Westerfeld

Malice by Chris Wooding

Pura Belpré Award

www.ala.org/alsc/awardsgrants/bookmedia/belpremedal

This award was presented biennially until 2008 and annually thereafter to a "Latino/Latina writer and illustrator whose work best portrays, affirms, and celebrates the Latino cultural experience in an outstanding work of literature for children and youth." The award is co-sponsored by the ALSC division of the ALA and REFORMA, the National Association to Promote Library and Information Services to Latino and the Spanish-Speaking.

2012 Medal: *Under the Mesquite* by Guadalupe Garcia McCall

2011 Medal: *The Dreamer* by Pam Muñoz Ryan, illustrated by Peter Sis

2010 Medal: *Return to Sender* by Julia Alvarez.

Quick Picks for Reluctant Young Adult Readers

www.ala.org/yalsa/booklists/quickpicks

This annual, annotated list is prepared by a YALSA committee for young adults ages 12 to 18 who do not like to read. The chosen titles are recommended for recreational reading, not for instructional use. Books are "evaluated by subject, cover art, readability, format, style and teen feedback."

Traditional fiction, pop culture titles, fantasy, and street lit are among the choices for this list.

2012 Quick Picks Top Ten

Enclave by Ann Aguirre

Whoogles: Can a Dog Make a Woman Pregnant? . . . and Hundreds of Other Searches That Make You Ask Who Would Google That? by Kendall Almerico and Tess Hottenroth

Pavement Chalk Artist: The Three-Dimensional Drawings of Julian Beever by Julian Beever

Bronxwood by Coe Booth

A Stolen Life: A Memoir by Jaycee Dugard

Chain Reaction by Simone Elkeles

The Zodiac Killer: Terror and Mystery by Brenda Haugen

Middle School: The Worst Years of My Life by James Patterson

D.C. Comics: The Ultimate Character Guide by Brandon Snider

Ghostopolis by Doug TenNapel

2011 Quick Picks Top Ten

This Is Why You're Fat: Where Dreams Become Heart Attacks by Jessica Amason and Richard Blakeley

Warriors Versus Warriors: Ten Fighters, Five Battles, One Winner by Catherine Brereton, Philip Steele, and Hannah Wilson

Rules of Attraction: A Perfect Chemistry Novel by Simone Elkeles

Sex: A Book for Teens: An Uncensored Guide to Your Body, Sex and Safety By Nikol Hasler

The D.U.F.F. (Designated Ugly Fat Friend) by Kody Keplinger

Yummy: The Last Days of Southside Shorty by G. Neri and Randy DuBurke

Scars by Cheryl Rainfield

Some Girls Are by Courtney Summers

Rikers High by Paul Volponi

The Tattoo Chronicles by Kat Von D with Sandra Bark

2010 Quick Picks Top Ten

Street Art Book: 60 Artists in Their Own Words by Ric Blackshaw and Lizarrelly

The Naked Truth: Young, Beautiful and (HIV) Positive by Marvelyn Brown

Perfect Chemistry by Simone Elkeles

Jumping Off Swings by Jo Knowles

Dope Sick by Walter Dean Myers

The Vampire Book by Sally Regan

Lockdown: Escape from Furnace by Alexander Gordon Smith

Show Me How: 500 Things You Should Know: Instructions for Life From the Everyday To the Exotic by Derk Fagerstrom and Lauren Smith

High Voltage Tattoo by Kat Von D

Paranormal Caught on Film by Melvyn Willin

Robert F. Sibert Informational Book Medal

www.ala.org/alsc/awardsgrants/bookmedia/sibertmedal

The Robert F. Sibert Informational Medal has been awarded annually since 2001 to the author of the "most distinguished informational book published in the United States in English during the preceding year." The award is sponsored by the ALSC division of the ALA and supported by the Bound to Stay Bound Books.

2012 Medal: *Balloons Over Broadway: The True Story of the Puppeteer of Macy's Parade* by Melissa Sweet

2011 Medal: *Kakapo Rescue: Saving the World's Strangest Parrot* by Sy Montgomery, photographs by Nic Bishop.

2010 Medal: *Almost Astronauts: 13 Women Who Dared to Dream* by Tanya Lee Stone.

Schneider Family Book Award

www.ala.org/awardsgrants/awards/1/detail

The ALA's Schneider Family Book Award honors an author or illustrator for a book that "embodies an artistic expression of the disability experience for child and adolescent audiences." The book must portray some aspect of living with a disability or that of a friend or family member, whether the disability is physical, mental, or emotional.

2012 Award

Middle School: *Close to Famous* by Joan Bauer
Wonderstruck: A Novel in Words and Pictures by Brian Selznick

Teen Book: *The Running Dream* by Wendelin Van Draanen

2011 Award

Young Children's Book: *The Pirate of Kindergarten* by George Ella Lyon, illustrated by Lynne Avril

Middle School: *After Ever After* by Jordan Sonnenblick

Teen Book: *Five Flavors of Dumb* by Antony John

2010 Award

Young Children's Book: *Django* by Bonnie Christensen

Middle School: *Anything but Typical* by Nora Raleigh Baskin

Teen Book: *Marcelo in the Real World* by Francisco X. Stork

Scott O'Dell Historical Fiction Award

www.scottodell.com/pages/ScottO'DellAwardf orHistoricalFiction.aspx

This award has been presented annually since 1984 to an outstanding work of historical fiction for children and young adults. The selection must be intended for children or young adults; be set in the New World, Canada, Central or South America, or the United States; be written in English by a U.S. citizen; and have a U.S. publisher. This award was established to "encourage other writers—*particularly new authors*—to focus on historical fiction. [Scott O'Dell] hoped in this way to increase the interest of young readers in the historical background that has helped shape their country and their world."

2012 Award: *Dead End in Norvelt* by Jack Gantos

2011 Award: *One Crazy Summer* by Rita Williams-Garcia

2010 Award: *The Storm in the Barn* by Matt Phelan

2009 Award: *Chains* by Laurie Halse Anderson.

Stonewall Children's & Young Adult Literature Award

www.ala.org/glbtrt/award

Established in 2010, the Stonewall Book Award for Children's and Young Adult Literature Award honors the best lesbian, gay, bisexual, and transgender literature and the authors who have brought GLBT experiences to light. The ALA's Gay, Lesbian, Bisexual, and Transgender Round Table sponsors this award.

2012 Award: *Putting Makeup on the Fat Boy* by Bil Wright

2011 Award: *Almost Perfect* by Brian Katcher

2010 Award: *The Vast Fields of Ordinary* by Nick Burd

Sydney Taylor Book Award

www.jewishlibraries.org/ajlweb/awards/stba

The Sydney Taylor Book Award is presented annually to "outstanding books for children and teens that authentically portray the Jewish experience." Gold medals are awarded in three categories: Younger Readers, Older Readers, and Teen Readers. Honor books are awarded silver medals, and notable books are named in each category. The Award is sponsored by the Association of Jewish Libraries (AJL).

2012

Younger Readers: *Chanukah Lights* by Michael J. Rosen, illustrated by Robert Sabuda

Older Readers: *Music Was It: Young Leonard Bernstein* by Susan Goldman Rubin

Teen Readers: *The Berlin Boxing Club* by Robert Sharenow

2011

Younger Readers: *Gathering Sparks* by Howard Schwartz, illustrated by Kristina Swarner

Older Readers: *Hereville: How Mirka Got Her Sword* by Barry Deutsch

Teen Readers: *The Things a Brother Knows* by Dana Reinhardt

2010

Younger Readers: *New Year at the Pier: A Rosh Hashanah* Story by April Halprin Wayland, illustrated by Stephane Jorisch

Older Readers: *The Importance of Wings* by Robin Friedman

Teen Readers: *Tropical Secrets: Holocaust Refugees in Cuba* by Margarita Engle

Teens' Top Ten

www.ala.org/yalsa

Teens "nominate and choose their favorite books from the previous year" for this award sponsored by YALSA. Nominations are made through members of teen book groups in 16 school and public libraries throughout the United States, and teens from ages 12 to 18 vote online for their favorite titles.

2011

Clockwork Angel by Cassandra Clare

Mockingjay by Suzanne Collins

Crescendo by Becca Fitzpatrick

I Am Number Four by Pittacus Lore

The Iron King by Julie Kagawa

Matched by Ally Condie

Angel: A Maximum Rise Novel by James Patterson

Paranormalcy by Kiersten White

Before I Fall by Lauren Oliver

Nightshade by Andrea Cremer

2010

Catching Fire by Suzanne Collins

City of Glass by Cassandra Clare

Heist Society by Ally Carter

Shiver by Maggie Stiefvater

Hush, Hush by Becca Fitzpatrick

Beautiful Creatures by Kami Garcia and Margaret Stohl

Along for the Ride by Sarah Dessen

If I Stay by Gayle Forman

Fire by Kristin Cashore

Wintergirls by Laurie Halse Anderson

2009

Paper Towns by John Green

Breaking Dawn by Stephenie Meyer

The Hunger Games by Suzanne Collins

City of Ashes by Cassandra Clare

Identical by Ellen Hopkins

The Graveyard Book by Neil Gaiman

Wake by Lisa McMann

Untamed by P. C. and Kristin Cast

The Disreputable History of Frankie Landau-Banks by E. Lockhart

Graceling by Kristin Cashore

YALSA Award for Excellence in Nonfiction

www.ala.org/yalsa/nonfiction

This nonfiction award began in 2010 and is sponsored by the YALSA to honor the "best nonfiction book published for young adults (ages 12–18)." The award is to "promote the growing number of nonfiction books published for young adults [and to] inspire wider readership in the genre."

2012 Award: *The Notorious Benedict Arnold: A True Story of Adventure, Heroism & Treachery* by Steve Sheinkin

2011 Award: *Janis Joplin: Rise Up Singing* by Ann Angel

2010 Award: *Charles & Emma: The Darwins' Leap of Faith* by Deborah Heiligman

Young Adults' Choices Reading List

www.reading.org/Resources/Booklists/ YoungAdultsChoices.aspx

The Young Adult Choices Reading List is sponsored by the International Reading Association (IRA). Beginning in 1987, this project has prepared an annual list of new books that will encourage adolescents to read. "The books are selected by the readers themselves, so they are bound to be popular with middle and secondary school students." "Each year approximately 4,500 students in grades 7 to 12 from different regions of the United States select 30 titles from new books donated by North American publishers." The following are a few examples from the 2011 list of 25 selections: *The Big Ideas that Changed the World* by Dorling Kindersley, *Incarceron* by Catherine Fisher, *Leviathan* by Scott Westerfeld, *The Necromancer* by Michael Scott, and *Out of My Mind* by Sharon M. Draper.

Young Readers' Choice Award

www.pnla.org/yrca

The Pacific Northwest Library Association sponsors the Young Readers' Choice Award. It is the "oldest children's choice award in the United States and Canada." Nominations are taken from children, teachers, parents, and librarians in the Pacific Northwest and include graphic novels, manga, anime, as well as traditional genres. Nominated titles are those published three years prior to the award year.

2011

Junior Division: *Amulet: The Stonekeeper* by Kazu Kibuishi

Middle Division: *Rapunzel's Revenge* by Shannon Hale

Senior Division: *The Hunger Games* by Suzanne Collins

2010

Junior Division: *Diary of a Wimpy Kid: Greg Heffley's Journal* by Jeff Kinney

Middle Division: *Schooled* by Gordon Korman

Senior Division: *City of Bones* by Cassandra Clare

Appendix B

CITIZEN'S REQUEST FOR RECONSIDERATION OF A WORK

Author _____ ○ HARDCOVER ○ PAPER

Title _____

Publisher _____

Request initiated by _____

Telephone _____

Address _____

City: _____ State: _____ Zip: _____

Telephone: _____

Complainant represents

○ Himself/Herself

○ (Name Organization) _____

○ (Identify other group) _____

1. Have you been able to discuss this work with the teacher or librarian who ordered or who used it? ○ YES ○ NO

2. What do you understand to be the general purpose for using this work?

   Provide support for a unit in the curriculum? ○ YES ○ NO

   Provide a learning experience for the reader in one kind of literature? ○ YES ○ NO

   Other _____

3. Did the general purpose for the use of the work, as described by the teacher or librarian, seem a suitable one to you? ○ YES ○ NO

   If not, please explain.

   _____

   _____

4. What do you think is the general purpose of the author of this book?

_____

_____

5. In what ways do you think a work of this nature is not suitable for the use the teacher or librarian wishes to carry out?

_____

_____

6. Have you been able to learn what the students' response to this work is?   ○ YES   ○ NO

7. What response did the students make?

_____

_____

8. Have you been able to learn from your school library what book reviewers or other students of literature have written about this work?   ○ YES   ○ NO

9. Would you like the teacher or librarian to give you a written summary of what book reviewers or other students have written about this book or film?   ○ YES   ○ NO

10. Do you have negative reviews of the book?   ○ YES   ○ NO

11. Where were they published?

_____

_____

12. Would you willing to provide summaries of the views you have collected?   ○ YES   ○ NO

13. What would you like your library/school to do about this work?

　○ Do not assign/lend it to my child.

　○ Return it to the staff selection committee/department for re-evaluation.

　○ Other (please explain)

_____

_____

14. In its place, what work would you recommend that would convey as valuable a picture and perspective of the subject treated?

_____

_____

Signature: _____   Date: _____

Reprinted with permission from the National Council of Teachers of English. Revised April, 2009.

GLOSSARY

accuracy   In realistic fiction, the exactness or correctness of the characters, situations, or settings.

acting   An actor's interpretation of character.

adventure story   *See* survival stories.

aesthetic   A stance taken when reading is done for pleasure in a "lived-through" experience.

affective fallacy   The phrase used by the New Critics for any consideration of a reader's personal interpretation in the study of a literary work.

allusion   Single or limited reference in a literary work to other literature or event in history, contemporary people and places, or popular culture.

alternate history fiction   A type of speculative fiction that explores an imaginary world that might have existed if circumstances were different.

anime   A Japanese style of animation often characterized by colorful graphics and incorporating adult themes.

antagonist   The person or force that is directly opposed to the protagonist; if a character, may be either round or flat.

archetypal literary criticism   A type of criticism based on Jung's belief that certain generalized models, or archetypes, are present in the psyche of all people, and these archetypes eventually recur so frequently in literature that they become a part of the literary experience as models or patterns of characters, situations, or actions, influencing a reader's expectations and interpretations.

archetypes   Generalized models present in the psyche, the mind or soul, of all people that represent patterns of characters, situations, or actions; a kind of universal figure often found in mythology and legends.

arrangement   The physical relationship or position of people, objects, and background in a single camera shot.

auteur director   A film director who develops a personal vision for a film by controlling all aspects of filmmaking.

authorial audience   General assumptions authors make regarding the characteristics of the audience for their books.

authority   In realistic fiction, the question of whether or not an author can write accurately about a cultural group if not a member of that group.

author's narrative strategy   The author's plan for how a story is told.

autobiography   An account of a person's life written by that person with the expectation that this personal history will be read by someone else.

backdrop setting   A setting that attracts little notice and could be changed without significantly altering the events of the story.

balloons   In a graphic novel, the graphic element inside a panel that contains words being spoken by the characters.

banning   *See* censorship.

biography   A genre of nonfiction that is a written history of a person's life written by someone else.

book pass   A book sampling method in which students gather in a circle and read a book for a few minutes. When the teacher calls out "book pass," students pass the book to the person on their right and receive a new book to sample.

book sampling An approach for matching readers and books in which students have a few minutes to look over a book to decide if they want to read it.

book sort A book sampling method for individuals or small groups in which each student receives 6 to 10 books, peruses each, then sorts them into piles of "no," "yes," and "maybe."

book talk A brief introduction to a book that strives to entice readers.

bottom lighting Light from below the face, making the face look distorted and ominous.

bridging An approach to literature study that pairs or groups literary texts for the purpose of creating intertextual connections.

Bunraku Intricate Japanese puppet theater that uses large puppets, up to four feet tall, and requires skilled puppeteers to handle the puppets.

camera angle The angle at or from which the camera looks at the action.

camera distance The relative distance from the camera to the action being filmed, usually in relation to the actor(s); may be extreme close-up, close-up, medium shot, or long shot.

camera movement The physical movement of the camera; may be a pan, tilt, zoom, or dolly shot.

categorical documentary A documentary that is intended to provide information in an analytical way.

censorship Removing or restricting access of a work from its intended audience.

challenge An attempt to remove or restrict materials from the curriculum or library based on the objections of a person or group.

cinema verite A French term for "truthful cinema." Also called *direct cinema documentary*.

climax The turning point in the story after which the eventual outcome is inevitable.

collective biographies A collection of individual biographies usually connected by a common theme or topic.

color saturation The intensifying of a specific color.

Commedia dell'Arte A form of Italian theater that observes the three unities but does not use scripts

and whose actors play highly recognizable stereotypes and enrich a simple plot outline with improvisation and "lazzi," practiced bits of clowning.

compilation film A documentary film that is produced by putting together images from archival sources.

conflict A struggle between the protagonist(s) and some other force.

conscious delight The stage of literary appreciation in which a reader gains additional pleasure by understanding the craft of writing.

contemporary literature for young adults Literature, including print and nonprint works, that brings pleasure and understanding to many readers between the ages of 10 and 18 by providing ways of exploring their own identities and of discovering their place in the contemporary world.

costumes Clothes characters wear that can suggest important aspects about characters or setting.

creation myth A myth that explains a people's origins.

creative journalism *See* literary journalism.

creative nonfiction *See* literary nonfiction.

creative nonfiction graphic novel A type of graphic novel that combines factually accurate events and real people, places, and/or times and the author's use of creative license to weave a story around the real facts and elements.

critical literacy A perspective that focuses on the ways in which texts are constructed in social, political, and historical contexts; such a perspective encourages readers to consider the ways in which these contexts position both readers and texts and how these contexts influence, and even endorse, particular interpretations of the text.

critical media literacy Literacy that focuses on analyzing media and related components; may include the production of media texts, in particular, media texts that challenge messages in the dominant discourse.

critical stance A stance in which readers consider the choices an author made in creating a text; helps readers become aware of how a text is influencing them.

cultural authenticity In realistic fiction, the ability of the author to portray all aspects of a story in an accurate light.

cut The simplest editing transition as one scene ends and another begins.

deep focus A camera focus where all objects in both the foreground and background remain in focus.

defamiliarization The process in New Criticism of focusing on how the "ordinary" becomes unordinary through literary or artistic language and images.

deity myth A myth that tells about the exploits of supernatural beings, usually gods, and features a human hero and panoramic scope.

denouement The final outcome of the story.

developmental significance Refers to literature that makes a successful connection to the common interests and concerns of adolescents.

diary An account of a person's life that usually has a day-to-day or week-to-week format and tends to be deliberately chronological.

diction The level of formality in the language used by the narrator and the characters.

diegetic sound Sound that can be heard by the characters.

direct cinema documentary A film that records an ongoing event as it happens with minimal interference from the filmmaker. Also called *cinema verite*, a French term for "truthful cinema."

dissolve A gradual transition in which the end of one scene is superimposed over the beginning of a new one and for a brief moment both images are visible at the same time.

diverse literature Works that help readers to cross boundaries and see the world from new perspectives and that reflect differences among people, including language, sexual orientation, and social position as well as ethnicity and cultural background.

documentary film A film that combines information and artistry in order to elicit both understanding and appreciation from an audience.

dolly The movement of a camera on a track, on wheels, or in someone's hand.

drama A type of literary work that requires both actor and audience to bring it to life; always includes human voices, facial expressions, and movement and may include art, music, props, and costumes as well.

dramaturgy The term used in the theater for information that helps the actors to create their roles and the audience to appreciate the play.

dynamic character A character who changes during the course of a story in response to the events that occur.

dystopian fiction In contrast with utopian literature, a literary work that imagines a world worse than the present one, often extending disturbing current trends to show how disaster, misery, and injustice may be looming in the future—often the near future.

editing A process that involves the selection of images and sounds for inclusion in a film and putting the shots together; *see also* cut, fade, dissolve, montage, wipe, flashback.

efferent A stance taken by a reader who is seeking to extract information.

epic Long narrative poem that tells the central events of a particular people and celebrates their ideas and values.

epic fantasy A sub-genre of fantasy that echoes the spirit and tone of ancient hero tales but creates entirely new characters, and often entirely new worlds. Also referred to as "high fantasy."

epilogue A structural device that summarizes events happening after the ending of a story in order to clarify the story or provide a sense of closure.

episodic plot A type of plot in which a series of loosely tied together incidents gradually reveal significant aspects of the setting or characters.

essay A short piece of literary nonfiction; may be written in several formats including letters, as a periodical serial, a political tract, or a newspaper or magazine column.

explicit theme A theme directly stated in the story by the narrator or by one of the characters.

exposition The background information often at the beginning of a story that may describe the setting, introduce the characters, and establish the protagonist's goals.

fade in fade out A transition where one scene gradually goes dark and the new one gradually emerges.

fairy tale A type of traditional literature having strong elements of magic.

falling action   Follows the climax and provides answers to unanswered questions.

fantasy   Imaginative literature containing elements that are nonexistent or unreal and events that are influenced by magic or the supernatural, creating worlds that reveal hidden truths and deeper realities.

feminist theory   A theory that focuses on issues of how women are portrayed in literature, female authors, and sexual politics.

figurative language   The use of words in a non-literal way.

first person point of view   The personal perspective of one character, usually, but not always, the protagonist, in which that character can tell only those aspects of the story that are experienced directly by that character and the pronouns "I" and "me" predominate.

flashback   A deliberate interruption in the main narrative that inserts a brief glimpse at a past event.

flash forward   A structural device that alerts the reader to an event before it happens.

flat character   A character about whom too little information is provided for that character to be well developed.

focus   The clarity and detail of an image, produced by the type of lens used and the distance between the camera and the object being filmed.

folk literature   *See* traditional literature.

folk tale   A narrative story handed down through the oral tradition with roots in a particular culture; likely to change with teller and the telling.

foreshadowing   The author's use of hints or clues to suggest or indicate what might happen later in a story.

formalist criticism   *See* New Criticism; also referred to as formalism.

forms   Art elements that are three-dimensional, having height, width, and depth, and serve to define objects in space.

fourth genre   *See* literary nonfiction.

framing   What is included and what is left out of a shot, or the "picture frame" around what can be seen.

front lighting   Light that is even across a face, creating a flattering effect of innocence or openness.

gay/lesbian studies   Literary studies that explore issues relating to sexual orientation and gender identity, usually focusing on LGBTQ people and cultures. Also called *queer studies.*

gender criticism   Criticism that seeks to broaden the underlying issues related to gender and includes questions regarding both femininity and masculinity.

genres   Groups of literary works related by form, style, purpose, or subject matter.

graphic novels   Book-length comic books that depict a sophisticated story told between two covers.

Greek theatre   Drama that originated in ancient Greece and was the source of the three unities of time, place, and action that Aristotle identified as the key to an effective plot.

guided literature study   A teacher-directed literacy routine that emphasizes literary concepts, vocabulary, and comprehension.

gutter   In a graphic novel, the space between panels; may indicate a transition when action jumps across place or time, mark a change in subject, or even represent a purposeful disconnect.

hero myth   Myths that features a hero figure, often male, who possesses supernatural abilities and performs extraordinary feats in the course of laying the foundations of human society.

high fantasy   *See* epic fantasy.

high key   A lighting style in which most of the scene is brightly lit, creating a lively mood and a sense of openness.

historical fiction   A fictional story set in the past. The setting will influence the events and characters in varying degrees.

hue   Gradations of color.

illustrated book   A book in which the narrative is predominately verbal and the illustrations fill a supportive or subordinate role.

imagery   A style device that creates a strong impression in the reader's mind by appealing to the senses through descriptions of sight, sound, smell, touch, or taste.

implicit theme   A theme that is not explicitly stated but emerges from what characters do, decisions they make, and the motives behind those decisions.

independent reading level   The level at which a reader can read fluently and with ease.

informational nonfiction A type of practical nonfiction "designed to communicate information in circumstances where the quality of the writing is not considered as important as the content" (Nordquist, n.d.; see Ch. 8).

integral setting A setting in which the time and place are essential to the story and have a major influence on the events, characterization, or theme.

intentional fallacy The phrase used by the New Critics for consideration of an author's intention in the study of a literary work.

interactive ebook An electronic book, often read on a tablet computer, that provides a multimedia experience incorporating sound, sight, and touch and allows the reader to interact with it.

interest survey Written questionnaire or inventory devised to solicit opinions about books, topics, and activities.

internal conflict A "person against self" conflict that occurs when a character is struggling with a personal issue such as a choice between opposing values.

interpersonal conflict A conflict that pits person against person.

intertextuality A process of interpreting any text in relation to another text. As a metafictive device, it implies that a new work is created and is understood largely through its relationship to a previous work or works.

interview documentary A film that records people's testimony about something.

journal A type of personal narrative that may focus on a specific experience or event and may include the observations, dialogue, and the private thoughts of the author.

Kabuki A type of Japanese dance drama with elaborate costumes, stylized acting, elaborate makeup, song, and exaggerated movement.

keys Lighting styles.

legend A type of traditional literature that usually memorializes a remarkable character who actually lived or an event that actually happened.

line An identifiable path of a point moving in space; can vary in width, direction, and length. Lines can be straight or curved, thick or thin, and horizontal, vertical, or diagonal.

literacy routine A pattern of materials, procedures, and activities used together to meet a literacy goal.

literary canon Literary works that have become part of a society's cultural heritage and that many, if not most, well-read individuals in that society will have read—or read about.

literary criticism A judgment about the value or worth of a literary work that is based on what a particular theory directs a reader to consider.

literary journalism A genre of nonfiction that challenges the traditional view of objective reporting by incorporating dialogue and dramatic action and other elements of fiction. Also referred to as *creative journalism.*

literary nonfiction A hybrid type of literature that blends the power of fact with literary techniques such as theme, setting, characterization, dialogue, and tone as well as stylistic devices such as metaphors and similes. Also known as *creative nonfiction, narrative nonfiction, literature of reality,* and the *fourth genre.*

literary significance Refers to literature that gives readers exposure to the forms and techniques of literary writing.

literary theory Theory that frames how a reader investigates assumptions, principles, and concepts about literature.

literature circles A literacy routine in which students carry on discussions about books they have selected or been assigned.

literature of reality *See* literary nonfiction.

low key A lighting style in which less illumination creates contrasts; can create an ominous feeling.

manga Japanese-influenced printed comics.

Marxist theory Literary theory that focuses on social and economic class, economic inequities, and the relationship between wealth and power.

mediated listening–thinking activity The technique in which the teacher reads up to a meaningful stopping point in a text, then asks students to make predictions or connections and to explain their reasoning.

medium The material and process used to create art, such as watercolor, acrylics, pencil, or print; choice of illustration medium impacts the mood of the story and the overall feeling that is conveyed by the illustrations.

memoir   An account of a person's life written by that person that usually focuses on a specific phase or event of the writer's life or encounters with certain people.

metafictive literature   Literature that intentionally reminds readers that they are reading and interacting with words and images, thus creating an awareness of the ways in which the text is playing with traditional beliefs and forms.

metafictive mashups   Mixing elements from multiple genres and formats in a literary work.

metaphors   Implied comparisons between two dissimilar things that have some trait in common.

mixed genre   Genre conventions are broken by using nontraditional structures or mixing genres.

modernism   An intellectual and artistic movement based on a preference for the new and the avant-garde over the traditional.

montage   An assembly of shots intended to condense or expand time or to develop a theme.

multicultural literature   *See* diverse literature.

multimodal texts   Texts that combine multiple modes of communication, for example, combining the language and structures of traditional genres with images and perhaps sound and links to online content, in the case of interactive ebooks.

multiple points of view   A metafictive device in which multiple narratives are told from different points of view.

mystery   A sub-genre of realistic fiction in which the protagonist is trying to solve a crime or find out why something has happened or who made it happen.

myth   A type of traditional literature that has come down anonymously from a remote time and that attempts to explain the origins of the world, including human society and culture.

narrative nonfiction   *See* literary nonfiction.

naturalism   An intellectual and artistic movement based on a belief that natural laws, not supernatural ones, govern the world.

neutral key   A lighting style that is even and balanced.

New Criticism   A literary theory that considers literary texts as complete works of art that should be studied without consideration of external influences, including readers, authors, or historical or cultural contexts.

Noh   A type of stately, classical Japanese musical production based on themes about heroes. Often the actors wear masks and the performance includes a chorus.

nondiegetic sound   Sound that cannot be heard by a character, often music and voice-over narration.

nonfiction   A type of literature that is not made up but rather is a gathering of facts presented through reason and logic.

nonlinearity   Rather than following a straight, chronological line through a series of events, the narrative veers in a different direction.

notebooks   *See* journal.

omniscient point of view   A perspective in which the thoughts and actions, past or present, of many characters are revealed.

oppositional reading   A reading that actively questions the ideological assumptions in a text.

oppositional viewing   A viewing that actively questions the ideological assumptions in a film.

oral literature   *See* traditional literature.

pan   A camera shot in which the camera moves left or right.

panel   In a graphic novel, the block of content with a visual or implied boundary around it; a panel may contain only words, only images, or both.

period fiction   A novel that is set in a past era but has a plot that addresses general and universal themes that are not specific to the period.

person against nature conflict   A type of conflict that pits a character against impersonal forces, particularly elements of nature such as a storm or rugged environment.

person against society conflict   A type of conflict that focuses on a protagonist's growing discomfort with the values and mores of society. Battling hatred, prejudice, or other forms of social injustice is a person against society conflict. This type of conflict also can occur on a grand scale with a large number of people demanding social change.

personification A form of figurative language in which human traits are assigned to nonhuman things.

picture book A profusely illustrated book that communicates through both verbal and visual elements and in which the visual elements are so pervasively intertwined with the text that the story cannot be understood without them.

plot The element of a story that involves what the characters do (actions), what happens to them (events), and the sequence of those actions and events (the narrative order).

poetry Literary works that are visual and auditory, are carefully crafted in miniature to communicate real feelings about things that matter, and create vivid mental images through the use of language.

point of view The perspective, the voice, or narrator an author uses to tell the story.

portrait documentary A film that centers on someone's life.

post-apocalyptic fiction A literary work that takes place in a world after near total destruction has occurred.

postmodernism Changes in attitudes, styles, and academic disciplines that occurred following World War II; postmodernism is characterized by an attitude of disbelief or skepticism, a reluctance to accept the official version of what is true or the prevalent rules regarding how things must be done.

problem novel A type of realistic fiction dealing with social issues and coming-of-age situations.

progressive plot A type of narrative structure that follows a sequence of exposition, rising action, climax, falling action, and denouement or resolution.

prologue A structural device at the beginning of the story used to briefly describe events that occurred before the plot begins.

protagonist The central figure in a story with whom readers typically identify.

queer theory *See* gay/lesbian studies.

rack focus Changing the focus on various aspects of a shot so a clear image becomes out of focus or something not in clear focus becomes clear.

readability The reading ability needed to read a particular work, usually expressed in a grade level by year and month such as 12.1, indicating a person who reads at the level typical of students in the first month of twelfth grade.

reader response theory A range of theoretical perspectives that focus on what literature "does," not what it is; contends that a literary work exists only in the moment that a reader transforms the symbols on the page into something meaningful.

reading workshop A literacy routine in which students select a literary work and read it independently. They may decide to read the same book as other students.

realistic fiction A genre of literature for young adults in which the characters behave in a recognizably human manner, and the situations and circumstances confronted by the protagonist are possible in real world settings.

reinventions Contemporary retellings of traditional tales that veer away drastically from the basic form, plot, or meaning of the original, often adding ideas that were entirely absent from the original.

Renaissance theatre Drama originating from the mid-16th to mid-17th centuries in Europe that often combined Greek source material and commedia stereotypes; some of these plays are the most famous and notable of Western theatre.

resolution *See* denouement.

retellings Updating and adapting a story to fit a new audience as the story passes from place to place and across generations. Retellings occur when an oral story is transferred to a new medium, such as print, where it can be illustrated, or when adapted for television or film. Retellings may transform some elements of a story, but they generally preserve the overall plot, theme, and spirit of the original.

reverse bridging An approach to literature study in which students read a challenging work with a great deal of teacher assistance, and that work then becomes a bridge to less challenging literature that the students read more independently.

rhetorical documentaries A documentary that is intended to make an argument and persuade viewers to a particular point of view.

rising action Further development of the conflict and additional complications.

romance   A sub-genre of realistic fiction that is characterized by a central love story and an emotionally satisfying and optimistic ending.

round character   A three-dimensional character that is portrayed as a complex individual with a range of traits, both strengths and weaknesses.

scene   An arrangement of shots of the same general action, time and location.

science fiction   *See* speculative fiction.

second person point of view   A perspective that makes the reader the main character of the story and uses the pronoun "you."

self-conscious development   The stage of literary development in which a reader's pleasure is enhanced by a growing ability to relate to characters and to consider what he or she might do in a similar situation.

self-referential   A stylistic device through which readers are made aware that they are immersed in fiction by exposing the process of making the book or by acknowledging the existence of the author.

sets   The location in which the action takes place and the props are contained; may be an existing or constructed location.

setting   The time and place in which the action of a story occurs.

shapes   Art elements that are two-dimensional, having height and width, and serve to define objects in space.

shared reading   The process by which students follow along in their own copies of the text while the teacher reads aloud.

shojo   The genre of Japanese manga intended for girls.

shonen   The genre of Japanese manga intended for boys.

short story   A form of literary narrative that can be read in one sitting and whose every aspect should function toward a particular effect.

shot   The basic unit of film construction; a consecutive series of film frames that shows continuous action; the image that remains on screen until it is replaced by another.

similes   Comparisons using "like" or "as."

slave narrative   A type of historical memoir usually written or dictated by a slave; a first-person account that provides insight into both slavery and personal narrative.

social significance   Refers to literature that is likely to give the reader new perspective about society and its diverse members.

soft focus   A camera focus that blurs images slightly; used on some occasions for close-ups.

space   An element of art that refers to the areas around, between, or within the different elements in a work, serving to create an illusion of depth or of being three-dimensional.

speculative fiction   A type of fiction based in established principles of physical or social science that form the basis for other realities that are suited to social and cultural speculations that may apply to our reality; should help readers achieve a new perspective on the familiar through its contrast with "the other." Also referred to as *science fiction*.

sports fiction   A sub-genre of realistic fiction that focuses on sports action, books that blend character development with sports, and stories where the main character is an athlete, but the sport is only loosely connected to the story.

stages of literary appreciation   A model that shows how a reader's appreciation of literature grows and changes.

stance   The way a reader approaches a text based on a purpose for reading the text.

static character   A character that remains essentially the same in personality and behavior and is, most often, a minor character.

steampunk   A hybrid genre inspired by the technological advancements made in the 19th century and by the pulp fiction of the 1920s, '30s, and '40s showing what the future would look like if it had come along during the Victorian era.

stereotype   A flat character that is reduced to a single trait, often by categorizing the character as belonging to a particular group.

style   The actual language used in a literary work; includes diction and word choice, sentence structure (syntax), and the tone an author uses. In referring to art, the manner of expression in a work.

survival story   A type of realistic fiction in which the main character may experience an internal struggle but will always face an external challenge that is often a matter of life and death, with the danger coming from the natural environment or from other people, and in which meeting the challenge provides opportunities for personal growth and self-discovery.

symbol   An image or words that go beyond a literal or concrete meaning to represent an abstract or figurative meaning.

symbolic setting   A setting that comes to represent something other than a literal time or place.

synthetic documentary   A film that combines several documentary film styles.

talking heads documentary   *See* interview documentary.

tall tales   A type of traditional literature in which the main character has superhuman attributes, that is light in tone, and that has events so exaggerated that they become humorously unbelievable.

teacher read-aloud   A literacy routine in which the teacher reads aloud to students.

texture   An element of art that is used to capture the surface quality of an object that a viewer senses through touch.

theme   The concept or proposition that gives a story its significance; it can be explicit and directly stated or implicit and implied.

third person limited point of view   A perspective in which the story is told from one character's perspective and the other characters' perspectives are unknown.

third person point of view   A perspective that can be recognized by use of the pronouns "he," "she," or "they."

thriller   A subgenre of realistic fiction in which the level of suspense is high because the protagonist is facing impending danger and waiting for something to happen.

tilt   A camera shot in which the camera moves up or down.

toneThe attitude the narrator has about the literary work and its intended readers, conveyed through word choice and perspective.

traditional literature   Stories that are part of the cultural heritage of a community or people, shaped and reshaped through ongoing telling to fit the needs of tellers and audiences of a particular place or time.

transaction   A term used in reader response theory to indicate that when the reader and the text come together they mutually affect each other to evoke an experience.

transcendentalism   An intellectual and artistic movement based on the belief that spirituality is gained through individual intuition.

transitions   *See* editing; *see also* cut, fade, dissolve, montage, wipe, flashback.

unconscious delight   The stage of literary appreciation in which a reader finds personal satisfaction in reading. It provides the foundation for later stages.

unit-centered literacy routines   Literacy routines in which genre units, author studies, or literary themes are organized to create connections among literary texts.

unreliable narrator   For various reasons, such as pretending, lying, or being mentally unstable, the narrator's truthfulness is questioned.

urban legend   A type of traditional literature rooted in the oral tradition told as "true stories" that usually tell about events that are incredible or bizarre.

value   Describes how light or dark a color is and its *intensity*, how bright or dull.

variants   Different versions of traditional tales that arise from the oral tradition as tellers refine the tales for local audiences.

wipe   A transition where one shot appears to wipe another from the screen.

zoom   Movement of a camera lens that gives the impression the camera is moving toward or away from the object and thus makes objects appear to grow larger or smaller.

AUTHOR AND TITLE INDEX

SUBJECT INDEX